The Rock Art of Norway

Trond Lødøen and Gro Mandt

WINDgather
PRESS

Windgather Press
is an imprint of
Oxbow Books, Oxford

Norwegian edition published by Det Norske Samlaget, Norway

English Language edition published by agreement with
the Hagen Agency AS, Norway

ISBN 978-1-905119-28-8

A CIP record for this book is available from the British Library

This book is available direct from

Oxbow Books, Oxford, UK
(Phone: 01865-241249; Fax: 01865-794449)

and

The David Brown Book Company
PO Box 511, Oakville, CT 06779, USA
(Phone: 860-945-9329; Fax: 860-945-9468)

or from our website

www.oxbowbooks.com

Printed in Hong Kong by
Kwong Fat Offset Printing Co Ltd

Contents

Foreword iv

1. Images in Rock – Enigma and Challenge (GM/TL) 1
2. The World Heritage Site in Alta (TL) 15
3. Aldon in Varanger (TL) 27
4. Rock Art of the Northern Tradition in Troms County (TL) 42
5. Forselv in Skjomen (TL) 56
6. Polished Rock Art in Nordland (TL) 69
7. Cave Paintings in Nord-Trøndelag and Nordland (TL) 84
8. Rock Art in Trøndelag (TL) 98
9. Rock Art at Bogge in Romsdal (TL) 112
10. Mjeltehaugen at Giske – A Glimpse of an Enigmatic Grave Monument (GM) 124
11. Vingen in Bremanger "Nature's own colossal museum for rock art!" (GM/TL) 139
12. Kårstad in Stryn – An Encounter Between Two Cult Traditions (GM) 162
13. Leirvåg in Askvoll – Boat Images Reflecting the Spirit of the Time (GM) 177
14. Cup Marks in the Sub-Alpine Regions of Southern Norway – Traces of Ancient Animal Husbandry (GM) 188
15. Berge in Strandebarm (TL) 200
16. Bakke in Jondal – A Sacred Site and Meeting Place in the Bronze Age (GM) 213
17. Etne in Sunnhordland – A Small and Diverse Rock Art Region (GM) 228
18. Revheim at Hafrsfjord – a Unique Context in the Rich Rock Art Region of Rogaland (GM) 239
19. The Rock Art of Lista – the Southernmost Outpost (GM) 253
20. Sporaneset in Rauland and other Rock Art Sites in Telemark (GM) 264
21. Rock Art of the Northern Tradition in Eastern Norway (TL) 279
22. Skjeberg in Østfold – an Abundance of Rock Carvings (GM) 297
23. Fading Images (GM/TL) 309

Key to Caption Credits 320
Bibliography 321
Index 330

Foreword

It is educational to write a book, and enlightening to approach old, familiar material and established interpretations with renewed queries and perspectives that are different than those used in the past. Moreover, the quest for new knowledge is challenging because deeper insight opens the way for countless new interpretational alternatives. Through an examination of rock art from all parts of Norway studied globally, we have been able to see patterns and diversities that studies of limited chronological periods of times and regional analyses have seldom seen before. In our attempt to understand and document the patterns we maintain are discernable within the geographic region called Norway, we have also drawn on material from and knowledge about rock art images from other parts of the world.

Not least, we have found inspiration for seeking new thought perspectives through the many academic dissertations that have been produced in the university environment. With undaunted courage, students have grappled with complex theoretical problems in order to find meaning in the mute traces of culture found by archaeologists. Their dissertations represent important new sources of knowledge, and the thoughts, interpretations and solutions that are presented have been a veritable treasure chest for us during our work on the manuscript for this book.

We owe a debt of gratitude to many people for their contributions in the writing process. Colleagues, friends and family members have contributed with useful comments on the draft texts and finished chapters. Special thanks go to Jenny-Rita Næss, Museum of Archaeology, Stavanger, who spent much time reading through and offering wise and insightful suggestions concerning large portions of the manuscript. Special thanks for comments on isolated chapters are also owed to Liv Helga Dommasnes, Sonja Innselset, Trond Linge and Tore Slinning, University of Bergen, Anne-Sophie Hygen, Directorate for Cultural Heritage, Marthe Pramli, Sametinget [Sami Parliament of Norway], Harald Johnsen, Troms county Administration and Tarjei Mandt Larsen, University of Stavanger.

Colleagues throughout Norway have helped us both in terms of practical tasks and by showing an interest in our book project, as well as by demonstrating a willingness to discuss the myriad of professional issues that have emerged along the way.

Illustrations – photographs, maps, drawings and tables – are important elements in the documentation of archaeology and not least of all the images on rock panels. Our gratitude is due to both institutions and individuals who have contributed illustrations for this book. Ragnar Børsheim and Morten Kutchera of Arkikon have the well-deserved credit for the maps that serve to introduce each chapter. Svein Skare and Hans Davanger, Bergen Museum, Lene Buskoven and Inger Marie Olsrud of the Directorate of Cultural Heritage, Sveinulf Heggstad, Bjørn Hebba Helberg and Knut Helskog of Tromsø Museum, Mari Høgestøl of the Museum of Archaeology, Stavanger, Rune Kyrkjebø of Bergen University Library, Kalle Sognnes, Department of Archaeology and Religious Studies, NTNU, Ingegerd Stenström, Umeå University, Svein Erik Ski, Vestre Slidre, Aud Beverfjord and Sally Skow of the Museum of Natural History and Archaeology, NTNU, have helped us in acquiring good illustrations. Photographers Arve Kjersheim, Arvid Sveen and Ragnar Utne are owed our gratitude for excellent photos of the rock images and the context in which they are found. Colleagues in archaeology have also contributed to the visualization of our text – thanks go to Jan Magne Gjerde, Heidi Handeland, Tom Heibreen, Sonja Innselset, Tore Slinning and Marit Wold Midtun for permitting us to use photographs they have taken in the field.

For the original edition of this book our thanks go to the Norwegian publisher *Det Norske Samlaget*, and in particular our editor, Sverre Tusvik, who was willingly flexible with deadlines, the number of illustrations and linguistic norms, and to designer Stian Hole, who listened to our concerns regarding the Norwegian version.

In the process of making an English edition an expression of gratitude goes to the Hagen Agency and to David Miles of English Heritage for their invaluable assistance in gaining acceptance of our manuscript by a British publishing company. At *Windgather Press* our thanks go to Richard Purslow and Clare Litt.

We are also thankful for the financial support provided by the University of Bergen and the Norwegian Directorate for Cultural Heritage for the translation of this work. Thanks are also due to translator Tim Challman who made the initial translation and to Jon Brokenbrow who has been responsible for the final proof reading. And finally, we would like to thank each other for a fruitful collaboration, regarding both the original version and the process of re-writing, adjusting and updating the text into English. This has involved many long discussions concerning rock images, problematical issues, methods for imparting information and formal presentation.

Bergen, January 2009,
Trond Lødøen and Gro Mandt

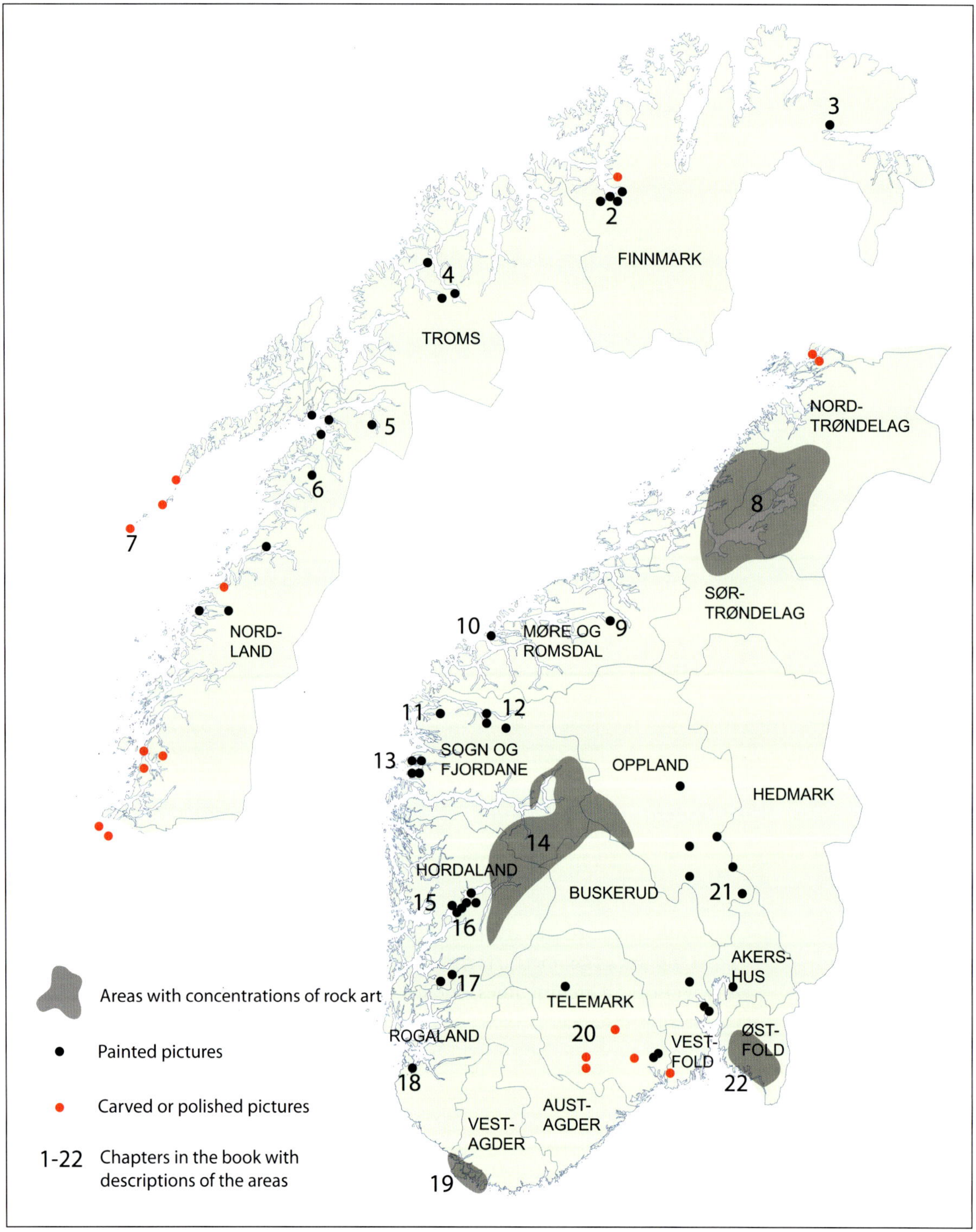

Location Map

Images in Rock – Enigma and Challenge

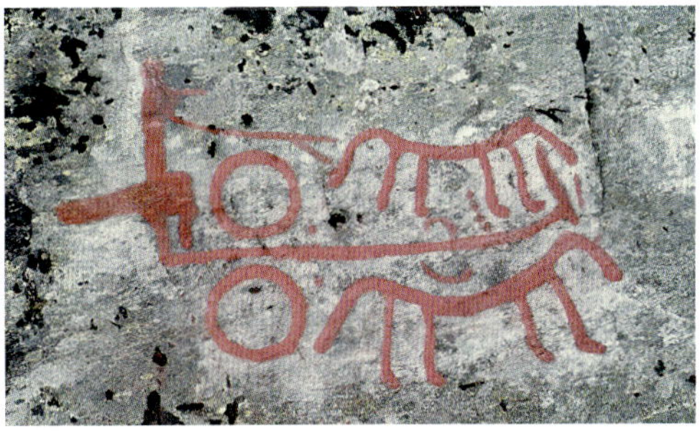

FIGURE 1. On the pebble beach at Staveneset in Sogn og Fjordane are several small rock carving panels and burial mounds. One of the panels has a motif that is unique for Western Norway: a two-wheeled cart drawn by two horses and with a figure on top of the coachbox. Depictions of carts with both two and four wheels are also known from Østfold in south-eastern Norway. Close parallels to the special type of cart motif found at Staveneset, however, where both horses are heading in the same direction, occur only in Southern Sweden, in particular in Scania. These cart figures date from the Bronze Age.
GM

For thousands of years people in all parts of the world have put their marks on rock panels and stones. Images can be found in dark and narrow cave passages, on barren rocks on the seashore, along the edges of cultivated fields, in rugged mountain terrain and on the walls of rocky mountain slopes. They are discovered on large, earth bound boulders, on smaller, movable stones or on rock panels in burial chambers. Most of them are engraved or painted on the surfaces – often in several colours. Some of them are scratched, carved, polished or cut into the stone. We find images of animals and humans, of objects used by humans, such as boats and carts, swords, spears and hunting implements. We nod knowingly when we find many of these, even though the species of animals or the shapes of the human figures vary according to where they are found in the world and how old they are. Some of the images of man-made objects bear strikingly similar traits from one part of the world to another. On rock panels we also find images that we are unable to associate with specific objects that we know from our own contemporary time or from previous archaeological discoveries. At times we are led to believe that the images depict objects that were used by those who created the rock art, but of which we have never found any traces, perhaps because these objects were made of wood, bone or horn material that is rarely preserved up until our own era. On other occasions we encounter images that we recognize as geometric forms or abstract patterns – circular and spiral figures, zigzagging and arching lines, chequered patterns and the like – images that leave us clueless as to their meaning.

Language without words

A distinctive trait of humans is that of being able to think and express oneself using symbols – signs that represent something other than oneself. Language is such a system of symbols which is essential for exchanging information and knowledge between individuals and groups. But human beings have also developed a great number of non-linguistic forms of expression that denote

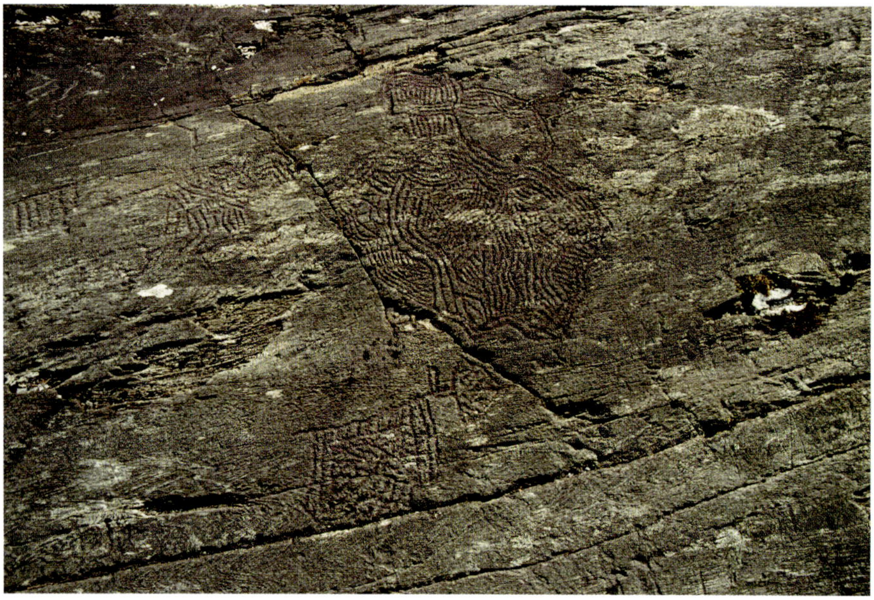

FIGURE 2. While many of the rock images seem recognizable for people of today, such as human beings, animals and human-made objects, other motifs are incomprehensible due to lack of comparisons. This, for example, is the case with the line patterns in a group of figures from Ausevik in Flora, Sogn og Fjordane. One of the great challenges in rock art research is how to approach an interpretation of these kinds of motifs. To a certain extent it may prove helpful to study the location of the images on the stone surface, the connection between cracks and uneven sections of the rock surface, the relationship with other figures, etc., but it is still uncertain whether the riddle can be solved.
GM

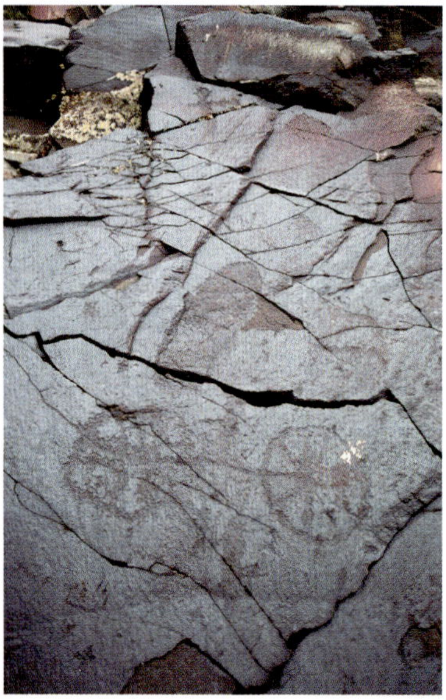

FIGURE 3. At Tamgaly in Southern Kazakhstan there are also rock carvings from the Bronze Age depicting horse-drawn carts. Tamgaly is a small ravine located midway on the expansive Central Asiatic steppes. For thousands of years the ravine has been a meeting place for people who have carved their symbols on the rocky slopes. Both the cart figures and a number of other motifs at Tamgaly bear striking resemblances to the Scandinavian rock carvings. Whether this reflects some form of contact between the two areas during the Bronze Age is an open question for the time being. It has been established, however, that Bronze Age societies in Northern Europe were influenced from many different areas, in the form of tangible objects as well as ideas.
GM

concepts about the human condition and people's relationship with higher powers – such as rituals, dances, music and art. It is this non-linguistic world of symbols that we encounter in rock art. As opposed to the ancient languages that researchers have managed to decode, the language of rock art images remains enigmatic. We have to interpret it based on our own modern era and our understanding of the world.

We who live in the 21st century are accustomed to interpreting images. We are confronted daily by the media in the form of images we see through films, television, advertising and cartoons, all of them requiring us to infer meaning, evaluate and perhaps be critical – with or without the aid of explanatory words. Therefore we have no problem imagining that the rock images from a past era may mean something entirely different than what they appear to depict – that they are symbols of more than physical references, of more than what we can touch and feel. Depictions of animals, humans and boats may be symbols of something more – perhaps even something completely different – than merely animals, people and boats. An animal figure may depict the game that is being hunted or represent the desire for a successful hunt, but it may also be a depiction of a mythological being. Human figures may represent divinities, participants in a cult or shamans performing rituals. Boat figures may portray warships or trading vessels, or they may be symbols of the kingdom of the dead, or the passage of the sun across the sky.

A worldwide phenomenon

One of the longest uninterrupted rock art tradition in the world is found in Australia. The oldest images are estimated to be more than 40,000 years old (Flood 1990; www.aboriginalartonline.com/art/rock.php), and up until the 1960s new images were painted or repainted on rock walls in the Australian continent (Chippendale and Tacon 1998). In other parts of the world it was also a custom to apply images on rock up until recorded historical time, for example in South Africa and on the American continent. In these places the indigenous population continued to produce rock images after Europeans had colonised their lands in the 1500s and 1600s (Lewis-Williams 1981). European rock art also has distant forbears: in the border areas between France and Spain, caves

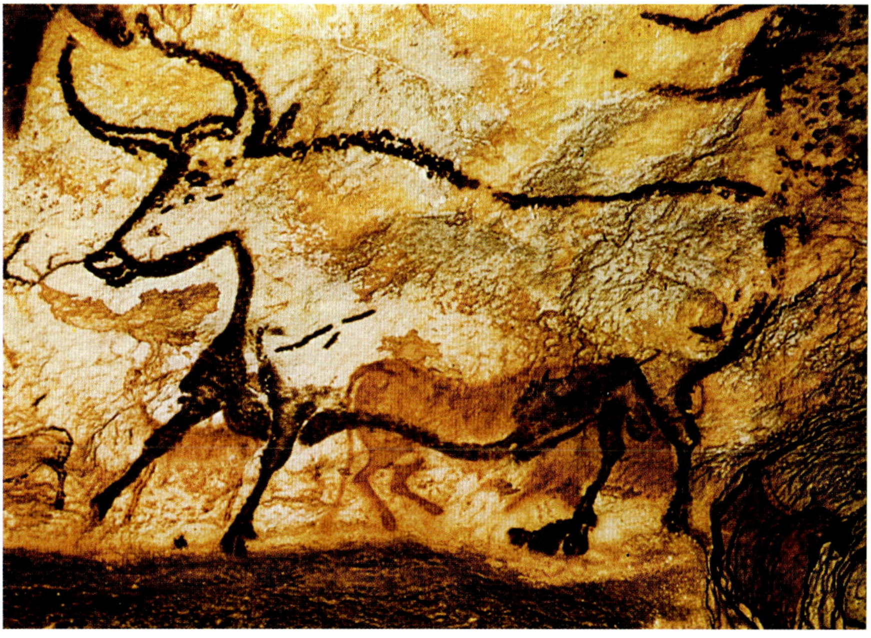

FIGURE 4. When the first cave paintings were discovered in Southern Europe in the 1800s, scholars were convinced that they should be explained as purely artistic expressions – that they were "art for art's sake", created by people living thousands of years ago in a society marked by an overabundance of wild game and who therefore had spare time for artistic pursuits – such as this impressive bull found at Lascaux in Southern France. This explanation probably reflects the view on art in the western world at that time, as decorations created to make homes, workplaces, parks and public facilities more pleasant, or to admire on visits to galleries and exhibitions. (Adapted from Leroi-Gourhan 1982).

have been found containing painted images – primarily depictions of various types of animals, some of which are extinct species – that are 30,000–40,000 years old. Scandinavian rock art is much younger. The oldest rock images in Scandinavia are probably about 9000 years old, while the youngest are dated to around 400 AD.

Focus on Norway

We know of more than 1100 places in Norway where rock art has been found. Each of these sites can comprise several panels adorned with rock art. From Finnmark in the north to Lista in the south, and from islands on the coastline in the west to the Swedish border in the east, we find petroglyphs and rock paintings on rock faces and boulders, under overhanging cliffs, on grave slabs, and occasionally in caves. They occur along the coast and on the shore of lakes, on riverbanks and in Sub-Alpine areas. In some parts of the country there are concentrations of rock art sites as well as great variation in both the numbers of figures found there and in the kind of images or motifs depicted, for example in Østfold, Rogaland, Sogn og Fjordane, Trøndelag and Finnmark. In the areas between these regions the sites are more scattered and the motifs more similar. Many motifs appear in all parts of the country – and also in the other Scandinavian countries – for example deer, boat figures and cup marks. Other motifs are less widespread, such as human figures, weapons, carts and trees. Both the design and the composition of the images vary in the different parts of the country. The reasons for such differences are in part that the sites occur in different eras, and partly that they were used for different purposes. It has been a common practice to group Scandinavian rock art into two main categories. The oldest – called *veidekunst* [hunter's art] or the *Northern Tradition* – is associated with hunter-gatherers from the Stone Age, in the period 9000–2000 BC. The other group is known as *jordbruksristninger* [agricultural petroglyphs], also referred to as the *Southern Tradition,* and associated with people of the Bronze and early Iron Age – from approximately 1800 BC until about 400 AD – who practiced farming as a livelihood. The distinction between the two groups is made first and foremost based on the kind of motifs that are depicted. The most common motifs in the Northern Tradition are animal figures – particularly of the deer family, such as elk, reindeer and red deer, and the large sea mammals such as whales, porpoises and seals – although human figures and abstract motifs have also been found. Those of the Southern Tradition have a wide range of motifs including, among others, humans, boats and other man-made objects, as well as circular figures such as rings, spirals and cup marks. Whether the images of the hunter nomads and the farmers represent two distinct and independent traditions, or whether they represent a continuous tradition encompassing changes in expression over time, continues to be an unresolved issue to this day

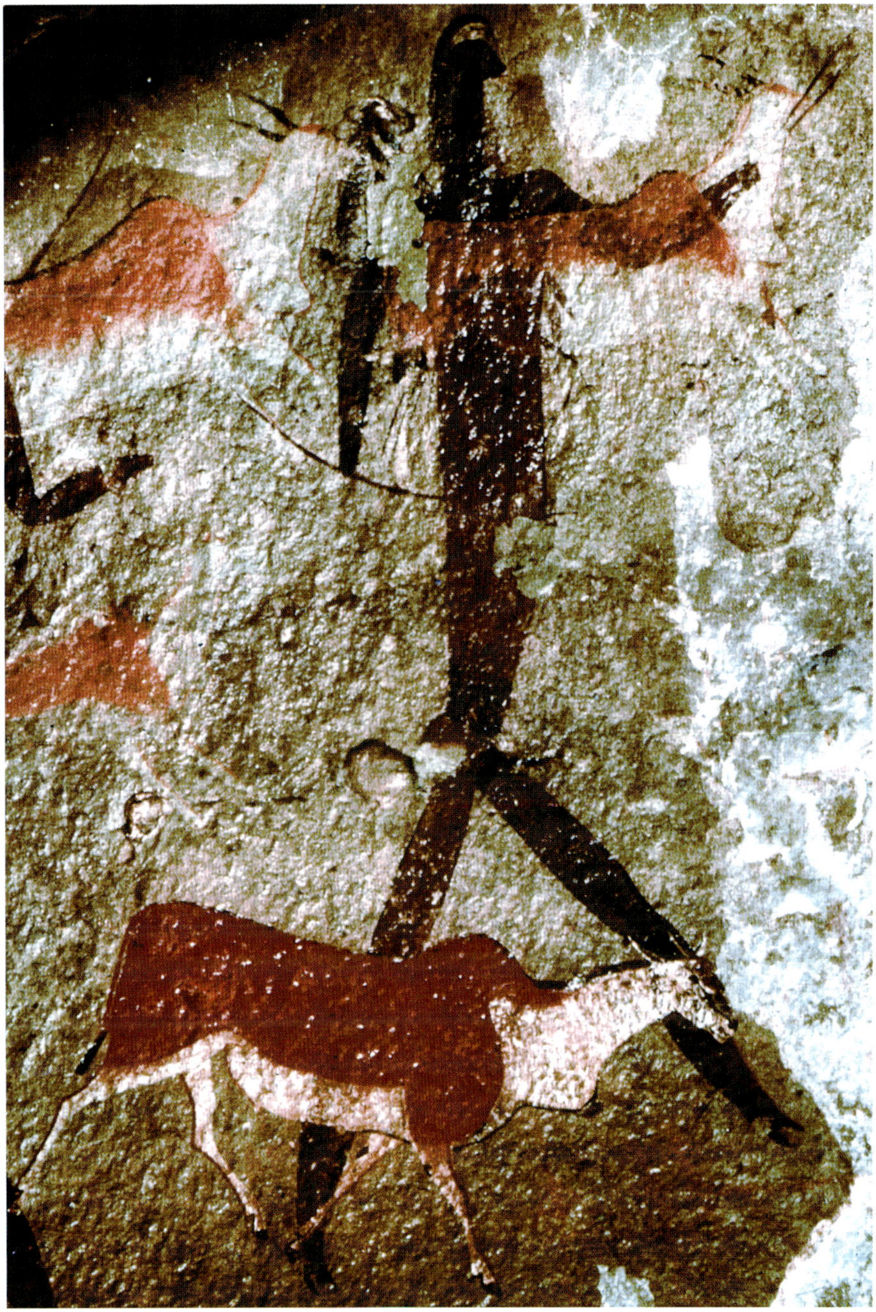

FIGURE 5. The eland is an important motif in many rock paintings in Southern Africa. The animal is often depicted together with humans in scenes that are associated with myths, rituals or shamanistic practices by the San people known from records made in the 1800s. The group of figures seen here is interpreted as a symbolic depiction of the kinds of experiences a shaman might have while in a trance – the feeling of being transformed into an antelope, or the dream-like visions of the animals themselves (after Clottes and Lewis-Williams 1998).

On the threshold between the past and the present

Why have humans carved and painted images on rock panels and stones for thousands of years? What did the images signify in ancient societies? What kinds of activities were carried out at the sites, and what were the stories that were told? These questions have fascinated and frustrated scholars and enthusiasts for hundreds of years. Ever since the first rock art images were discovered and described in the 1600s and 1700s, many different and often contradictory interpretations have been proposed. The divergent interpretations of rock art illustrate how each new generation of researchers studies and interprets collected data based on the professional issues that they find interesting and important to analyze, based on the knowledge, insight and professional experience they possess at the time. At the same time, we see how interpretive models are largely determined by contemporary factors in the researcher's era: by political and religious factors, conflicts of interest and issues up for debate, not to mention gender and social background.

This is the way things must be, because the remnants of the past only reveal to us a fraction of how life was once lived, and the full truth concerning how things really were will forever elude us. We can never reconstruct the past as it once existed – our interpretation will be only a construction of the way things may have been, grounded in our ballast of professional knowledge and our own, western contemporaneity. We must acknowledge how important our own era and our individual theoretical perspectives are as influences in the interpretive process. In other words, we read the present into remnants of the past.

Making images speak

The varied and enticing images seem to link the past with the present to a greater extent than other archaeological material does. The swarm of images tell us something, even though we are unable today to fully understand the original meaning they imparted. When we stand before a rock art site in the open air, or when we are inside a dark, cavernous passage and spot images flickering before us in the light of a torch, it is almost as if we are in the presence of a world of thought from the ancient past.

We believe that the images on the rock communicate concepts that were once so important for ancient society that they needed to be preserved through the permanent and powerful medium of stone. However, over the millennia, knowledge of the meaning of the images has been forgotten. What, then, are the odds that we can get these mute images to speak to us? In contrast to anthropologists, who study living societies, archaeologists do not have informants who can reveal how the remnants from another age were used and what they meant. In the northern part of Europe we lack both written historical sources and continuous traditions that may shed light on the meaning of the rock images. In those parts of the world where rock art traditions have survived practically up to our own era, we nevertheless know a little about why people inscribed images on rocks. Perhaps we can use what knowledge we do have as a basis for comparison in order to interpret the rock art in Scandinavia?

Fragment of a reality

Traces of human activity in the past reflect an infinitesimal portion of the living reality that once existed. The archaeological remains – the man-made items that were used and the manner in which humans affected their physical environments – are the results of acts carried out by people. The finds, however, represent a small and random selection of the infinite number of acts that occurred in a given society, and as a rule, only a few small physical details for each act have been preserved up until the present time. We call these fragmentary, physical remnants of past actions material culture. Often items from the past are shrouded in mystery; they are different from things we have in our modern environment, while at the same time there is something familiar about them. By comparing the archaeological remains with items from the modern age or from the not-so-distant past, we can gain knowledge about how artefacts may have been used and about their meaning in the era to which they belonged. Comparisons can help us to understand how people in prehistoric times lived and how they organized their lives, as well as how people related to one another. Such explanatory frames of reference consist of analogies.

In dialogue with analogies

Extensive expeditions as part of the European colonization of other parts of the world during the 1700s and 1800s led to the documentation of other societies and the customs of native peoples through an increasing number of written ethnographic studies. These descriptions also contain information about the painted and carved images on rock panels and stones that so fascinated the early ethnographers. In the American continent, from the 1600s onwards, ethnographic and ethno-historical materials were compiled on the religions and use of symbols by indigenous people, including their association with rock art (Barnes 1982, Schaafsma 1992). In southern Africa, extensive studies were carried out into the customs, traditions and myths of the San Bushmen, and this material has been used by scholars today as an explanatory model for interpreting the many rock paintings in the same area (Lewis-Williams 1981). In Australia the myths of its indigenous inhabitants – the Aborigines – were recorded from the time the white settlers first arrived some 200 years ago, and ancient myths and conceptions that can be linked to the rich rock art artefacts on the Australian continent are still a living tradition today (Flood 1990).

We are never able to draw direct analogies between rock art in Norway and, for example, rock paintings made by the San Bushmen in southern Africa or those made by the Aborigines in Australia. However, the analogies can function both as corrective factors and as sources of inspiration when we wish to interpret the rock art in Scandinavia. The analogies demonstrate perhaps that rock art sites did not all have the same significance, nor were they used in the same manner. Some of them may have been sacred sites for only a few members of society. Some sites were possibly accessible only to women; others were restricted only to men, and still others were open to the population at large and were available to all members of the group. The images reveal much about mythology and notions of faith, about the relationships between women and men, about life and world-views, taboos and hierarchies. Some sites may have been part of rituals and cult events designed to establish a sense of community and belonging among the members of the group, or they may have been used in conjunction with education of young people, perhaps in order to usher them into the world of adults and inculcate the mysteries of life.

Analogies are able to show us how complex and ambiguous the meaning of the rock images may have been. The most frequently depicted animal figure in San rock art – the eland – may be associated, based on myths, to rituals as diverse as hunting initiations for young boys, girls' first menstruation, marriage ceremonies and the ceremonial dance of shamans (Lewis-Williams 1981). Could it be, perhaps, that the deer and sea mammals depicted in the Northern Scandinavian tradition also had as many alternative meanings? Analogies can also make us aware of what we should try to see in our own rock art – the traits in the images, the rock they are applied to and the context in which they are found, which in turn can help us to interpret the meaning behind them.

The complex context

The images on stone were produced and used in a living society. If we are to discover the meaning behind them, we need to study them in context with other traces of the same society. Interpretation must be based on the context of which the images are a part, as well as the patterns that the scant traces form in time and space.

An entire range of elements comprising the context in which rock art is found are important for interpretation: the form of the rock, the quartz veins that separate groups of figures, proximity to water, the vegetation around the site, the distance to other rock art sites, the burial mounds on the nearby hillside, the sacrificial site in the adjoining peat bog, the dwelling remnants a few hundred metres away, the view of a mountain peak or an island on the ocean horizon, the first rays of spring sunlight that fall on the exact rock art site. Or perhaps the sound of the nearby gushing waterfall provides a clue to the meaning of the rock art image, or maybe also the echo that is reflected off a mountain wall, or the sound made when a figure was pecked into the stone, or the pigment chosen to apply colour to an image.

The hidden traces

Remnants of human activity in the past are not always visible in the landscape. Hidden below the earth are accumulated remnants of dwellings, graves, discarded objects, tools and other materials that humans have left behind throughout the centuries, some perhaps surviving millennia, and which served either a specific purpose, such as sacrifices or votives to the gods, or were simply discarded, lost or forgotten. Archaeological excavations have also uncovered artefacts concealed in the ground close to or around the rock art sites. Objects, rubbish, hearths and layers of charcoal have been found. If such traces reflect activities in the area that were contemporary to the time the images were made, they can be an invaluable source of knowledge about both the age and meaning of the images themselves. Research into these types of cultural traces has only just begun. Few radiological datings (C_{14}) have been carried out, and we do not yet have a sufficient overview that allows us to date and interpret archaeological artefacts in the soil around rock art sites. Both the objects and the hearths may date from hundreds, perhaps thousands of years before or after the rock images were made. It is possible, for example, that it was the images themselves that attracted people to the site many generations after the symbolic meaning of the images was forgotten. Perhaps the strange, semi-eradicated symbols on the rock panels were explained as distant traces left behind by ancestors from the dawn of time?

In order to corroborate that rock images and archaeological remains in the soil near the rock art sites were contemporary in time, we have to be able to establish recurrent patterns – for example that certain traces of activities are repeatedly found near certain types of rock art. Or we might find objects that in all likelihood were used to make the rock images – for example tools used to peck rock carvings. With luck, these objects are found in layers of earth that can be dated, among other ways by using radiological dating of charcoal or other organic material. This in turn may result in a more precise dating for the rock art, giving us the opportunity to situate it within a chronological framework that coincides with the other cultural materials found. In this manner we also obtain a better basis for interpreting the society, religion and world-views of the people who created the rock art.

New knowledge gained through patterns

The search for meaningful patterns in the fragmentary body of traces from the past can be likened to the investigation of an unsolved crime. Each individual clue provides only a part of the overall solution. In order to be able to form a plausible notion of what actually happened, we collect and analyze the many small pieces of evidence and study how they interrelate. We need many concurrent observations to be able to discern a meaningful pattern. However, in contrast to solving a crime, the riddles of the past can never be fully solved. We never know if the more or less plausible explanations we propose result in a true solution to the riddle. More often than not, the questions that emerge outnumber the answers we are able to give. In many cases we are able to see patterns in rock art materials, but we are unable to interpret their meaning – perhaps because some of the pieces of the puzzle are missing and this defies interpretation of the whole.

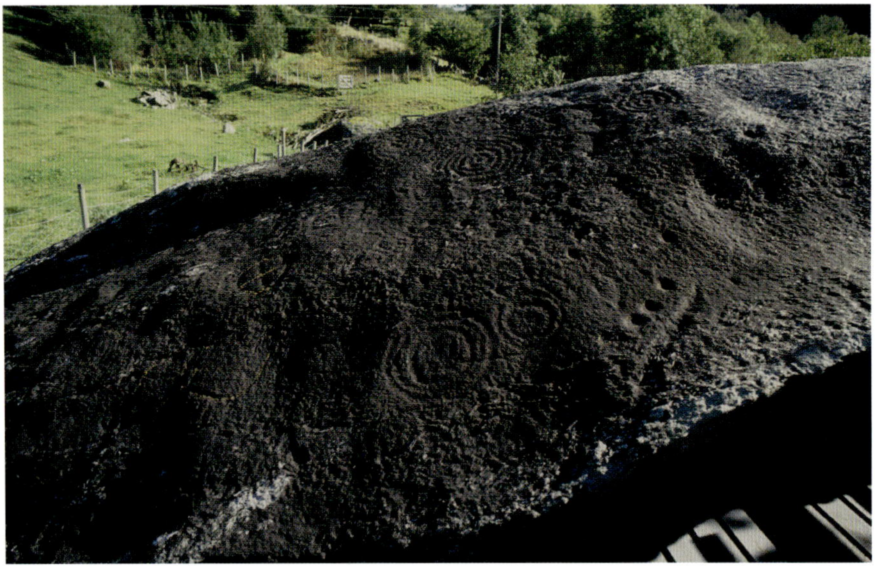

FIGURE 6. When slanted sunlight falls on the rock carvings of Duesteinen in Etne in Hordaland, the man-made lines of the images are clearly discernable. Slanted rays – in early morning or evening sunlight, or artificial light in darkness – bring out the relief created by the pecked grooves. With changing light, the images on the stone surface also change, giving the spectator the impression that the rock comes to life. This is a much more impressive experience than simply seeing a collection of figures highlighted in red paint and seemingly "glued" to the surface.
RU

For example, it is perplexing that rock art sites often occur in concentrations, while there are expansive surrounding areas in which one finds no rock art images, or perhaps only a few, sparse and scattered. We can speculate that the places containing many sites and figures were central gathering places where groups of people from a wide area assembled at certain times of the year. Another explanation may be that the stone images were not publicly shared, but were the domain of certain social groups or persons holding special religious or cult functions. Or perhaps it was events in society – crises, conflicts of interest and the like – that motivated people in specific areas to express themselves through rock art. It may also have been distinctive qualities of the landscape – mountain formations, proximity to water, communications junctions – that motivated people to create petroglyphs in exactly the places where we find them.

The rock panels that were chosen for rock art are also a frequent source of speculation. Some of the rock surfaces are covered with an abundance of figures, while large, even and smooth rock surfaces nearby do not have a single figure. What made the artists use only this one rock panel – perhaps over and over again? At other times, we find sites where the rock surface is so weathered and covered with pits and cracks that the images are scarcely visible. Why was this isolated rock panel so important that it was chosen for rock art even though the rock species – based on our present-day views – is of poor quality?

The meaningful rock

The manner in which the images appear on the rock panel can also be significant for interpretation. The images are ambiguous: we see them as indicative rather than as something absolute and comprehensible. At times it can be difficult to determine which marks on the stone's surface were man-made and which were created by natural forces, such as ice scouring. In many cases the creator of the image took advantage of the natural lines and incorporated them into the image, and it is possible that some of the lines and hollows in the surface were the very source of inspiration or reason why the figure was placed in the position where we find it on the rock panels.

Fluctuating light and weather conditions reinforce the ambiguity and elusiveness of the images: we see them, but at the same time we do not see them. In direct sunlight or when the sky is overcast it is often impossible to make out the images. Under oblique sunlight or artificial lighting at night, however, the rock images come alive: suddenly a multitude of figures appear on a previously void and barren rock surface. Lines that earlier were barely perceptible, or which perhaps could only be sensed with the fingertips, appear clearly and well defined, and it is easy to see the many chipping marks in the rock surface. But with an inopportune change in lighting the image disappears again, and the elusive nature of the medium once again takes the upper hand. Applying water, in addition to proper lighting, can coax an image into view from a seemingly barren rock surface. Beneath a veil of water the relief of the lines is reinforced and highlighted.

Was it perhaps intentional that the images should not be seen at any given time of day – by all people and in all situations? Maybe a shaman or priestess was meant to invoke them at sunset or by torchlight – or when life-giving rain ran over the surface of the stone? Perhaps all the images should not be seen together at the same time. The carved figures were undoubtedly easier to see when they were first cut into the stone, with clear-cut, light lines in contrast to the darker rock surface. Perhaps certain figures were re-carved so that they were made more visible on specific occasions – when special stories were to be told – whilst other figures went left un-retouched to recede, so to speak, into

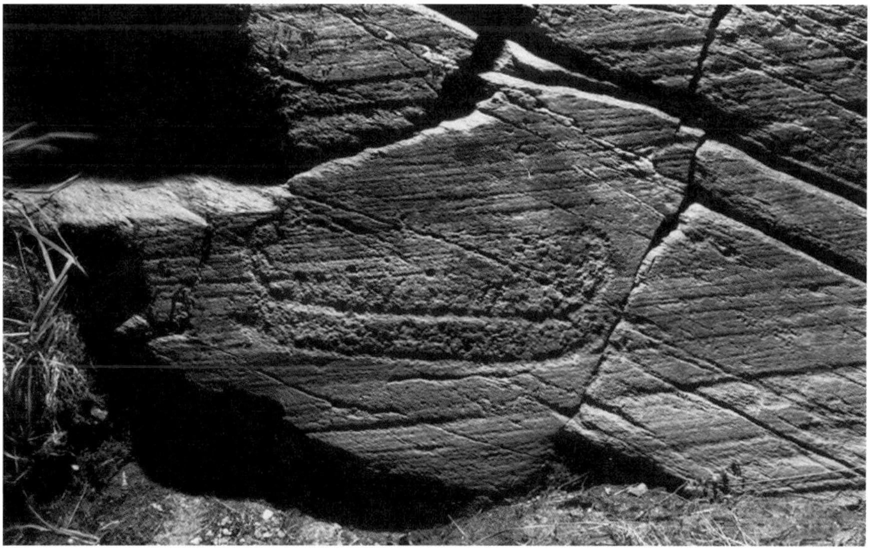

FIGURE 7. At the time the rock carvings were made, the grooves undoubtedly emerged as light lines against a darker rock surface. Time has worn down the figures, however, so that today it is often difficult to see them. By means of slanted light it is possible to make out the relief created by the grooves and bring the image into view. This boat image from Bakke in Jondal in Hordaland was discovered by chance some years ago on a late evening under slanting sunlight and was later photographed using artificial light at night.
JMG

the stone. In this way, some of the figures were possibly allowed to remain in the background for a time – until new stories were to be told, and the images reawakened.

The hundred tales

When we encounter a rock art site, we are filled with a sense of wonder, while at the same time feeling a sense of proximity to the artists who once carved or painted the images on the rock panels. Images in stone are spectacular and often beautiful; they appeal to our imagination and emotions. They tempt us to look into the past and to wonder about what people from a distant era believed, about how they regarded their own existences. It is no wonder, then, that rock art sites have become increasingly popular as tourist attractions and stops for tour operators. Images inscribed in stone have inspired artists. They have been the models for the logos that were designed for the Olympic Games hosted by Lillehammer in 1994, and for a large number of souvenirs designed on the many images borrowed from rock art sites.

A theoretical framework that entails a large number of topics, issues and debates characterizes the status of research on rock art at the turn of the millennium. New issues, new methods making it possible to understand what archaeologists do when they interpret traces from our past, and how they do what they do, have opened a fascinating and wide-ranging – but perhaps also highly complex – field of prehistoric research. Re-thinking and experimentation are applauded, and the boundaries between professional fields are becoming increasingly diffuse.

We do not know what different kinds of stories were told at the many different rock art sites. Perhaps some of the stories were associated with special events or activities, whilst other stories were told on other occasions? In our own time both professionals and laymen tell stories at the rock art sites. They are most certainly not the same tales that were told in the distant past. But the stories we tell are the best we can relate, based on our sparse knowledge of the past.

The stories we tell in this book

The rock art sites that we present in this book, as well as the stories we will tell, represent a voyage in time and space – from the oldest images to the youngest, from very north to the very south of Norway. The sites are chosen with consideration for the many, varied archaeological issues associated with dating and interpretation of the rock art. We have chosen to focus on areas with concentrations of sites and to include examples of isolated and more unobtrusive panels. Each of these illustrates in its own way the differences and similarities in the wide range of rock art. We highlight tales of discoveries that illustrate how chance often plays a decisive role when new rock art sites are found. We also include stories and traditions that are associated with some of the sites.

FIGURE 8. Postglacial Chronology of Norway. Please note the differences between Northern and Southern Norway in both chronological periods and terms e.g. Early and Late Stone Age *vs* Mesolithic and Neolithic, and Early Metal Age *vs* Bronze Age. The timetable for Northern Norway is based on Olsen (1994) in combination with Hesjedal *et al.* (1996), and the timetable for Southern Norway is based on Bergsvik (2002).

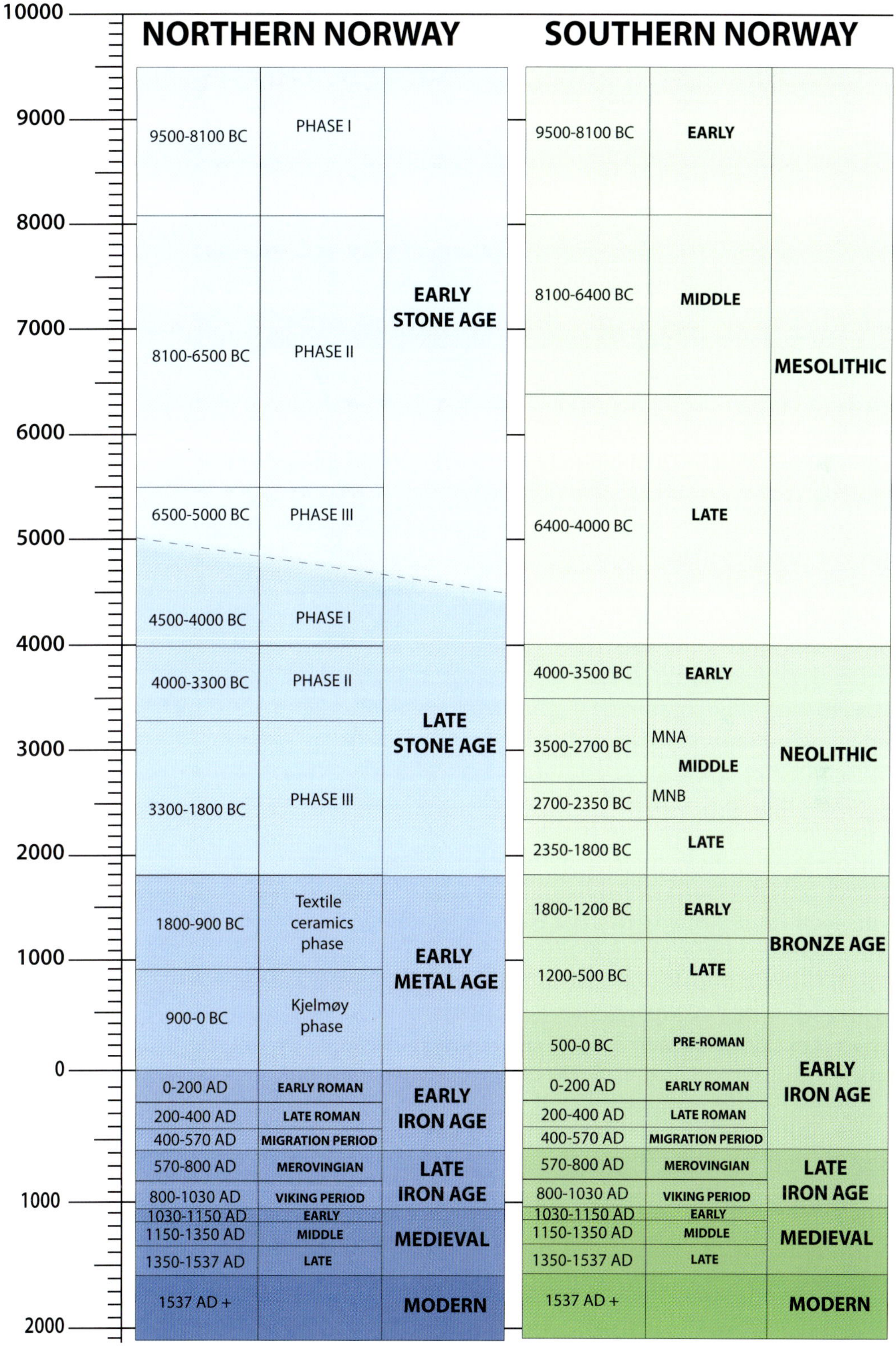

10000
9000
8000
7000
6000
5000
4000
3000
2000
1000
0
1000
2000
NORTHERN NORWAY
9500-8100 BC
PHASE I
8100-6500 BC
PHASE II
6500-5000 BC
PHASE III
EARLY STONE AGE
4500-4000 BC
PHASE I
4000-3300 BC
PHASE II
3300-1800 BC
PHASE III
LATE STONE AGE
1800-900 BC
Textile ceramics phase
900-0 BC
Kjelmøy phase
EARLY METAL AGE
0-200 AD
EARLY ROMAN
200-400 AD
LATE ROMAN
400-570 AD
MIGRATION PERIOD
EARLY IRON AGE
570-800 AD
MEROVINGIAN
800-1030 AD
VIKING PERIOD
LATE IRON AGE
1030-1150 AD
EARLY
1150-1350 AD
MIDDLE
1350-1537 AD
LATE
MEDIEVAL
1537 AD +
MODERN
SOUTHERN NORWAY
9500-8100 BC
EARLY
8100-6400 BC
MIDDLE
6400-4000 BC
LATE
MESOLITHIC
4000-3500 BC
EARLY
3500-2700 BC
MNA
MIDDLE
2700-2350 BC
MNB
2350-1800 BC
LATE
NEOLITHIC
1800-1200 BC
EARLY
1200-500 BC
LATE
BRONZE AGE
500-0 BC
PRE-ROMAN
0-200 AD
EARLY ROMAN
200-400 AD
LATE ROMAN
400-570 AD
MIGRATION PERIOD
EARLY IRON AGE
570-800 AD
MEROVINGIAN
800-1030 AD
VIKING PERIOD
LATE IRON AGE
1030-1150 AD
EARLY
1150-1350 AD
MIDDLE
1350-1537 AD
LATE
MEDIEVAL
1537 AD +
MODERN

There is no definite knowledge of archaeological material existing from the Paleolithic within the geographical area that today comprises Norway. During the Late Ice Age, most of Scandinavia was covered with ice that gradually melted but did not make it possible to live here until some 11,000 years ago. As a result, our oldest known archaeological remnants date from the Mesolithic. It is important to note, however, that in Nordland and Troms, amongst other places in the Salten and Ofoten areas, there are large concentrations of limestone caves which are hundreds of thousands of years old and in which fauna material has been found that is much older, including the skeleton of a bear some 120,000 years old (Lauritzen *et al.* 1996). This opens the theoretical possibility that in time, traces of human beings may be found in these caves, and perhaps even rock art dating from a period of time prior to the Mesolithic. Although the oldest archaeological remnants are some 11,000 years old, it is presently unclear how far back in time we can date our oldest known rock art, but it is assumed that the polished rock art in Nordland may perhaps be traced back as far as the Early or Middle Mesolithic. From the Late Mesolithic and onwards, there appears to be a dramatic increase in occurrences of rock art of the Northern Tradition, primarily depicting large mammals – a tradition that seems to have continued into the Neolithic. From the end of the Neolithic, the Northern Tradition appears to have been succeeded by the rock art of the Southern Tradition, which results in an entirely different pictorial expression, featuring boats, circles, spirals and cup marks.

The selected viewpoints, explanatory models and dating methods that we present are products of our own interest in research, and they are in part based on studies of rock art found in other parts of the world. Rock art research is international in scope in the sense that theoretical and methodical references and approaches are common throughout the world, while theories and methods must at the same time be applied to the specific regions, sites and images.

In this book we provide more questions than answers. Some of these questions can perhaps be answered through more detailed analyses of the rock art and the local context of which it is a part. Other questions will never be able to be answered, because the past as it existed will forever remain elusive to us. Despite all of the challenges that rock art presents, despite our lack of certainty, despite the fact that we are unable to provide answers, we nonetheless allow ourselves to be fascinated by the past and the stories we are able to create, based on the scant and scattered materials that have been discovered.

The World Heritage Site in Alta

At the head of Altafjord in Finnmark is the largest group of hunting art sites known in Norway. Most of the figures were not discovered until well into the 1970s, and research on the rock art in this area therefore began relatively recently. Nonetheless, comprehensive documentation has been completed. The oldest sites and figures are well over 6000 years old, whilst the youngest are barely 2000 years old. In all likelihood the rock images were left behind by a nomadic population that subsisted on hunting, trapping and fishing, or by groups living in the surrounding areas who gathered here at regular or irregular intervals. The figures on the individual subfields are very similar to each other, a fact that suggests they were not carved by random visitors. They were more likely created by a chosen few who had exclusive rights to make images in rock. The motifs are largely four-legged animals, such as reindeer and bear, in addition to figures of humans, fish, boats, tools and geometric patterns. The figures occur either in isolation or as parts of a larger context. Although it is tempting to see the images as direct denotations of hunting and fishing, it is just as likely that the motifs represent mythological, spiritual or religious conceptions.

The discovery

The very first rock art site in the Altafjord area was discovered in 1950 when a small stone block was uncovered by a farmer's plough in a field at Langnes, situated some distance out along the fjord. Following this discovery, a number of rock art images were found during the 1960s on a vertical mountain wall in Transfarelvdalen farther into the fjord basin. During the 1970s discoveries became more frequent. In 1973 the rock carvings at Storsteinen in Bossekop and the rock paintings in Jiebmaluokta/Hjemmeluft were discovered. Both sites are located near the town centre at Alta. In 1977 figures were also found near the centre of Amtmannsneset, and in 1978 in Altafjord, at the head of the narrow Kåfjord (Helskog 1988). At steady intervals, new figures have been discovered, particularly at Amtmannsnes and at Jiebmaluokta/Hjemmeluft. In 1998 yet another block of stone was discovered at Langnesholmen, and as recently as 2000 several painted panels were found in Tollevik by the Komsa Mountain, between Amtmannsnes and Bossekop. Other recent discoveries include several rock paintings in Transfarelvdalen (Simonsen 1969). Apart from the two stone blocks mentioned above, all of the discovered sites are located at the head of Altafjord. Several of the localities display striking similarities in terms of

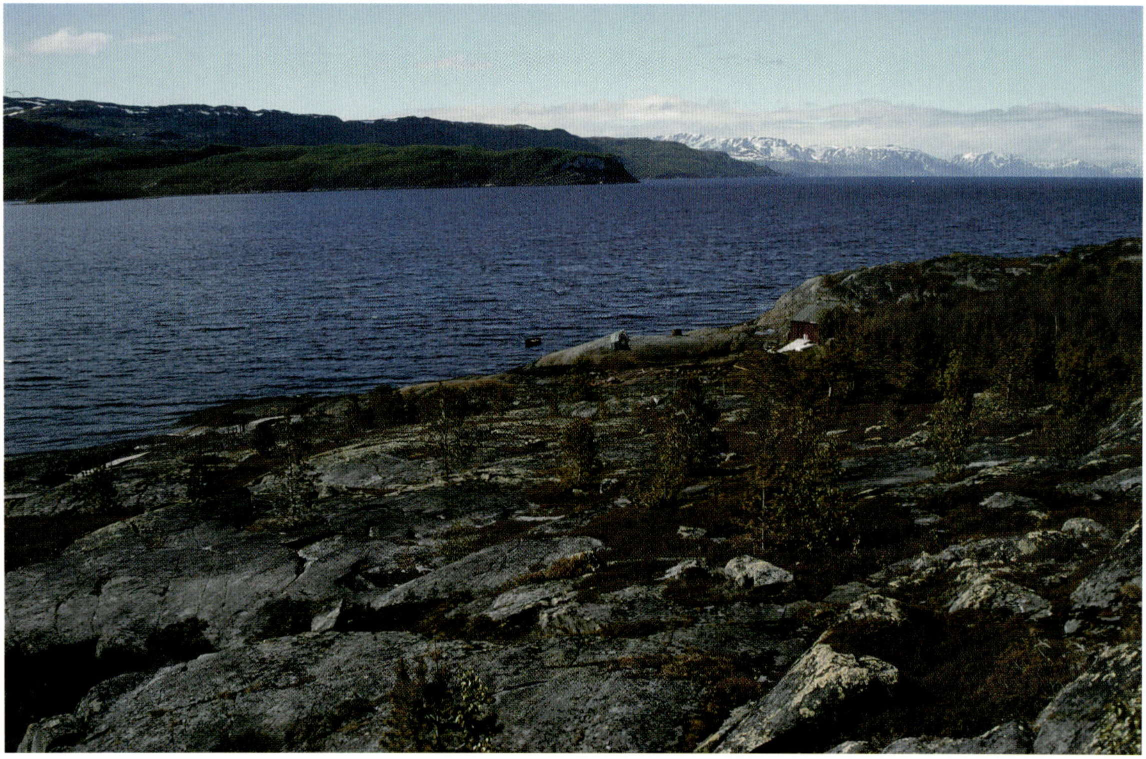

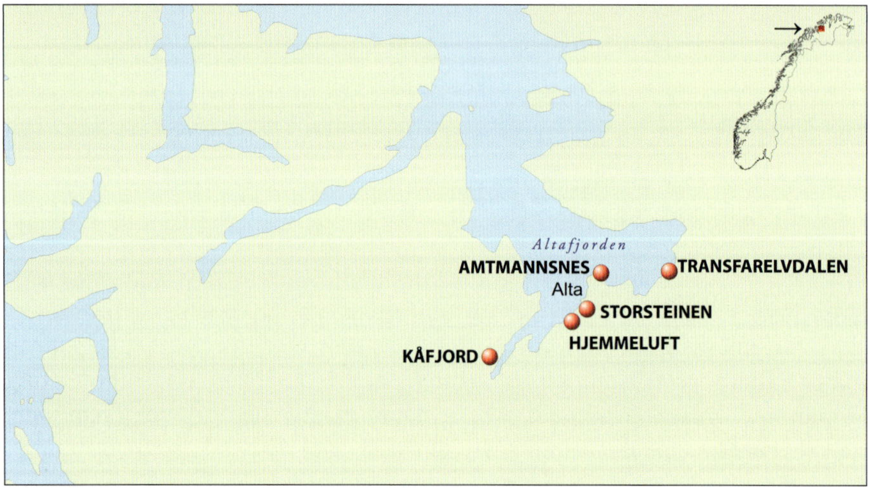

FIGURES 9–10. The sites in the World Heritage area are all located deep inside the Altafjord basin. *Above*: The eastern side of Jiebmaluokta/Hjemmeluft with a panorama of Altafjord.
MAP AI, ILLUSTRATION TL

individual figures, choice of motifs and composition of motifs, whilst others have few or no common characteristics. With the exception of the paintings in Transfarelvdalen, all of the figures in all of the sites were created by point chiselling, probably using a sharpened stone of a harder type than the base rock, to form the lines of the figure with countless chisel marks made on the surface of the stone. In many places we can see that the chisel marks differ, probably caused by the fact that the tools used had to be constantly re-sharpened or replaced with new ones. This resulted in the chisel marks being of a somewhat different nature as the figures took shape.

UNESCO

In 1985 the fields that had been discovered up to that time in Altafjord were included as the fourth Norwegian cultural monument on UNESCO's World Heritage List. Taken together, the site represents the largest concentration of rock art associated with prehistoric hunting societies in Northern Europe. The World Heritage site comprises a total of five areas where rock art was discovered, all of which are in the Altafjord basin: Jiebmaluokta/Hjemmeluft, Storsteinen, Amtmannsnes, Transfarelv and Kåfjord. Along with the rock art in Tanum, Bohuslän in Sweden, this is the only Scandinavian rock art site to be included on the UNESCO list, which altogether has about 878 areas (September 2008) characterized as distinctive cultural and natural heritage sites in the world. Other rock art areas in Europe on the World Heritage List are found in Portugal, Spain and Italy. Inclusion on UNESCO's list is an acknowledgement that the cultural monuments are particularly important in a global context. The rock art in Alta shares this feature with six other cultural monument areas in Norway: *Røros Mining Town, Urnes Stave Church, Bryggen, Vegaøyan – The Vega Archipelago, Struve Geodetic Arc, Western Norwegian Fjords – Geirangerfjord and Nærøyfjord.*

Transfarelv

In 1966, Tromsø Museum was informed that a number of rock paintings existed at the bottom of the Transfarelv valley, some kilometres to the northeast of central Alta (Simonsen 1969). The valley is quite narrow, beginning at the head of Rafsbotn and stretching due east and upwards towards the open plain. At the mouth of the valley, not far from the fjord and only some 20 m above sea level, the first figures were discovered on a vertical mountain wall. The figures were well known by local residents, but were now made known to the general public. There were a number of figures on the mountain wall representing human and animal figures, as well as some shaded areas. All of them were well sheltered, since the mountain wall slants outwards and creates a natural, protective overhang sheltering the figures from precipitation. Many of the figures are somewhat indistinct and blurred, and it is difficult to determine what they represent. All of the figures are painted in a reddish colour, most likely iron oxide mixed with substances that served as binding agents for the pigment. They are painted with finger-thick lines, and it is likely that hands and figures were indeed used to apply the paint. By the 1960s, these line figures had already been compared with the strikingly similar rock paintings at Kjeøya in Troms and the cave paintings in Solsemhola and Fingalshola in Nord-Trøndelag.

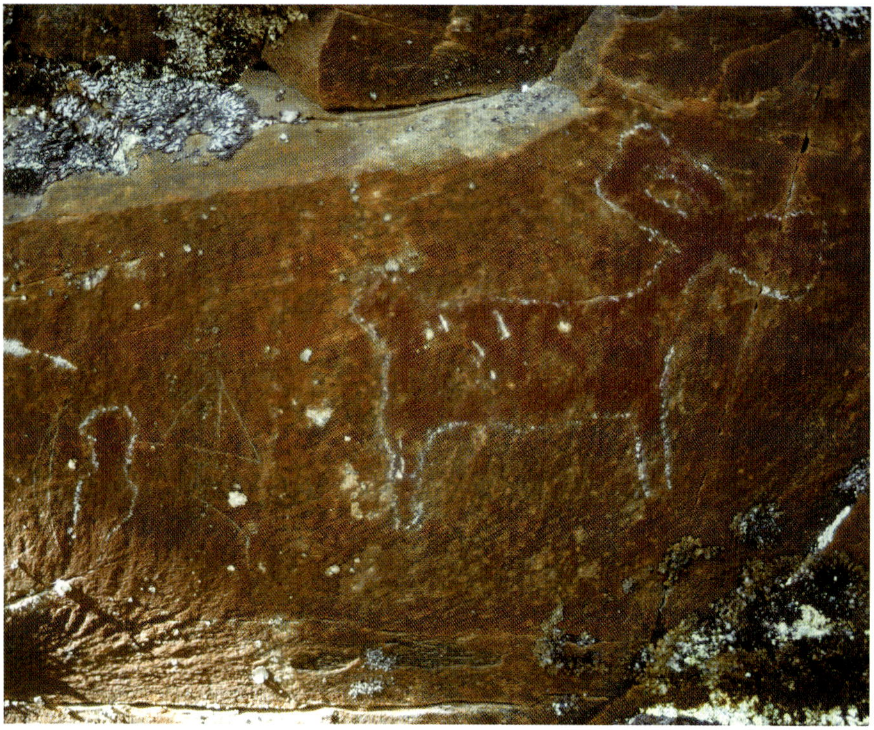

FIGURE 11. Painted image on a sheer rock wall with an overhang in Transfarelvdalen.
AK

During the following years more figures were found a little further up in the valley, consisting of both geometric motifs and depictions of animals. As recently as 2002 and 2003, even more figures were discovered. There are close to 50 figures concentrated in the area, but it is likely that there are many more higher up in the craggy valley strewn with boulders and scree. Images of this kind are normally dated to a period from 2000 BC up to the beginning of the Christian calendar. The line figures are notably similar to the many human figures that are found in the caves along the coast of Nordland County and Nord-Trøndelag (Bjerck 1995).

More recently, painted animal figures have been found among other places in Northern Sweden, which date from a much earlier era and are interesting in terms of comparison with the images in the Transfarelv valley. Datings reveal that these rock paintings may be as much as 5000 years old (Lindgren 2002). The implications for Altafjord are that there may have been concurrent traditions for both painting and carving images. The reasons why these images were localised in this particular valley are of course an open question, but it seems that rock paintings were not as rare as previously thought. They are often difficult to see, and it is only in recent times, with an increasing focus on this category of rock art, that more and more panels containing painted figures have been discovered throughout Norway.

Storsteinen (The Great Rock)

Events took a new turn in 1973, with the discovery of the rock carvings at Storsteinen. In this year a professional blaster was hired to assess the removal of a potentially dangerous boulder in Bossekop at Apanes, situated to the west of Alta's city centre. The boulder was considered a threat to two gardens in a residential section, and was to be removed. The blaster surveyed the boulder thoroughly in order to assess how best to remove it without causing damage to the adjacent houses, and in the process he came across several carved figures on the top of the stone. He then turned down the job, notified Tromsø Museum, and the boulder was kept intact. Today it is incorporated into one of the two residential gardens, and with its height and volume, truly lives up to its name [The Great Rock]. It stands two to three meters high and has a surface area of well over 60 m^2. Further investigation revealed that it has between 500 and 600 figures on its surface (Helskog 1988). Most of them were found on top of the stone, but there are also a few on the side of the rock. On the top there is a profusion of figures that are carved close to one another, and some overlapping others. They are mainly depictions of reindeer and elk, but also include human figures and geometric patterns. One of the most curious depictions is a human figure that appears to be riding a reindeer. This trait is paralleled in other places in Norway, including Vingen and Ausevik, Western Norway, where several human figures are depicted riding animals that have been interpreted as representing red deer.

The rock carvings that are carved on Storsteinen give the impression of being a part of an epic scene that may once have taken place, or of a mythological, imaginary world and framework of perception that has been visualised and made more tangible. The figures find their parallels at Amtmannsnes and Jiebmaluokta/Hjemmeluft, and they are estimated to date from the period between 4200 and 1800 BC.

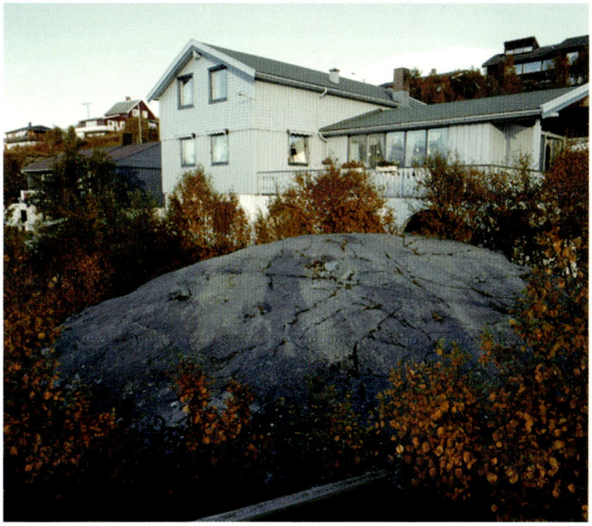

FIGURE 12. A huge stone outcrop, known as Storsteinen (the Great Rock). It is also difficult to photograph, and when the photographer climbed on top of the neighbouring garage with the sun behind him, his shadow was cast on the stone.
AK

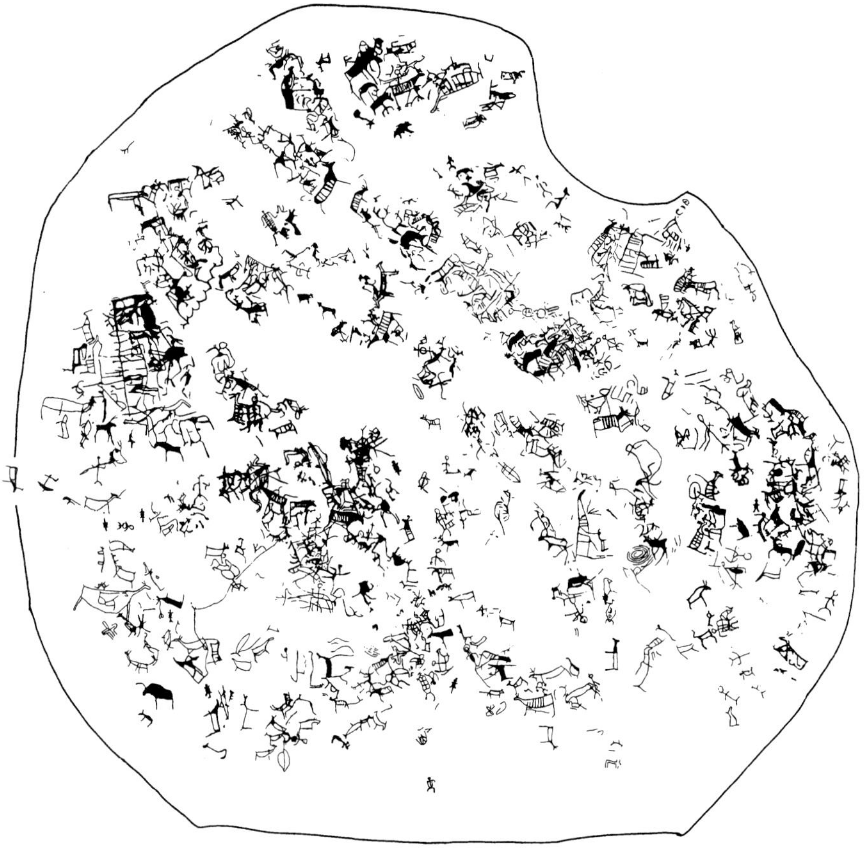

FIGURE 13. Storsteinen contains some 600 figures. They are part of what could be referred to as a gigantic scene.
KH

Jiebmaluokta/Hjemmeluft

Just after the figures on The Great Rock became known to the public, many new discoveries were made around a wide, open bay farther west along the shoreline from Bossekop. The bay is known as *Jiebmaluokta* in Sami, or by the Norwegian name Hjemmeluft. Here the figures appeared in the evening sunlight, beneath uprooted trees, on open rock panels, often in places frequented for decades by people who never saw them (*ibid.*). The discovery of the figures on The Great Rock had made people aware of the potential presence of other carvings in stone, and more conscious of what they could look for. It is also interesting to note that the archaeologist Anders Nummedal, who, in the late 1920s, was responsible for comprehensive archaeological excavations throughout Norway, had already completed one of his dwelling site investigations in precisely this area. The excavation was carried out very close to one of the extensive rock carving fields in the bay, but he did not discover any of the rock images here. As is often the case, it is frequently perceptive and attentive laymen who make important discoveries, and this will be amply illustrated in other chapters in this book.

Jiebmaluokta/Hjemmeluft may be generally described as a relatively wide bay located on the western outskirts of the town of Alta, at the foot of Skoddevarre

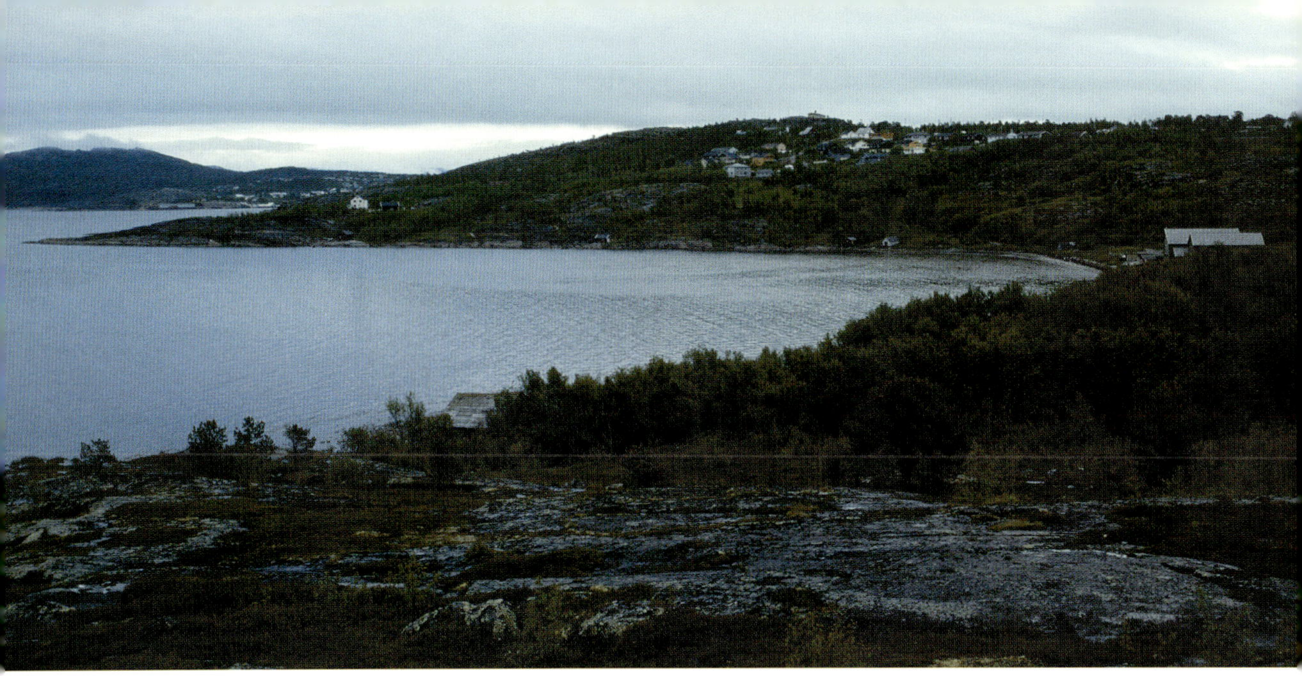

FIGURE 14 *(above)*. Jiebmaluokta/ Hjemmeluft, the site of large concentrations of rock images on both sides of the bay, at a height of between 26 and 8 metres above sea level.

TL

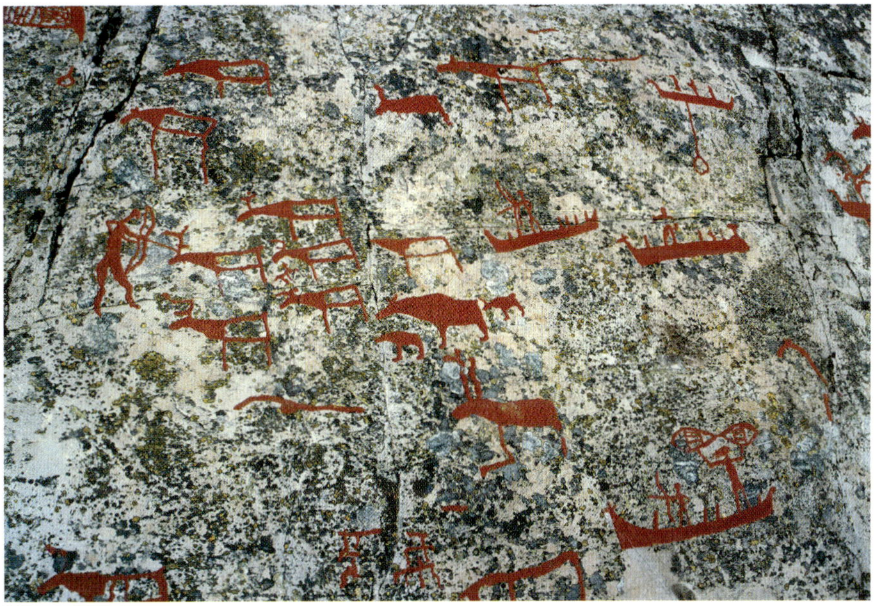

FIGURE 15 *(right)*. One of the many scenes found in Jiebmaluokta/ Hjemmeluft that may be depictions of specific events in prehistoric time, or visualisations of mythology.

TL

Mountain. The area containing rock art is delineated by the Altafjord on the northern side and Europe Route 6 to the south. The bay is located more or less centrally in the inner, quite broad head of the fjord. There is also a good panorama out along the entire fjord, with views to the islands in the north, to Stjernøya and Seiland. This area is characterized by coastal rocky slopes and rocky knolls interspersed with grassy and heath-covered flatlands. The entire area is covered with deciduous and pine woodlands, which in some areas are quite dense. In this area more than 2000 carved figures are known to exist, concentrated within subfields at various altitudes on both sides of the bay (Helskog 1988). The most common motifs are animal and human figures, as well as depictions of boats. The predominant animal species are reindeer, elk and bear, as well as isolated figures of birds and fish. The human figures are depicted either alone or together with animal figures, in what we may interpret as hunting scenes or ritualistic ceremonies. The human figures are also involved in other types of social interactions that have been interpreted as dances or ritualistic performances. The boat figures are with or without crews, and occur in groups or alone, in what may be interpreted as hunting or fishing scenes. Together with these motifs, there are abstract patterns in the form of linear networks and wavy patterns, as well as figures that are difficult to identify and interpret.

On many of the panels, it seems that bears are the centre of attention, often depicted migrating from their dens to other areas, with footprint markings in the form of small circular points chiselled into the rock. The footprints cover great distances. These depictions appear to emulate the seasonal progression from the time the bear leaves its den in the spring up until it goes into hibernation underground during the late autumn (Helskog 1999). Sami ethnography teaches us that bear have functioned as links between the superficial world and the underworld. Still in the modern historical era, there are many notions associated with bears. Examining other sources, mythological conceptions and not least history itself, we find many references associated with bears, the way they can be hunted, and generally how humans relate to them. These notions are interesting to assess in relation to modern conceptions.

The rock art at Hjemmeluft/Jiebmaluokta can undoubtedly be closely associated with the prehistoric shoreline level, a factor that makes it possible to date the art in relation to land upheaval that has occurred since the first Ice Age and up until the present day. The rock carvings are delineated within four defined and separate elevation levels, which each display stylistic and formal similarities between about 8 and some 26 meters above the current sea level. These differences in elevation are separated from one another by broad zones that do not contain rock carvings. What supports the concurrence between rock art and the prehistoric shoreline levels is that the stylistic traits correspond with the same elevation above sea level

FIGURE 16. Two bears from Jiebmaluokta/Hjemmeluft. In slanted sunlight they are clearly visible.
TL

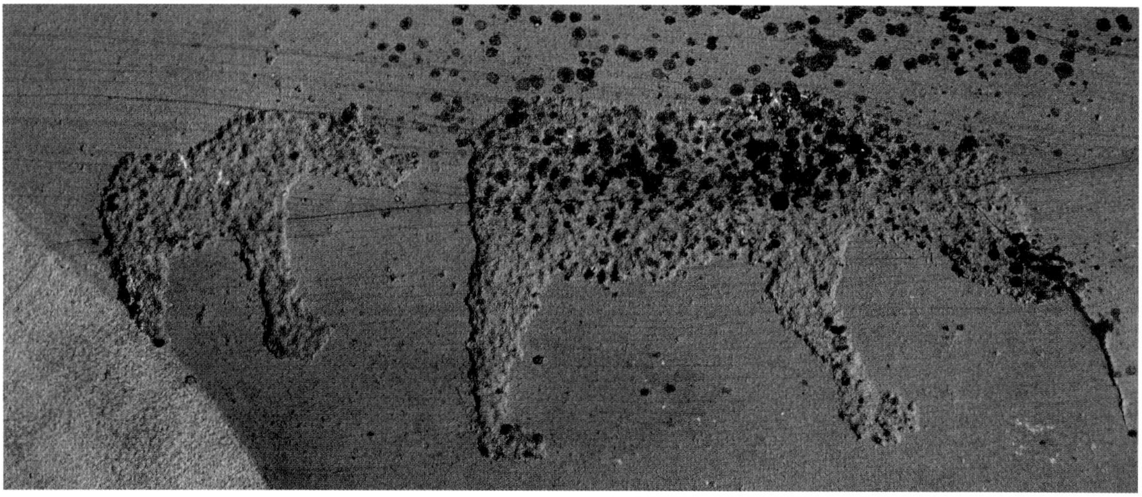

on both sides of the bay (Helskog 1988). We can therefore deduce that the rock art was created on rock panels near the water whilst the rock was barren and not covered by lichens, moss and vegetation. As the earth rose in relation to sea level, the rock art was elevated further and further up from the shoreline. Based on geological shoreline displacement data and the probability that the oldest rock carvings lie at the highest elevations, we have attempted to place the rock images at Hjemmeluft in chronological phases. The chronology for rock art in Alta has been revised recently, and appears to be dividable into five separate phases:

Phase 1: 4200 to 3300 BC
Phase 2: 3300 to 1800 BC
Phase 3. 1800 to 800 BC.
Phase 4: 900 to 100 BC
Phase 5: 100 BC to 200 AD. (After Helskog 2000)

In the vicinity of the rock art, a series of archaeological excavations and test investigations have revealed materials and tools from a prehistoric settlement that dates from the same period as the rock art. Several dwelling features are also known to exist in the area and can be chronologically situated, based on their elevation above sea level, their shape and size, to coincide in all likelihood with one of the phases mentioned above, or to those indicated in the table below.

FIGURE 17. The chronological development of rock images in Alta can be divided into five phases. KH

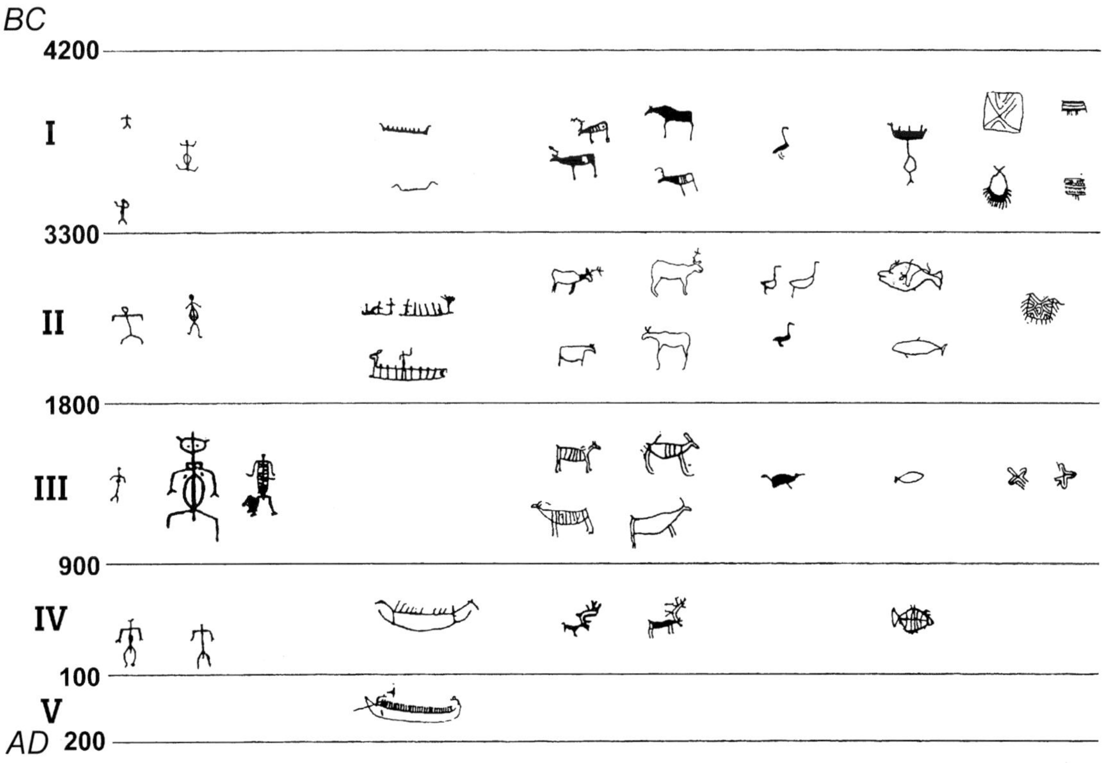

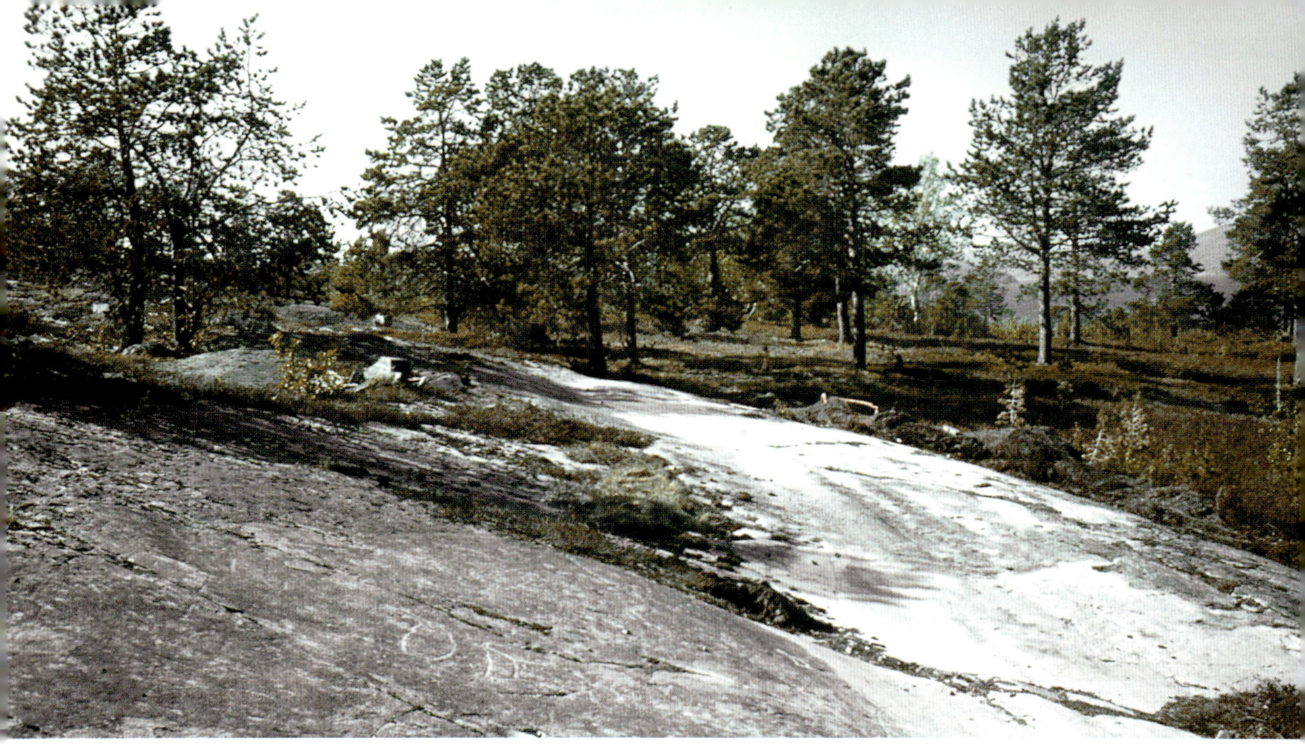

Amtmannsnes

FIGURE 18. The rock-faces with images here at Amtmannsnes are extremely worn and weathered.

TM

In 1977 another panel of rock carvings was discovered at Amtmannsneset on the eastern side of Komsa Mountain, directly north of the town of Alta. The following year yet another panel was found in the same place. The figures are very weathered, obscure and difficult to identify. Altogether there are more than 600 figures here, and they are clearly different from those of the other Alta fields (Helskog 1988). There are numerous prominent human figures, although the majority are animal figures. All of the human figures are quite different. At least one is depicted with an animal in its stomach. Some researchers have situated this within a mythological context that may serve to explain why animals are so frequently depicted in rock carvings. One of the explanations that has been put forward is that there was a common conception among the creators of the images that both humans and animals, in this case probably reindeer, were born of a common female progenitor (Engelstad 2001). Similar notions of common origins for both people and animals are known from ethnographic studies. This underpins the mythological interpretation of certain animal figures, and explains by extension the role and place they held in rock carving sites. In this respect, the creators of the images attempted to interpret, explain and understand the roles and positions of the animals and humans in relation to one another at a given contemporary point in time.

The rock carvings are located between 14 and 17 meters above sea level. Based on what we know about land emergence, the rock art here – assuming it was carved just near the shoreline zone – would have been created around 1800 BC (Berg 2003). However, in the case of Amtmannsnes we do not have a localization in relation to the shoreline that is as convincing as that of Jiebmaluokta/Hjemmeluft. Furthermore, the composition of the Amtmannsnes images is so particular that

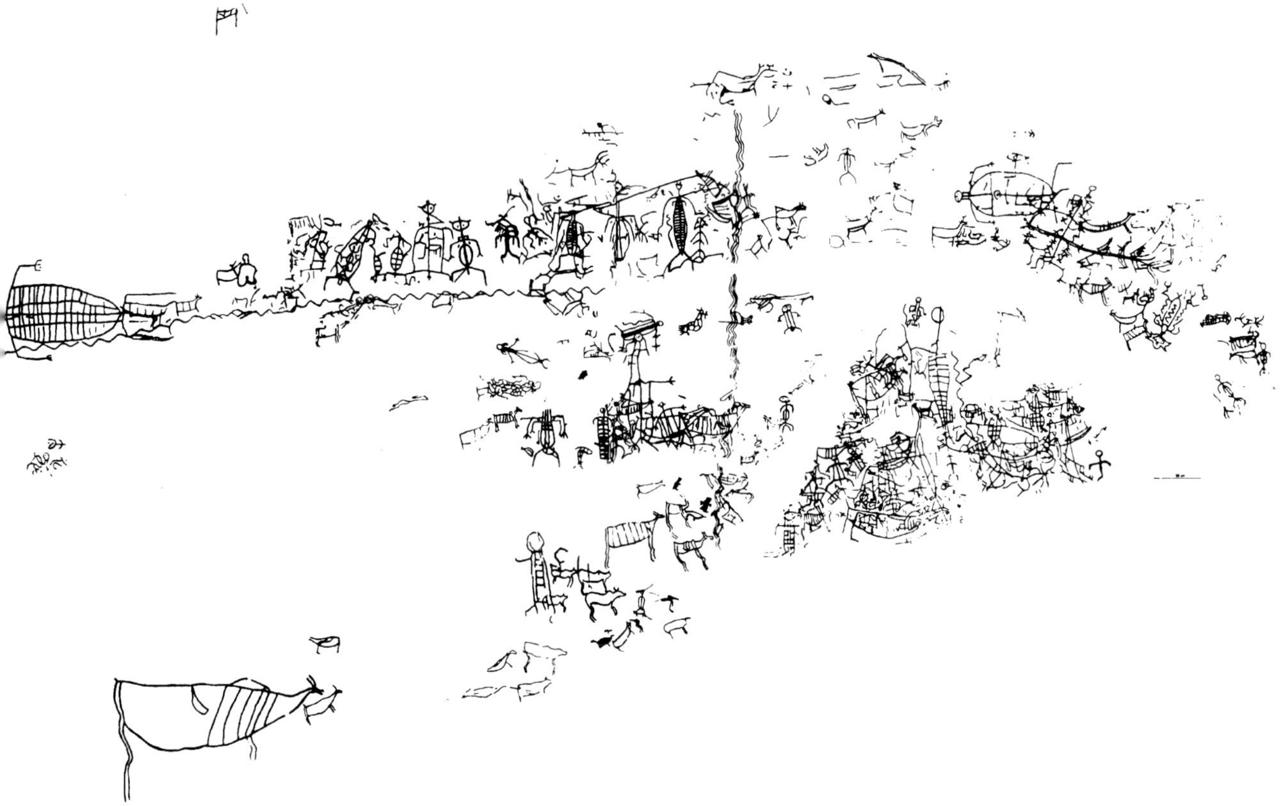

FIGURE 19. The numerous human figures at Amtmannsnes are particularly stunning.
KH

it has been difficult to find a basis for comparison in other places, although it has been argued that some of the figures have parallels at Storsteinen. Another dating method is to associate the carvings with remnants of settlements found just below the panel, which are estimated to date from 1800 BC. The dating of these settlement traces, however, is also uncertain, which in turn entails the possibility that the images may be even younger. It has been argued that they may date from a later era, perhaps as late as about 900 BC (*ibid*).

Today it is extremely difficult to identify the figures at Amtmannsneset. They have been exposed to weathering and wear from both grazing animals and vehicle traffic. It has even been documented that vehicles with studded tyres have driven over the rock. In order to gain an insight into the many images that were carved here, comprehensive and detailed studies have been required, during which it has been necessary to use chalk and oblique lighting – both artificial and natural – in order to highlight the lines and relief in the rock and thereby retrace the composition. Finally the images were traced on foil and photographically reduced to a workable size.

Kåfjord

In the same year when the last panel was discovered at Amtmannsneset, yet another panel was found in Kåfjord, inside Altafjord. In contrast to Amtmannsnes, many of the same styles and types of figures as those found in Hjemmeluft were present in Kåfjord, associated to both the oldest period and to the subsequent period (Helskog 1988). Taken together, this would indicate that the tradition of carving images in Kåfjord stretches from 4200 to 1800 BC. Here we find herds of reindeer, large images of bears, and also human figures wearing snowshoes and carrying tools. The size of the field in Kåfjord has not yet been determined, since we assume that there are many more figures still beneath the turf. Major efforts made in recent years to survey and document this area have led to the discovery of individual figures that currently number around 1000.

Making the World Heritage Area accessible to the public

The rock art in Alta is the only prehistoric cultural monument of the four Norwegian sites on UNESCO's list. From the five areas in Alta that comprise the World Heritage site, only Jiebmaluokta/Hjemmeluft has been made accessible to the public. Efforts have also been made to provide visitors with the best possible insight into the numerous periods that are represented by the images. The site has been adapted with walkways that lead the many thousands of visitors through the area in a way that leaves the rock carvings completely undisturbed. If visitors keep to the walkways from one field to the next, following the posted signs and using the guide folder (printed in several languages) along the way, the tour provides a proper introduction to the rock art found in the area. There are also professional guides who speak a number of languages. In the early 1990s a museum building with exhibits was opened, providing visitors with an insight into the scope and size of the World Heritage area, the age of the images and explanations of what they may represent. These measures have helped to reduce to an absolute minimum the urge vistors may have to explore the area on their own. By making the area accessible to the public, it has been possible to keep other, more vulnerable sites safe from traffic, and thereby preserve them for the future. The strategy of focusing on just one area, Jiebmaluokta/ Hjemmeluft, has played an important role in protecting the other sites.

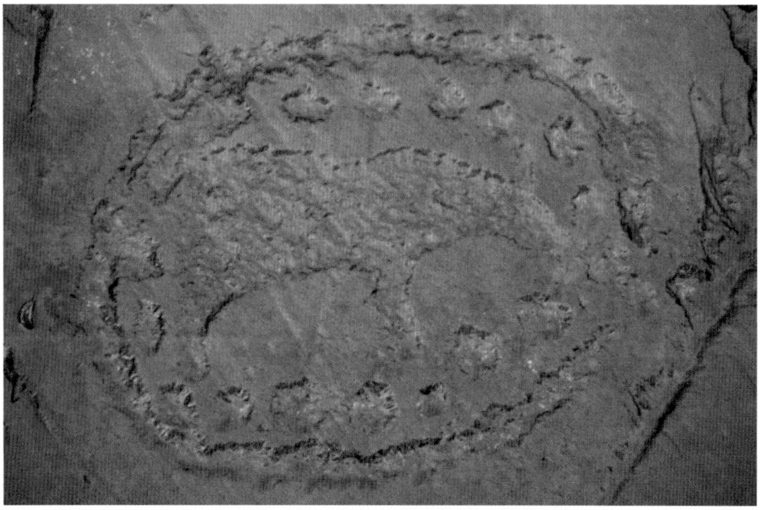

FIGURE 20. A moistened rock surface in Kåfjord, where a bear is encircled by pawprints around the den.

TL

Aldon in Varanger

Close to the northernmost point of Finnmark, at the very top of Norway, there is a small field of rock carvings. The rock images that are located on the distinctive Aldon Ridge in Unjárga gielda/ Nesseby municipality on Varangerfjord can by no means be called particularly spectacular in terms of numbers, since only two small four-legged animal figures are known to exist. Nor can they be conveniently placed in any one stylistic tradition known from other parts of Finnmark, Northern Norway or elsewhere in Scandinavia, and this presents a challenge in terms of finding other figures with which they may be compared. One peculiarity is the fact that the rock images are located at an unusually high elevation. At the same time it is more difficult to relate them to earlier shorelines and to defined time periods. Interpretation is made even more complicated by the fact that we lack archaeological finds in the vicinity that might otherwise be related to the images and thus allow us to deduce a larger cultural and historical context for their occurrence. Nevertheless, what is unique about Aldon is that written references exist revealing that sacrificial ceremonies were held on the summit of the ridge (Vorren and Eriksen 1993), and this permits an entirely new comprehension of what this rock art may have represented.

Location

Aldon is best described as a pronounced plateau located deep within the northern side of Varangerfjord, about five kilometres east of Varangerbotn (Simonsen 1970). Between the villages of Gornitak and Bunes is the mouth of the Mesk River, or *Alddajohka*, as it is also known. The summit of Aldon is located on the eastern side of the river about one kilometre from the fjord. The ridge slopes gradually upwards from the fjord side, but towards the summit it becomes steeper and almost impossible to climb. Approaches from the other side are considerably less steep, but still challenging enough to make it difficult for climbers whose goal is to reach the summit. Deciduous woods and undergrowth cover the slope towards the summit and appear to increasingly dominate the landscape. On the rear side and below the summit, the woods form an even and continuous ground cover that gradually rises northward towards the barren plain further along the Varanger peninsula. A hollow in this vegetation reveals the meandering Mesk River curving through the fjord basin. From the summit where the rock art is located, one becomes aware of the fact that the steady murmur of the river competes with the pervasive noise of today's traffic from the main road along the fjord. The presence

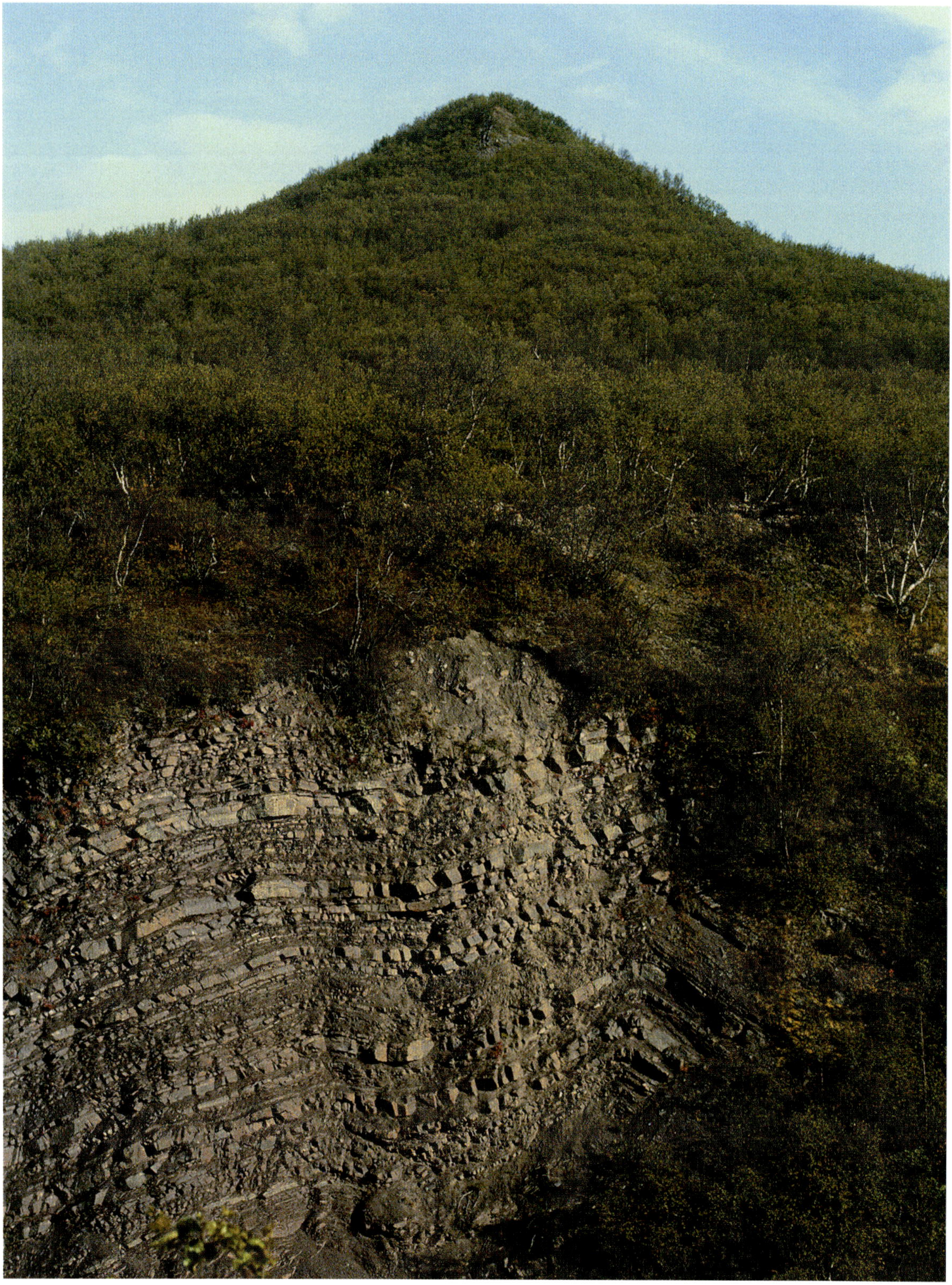

of power lines has also strongly marred the slope down towards the fjord and stand in garish contrast to the respect people in previous eras must have had for both the rock images and for Aldon in general. From the plateau on the summit there is an open and wide panorama out across the otherwise low-lying landscape within the Varangerfjord basin. From here it is possible to see many of the areas known for concentrations of cultural monuments dating from the Stone Age and from the Sami Iron Age, but also from the Middle Ages and Modern era. Towards the west there is a view down to the Varanger basin, and to the south and southeast the elongated Selenjárga/-Angsneset promontory. Further along in this direction it is possible to see the southern side of the Varangerfjord, with the cultural monument areas of Oddajohka/Nyelv and Rissebákti/ Gressbakken (Olsen 1994). Out across the fjord towards the east the view stretches all the way to Ceavccageadgi/ Mortensnes, a continuous cultural environment that is in a class of its own in terms of Stone Age dwelling sites, sacrificial ceremony grounds and sacred stones, and a large scree burial site (Schanche 2000). Out across the open skies to the east it is possible to see as far as Murget, a well-known offering site, with its steep cliffs towering above the shoreline just west of Ceavccageadgi/ Mortensnes. There are also a number of well-known and important Sami offering sites lying in succession along the fjord. Many of these were still in use until relatively recent times.

The rock carvings located on the south-western edge of the plateau may be viewed from this perspective. It seems as if they represent some clear connection to several of the previously mentioned places, and they appear to emphasize the importance that the rock art itself and Aldon in general had for the people in the area. Although they are difficult to date, the figures may have their origins far back in time. Most of the lines comprising the figures are the products of pecking, which is the prevalent technique used for prehistoric rock art and is

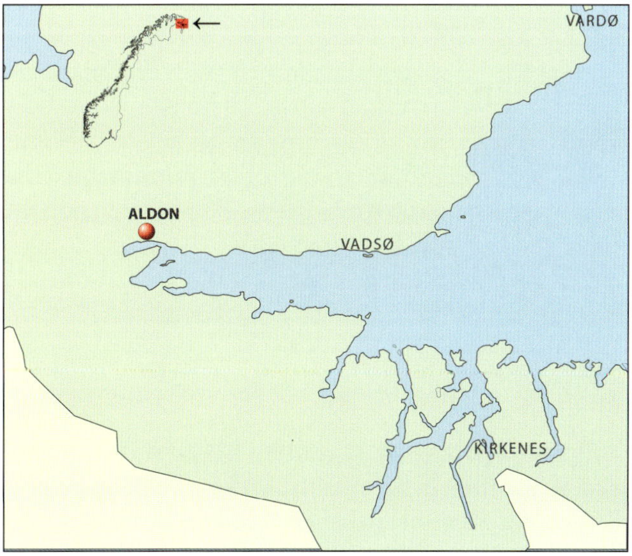

FIGURES 21–22. *Opposite*: Aldon with the river gorge above Meskelva in the foreground. Aldon is located deep inside the Varangerfjord basin, on its northern side.

MAP AI, ILLUSTRATION TL

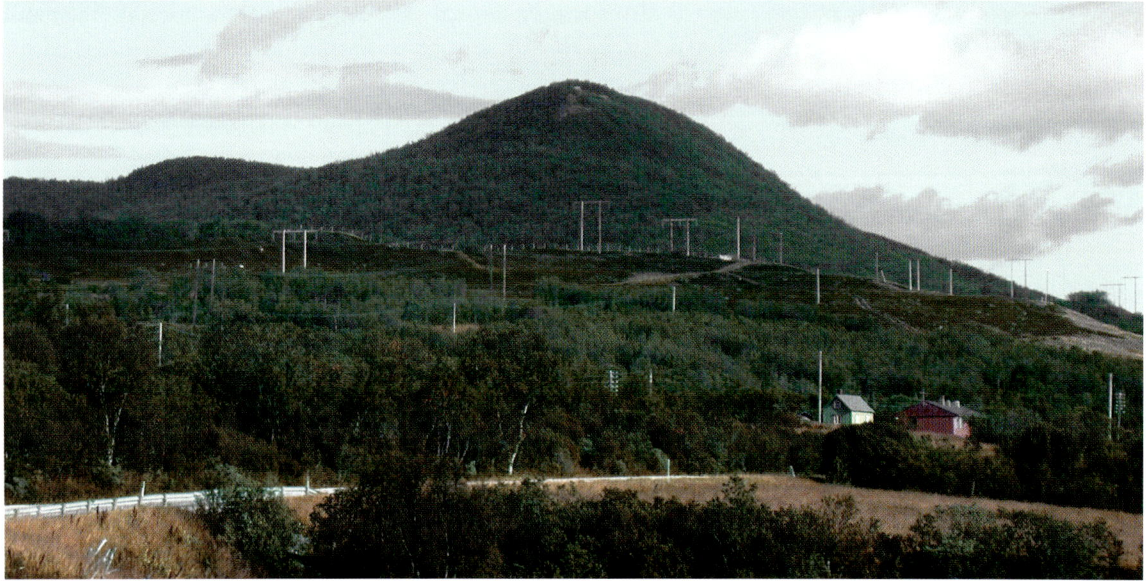

FIGURE 23. The immediate surroundings of Aldon are marked by modern features, such as fences, high voltage lines, roads and settlements.
TL

often helpful in distinguishing older from more modern images. However, it should be noted that some of the lines appear to be scratched into the rock. Aside from the pecking itself, there are few clues that allow us to date the figures, but several factors support the theory that they are very old. The rock appears to be just as worn and patinated in the furrows as the surfaces around the carvings. According to sources, they were well covered with vegetation and sedimentary gravel when they were found. The processes that led to the figures being covered with sedimentary gravel remain unexplained. They may have been covered with uncompacted materials as a result of a combination of human activity, erosion and weathering. If erosion alone is the cause, the gently sloping terrain may indicate that the process occurred over a long period of time, and thus suggests that the images are relatively old. Earlier it was suggested, based on similarities to the rock paintings at Transfarelvdalen in Alta, West Finnmark, that they may date from the period between 500 and 300 BC (Simonsen 1969). The comparison was substantiated by certain similarities in image expression between the rock art at these two sites. New interpretations of the rock paintings in Transfarelvdalen suggest that they are older, perhaps from the period between 2000 and 500 BC, or even much older, and this would in turn indicate that the rock images at Aldon are equally old. It should be noted, however, that comparisons of pecked and carved images with painted ones is nonetheless problematical.

The discovery

The site was discovered in 1961 by Y6 and Y7 pupils of the former Mesk River School, located at the time in the fjord basin below Aldon. The teachers and students had chosen a September day for an autumn ramble to the summit.

While they enjoyed their packed lunches and the view, one restless pupil began to kick at a loose piece of turf on the outer edge of the summit. Many of the former pupils who live in Varanger and who were part of the excursion remember their surprise when the figures came into view. Someone had engraved images of animals here at the summit of the mountain, and the turf had totally concealed them! It is unclear as to whether both figures were discovered at the same time, or whether one of them was found later. The pupils who made the discovery were nonetheless unaware of the importance of the find, and it did not occur to them to tell anyone. As a result, several years passed before local residents informed Tromsø Museum and made the find known to the public.

Unusual location

The information received by Tromsø Museum in the autumn of 1964 was met with considerable scepticism. The occurrence of rock images in the Varanger area was extremely rare, let alone at an elevation of nearly 200 metres above sea level. The report was nevertheless investigated in order to substantiate or perhaps repudiate it. The fact that the images were reported from an area of Eastern Finnmark where hardly any rock art had been found was nonetheless exciting. In fact, large concentrations of rock art had indeed been found further east in Russia and further south in Finland. A rock painting on a panel in Oddajohka/Nyelv, Varanger, was also known to exist, having been found after excavation of a stone pile in the 1930s (Simonsen 1958).

Investigations in the field confirmed that the information was correct. A rock carving site unknown until that time was located high in the terrain, close to 200 metres above sea level, but nevertheless at unusually high elevation. Pecked in tillite, the local bedrock, two relatively small animal images were documented through tracing and photographing. The figures were not more than 30 centimetres long with a space of just under two metres between them. Both were very stylised, with their hind ends towards one another. The heads of the figures had two straight lines, diagonal or vertical, and may be interpreted as depicting antlers or ears. There are few indicators of the type of animal depicted. Based on its long legs, it is likely that one of the figures represents a type of deer. The other figure is much more difficult to interpret. Some have claimed that it is a hare, seeing the two close-set, parallel lines as ears. Others consider that this figure also represents a member of the deer family, in all likelihood a reindeer.

Other figures

One of the reasons why the turf cover concealing the figures was so easy to remove is that erosion, after a heavy rainfall, had washed away some of the grit and vegetation in the immediate area. It cannot be discounted that there may still be other figures concealed beneath the turf surrounding the figures; these may provide images that could help us to see contexts and similarities with other

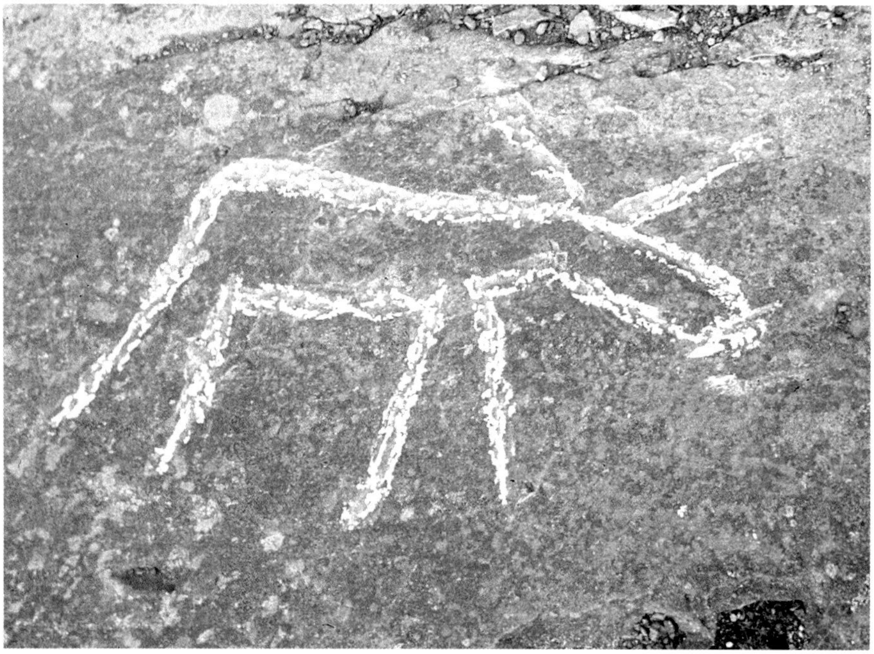

FIGURE 24. The most distinct animal image is a stylised and very simply shaped reindeer.
TM

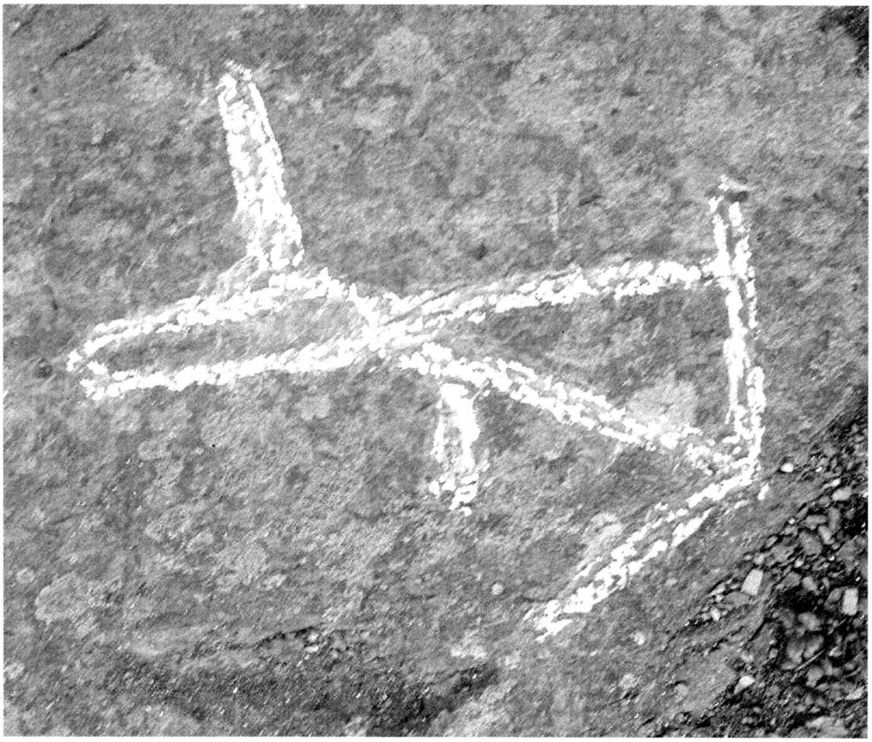

FIGURE 25. This figure has been interpreted as both a hare and a reindeer.
TM

rock carving sites. One sign suggesting the animal figures are not the only ones in the area are pecking marks on a large stone a little to the east of Aldon. It is not possible to discern what was once pecked into the stone, but there are several fragmentary lines that are very likely the remains of weathered images, and which may have some association with the other two animal figures.

Long-term tradition of images?

In the vicinity of the animal figures there are other figures that are probably far younger. These are located on the north-eastern side of the summit, a little more than 150 metres east of the animal figures, on an exposed rock panel (Vorren and Eriksen 1993). Here the depiction is of a human dressed in what may be a woven jacket and cap, and holding a spear pointed at an animal. It has been claimed that the animal must represent a wolf, but another interpretation suggests it is a member of the seal family. This latter interpretation is supported by the fact that only a few metres away are chiselled lines that represent a boat with a sail. The type of sail resembles a kite and suggests that the figure must be relatively young. As with the other rock carvings, the age of these figures has not been determined. The relatively recent age illustrates a challenge in the fields of archaeology and rock art research. How far in time does rock art extend? What is rock art, actually, and what delineations do we have for the figurative carvings, often modern in appearance, that we find in many other places? It is tempting to compare the boat figure in Aldon with the carved boat figures found on rocks in Padjelante, Northern Sweden (Mulk and Bayliss-Smith 2001; 2006), in the border area near Salten in Nordland County, Norway. It has been suggested that homogeneous images of boats may extend surprisingly far back

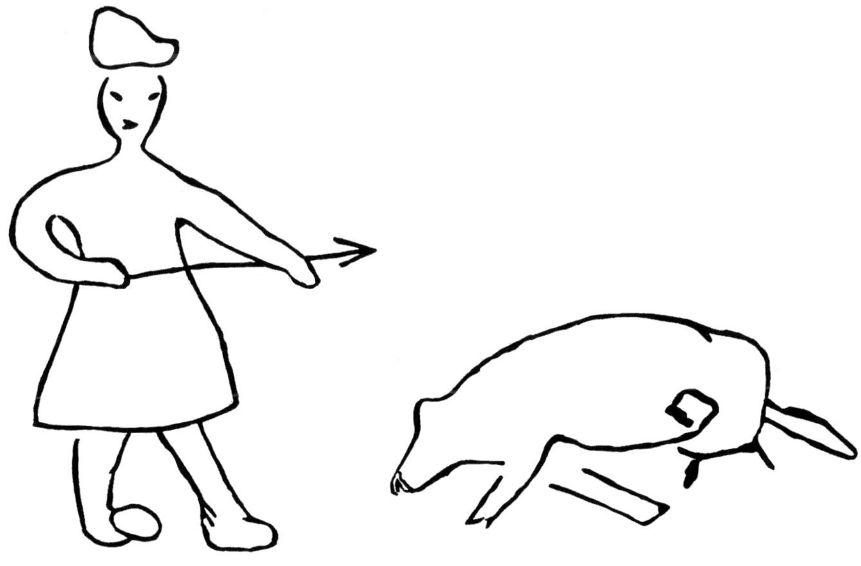

FIGURE 26. It is uncertain whether this is a wolf or a small seal being harpooned by a human.
ØV

in time, to the Viking era/early Middle Ages. As in Aldon, the figures are also located in an area with strong Sami traditions. We will not go into any further detail here about these figures or this issue, but we would add that it appears as though Aldon has a lengthy tradition of pecking and carving images into rock. In several places both at the summit and on the slopes below, there have been recent reports of the existence of carvings and line fragments. These should be investigated more thoroughly in the future so that we are able to identify contexts and the course of traditions over time. Archaeological surveys of the subsoil near the animal figures may also reveal objects and materials that will permit us to determine the age of the rock art.

Sami offering site

One indication that calls for a deeper analysis concerning both the place and the rock art itself is the close association between the place name, Aldon, and the Sami word *alda*, meaning place of sacrifice. In addition, there are a number of accounts telling of offerings on the summit, and these tend to corroborate the association between the names. Already in 1694, Niels Knag mentioned in "Jordeboeg og Mandtal ofuer Nordmend og Finn" [Cadastre and Census of Norwegians and Finns] that a large stone – a *seidestein* [sacred stone for offerings] – was located at the summit of Aldon and was used for sacrifices of reindeer (Vorren and Eriksen 1993; Sveen 2003). He tells that there were large accumulations of bones around the base of the stone, suggesting repeated offerings over time. The *seidestein*, which had been known as the *Storjunkeren*, was undoubtedly toppled and pushed over the cliff during the 1700s, when Christian missionaries in Copenhagen implemented a wholesale purge of all pagan practices. Information about the sacrificial activities and the subsequent attempts to ban them prompted local residents to search for the sacrificial stone in the undergrowth and wooded areas lying beneath the summit. A few years ago, some 100 metres down the rear side of the mountain, a large boulder was

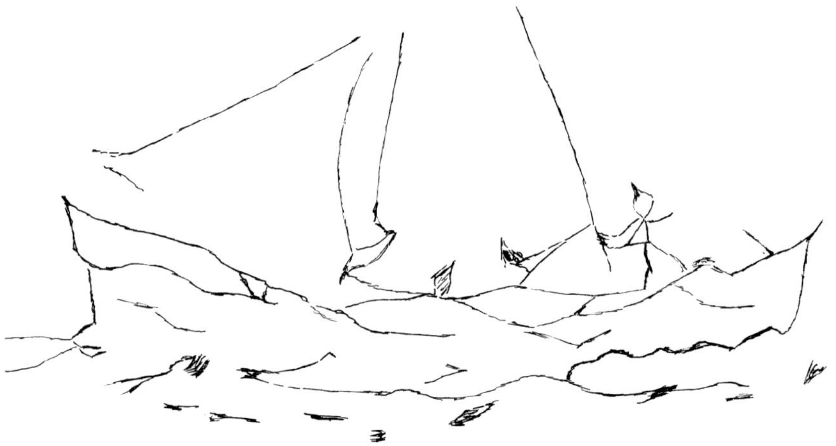

FIGURE 27. The boat is partly pecked and partly carved next to the human and animal figures on the stone, see FIG. 26.
OMD

found matching the description of the once sacred *Storjunkeren* (*ibid.*). Still resting on the slope, the boulder is nearly two metres long and is embedded in the forest floor. Just above it there is a deep furrow in the soil, which suggests that this is the stone that was pushed over the ledge above, landing with great force on the incline and then sliding a short distance before coming to rest.

Dubious written sources

Several written sources refer to Aldon as one of the classical sacrificial sites (Vorren and Eriksen 1993; Qvigstad 1927), with large accumulations of bones surrounding the *Storjunkeren*, although there is little information concerning specific sacrificial rites. Nevertheless, this information would be quite unreliable, since it would have been recorded by missionaries whose primary goal was to combat these religious practices, which they considered as devil worship. Also, the missionaries were rarely or never first-hand witnesses to the sacrifices or cult celebrations. Information was normally recorded in second-hand or third-hand accounts that were likely to portray the customs in a different light, and not correspond to reality.

None of the written sources mention the rock carvings. It is possible, therefore, that they are older than the place of sacrifice. However, we cannot dismiss the possibility that they were created after the place of sacrifice had been established, or that the easily degradable bedrock misleads us into thinking they are older than they really are, that they are not a part of some prehistoric rock art tradition, but are rather of later date, and that they have counterparts in other places purely by chance.

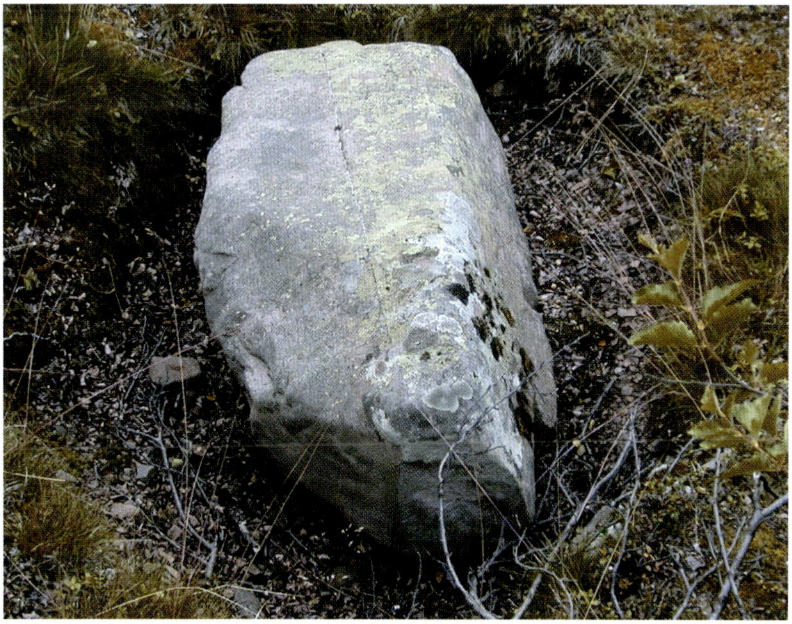

FIGURE 28. Several stones on the hillsides below the summit fit the description of Storjunkeren.
TL

What we do know about the sacrificial rite is that the stone was coated with fish or animal fat so that it became slick and shiny (e.g. Bäckman 1975; Rydving 1993). There were often separate sacrificial sites for different animals. Taking all of these factors into account, the *Storjunkeren* was used only for sacrificing reindeer and was coated with reindeer fat. However, evidence that blood, horns and bones were sacrificed explains the large accumulations of rotten bones and horns that are described in written sources (e.g. Vorren and Eriksen 1993). Religious and historical studies of these types of rituals suggest that an important aspect in the sacrifices was to display respect for the underworld – *Jábmeáibmu* – which was the realm of the dead, but in which gods that were associated with fertility and birth also resided (Bäckman 1975; Rydving 1993). The sacrifices also served other purposes. By offering bones and horns from wild reindeer, the hunters honoured the animal and invoked forgiveness for the kill. The reverential treatment of bones ensured that the animal would be resurrected, as the recipient of the sacrifice would then create new animals based on the offered bones. Additionally, the animal's soul would intervene to persuade other animals to submit to slaughter. Sources suggest that the resurrection of animals was not only intended for the world of the living, but also for those who had passed on into the realm of the dead. In this manner both the gods and deceased relatives of the hunter benefited from the sacrifice.

FIGURE 29. It can be difficult to make out the entire animal image in natural light without moving and changing your perspective. The front portion of one of the animals is clearly visible, while the back of the body and the hindquarters can hardly be seen.
TL

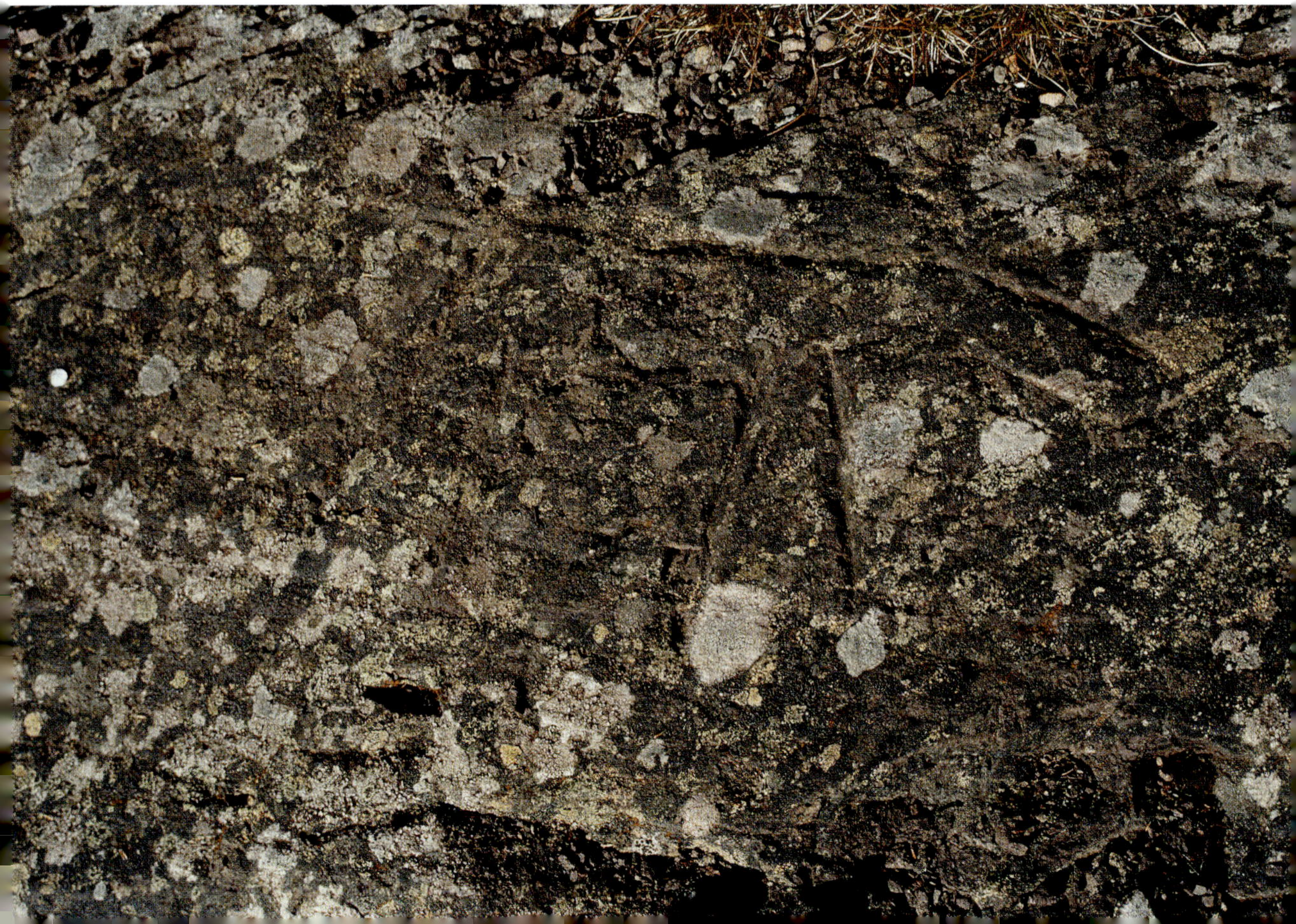

There is also the concept that the sacrifices ensured that the soul of the dead animal would not seek revenge against its hunter.

The religious and historical sources that make it possible to understand the sacrificial rituals date from an era when reindeer herding and the domestication of animals were common practices. They can therefore be difficult to apply in order to understand an earlier historical moment. Nevertheless, it has been claimed by historians of religion that the sacrificial ceremonies were undoubtedly grounded in the ideology of the hunter society, a factor that supports applying the sources to a much earlier period of time. It is important to remember that the herding of tame reindeer, a practice of various inland Sami groups, was increasingly prevalent during the 1600s (Hansen and Olsen 2004). Before this period, a combination of fishing and hunting was most common. Wild reindeer hunting in Varanger was a very widespread practice up until the 1600s, indicated by a noticeable and marked decrease in the reindeer stock (Vorren 1998). In many places we find the remnants of hundreds of large hunting pits, which bear witness to how extensive this practice really was. With this perspective, it is possible to imagine that the sacrificial rituals became dramatically more intensified as the wild reindeer stocks were overtaxed.

Another critical issue concerning sources is the influence of the Catholic prohibition campaign that was advancing rapidly at the time. The Sami religion was affected, to such an extent that it is difficult to distinguish the reactions to extensive missionary efforts from the basic, original views. There are, however, written sources recorded by people who were less critical of the Sami religious practices, and these permit us an insight into the true origins of the sacrificial ceremonies. In any case, Christianity did not take root in the Sami societies. The Sami religion had several gods, and while the Christian element was accepted, it failed to replace the Sami gods, and was instead incorporated into contexts that entwined Christianity with the original, pagan gods and spirits. For this reason, many people continued with religious practices involving sacrifices far into the modern age.

Indications of the individuals who could make sacrifices are somewhat contradictory, but some maintain categorically that most sacrificial rituals were performed by *noaides*, or Sami shamans. The *noaides* were intermediaries between this world and the afterlife, and were able to dissociate body and soul in order to make spiritual journeys into the realm of the dead. In this way they were capable of communicating with spirits and become enlightened as to what was required in times of crisis. During journeys to the spiritual world, the *noaides* invoked the aid of animals such as reindeer, fish and birds (Bäckman 1975; Bäckman and Hultkrantz 1977).

It is difficult to say how far back in time Sami ethnicity and the customs of sacrifice reach. The information we do possess reflects great changes over time, as well as many local variations, in particular between the Coastal Samis and the inland Sami groups. Due to the continuity of archaeological artefacts, there is much that suggests that Sami culture, ethnicity and identity originated far back in time and developed from the end of the Late Stone Age and throughout the

Early Metal Period (Olsen 1994), although we do find major similarities between Sami ethnography and archaeological material that extend even further back in time. At any rate, it is reasonable to believe that the practice of offering sacrifices underwent constant change as a result of internal factors within groups, contact with other groups and influences from other geographical areas.

The age of the sacrificial sites

The determination of the age of the sites is a difficult issue in itself, as in many of the places only vestiges of highly perishable materials remain, and these cannot be traced. Apart from this, many of the offering sites may have been part of contexts that did not result in artefacts of a material nature being left behind. An attempt has been made, however, to ascertain the age of a few of the sacrificial sites in Varanger through the radiological dating of organic materials. To the extent that these types of materials could be found in the subsoil, datings suggest a period of use extending from about 1000 to about 1650 AD (Vorren and Eriksen 1993). The reliability of these results, however, is limited, as it was neither possible to clearly determine a period of usage based on subsoil stratification, nor to obtain any assurance that the results accurately date the oldest of the sacrificial rituals. The datings are largely based on charcoal, most likely from abandoned fire pits, and we are also uncertain as to whether these have any connection with the sacrifices. If the only items left behind at the sites were fat or blood, it will be impossible to trace these materials, and equally impossible to date sacrificial activity using traditional radiocarbon dating. There is an obvious possibility that the places of sacrifice date from a much earlier period.

Based on the suggested dates for the rock art – from 2000 to 500 BC – we may be tempted to conclude that Aldon was chosen as a site for sacrifices because it had rock art. Also, prominent and eye-catching mountain formations were often chosen as sacred places and sacrificial sites, and this tends to refute the idea. It is preferable to believe that the rock art was created at a place that already was firmly established within the prevalent system of beliefs. Lacking written sources, it is difficult to clearly determine the sacred meanings that were attributed to the landscape. However, there is much to suggest that from an early period of time the landscape and its many natural features, mountains and summits, were already attributed with mythical and religious meanings. From far back in the Stone Age we have reliable indications of this type of adaptation of the environment for the purposes of worship, including findings that we interpret as the remains of sacrifices. These are often found at or near prominent natural features of the landscape, near large boulders, cliffs or mountain formations, to name but a few. It is tempting to conclude that these were chosen as holy grounds or places for sacrifices because they were distinct features in the landscape.

FIGURE 30. Opposite: The figures have become overgrown in the 40 years since their discovery, and they are often hard to see. This figure has been highlighted in chalk, with the mouth of Varangerfjord in the background.
AS

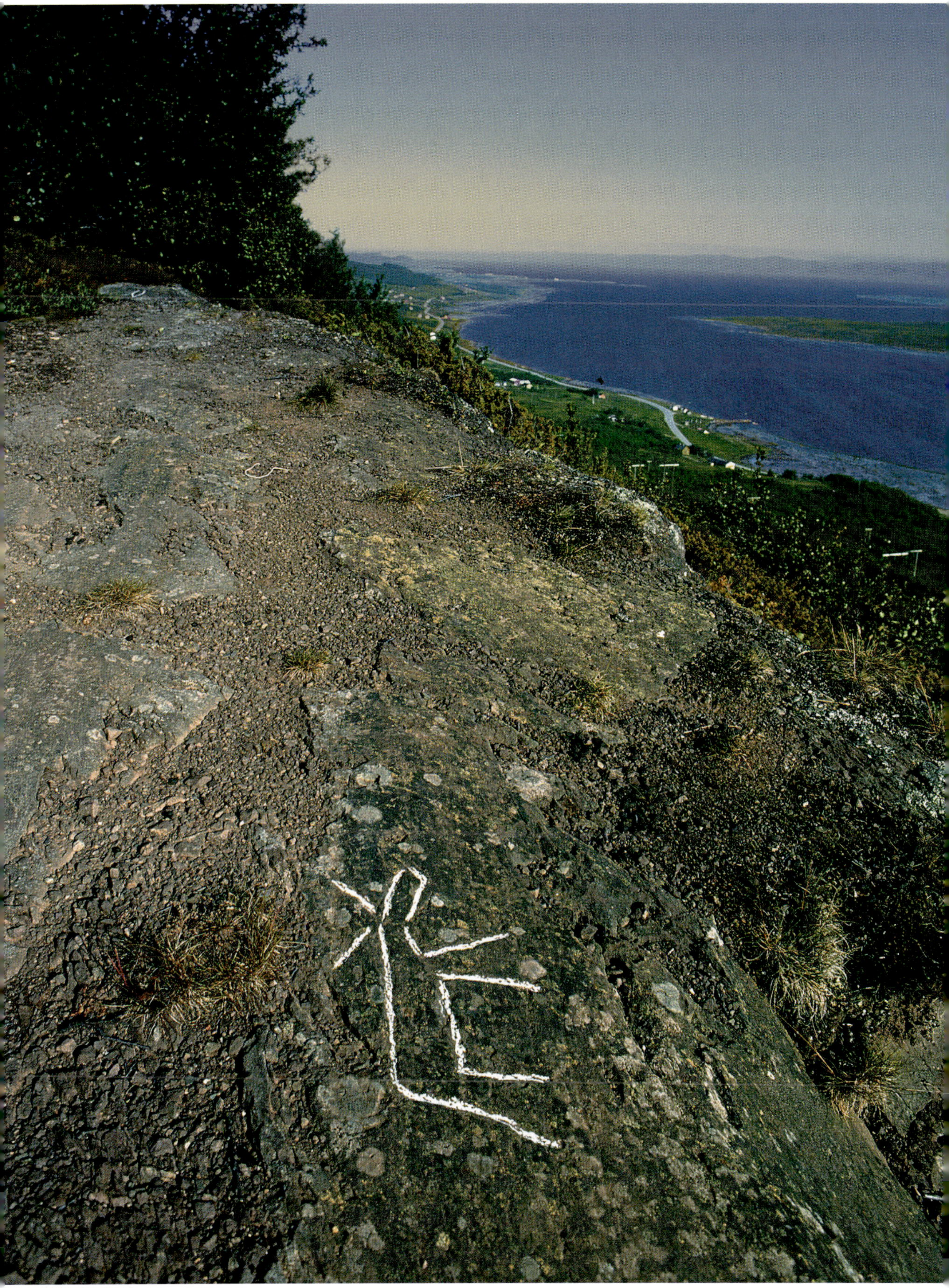

Contexts

All of this represents only somewhat vague and limited evidence, although it is interesting that we have rock art depicting reindeer at a place where we know reindeer were sacrificed, or if not the whole animal, at least the bones. Written sources mentioning the tall *Storjunkeren* at the summit of Aldon provide no indication of how long it may have been there, whether it was raised by people or was a fixed, natural feature from the outset. Nor do we know if the stone may have taken on the role of a sacrificial site after an even older place of sacrifice, which well may have been the rock art images. Although none of the written sources mention the rock images, it is interesting that they were found in such close proximity to the place of sacrifice. There appears to be a connection here that should be investigated more thoroughly. This is a challenge that needs to be undertaken in order to better understand not only the rock art, but also Aldon as a place of sacrifice.

Sources from the 1700s mention Aldon as a sacred mountain, and sacred mountains also contain a spiritual world, *Saivoáibmu*, an important factor in obtaining a clearer understanding of the images (Bäckman 1975; Hansen and Olsen 2004). Just how long concepts of the spiritual world have existed is of course difficult to determine. However, there is little to suggest that its origins date from recent centuries, or that it is a new phenomenon. Spiritual worlds have been an entirely natural part of human belief and knowledge in most societies since time immemorial.

From various ethnographical studies carried out in areas where living rock art traditions are still present, we have indications that the rock surfaces are often seen as a 'membrane' to another dimension or spiritual world, and not merely as the surface of a stone (Lewis-Williams and Dawson 1990). Through these privileged rock surfaces it was possible to come into contact with the spiritual realm. The structure, form and shape of mountains are therefore important to the depiction, and in many places these factors are decisive for the type of images that are created. This is a basic, essential perception of rock art that amply explains why lines were drawn and images were created. In many places we find that the natural lines in the rock surface were used as part of the image created; a natural, curved line may form the outline of an animal's belly, a scrape in the stone's surface may be used to depict a leg, and natural cracks in the stone may be incorporated in an image of reindeer antlers. At times it may appear that the rock surface in itself prompted the images created on it, as if a human being or an animal is partially revealed on the surface and is then made whole by the lines added by the artist. It may be a case of evoking something that actually belongs to another world through depiction, and drawing it into the world of the living through lines applied to the rock. In line with this notion, the natural features in the rock coincide with several of the pecked lines in both animal images at Aldon. In this way, the surface of the rock here may have functioned as a membrane between our world and *Saivoáibmu* or a similar, older spiritual realm. The image of a reindeer may therefore have been developed on this membrane in order to have more open, direct contact with the spiritual world during the sacrificial ceremonies in which reindeer were the central point of focus. At the same time the images, carved in stone, emphasized the power and significance of the sacrifice. If the society at the time was in a state of crisis, this may have been a means by which to emphasise the significance of the sacrificial ceremony.

In the more than 40 years that have passed since the images were discovered in Aldon, there has been dramatic increase in the number of new images and panels found, particularly in Finnmark County. Many of these have striking parallels to Sami mythology and traditions, not least the rock carvings in Alta and Kåfjord (Helskog 1999). As recently as 2000, rock paintings were discovered on an outcrop in Ruksesbákti, Inner Billefjord, on the Porsanger fjord, including a striking parallel to images that have been found on several of the well-known Sami shaman's drums. It is tempting, therefore, to regard the depictions on the shaman's magical drums as an extension of an older tradition involving painting and pecking images into stone.

Many other images now concealed by overgrowth may yet be found on mountaintops similar to Aldon, not only in Finnmark, but in Northern Norway and the rest of the country, and these may provide valuable clues when put in context with the discoveries we describe here. Discoveries may be made in places where there is written mention of sacrifices and sacrificial stones, but where knowledge about how the rock art was produced has been forgotten or lost. These are places we have yet to discover, and which may possibly clarify the connections between ancient sacrificial ceremonies and rock art.

Rock Art of the Northern Tradition in Troms County

Traces in Copenhagen…!

Between the years 1787–1788, Martin Vahl was the first professional botanist to complete a journey to North Norway. He was a professor of botany at the University of Copenhagen, and he left in its archives a collection of notes entitled *Anmærkningen paa Reisen til Nordlandene og Finmarken* [Notes on a Journey to Nordland and Finnmark]: *natural history, economics, geography.* His notes reveal that he visited Balsfjorden, one of which states: "*On a farm in Balsfjorden there is a slab of stone on which a large number of images are engraved; a farmer drew one of these for me*" (Holmboe 1916). The note was illustrated with a simple sketch of an animal. It is uncertain whether Vahl actually ever saw the image himself, or whether it was the product of second-hand information, or if the accompanying sketch was the work of the farmer he mentioned. When archaeologists became aware of this note around 1915, a number of them took an interest in it, in particular the Swedish archaeologist Gustaf Hallström, who was planning to write a general survey of Scandinavian rock art (1938). He was already in the process of calculating how much time it would take to thoroughly examine Balsfjorden, when he received unexpected help from local residents in Troms. There was obviously a limit to the number of farms that

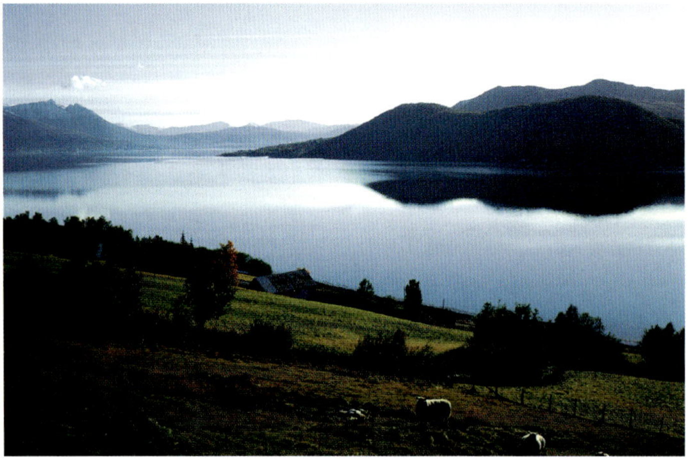

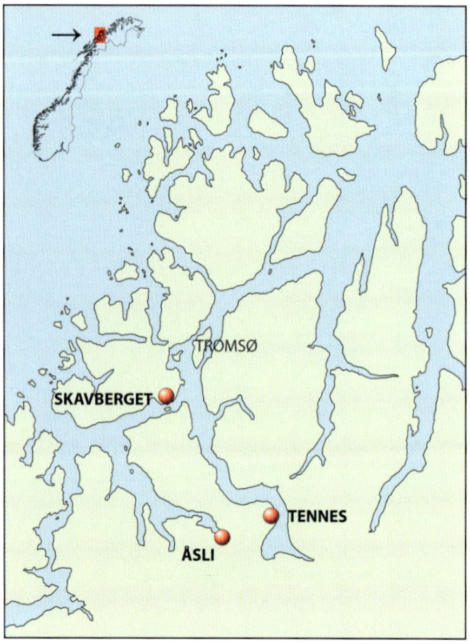

FIGURES 31–32. The Balsfjord landscape with Tennes in the background. The sites are mainly found in Straumsfjorden, Balsfjorden and Malangen.

MAP AI, ILLUSTRATION RU

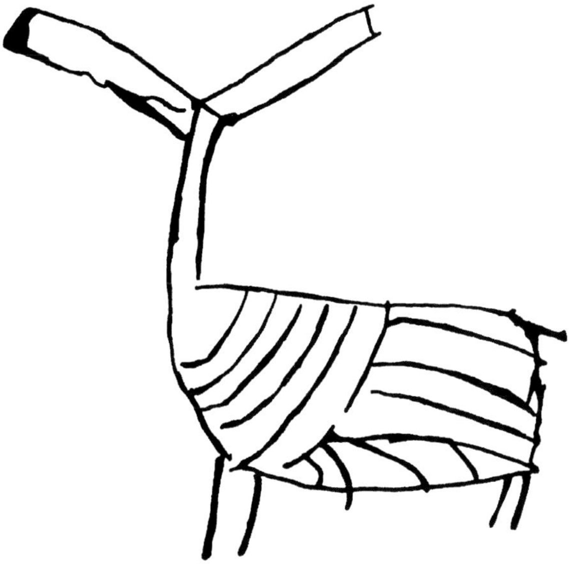

FIGURE 33. The depiction of an animal on Bukkhammarn (Goat Bluff), initially interpreted as a goat or a billy goat and sketched by a farmer.

had existed in Balsfjord at the time of Vahl's travels there, and this significantly reduced the search area, so that soon after his arrival in Troms, Hallström very quickly made his way in through Balsfjorden to Tennes. It turned out that an elderly gentleman was familiar with the discovery that had lain in obscurity in Copenhagen for more than 125 years. From the pier at Tennes, Hallström was led some hundred metres up to Bukkhammarn, already then a namesake after the image of a what was earlier interpreted as a goat, and long ago, sketched by a farmer from Tennes. It also came as a surprise to the elderly gentleman that the images were still intact, since stone had been transported to the parsonage farm from Bukkhammarn, but the image was found higher up. It did not take long before Hallström, who had a trained eye for rock art, found the images at Gråbergan and the slabs of stone with images, which had been used as stepping stones across a nearby stream (Hallström 1938). He carried out an extensive search of the area but was unable to find any more images.

A fjord system with many rock carvings

The Tennes image was the first known rock carving in Troms and the first documentation of rock art discovered in Norway, although it had been concealed from the public for a very long time in an archive in Copenhagen. Tennes is one of three areas in Troms with rock carvings of the Northern tradition, situated close to each other and associated with the same fjord system, which comprises Straumfjorden, Malangen and Balsfjorden – in other words, the fjords just south of the city of Tromsø. Furthest north are the rock carvings at Skavberget (Simonsen 1955; 1958), which is located on the southernmost side of Kvaløya, at the narrowest point of the Straumsfjord. Furthest south is

Åsli (*ibid.*), reached by travelling to the end of Malangen and continuing on through the narrower Nordfjord. The rock art panel is located at the mouth of Nordfjord Lake, just inside the head of the fjord. The last panel is Tennes (Gjessing 1932; Hallström 1938) itself, found by continuing eastward, across the isthmus to the head of Balsfjord and then several kilometres further north. The areas of the rock carvings have their own distinctive traits and qualities. In particular, the fact that they lie in close proximity to each another has led many people to consider these rock art areas as being in conjunction with one another. This view has been reinforced by the fact that four-legged animal images have been found at all of the panels and that the locations in the terrain correspond with known migratory paths for reindeer, or which we are able to deduce were present based on the features of the terrain. However, it is important to note that many of the animal figures are so stylized that it is uncertain whether the images represent reindeer; some of them clearly appear to be depictions of elk or bear. In addition to these, there are numerous sea mammals on several of the panels, such as seals, small whales and in particular porpoises, as well as humans and boats.

Skavberget

The rock carvings at Skavberget were discovered in the spring of 1950. It was the owner of the property himself who had come across the images on the face of a mountain wall facing south, and he immediately contacted Tromsø Museum. A large amount of leachate that had flowed over the steep, two to four metre-high rock face made documentation difficult, and it was not until 1952 that a thorough examination was completed (Simonsen 1955; 1958). Many of the images were also partially covered with soil and sediment. The soil was carefully removed, but no archaeological material was found that could be put in context with the images. Not long after the documentation of what was thought to be the entire site, several other images were discovered further east on the mountain wall. Altogether some 30 images were discovered at Skavberget. All of them are quite different in character, size and most probably in age as well, distributed in three sections of the mountain wall, which has some sections that are less steep and pronounced than others. The last panel was found to the east, almost alongside the main road and quite low on the rock surface, with fourteen images. Most of them were simple, stylised depictions of deer; some possibly represent dogs, a seal, a porpoise and an unusual human figure. One of the deer images is placed

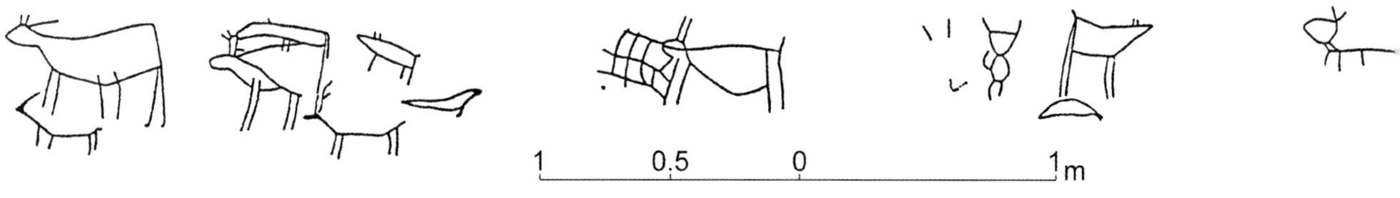

FIGURE 34. Simple and varied figures found at Skavberget. On the left, a group of animals, one with six legs. In the centre is an animal with a lattice pattern in front of it. To the right we see human figures, a porpoise and a reindeer. On the far right is an unidentifiable figure. The most distinct of all of these is the seal on the left in the series of images.
PS

FIGURE 35. For many years, a barn stood in front of this panel, where the animals had direct contact with the rock wall. This explains why the panel is extremely worn.
PS

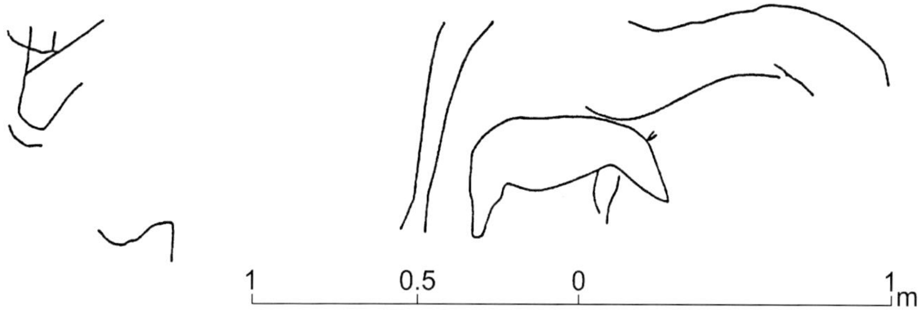

very close to a frame, or cage-like image that has been interpreted as a trap. It is also interesting to note that the largest animal image on the western side of this surface is depicted with six legs. The images are all quite small; the largest of them are only about a half metre long. Here as well, the images were partially covered with soil and sediment, but no other archaeological material was found. It is likely that the covering material was the result of land cultivation and deposits of fallen mass from overhanging ledges.

Some 75 metres further to the west there are remains of another panel with four or five animal images that are quite weathered. One of these is most likely a bear. A barn once stood in front of the images, and the rock wall itself was used as the building's northern gable wall. This meant that the animals kept in the barn had direct contact with the wall surface, rubbing against it and licking the surface so that the rock carvings became quite worn over the years. This is the most likely explanation for why the images are so indistinct.

The panel that was first discovered is located another 15 metres to the west. It extends over between four and five metres of the mountain wall. On the far westeren surface there are two very distinct human figures that stand about 60–70 centimetres tall. The legs, thighs, arms, body and head all have their own distinctive features. Both figures, which are very similar to one another, have different body decor, leading some considering them as depictions of a man and a woman, although there are grounds to doubt this. Another special trait of these figures is that the one standing farthest to the west is holding some kind of object in its hand. This appears to be a y-shaped shaft holding up a circular disc. Interpretations of the object have ranged from a drum, a sun idol, a bird or

FIGURE 36. Here human figures have been given a prominent position, surrounded by animal images.
PS

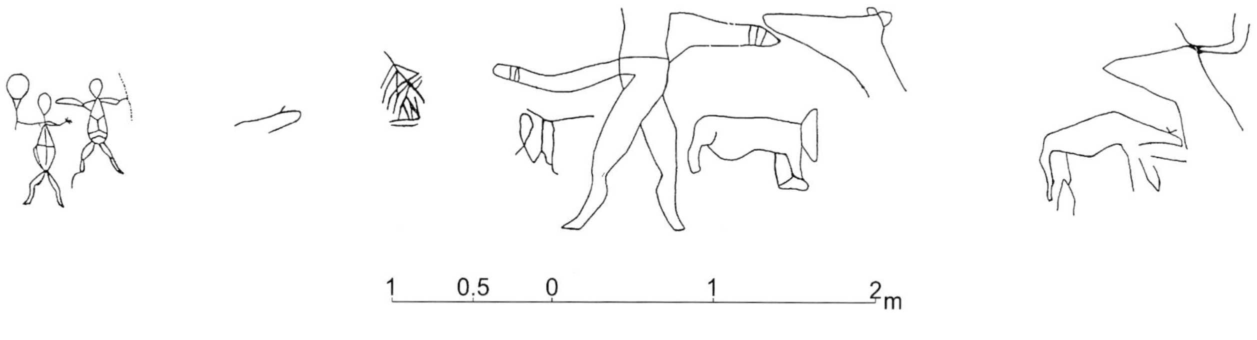

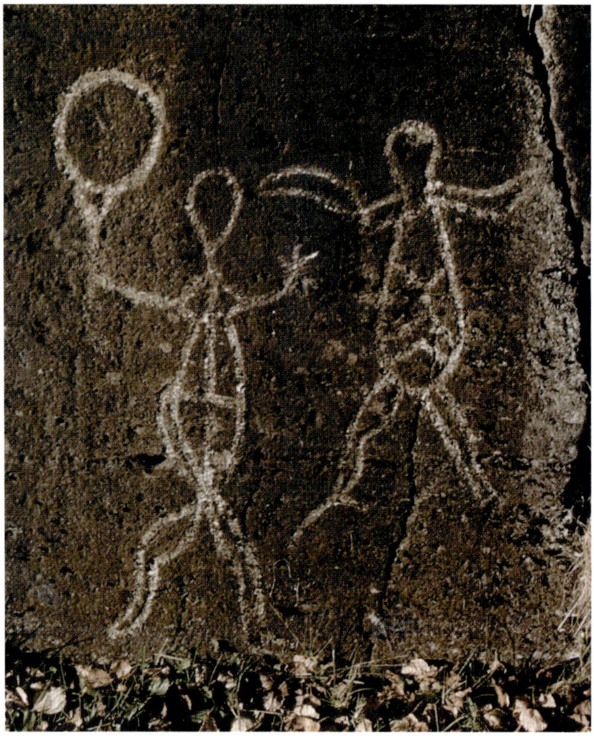

FIGURE 37. Distinctive human figures depicted carrying out activities that are open for many different interpretations.
TM

fish head. There are many possibilities, however. The hand of the other human figure has been destroyed by exfoliation, and it is conceivable that this figure was also depicted holding a similar tool. A little further to the east there is a simple image of the head of an unknown species of animal, and a compact confluence of overlapping lines. There is also an image that has been described as a depiction of a human with a large phallus, with parts of the torso and head missing. If we examine the legs, they appear to belong to two different individuals, with the characteristic thighs and legs depicted in profile. This is further supported by the fact that the figures do not have one phallus but two, each pointing in a different direction. Everything would seem to suggest that the image is not meant to depict one human figure, but two, one overlapping the other. There is also a bear with a strangely deformed head, and two individual animal heads which seem to represent reindeer. Since no lines were found outlining the bodies of the latter, an explanation has been put forward that these animals were depicted as swimming, which naturally entails that only the heads are visible. Similar depictions of what must be swimming reindeer are known from Jiebmaluokta/Hjemmeluft in Alta (Helskog 1988). It is also natural to see these images in context with their location here in Rystraumen, which is the narrowest strait of the Straumfjord between Kvaløya and the mainland, a natural crossing point for animals migrating across the fjord.

On the flatlands close to the eastern panel, Stone Age tools were discovered long before the images were found, including several sharpened slate arrowheads.

There was probably a settlement at this point. It has been partially obliterated by roads and later settlement, but some of the arrowheads have been preserved in Tromsø museum. They were found on a small stretch of flat land in front of the mountain, generally at the same elevation in the terrain as the most easterly rock panel, approximately 11 metres above sea level. The location at the same level may suggest that the settlement and the rock carvings on the far eastern side are contemporary. Based on studies of land uplift in the area, it is estimated that both the rock art and the artefacts are about 5000 years old (Hesjedal 1990), and this coincides with the arrowheads that were found, amongst other elements. The images further west at Skavberget are located six to seven metres higher up, and based on the land uplift, it is likely that they may be several thousand years older.

It is otherwise difficult to draw parallels between images and panels, but it is likely that the location of the rock images at Skavberget is associated with the natural crossing point between Kvaløya and the mainland, both for people using boats and for animals swimming across.

Åsli

The rock carvings at Åsli at the far end of Malangen were found in 1948 by the landowner, who notified Tromsø Museum a few years after finding them. He had been clearing some moss from a mountain slope just south of the waterfall that has its source in Nordfjord Lake, when he came across the images on the rock surface (Simonsen 1955; 1958). A comprehensive clearing effort was necessary to uncover the entire panel. The lower portion of the rock surface was covered only by moss, which was easy to remove, but the upper portion was covered with a half-metre thick layer of soil and turf. When large portions

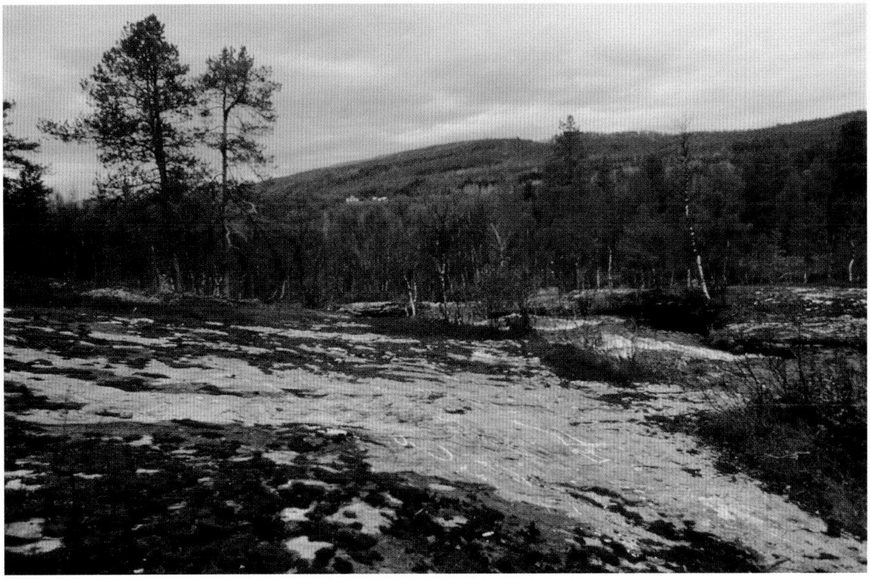

FIGURE 38. The Åsli panel is located just south of the waterfall that flows out of Nordfjordvatnet at the far end of Malangen.
TM

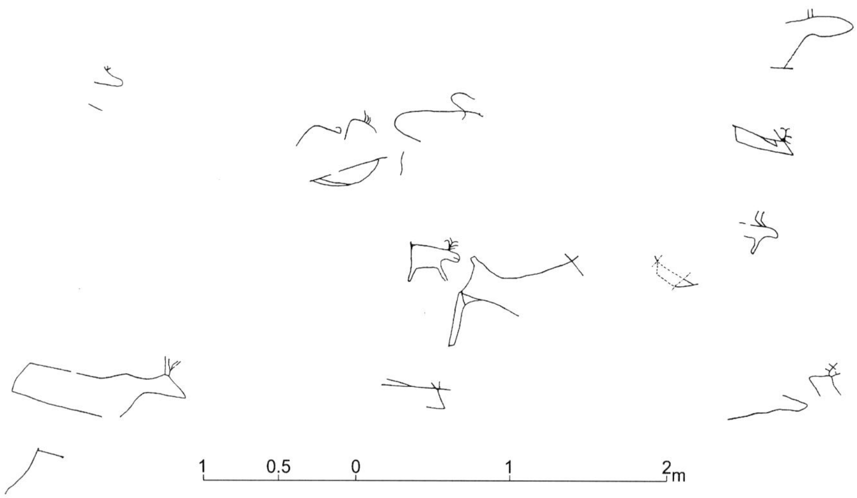

FIGURE 39. Most of the figures are heavily damaged due to exfoliation and weathering.

PS

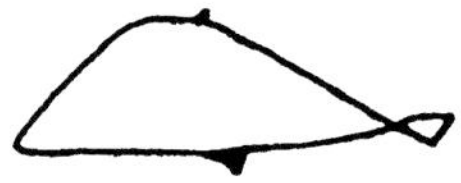

FIGURE 40. A small whale or porpoise located further north on the rock surface.

PS

of the rock surface were uncovered and made visible, it was discovered that there were many more images. The panel is located in a prominent and visually appealing position alongside the waterfall, but the rock is now very weathered, and many of the images have been destroyed and are difficult to discern. All of the rock images are distributed across a 20-square-metre stretch of flat land and comprise at least 15 small, stylised images, along with a number of lines that are difficult to associate with the whole. At least eight of the images appear to depict reindeer, but there is also a porpoise, a boat and a figure that may be an elk. The figures are small, and only one of them is longer than one metre. The lower part of the rock art panel is located just short of 20 metres above sea level, and at a distance today of about one kilometre from the bottom of the fjord. The images were undoubtedly carved in the Stone Age during a period when the water level would have brought the fjord almost to the edge of the waterfall. It is interesting that the images were placed close to the waterfall. It was perhaps because of this prominent landscape feature that the images were created exactly here, in addition to the fact that the area just below the waterfall would have been a natural wading point for migrating animals, a factor that corresponds with the placement of images at Skavberget.

Tennes

In the Tennes area, which we have touched upon earlier, there are a total of four panels with rock art. Two of these lie within the property limits of the old parsonage farm and are known as Bukkhammarn and Gråbergan. A third panel is located about one kilometre further north on the Kirkely property. That last panel that was discovered is located at Venset farm.

Bukkhammarn

Bukkhammarn lies at the edge of the forest above the settlement at Tennes. The panel on which the images were found is quite steep, seven to eight metres long and more than two metres tall. It comprises nine reindeer images that in all likelihood represent elk, probably eight adult animals and a calf (Gjessing 1932; Hallström 1938). There is also a single, curved line near one of the images at the northernmost end of the panel. The largest image is a little more than one metre long. The animals are heavily stylised, and the bodies are filled in with lines that may represent ribs. Half of the images lack body decor. At the lower edge is the image that the botanist from Copenhagen described in his notes. It has a strikingly long head and a more complete body decor than the other images. The legs that were shown on the sketch Vahl had in his possession can no longer be seen on the rock panel. The figure is facing south, while all of the others are facing in the opposite direction. The lower portion of the panel is located about 28 metres above sea level, which would indicate – based on land uplift data – that the images were created some six and a half thousand years ago (Hesjedal 1990).

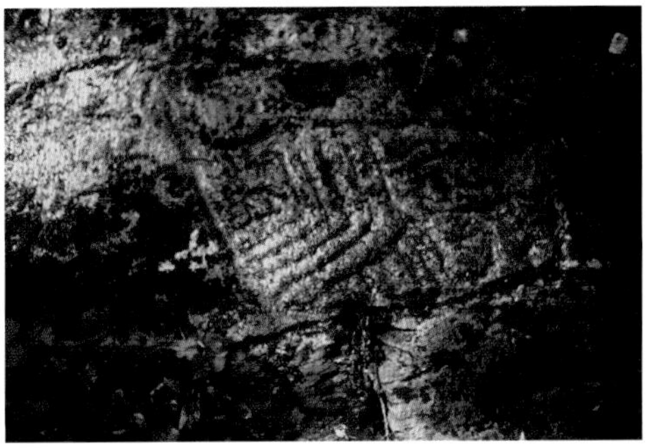

FIGURE 41. The image interpreted as a billy goat at Bukkhammarn was once sketched by a farmer. The panel has become heavily overgrown in recent years. The legs of the animal can no longer be seen due to weathering.
TM

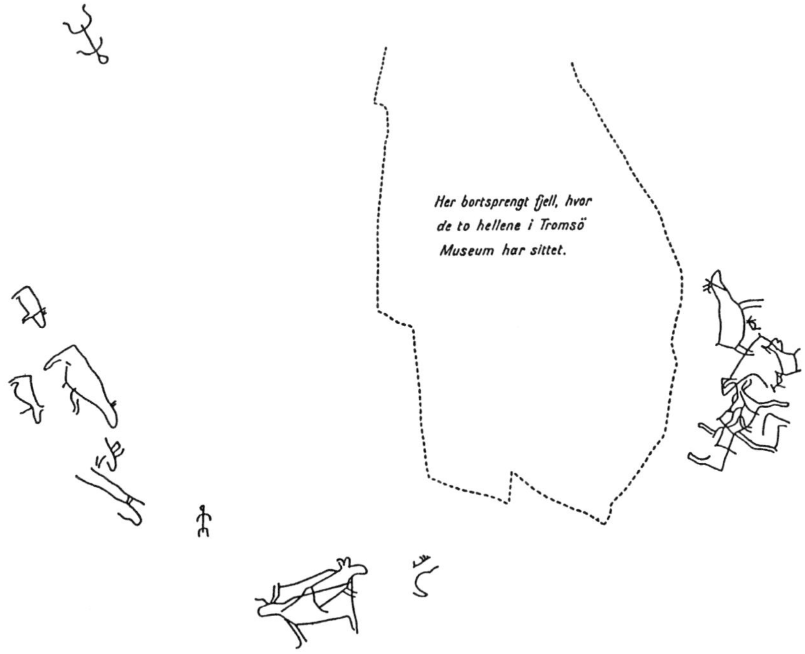

FIGURE 42. Several of the animals are superimposed on top of one another in a semicircle around the larger animals, nearly all of which were blasted away and removed from the Gråbergan site.
GG

Gråbergan

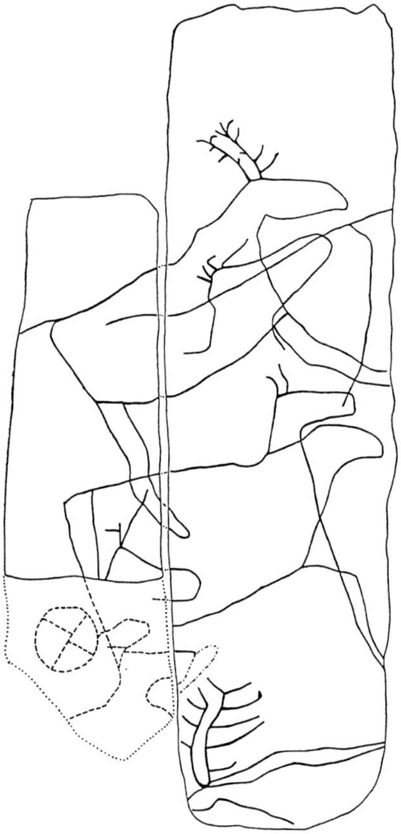

FIGURE 43. Stone slabs blasted out of Gråbergan. The slabs are now preserved at Tromsø Museum.
GG

A few hundred metres below Bukkhammarn, in fields and on the opposite side of the stream, is Gråbergan, a rounded, dome-shaped knoll with images on several points. As many as nineteen images – seventeen animals and two human figures – have been identified (Hallström 1938). The animal images are difficult to identify as species, and are almost devoid of body decor; only one transferring line can be seen in two of the figures. The human images are simple stick figures. Otherwise, a common trait here is that the animal figures overlap one another. The upper portion of the knoll has been destroyed. Oblong slabs were found here that were removed and used as a bridge over the stream between Gråbergan and the settlement at Tennes. On two of the panels there are two complete animal images, both much larger than those that have been found elsewhere at Gråbergan. As a number of scholars have maintained that rock art developed from large, naturalistic figures to smaller and more schematic images, it could be suggested that these figures are the oldest. This theory is supported by the fact that the slabs that come from the top of Gråbergan may have been the natural place to begin when a knoll was to be decorated with images. Also there is at least one animal head without a body; another head merges into the edge of one slab but lacks a body, as not all of the stone slabs were found. In one of the complete images, the animal appears to have an extra head, unless it belongs to another animal standing behind the first. There are indications from Hallström's time that there was a circular image on the southernmost end of the shortest rock panel, but this portion is no longer present. The panel is located about 19 metres above sea level and based on land uplift data, can be dated to being between 4000 and 5000 years old (Hesjedal 1990). Today the slabs form part of the Tromsø Museum collection.

Kirkely

More than twenty years after Hallström arrived in Balsfjord, even more images were found in the area. The parson's wife at Tennes had shown some books on rock art at Bukkhammarn and Gråbergan to one of the women from the neighbouring Kirkely farm, situated less than one kilometre further north along Balsfjord. This caused a strong impression on the woman from Kirkely, and she set about scraping away moss from stone surfaces to see if she could find images on the family property. It was not long before she found the largest concentration of images in the area, some forty figures on a flat stretch of land less than 100 metres northwest of the farmhouse (Simonsen 1958). The lower

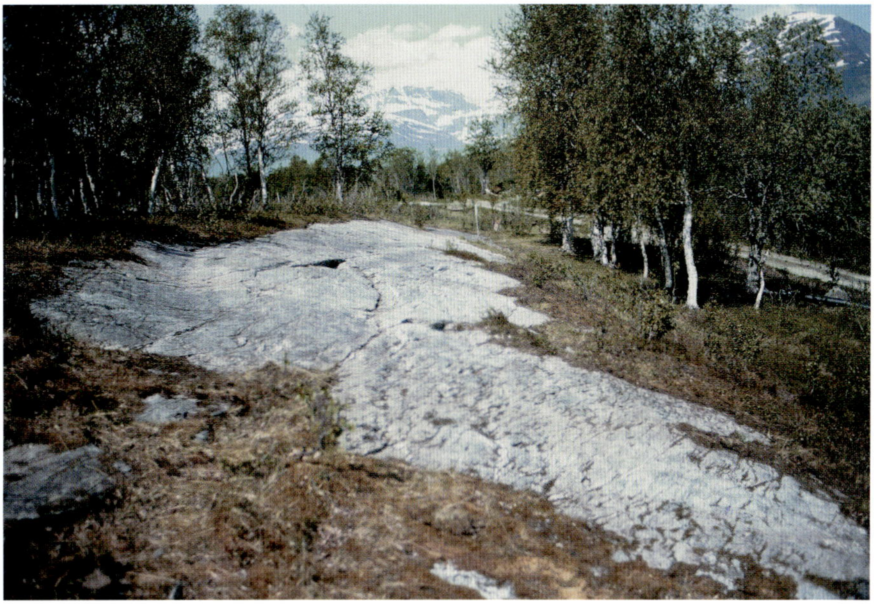

FIGURE 44. The largest collection of figures in the Tennes area is located here at Kirkely.

TM

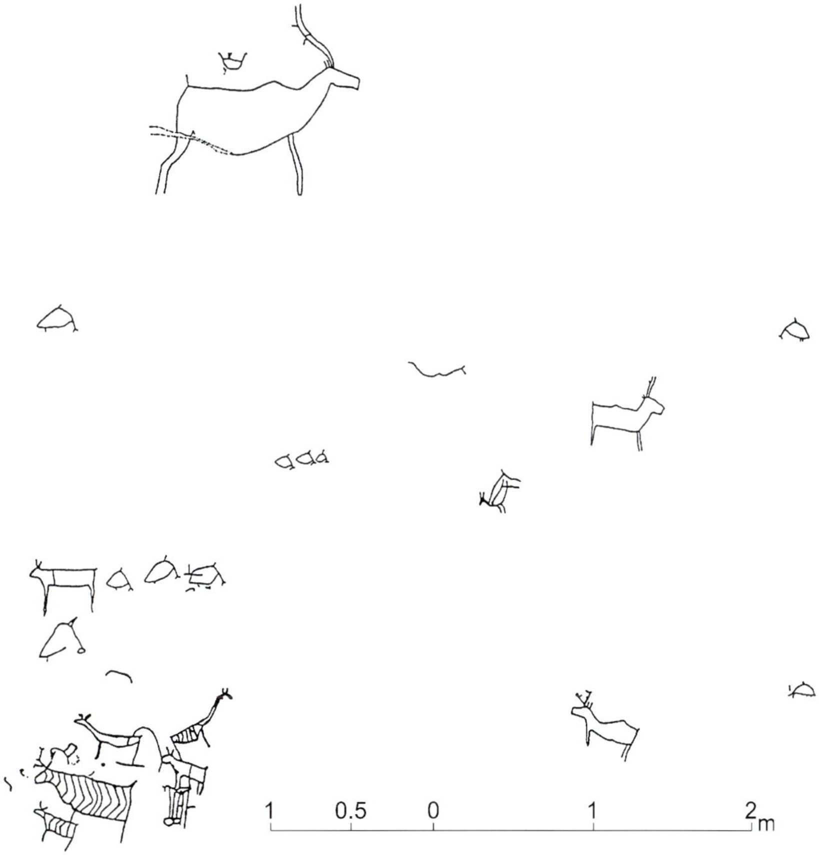

FIGURE 45. Tracing of the Kirkely panel. The top image is a little more naturalistic and carefully made than the animals further down on the panel. At the very bottom, on the other hand, the animals have hatching as body decorations.

PS

portion of the panel, like Gråbergan, is located about 19 metres above sea level. Many of the images, mainly sea and land mammals, are quite weathered. A large number of deer are depicted, and as many as thirteen images of porpoises or smaller whales. The panel also has images of boats.

On the top of the panel is a large deer with long horns and a prominent hump on its neck. The figure is not depicted in any way as naturally as in other locations in North Norway, but it is definitely the figure that has been given the most natural expression here at Kirkely. Also, the animal lacks any body decor. In addition, there are several scattered, smaller images of deer running down and across the panel. Interspersed here and there we find groups of porpoises or small whales that seem to follow one another as if they form part of a pod, and in close association with a deer. At the bottom there is a collection of more stylised animals carved in close proximity to one another, some with shaded bodies. One stands out in particular due to its highly marked body decor in the form of an angular rib pattern, covering the entire body all the way up to the neck.

One particularly interesting feature of the images on the lower portion of the rock is that they are very worn (*ibid.*), probably the result of wave impact, a factor that is also supported by the fact that the images were found partly covered with sandy sediment containing the remains of shells. Taking all of these factors into account, the figures may have been carved very far down near the fjord waterline, perhaps even at low tide, and storms or spring tides may have

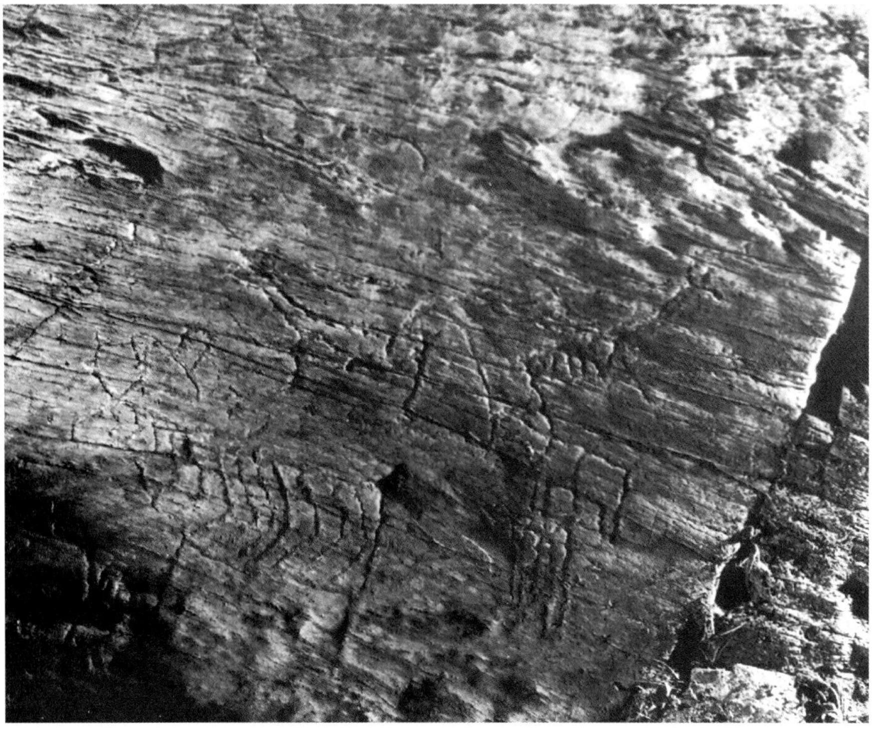

FIGURE 46. These figures are very worn, probably due to wave impact. The weathering has not affected all of the lines, however. The horns of the largest animal, for example, appear to have been pecked at some time after wave erosion was no longer a factor.
EB

subsequently washed the sandy sediment up against the rock. Some researchers have posited that these images may have been exposed to the so-called Tapes transgression, but the transgression must have taken place long before the rock carvings at Kirkely were created.

Changes in ocean conditions

The Tapes transgression was a direct result of a warm period as early as 9000 years ago (Bjerck 2008). After land had risen and emerged for several thousands of years in pace with the melting of the ice, the world's large inland glaciers also began to melt. The oceans began to rise as the glaciers melted more quickly than land emerged, a situation that is referred to as a transgression. The result was that land became flooded. This situation was normalized about 7000 years ago, during the mid-Early Stone Age, and from that period we often find terraces and shoreline embankments at the level at which the ocean stood for a period of well over a thousand years – the so-called Tapes maximum period. Following this period, land uplift accelerated more rapidly than the influx of water from the world's oceans, and a regression occurred. The name Tapes comes from a mussel of the same name that was very plentiful at the time. At Kirkely there are clear traces of the Tapes maximum at about 30 metres above sea level in the form of large embankments, physical proof that the ocean stood at this high level some 7000 years ago (Engelstad 1925). If this transgression were the cause for the wear caused to the rock carvings, then it must have occurred at some stage before the rock surface was inundated, which would in turn suggest that the rock images were extremely old. If they were indeed so old, it would also entail that the remainder of the images on the surface would have been exposed to an equal degree of wear, and there is no sign of this.

It therefore seems clear that the rock carvings at Kirkely must have been produced after the Tapes maximum period and after the water level had fallen by some 10 metres, so that the rock was once again exposed. Based on our knowledge of how quickly land emergence occurred, it was not until just under 5000 years ago that the ocean had receded enough to bring the rock up above the surface again (Hesjedal 1990).

The explanation for the lowest images being so weathered must therefore be that they were affected by the fjord during the time when they were created. Perhaps they were pecked out at the water line, which would in turn explain that the images were exposed to storm surges, spring tides and ice erosion over a period of hundreds of years, and before the land emerged to the point where the images were no longer exposed to the impact of waves and erosion. It is interesting to note that certain parts of the images affected by water erosion were later retouched with pecked lines, including one of the large animals, whose ears were transformed into horns (Gjessing 1938; Simonsen 1958). The lines that are pecked into the stone are very visible, and we can clearly see each pecking mark, in sharp contrast to the lines in the rest of the animal image.

The time perspective that emerges reveals that the rock art, at least at Kirkely, must have been in use or important for several generations, as the changes in sea level amounted to a few centimetres per year. In this case it is interesting to consider that a long period of time must have passed before the land had risen enough to situate the images at a safe distance from the waves, and the artist was able to transform ears into horns and to peck out additional lines that remained totally unaffected by sea wash. This suggests that even though the rock carvings may have been created by one or more humans during a given period, they were maintained and 'refreshed' by many subsequent generations.

Venset

Although Hallström carried out a thorough and lengthy search in the area around Bukkhammarn and Gråbergan, even more images were discovered in the area during the 1980s, this time at the Venset farm to the north of Bukkhammarn. If we take Bukkhammarn as a point of reference, the distance to Venset is approximately the same as to Gråbergan, only in the opposite direction, to the north. The panel is located in the farmyard of Venset and is today overgrown with turf and moss. About ten animal figures, mostly bears, were discovered on a rock surface, together with a few deer. The panel has become covered by undergrowth in just a few years.

Other panels in Troms

The sites mentioned here comprise the majority of the rock carvings of the Northern tradition in Troms, at least if we only take images into account. Further south in Troms, close to Harstad, there are a few more panels. One of these is on the island of Rolla in Ibestad municipality, just east of Harstad, and shows the outlines of at least five figures at eye level pecked into a steep mountain wall (Simonsen 1958). Two of the figures most probably represented naturalistic depictions of elk. The best preserved is almost one and a half metres long. There are also two geometric motifs and an image of what may be a boat. The images are so weathered that they are difficult to discern. Further north, in Kvænangen near Lillestraumen, a boulder was found some years ago engraved with two bear figures. The boulder was found on a terrace where there are many dwelling features left from settlement during the Late Stone Age, which are in turn natural to examine in context with the rock art on the boulder.

In conclusion, it is also necessary to mention a more curious discovery made on the island of Skjervøy in the early 1980s. A rock art panel was found in the cellar of a private home, when an extension was built on one of the existing houses along the Hamne road on the island, and the owner began to excavate earth from beneath the building in order to add a cellar. It was then that the figures were unearthed. They were discovered on a large, well-worn stone slab that extended out from the foundations of the cellar. A pecked figure of a human, an animal and a few disassociated lines were found on the rock. It is likely that there are more images beyond the cellar's foundations.

Apart from the rock art of the Northern tradition mentioned here, there are also two panels containing painted rock art in Tromsø. One of these is located on the tiny island of Kjeøya north of Harstad (Simonsen 1958). The panel is part of a steep mountain wall on the south-western side of the island. It has ten human images, a geometric pattern and an image of what may be an elk painted in red. The images are small, and the colours are extremely faint. Recently, painted images were discovered on an overhanging rock at Bakkejordberget in Sørreisa. These paintings were originally discovered during the 1960s by some enthusiastic fourth-year pupils after they had studied the Stone Age in school, but it would not be until 40 years later that they were taken seriously, and the information would finally reach Tromsø Museum. Taking all of the relevant factors into account, these last two panels are considerably later than the rock art of the Northern tradition, and probably date from the early Metal Age, between 2000 BC and the beginning of the Christian Era.

Forselv in Skjomen

Deep within the Ofotfjord, very near the city of Narvik, narrow Skjomenfjord curves some 20 kilometres southwards between tall, steep mountains and ends only a few kilometres from the Swedish border. Already at the inlet to the fjord one can glimpse the tall, smooth mountain peaks and precipitous fjord banks farther in. Towards the head of the fjord, on the western side, Frostisen glacier towers over the landscape at heights of 1200 to 1700 metres above sea level and from time to time calves bluish green blocks of ice down into the fjord below. Halfway to the fjord bottom in Skjomen, almost directly beneath the glacier but before the fjord becomes bordered by its steepest banks, we find the Forselv rock carvings (Gjessing 1931; Hallström 1938). Since the entire western side of Skjomenfjord plunges steeply into the fjord from the mouth all the way to the far end of the fjord, Forselv stands out as one of the last places on the way in where it is possible to go ashore. Today the place bears the name of the river that carries melted ice down from the glacier, ending in a mighty waterfall just above the surface of the fjord. Immediately below the falls, a low-lying stone outcrop stretches inward, parallel with the fjord, and forms a natural border between what today are infields and the embankment sloping down to the water. Proceeding from the river and along the outcrop, which gradually slopes upward over the surrounding landscape, we arrive some 300–400 metres further on at the rock art panel, which is located at an elevation of some 30 metres above the fjord at the point where the mountain ridge begins to recede into the plateau. Here the rock is smoother and more even than elsewhere along the ridge. Many attempts have been made to find rock art images along the entire mountain ridge, but in vain. Over the last few centuries the shoreline has been cultivated all the way up to the rocky inclines, as revealed by several large piles of cleared stones. Today the area is no longer cultivated, and grazing is limited, with clear signs that the forest – both pine and deciduous trees – is beginning to dominate. Nevertheless the view from here to the fjord is still open in both directions as well as towards the sheer, desolate and precipitous mountainsides. In spring and summer it is possible to hear the constant roar not only of the Forselv River, but of the countless streams and smaller falls that cascade down the mountainsides on the other side of the fjord.

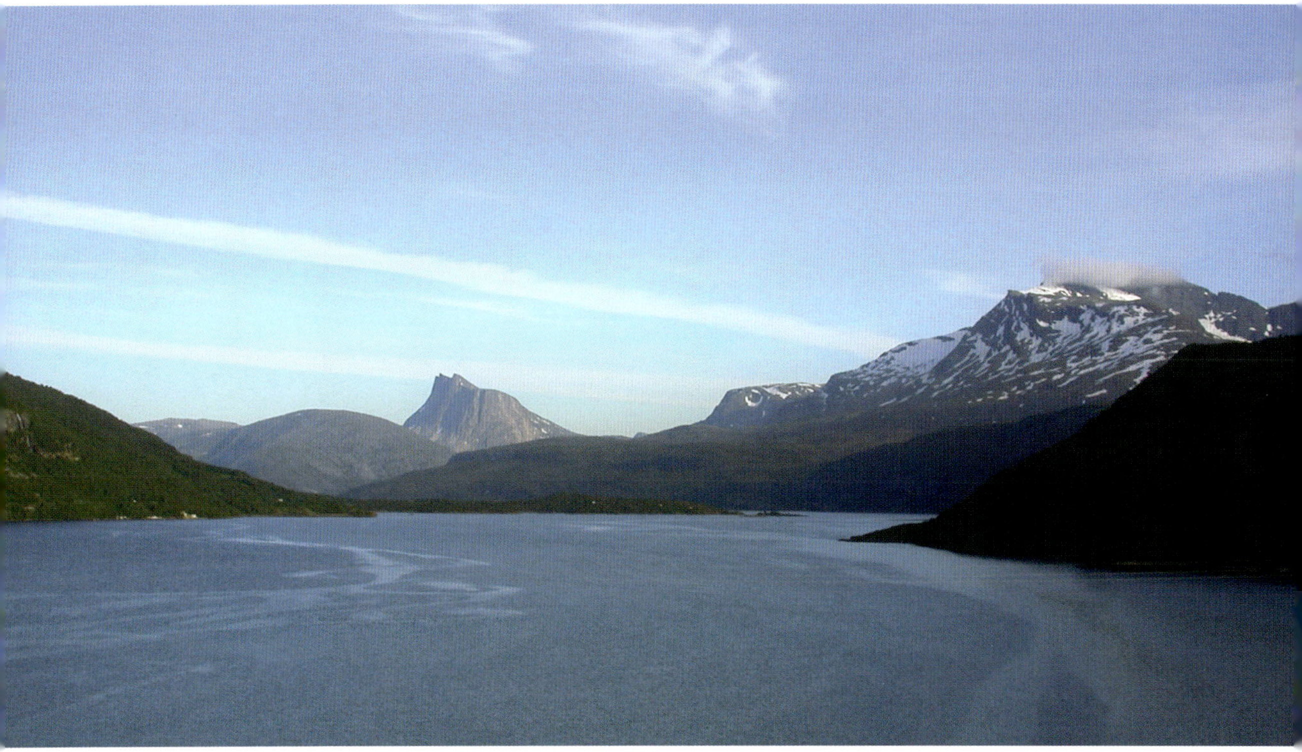

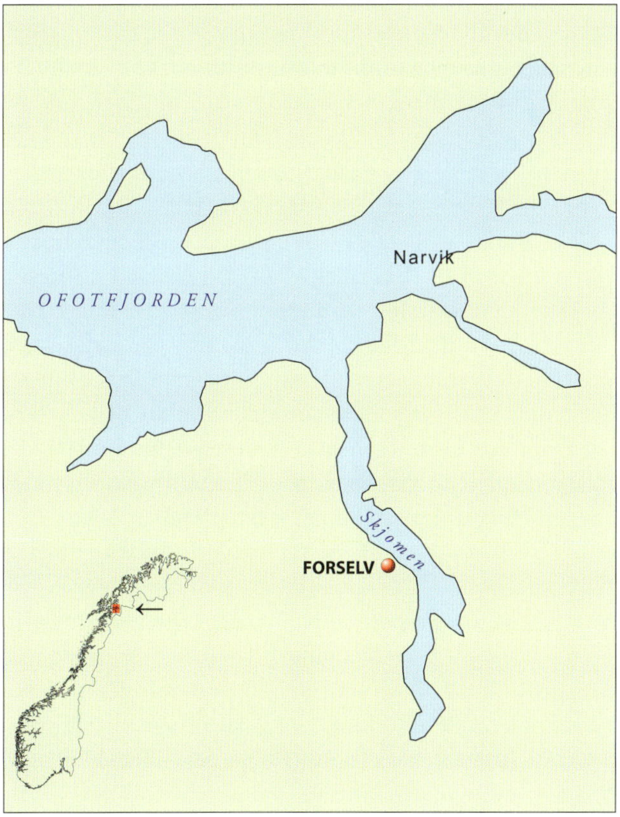

FIGURES 47–48.
Above: The inlet on Skjomenfjord with Lappviktinden peak as the landmark in the distance. Forselv is situated about half way between the mouth and the end of Skjomenfjord.
MAP AI, ILLUSTRATION TL

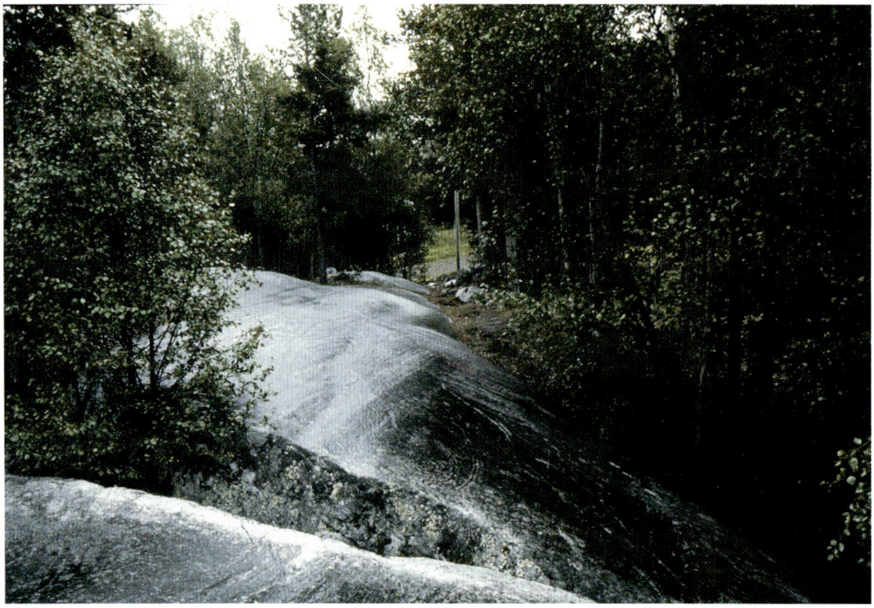

FIGURE 49. The Forselv rock panel. Today the forest is gradually surrounding the panel. TM

The myriad

Altogether there are more than 40 images on the rock panel, and all of them are created by pecking. It is not the naturalistic character of the images that is most impressive, but instead the great variation in motifs on a relatively small surface. The impression is of a throng of images resembling a surrealistic parade across the rock: humans, land and sea animals, fish, boats, as well as circular and geometric figures and a number of more or less quadratic and rhombic box images filled in with carefully considered and well-developed pattern work (Gjessing 1931; Hallström 1938). All of the images stand close to one another, almost aligned, along a 12-metre-long segment of the panel which is bordered at both ends by two clefts. The compact concentration of images within this limited space has prompted many researchers to describe the images and rock surface as a frieze. Outside of the bordering clefts, there are only three images. On the outside of the northern cleft there is only one image of an animal. It seems that the image was never completed, or that it has been worn away over time. Just south of the other cleft there are two reindeer images, one of them only a half-image. The latter was probably exposed to erosive weathering. Severe weathering has obviously affected the main panel as well. Amongst the more of less whole and distinct images, there are a number of fragmentary lines that are difficult to make out today. In many places it is entirely impossible to properly explain or interpret what the lines may have represented. This situation is challenging for researchers, since what once was a whole is no longer available in its entirety. The combinations that remain, therefore, give rise to practically countless, inexhaustible explanatory models. Judging from the way the images are arranged, we are nonetheless convinced that the rock was used as a gateway to the beyond.

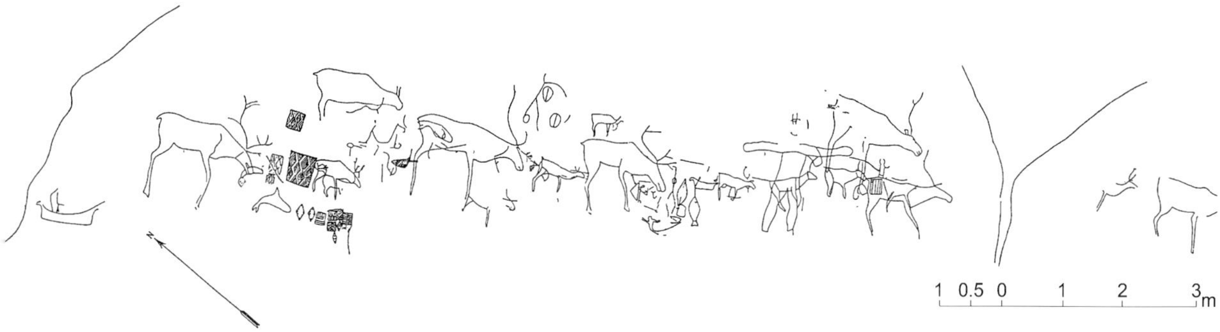

FIGURE 50. A large number of figures, some of them superimposed, including humans, land and sea animals, fish, boats and several geometric figures.
GG

Dating difficulties

The dating of the images is problematical. We lack knowledge making it possible to substantiate dwelling sites near Forselv, which would naturally allow us to place them in context with the images. Like many other fjords in Northern and Southern Norway, human activity in Skjomenfjord in prehistoric times is insufficiently substantiated. There have been some scattered finds in along the fjord, including slate arrowheads from the Late Stone Age, but it is far too risky to use these as a basis for dating the images. When the images were discovered in 1929, it was also known that a number of old hearths and charcoal deposits had been found in the field near the panel, although all of these remains were lost when the area was cultivated. Today there are some indications that there were areas where cultivation was less intensive and where it is plausible that some archaeological material may still be found. The area has not yet been investigated. The site was also cultivated at an early stage, as there was a large pile of cleared stones up near the rocky plateau. The stones were partially removed at the same time as the images were documented, although additional images were not found.

For a long time it has been uncertain how land uplift occurred at this point. It was very relevant, therefore, when some years ago a number of tree trunks were uncovered during excavation in an old river delta in Skjomen, located between 20 and 30 metres above the current tree line. Dating of the tree trunks found at this point in the delta area proved that the water level had stood at this height some 6000 years ago, towards the end of the Early Stone Age (Dahl 1993). Perhaps the site was in use at that time. The lowest-lying images are located about 31 metres above sea level, and would have been near the fjord's water level at the time. This would have been an ideal moment for landing boats at Forselv. There would have been a small bay on the fjord near the inner side of the mountain ridge, and the ridge where the panel is located would therefore have been well sheltered from strong winds and turbulent waters. The images could then be made practically hidden from view from the fjord, while at the same time the creators of the images would have had a good view and control over the approach from the fjord. It is another question altogether as to whether the images were pecked out during roughly the same time period. Relatively few refreshed lines and a generally homogeneous creative technique suggest that most of the images were made at approximately the same time. Neither do differences in pecking techniques help, as the panel is relatively weathered and the lines are generally uniform. A large human figure almost at the southernmost tip of the panel was perhaps superimposed over several other figures, perhaps much later than the other figures, although it is difficult to be certain.

The terrestrial animals

At first glance we are attracted by the large images of at least six reindeer, about one metre long. They appear to be migrating southward over the panel. They are impressively naturalistic, and most have large antlers. After this, our attention is drawn to the many smaller animals, also including reindeer, which are abundant. A couple of these, at the southern edge, stand out from the others by the manner in which their heads and more stocky bodies are depicted. The fact that their hind quarters extend all the way up to their backs makes them all the more distinctive. Some researchers have suggested that these were meant to represent dogs, but others have been quick to point out that these animals have antlers, a fact that would tend to exclude any animal other than reindeer. The discrepancy in size may be the result of a desire to portray depth in the image – to indicate quite simply that the animals are farther away. This said, some do appear to be calves.

Amongst the animals in the southern part are two peculiar images that are close to each other, practically overlapping. One of these appears to be a reindeer, the other a bear. Judging from the way the animals are placed, it seems as if the larger animal image was created first, and that the creator of the second image has taken advantage of the reindeer's belly line and used it as the upper outline of the bear's back. What is perplexing is that the line for the head and

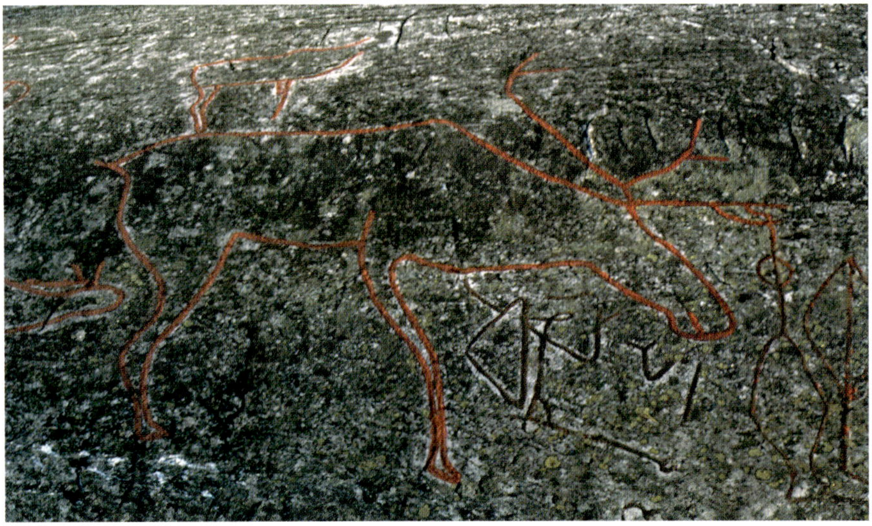

FIGURE 51. One of the largest reindeer images placed in the centre of the panel.

TM

neck of the bear has been misaligned and runs parallel higher up in the image. It almost seems as if the work was interrupted for some reason, and that when it was resumed, the engraver accidentally or intentionally extended the bear's head into the reindeer's neck (Gjessing 1932).

Since the majority of the images are created with a high degree of precision and careful consideration, it seems strange that the position of the bear's head would be the result of carelessness. However, it may have been an intentional act that we do not understand in our modern age. If we look more closely at the reindeer superimposed over the bear, we find that the hind leg is placed as if it is pushed forward on the body. Several of the other images have similar traits, which appear to form a pattern. It is as if an attempt has been made to manipulate the natural lines of nature, and this should perhaps be seen in the light of the intended purpose of the rock art.

Sea mammals and fish

The viewer's attention is gradually drawn towards other motifs. Just below the reindeer in the northern section, there is a clear image of a porpoise or small whale with a distinct tailfin. The whale is depicted in the characteristic, arched position, as if it had just surfaced for air and was about to plunge back into the deep. It appears alone, apparently without any other connection to the whole. On other panels with which this panel could be compared, it seems as if there are connections or contrasts between sea mammals and large land animals that have been intentionally expressed through the images. We find examples of this, among other places, at Bogge in Møre og Romsdal and on panels with polished images, in both Leiknes and Klubba.

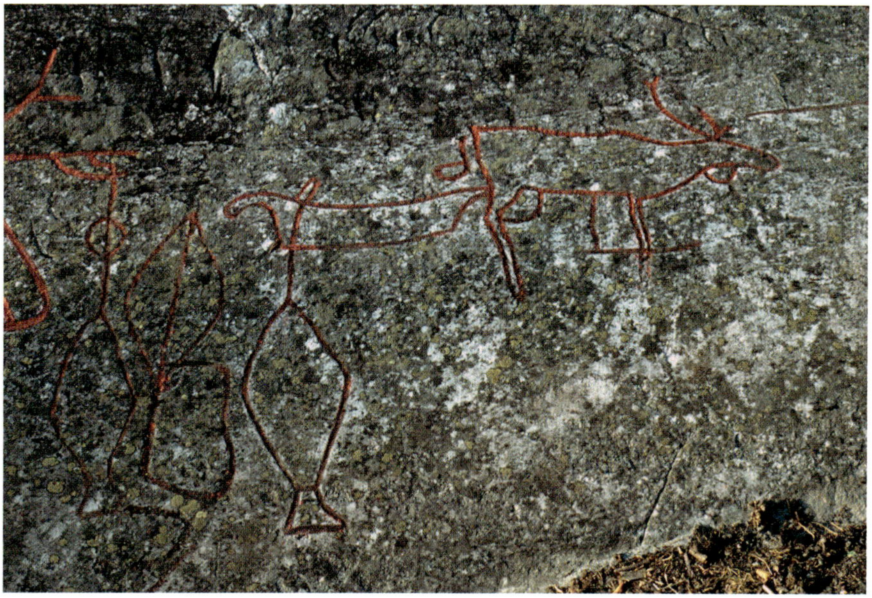

FIGURE 52. Halibut are a recurring subject on many rock art panels. It is likely that there were many conceptions associated with this fish species.

TM

Amongst the animals further south on the panel there are several halibut. At least one of these appears to be hooked on a line beneath a boat. The line clearly extends up to the boat, but there is no human figure on board. It is possible, of course, that there once was a human figure in the boat, but that it has been erased by weathering. However, it is also possible that there was never an intention to depict a human, and that the aim was to emphasize other factors beyond the human, factors and elements that would thereby be elevated to a more reverent level. There are countless ways in which this may be seen. The other two halibut are shown adjacent to the first, and are in the same vertical position. One of them is hanging on a line that extends directly upwards and has a circular figure that probably represents a weight on the line. But there is no boat – only a horizontal, scoured line. In all probability this was intended to represent the bottom of a boat, which was then left incomplete, or else other lines may have been weathered away.

It is interesting to find halibut interspersed with reindeer. Based on other comparable panels, including some in Alta (Helskog 1988), it seems that halibut are closely linked with reindeer. Even today there is superstition associated with halibut, also known as "hellefisk", a rewriting in Norwegian of the term meaning literally "holy fish". It is the largest of the flounder family and one of the largest bony fish we have in Norway. It can grow to be very large; in modern times halibut weighing more than 300 kg and longer than three metres have been caught. It is particularly its size that has made it prominent, and we know that their guts were used to cure illnesses before the advent of modern medicine. However, halibut is particularly associated with the drama of landing such a large fish. It is not difficult to imagine that the work involved in landing a halibut could quickly develop into a life-or-death struggle, particularly when we consider the simple boats that must have been in use during the Stone Age.

Perhaps the most peculiar feature of the rock art at Forselv is that the largest of the reindeer, at the northern portion of the panel, is depicted clutching what is either a whale or a large fish in its jaws. This is an extraordinarily unusual element in terms of normal reindeer behaviour, and is probably of mythological nature. It is only possible to speculate on the meaning of a reindeer holding a fish in its jaws. It is an entirely inconceivable situation which must be attributed to spiritual or mythological factors, unless it is a figment of the imagination of the image's creator. It is difficult to identify the species. If it is indeed a fish, it is tempting to interpret it as a salmon. In early times the salmon held an important position in our culture and was seen as the king of kings among fish. The salmon's ability to survive in fresh water, saltwater and brackish fjord water may have earned it a special status. Obviously it is difficult to trace historical perceptions of fish and animals far back in time, but such projections may offer some insight into the status that various species may have had. Others have interpreted the image as representing a porpoise, which in turn renders the other porpoise in the image – splashing in the waves beneath the reindeer figure – more important, as if the reindeer has caught one of the two porpoises.

Another special feature of this panel is that one of the large reindeer is depicted with what appears to be a fish incorporated in its hindquarters; this is yet another indication of the connection between land and sea.

Boats

The knowledge we have about boats from this early period of time is based on what we are able to deduce from the rock art. We have yet to find any remains of boats dating from the Stone Age in our part of the world. It is obvious that boats must have existed very soon after the last Ice Age. If they did not exist, then many of the islands off the outer coastal areas would have remained unsettled, and it is an established fact that people made their way to these islands within a short time of the ice receeding (Bjerck 2008). There are many different perceptions of the types of boats that may have been used, depending on where they were used and for which destinations. In Denmark, for example, we have found hollowed-out tree trunks that were viable in sheltered areas without heavy currents, wind and waves (e.g. Malm 1995). Another alternative in more northern regions may have been rib-frame boats covered with stretched hides. Several of the boats seen in rock art have vertical lines that we are logically led to interpret as ribs. At Forselv, there are two clear depictions that are quite similar, one at the top and one in the centre of the panel. It is difficult to determine how these were constructed, but in some of the boat images in areas of northern Norway we find examples of vertical lines and dashes in the hull, which can be interpreted as ribs on a boat frame that were then covered with stretched hide.

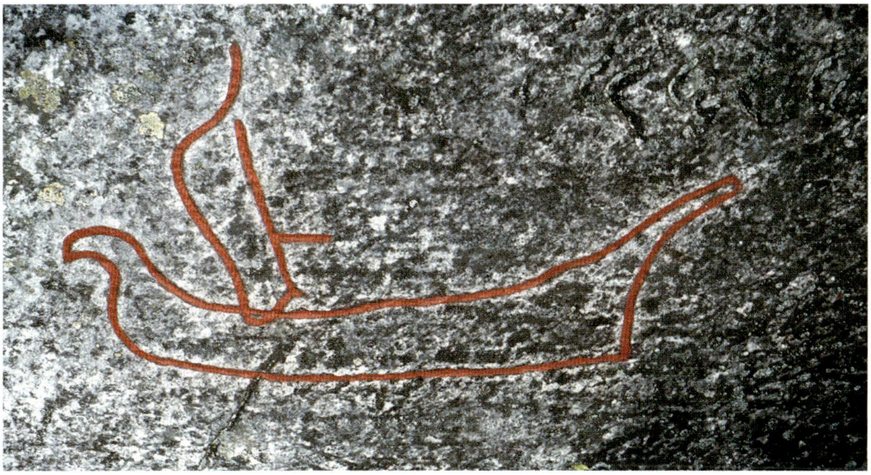

FIGURE 53. A boat image at the northernmost end of the panel. The lines on board are perhaps intended to illustrate a person.

TM

People

Amongst the animals in the southern portion of the panel is the aforementioned human figure, highly stylised, without distinct hands, feet or head, while the rest of the body is relatively well proportioned. It is somewhat uncertain whether the head was simply worn away, but the lack of hands and fingers suggests nonetheless that the body itself was the centre of attention, and that the intention was to emphasize bodily qualities. The figure is depicted as standing and facing the viewer, with its hands stretched out in opposite directions. It was pecked on top of one of the smaller reindeer and the legs of a larger reindeer. This gives rise to the speculation that it may have been created at a later period. This said, it is important to note that there are many cases in which images appear to be contemporary, even though one is superimposed over another. The relatively naturalistic manner in which these images were depicted may suggest that they are contemporary to one another. It is natural to compare the image with the human figure at Skavberget in Troms, where the body also appears to be the emphasized feature, even though the two images are somewhat different in design (Søborg 2006). As previously mentioned, there is no human presence on board the boat, which is located in the centre of the panel. In contrast, there are a few lines on board the boat at the far north of the panel, and these may be construed as representing a person.

Mythological associations and spiritual factors

The animal images carved on rocks, as we have found in many other sites, have been interpreted as hunting scenes and an invocation to ensure a successful

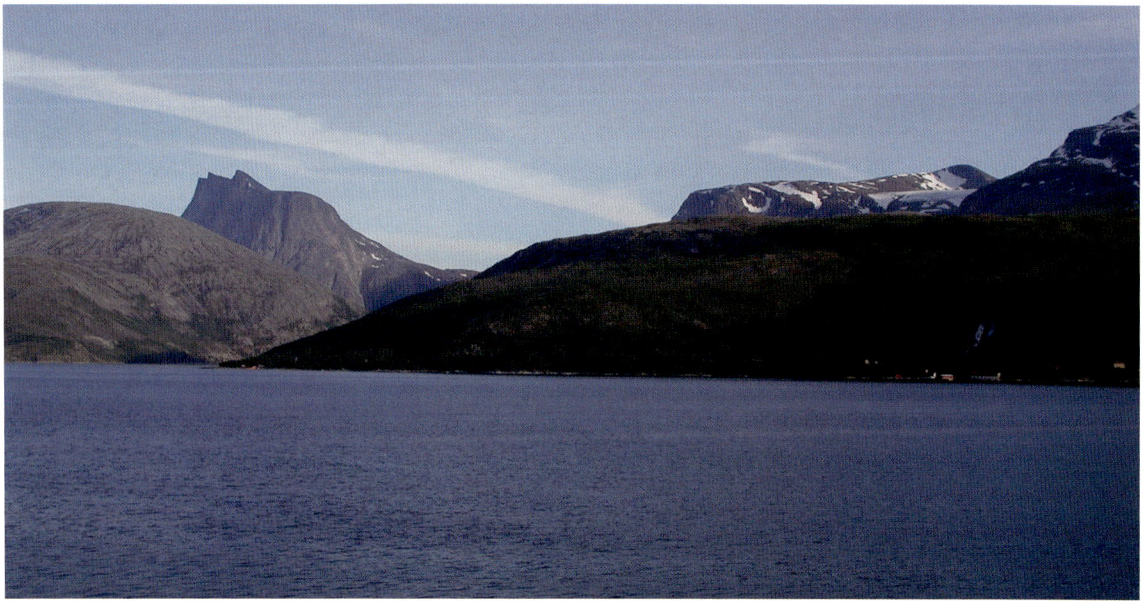

FIGURE 54. Lappviktinden peak at the far end of the fjord, and Forselv to the right. The rock carvings are located about 300–400 metres inside of the waterfall
TL

hunt. There are also depictions that cannot be interpreted as more than mere hunting scenes, including the panels at Hjemmeluft in Alta, where we see people carrying bows and arrows or spears in close contact with animals (Helskog 1988). On the Skjomen panel, the closest we come to hunting is the hooked halibut hanging on a line beneath one of the boats. In reality, it is not the catch that is the focal point, but instead the relationship between fish and boat. The other boat, however, is depicted without any close relationship to halibut or other fish. Neither do the reindeer appear to be a part of any evident hunting situation. On the contrary, they represent situations that can hardly be anything other than spiritual or mythological. The societies in question here never had a marked delineation between economy and religion. All aspects of existence were most likely intertwined, so that hunting and fishing were one with spiritual and religious life. In comparison with other societies, we know that it was essential to take ritualistic and spiritual precautions when setting out on a hunt, a fishing outing or a foray to gather resources from nature. Most actions were probably ritual actions. Similarly, most of the natural environment during the Stone Age must have been regarded as animated. We can easily imagine, based on ethnographical studies, that there would have been established measures and perhaps ritualistic sacrifices for all of the practices that we associate today with the exploitation of natural resources (Zwelebil 2008), whether hunting land animals or gathering herbs and berries. The person or persons who created the rock images at some point during the Stone Age made a very different distinction between the animal and the human world that we have today. Of course it is impossible for us to definitely determine the kind of perceptions that were associated with the individual animals; we can only suggest possibilities based on interpretation. One logical explanation is that each type of animal was perceived in a special way, and that some animals were considered as being more important and more vital than others.

We know that the frames of reference that we consider as normal today and that are well founded in scientific research were not the same as those of people living only a few centuries ago. Therefore we cannot expect that Stone Age people would have had the same so-called rational view of their environment as we have today. Theirs was certainly a world-view that mirrored the close contact with nature that we can perhaps glimpse through the depictions of the rock art images they created. For example, it seems clear that there was a conscious and probably antagonistic perception of the relationship between land and sea animals, and between land animals and fish. Even today many people hold that there are higher powers governing everything that occurs around us, despite generally accepted scientific explanations. As we have only researched prehistoric religion to a very small degree, these aspects of society have been neglected in the literature (*ibid.*). This has prolonged the tendency to conceive prehistoric people as being as simple and rational as we are today, continually hunting for new resources to exploit. Today we make a clear dichotomy between nature and culture, but it is entirely unclear whether

Stone Age people made such a categorical distinction, or if they made any distinction in the way we do today. Inasmuch as they distinguished themselves and distanced themselves from animals, this was quite certainly done in a different way. In addition, we have explanations for most phenomena and no longer raise questions about obvious circumstances, such as the seasons of the year, that a 24–hour period brings both daylight and darkness, that the coastline experiences high and low tides, or that the weather brings rain, snow, wind, lightning and thunder. Basically, we no longer question natural phenomena that even until quite recently were still attributed to mythological occurrences.

Today, we understand the migration patterns and special behaviour of animals in our own way. The same behaviour may have been perceived, experienced and interpreted in an entirely different way during the Stone Age, and may have had explanations that must be seen in the light of the society and world view of that time, with interpretations in the context of their religion and mythology.

We know that animals were slain, but we do not know what steps had to be taken before animals could be killed. Ethnography is full of examples showing how certain societies and individuals organise the hunt and the kinds of taboos that exist. In some places it was necessary to emulate the animal being hunted as closely as possible; in other places it was necessary to avoid contact with other members of society. In this respect the alternatives are inexhaustible. It is likely that a number of taboos were associated with land animals, sea mammals and fish, and that it was necessary to be wary of breaking these rules. It was thought that to do so could seriously affect the chances for hunting game or catching fish. An even worse consequence may be that animals and the souls of animals would cast a spell on their hunters, leading to poverty, illness and death.

The reason why some animal features were deliberately manipulated is also an open question. Ethnographical studies show that there are many cases where people who undergo rites of passage, often from puberty into adulthood, are shown grotesque masks and images of animals and humans whose natural features are heavily manipulated and distorted (e.g. Turner 1970). The purpose for this is to raise the consciousness of ritual participants who are to be born anew into the world, so that they will be better equipped, in a figurative sense, to distinguish between the natural and unnatural features and therefore develop into reflective individuals. This perspective helps explain why animals were intentionally depicted with distorted proportions.

Quadratic figures

Perhaps the strangest feature of the rock art at Forselv is the fact that there are quadratic figures included amongst several of the animal images. There are at least eight quadratic and four rhombic figures, all of varying sizes, some of which are severely weathered. The inner cross-hatching has nevertheless been preserved in many of them. Some are filled with vertical and horizontal lines,

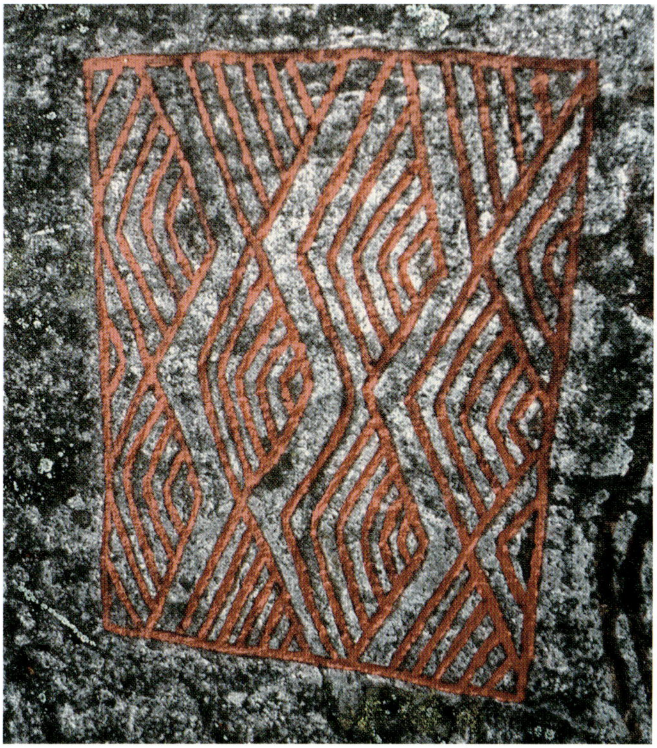

FIGURE 55. Among the more spectacular images are the framework patterns. Their meaning is unknown, but exact parallels in terms of both shape and decoration are known to exist, among other places in Trøndelag. TM

although a couple of them are filled with an attractive and fascinating pattern of rhombic figures that are in turn cross-hatched with angular lines. These figures are concentrated almost at the bottom of the panel, and are set apart from the other images. One of the figures, however, is pecked into the hind hip of the southernmost animal in the centre section. The first impression is that these figures represent a very recent feature. For this reason, they are also placed in context with ceramic decor from the Late Stone Age or the Neolithic. Similar figures are not known to exist in other local panels, but there are a number of counterparts in other places relatively far away. The characteristic decor in the rhombic figures is found, among other places, at Hell and at Bardal in Trøndelag (Gjessing 1936). The similarities between the quadratic figures at Bardal in Trøndelag and those at Forselv are particularly striking, especially when we consider the great distance between the two panels.

Relationship with other areas

There are also other areas in which similar quadratic figures have been found, one of which is in Finland (e.g. Lahelma 2008). It is a painted image, but the resemblance to the figures in Skjomen is striking. Another interesting item in this context is the fact that many Stone Age dwelling sites have been found in the mountains above Skjomenfjord, as well as in the mountains farther to the east. This may suggest that there was contact between the Skjomen dwellers and these areas. In the Christian era, the fjord was a gateway to the mountain range and contact with the land areas that are now in Sweden, as well as with other areas even further to the east. This in turn may have been built upon much older, established routes and contacts that had existed already from the Stone Age.

It also seems clear that the creators of the Forselv images left behind artistic expressions in other places within a reachable distance in the local area. This becomes particularly clear when we examine one of the animals in the southernmost section of the panel, where we see that the contour lines of one foreleg and one hind leg are extended further down than the others. Archaeologists would have continued to show little interest in this feature if it were not for the fact that a short distance further north, on the northern side of Ofotfjorden at Herjangen (Gjessing 1932), there is a reindeer image shaped in precisely the same way, suggesting that these two animal images were created by the same person. In further support of this possibility, there are two identical, small circular figures divided in half by a vertical line at both Forselv and Herjangen. It is uncertain what they were meant to illustrate, but their similarity is undeniable, and serves to link the Herjangen figures with those at Forselv.

This also suggests that rock art was the domain of a chosen few in society, most probably religious specialists who invoked higher powers on behalf of society in various geographic areas, and who carved their invocations on stone as they moved from place to place as a result of changes in society, or other factors.

It is still unclear why Skjomen in particular was chosen as a site. However, it is interesting to note that inner fjord areas were often chosen as the location for rock art production, as opposed to the open coastal areas. Explanations could be found along the shores of Skjomenfjord, where future archaeological excavations may reveal the answers to many questions. Recently a few more images have been documented at the site by Tromsø Museum, but the tracings have not yet been published.

Polished Rock Art in Nordland

One of the most extraordinary types of art from the Northern Tradition in Norway is found in a limited area in the centre of Nordland. The rock art is normally described as polished images, the name given to the special technique used to create the images on stone. Only seven sites are known to exist, between Glomfjord and the Svartisen glacier plateau in the south and Vestfjorden in the north. The images, all of which are of animals, are generally contour-polished, meaning that we only see the outlines of the animals depicted. Large mammals are the most commonly depicted subjects. In most cases these are land animals such as reindeer and elk, although birds, whales, seals and even fish are also found in certain locations.

The size of the animals is frequently exaggerated, and it is not uncommon to find reindeer as long as four metres. In many places they are vividly expressed in what appears to be an individual style, a personal form of expression or a type of impressionism from a bygone era. On the panels with this type of rock art, we find either compositions with numerous images, or depictions of individual images. In some places the images are also polished on top of one another. Initially, it may be thought that this was an attempt to bring out depth and perspective between the natural subjects. However, when we find sea mammals overlapping land animals, this does not appear to hold true. Neither is the possibility that the artists were unaware that there were other images present on the rock when they began work on a new one a plausible explanation, as the images are quite clear-cut even today. When one of the bear images on one of the southernmost panels is depicted with the head of an elk, and a whale was polished over a land animal, it is tempting to conclude that these choices were made based on some mythological rationale. Portrayal techniques vary from the naturalistic to the more schematic. A characteristic trait is that these polished rock art images were applied to smooth, barren stone surfaces. It is possible that such surfaces were physically attractive when the images were made, and that they had features that made them stand out, even at long distances, as well as providing a suitable flat surface on which to polish images. At the same time it is true that many other, equally attractive and suitable surfaces in the immediate vicinity of the rock art images were not chosen. We have so far been unable to break the elusive code that may explain why rock art was placed where we find it. This applies to all rock art wherever it is found. It is likely that numerous factors related to spiritual factors and worship came into play when a surface was chosen for decoration.

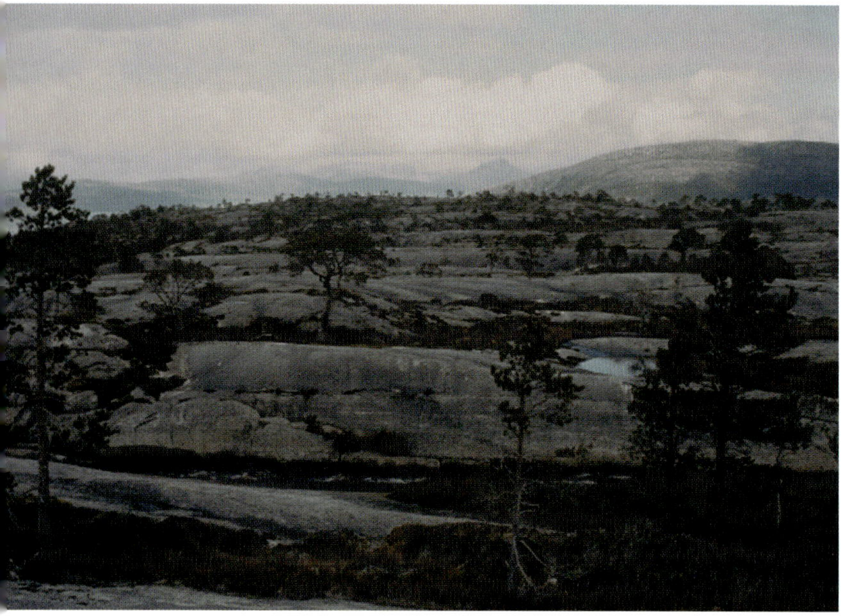

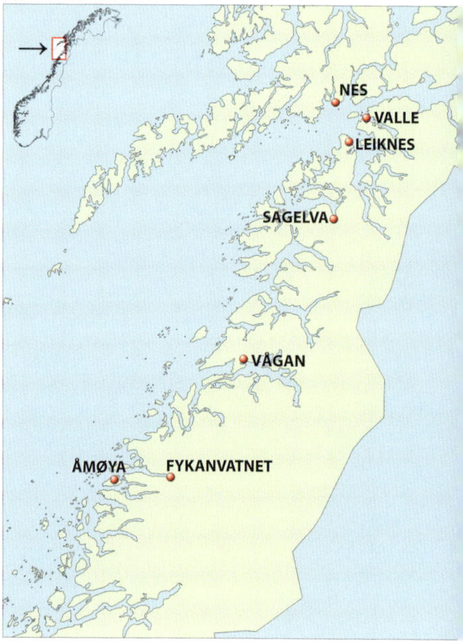

FIGURES 56–57. Polished rock art is found in a limited part of the county of Nordland. It is typically found in barren areas devoid of vegetation, on highly exposed, smoothly weathered rock. The photo is from Valle in Efjorden, where polished figures are found on at least two of the ridges in the centre of the picture

MAP AI, ILLUSTRATION TL

Techniques

Neither are we any more certain of the type of tools that were used to create these images. This said, it has been established that the images were created using some type of polishing technique. Polishing is done without cutting grooves, but merely polishing contours on the upper surface of the rock panel. The lines of the images emerge on most of the panels as light streaks against the darker rock surfaces, which are mostly granite or gneiss. If we run our hands over the lines, it is possible to feel that the surface is smooth in contrast to the unpolished surfaces inside and outside the contours. Surprisingly, whenever artificial light has been used at night, the lines have emerged almost with the brilliance of a reflective strip. On some of the panels there are lines that appear to stand out three-dimensionally from the rock surface. It seems that the polished lines have been more resistant to weathering than the remainder of the surface. In some places the images are also somewhat overgrown with lichens, but the lines still emerge clearly, probably because lichens and moss do not attach themselves as firmly to polished rock surfaces.

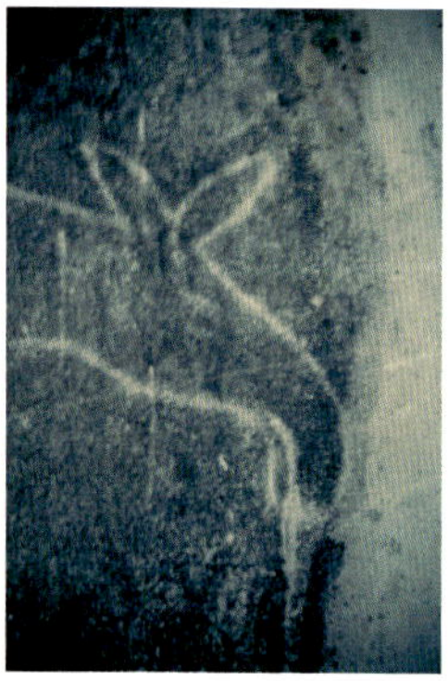

FIGURE 58. Representation of the head of an elk from Vågan. The very smooth, polished lines stand out from the surrounding surface.

TL

Age

As previously mentioned, the usual method for determining the age of the images of the Northern Tradition in coastal areas is based on geological surveys of land uplift after the last Ice Age. Based on similar studies it has been argued convincingly that the rock art must have been created on stone surfaces near the seashore and not long after land emerged from the sea, before these surfaces became overgrown with lichens, grass and other vegetation. Knowledge of the rate of land emergence makes it possible to calculate when the rock art, today located high above sea level, was located at shoreline level. The method is supported by the fact that rock art of the Northern Tradition found inland has been unaffected by land upheaval after the last Ice Age, and is still today located at the waterline along rivers and watercourses (Bakka 1973). The coast of Nordland was forced downward during the last Ice Age, and rose dramatically after the ice receded. The polished rock art in most cases lies at such high elevations that it can be dated all the way back to the first millennia after the last Ice Age, when the particular panels with rock art were at shoreline level. These rock images are therefore considered to be the very oldest rock art in Norway and perhaps bear witness to the pioneer settlers who first migrated to the land after the last Ice Age. The different elevations at which the figures are located may also be indicative of great differences in age between the various panels.

The placement of rock art above today's sea level varies between a little less than 40 metres up to 90 metres. This difference in elevation, however, is not in itself a basis for deducing time differences. The inland was compressed downward during the last Ice Age, so that the images that are found at high elevation inside a fjord may very well be contemporary with images that are at a lower point further out towards the coast. Based on what we know about land emergence, this elevation allows us to date it back to a period between eight or nine thousand years ago, when the rock images were located along the shoreline.

Klubba at Åmøy

Along the rugged western coast of Nordland, about 25 kilometres north of the Arctic Circle, we find the most southerly rock art of this type. It is located at Klubba at Åmøy, between Meløyfjorden and Skardsfjorden. The rock art site itself is to the north, some 300 metres from the shore and about one kilometre west of the eastern tip of the island. While the shoreline and the lower-lying portions along the northern side of Åmøya are characterised by moors and scree, at the foot of Skardstinden there is a change in terrain and an area of smooth and barren rocks. Here the landscape is more desolate and dramatic, offering a panorama of craggy mountain peaks. The fact that the rock art was originally discovered by people looking for eagles' nests reveals something about its location.

On many of these smooth surfaces, most of which face north, there are some twenty or so images, all of them of the polished type (Hallström 1938). They lie in concentrations across the shiny rock surfaces, either individually or in groups. The images are depicted with a varying degree of naturalism. Some are very well executed, while others appear to be almost stunted, with major disproportions in the bodies of the animals. On several of the figures we also find lines that

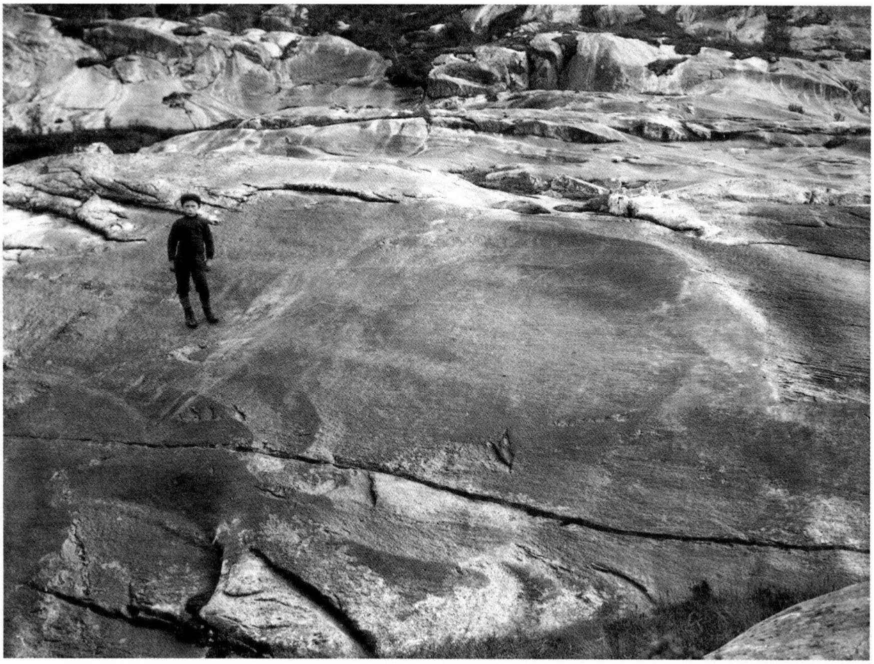

FIGURE 59. One of the panels with images at Klubba, photographed by Gustaf Hallström in 1913.

were obviously errors and which were corrected. Some of the images were also polished overlapping one another. Most of the images are meant to represent elk or reindeer, but at least one of them is of a bear. One large elk at the bottom of a panel is executed in a very naturalistic and impressive manner. It is almost four and a half metres long, and partially overlaps a smaller reindeer. Among the many land animals there are also two whales, probably orcas or killer whales. A special feature of one of these figures, which is almost seven metres long, is that it was applied on top of three elks, a feature we find in one of the panels further north. Not all of the images are as distinct, and in many places the lines are the same colour as the background stone. These are hard to make out, but the lines can still be felt by running your hand over them, as they are smoother to the touch than the background rock. In several places the images are badly weathered, and some are marred by graffiti, which had already begun to be a problem by the early 1900s, increasing as the years went by (*ibid.*). Curiously, apart from scratching their names and initials, some people have carved human figures wearing trousers and dresses, which clearly belie their modern origins, and which stand in garish contrast to the prehistoric images.

Fykan Lake in Glomfjord

Leaving Klubba and following Meløyfjord eastward until we reach the end of the narrow Glomfjord, we arrive at the next area with polished rock art. Here the mountains to the east are marked by numerous scoured and smooth sections, a trait that emphasizes the massiveness of the mountains and the alpine

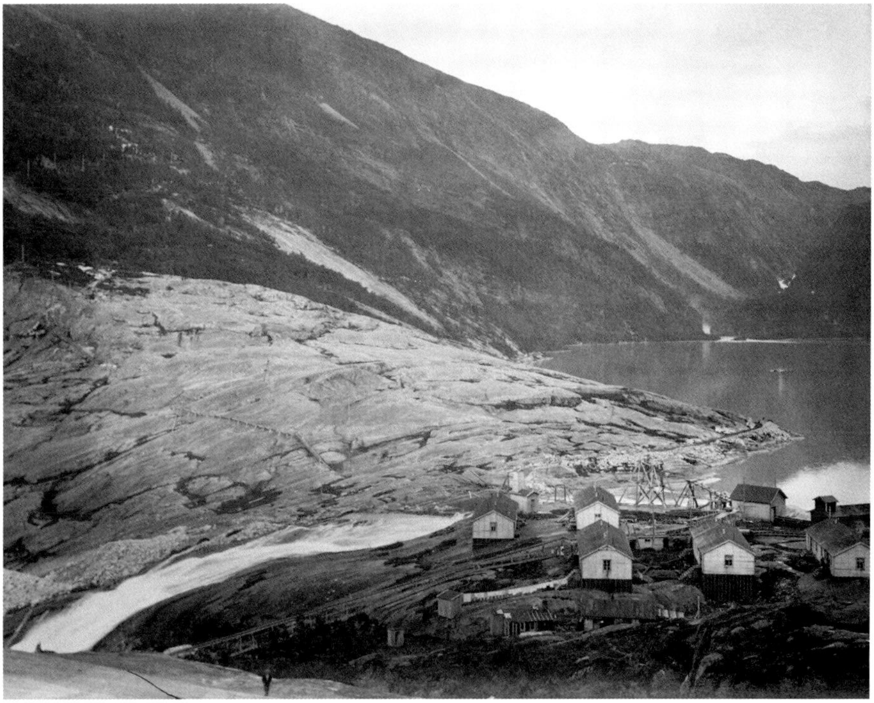

FIGURE 60. The images are distributed across the weathered panels shown in the photo, with Fykanvatnet on the right. In 1917, when this photo was taken, industry was already visibly present in the environment.
GH

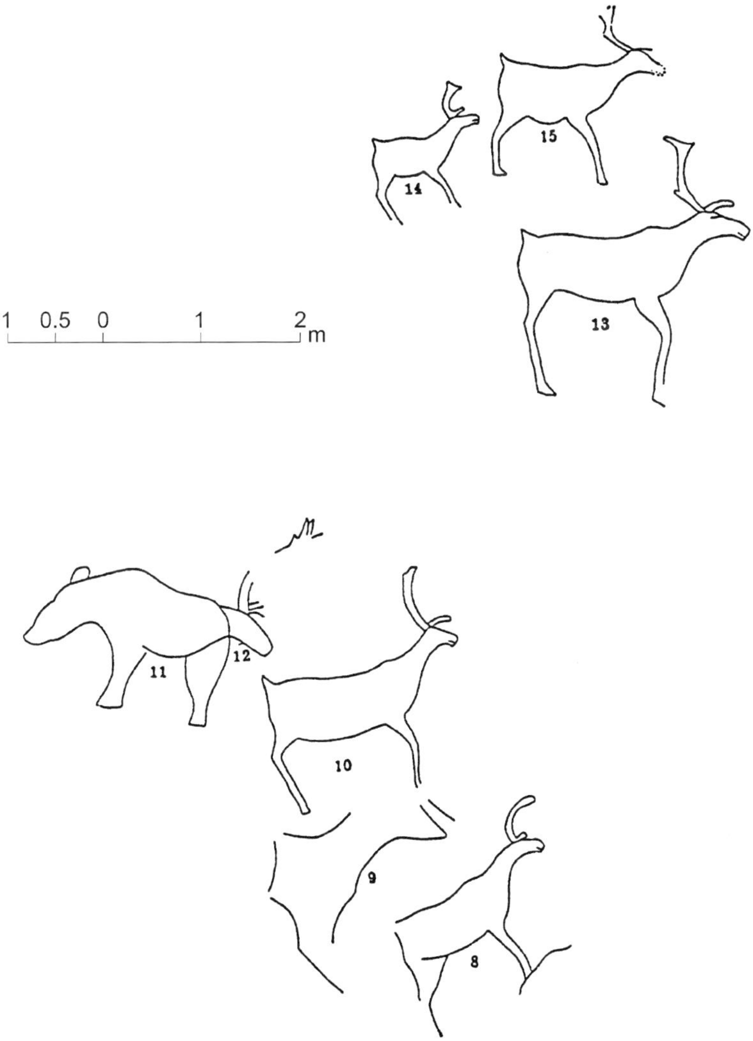

FIGURE 61. Some of the figures on the shores of Fykanvatnet. There is a peculiar combination of a bear and a reindeer in the middle of the panel.
GG

desolation. The rock art is located some hundred metres inside the head of the fjord, on a ridge between the fjord itself and Fykan Lake further in. Before the advent of industry, the images lay untouched and practically isolated above the rushing waterfall. Today the water is regulated, the waterfall has been harnessed with pipes, and Route 17 runs right alongside the rock art site. Despite efforts to protect the rock art, spillages and pollutants from industry have seriously harmed the images. In many places it can no longer be found. More than twenty-five figures were found here, most of them reindeer, but also bear and elk (Gjessing 1932; Hallström 1938). What was probably meant to represent a halibut is also found in amongst the images of land animals. Depictions of fish are uncommon, and there is only one other known case where they are found on panels of polished art of the Northern Tradition. Some of the figures are difficult to identify as elk or reindeer. The animals that can be clearly identified as reindeer all have easily distinguishable antlers. At least two animal figures have been created overlapping one another. Here, too, we find the peculiar depiction of a bear with an elk's head. The head is placed at the hind part of the bear in such a way that both animals share the same belly contour. The intention of this kind of fusion is of course uncertain, but it is tempting to conclude that it had its origins in mythological notions of animals at the time it was created. The figures are very naturalistically depicted, making it a simple task to identify their species. Apart from the fact that the area has lost much of its pristine atmosphere as a result of industrialization and road construction, the attention the rock art has received and its attractiveness here, as at Klubba has resulted in a great deal of damage caused by graffiti signatures and other scribbling that has been added to the surface of the rock immediately alongside the images.

Vågan at Skjerstadfjorden

To reach the next panel containing polished rock art, we have to travel considerably further north, to Vågan at Skjerstadfjorden in Salten, midway between Fauske and Bodø. Here at Mjønesfjellet, some distance north of Saltstraumen, there is a single image of an elk polished onto a slanting stone surface. The image is naturalistically depicted with a prominent hump on its neck and its head lowered (Hesjedal 1990), and is about three metres long. The desolate atmosphere of the area, with its countless smooth and barren stone surfaces up near Mjønesfjellet and Mjønestindan, is convincing enough to suggest that more polished figures are still waiting to be discovered in the area. In the meantime, only one is known to exist, despite the efforts of archaeologists and laymen who have searched for rock art images on the stony surfaces in the area. It is interesting that the area is only a short distance from Saltstraumen, where several dwelling sites dating from the earliest years of the Early Stone Age have been found, and which may be as old as the elk image. Perhaps the person or persons who created the image resided more or less permanently next to the Salstraumen rapids. Why the figure was polished into the stone at exactly

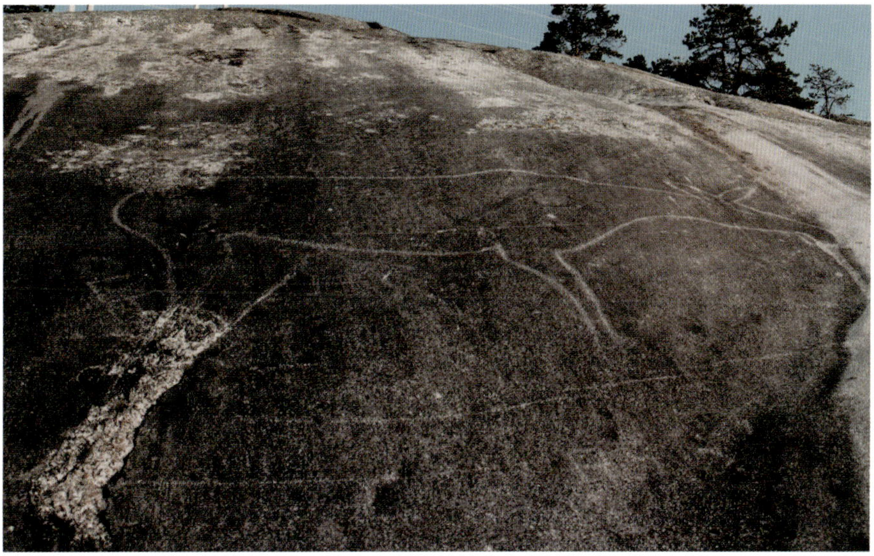

FIGURE 62. An isolated elk at Vågan (Cf. p. 70). Despite persistent searches for other figures in the area, this appears to be the only one present. It is interesting that the natural structure of the rock has been incorporated into the hind leg of the elk.
TL

this spot is obviously an open question. It may have been necessary, however, in the case of this image and for most of the others, that the creator needed to distance himself from the rest of the group when the ritualistic act was to be carried out, polishing a new image into the surface of a carefully selected rock. One particular feature at this site, however, leads to much wider explanations. A closer examination of this figure reveals that the hind leg coincides with a rather long quartz intrusion on the surface of the rock. It is obvious that the quartz vein must have been the point of departure for the whole figure. Prior to the creation of the rock art, the natural character of the vein was most likely perceived as the hind leg of an elk, partly exposed in a visible membrane, and an opportunity to be seized. Both the surface of the rock and the partly visible animal may have been regarded as an opening to an underworld, and the animal as a sacred messenger operating beyond the surface. In order to embrace, accept or control this potential force in the world of the living, it was enhanced to a point that extended beyond this membrane by adding further polished lines, creating the large elk. We will explore other issues related to this in the coming chapters.

Sagelva in Hamarøy

In order to reach the next panel with polished images, at Sagelva in the northernmost point of Hamarøy, we need to travel roughly the same distance. Here we find two reindeer depicted on a steep rocky slope at the point that was originally the overflow from Rotvatnet (Gjessing 1932; Hallström 1938). Today the lake is regulated, and the once mighty Sagelva, with a water level that has sunk much lower than when the rock art was discovered, barely trickles past the site. The roar of the rapids once heard here has been supplanted by the noise

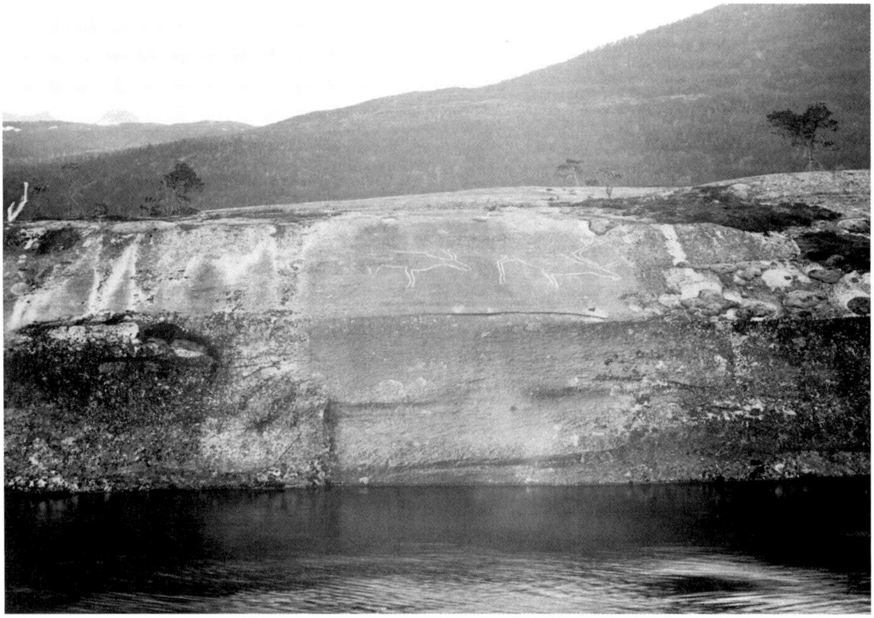

FIGURE 63. Two reindeer are depicted on the sheer rock wall rising out of Sagelva.
GH

of road traffic along Europe 6, which was rerouted past the rock art a few years ago. Both animals depicted have lowered heads in exaggerated dimensions. It seems that the animals were never completed, as some of the contours for the backs are missing. It should not be overlooked, however, that the passage of time may have eroded away lines that were formerly present.

Even further north are the three most northerly points with polished rock art, situated at the points of a triangle running north and south of Vestfjord, where the fjord gradually runs across towards the Ofotfjord. The panel on the northern side is located on the island of Hinnøy, about five kilometres east of the community of Lødingen, and has been named after the small village of Nes on the Kanstadfjord. Just south of Nes, on the other side of Vestfjord and west of the mouth of Tysfjord, is the Leiknes panel, one of the largest panels with polished rock art of the Northern Tradition, and on the eastern side of the outlet is the rock art at Valle, on the inlet leading to Efjorden in Ballangen.

Nes on the Kanstadfjord

The Nes locality is named in written sources after the village of the same name, but it is located about three kilometres to its north. The two places with rock art also have local names. The first images were discovered in 1967 at the foot of Lødingaksla, a little more than 300 metres from the narrow Kanstadfjord. On a steep rock wall in an impassable and stark, bedrock-dominated area with the peculiar name Josarsaklubben, several figures were found (Hesjedal 1990). They were visible even at a considerable distance, and were surprisingly well preserved despite the thousands of years they had stood there. In the centre of

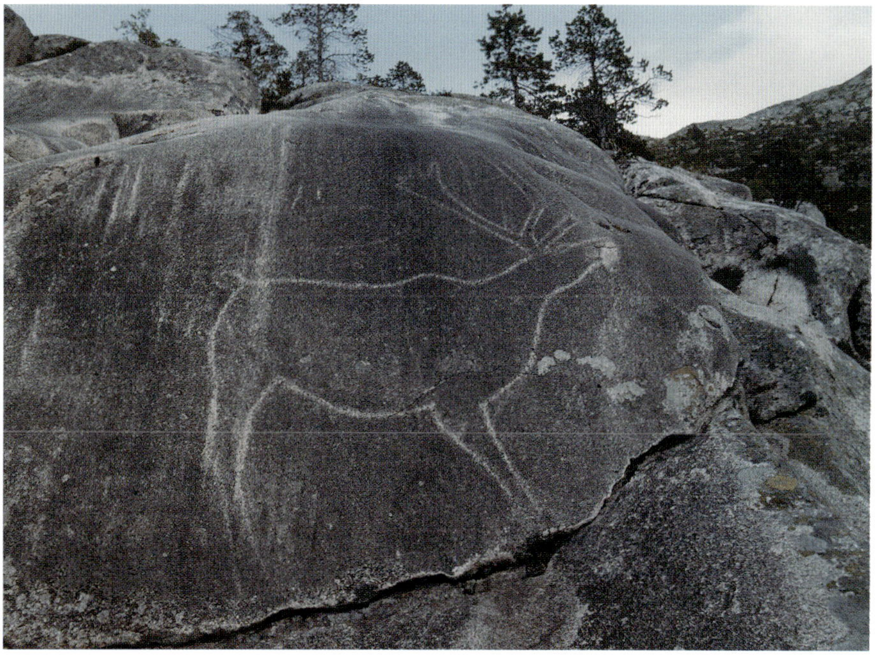

FIGURE 64. Shiny polished lines make the figure visible from a long distance. This reindeer on Josarsaklubben at Nes displays boisterous behaviour typical of the autumn mating season. BHH

the surface and clearest of all, is a large reindeer. It is depicted with a raised head, and appears to be demonstrating its strength as stags do in autumn (Figure 64). Less clear, perhaps because it was not as thoroughly polished, is the head of an elk with antlers, together with the forequarters of another reindeer. There are also other images that are even less distinct, including some that may represent fish. As recently as the mid-1990s, several more images were found on a surface 250 metres further north in Fjellvika. These were a large porpoise and the head of an elk. The porpoise has a definite counterpart at Valle in Efjorden, and therefore connects these two panels. It is possible that the same person created the images of both sites. The rock art at Nes is the most northerly example of the polished type known to exist. The images are surrounded by an area dominated by bedrock that is highly exposed and stretches over a wide area, particularly northwards along Kanstadfjorden. Therefore, it is wholly possible that even more panels may be discovered, and that the northern border for polished rock art will be pushed further north. Recently, a few more images has been documented in this area, but have not yet been published.

Leiknes in Tysfjord

Perhaps the best-known panel containing rock art of the polished type is found at Leiknes, a small promontory that juts out in an easterly direction into Tysfjord (Gjessing 1932; Hallström 1938). Most of the figures were polished onto a large, continuous stretch of flat rock that slants steeply down to the road, which today runs along the fjord in the direction of Korsneset at the outermost section of Vestfjord. The panel is surrounded by many other smooth slopes and barren sections, which were in all likelihood completely bare at the time the rock art was created. Nonetheless, one surface stands out for its smoothness and brilliance, and this was without doubt the reason why it was chosen. Polished into the surface here are reindeer, elk, bear, whales, birds and a figure that is probably a hare. Many of the figures have been placed overlapping one another. One very special feature is that several of the figures have their heads turned backwards, as if they are looking at something behind them. This almost certainly has some significance, but it eludes us today. There is also a very large depiction of a whale, probably an orca. This one is also close to seven metres long, and like the one at Klubba, has been superimposed on top of the other

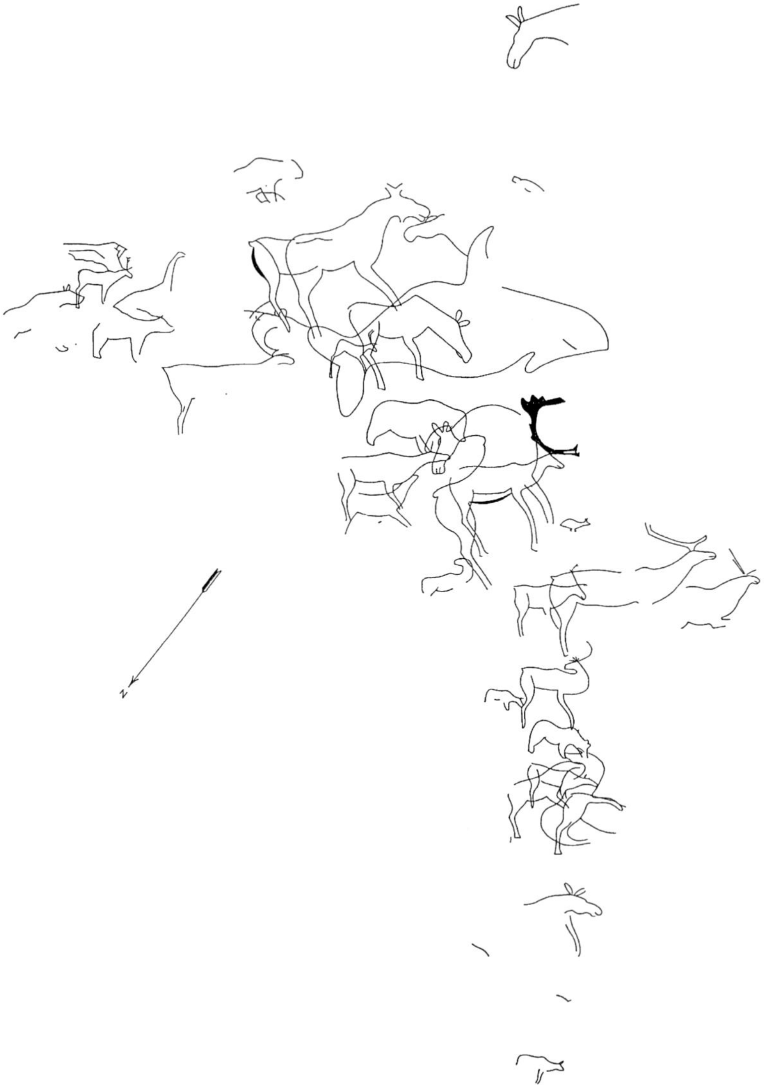

FIGURE 65. Tracing of rock images at Leiknes. The animals on the large panel gradually diminish in size as the viewer moves down the slope.
GG

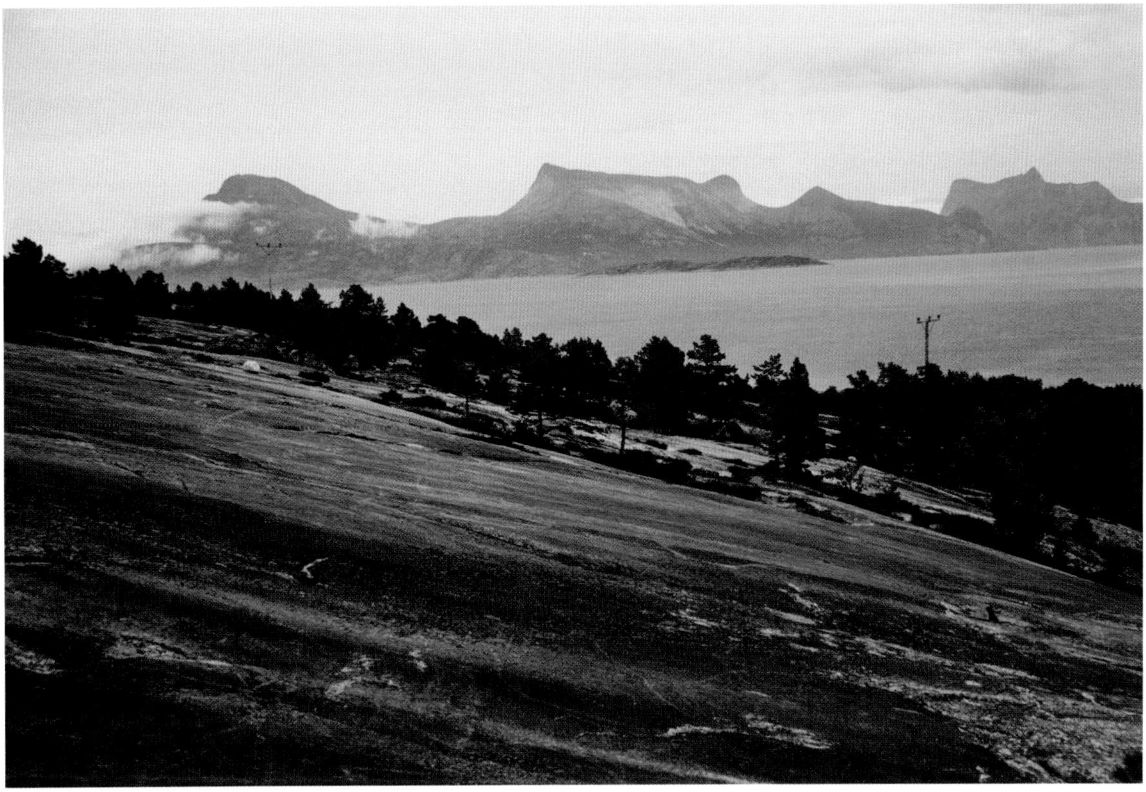

FIGURE 66. The large rock panel with animal images at Leiknes in the foreground, with Tysfjord in the background. Polished images are also found at Valle, located behind the mountain to the left in the picture.
GH

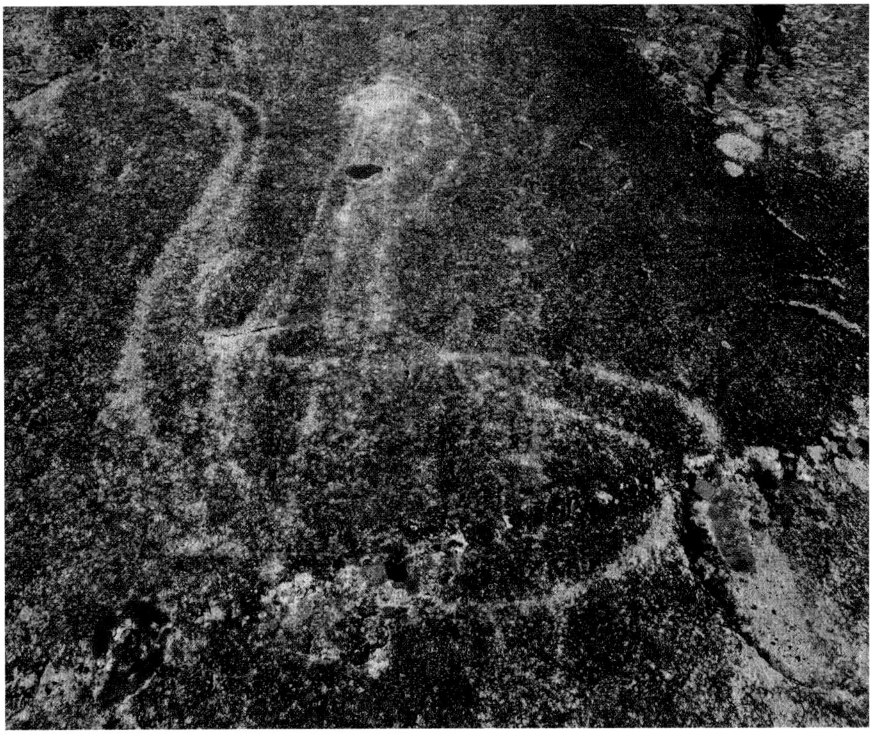

FIGURE 67. A pair of swans on the lowest section of the rock surface at the Leiknes site.
TL

animal images. It is interesting to note that one of the elks has been placed almost inside the body of the whale.

These virtually identical forms of expression at Klubba and Leiknes are separated by great distances, and immediately raise the question: What relationship may have existed between the two sites? Or was it an integral part of the culture and custom of the creators of the images that whales were to be superimposed over other animals? Normally, only the contours of the animal images are polished, but here we find certain sections of some of the figures that are completely polished. This is the case of an impressive set of antlers on a reindeer stag, making it prominent in the setting with its dazzling adornment shining out amongst the other, more subdued figures. Another trait worthy of note is that the figures diminish in size, from large figures at the top to successively smaller images descending down across the slope. Just to the east of the main concentration there is a smaller cluster of additional images. They are less distinct, but judging from appearances, two of them represent a seal and a reindeer. Some distance below them are two long-necked bird images, probably swans, which have been polished onto a small surface using the same technique. The contours of the images overlap one another, and some scholars have suggested that the figure represents the same swan, but portrayed in two different postures, ostensibly to present the illusion of movement in the image.

FIGURE 68. Only two of the countless rocky ridges at Valle are known to have rock art images. In the centre of the photo is a seal above a porpoise and just behind a reindeer. A little further along the ridge is the vague image of a seal.
TL

Valle in Ballangen

The last of the panels we will refer to here are located at Valle, on the inlet to Efjorden in Ballangen, and at Valletindan, which can be seen to the northeast from Leikneset. Inside the south-eastern side of Valle Bay at the foot of the Valletindane range, there is a sensation of travelling back in time to when the images were created. A special aspect of this area around the rock art images is that there has not been a single modern incursion anywhere on the landscape. No construction of any type, in any direction, bears witness to the century or even the millennium in which we live. The landscape is characterised by pristine, smooth rock surfaces occasionally interrupted by grassy hollows running lengthways. This type of landscape dominates a large area, and is only interrupted by the towering Valle peaks to the south, and the fjord and bay to the north. Spread across the low-lying areas are gnarled pine trees, evidence of the strong gales that ravage the landscape.

There are two groups of figures of the Northern Tradition here (Hesjedal 1990). One of them is a series of aligned images on a circular stone panel just above a stream. Facing against the current of the stream, the first images represent a seal and a whale-like shape (probably a porpoise) that overlap one another. A little less than a metre and a half away is a reindeer. Only the head with antlers and the line of the hindquarters is visible, as if the reindeer were left unfinished. It should be noted that the stone is not as thoroughly polished further down, and this makes it difficult to discern the lines. A metre and a half further away there is

FIGURE 69. This bear, also in Valle, can be seen from far off. Further to the right on the rock surface, a reindeer's head was once seen, but in recent years it has not been found.
TL

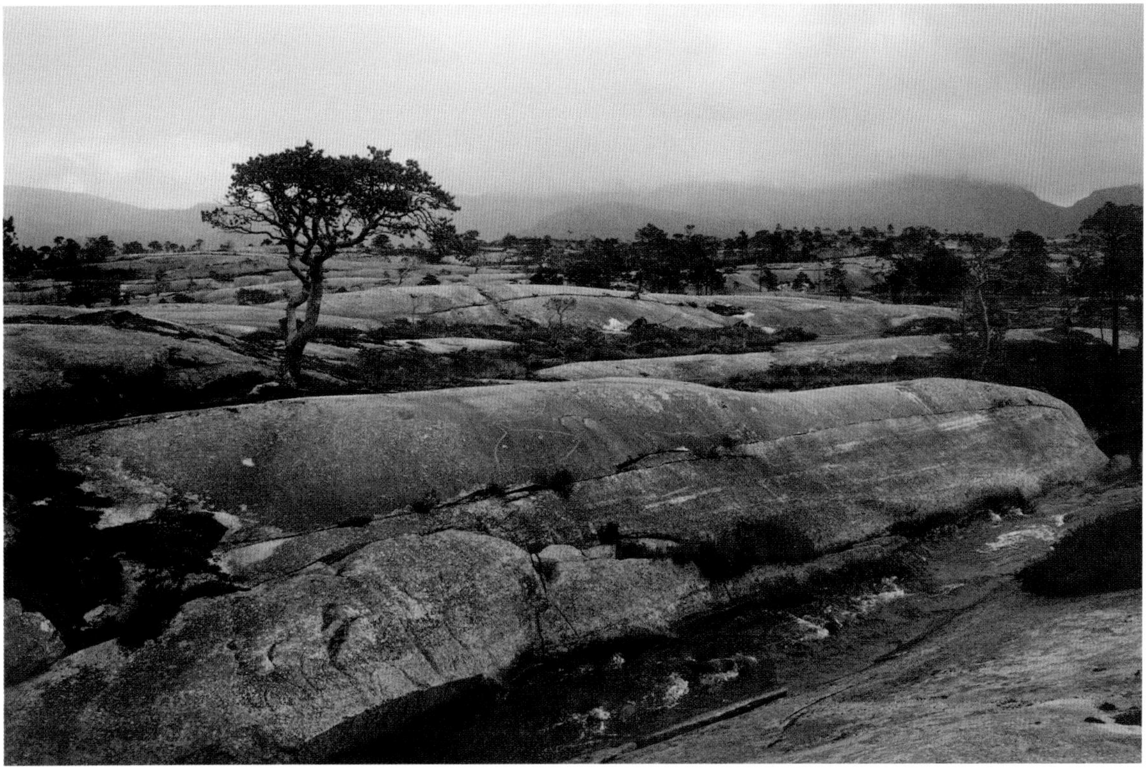

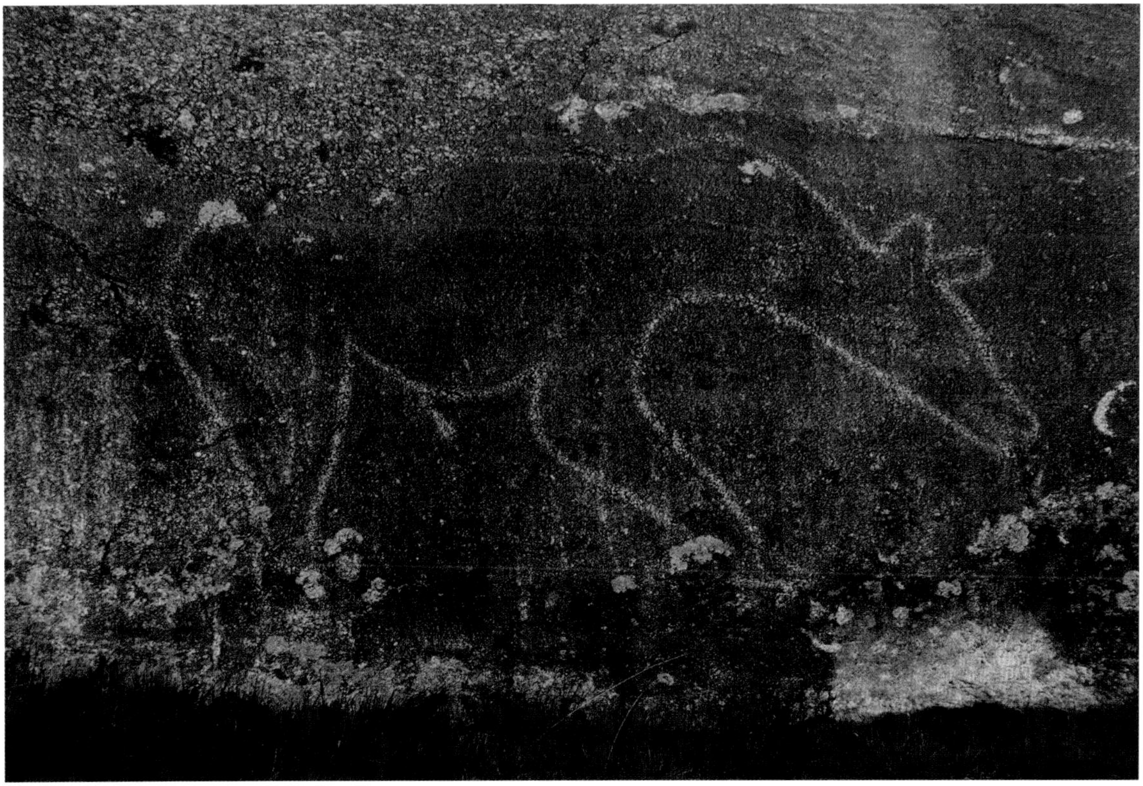

yet another image of an animal, even more indistinct, although there are grounds to believe it is a reindeer. At the most easterly point of the rock panel there is another seal, but significantly larger than the first. Leiknes and Valle are the only sites within this group with depictions of seals. The figures were probably polished into the stone at shoreline level as a procession of seal, porpoises and reindeer, all of which migrated near the shoreline here. It is interesting that both sea and land animals are included in this context. This breaks with natural delineations, but the relationship between sea and land animals here nevertheless lacks the same contrastive expression seen in Leiknes and Klubba, as none of the figures here overlap one another. Although all of the species may at one time or another have been in the water, occasionally surfacing out of the same fjord, there is undoubtedly a deeper meaning here which, if revealed, could lead us to a closer understanding of the world-view and mythology of this bygone era.

About 150 metres further east, on a more horizontal rock panel, there is a large, meticulously portrayed bear. Examining it closely, it can be seen that some modern passer-by was unable to restrain himself and added an appendage to the bear. Less than 25 metres from the bear are the polished contours of the back, head and chest of a large reindeer. As with the images near the stream, it is curious that the belly and legs were not completed. This said, it is plausible that the animals were depicted as swimming, in the same way seen on other panels. This interpretation, however, does not seem logical, as too much of the hind section of the reindeer is visible. It has been suggested that the image of the bear represents a polar bear, although there is no basis for distinguishing the two species of bear. We are also uncertain whether there actually were polar bears here as late as the period following the last Ice Age.

Unity of form, choice of subjects and design

No other images have been found at Valle, and no panels containing rock art of the Northern Tradition are known to exist other than those described here. The polished images stand out as a distinctive and unique group, despite the distances between the panels. Not only does the polishing technique closely link the panels and images, but the choice of subjects and compositions also leads us to speculate that the same person may have been active at several of the sites. It is also possible that a single individual, one who had superior talent and was probably endowed with a unique status, created all of the images. This would have been possible over a long lifetime, but also over a considerably shorter period of time. If the images were created during a very limited period of time, it logically follows that the use of the shoreline level as a method for dating the rock art is too imprecise. Even though it has been claimed that the rock art was produced over a longer period of time, it has already been established that there are major margins of error in this method. The images may very simply have been polished into the stone at a point high above the shoreline at the time they were made.

The people who lived in these areas at the time appear to have led very nomadic lives, seasonally and annually, taking them across the kind of distances we refer to here, either singly or in groups. It is impressive that they were able to portray the animals so naturalistically, and often in large dimensions. It is also incredible that many of the figures are still so distinct today, after many thousands of years. It is interesting that certain animals are recurrent in the images, that the figures on several of the panels are superimposed, and that both land and sea mammals occur in these overlapping images. Current opinion holds that there were unique notions or ideas behind this, and these factors provide food for thought for future analysis and interpretation of archaeological materials from the same period, as well as for descriptions of prehistoric societies.

It is impossible to know how many panels and images of the polished type may have existed, and how many may still lie waiting to be discovered. It is likely that more polished rock images will be found in the future. If we consider the kind of relationship that may have existed between the places where we know that polished images were present, it is obvious that the short distance between Klubba and Fykan Lake would have allowed a high degree of contact. It is also likely that there was a connection between Valle, Leiknes and Nes, while both Vågan and Sagelva seem to have remained isolated. If we try to imagine how the geography looked at the time when the land was still compressed and forced down by many metres after the last Ice Age, it becomes evident that it was much easier to travel between several of the sites. At the time many of the fjords were connected by what are today isthmuses and watercourses, and people did not need to make their way around fjords and exposed peninsulas. It is probable that the people who created the rock art travelled by boat, although no remains of any vessels from the period have been found. It would therefore be interesting to try to find more rock art along what may have been routes between the different panels, paths that would have been completely different than those we may propose today. There must have been some connection: the unique polishing technique and the similar figurative and compound-subject form of expression could not have occurred independently of each another at these seven different locations.

Cave Paintings in Nord-Trøndelag and Nordland

The discovery

In 1912 a series of peculiar paintings of human figures were discovered on the wall of a deep and narrow cave passage on the island of Leka in Nord-Trøndelag. Some young people from Solsem, the village that the cave was later named after, had come across the images. They found the entrance to the cave almost 80 metres above sea level in a boulder scree area, where there was a good view of the small village and open sea beyond it. The cave was almost inaccessible, and in front of the entrance was a large boulder that was difficult to move aside, and which was in all likelihood the reason why the cave had not been investigated before. It was also unknown in the local area if anyone had ever been inside the cave before this particular day in May, 1912. The young people used a rope and ladder to descend into this unknown landscape, and only carried a small lamp. Once inside and at the foot of the large boulder that partially blocked the entrance, they lowered themselves some 8–10 metres down a steep underground scree slope to the bottom of the cave. As they descended, there was still a little daylight from the entrance to the cave, but the passage became darker and darker as they made their way downwards. Gripped with excitement and highly alert, they continued on for a further 15 metres through a smaller passage that opened onto a much larger, taller cave. At this depth, the cave veered off towards the west, thus preventing any daylight from reaching the passage leading inwards. From that point on, the passage was pitch dark, and they had to resort to the lamp they had brought with them. The cave floor was covered with water-worn pebbles in many places, as well as angular boulders that had fallen from the roof, making it even more difficult to make their way further inside. Their eyes had only just adjusted to the darkness when, to their disappointment, they discovered that the cave ended abruptly just 15 metres away. Their sense of adventure was far from exhausted, so that they began to investigate their surroundings – first the floor, then the walls. It was then that they came across the strange paintings, a number of simple but very distinctly lined drawings of humans painted in red, standing out in stark contrast to the plain, grey cave wall (Petersen 1914; Hallström 1938).

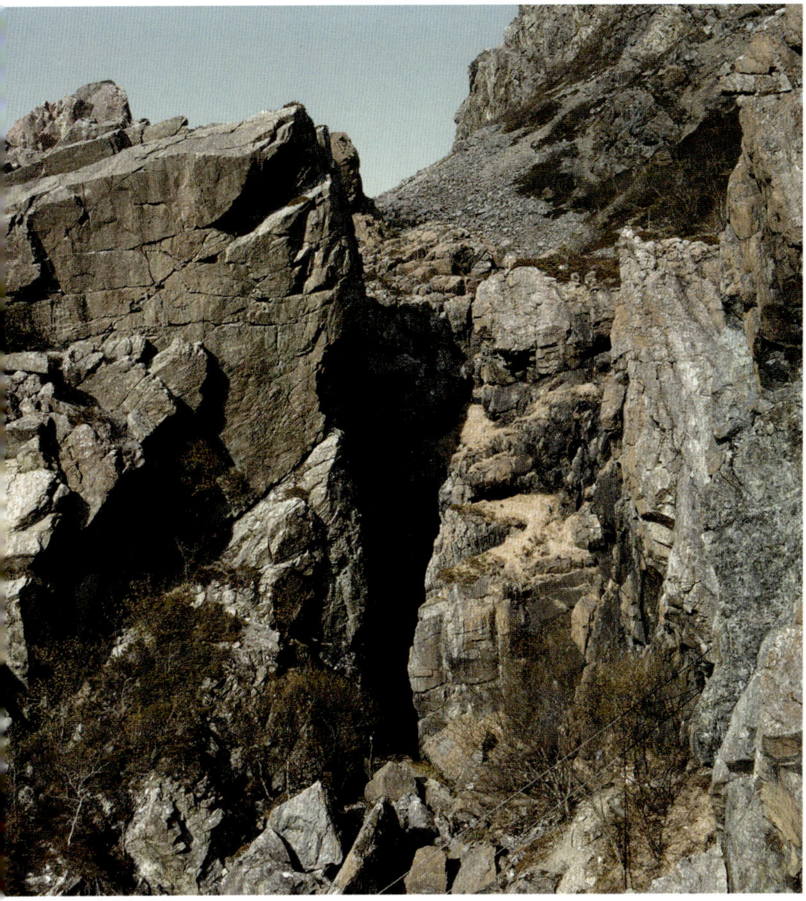

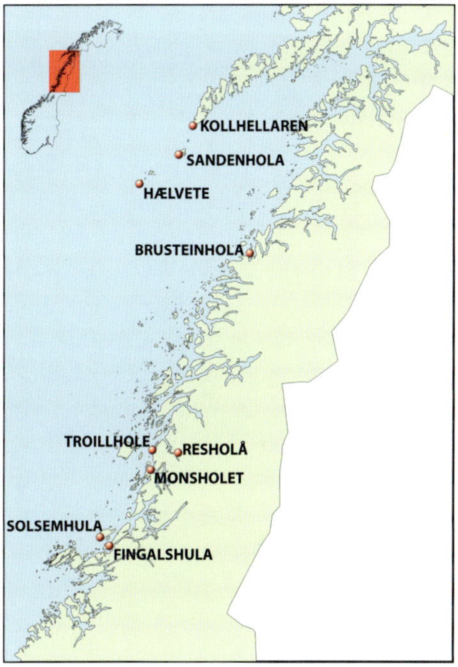

FIGURES 70–71. The narrow entrance to Solsemhola, made accessible today by a staircase down to the first narrow section. Cave paintings are found spread from Nord-Trøndelag to the Lofoten islands.

MAP AI, ILLUSTRATION AK

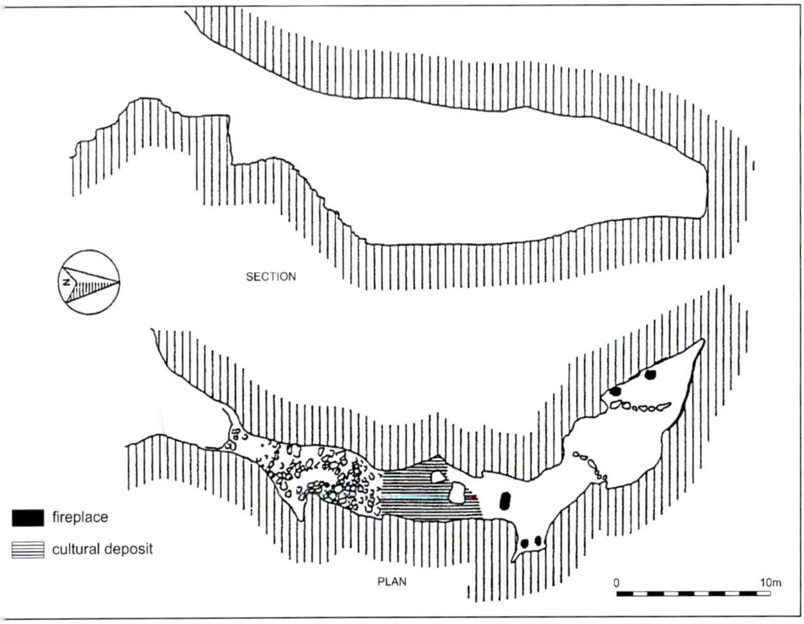

FIGURE 72. A side plan in cross-sectional view shows the scope and character of Solsemhola.

KS

The images

Det Kongelige Norske Videnskabers Selskab, today known as the Museum of Natural History and Archaeology, in Trondheim, was notified immediately after the discovery, and archaeologists visited the cave in the same year. By the following year, the images were well documented and the rest of the cave had been explored. All of the images were found deep inside the cave, a total of 21 figures on three panels, two on the western wall and one on the eastern wall, with the groups facing each other at the bottom of the cave (Petersen 1912). The innermost figures are only about half a metre from the end of the cave. All of the human images have arms and legs that jut out considerably from the body, and small, circular heads. Many of the figures have a line drawn hanging between their legs, interpreted by some as phalluses, denoting that the figures are male, and that those without them are women. Identification of gender on this basis, however, must be carried with a considerable degree of caution. For all we know, the line may well have been part of the subject's clothing. Three of the line figures stand out in contrast to the others. One is carrying a long object in one hand, perhaps a torch or a club, and appears to be holding one of the other human figures by the hand. Another is distinguished by having a more proportionately shaped head than the others. The third of the figures, located on the far side of the largest cluster of figures, extends its arm in a long, horizontal line that is intersected midway by a similar long, vertical line, so that the two together form a cross. The tallest of the human figures is well over half a metre tall, although the length of the others varies. Also, the images are positioned at different levels above each another, perhaps to give them a perspective of depth. In any event, they are portrayed in a quite unique way.

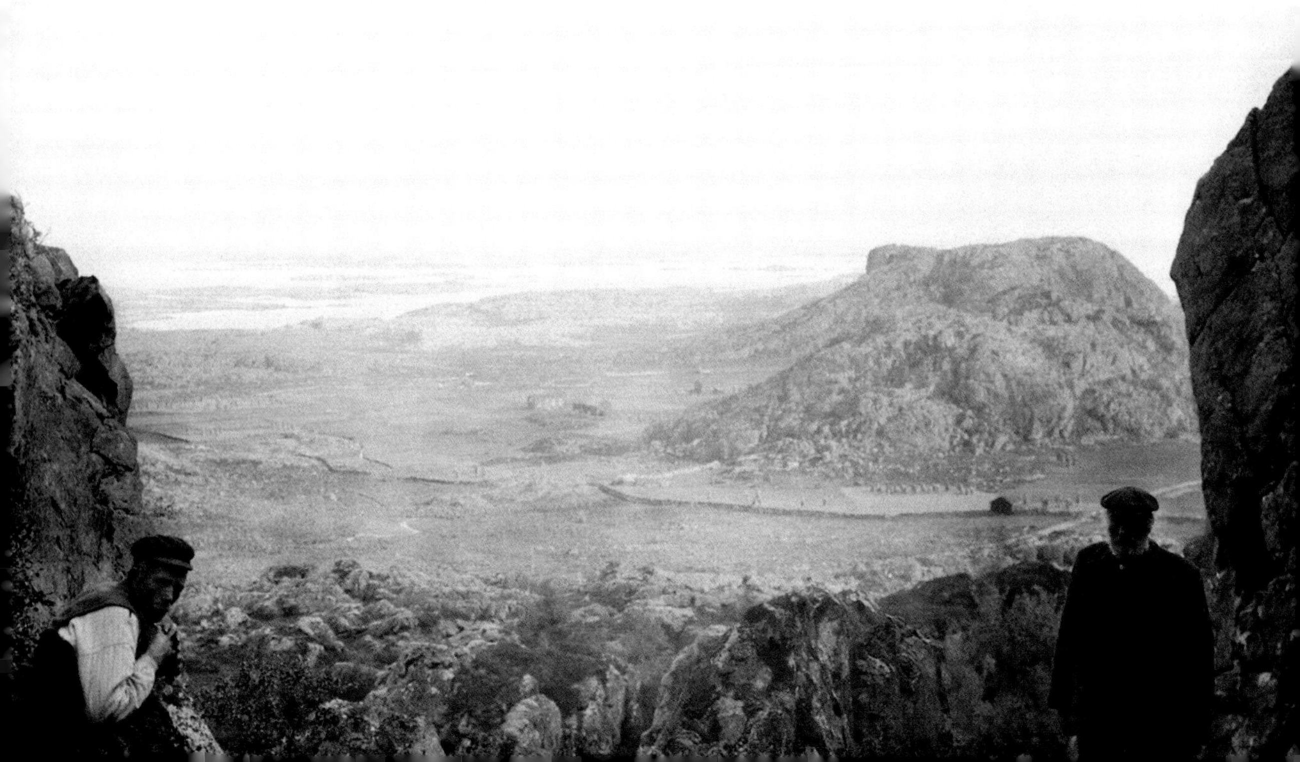

FIGURE 73. View from the inlet towards Solsem and the open ocean in the background. The photograph was taken the year after the cave became known to the public, and the people are local residents of Solsem.
GH

FIGURE 74. Easily distinguishable human figures against the background of the grey, stained cave wall.
AK

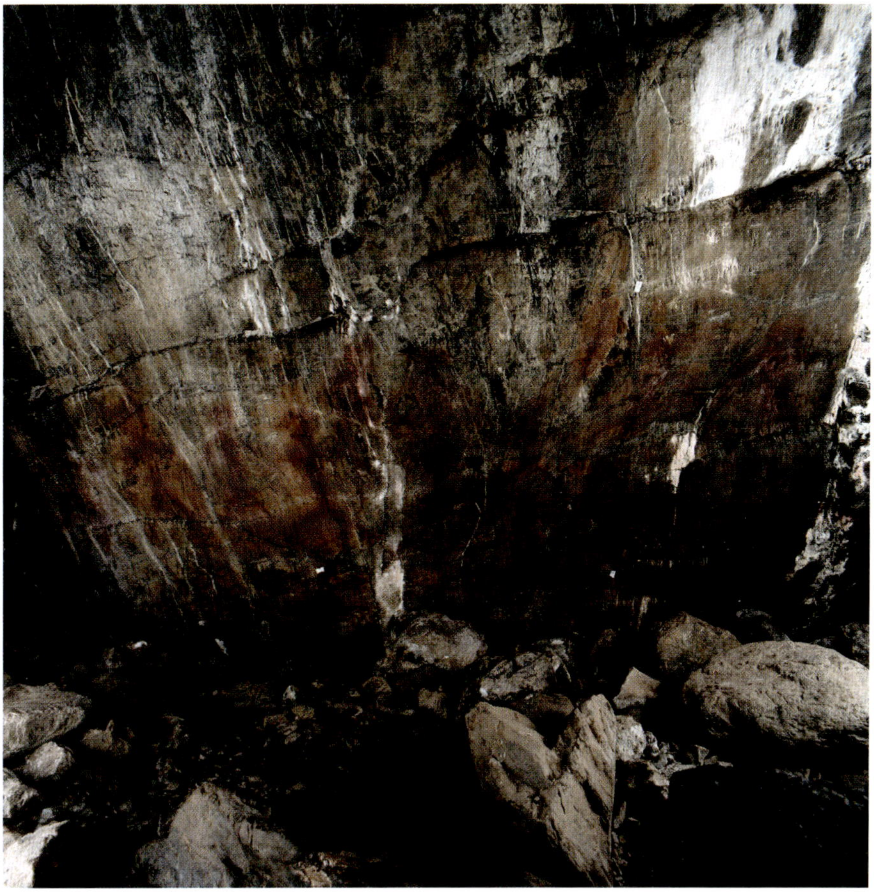

FIGURE 75. Tracing of the images on the eastern side. We can clearly see the figures that stand out from the rest. One of these is carrying a flaming torch, another has a pointed head and the third has one hand bound to a cross.
KS

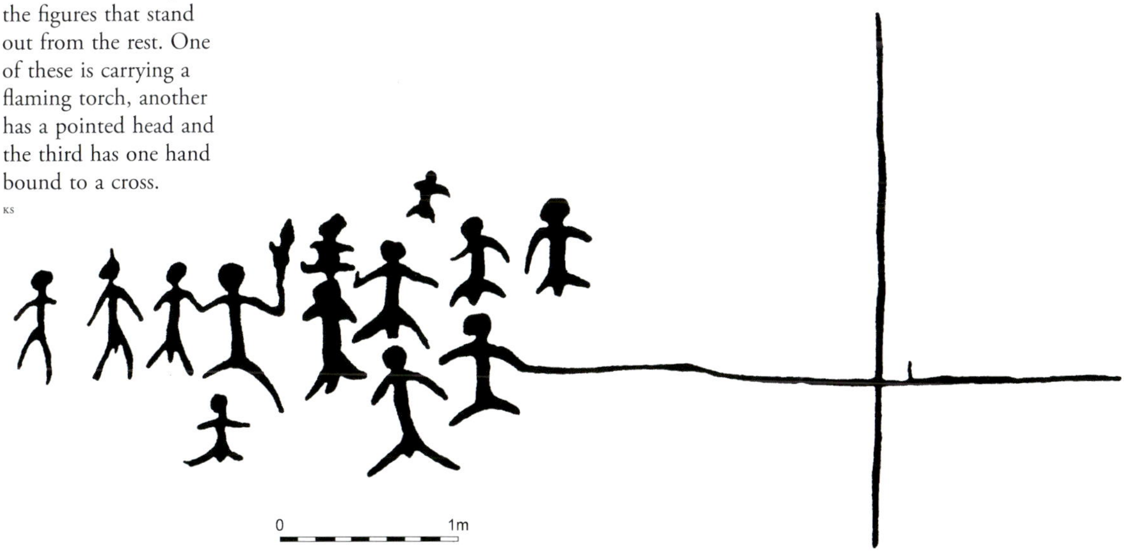

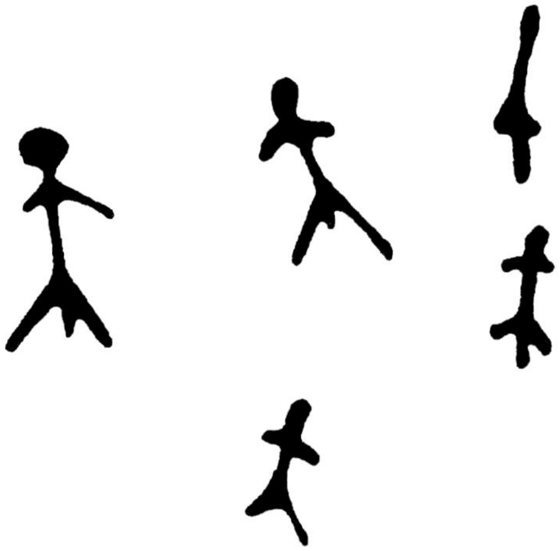

FIGURE 76. The larger of the two surfaces of the cave's western side.
KS

Other finds

Surveys in 1912 and 1913 revealed that there were also a number of large stones aligned across the passage in the inner half of the cave, and that these were evidently placed there with the aim of dividing the cave into a number of compartments. We do not know why this was done. The floor of the cave was also investigated, and parts of it were excavated (Petersen 1912). A number of loose items were also collected from the surface of the floor, and bones and skeletal fragments were found all over the bottom of the cave. In the outer area, a layer of charcoal was also found. From this section and the rest of the cave floor, almost 2000 bones and fragments from various animal species were collected. Fish bones were from cod, herring and flounder; bird bones were dominated by ptarmigan, seagull, little auk, great auk and white-tailed eagle. The mammal bones found came from sheep, seal, goats, bulls and horses. There were also bones of humans, including children and adults. Few artefacts were found, and there was no sign that tools had been made in the cave. This indicates that activity in the cave differed from that found in numerous outdoor dwelling sites. No more than four artefacts were found in the outer area: a harpoon point, a small bodkin made of bone, a whetting disc, and what may have been a jig-line protector made of bone. The investigations were unable to confirm or reject whether the human bones came from a grave, or if they came from a human that had been devoured. If we want to dwell on the latter possibility, it is hardly likely that cannibalism was performed out of a need for food, but instead out of ritualistic necessity. Cannibalistic rituals are documented in historical contexts, and have also been considered likely in prehistoric times. We know, for example, of beliefs that by eating the flesh of dead companions, it would be possible to acquire their skills and knowledge. Of course there is always the possibility that the person may have died in the cave, or been buried here, and that rodents or other animals scattered the bones at a

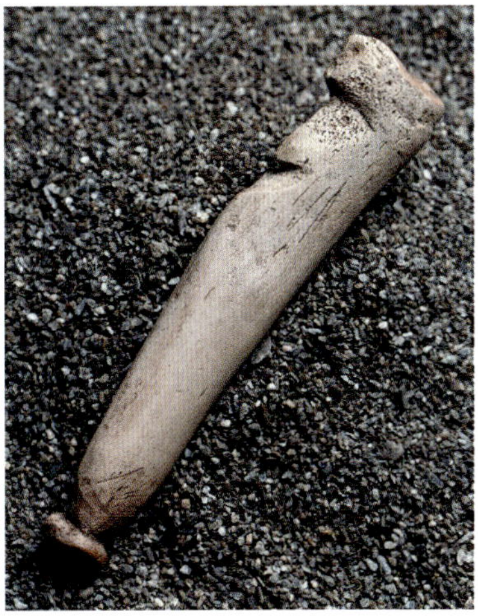

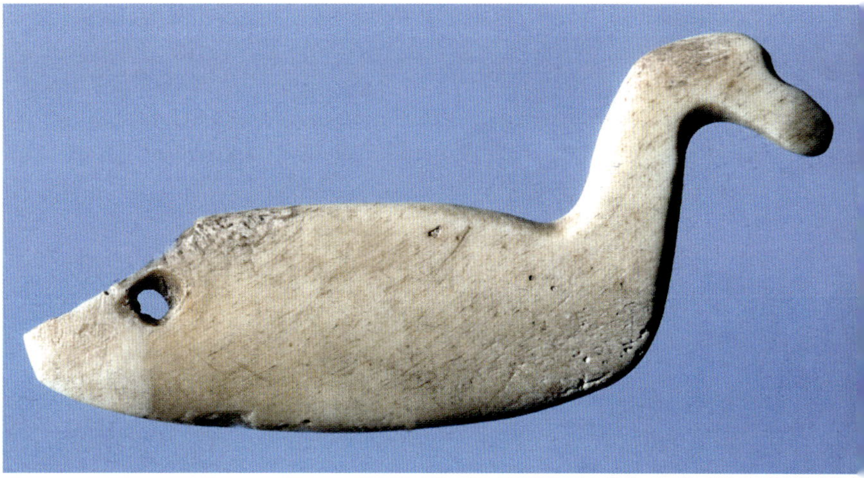

FIGURE 77 *(left)*. A whalebone carved to resemble a face. Its meaning and use are unknown.
NTUNUV

FIGURE 78 *(right)*. A handsomely carved bird, also from Solsemhola. It is probably a great auk, which we know was hunted in both prehistoric and historical times. The species is now extinct.
NTUNUV

later stage. Many of the animal bones show clear signs of teeth marks that may have been from predators or dogs, while others show scrape marks indicating that tools were used to cut up the body or to scrape the bones clean.

No cultural layers were found in the inner area where the rock paintings are located. However, a number of special artefacts were found (*ibid.*). These are objects that are inviting to see in context with the paintings, and that suggest the kind of special activity that took place here. One of the finds is a toe joint from a seal that was reshaped by smoothing the sides flat, although its purpose and use is unknown. Another find is a leg bone from a seagull, hollowed out and bevelled, with a small hole at one end. It is unlikely that this is anything other than a flute. There was also a finely carved bird made from the bone of a bull. The figure is probably meant to represent a great auk, a species we know was abundant at the time, but which is now extinct. The last artefact found was a meticulously made arrowhead of dark slate. The arrowhead is classified in archaeological terminology as the Sunderøy type, which we know was in use in the early Metal Age or Bronze Age, during the period between 1800 and 900 BC (Olsen 1994). The lack of other material suggests that the cave must only have been in use for a relatively brief period. At the same time, the cultural layer, charcoal and bones suggest that people must have congregated and spent a considerable amount of time here. The cave was probably used at more or less regular intervals. Judging from all of the materials that were left behind, it is logical to assume that the cave must have been used for ritualistic activities.

It is easy to imagine how the surroundings in the cave created a special atmosphere, totally isolated from the outside world. The darkness and the echo were almost certainly conducive to manipulating the senses. Torches, light sources and open fires that were lit in here also must have added further effect to the atmosphere, and set the stage for special states of consciousness in which flames, smoke and sound played an active role. It is also possible to imagine how the shadows of the people participating in the rituals must have been cast on the walls to create an eerie impression, while wet paint was applied to the bare cave walls. The images created would also have contributed to the desired state of mind. Of course it is necessary to be cautious when trying to interpret who and what is depicted in the images, but it is not implausible that the same people who took part in the rituals were also portrayed on the walls.

Unique images

At the time they were discovered, the paintings in Solsem Cave were the first known cave paintings in Northern Europe, and attracted a great deal of attention. For a long time they remained a unique cultural monument, and it would not be until half a century later, in 1963, that another cave containing paintings was discovered. In this year it was revealed that paintings had been found in the Fingal cave in Gravvik (Marstrander 1965), also in Nord-Trøndelag, just 10 kilometres southeast of Leka. This cave is also located at a high elevation in a stone scree slope, approximately 90 metres above sea level. As in the Solsem cave, the entrance was narrow and difficult to access, and ropes or ladders were required to enter. There were other striking similarities, such as the nature of many of the images, in terms of both their shape and colour. The images here, however, were more widely distributed, over several different walls. On both sides of a very narrow passage half way into the 100-metre long cave, there were two panels, while a third was found at the end of the equally long and narrow passage leading to the back of the cave. A total of twenty-one images

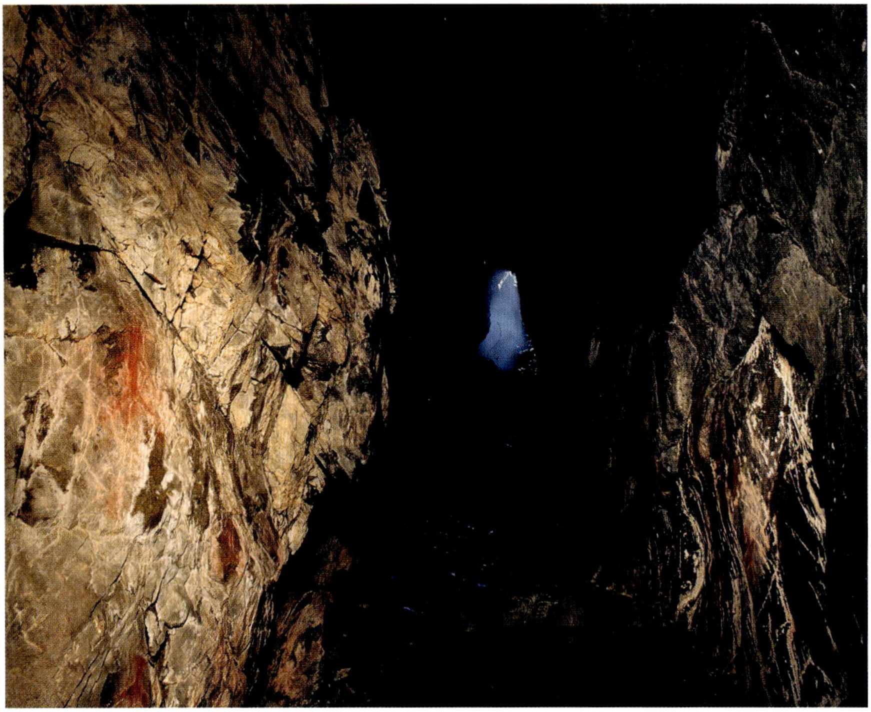

FIGURE 79. Inside Fingalshola there are images on both sides of the passage facing the inner part of the cave.
AK

were found in the cave, seventeen of them clearly human figures, but a few that perhaps represent animals (*ibid.*).

Several more decades would pass before cave paintings were discovered in the Skåren-Monsen cave, a little further north in Brønnøy, Nordland (Sognnes 1983). This is a very long cave, stretching some 120 metres, and again with its entrance in a stone scree slope some 150 metres above sea level. In contrast to the caves mentioned above, the entrance here was wide and imposing, almost 25 metres high. At the very end, in the deepest and darkest area, five figures were found. None of these can be definitely identified as human images, although they were all painted with simple, red strokes. As far as identification is possible, several of them seem to represent animals. One of the images is most likely a deer, painted in profile and with two long lines extending up from the head and probably representing antlers or ears. Two other figures are quite similar and resemble stylised reptiles depicted from above, with a line running from

FIGURE 80. The impressive arched entranceway to Kollhellaren. The person standing in the sunlit entryway provides perspective in terms of proportions.
TN

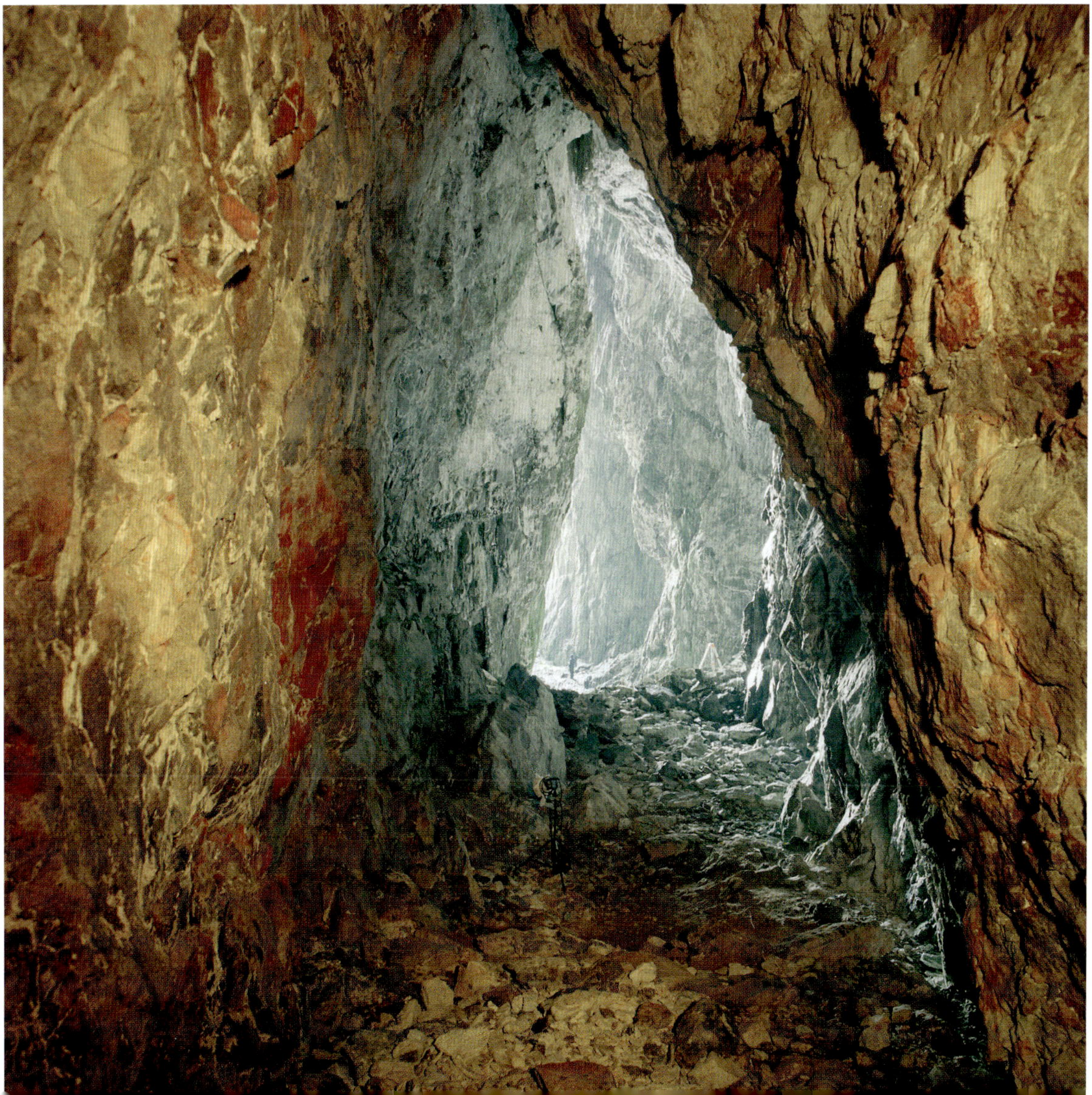

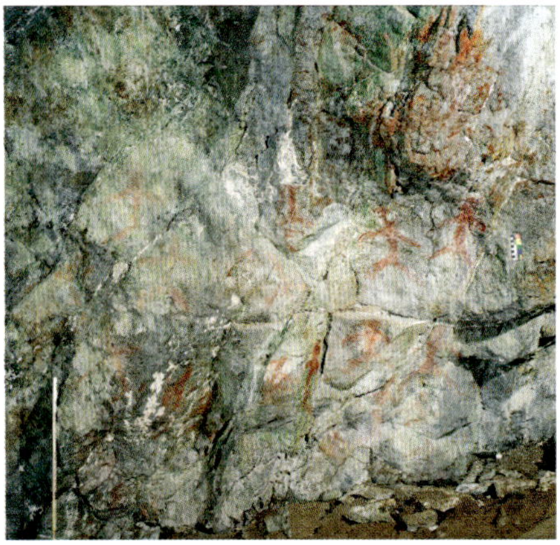

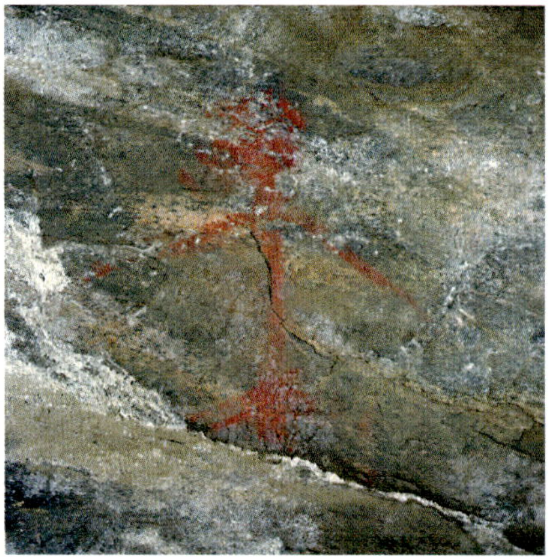

FIGURE 81 *(left)*. One of the rock surfaces inside Kollhellaren, with distinctive human figures.
TN

FIGURE 82 *(right)*. A very clear image of a human, found in Sandenhola.
AK

the tail through the body and up to the head, with two intersecting lines that denote the front and back legs.

More cave paintings were discovered further north along the coast over the following years, all in Nordland. In 1987 a large number of painted images were found inside the impressive Kollhellaren in Moskenes, on the western side of the Lofoten promontory (Hauglid *et al.* 1991). The cave had been known for a long time, as it was impossible for travellers passing in boats not to notice it: with a 50-metre-high opening and width of some 12 metres, it can be seen from far away. However, it is difficult to access; although only 25 metres above sea level, the crashing waves and swells from the open ocean below it are a danger to even the sturdiest vessels, and seafarers risk being dashed against the mountain wall unless they exercise extreme caution. The cave is about 100 metres long, and the ceiling remains impressively high all the way into the cave. Entering through the passage, half way there are two transverse passages that run 20 and 35 metres to the left and right. The paintings are located in three points. Two panels are just inside each of the two transverse passages, and the third is located at the very end of the main passage, which ends in a narrow crevasse. A total of thirty-four images were found, twenty-eight of which are clearly human images, and closely resemble those found in the other caves. The others were also probably depictions of humans, but have partially deteriorated. One of the images stands out as holding a long pole or rod in its hands.

Just after the paintings in Kollhellaren were discovered, it was announced that images on the walls of a cave at Hamnøy in Vevelstad had been known of for many years. We can only speculate as to the origins of the mysterious name Troillhåle [Troll Cave] and its possible connection with the prehistoric paintings, rituals and other traditions. Like many of the other caves, this one is located high up in a steep scree field, 100 metres above sea level, and it is quite narrow, with a length of 20 metres. The two images are at the far end, inside a transverse passage that narrows to such an extent that it is necessary to crawl the last few metres (Bjerck 1995). One image depicts a human, while the other appears to be a cross-like figure. There are also a number of smears and lines that may be the remains of images that have disintegrated or weathered away. Based on these observations, we cannot exclude the possibility that the cross-like figure may have been a human image.

The early 1990s were also a good period for cave paintings. In 1992, cave paintings were discovered at Trenyken far out on the open ocean, a few miles from the island of Røst. Inside a cave more than 100 metres deep with the evocative name Hælvete [Hell], seven distinct human images were discovered, along with the remnants of what may have been an eighth (*ibid.*). Numerous smears of colour that may be the remains of other figures were also documented. One of the human images is distinctive in size and shape. It is almost 90 centimetres tall, has clearly extended fingers, flexed knees and a head with horns. There are also remnants of another hand, also with extended fingers that may have belonged to a similar human figure. The other human images are very simple, like those found in the other caves. Unfortunately, the images have been marred by graffiti in recent years.

In the same year, a number of images were found in Reshåla, a cave in Vistnesfjorden in Vevelstad. These are mainly comprised of lines and circles, and are different from any of the other cave paintings (Berglund 1993). The figures appear to have been sketched with charcoal or a black stone. Both this factor and the place where the cave is located, far inside a fjord, suggest that the images belong to another form of expression and another social tradition.

Two years later, eight or nine human figures were found in the 130-metre-deep Sanden cave on the island of Værøy (Bjerck 1995). The entrance is quite narrow between the scree and the foot of the mountain, but the cave widens just inside the entrance. Climbing down the steep scree inside the cave, the passageway at the foot of the scree narrows considerably and continues inward as a narrow crevasse. At the entrance to this crevasse, the paintings are on both sides of the narrow passageway. Only a few months afterwards, paintings were found in the Brusteinar cave in Gildeskål, further towards the mainland (*ibid.*). This cave has a large tunnel-shaped entranceway located close to 100 metres above sea level. At the far end of this 120-metre deep cave, twelve human images

FIGURE 83. Brusteinhola on the left in the photo. The distinctive peaks are Breistjerna in the foreground, with Høgstjerna in the background. In recent times there have been a number of boulder falls inside the cave, and it is now extremely dangerous to enter this area. The boulder falls have damaged the rock paintings, and a large slab with several images has been transferred to Tromsø Museum.
AK

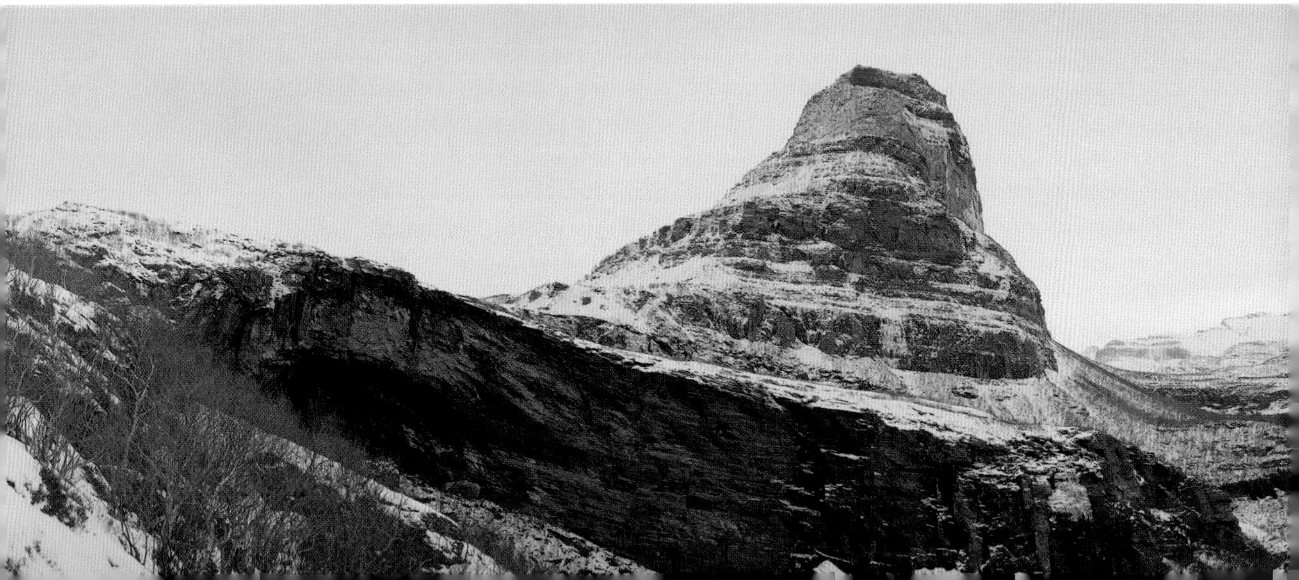

were discovered. Their position contrasts with the other caves, as the figures are painted on the ceiling and on a raised stone slab at the far end, where the cave splits off into smaller passageways that make it difficult to proceed.

Very recently, two more sites with cave paintings were discovered in Lofoten: a number of human images in the Bukkhammer cave, not far from Kollhellaren, and some images of what may be animals in the Simon Krane cave in Kabelvåg. At the latter site, a number of pecked or polished images of bear and elk were also found. The arrangement is unique, as rock carvings and rock paintings have only rarely been found in the same location in Scandinavia. The cave paintings have still to be fully documented, and their authenticity was recently questioned.

The paintings

With the exception of Reshåla, red pigment was used as in the other caves, with general variations in colour and character (Norsted 2008). Analyses show that the pigment in this paint is iron oxide, which is found in nature as haematite and in several places inside the caves as iron deposits from crevices and leachate deposits. Iron oxide was probably used as the main ingredient in the paint. Red marks on the floor in the Solsem cave, clearly the result of dripping, reveal that the paint was in liquid form when it was applied. Perhaps it was not as fluid in all places. In the Fingal cave, for example, "palette stones" were found on which the paint may have been mixed. These stones, however, may have been used to crush and grind iron oxide before it was mixed with liquids that acted as binding agents. It is not known at this time if the paint contained any other ingredients. It was probably made just by mixing iron oxide with water. Water inside the caves is often rich in lime, making it an acceptable binding agent for application to the damp cave walls.

The width of some of the strokes suggests that the paint must have been applied using fingers, most probably two fingers held together. However, clear gaps in some of the lines, including those seen on the cross-like figure in the Solsem cave, indicate that a brush-like tool was also used.

Age

Like all other rock art, it is a challenge to determine the age of the cave paintings. All of the caves are too elevated in the terrain to permit dating using the shoreline method. It is important to note that after the last Ice Age, the sea level was never higher than 10 metres above today's sea level in Lofoten (Hesjedal 1990), while the caves here are situated between 25 and 40 metres above sea level. Attempts have been made to date the paintings by comparing stylistic expressions in the various caves, and at the same time comparing the paintings with human images found in the more open sites, also taking into consideration the contexts that have been associated with them. Attempts have also been made to draw parallels with archaeological finds in the immediate vicinity of the caves. However, in most places there have been finds from so many different periods that they, too, do not allow us to clearly determine the age of the cave paintings.

For the time being, attempts to date the paintings have been unfruitful. If analyses reveal that the paint contains organic material, and we are able to extract and isolate this material in its purest form, we may be able – with the aid of advanced radiological methods – to determine the exact time when the paint was applied to the rock wall. Obviously, it is not possible to take samples from the paintings themselves. However, there may be fragments or residue that has peeled off and fallen to the floor. One of the methods that offers the best results in terms of determining age is dating based on other finds in the caves. Nevertheless, it should be noted that for the time being there are only a few caves in which datable material has been found. This is the case in the caves of Solsem and Hælvete. In the Solsem cave, for example, a comparison of the arrowhead that was found there with similar arrowheads from dated cultural layers and contexts in other places shows that they were used during the period between 1800 and 900 BC (e.g. Olsen 1994). In recent years, a piece of bone found in the cave has been analysed and dated to between 800 and 500 BC (Bjerck 1995), as well as a shell from the cave floor, dated to between 1870 and 1560 BC (Sognnes 1983). Additionally, a dating of a sheep bone with scrape marks situated it somewhere between 390 and 120 BC (*ibid.*). The datings differ substantially over a relatively long period, nearly 1800 years. However, it cannot be discounted that both the bone and the shell may have been brought into the cave at a later point in time, or that contamination of the samples may have affected the datings. It is therefore necessary to base surveys on as many datings as possible from different, but presumably contemporary categories of sources. The results mentioned here are all within the Bronze Age or Early Metal Age, and therefore give us a fairly clear indication of their age.

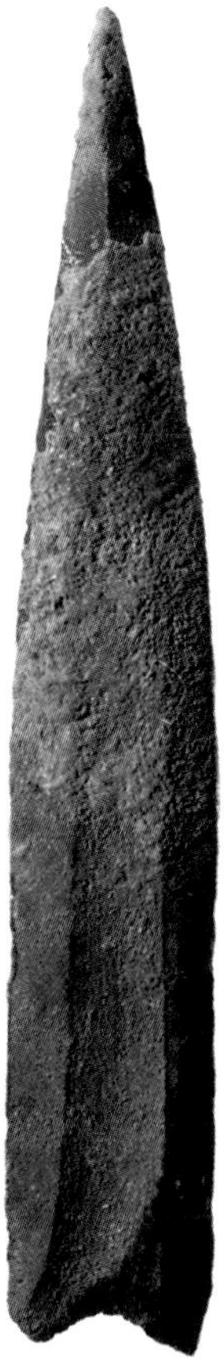

FIGURE 84. Arrowhead of the Sunderøy type, found inside Solsemhola. Probably in use during the period 2000–500 BC. NTUNUV

At the very end of the Hælvete cave, bones from a species of grey seal revealed clear marks from a cutting tool. The bone was dated to approximately between 1600 and 1400 BC, a period that coincides well with the oldest datings from the Solsem cave. Also, in the Fingal cave, a hearth was discovered many years earlier which, like the rock paintings, had been covered with a layer of calcite deposits. This may have been an open hearth that was lit at the same time as the paintings were created. Unfortunately, the calcite layer was removed before it could be analysed and dated. It is not known if any charcoal remains that has not been destroyed or contaminated.

Similarities and differences

Geological investigations of the caves have revealed that they were all created through continual wave erosion and thermal erosion against faults and other weak zones of the bedrock during the last Ice Age. In addition, frost processes and other types of erosion have caused rock falls from overhanging ledges, and these have partially blocked or reduced the cave entranceways, meaning that many of the caves are unsafe to visit. Regularly visiting the caves would have been a dangerous experience, a factor which undoubtedly contributed to their eeriness and was interpreted in a religious, spiritual or mythological context.

The similarities between the various caves and the situation of their images has been the object of some debate amongst scholars. Obviously, all of the caves are different, varying in their length, height and width. Nevertheless, something that may be considered a common feature in most of the caves is the presence of paintings depicting similar human figures that are organized in such a strict manner – standing side by side or in groups – that they must belong to a commonly shared societal tradition. The images are usually found in groups assembled on several panels, varying in the caves from one to four. There is also a clear tendency for the images to be located in the transition zone between lightness and darkness. Some are situated near the exit, while others are found in absolute darkness in the same cave. Another obvious common feature is that the images are situated in points where their more commonplace expressiveness is overshadowed, in areas where it is quiet, dark, cold and damp, and where sounds and voices take on a resonance that is unexpected and unusual. Some senses are inhibited; others are heightened. This must have provided the backdrop for inducing a state of altered consciousness, visions, trances and dreams.

Ritual and religious practice

There may be many reasons why the images were created inside caves. One possible explanation is to consider them in terms of a rite of passage. We know that in many societies with which it is natural to make comparisons, there are institutionalised stages of life through which members of society had to pass on their way from puberty to adulthood, and there were more arbitrary rituals when people were assigned new social roles. It is tempting to think that similar rituals also existed in prehistoric times. One common trait in such rituals is that the subjects were sequestered away from the rest of society, being ostracised for a period of time before they were allowed to return to the group. In some places these rituals were performed in deep secrecy. Such rituals often rely strongly on symbolic aspects that may be compared with being reborn, as the person would return to society with a newly acquired status. In this respect, it is interesting that the images are situated in the transition zone between light and darkness, as if to emphasize the symbolic duality. Even in our own modern society we find rituals such as baptism, confirmation and marriage, all of which contain some of the same elements. The atmosphere of the caves makes them particularly well suited as venues for rituals of this kind, as the symbolic aspect is so heightened, with the subject leaving the cave and being reborn into society. Another common feature is that the rituals are often initiated and performed by specialists. It was perhaps the tools and accoutrements of such a specialist that were found at the far end of the Solsem cave.

The underworld

As we have suggested in the preceding chapters, the placement of prehistoric sacrificial offerings indicates that there was a notion that the spiritual world existed within the realm of stone and mountains. Taking this kind of world-view into account, it is tempting to see crevasses and caves as openings onto, and passages into the underworld. It is easy to imagine that if contact was sought with forces of the underworld, specific gods or forefathers, the caves were the natural approach to them. Deep inside, individuals would be wholly surrounded by the forces that inhabited these underworlds. Inside the caves, each overhang, each boulder and each flat surface may have been interpreted in terms of the accepted faith. It is highly likely that only individuals with unique skills and special status were allowed to visit such sacred places, perhaps for the purpose of achieving some specific societal change, or for finding answers to elusive, existential questions (Lewis-Williams 2004). The images were painted as part of this "mission".

Another interesting question is the subjects that are depicted in the images. Naturally, we cannot provide a definitive answer, although we can reason that they must either represent those who were initiated to perform the secret rituals, those who were to undergo certain rites, or creatures associated with the underworld. One clue that can be pursued, of course, is the fact that all of the portrayals of humans are quite similar, a fact which in turn suggests that there was something permanent and institutionalised in the way depictions were to be made in the dark cave passageways in order to achieve their desired purpose.

With the exception of the Solsem and Fingal caves, the paintings were discovered quite recently. It is therefore reasonable to suppose that many more images will be found in the near future, both in the countless other caves along the coast and in the many limestone caves further inland. The discoveries will undoubtedly help to shape our understanding of these paintings, and allow us to answer some questions. Indeed, new discoveries are still being made inside the earlier known caves. Recently a systematic documentation was carried out in the Fingal cave of both the paintings and the environmental factors within the cave, also assessing the condition of the paintings. While this work was being carried out, an entirely new panel was discovered containing twenty to thirty new images, in addition to those previously known to exist (Norsted 2008).

Rock Art in Trøndelag

Along the central and inner area of the Trondheimsfjord basin, there are numerous rock art sites. If we consider Central Norway as a whole, it is true to say that most of its rock art panels are found in this area. The most frequently mentioned panels include Bøla, Bardal, Hammer, Hell and Leirfall, but when we single out these few panels, we do injustice to many others. Others deserve our attention, and we will mention them here. Many of these sites represent important cultural monuments in terms of their scope, diversity, abundance of images, and not least the many expressive scenes and other depictions that may be considered as visualisations of prehistoric mythology. Sometimes, specific events may have been depicted. It is difficult to be certain, however, and it is important not to discount the possibility that documentation of specific events may have been combined with a general, mythological notion, and that it was this framework of perception that was portrayed on the rock surfaces.

The Trøndelag panels can be divided into three separate categories. The first includes panels that are in the purely Northern Tradition; the second, panels that are in the agro-pastoral tradition, known as the Southern Tradition. A third category that is unique to the Trøndelag area due to its relative abundance here includes panels where both the Southern Tradition and the Northern Tradition are found on the same rock surface, in many cases including figures that have been superimposed on top of one another. During the 1800s, when we began to gain an overview of, and insight into the many panels with boats and cup marks, discoveries of large, naturalistic animal images concurrent with motifs from the agro-pastoral tradition, such as boats, soles of the feet and people led to the realisation that two different rock art traditions must have existed, and this subsequently resulted in the division of rock art into the Northern Tradition and Southern Tradition. The site of Bardal played an important role in this process (Gjessing 1936; Hallström 1938).

Apart from those mentioned here, more and more rock art paintings have been found in recent years in this geographic area. Although it is indisputable that pecked art dominates, this category is nevertheless only a part of the diversity. For the time being, they are limited to the Fosen peninsula and the municipalities of Bjugn and Åfjord, and the motifs are mainly comprised of animal images and geometric designs (Sognnes 1999).

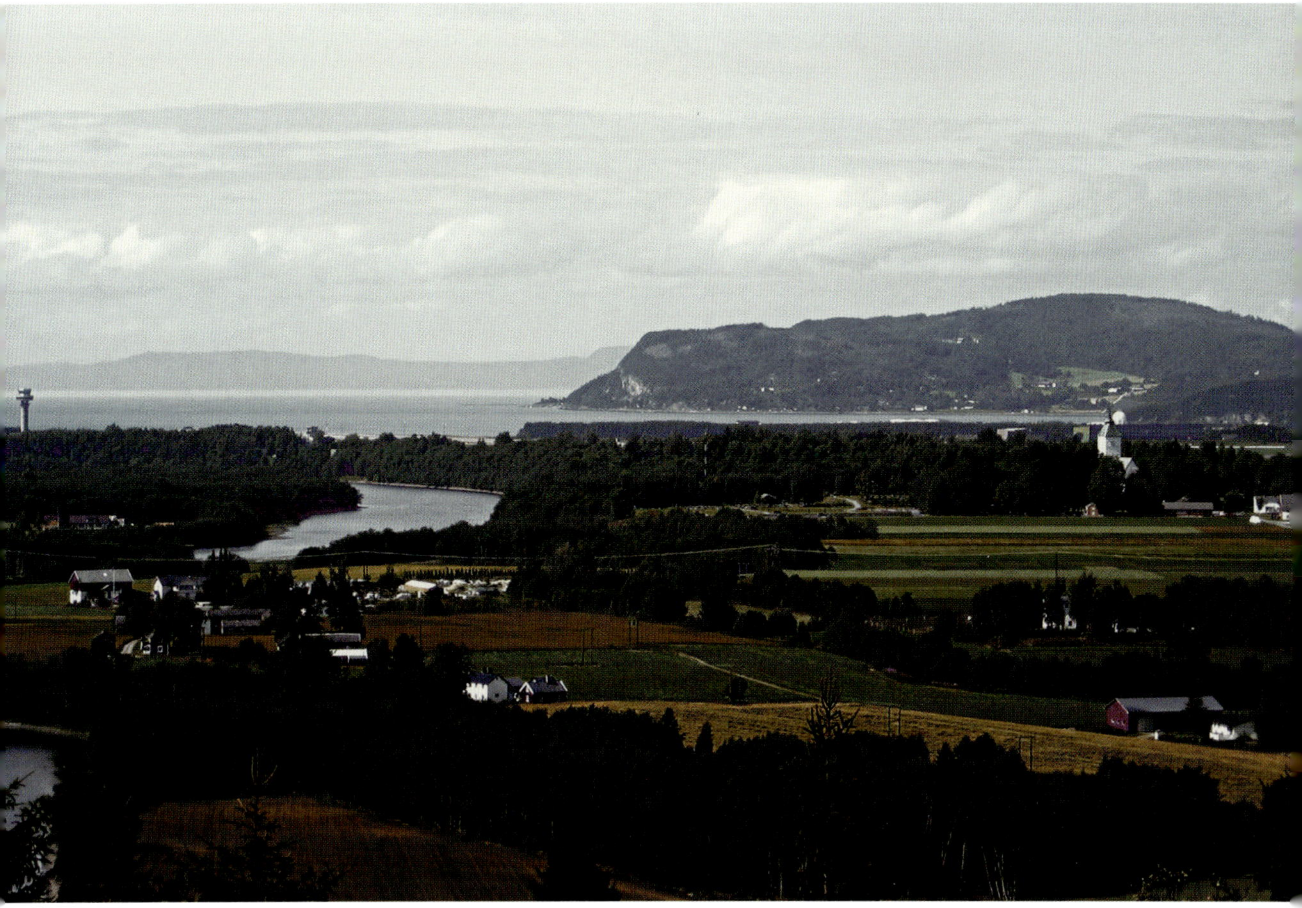

FIGURE 85. The southern side of the Stjørdal valley leading out towards Trondheimsfjord. The promontory in the background is Skatval, an area where a large concentration of rock carvings from the Bronze Age is found. In addition, rock carvings are found at close intervals along the entire northern side of the valley.

CO

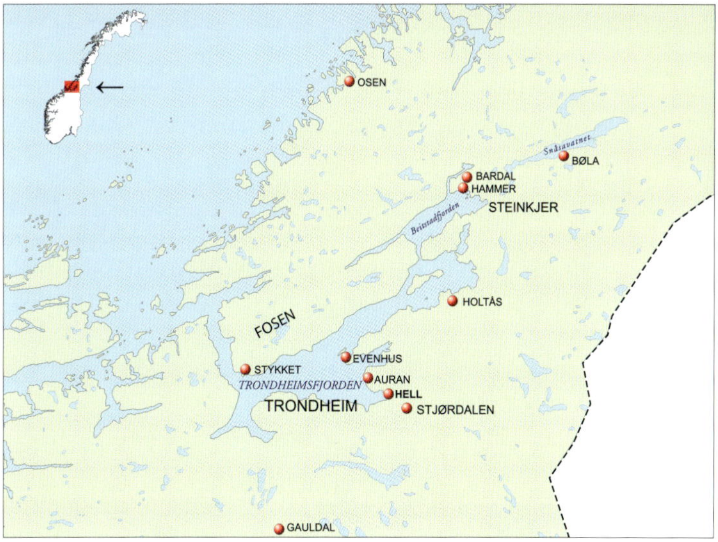

FIGURE 86. Along the mid and inner portions of Trondheimsfjord in Central Norway there are several rock carvings.

AI

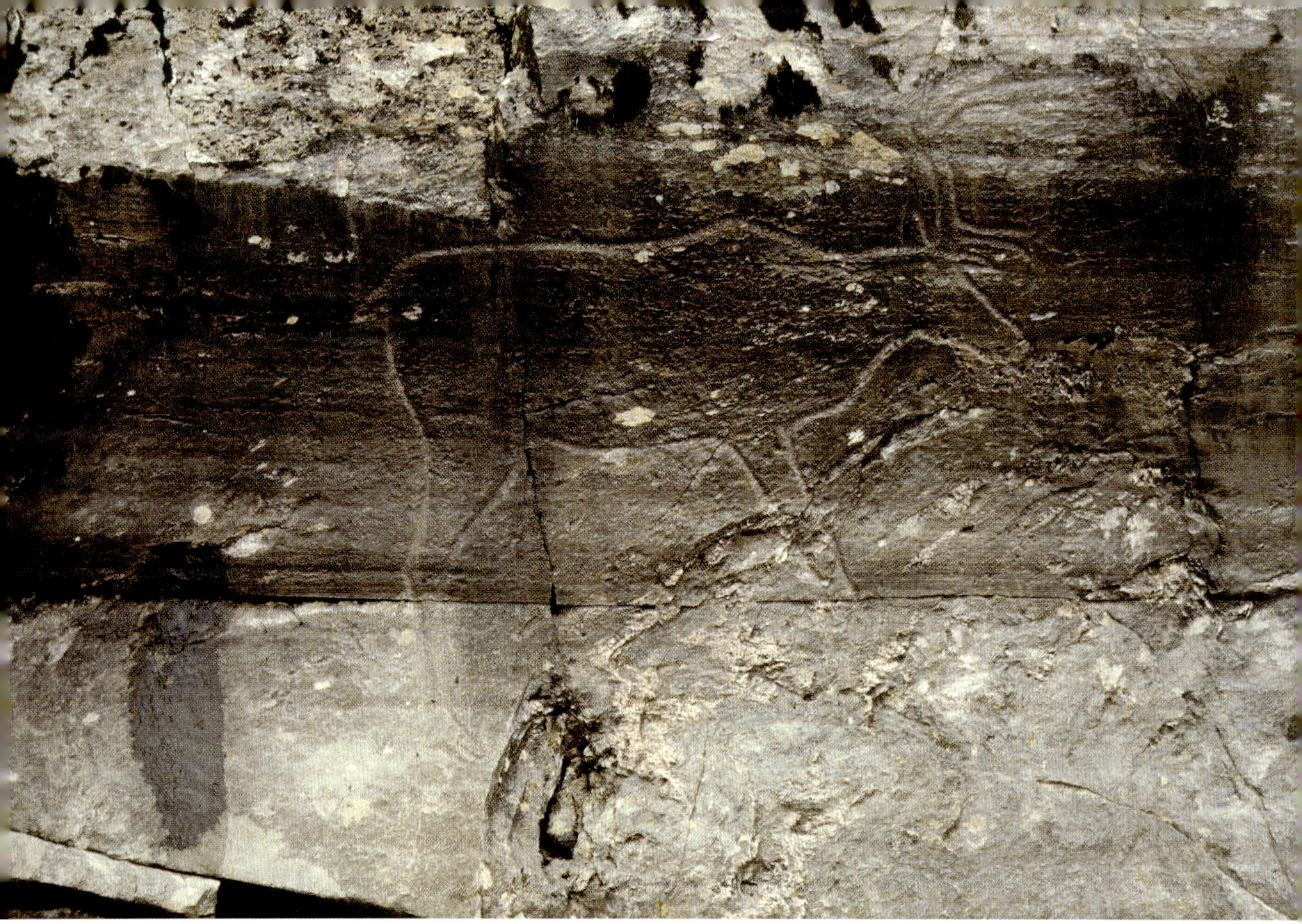

FIGURE 87. The very naturalistic and frequently mentioned Bøla reindeer.
TL

Panels of the Northern Tradition (Hunters' Art)

The oldest images in this area are mainly represented by the naturalistically depicted reindeer at the Bøla River, in the centre of the waterfall above Lake Snåsa (*ibid.*; Gjessing 1936). The image is perhaps the most true-to-life depiction of a reindeer that exists in Scandinavian rock art. It is formed by clearly pecked contour lines, and is a little less than two metres long. The lines are about two centimetres wide and one centimetre deep. The body area is partially shaded by pecking – perhaps in an effort to simulate the reindeer's pelt. The figure has been known locally since 1842, when moss was removed at the waterfall while work was being carried out to provide a water supply for a mill near the river. Subsequently other figures were discovered, including a bear, and more recently a human on skis. Today the images are at a considerable distance from the fjord. When the oldest of the images was created, however, probably some 6000–7000 years ago, Lake Snåsa was a part of the fjord and extended past the area where the rock art is today.

Other figures exist produced in a similarly naturalistic manner as the Bøla reindeer at Stykket in Stadsbygda on the far southern end of the Fosen peninsula, at Berg in Verdal and at Bardal in Beitstad. At both Berg and Bardal there are depictions of large elk. At Stykket we also find the remains of one large and two smaller elk images. The smallest of these is depicted facing the

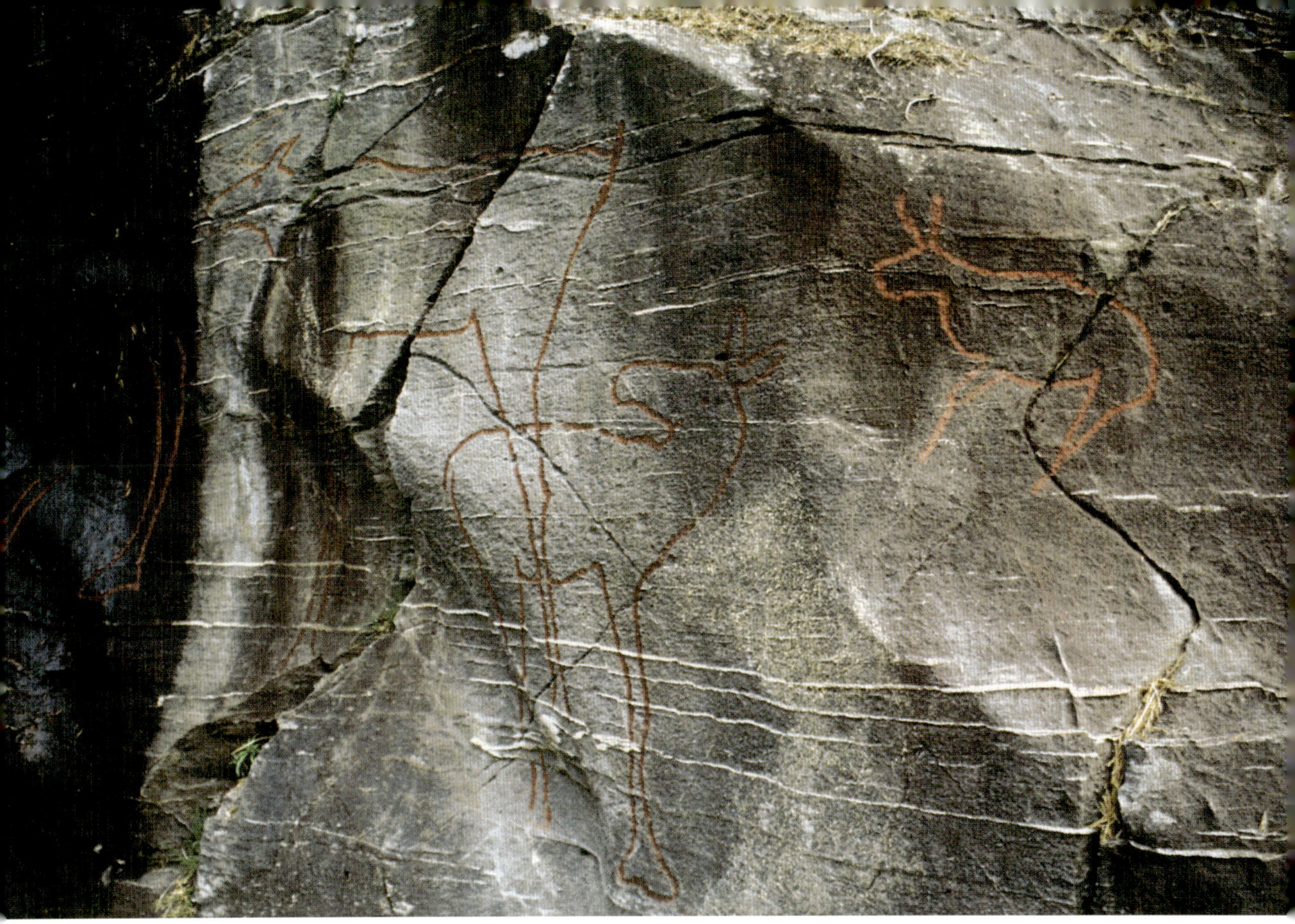

FIGURE 88. Large elks at Stykket, at least five in number. The rock surface is cracked and weathered, making many of the animals difficult to see. The stance of some of the animals, as well as the manner in which the elk turn their heads backwards, brings the images to life and gives a sense of movement.
KS

opposite direction from the others, but with its head turned back alluringly and looking at the other two. A panel further north on the western side of the Fosen peninsula, not far from Osen, also contains an interesting figure. Here a large whale figure, most likely a pilot whale, was found a few years ago, when workers dug out gravel from beneath a mountain wall (Sognnes 1999). The whale image is located more than 25 metres above sea level today, but it was undoubtedly created at a time when the sea was practically level with the image. A few more figures are also present on the rock surface, although they are overshadowed by the three-metre-long whale.

Other rock art panels of the Northern Tradition are found in Holtås, in Buvika and in Kvernavika, respectively in Steinkjer and Levanger (*ibid.*). On these panels, the figures are somewhat smaller and more stylised than the figures on the panels described above. In Buvika there are three relatively true-to-life depictions of whales pecked into a small rock surface not far from the grounds of the Steinkjer Museum. From the mouth to the tailfin there is a groove that expands into a pouch half way down the body. This can perhaps be interpreted as representing a lifeline, which will be discussed in more detail in the chapter on the Northern Tradition in south-eastern Norway. In Kvernavika on the western side of Skarnsundet near the Beitstadfjord outlet there are other marine species, a total of 15 quite realistic halibut arranged in a semicircle on the rock surface (Gjessing 1936). Apart from the contour lines, the bodies of the fish are

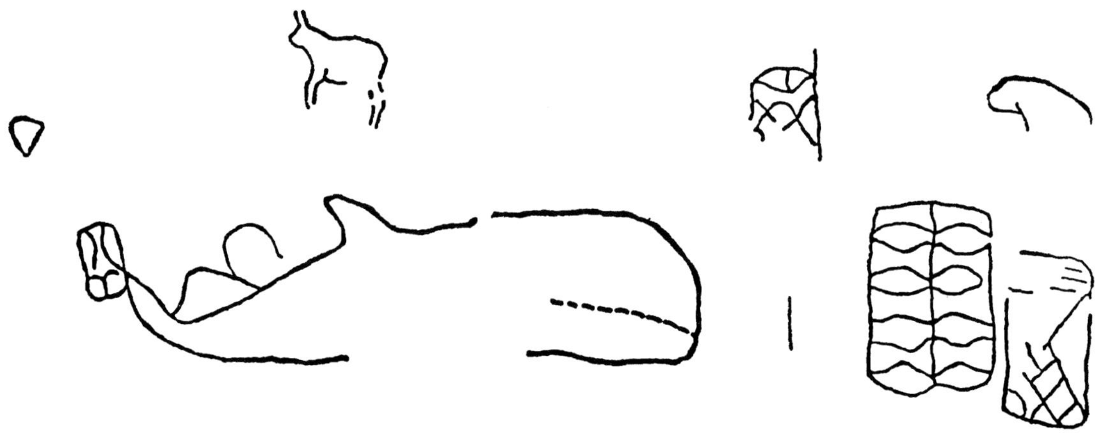

FIGURE 89. The large whale at Osen, surrounded by several smaller images, including several rectangular framework figures.
GG

divided by a central line that ends in a Y shape at the head. The largest image is well over half a metre long. At Holtås there are more than 100 images, most of which represent animals with patterns in the body, or animals whose bodies and legs are drawn using only single lines. Apart from the numerous small, stylised figures here, there is a characteristic feature where the bodies of the animals are shaded with lined patterns. The largest of the figures is just under 80 centimetres long. In addition to the animal images that perhaps depict deer, there are a number of zigzagging lines, ribbons with fringes, fragmentary lines and abstract patterns. The rock is heavily weathered and many of the images have deteriorated, and it is likely that others have exfoliated and are lost.

One of the panels of the Northern Tradition that stands out from the others is located at Hell in Lånke, Stjørdal (Hallström 1938; Sognnes 2001). On the steep mountain wall there are 11 animal images, a row of uniform rhombuses and some lines that seem to lack any real coherence. The animals are depicted in a less animated manner than those at Bøla and Stykket, but the creator put effort into portraying the antlers and shaggy fur along the neck. Two of the animals are noticeably larger than the other two. In particular, it is the technique used that distinguishes them from other rock art. The images are neither painted, polished or pecked, but are instead cut into the slate rock surface using deep grooves. The animals vary somewhat in style and size, but have many features in common. The longest figure is almost as long as the Bøla reindeer, just under two metres long, and the smallest measures about 20 centimetres. As far as it is possible to identify the species, they seem to be reindeer. The images are outlined in profile, and the body areas are divided into sections using vertical or diagonal grooves.

The rock images at Hell were mentioned in written sources as early as 1898, and have been the object of a number of analyses (*ibid*). The creative technique used has long been regarded as unique to Hell, but it has now been established that it was used on other panels in Central Norway, as well as in Jämtland in Sweden. This illustrates the risk of only focusing on one's own national borders when studying the spread of creative techniques and forms of expression in prehistoric times.

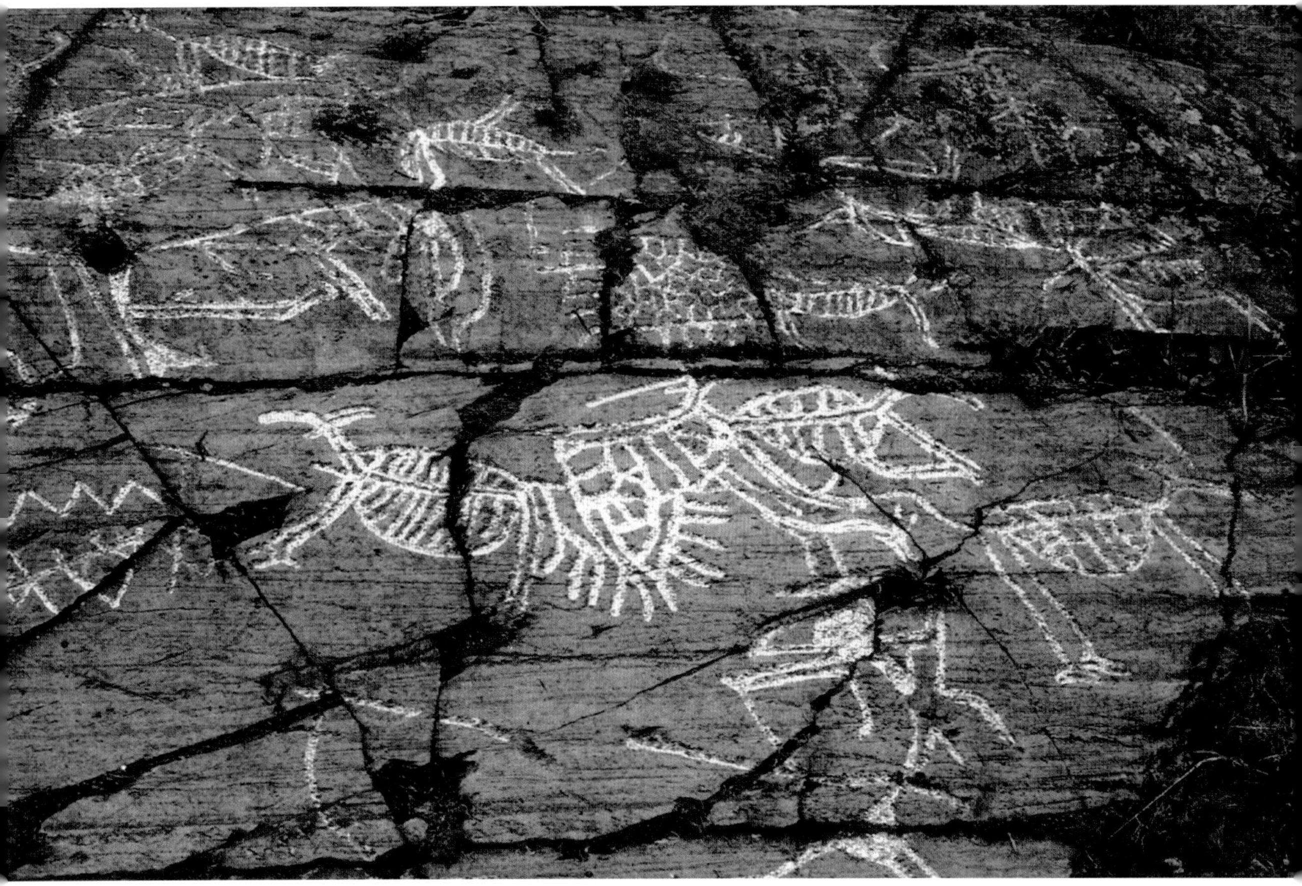

FIGURE 90 *(above)*. Figures highlighted in chalk at Holtås. The animal figures are highly stylized. The lines of their backs, pairs of legs and body decoration on their distended bellies are distinctive.

NTNUV

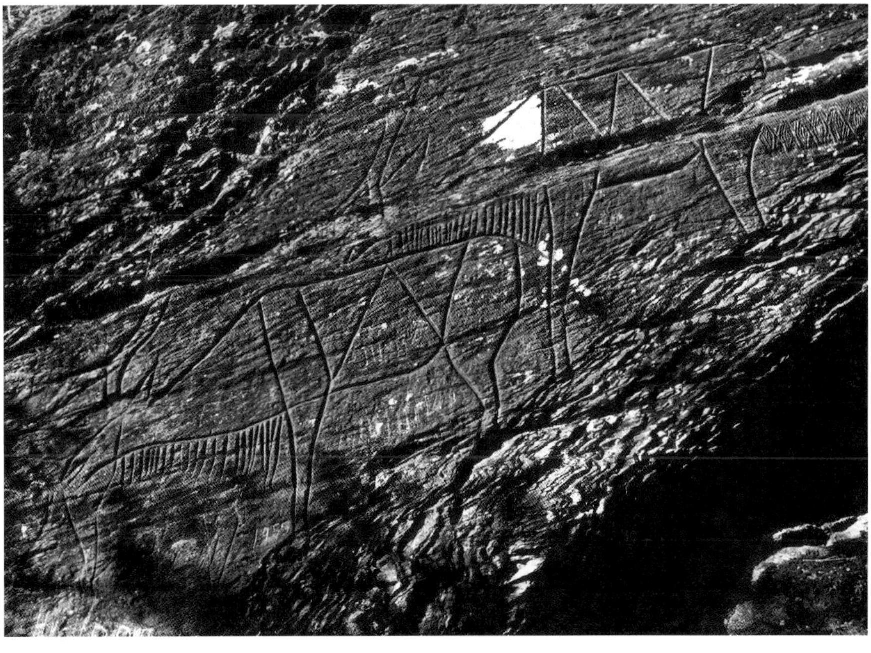

FIGURE 91 *(right)*. The figures at Hell were evidently carved into stone using sharp tools. The matted tuft on the lower neck of the reindeer is clearly visible. Directly behind the upper figure is the rhombus pattern. Similar patterns are found in Forselv in Sjomen and Bardal.

RU

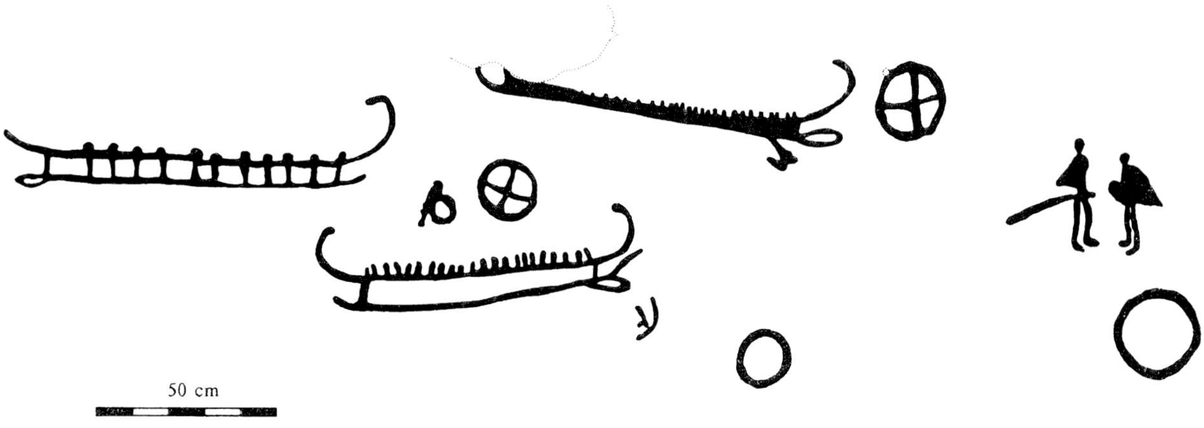

FIGURE 92. Panel VII at Hegra showing well executed boats, circles, crosses and human figures.
KS

Panels of the Southern Tradition

Panels with rock art from the Southern Tradition in the Trøndelag area are equally numerous. The Stjørdalen region is particularly noteworthy, as it is where most of the panels have been found. The largest groups of images are found at Auran, Ydstines, Hegra, Bjørngård, Leirfall and Fordal, which lie in succession along the valley, interspersed with a number of smaller panels (Sognnes 2001).

At the lower end of Stjørdalen, on the edge of the Skatval peninsula, rock art images have been discovered on the Auran property since the early 1900s. The area contains the largest concentration of single images in all of Central Norway, with more than 1300 figures (*ibid.*). A large number of them are cup marks. Further north is Ydstines, the first panel in Trøndelag to come to the attention of the general public. The panel was described as early as 1863, close to the Nesaunet farm, and was probably known to exist many years before. Along a low-lying knoll, over a surface area more than 20 metres long, a number of boats, foot soles, rings and cup marks were engraved into stone. Further up in the valley, at Hegra, several large panels with boats and rings have been found. Some of the boats are quite large, one of which is more than two and a half metres long. Today the panels are in the middle of a cultivated field and a densely wooded area. One of the panels was blasted with dynamite in the early 1900s, and the loose rocks were removed. One boulder with rock art now stands close to Hegra Church, probably originating from the blasting site. Many of the boat images here are practically identical to the boats at Bardal (*ibid.*).

Further up in the valley is Bjørngård, where there are ten to twelve scattered panels, many in densely wooded areas. Most of the panels are small and only have a few rock art images. The slopes are considerably steeper than those at other points in the valley. The first panels were also known to exist early in the 1900s, but more comprehensive documentation was completed in the 1980s. Some of the first panels that were investigated were never found again. The

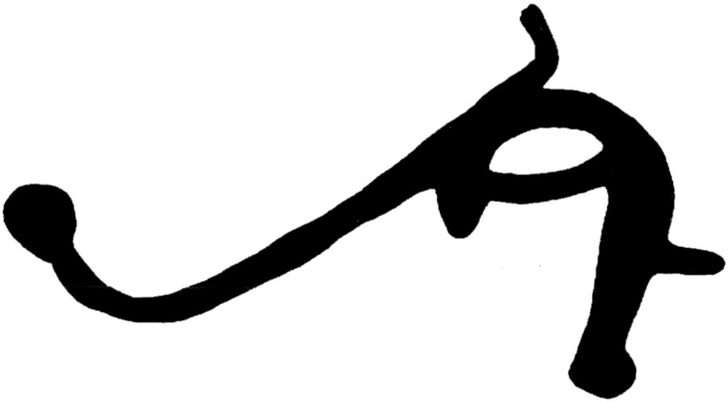

FIGURE 93. A depiction of what is probably a bronze trumpet, carved in the rock at Bjørngård. KS

panels are located at three different heights above the valley floor. One of the largest – often referred to as the main panel – is at the top. The panels at the lowest level are dominated by boat images. Above these are three panels nearly side by side with boats, quadratic figures and undulating lines. The top of the main panel is dominated by boats and human images, including a large human figure, numerous rings and an image that probably depicts a *lur*, a type of Scandinavian wind instrument.

Just under two kilometres south of Bjørngård is Leirfall, where a number of images have been discovered over the years on one large and several smaller surfaces. These feature large numbers of boats, circular figures, undulating lines and, most abundantly, foot soles, with many on all of the panels. The soles are often depicted in pairs, but single soles are found everywhere, as if they are traces of creatures or people who have walked across the rock, or were perhaps thought to reside inside the stone. There are also processions of human figures standing in single file. The panel was discovered in the 1920s near a stream. During the spring thaw, the stream swells and floods the terrain, eroding the rock surfaces. Many of the images are quite weathered as a result. Even further into the valley there are rock art images at Fordal, known to exist since the early 1900s. The images are on four separate panels dominated by four-legged animal figures. These are most probably horses, depicted as elsewhere with their heads turned towards one another. On two of the panels they are depicted almost in a circle around a spiral. The horses are arranged at some distance from the spirals, and appear to be part of an intentional composition. Apart from these images, there is a boat and a number of foot soles on the Fordal panels (*ibid.*).

There are also a number of areas outside of Stjørdalen containing rock art from the Southern Tradition. These include Tessem at the northernmost edge of the Beitstad peninsula, where there are several panels spread over a large area and featuring boats, foot soles, human figures and several *lurs*. Another is Gauldalen, just south of the Trondheim fjord, an area that stands out for its rock art on embedded boulders or smaller barren rock surfaces. The motifs include cup marks, foot soles, human figures and boats (Sognnes 1999).

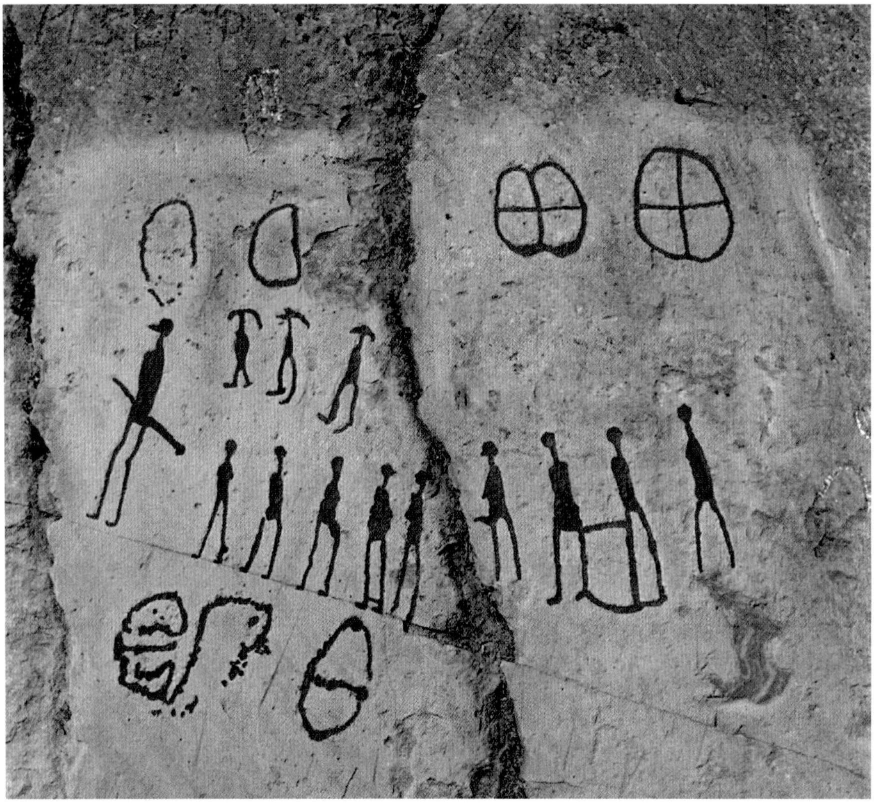

FIGURE 94. A photo taken at night of a procession of 13 people surrounded by foot soles. The procession is perhaps associated with ceremonies conducted at Leirfall. Leading the procession is what could be a ceremonial master, followed by two rows of people.

RU

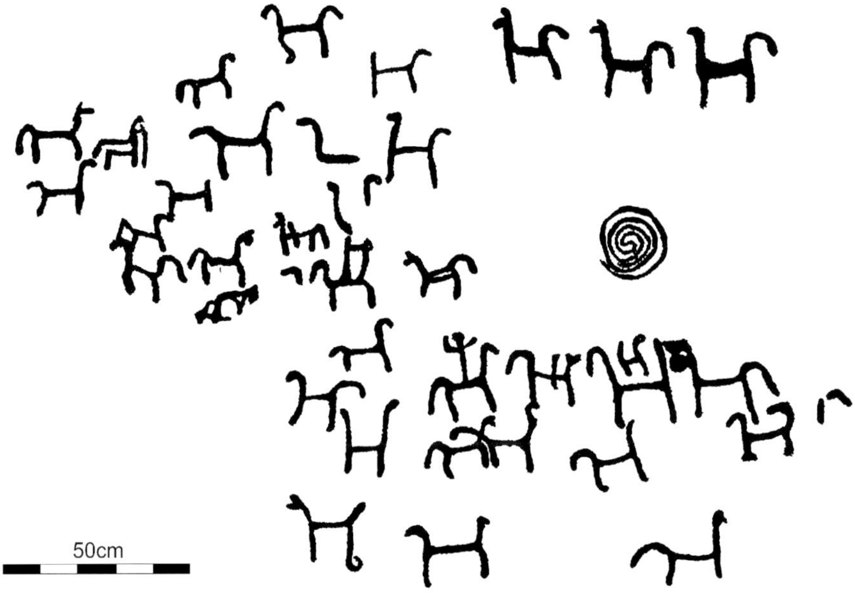

FIGURE 95. Stylized horses at Fordal, encircling a spiral at a safe distance. In the centre of the scene is a figure that is very likely a rider. Several of the vertical linear fragments crossing the body-lines of the animals may be the remains of other riders.

KS

Panels with both rock art traditions

As mentioned above, one characteristic of the Trøndelag area is that there are numerous panels on which rock art from the Northern and the Southern Tradition occurs together, such as in Bardal, Hammer and Skotrøa, all of which are in Beitstad, close to the city of Steinkjer, as well as at Evenhus a little further south, to name only the most well-known (Gjessing 1932; Hallström 1938). Many of these panels are dominated by rock art from the Southern Tradition, although initially the panels must have been used for depictions in the Northern Tradition. In several cases they were undoubtedly used for Hunters' rock art thousands of years before they were engraved with images from the world of ideas or the mythology of the agro-pastoral societies. In several places there is a noticeable contrast between the naturalistically depicted animal images and the stylistically expressed human images and ships.

One of these panels is on the Bardal farm, which is also the site of Scandinavia's largest concentration of rock art images. The main panel, situated in the farmyard, contains nearly 400 images carved onto one rock surface. Most of the motifs belong to the world of ideas of the agricultural society, and consist of boats, circles, spirals, a few human figures and individual animals. About sixty figures belong to the Northern Tradition, dominated by naturalistically depicted elk. There is also a six-metre-long image of a whale, which is the largest figure known to exist in Trøndelag (Gjessing 1936).

A short distance south of Bardal, at Hammer, a number of sites of varying sizes featuring different kinds of rock art were found. Here both generic forms of rock art – the Northern and the Southern Tradition – are represented concurrently. The panels at Hammer are on the borderline between wooded

FIGURE 96. A photo from 1908 of figures highlighted in chalk at Bardal. To the left in the photo, several large animal figures are surrounded by numerous boat images.
GH

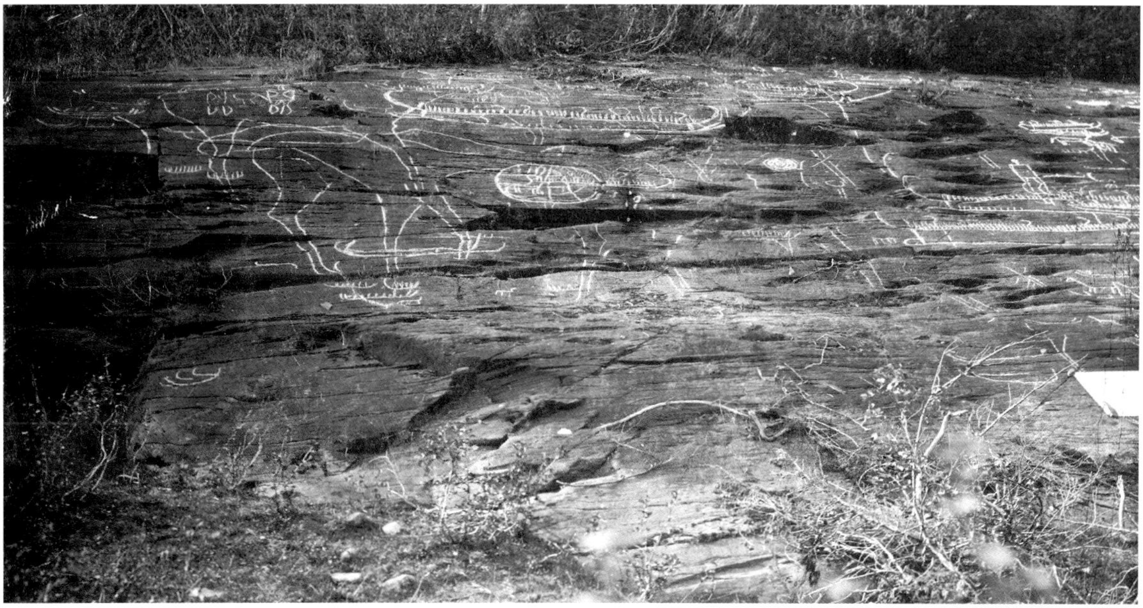

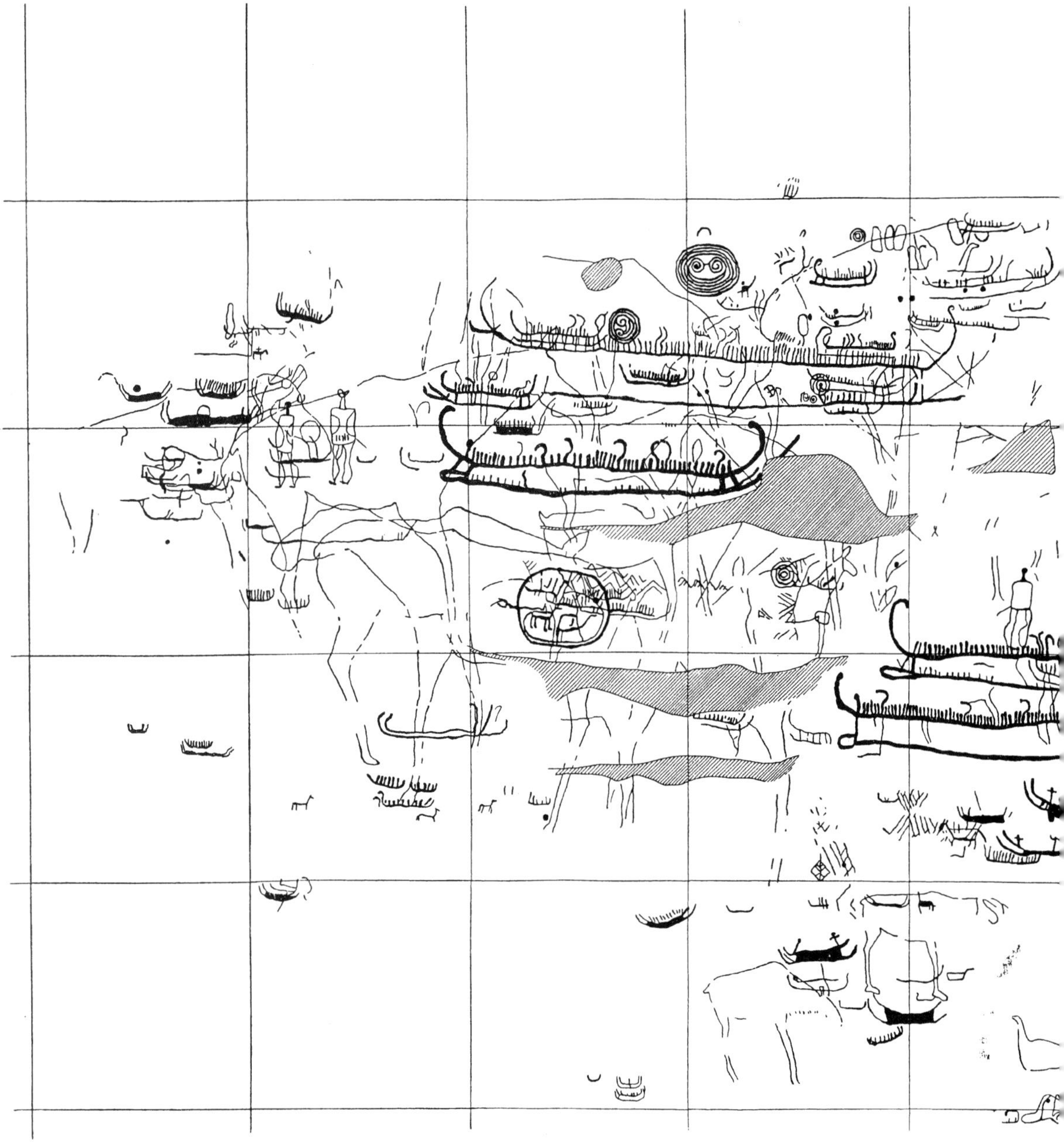

areas and cultivated fields, some 100 metres from the sea, and between 35 to 40 metres higher than the present shoreline. In all, nearly 300 figures and remnants of images have been studied. The Southern Tradition is represented by a number of boat images and numerous small, simply depicted animals. Among the many figures from the Northern Tradition, there are numerous portrayals of long-necked, strangely decorated birds, different types of whales, such as porpoises,

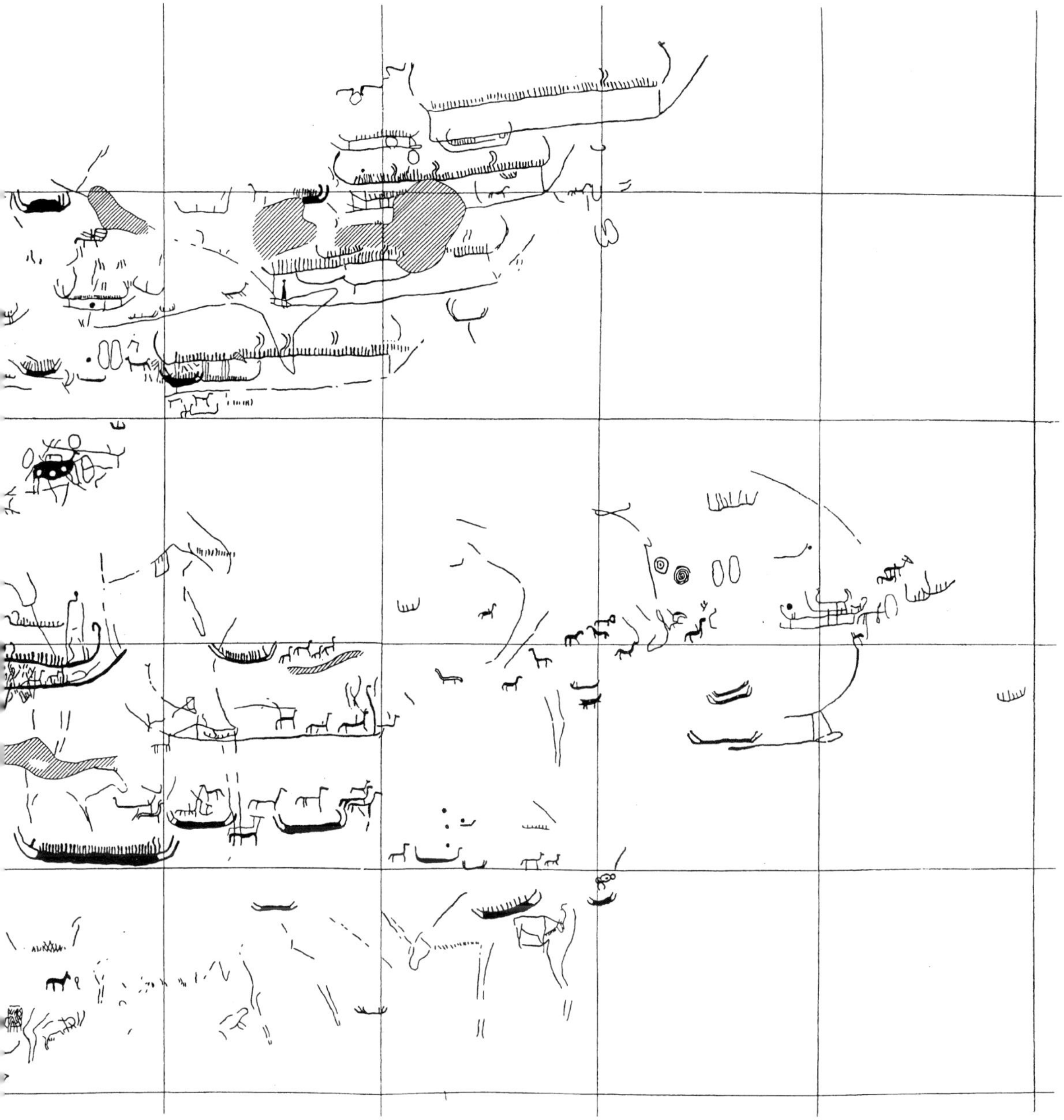

FIGURE 97. Tracing of the entire Bardal site, showing the extent of the various traditions and expressions that are found here. (The squares measure 2 × 2 m.)
GG

orcas and pilot whales, halibut, boats, humans and elk, the largest of which is some two metres long. At the bottom of the panel there are also a number of quadratic and rhombic figures.

It is interesting to note that both the characteristic rhombic patterns beneath the two large animal images at Hell and the quadratic figures here at Bardal have identical counterparts at Forselv in Skjomenfjord, Nordland (Gjessing 1932).

Even further east, very close to the city of Steinkjer, there is yet another panel with both main groups of rock art represented. The rock art is located on an adjacent property to the Østre Homnes farm, and is known as Skotrøa (*ibid.*). Here there are a total of 75 figures, with motifs from the Southern Tradition dominating most of the images: boats, circular pits, foot sole symbols and horses. The Northern Tradition is represented by five quite large animal images, probably representing elk, together with a long-necked bird. The remainder are groups of lines and unidentifiable figures, which in many cases are heavily weathered.

At Evenhus, located almost on the outermost edge of the Frosta peninsula, which juts out into the Trondheim fjord, there is yet another relatively large panel where both main groups of rock art are represented. This site is quite far out on the Frosta peninsula, not far from the village road and about 750 metres from the seashore. It now contains well over one hundred images, but originally there must have been even more. There are some forty boats, twenty elk and images of what must be deer or reindeer, at least ten whales and whale-like figures, around thirty cup marks, some circular patterns and a pair of human figures. Most of the figures are from the Northern Tradition, although there are also some features that are related to the world of ideas of the agricultural society – circles, boats with lines denoting keels and crews, and cup marks. The animal images are relatively natural in appearance, and are up to half a metre long (Gjessing 1936).

Traditions and contexts

Interesting perspectives are found in the way in which rock art from both the older and younger eras was engraved onto the same surface. We wonder how

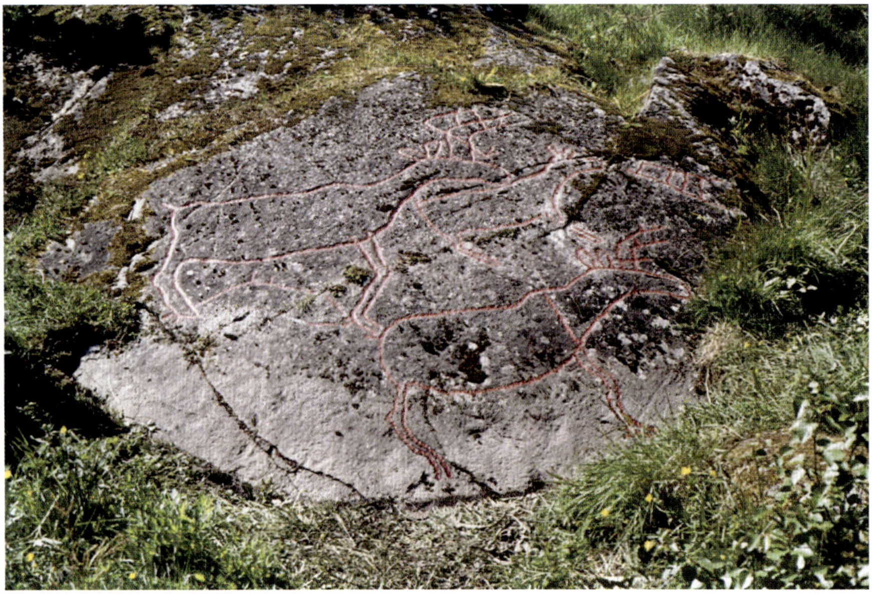

FIGURE 98. One of the panels found at Evenhus. The body and humped neck are clear indications that the images depict elk.
NTNUV

the people who created the youngest of the figures must have regarded the older images. What kinds of notions and thoughts would they have had about the origins and meaning of the older images, and to what extent were the older images an incentive for creating the newer ones? Of course, it is difficult to be certain. Initially, we may imagine that the oldest images were not visible to those who pecked out the later images: that during the process of engraving images from the Southern Tradition, the older, original images of the Northern Tradition were already heavily weathered and faint. However, this does not seem to be an acceptable explanation, as both the older and the younger images are still clearly visible today.

As there are so many panels containing rock art from both traditions, there seems to be a regular pattern at play, whereby the surfaces with art from the Northern Tradition seem to have been consistently re-carved with images from the Southern Tradition. Perhaps the Hunters' art on the panels was considered to be such a threat to the later society, with surfaces that displayed naturalistic animal images, that it became important in the Bronze Age to provide the surfaces with images from the contemporary society of the time, in order to promote and preserve its own ideologies, societal norms and culture. Today, property rights and land are regulated by a materialistically-oriented right to private ownership. Prehistoric societies most likely had their own means of protecting rights to property used for settlement, grazing and cultivation. There are grounds to believe that rock art itself was an important ideological and religious vehicle, and a necessary means of transmitting culture. It was undoubtedly important to base uses and traditions on the religion of the time.

Perhaps the older rock art images from the Northern Tradition contrasted too sharply with the newer norms of the age, so that they were unacceptable in an area that had been taken over by people with another set of values, and for this reason the images could not be left uncommented and untouched.

In addition, several examples exist from the Christian era where art has been destroyed or manipulated by new sovereigns for the purpose of imposing new ideologies (e.g. Tansey and Kleiner 1996). Perhaps we can consider the panels containing art from both the Southern Tradition and the Northern Tradition as an echo of the same development – that new ideas and new world-views overturn the old.

Rock Art at Bogge in Romsdal

South of the city of Molde, the broad Romsdalfjord branches off into several narrow fjord arms that cut inland across the country. Almost at the bottom of the longest of these fjords, Langfjorden, the considerably shorter Eresfjord arm extends southwards. On the eastern side of the mouth of this classic fjord landscape is the Bogge farm. Here, not far from the cluster of farm buildings, is the largest concentration of rock art in upper north-western Norway. If we follow Langfjorden inland from the coast by boat, the transition to more barren wilderness is striking on reaching the mouth of Eresfjord. The steep mountain slopes along the fjord appear uninviting and inaccessible, with their piles of fallen rock beneath smooth, vertical slopes where only stubby vegetation has found a foothold here and there. The gushing of countless streams and rivulets flowing down the slopes is a constant reminder of the precarious nature of the surroundings. Under certain light conditions, Eresfjord may seem quite inhospitable, particularly as the fjord is often in cold shadows. In contrast, the majestic mountains with their sunlit, snow-capped peaks beckon the visitor onwards. However, in order to reach the rock art it is not necessary to continue any further into the fjord. All that is required is to moor on the eastern side of the Eresfjord inlet. The immediate impression is that this is the last place where it is possible to go ashore before the fjord continues to its head, flanked all the way by sheer and insurmountable mountain walls. A closer examination of the passage, on the other hand, does reveal that there are several promontories and flat areas that once provided fertile conditions for settlement here. Today it is possible to reach Bogge by car from the head of Langfjord. Road construction here must have been a major challenge, as the steep escarpments and cliffs of the mountainside plunge almost vertically into the dark fjord below.

Although overgrowth has remained unchecked in recent times, the fjord inclines are generally barren, and are either smooth and bare or incrusted only with moss and lichens. A total of three panels containing rock art have been found here, both from the Northern and Southern Tradition, amongst cultivated patches of land on the fjord's slopes.

The best known panel is the highest in the terrain. Local people have known of its existence for many years, but it was not made known to the public until it was mentioned by Lieutenant Colonel Reinhold Ziegler in 1901, in the annals of *Det Kongelige Norske Videnskabers Selskab* [today's Museum of Natural History and Archaeology] (Ziegler 1901). The news brought many inquisitive visitors to Bogge in the following years. Among those who followed

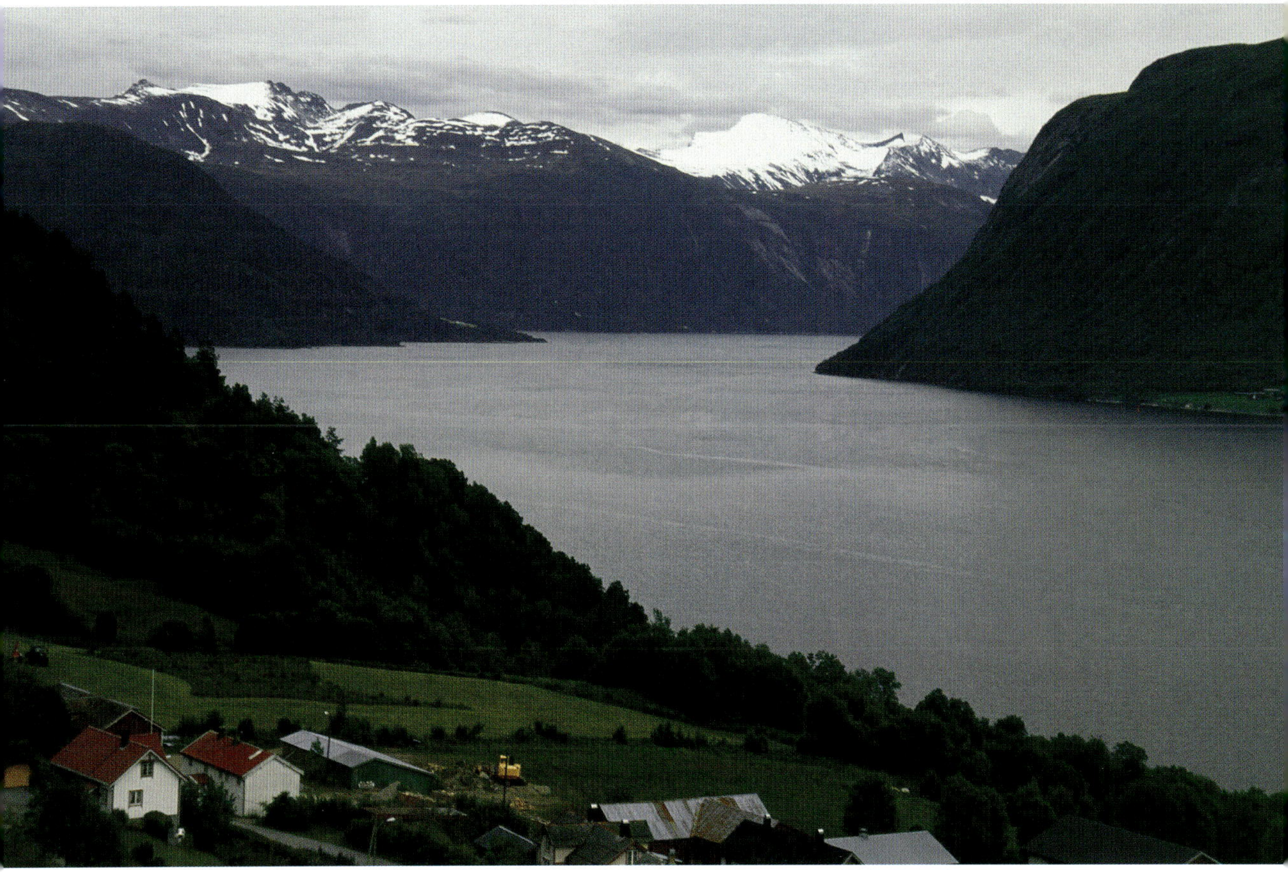

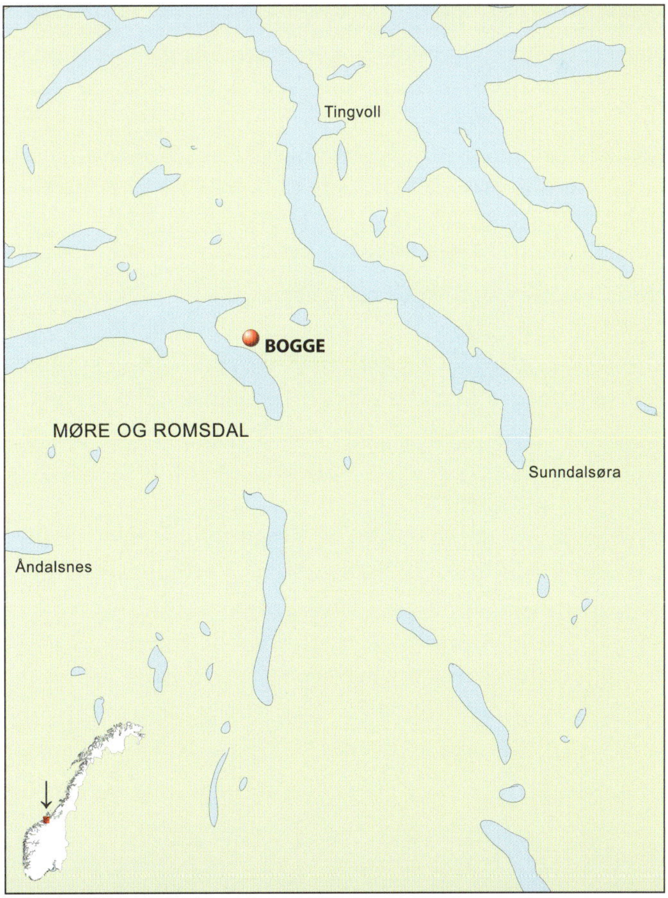

FIGURES 99–100. Bogge is situated at the mouth of Eresfjorden at the very end of Langfjorden, behind the promontory at centre left.
MAP AI, ILLUSTRATION TL

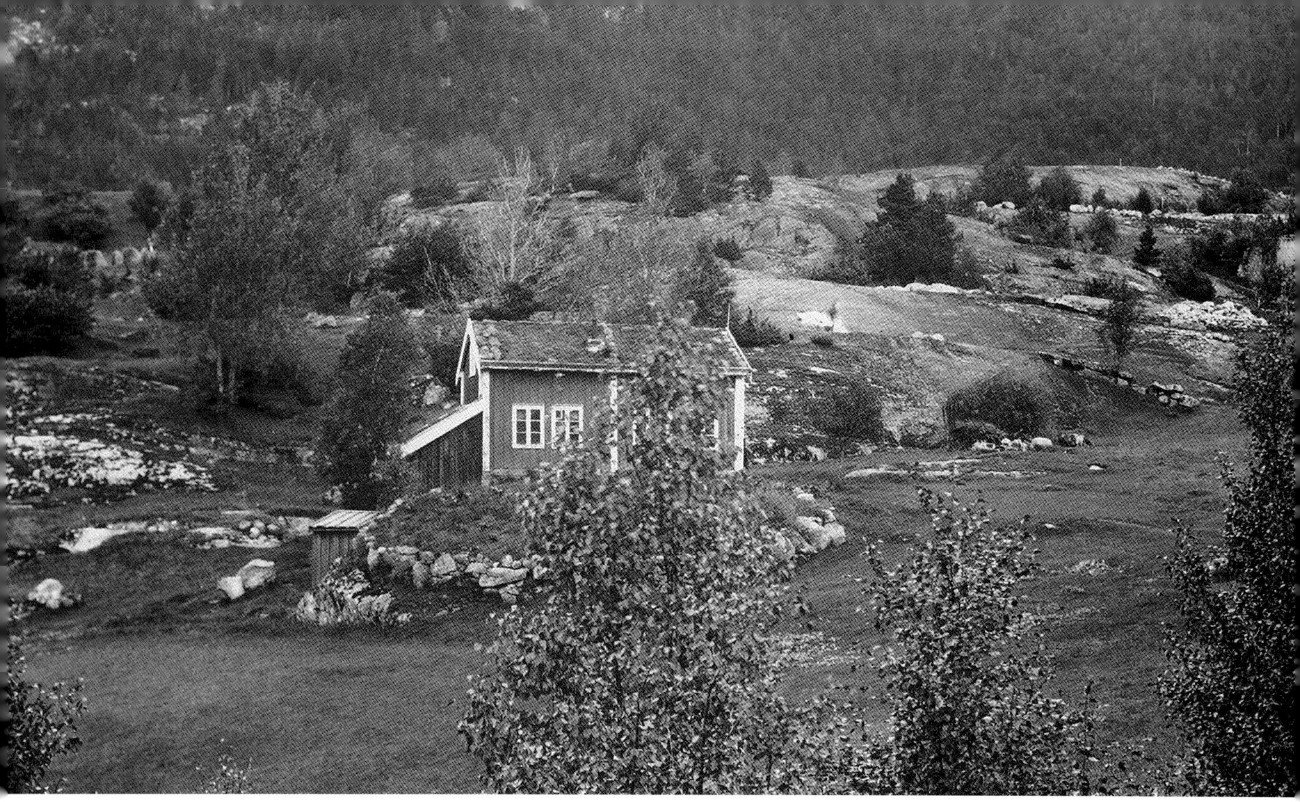

up Ziegler's documentation with a series of new discoveries was Swedish archaeologist Gustaf Hallström. He carried out comprehensive investigations here in 1908 and 1913 while researching for his large volume on rock art in Sweden and Norway (1938). Hallström was particularly interested in the superimposed images, where several images were pecked on top of older ones. This made it possible to determine which of the figures were the oldest, and by extension to acquire information that would make it possible to establish a relative chronology to more precisely determine the age of rock art. During his last visit in 1913, he discovered two other panels of rock art further down by the fjord that were previously unknown. Hallström's interest was first and foremost in the oldest rock art from the Northern Tradition, and it was while he was calculating the elevation of these images above sea level that he came across a dark, smooth and slightly concave rock panel at the edge of the fjord. He recorded in his description of the discovery that he thought to himself, as he was taking measurements, that the rock surface he saw at a distance would be a typical place where rock art from the Bronze Age may be located. It was not until later that he took the time to examine the panel more closely, and he was surprised that his suspicions were confirmed, finding a number of images depicting boats. Thrilled by the discovery, he began to investigate many of the other rocky knolls in the area. As a result, he found yet another panel with a number of whale images on a sharply slanting slab of rock further up in the terrain. It is unusual for an archaeologist to make a find of this kind, as more often than not they are discovered by laymen.

FIGURE 101. This was how the area looked when Hallström visited in 1908. The uppermost panel is located just behind the building.
GH

Rock art from at least three different prehistoric periods

Based on the locations of the panels high on the side of the fjord and the various motifs they feature, there are grounds to assume they were produced over at least three different, clearly defined prehistoric periods. All of the rock art was probably created on rock surfaces that were situated on the shoreline, uncovered by moss or other vegetation, in an environment similar to the one we find along the fjord today. Just after the end of the last Ice Age, land uplift began, and the panels were raised higher up in the terrain. Today the shoreline offers a good representation of the environment in which the creators of the rock art must have worked. Here we find shiny, rounded and barren rocks, almost plastic in their undulating forms, created by the ice that once scoured out valleys and fjords. In many places they are conspicuous and inviting, as if they were deliberately placed there so that someone would decorate them with rock art. This, however, cannot have been the case. There are many other rock surfaces nearby that are hardly distinguishable from those that have rock art, but do not have a single man-made mark on them. Or could it be that they are not as identical as we think? Perhaps we are unable to appreciate the qualities that once attracted people to adorn rock surfaces with images. What was important was perhaps not the technical quality of the rock surface that we tend to consider as important when we evaluate stone today. There may have been other spiritual and mythological factors that had to be present before a person would create rock art on a given surface. One explanation for why both the hardest granite and the most fragile phyllite have been used as surfaces for rock art in Norway is that our modern criteria for quality did not apply in prehistoric times. The main type of rock found at Bogge is micaceous gneiss, which is not one of the softest varieties of stone, but which nonetheless offers few problems for creating rock art. To do so, as at other sites, a hard and sharpened pecking tool was used. In several places there are clear marks left by the hard tip in the lines forming the images. These details are often weathered away. Unfortunately, the rock art images have also inspired people in modern times to add their own graffiti. In many places we find inscriptions, signatures and initials that mar the prehistoric rock art. This said, one consolation lies in the fact that the prehistoric images were cut more deeply than the modern inscriptions, and are therefore still clearly visible.

The lowest-lying panel – Bronze Age rock art

The lowest-lying panel, which Hallström discovered first, is situated on a gently sloping surface that has been eroded by leachate from a peat bog higher up. The panel is just above the shoreline, and is gradually becoming overgrown with vegetation. A total of 12 boat images were found here, all of which were marked with contour lines, meaning that only the outlines of the boats were pecked into the stone, generally depicting the double prow and single stern.

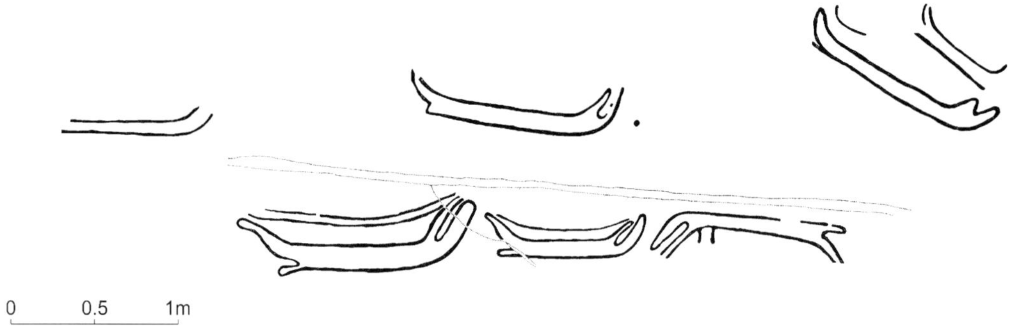

FIGURE 102. The figures located to the far west on the lowest panel.
GG

They are nearly equal in size and are arranged close to one another over an area slightly less than 12 metres wide. In amongst the boat images there are a number of rings, a double spiral, a pair of heart-shaped images and some cup marks (Bakka 1987). The horizontal lines of the boats follow the layering in the bedrock, and in many places they cannot be distinguished from the natural grooves in the stone. It is likely that the bedrock layering itself was seen as an important feature in the choice of this surface for the rock art. Many of the boat images are placed in sections over which water trickles continuously. It is plausible that placing the boats in their proper, aquatic element was intentional. A latticework of cracks just above the figures collects trickling water, and tends to support the theory by leading the water down to the boats lower on the panel. Images in a similar position are found in other locations, further supporting the likelihood that water running over the rock was a factor for creating the rock art in these areas. The peat bog that is the source of the water today may not have been here when the boat images were made, although the watercourse is very probably the same. Many of the boat figures have lines that are rounded at the edges and quite vague in nature; in other places we find only fragments and traces of lines that are probably the result of prolonged erosion from running water. Although today we know of more images than Hallström found here in his day, several of the most easterly images he recorded have never been recovered. If we take into account the information we have about land uplift in the area, it is likely that the images now situated 6 metres above sea level were created more than two thousand years ago. This corresponds with the end of the Bronze Age or the beginning of the Iron Age. It is difficult to form an opinion about their meaning. However, as the boat images are so recurrent and found in so many places, it seems clear that boats must have had strong symbolic and mythological values.

The mid-panel – a large number of whale images

Some way further up from the shoreline is the other panel found by Hallström. Here, a steeply sloping surface facing southwest was chosen for rock art. The

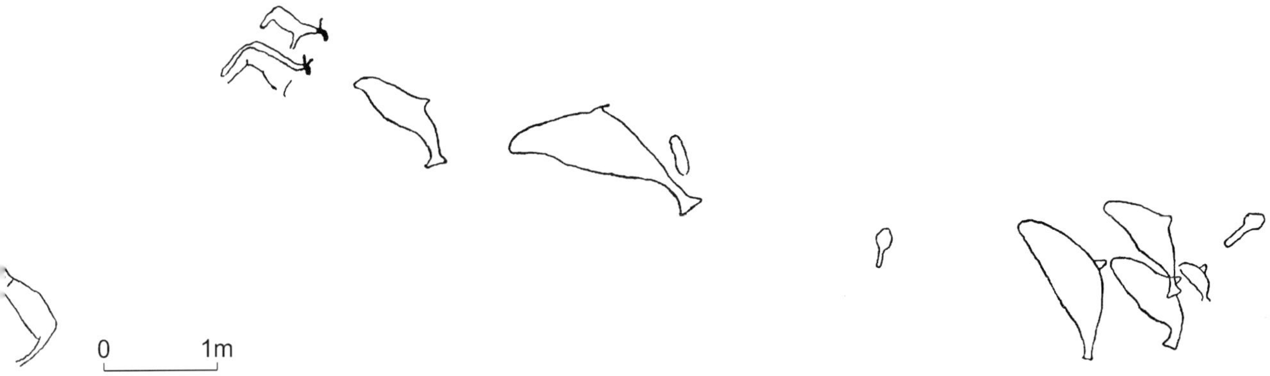

FIGURE 103. Whale figures – possibly pilot whales – in an encounter with some animal figures. Also, a few club-like images that are difficult to identify. GG

primary motifs seen on this panel are relatively large-sized whale images. There are also some smaller animal figures probably representing deer, although the schematic manner in which they are depicted makes it difficult to identify their species. The whales are quite stylised, and several scholars have claimed that they must be porpoises. However, if they are seen in context with the other animal figures, they are too large to support this claim. It is more logical to see them as larger species of whale, perhaps pilot whales, which we know are still found in local waters. Four of the whales are placed close to one another, as if to emphasize a close relationship between them. One is even superimposed over another, although they are almost identical, both in the technique used to depict them and in shape, and it is therefore probable that they are contemporary to one another. The other two whales are situated further west on the surface, one following the other. They appear to be met head-on, or confronted by two four-legged animals, as if to illustrate some kind of relationship, mythological or spiritual, that the creator of the images may have intended. Seen in context with the polished images in Nordland, the images here can be seen as a relationship or opposition between land animals and sea mammals that the prehistoric artists considered worthy of illustrating. This may be an important point that can provide a clue to the world of ideas shared by people of the age. Apart from these images there are two or three depictions that some scholars have interpreted as clubs, although we are far from certain as to what they were intended to be. There are also several fragmentary lines that may have originally been parts of animal images or inanimate objects, but which today are too vague and weathered to be identified. The lowest images are found less than 19 metres above sea level. Based on what we know about land uplift in the area, this would indicate that the images were created nearly 5000 years ago (Ramstad 2000).

The upper panel – the earliest known rock art

Still further up in the terrain, some 50 metres east of the mid-panel, we find the rock art that was the earliest known and that comprises the largest concentration

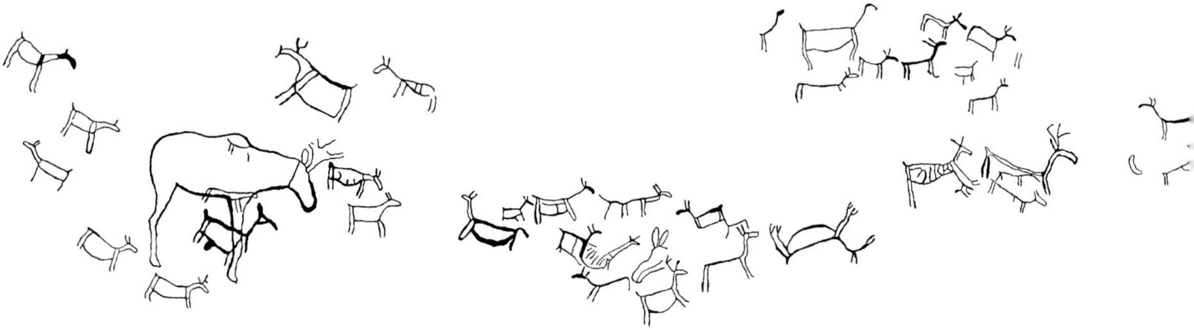

FIGURE 104. Tracing showing the majority of the figures that occur on the largest and earliest discovered panel. Two additional figures are located more than six metres away from the animal on the far left.
GG

of images at Bogge – the rock art that was made public through Ziegler's documentation (1901). They are located on a markedly rounded slab of rock. A farm road runs past the edge of the panel, and a part of the rock was blasted away in order to widen the roadway. It seems as though an effort was made to avoid destroying the images, although we cannot discount the possibility that some were lost. With the exception of an small, oblong figure, here there are only images of four-legged animals. A total of fifty-five figures are recorded, although more may still be concealed by soil deposits on adjacent sections that are covered with vegetation. On this panel, which faces in a south-westerly direction, there are several groups of animals that appear to be interrelated, as if the scene is meant to depict some prehistoric event. The arrangement of the animal images, however, provides few clues as to what they may have meant. Scholars have debated whether the figures are elk, deer or reindeer. Several researchers have reached a consensus that most of the images are deer. Moreover, it is difficult to determine whether the various figures represent stags, female reindeer or perhaps denote chronological differences. The similarities between many of the figures tend to indicate that the majority of them are contemporary to one another. It does appear beyond all doubt, however, that there are images on this panel that date from at least two different periods. Two of the larger images stand out from the rest. The clearest of these, an elk, is in the centre of the panel. It is almost two metres long, and is more than twice the size of the other images. The incised lines are broad and deep, in some places heavily weathered, but nevertheless even and distinct. The lines outline the entire animal and give it a very lifelike and naturalistic appearance. The antlers are indistinct, however, and it is likely that they were pecked or carved more faintly, perhaps at a later time. In amongst the other figures further towards the east, there is the head of an animal that also has the same dimensions as the large elk. The head alone is almost half a metre wide, and strangely is the only part of the body depicted. Even under optimal natural or artificial light conditions, it is impossible to detect any other perceptible lines. It therefore seems that the animal was left unfinished, or that there was never any intention

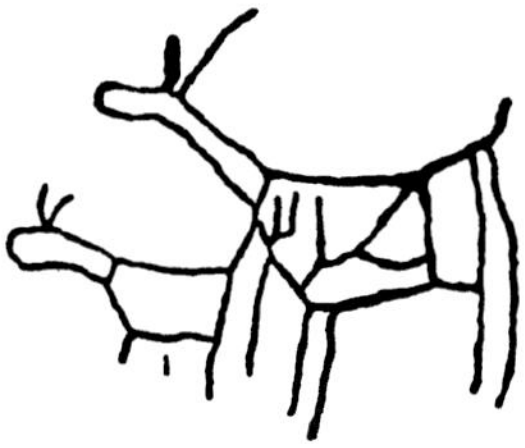

FIGURE 105. Two figures stand some six metres apart from the others.
GG

to depict more than its head. Also, the large images were made using a different technique than the others. While the contours for most of the images are cut only a few millimetres into the stone, the lines for the largest elk image are some two centimetres deep and are much broader. Whether the width is a result of weathering is difficult to say. However, it is interesting to note that Hallström was told that local people had "refreshed" the images using sharp objects so that they would remain distinct. If this was indeed a common practice, it may have significantly affected the depth of the grooves. Several scholars have suggested that these large, naturalistic elks must have been based on ideas and stylistic guidelines that were imported from the north, from Trøndelag and Nordland, and that they – like the latter – must be very old. The theory that the larger figures are older than the others is supported by the observation that many of the smaller figures seem to be superimposed over the larger, whole reindeer, and would therefore be younger. If we follow this rationale to its logical conclusion and state that the oldest figures are contemporary with the rock art in Trøndelag and Nordland, it would appear that there are major time intervals between these figures and the others. They do appear to be younger, all things considered, and we are therefore confronted with a problem in terms of the shoreline level. If we attempt to date them based on the prehistoric shoreline level, we are able to place the figures, all of which are about 24 metres above sea level, to around 6000 years ago. This panel is definitely problematic in this sense, and clearly illustrates the objection against using the shoreline level as a basis for dating rock art. Is it the oldest or the younger, superimposed images that are 6000 years old, or is the time interval between them so negligible that both stylistic traditions are approximately 6000 years old?

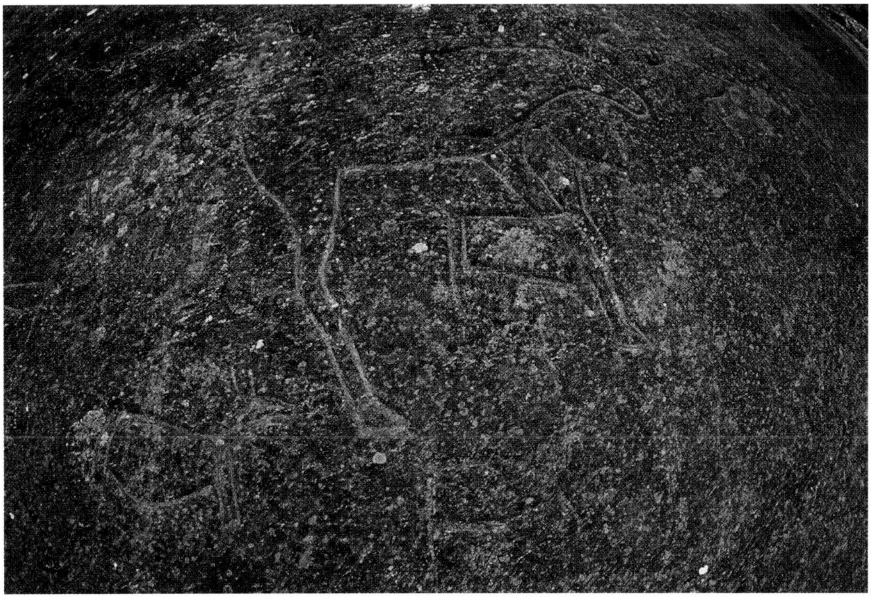

FIGURE 106. The large elk surrounded by smaller animal images. As the photo shows, several of the smaller animal images have been pecked over the larger one.
TL

The stylisation of the other figures is more schematic. In most points, the legs of the animals extend directly down from the back. In some places the back is only shown by a line, and the fore and hind legs descend perpendicularly from it. The way in which the legs are depicted also varies significantly in comparison with the oldest figure, which only has one foreleg and one hind leg, as if the other two legs were concealed behind those shown. The other figures are depicted with four legs, indicated by two simple lines at the front and two at the back. Two of the images have patterns in the body. In terms of arrangement, they are placed in what appear to be clusters or groups, where one group seems to be a flock migrating in the same direction. Another group has animals facing in different directions, with their forelegs and hind legs slanting out from the body, perhaps to illustrate that they are scattering, as if frightened, in different directions. Still others are depicted as though they are tense, on guard or are alert to some kind of danger. Several of these images are superimposed over the large elk figure, intersecting the forelegs, belly and line of the back. These animal images are arranged in groups from the centre and southwards on the rock, although two animals stand out as a result of being situated alone and on the most westerly point of the exposed rock surface, some six metres from the nearest cluster of figures.

Contact with the otherworld

Within the large concentration, there are two other animals that also stand out as a result of having appendages at the ends of their legs that resemble toes. On one of these, only the foreleg has this feature. The other is even more unusual since it is depicted upside down, a feature that attracted the interest of the Norwegian author Alexander Kielland, who visited the site only a couple of years after it became known to the public. He believed that the prehistoric artists had done this on a whim, or as an ironic commentary:

> But what I admire above all else is that this artist chose to place one of the animals on its back with its legs extended in the air.... And I imagine uproarious laughter that has rolled out across Erisfjord prompted by this fat animal lying on its back with its legs in the air; a whim of the artist, which for its time undoubtedly was on a par with comedy that would later become renowned in art or literature. *(Author's translation)*
>
> *(*Alexander Kielland, Molde 15 October 1903*).*

It is quite doubtful that the feature was added as a prank by the person or persons who created the image. It probably had a much deeper rationale behind it. The rock art was not made for the purpose of adorning stone, but more probably for important religious, spiritual or mythological reasons that would not have admitted such frivolity. True enough, we have few clues to follow in terms of the religion of these prehistoric people. However, through archaeological material and ethnographical sources which permit relevant comparisons, we are also able to increase our knowledge of this area. Some of the best sources for understanding religious notions are the finds from sacrificial

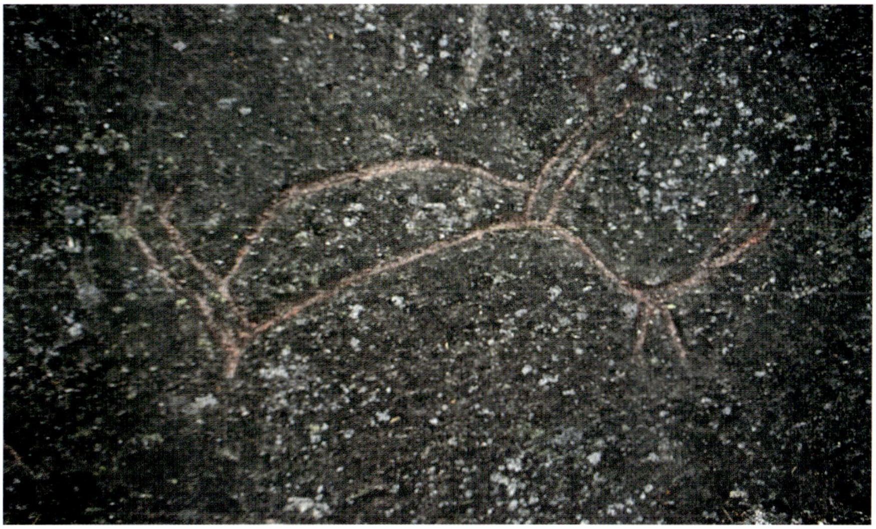

FIGURE 107. The animal depicted upside down which captured Alexander Kielland's imagination.
TL

sites from the same period. As votive offerings were made, beliefs must have existed in divine or perhaps spiritual worlds to which the sacrifices were offered, and to which the believers had to show deference through their acts. And as offerings, often stone axes, were buried beneath stones or rock slabs, this may be an indication that spirits and gods were presumed to belong to the underworld beneath the ground or inside rocks. The ways votive offerings were deposited, often in conspicuous places, may indicate that these forces were seen to be present in many parts of the landscape, with the result that believers showed great respect for the environment. Supported by ethnographical material, it is possible to imagine that these people must have regarded their surroundings as being animate, possessing souls, and that there were worlds beyond their own where both animals and humans, or their spiritual counterparts, dwelled. In the depiction of one animal in an upside-down position, we may be seeing an expression that this animal is different from the rest, belonging to another world, the great beyond. Perhaps the position simply symbolized the soul of animals. At other sites with which it is both interesting and relevant to make comparisons, such as a number of panels in Vingen, Bremanger, we have examples of animals that are depicted in pairs, muzzle to muzzle, where one of the two is the distorted, mirror image of the other. Of course we cannot completely discount the possibility that this was an effort to present another visual perspective or a different physical position taken by an animal from the natural world, such as when an animal dies and falls inside the herd. However, based on a number of ethnographic sources, we know the concept of an inverted world of the dead where all actions and all occurrences were mirrored and turned upside-down in relation to the world of the living. It is wholly likely that a notion of this kind existed far back in time. By extension, there may have been a belief that both people and animals walked above ground against the mirrored underworld, heel to heel. This notion undoubtedly played a role in the choice of stone surfaces on which images were to be depicted. As we have mentioned elsewhere, the rock surfaces may have been regarded as membranes between this world and the world beyond, a contact that could only be enabled by choosing certain surfaces (Lewis-Williams and Dawson 1990). In all likelihood, rock art represents the vestiges of religious acts and communication between this world and the next. Considered in this way, it may seem strange that the figures were superimposed over one another. The larger elk is so distinct and prominent on the stone that it is out of the question that it could not be seen when the other figures were made. It is probable that the privilege of creating rock art was delegated to an elite few, for example specialists in rituals, and that rock art was created only on special occasions or when circumstances demanded it. At times it may have been regarded as necessary to communicate with these other worlds in order to find out what was required of the society in the world of the living. This contact may have been delegated to the certain chosen few, perhaps shamans, through visions, which as we know have been practically institutionalised in many societies. Only through visions, which in turn can be seen as the result of negotiations with the other world, was it possible to determine what offerings or changes in society were expected, in order to maintain the norms of the existing society. In order to make contact, it may well have been necessary for the "chosen one" to alter their state of consciousness. This could have been achieved through various means – dancing, drumming, intense fasting, ingesting hallucinogenic substances or other means. The change in consciousness may have been regarded as the soul being released from the body and sent on a spiritual journey to destinations beyond our world. We know that this has been an important function and means used by shamans and *Noaides* in historical times, and it was certainly used by people of corresponding status in prehistoric times. On returning to normal consciousness, it may have been believed that the soul returned to the body, bringing a message from the world beyond, and the images could then be recorded in stone.

For the actual production of the rock art, it was perhaps the stone itself and its qualities, combined with the state of consciousness the artist was in, that jointly created the proper circumstances and expressions. During this process it would have been totally irrelevant whether they created new images over the older ones. At the same time, however, it seems that older images inspired the newer ones, as if the creators had found a stone or an area where contact with the otherworld was already possible, a channel that was already open to the beyond or to a divine world for the people who had come to the area at an earlier time. This also helps to explain one of the most curious circumstances at Bogge, namely that they chose to depict images in stone over such disparate prehistoric periods. The creators of the rock art in the Bronze Age or in the Early Iron Age may have perceived the older images as a surface in contact with the spiritual world, or interpreted the older animal images several thousands of years later in a religious and mythological context which, in the contemporary period, made it necessary to create boat images. We are a long way from being able to draw any final conclusions, although it is tempting to think that the tradition of using rock as a source for comprehension and contact with other dimensions has survived for hundreds and thousands of years, and that this explains why we find figures from earlier and more recent periods of prehistory in the same place. Nevertheless, this contradicts the enigma in Trøndelag, where so many panels from the Northern Tradition of rock art have been re-carved with art from the Southern Tradition.

This said, there may well be another explanation that we are no longer capable of understanding, and which may be associated with natural circumstances at Bogge in particular. We are only able to speculate whether this particular area, with its tall mountains and deep fjords, probably isolated in relation to the rest of society, may have created the basis for seeking the necessary visions.

Other archaeological material in the area

As well as the panels and figures that are mentioned here, other solitary images have been found. Some distance to the west of the upper panel, a figure was discovered in the 1930s at the same height as the upper panel, and in the same style as most of the images on this panel. Why this figure remained isolated is, of course, unclear. However, it is possible to conclude that other rock art exists or once existed on many of the other panels as well as those known to exist today. It may be overgrown, covered with earth or simply obliterated by weathering. Cultivation of agricultural areas has been intense in recent centuries, with fields tilled all the way up to the stones bearing rock art images. In turn, this has also led to the discovery of a large amount of archaeological material dating from the Mesolithic to the Bronze Age, and which therefore coincides with the datings of the rock art. These basically represent stray finds, but which nonetheless are indicative of the activity that has occurred at Bogge. The amount of materials appears to be unique in comparison to that found at other places in Eresfjorden, Langfjorden and other fjords in the area. If cultivation has not totally destroyed all remains in the sub-soil, it will be important in the future to complete archaeological investigations focused of the sub-soil in order to obtain even clearer answers regarding what the archaeological material and rock art images may have represented.

It is quite unlikely that Bogge was permanently settled when the two oldest panels were created. It is more probable that the Stone Age people who created the two oldest panels belonged to groups who migrated on a seasonal basis, but who had permanent ties with specific geographical areas. When the younger boat images were made, the people may have settled more permanently within the fjord basins. A burial mound close to the fjord, probably dating from the Bronze Age, may indicate, in contrast to earlier periods, that settlement was more permanent during this period. The world-view held by fishermen-hunters during the Stone Age and the farmers during the Bronze Age and Iron Age may have allowed them to seek answers to existential questions precisely in this location, in a place where they had direct access to the otherworld.

Mjeltehaugen at Giske – A Glimpse of an Enigmatic Grave Monument

The sailing route along the coastline of Sunnmøre is broken by long fjords with sounds and islands of various sizes in the open ocean off the shore. Most of the islands are rocky with strips of flat land along the shoreline like the green brim of a hat encircling the central mountain peaks, but on the tiny island of Giske northwest of Ålesund, the flat shoreline extends across the entire island. The island only has rock formations to the north, and has been described as "a ring of gravel and stone around a central moor" (Fett 1950). In the Middle Ages the island was the seat of the powerful Giske lineage, who owned properties all over large parts of Norway during the 1500s (Kvamme 1994). We assume that the manor farm belonging to this land-owning gentry was located on the southern side of the island. Here there is a small marble church built by a member of the family during the second half of the 1100s (Kloster 1957). Excavations close to the church have revealed foundation walls of what was probably the headquarters of the Giske family, dated to the end of the 1100s (Larsen and Reimers 1994). On this tiny island in the Sunnmøre shipping channel, archaeological remains were found dating from even earlier times that are just as noteworthy as those from the Middle Ages. About one kilometre east of the church, on the Giskegjerdet Farm, is a large burial mound known as Mjeltehaugen. It is 30 metres in diameter and about two metres tall, but it appears much taller because it is built on a natural sand bank. The towering mound is distinctly visible on the flat countryside at Giske.

"... of the greatest interest for antiquarians"

In the early summer 1847, landowner Christopher Hagerup decided to excavate the Mjeltehaugen mound. The large mound had attracted treasure hunters before, as traces of digging were found in several spots. There is no record of anything being found during these earlier excavations, but the landowner's dig uncovered relics that are unparalleled in Norwegian prehistory (Christie 1847; Lorange 1879). At the time there were no preservation regulations applying to archaeological remains or prehistoric relics, and property owners were free to remove items and to sell them at will. It is an open question as to what would have happened to the finds made at Mjeltehaugen if Hagerup had not been visited during July of the same year by a member of the administration of Bergens Museum, Wilhelm Frimann Koren Christie. It was Christie who had taken the initiative in 1825 to found Bergens Museum, and he worked tirelessly

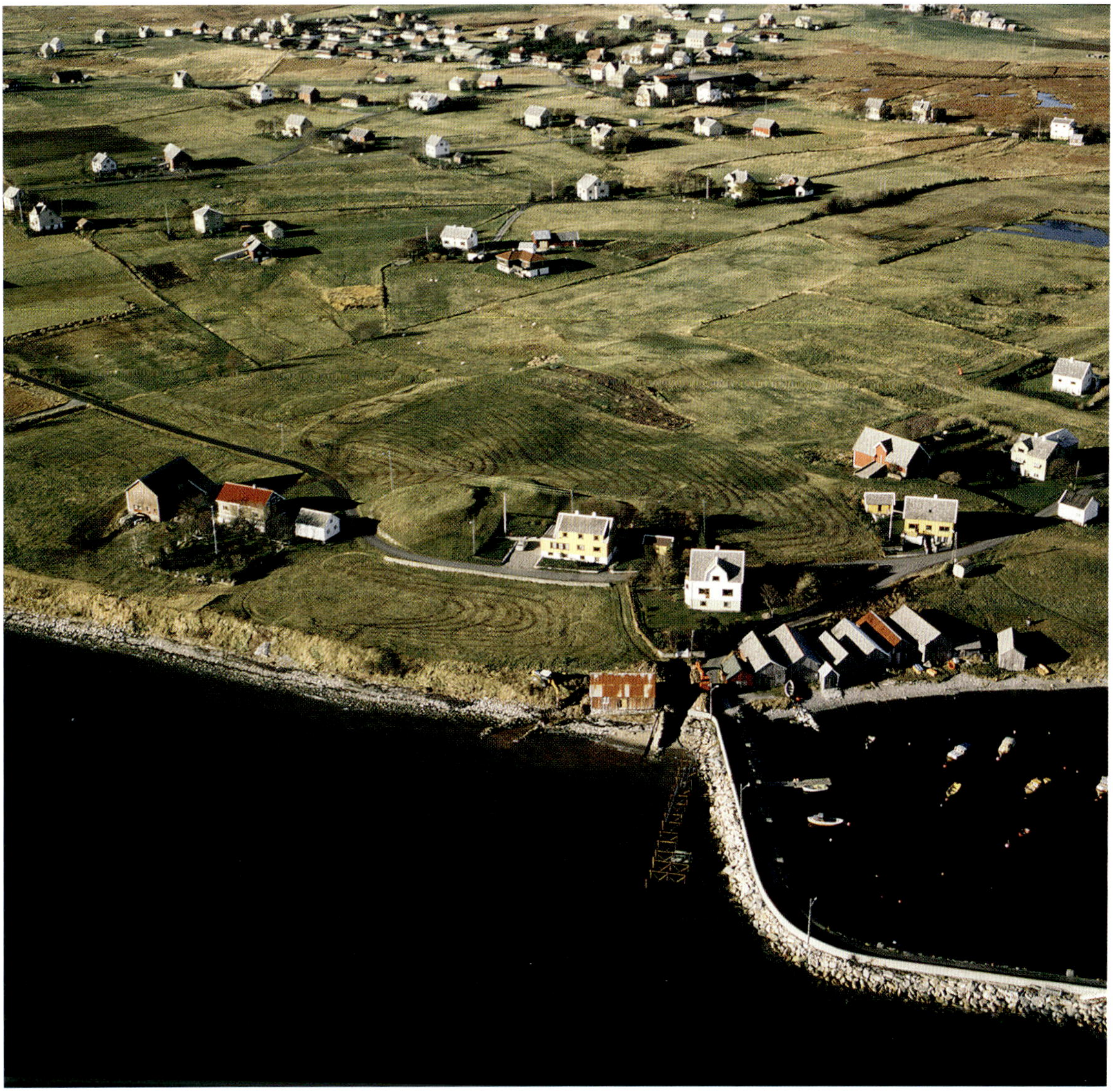

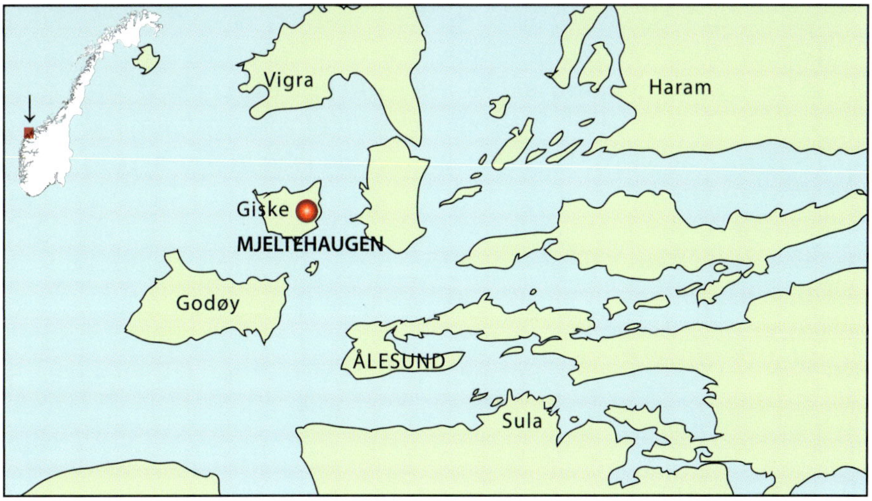

FIGURES 108–109. Aerial photo showing the southern side of the island of Giske. Mjeltehaugen is located close to the centre of the photo, alongside the road that runs between a large yellow house and a smaller white house. The mound is easily visible on the flat terrain of the island, and it is easy to see why it has attracted so much attention over the years.

MAP AI, ILLUSTRATION SS/BM

for many years collecting archaeological pieces and other exotic objects for the museum (Haaland 1996). He made yearly journeys in the rural areas north and south of Bergen, and fortunately for Mjeltehaugen's posterity, one of his journeys took him to Giske in 1847.

Proprietor Hagerup told Christie of the excavations in the burial mound and showed him the objects that had been found, or more precisely, the remnants of what had been found. Christie realised immediately that these were "... of the greatest Interest for Antiquarians" (Christie 1847). In the report he wrote to the museum administration later the same year, the frustration he felt standing at the edge of the excavation site is palpable:

> "It is unknown whether, during the earlier Excavation, anything was found, but during the most recent one Relics were uncovered that would have been of great Interest, if only an Expert had been present, had recorded, sketched and examined them, as well as seen to it that they were Preserved as much as possible." (*ibid.).*

If Christie had not intervened, the archaeological remains found at Mjeltehaugen would have existed in posterity only as a short written report to Bergens Museum. As chance would have it, he was present in person at the site and recorded first-hand information from the persons who did the excavation, and he saw to it that the finds were preserved in the public interest.

Excavation and salvage operation

The workers had dug a two-metre-deep trench running from the top of Mjeltehaugen, removing soil and a metre-thick layer of rubble before they reached fine-grained sand. In the layer of sand they found eight stone coffins standing side by side, arranged east to west. The long sides of the coffins were made of wide, thin slabs of slate, while the ends were made of thicker stones, and the ends facing east were a little wider than those facing west. The coffins were covered with large slabs that were difficult to pry loose from the walls. Most of the coffins broke into pieces when they were pulled out of the gravesite, but some remained intact and measured 1.20 × 0.60 metres. It was recorded that on the underside of the lids there were "engraved Embellishments, consisting of Circles, Tracery, horizontal and longitudinal Lines and Leafwork", while the wall slabs were undecorated. The coffins were filled with sand, and there were charred human bones placed directly on the sand bottom. However, no other objects were found.

Fragments from the slate slabs were placed at the edge of the excavation site; others were taken to Hagerup's house. Here the proprietor's children were permitted to play with them, with the result that they were broken into even smaller pieces. In order to save as much as possible, Christie gathered as many fragments as he could find – "particularly those upon which engraved Figures could be seen" – and he saw to it that they were sent to the museum in Bergen. On Christie's initiative, Bergens Museum purchased Mjeltehaugen in August of the same year (Christie and Hagerup 1847). The purchase entailed that the

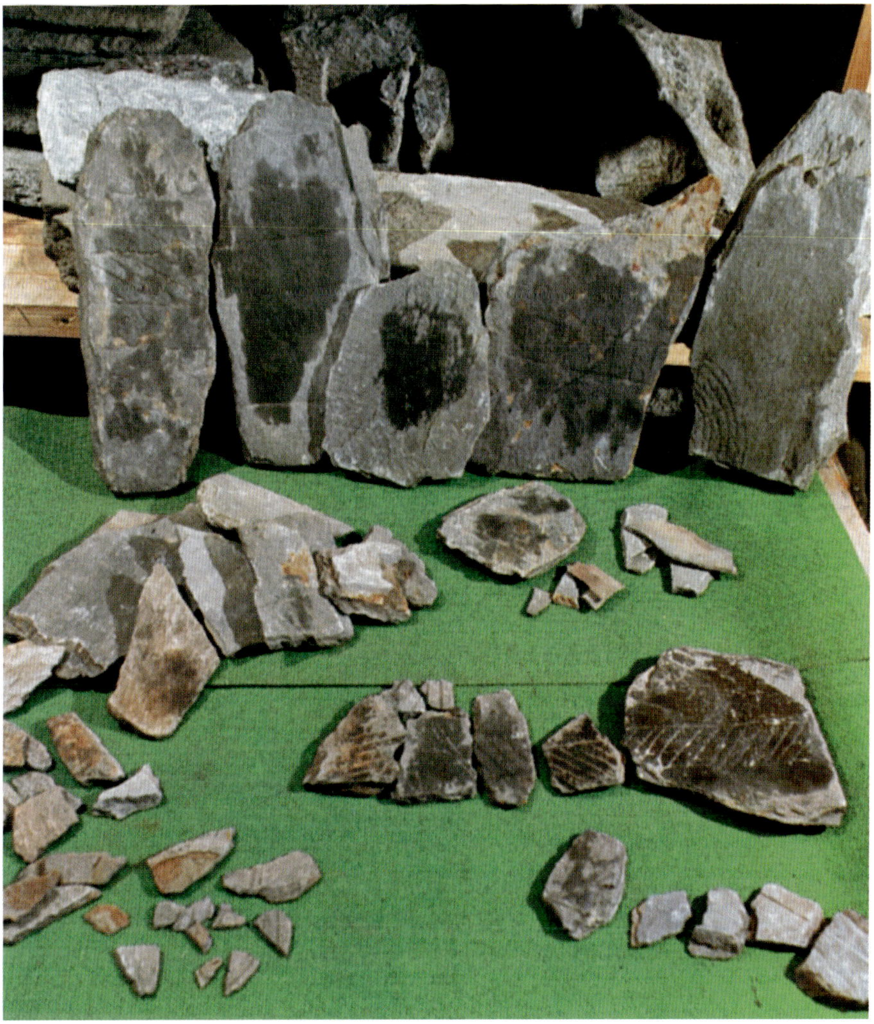

FIGURE 110. The stone slabs used to make the coffins broke into many large and small fragments when they were removed from the graves. The species of stone from which the slabs were cut is schistous and very fragile, and the large, heavy coffin lids, only a little more than three centimetres thick, were difficult to pry loose from the coffin walls. A total of about 300 fragments with rock carvings were preserved, but many are so small that it is not possible to piece the puzzle back together.

BJ. SKARBØVIK, SP

museum secured the rights to excavate the mound and to keep whatever finds were made. The rationale given was that the mound was regarded as "containing highly valuable and unusual material, among which truly antiquarian Treasures lie concealed" (Christie 1847). During the mid-1800s, this was the only recourse that antiquarian authorities had when they wished to protect a unique cultural monument such as Mjeltehaugen.

The treasures of Mjeltehaugen

In particular, it was the "engraved Figures" on the slabs from Mjeltehaugen that intrigued Christie. When reading his report, it is as if we hear his own voice when he reflects over the unusual linear patterns and speculates whether some of the figures perhaps represent boats. He also noticed that the fragments

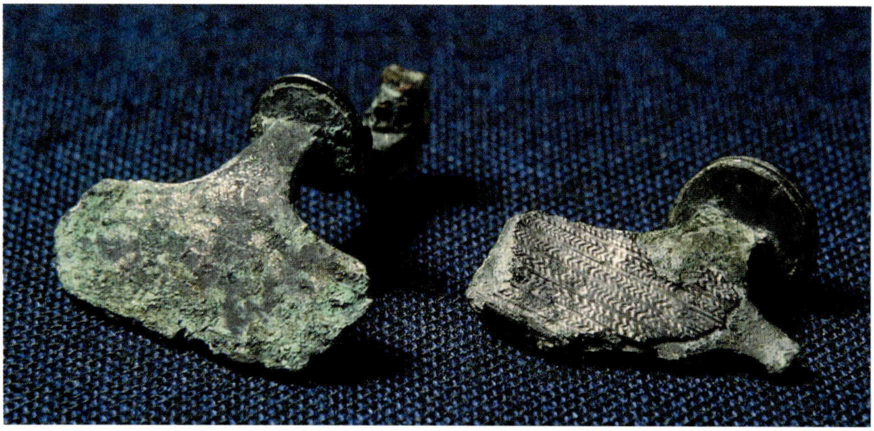

FIGURE 111. Two bronze fibulae were discovered in Mjeltehaugen at intervals of six years – the one in 1872 in gravel removed from an earlier excavation, the other in 1878 during Lorange's investigations. The brooches are so similar to one another that they are believed to be a pair from a woman's grave during the Roman era (about 200 AD). Both fibulae were silver-plated, and they probably belonged to a woman of high social rank.
AMO/BM

of several of the smaller pieces appear to fit together, and he looks forward to "when Time allows, having the Opportunity to gather all of the acquired Pieces and place them in front of you on a suitably large Surface so that from the different acquired Smaller pieces one can piece together larger ones and thereby obtain a clearer and more complete Notion of the Figures' Diversity, Character and possible Meaning" (*ibid.*).

Christie himself never found the time to put the puzzle together – it was not until the beginning of the 1900s that the task was accomplished (de Lange 1921). Before that time, Bergens Museum had completed several excavations of the mound. The survey that would come to be most significant for Mjeltehaugen's renown in posterity, in terms of both dating and interpretation, was conducted in 1878 by the newly appointed curator of Bergens Museum, Anders Lorange. He was the first permanently employed curator at the museum, and had long experience with excavation of grave mounds (Hagen 1997)

It was Lorange who established how Mjeltehaugen was constructed, discovering among other things that it was built on a sand bank (Lorange 1879). At the bottom of the mound he found dark, burnt sand, and he concluded that this was a remnant from an open fire that had been made here before the grave containing the decorated slabs was constructed. Over it was piled a heap of stones and on top of a layer of sand the mound was created. He found burnt bones and a large number of slab fragments, and together with those that had come from earlier excavations, including some with rock art on both sides, the number of smaller and larger fragments totalled about 300 – many of these with traces of rock art.

During Lorange's excavations no artefacts originating from the gravesite with the decorated slabs were uncovered. However, on top of the stone layer he found a bronze fibula in situ, similar to a fibula which emerged accidentally in 1872 in gravel from the mound. Consquently Lorange maintained that Mjeltehaugen had comprised two burial-faces, the older one represented by the decorated slabs and the younger by the two fibulae. He regarded the brooches as a pair belonging to a female burial from about 200 AD, placed near the top of the mound. He presumed that the burnt bones found by him and earlier excavators belonged to this secondary grave. He found the primary burial more difficult to interpret – not only in assigning a date to it, but equally in terms of its very construction.

Unusual rock art in an unusual context

The majority of the rock art motifs on the slabs from Mjeltehaugen are different than those that occur on bare rock-faces and boulders found in outdoor settings. The dominant motif on the slabs is linear ornamentation covering the surface and arranged in parallel strips: double and triple zigzagging lines and wavy lines, fishbone patterns and rows of quadrates in a chessboard pattern (de Lange 1912; Mandt 1983; Linge 2007). Nevertheless, Lorange thought that the motifs from Mjeltehaugen belonged in the "Age of Rock Art", a period that corresponded in his time to the Bronze Age. The fact that there were also more usual rock art motifs on the slabs perhaps supported this dating: four complete and several partial boat figures, as well as parts of a concentric ring figure.

During the second half of the 1800s, only one other gravesite in Scandinavia with the same monumental character as Mjeltehaugen was known to exist. It is a large grave mound in Kivik, Skåne called Bredarör (Randsborg 1993; Goldhahn 2004). It was discovered in 1748 and during Lorange's time dated to the Early Bronze Age. The mound contained a coffin that was a little more than three metres long and constructed of stone slabs – four on each of the long sides and all of them engraved with rock art. Bredarör and Mjeltehaugen are unique, each in its own way in their respective geographic areas, but they do have a number of common features that were given weight in Lorange's interpretation of Mjeltehaugen (Lorange 1879). Both are monumental sites, and both have contained coffins constructed of slabs decorated with rock art. It is true that only some of the motifs in the Kivik grave are of the same character as those of Mjeltehaugen, for example zigzagging lines, but it was the design of the coffin in the Swedish grave mound that particularly interested Lorange.

Lorange had difficulty accepting that the oldest burial site in Mjeltehaugen

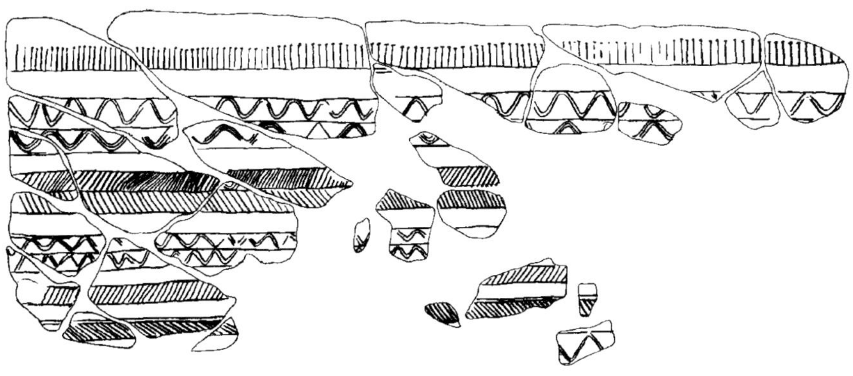

FIGURE 112. At the beginning of the 1900s, several of the slab fragments from Mjeltehaugen were pieced together. The reconstruction was based on what was believed to have been the original length of the decorated slabs, about 1.2 metres. AMO/BM

had contained eight coffins with carvings only on the lid slabs and undecorated side slabs. If this were true, he argued, then many more fragments without rock art should have been found. He therefore drew the conclusion that the information from the unskilled diggers had been a misunderstanding and that they actually had found "one Coffin constructed of 8 Slate slabs" (*ibid.*). Lorange was of the opinion that the grave had contained only one large coffin. He accepted the information that the slabs originally had been 1.20 × 0.60 metres, and that thick, undecorated stones had been used for the short sides. On the basis of this, he reasoned that the coffin had been 2.50 metres long with two rectangular slabs on either long side and four laid crosswise as a lid. He also concluded that both the side slabs and the lids had been decorated with rock carvings. Lorange's proposed reconstruction of the primary grave in Mjeltehaugen is not unlike the decorated coffin in the Kivik grave. He thought that this supported dating the Giske burial mound to the Bronze Age.

A controversial memorial

During the 150 years that have passed since the secrets of Mjeltehaugen were uncovered, the site has been frequently debated in professional circles. There has, however, been little debate over Lorange's reconstruction of the primary burial in Mjeltehaugen. Most scholars in recent years appear to have accepted that there was only one, and not eight coffins in the mound. The arguments for supporting Lorange's interpretation of Mjeltehaugen are based on his keen observation ability and vast digging experience (Bøe 1942; Marstrander 1963). Lorange's reconstruction, therefore, has also been consequential for the dating of the site, since one large coffin covered with a monumental stone pile or earthen mound is still considered to be typical of burial practices in the early Bronze Age, probably around 1500–1300 BC.

The rock art on the Mjeltehaugen slabs has been more difficult to place in terms of date and rock art tradition. The linear patterns of the type that is found in Mjeltehaugen is practically unknown in outdoor rock art traditions. A number of grave slabs engraved with rock art have been found in Rogaland and Trøndelag with motifs that resemble those of Mjeltehaugen: parallel bands, fishbone patterns, and double wavy lines (Fett and Fett 1941; Mandt 1983). Some of the slabs have been dated to the Bronze Age, but datings are more uncertain for some of the others.

In an attempt to place Mjeltehaugen within a larger regional context, comparable material from Central Europe has been introduced. In this geographic area there is a burial custom from the Late Stone Age where large coffins built of split slabs and lid slabs laid crosswise are decorated with linear patterns. In particular, attention has been drawn to a small group of grave cists with decorations of a striking resemblance to the linear ornaments of Mjeltehaugen (Marstrander 1963, 1978). The ornamentations sometimes cover the surfaces and are sometimes arranged in parallel bands such as in

Mjeltehaugen, and they consist of zigzagging lines, diagonal lines in a fishbone pattern and shaded triangles. The problem with associating these grave cists with Mjeltehaugen is, on the one hand, that they are several centuries older than the finds at Giske, and on the other that there is no substantiated archaeological material from Sunnmøre that might suggest any contact with Central Europe during the same era (Mandt 1983; Hagen 1983).

In addition, boat images of the type found on the Mjeltehaugen slabs are not known to exist in the material from Central Europe. On the other hand, boat figures like this frequently occur on a number of rock art panels along the entire western coast of Norway, from Rogaland in the south to Trøndelag in the north, and are seldom found in the eastern parts of Scandinavia, thus indicating that this boat type is a western phenomenon (Mandt 1983, 1991). It has been suggested that this also applies to the types of linear patterns found at the Mjeltehaugen slabs, and that these motifs represent a local tradition associated with the coastal areas (Fett and Fett 1979). Some scholars are of the opinion that the boat images of the "Mjeltehaugen type" are based on boat depictions from the Northern rock art tradition, and that, like the burial custom itself, this may support dating of the primary grave in Mjeltehaugen to an early period of the Bronze Age (Marstrander 1963).

An arduous and time-consuming task

The construction of a mound with the dimensions of Mjeltehaugen – 30 metres in diameter and at least two metres in height – must have required enormous effort, both in collecting stones along the shoreline and piling them onto the gravesite. The amount of time this took would have depended on the number of workers involved (Mandt 1983; Linge 2007).

Finding and shaping the slabs for the coffin – or coffins? – must also have been costly in terms of planning, work and time. Geologists have been able to establish that the species of rock that the Mjeltehaugen slabs are made of is not found at Sunnmøre (Askvik 1983). The closest deposits of this kind of rock species are in Trøndelag to the north and the outer part of Sunnfjord to the south. It is interesting in this respect that the boat images of the Mjeltehaugen type occur on rock art panels in both of these districts, and in Trøndelag there are also grave slabs decorated with a linear pattern similar to that of Mjeltehaugen (Mandt 1983, 1991; Linge 2007).

It has not been established from which of these two areas the Mjeltehaugen slabs came. Whatever the case may be, the journey was a long one – about 100 nautical miles from Giske to outer Sunfjord, and about 150 miles to Trondheim. Seafarers also had to cross dangerous stretches of open sea along the way – Stadthavet (The Stadt Ocean) in the south and Hustadvika (The Hustad Bay) to the north. We do not know what kinds of boats seafarers from Western Norway used during the Bronze Age, but they were undoubtedly rowing boats, since the engravings of boats from this period lack sails. They must at any rate have

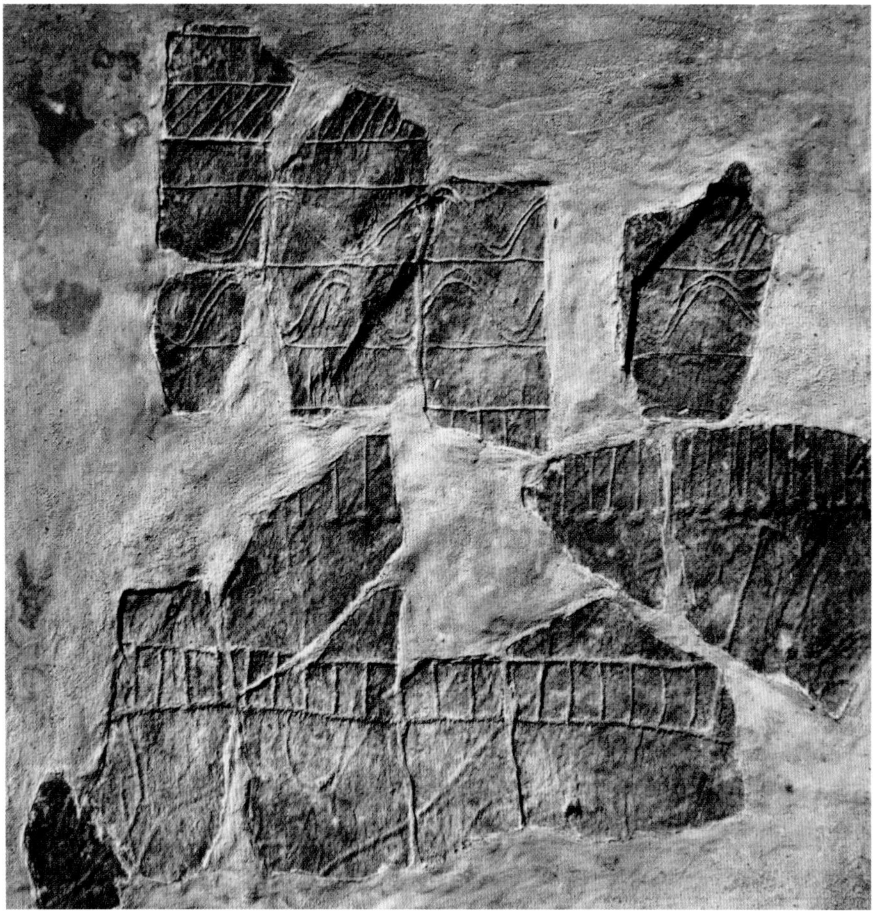

FIGURE 113. The boat images on the grave slabs from Mjeltehaugen are simply shaped, with the lines of the stem practically perpendicular to the longitudinal lines marking the gunwale and keel. Where the stem section is preserved, the keel line extends slightly beyond the hull, and at the top the stem is curved. The hull is shaded with vertical, parallel lines. The geometric patterns extend across the boats – on these fragments only a few of the fringe-like motifs can be seen. AMO/BM

been seaworthy and robust craft, because the cargoes they were to carry were not light. Calculating only based on the eight slabs that had ornamentation, according to Lorange's reconstruction, the weight may have been about 500 kilograms, and added to this would have been the weight of the undecorated slabs. The sea voyage back and forth to Trøndelag may have taken at least three to five days, somewhat less time to Sunnfjord – depending on wind and currents and the number of crew (Linge 2007). Once ashore, the slabs had to be shaped by hand, and the Giske workers would perhaps have to negotiate agreements with the local owners. From the time the slabs began their journey south or north until the mound was completed months may have gone by – depending on the number of workers who participated in the building of the mound. If weather conditions were stormy – and the construction was delayed – it may have meant that work had to wait until the winter storms had passed (Mandt 1983).

The Giske burial mound in a local perspective

The great effort that had to be mobilised in order to build the monumental grave mound at Giske reflects the fact that society was well organised, and that there was no scarcity of essential commodities. If not, it would have been impossible to keep a group of workers occupied with the building of a monument, while the daily supply of food essentials was delegated to other members of the society. The islanders at Sunnmøre during the Bronze Age had access to a rich supply of natural resources. With easily tillable and fertile soil combined with fishing on the sea, they developed a combined subsistence that not only provided for their daily needs but also brought wealth that could be exchanged for goods and services associated with prestige and social status (Mandt 1991). Equally as important as natural resources was the shipping channel for the people who settled on the Sunnmøre islands and the outer fjord regions during the last millennium before the Christian era began. The shipping channel was a link with the outside world. It opened for contact and relations far and wide, and it was the route through which impulses from both north and south reached the island society along the northwestern coast. The interplay between rich natural resources and lines of communication with the outside world was at the core of this surplus society of the Bronze Age that is reflected in Giske.

The network of contacts that can be traced through the finds at Mjeltehaugen – reflected initially in the similarities between some of the rock carvings on the grave slabs and open-air rock carvings along the coast – also bears witness to interaction and cooperation over great distances. Whether the Mjeltehaugen slabs came from the slate fields in Sunnfjord or in Trøndelag, the long distances reveal that people who lived along the coast had contact with one another and that they had well developed knowledge of local geography. It is difficult to imagine that the Giske dwellers set out haphazardly in quest of a heavy cargo of slate slabs; either they had planned to extract them themselves, or trade with those who had rights in the quarry.

Mound building for whom – and for how many?

For whom was the burial mound at Giske raised – and in whose memory? Since the people of Giske invested so much planning, so many resources and work hours in the construction of the monumental grave mound, it is logical that a person of stature was laid to rest there – someone with status and power whose memory was to be preserved beyond death (Mandt 1983). Another explanation for the special circumstances surrounding the building of the mound may be that the gravesite concealed not one, but several prominent persons who were buried there (Linge 2007). In 1878, when Lorange doubted the observations of the unskilled diggers, he based his scepticism on what he perceived as a misunderstanding about the number of slab fragments that were decorated as opposed to those that were plain. It is almost as if he had completely forgotten

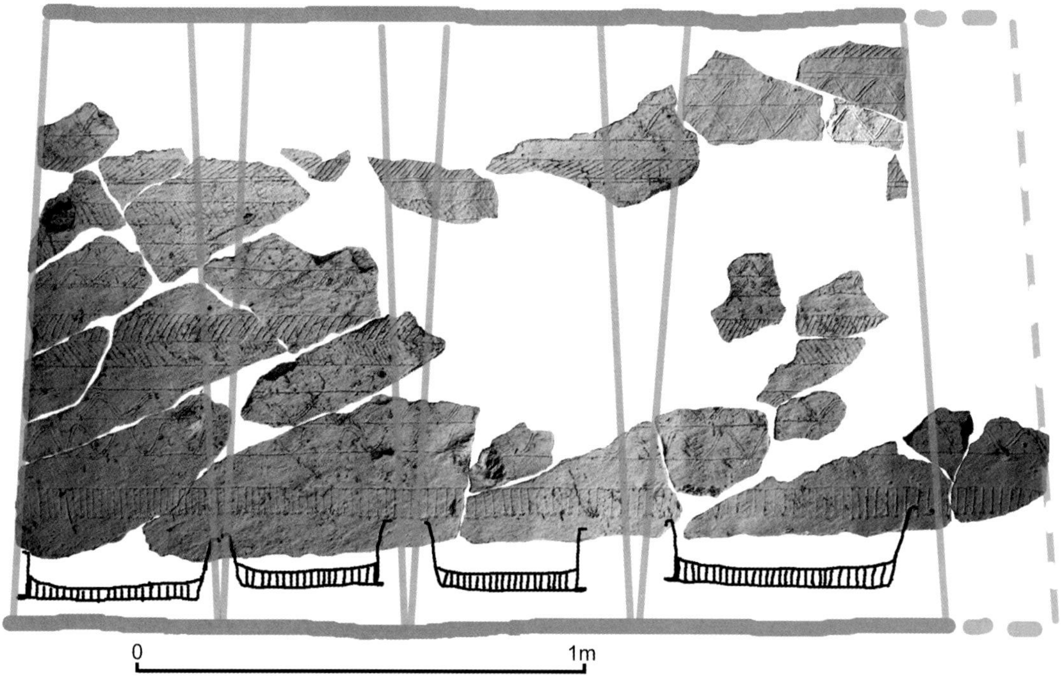
0
1m

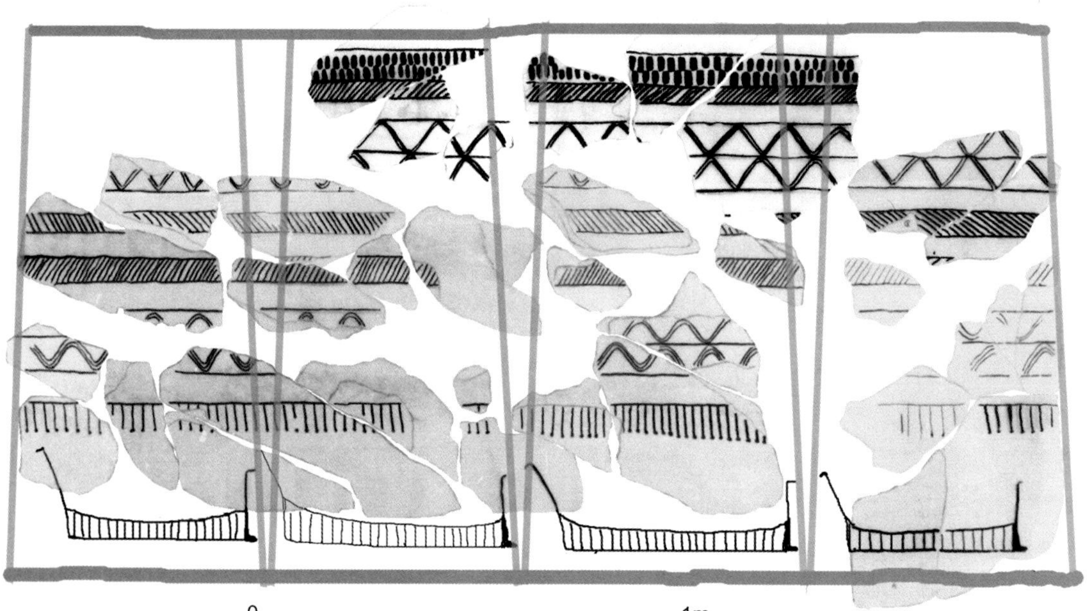
0
1m

FIGURE 114. An alternative arrangement of the Mjeltehaugen slabs supports the probability that there actually were eight coffins in the primary grave. The interpretation is based on a jigsaw puzzle of tracings and casts made of the numerous slab fragments, in dialogue with the written sources from Christie and Lorange, and it entails that the majority of the carvings were placed on the down-turned sides of two large coffin lids that each covered four coffins placed side by side. (After Linge 2007).

what Christie had pointed out 30 years earlier, namely that the fragments of slate he had collected were "particularly those upon which engraved Figures could be seen" (Christie 1847). It seems that the time is now ripe for taking Christie's observations seriously and for accepting the facts that his informants provided.

Recently an alternative arrangement of the slab fragments from Mjeltehaugen has been put forward, that supports the probability that there actually were eight coffins in the primary grave (Linge 2007). The interpretation entails that the majority of the carvings were placed on the down-turned side of two large coffin lids that each covered four coffins placed side by side. In addition, one of the lids had carvings on portions of the side that was turned facing up.

If this interpretation is correct, Mjeltehaugen is indeed a unique burial mound, and it raises more questions than it answers. What was the reason behind eight persons being buried at the same time – had they been the victims of a tragic accident, had they been killed in battle (Fyllingen 2002), or had they died of a contagious disease? Were those who were buried together members of a family? Was perhaps only one coffin made for the person of highest status, while the other coffins contained people who were sacrificed in honour of the dead chieftain (Linge 2007)?

Human sacrifices are not an unknown phenomenon in Bronze Age gravesites, among other places in Denmark (Kyvik 2002). In the archaeological material and written sources of later periods there are also examples of prominent persons being followed to the grave by people who were either voluntarily or involuntarily sacrificed (Brøndsted 1961). The custom probably has its origins in the notion that demise and death are closely related to creation and life. Life-giving forces are released through the destruction that a sacrificed victim represents, and a human sacrifice is the strongest symbol for the recreation of life (Kyvik 2002).

The long preparation

Regardless of who or how many people were buried in Mjeltehaugen, the question still remains: Why did it take so long from the time the mound was begun until it was completed? There may be practical causes for this. From our recent past we know, for example, that it was not uncommon in rural areas for the funeral to take place several months after the death. A person who died in the middle of winter often had to be laid out temporarily, for example in a barn loft, until the spring thaw, so that a grave could be dug. It is also plausible that the planning and construction of the grave monument was supervised by the very person whose final resting place it was to be.

Another explanation might be that the burial was completed in two phases, the first being a temporary burial, while the second and final funeral was carried out at a later point in time (Linge 2007). This kind of "double" burial practice, which is known to exist in other parts of the world, is associated with the view that death is part of a process. The death itself – meaning the end of biological life – is the start of a phase during which the deceased is in a chaotic transition state between life and death – no longer of this world, but not yet admitted in the realm of the dead. This liminal neither-nor situation is also critical for those left behind; it creates disorder in daily existence. It becomes necessary, therefore, for survivors to see to it that the deceased is initiated to his or her new status in death, and at the same time they are able to re-establish order and continuity in their own world (Turner 1967). The deceased is first separated from the living, perhaps by incineration or exposure in the open air so that the body will rot. After an interim period that might last several years, the final burial ceremony is performed – the deceased is transferred to a grave and is thereby separated for all time from the society of the living and transferred to the world of the dead. The deceased is now also socially dead, and social order is re-established (Bloch and Parry 1982).

If we entertain the notion that such a double burial might have been the custom of the Bronze Age society at Giske, it is easier to understand why the preparations for the grave mound took such a long time. It would have occurred in the interval between the temporary and the final burials. In conjunction with this, one might consider the burnt sand that Lorange found at the bottom of the mound, which he thought was left after a large open fire. Could this not be a remnant from the first, temporary burial of the body – or bodies? (Linge 2007)?

The extent of the crisis that results after the death of person is dependent on the position the deceased held in society. If the person had great political

FIGURE 115. Mjeltehaugen as it looked in 1922 when Johs.Bøe photographed the site. The mound must have appeared even more massive in prehistoric times, situated at the top of a natural sand bank several metres high, in the centre of the flat terrain at Giske.
JB

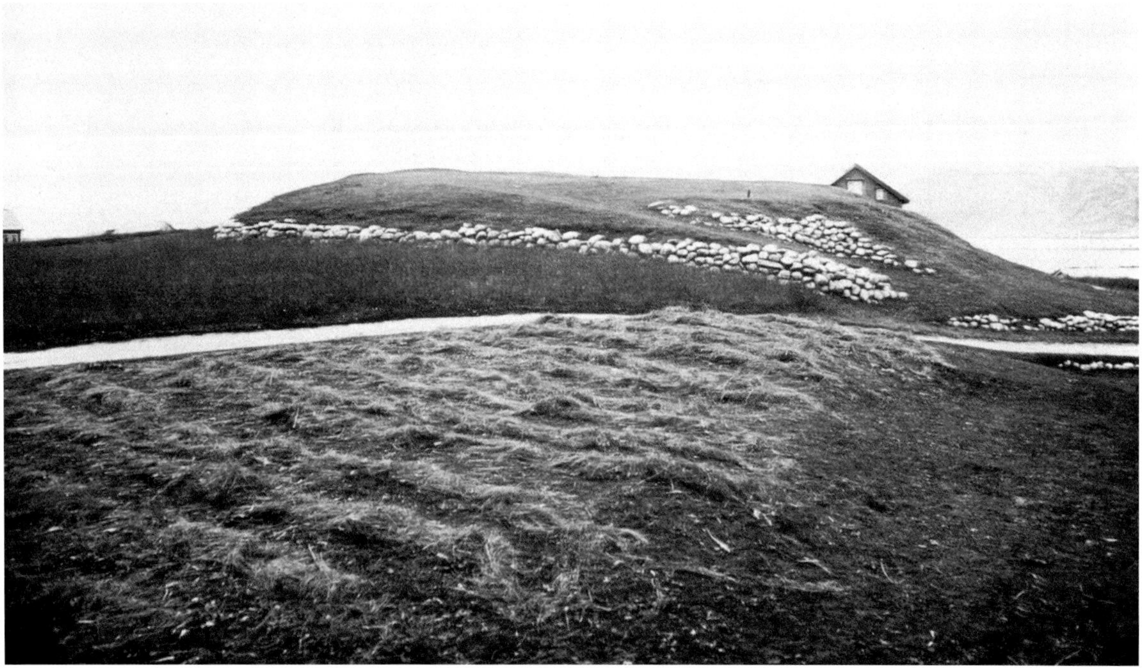

or religious power, the death affects all of society, and it is reasonable to assume that funeral rituals were of proportional scope, as the size and design of Mjeltehaugen amply express. It is also possible that the monumental mounds of the Bronze Age must be understood as something more than merely gravesites (Larsen 1996). They are normally situated in prominent places in the terrain, easily visible and with a wide panorama – exactly as Mjeltehaugen is placed atop a sand bank on a flat stretch of land at Giske. The mounds may have served as gathering places; they were perhaps holy retreats where contact with forefathers could be maintained. This may explain the monumental aspects of the burial mounds, but how are we to explain the engravings inside the monument, and for whom were they created?

Engraved art for the living or engraved art for the dead?

Lorange and the diggers from 1847 were in agreement that the engravings on the slabs at Mjeltehaugen were turned downwards in the burial chamber, perhaps with the exception of the few fragments that have markings on both sides. The theory that this applies to engravings in gravesites in general is supported by an analysis done in Rogaland, the area of Norway that has the largest number of gravesite engravings (Syvertsen 2002, 2003). Here it has been emphasized that the peculiar aspect associated with engravings buried at gravesites, in contrast to rock art in the outdoors, is that the former are entirely inaccessible to the living. They are permanently sealed in the graves, hidden beneath large amounts of soil and stone, invisible from the outside of the grave monument. They are not turned towards the next of kin or participants in the rituals, but rather towards the deceased in the grave. Most probably, the grave inscriptions were exposed above ground only for a limited time – the time it took to make them and place them inside the grave. Afterwards they remained – or at least they were meant to remain – concealed from the living for all time. Perhaps the engravings destined to be sealed in the grave were seen by only a few people – perhaps only by the creators of the figures, or by those who performed the burial rituals. The period of time during which the engravings were visible to the living might correspond to the transitional phase of the deceased, between the temporary and the final burial ceremony. In this neither-nor state, the engravings may have been associated with notions of taboos and danger, but also with magical forces (Linge 2007; Syvertsen 2003). The fact that the engravings were turned downwards in the burial chamber, and were later covered by the mound, may have been thought to preserve forces and at the same time protect the living (Syvertsen 2003).

An eternal memorial

The towering mound on the flat island landscape in the centre of the Sunnmøre shipping channel must have been regarded with great respect and perhaps awe in its time – whether or not it was a monument to one or more prominent persons or a sacred memorial and gathering place for many people – or perhaps both. We will never know whether the islanders knew of the engravings that were concealed inside the mound. We can only speculate as to whether rumours circulated about them for many decades – maybe even generations – after the mound was built. As far as we know, there are no traditions associated with the mound in the Christian era. Christie referred to the mound as "Mintehougen" – a name he found difficult to explain, but he guessed that it may have been a distortion of "Minnishaugr" – "a Mound erected to the Memory [Minde] of the Deceased". In retrospect we might suspect that this explanation was tinged by the discoveries he had just rescued for the museum in Bergen!

Vingen in Bremanger "Nature's own colossal museum for rock art!"

One of the landmarks along the outer coast of Nordfjord is the Hornelen massif on the far eastern side of the Bremangerlandet island. The mountain towers over the shipping channel between Florø and Måløy. Its dark, imposing shape rises 860 metres directly up out of the sea (Tveit 1983). Many tales and superstitions are associated with this monument of a mountain. According to local beliefs it was the realm of a band of trolls, and on Midsummer's Eve the witches were said to gather here to feast with the Grim Reaper. In the Sagas of the Kings, Snorre Sturlasson relates the tale of Olaf Tryggvason, who accomplished the manly feat of climbing the cliff-like eastern wall. It was this exploit that superior court barrister Kristian Bing, from Bergen, wanted to replicate when he travelled to Nordfjord around Easter in 1910 (Bing 1912). Little did he know that another formidable challenge awaited him in the neighbourhood of Hornelen.

"... a large number of heretofore unknown rock engravings"

It all began when Bing's local guide happened to mention that the summer before, as he was fishing, he had seen "some drawings of animals on a stone" at Vingen – an isolated smallholding a few kilometres southeast of Hornelen (*ibid.*). The barrister was not only an avid mountain climber; he was also interested in archaeology, and he considered these "drawings" to be worthy of closer examination.

And so, on the eve of Easter, he went to Vingen and was given lodging at the farm of Thue G. Vingen. His suspicions were confirmed – here there were actually previously unknown rock carvings! Thue showed him some twenty images of deer that people on the farm had discovered already in the late 1800s, but without attaching any significance to them and without making their existence known to others. Bing, who knew just what to look for, found many more images already during his very first visit to Vingen, despite the heavy snow cover on the ground that Easter. During the next few years the Vingen family found increasingly more images, so that by about 1912 some 100 animal figures and "a large number of other curious figures" were known to exist in Vingen and at neighbouring Vingelven, further west along the fjord. They were spread over an area of a couple of kilometres. Bing assumed that much more rock art would be found in this area, and he enthusiastically characterised Vingen as "a veritable museum, a colossal natural museum of rock art!" (*ibid.*).

Bing's prediction came true. From the time when the first deer images

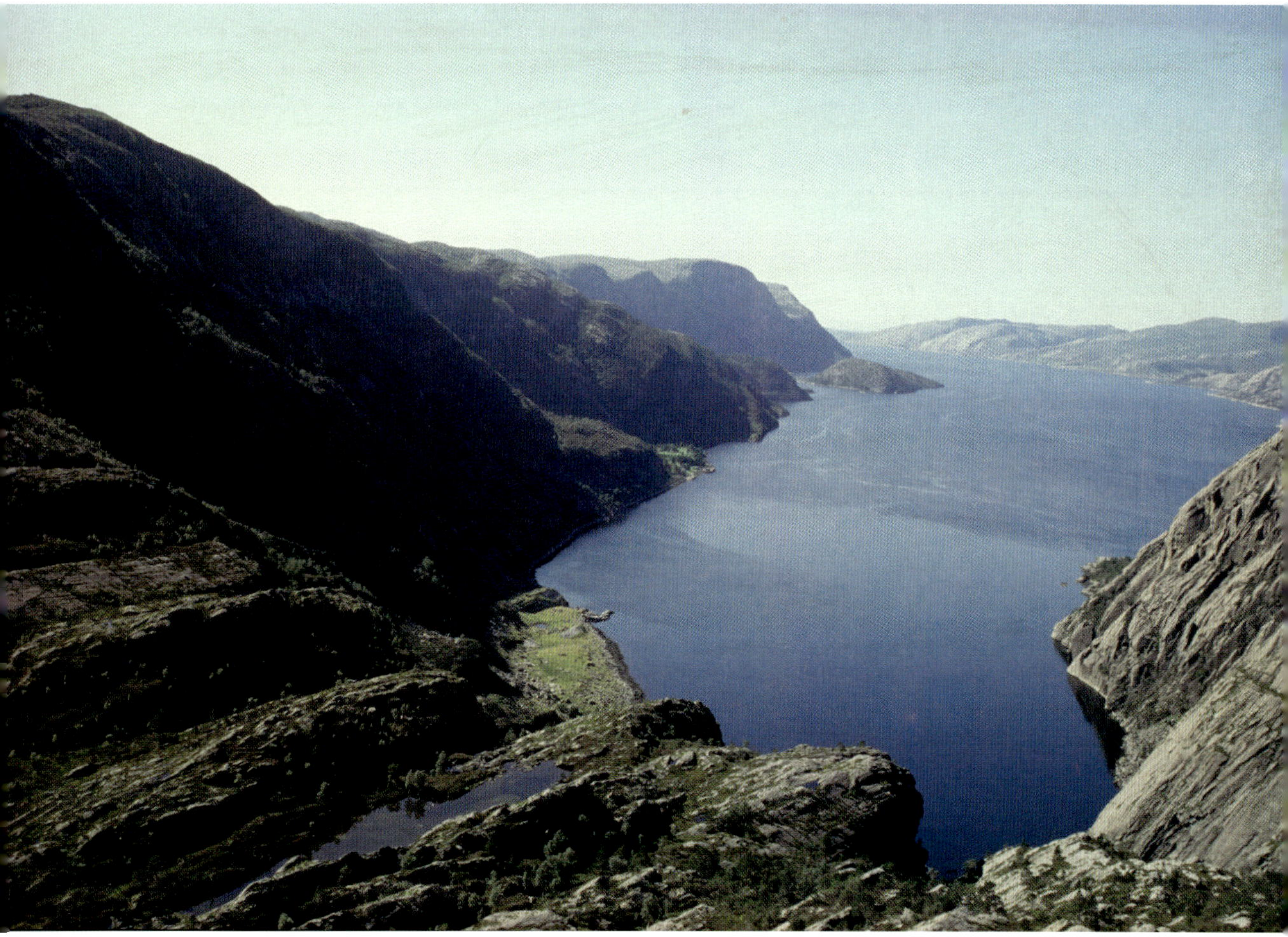

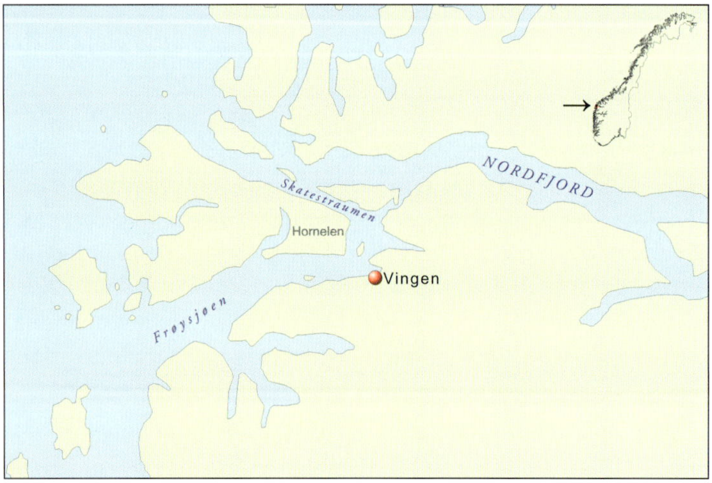

FIGURES 116–117.
At the far end of Frøysjøen, the tiny fjord arm Vingepollen cuts in between sheer mountainsides. To the left in the photograph is the narrow strip of land where Vingen and the majority of the rock carvings are found. The green spot seen farther out along the fjord is the Vingelven farm.

MAP AI, ILLUSTRATION TL

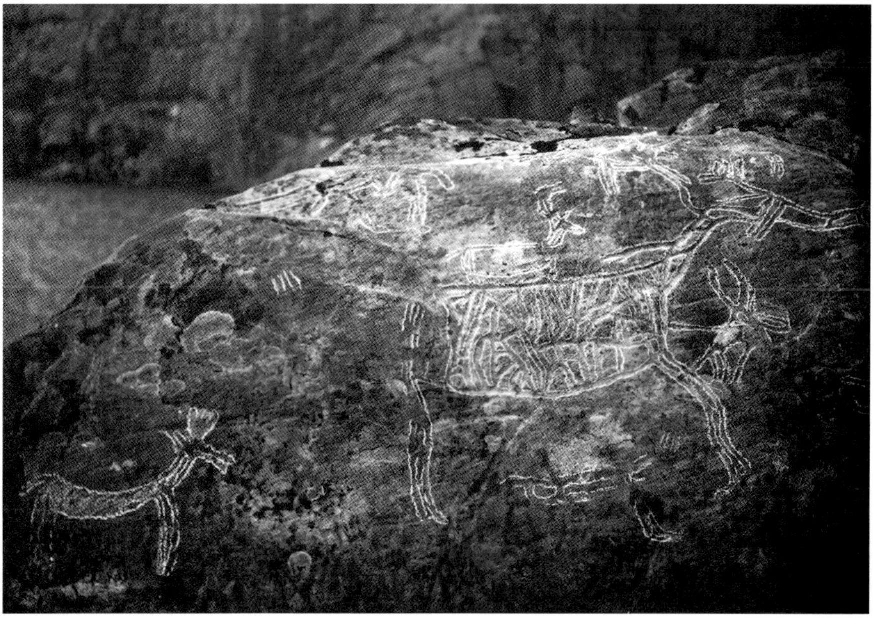

FIGURE 118. One of the first rock carvings Kristian Bing saw when he came to Vingen in 1910 were these animal figures pecked onto a sheer rock wall facing south on a long stone ridge called Hardbakken. The name is said to originate from the hard work required to cut the grass that grew on the northern side of the ridge at the time. Neither Bing nor the Swedish archaeologist Gustaf Hallström, who photographed many of the rock carvings at Vingen in 1913, were aware that more than 100 carved figures lay concealed beneath the turf on the section of the ridge facing north.
GH

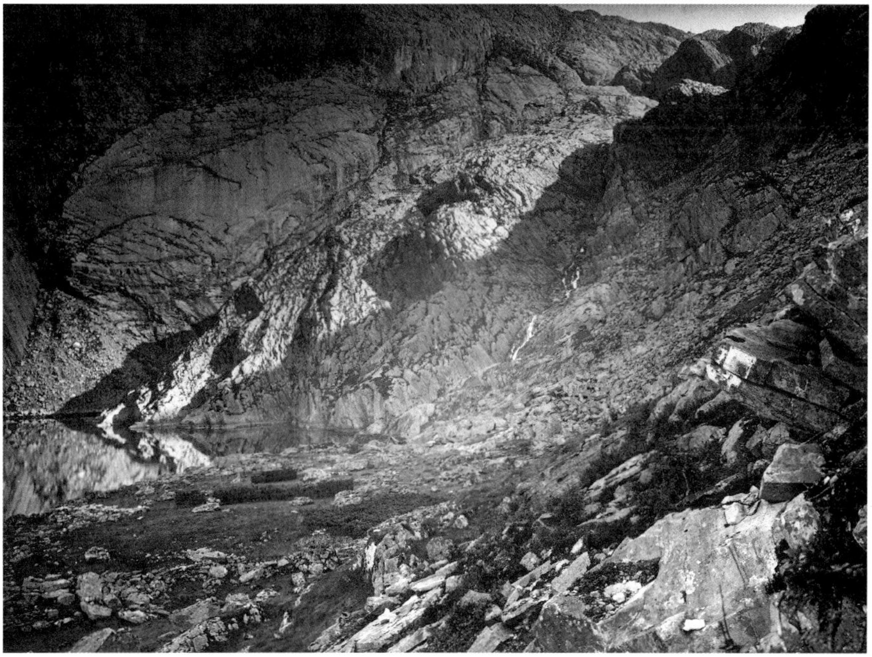

FIGURE 119. At the beginning of the 1900s a combination of fishing and small-scale farming provided a livelihood at Vingen – as illustrated by the hay-drying racks that Hallström captured in this photo. Just visible in the background are the Vingen farm buildings, sheltered at the far end of Vingepollen.
GH

became known in 1910 and up to the turn of the new millennium, more than 2100 rock art images distributed over some 300 panels of various sizes were recorded, in an area, excluding the Vingen farm itself, that comprises the neighbouring smallholding at Vingelven and the cotter's property at Fura, in addition to Hennøya some kilometres further west along the fjord (Lødøen and Mandt *in prep.*). As the largest rock art locality that is so far registered in

Southern Norway, Vingen has truly become the "colossal museum" that Bing foresaw.

A western Norwegian cultural landscape

What kind of place is Vingen? Bing described it as "... a barren and untamed place". Archaeologist Jan Petersen offered a more poetic description after his first encounter with Vingen, when Bergens Museum assigned him the task, in 1913, of recording the newly found rock art images (the author's translation):

> "And so we head into this most desolate of desolate places. It is Vingen. All around a small, narrow bay, hundred-metre-tall, bare, grey mountains rise almost directly up out of the sea. Waterfalls upon waterfalls form white cascades down the mountainsides, and at the southern side of the bay on a narrow terrace lie the Vingen farms, their buildings standing in these overwhelming surroundings like small dollhouses. – It is here that the rock art is located" (Brøgger 1925).

Vingen is situated within the Frøysjø basin in Bremanger municipality, at the tiny Vingepollen fjord arm, and with an open panorama of the Hornelen massif and the busy traffic along the main shipping channel. Vingepollen is about one kilometre long and some two hundred metres wide, surrounded by steep, 800- to 900-metre-tall mountains that belong to the great Devonian Hornelen field. At the far end of the fjord in the east, the Vingen waterfall rushes down through a steep mountainside ravine from the Vingen Lake 400 metres further up. On the northern side of the fjord, Tussurfjellet juts up out of the sea – a dark and sheer wall that ends in the lower Vingeneset area to the west. On the southern side of the fjord basin, a narrow strip of land stretches from the inner basin westwards to the expansive and steep rock-face called Vehammaren located at the mouth of the fjord. Further west towards Vingelven the terrain is steep, rocky and difficult to access.

From the mid-1600s herring fisheries provided a profitable living for the permanent residents in Vingen (Vanberg 1988). Subsistence was based on making full use of scant resources through a combination of fishing and limited agriculture – the combination that has been the subsistence pattern for coastal dwellers since time immemorial. Patches of arable land in Vingen were so limited that the fishermen-farmers had to put layers of soil on top of large boulders in order to expand the area that could be tilled. One reminder of these "Vingen fields" is found in the name of one of the stones containing rock art: "the turnip stone". Here turnips were grown many thousands of years after the rock art was created. When the herring fisheries failed during the 1870s, the result was crisis and poverty for the people of Vingen. The smallholders were in debt to local merchants, and many were forced to abandon their homes (*ibid.*). After the last permanent resident moved away from Vingen in 1936, the neighbouring smallholding at Vingelven used the Vingen area for hay and pasture for sheep and goats. The shallow, low-nutrient soil, with elements of peat and coastal heather, was suitable for age-old cultivating practices involving clearing, sowing and active harvesting. The grounds around the houses, the cultivated terraces, the stone fences, piles of cleared stone and old drainage ditches bear silent witness to the type of Western coastal culture that dominated during the past 250 years (*ibid.*).

Rock art on every rock and stone

The barren and dramatic coastal landscape is the backdrop for the abundant rock art heritage in Bing's "colossal museum". The landscape is characterised by long, parallel rock ridges running in an east-west direction, broken by smaller knolls and outcrops, tiny patches of grassy land and moors. Large numbers of boulders and stones of various sizes lie along the foot of the mountain and on the flat areas; these are fallen rock and erratic blocks left from the last Ice Age, including an expansive scree area with enormous boulders at the inside end of the bay.

Rock art images are found on practically all of the stones and rock faces that have an exposed surface: on the wide sloping sides of the ridges, on outcrops and flat rock surfaces, on earthbound boulders and on rocks small enough for a person to lift. One of the first people who completed a thorough and detailed documentation of the rock art at Vingen in the 1920s, Johs. Bøe, was convinced that there were probably rock art images on every single stone surface in Vingen! (Bøe 1932).

Most of the panels with rock art are located on the narrow stretch of land on the southern side of Vingepollen, although at the inner end of the bay and at Vingeneset the ground is covered with an abundance of panels of various sizes. The number of images on the individual panels varies greatly, from 200 on the long ridges to one or two on the smaller stones. In many places the images are found on the underside of large rocks in cavities and passages beneath large, erratic blocks. On the boulders in the scree there is rock art on the exposed, flat sections, and in the passages between the stones. In all likelihood there are many images that remain undiscovered, partly because the lines of the images are faint and shallow and therefore difficult to make out, and partly because many boulders and stones are covered with a thick layer of lichens or turf. Over the years weathering has also obliterated many of the images.

The predominant rock in Vingen is sandstone. The images were created using the pecking technique, whereby each mark made by the point of the pecking tool created a tiny depression in the stone. The pecked grooves are generally narrow and shallow – and in some cases entire areas, for example the bodies of animal images, are entirely filled with pecking marks. A few years ago, a pecking tool made of diabase, a much harder rock than sandstone, was found during a survey of the sub-soil. The tool was pointed at one end, and the size of the tip matches the width of the pecking marks that make up the rock art images (Lødøen 2003; 2007). It is likely that this is one of the tools used when the rock art was created. Analyses of the tool have established that it came from a quarry located much further south, in the vicinity of Florø – the Stakaldeneset quarry. We know that this quarry was used as a raw material source for to make axes and similar tools over a lengthy period of time during the Middle and Late Mesolithic (Olsen and Alsaker 1984).

Myriad of motifs

The dominant motif in Vingen is deer – the majority depicting red deer, while some may represent elk and, in some cases, reindeer. The deer motif comprises at least 40 percent of all of the images (Viste 2003). The animals occur in many sizes and varying shapes, all of them depicted in profile. Some of them have antlers; others do not, and many have an intricate linear pattern in their bodies. A number of the four-legged animals appear to depict wolves or dogs. A few sea mammals, such as whales or porpoises, are depicted, as well as an occasional bird and possibly a few snakes. Human figures are also present in various shapes, and comprise about three percent of all of the images (*ibid.*). All of the humans are seen frontally; some have male or female genitalia, but the majority of the images cannot be distinguished in terms of gender. Like the deer images, several of the human figures have patterns in their bodies, and some are depicted as skeletons. Different abstract and geometric designs also occur – notably zigzagging lines, oval shapes and lattice patterns. Hook shaped

FIGURE 120. From the summit of Tussurfjellet on the northern side of Vingepollen there is a good panorama of the numerous rocky ridges and boulders with rock carvings found on the rim of land.
TL

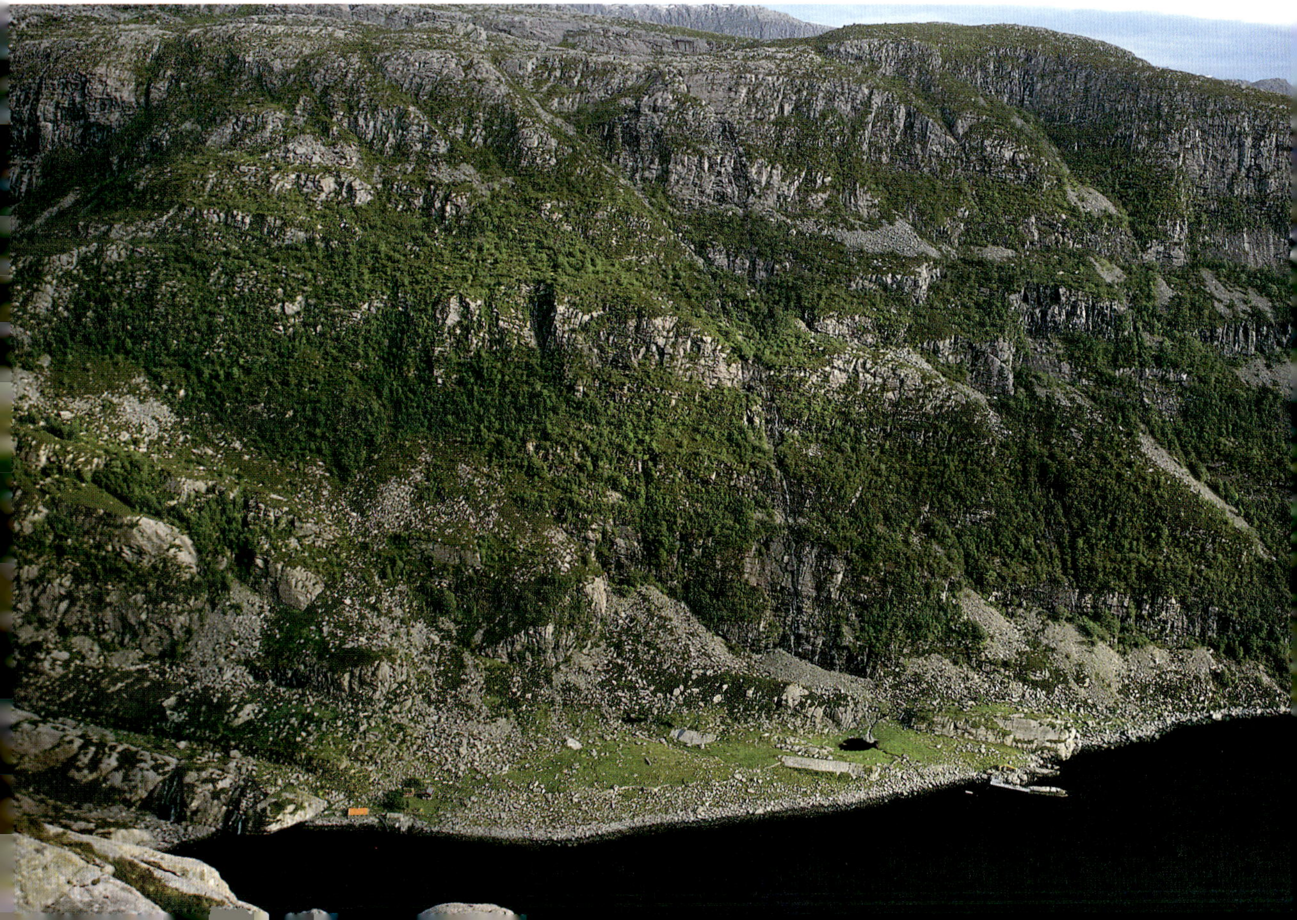

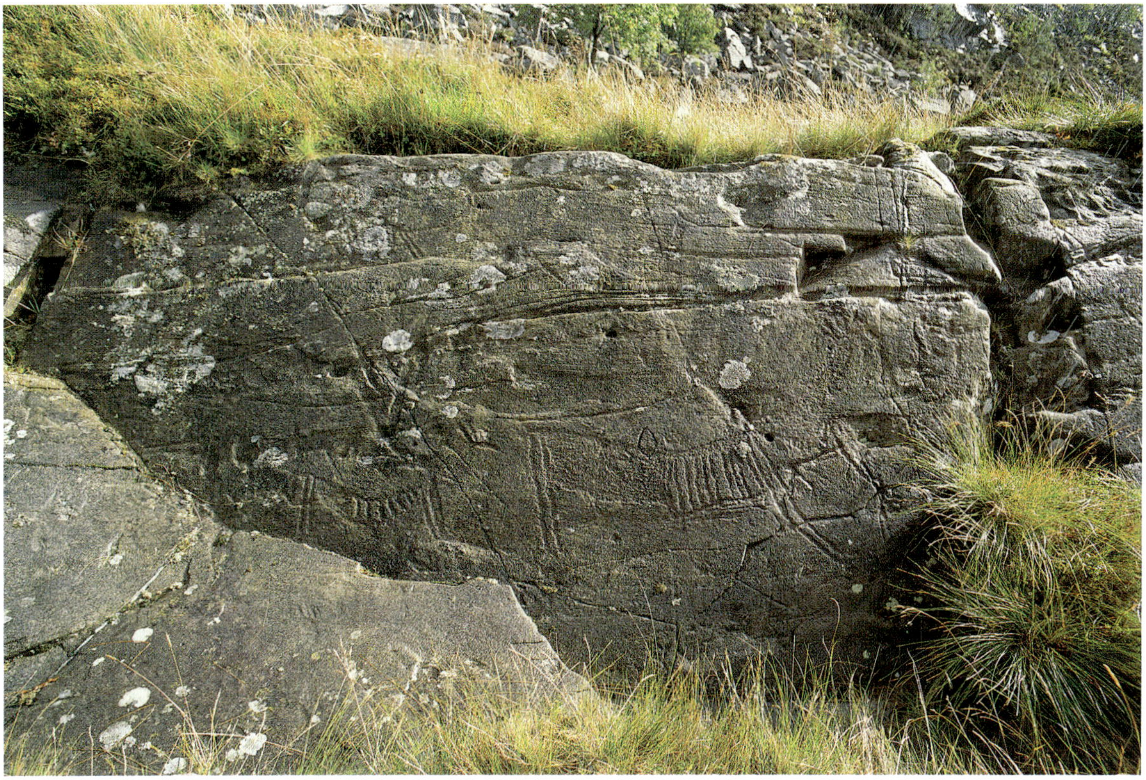

FIGURE 121. This group of figures located high on the most westerly mountain ridge at Vingen – Vehammaren – was discovered in 1913. The tiny oval pecked in above the contour line of the largest animal's back does not appear in the photograph that Gustaf Hallström took at that time. It is included, however, in a photo that Johs. Bøe took at the end of the 1920s. It is probably a mark of ownership that someone carved sometime during the interval of a decade – an example of modern man's penchant for making his mark on the rocks and stones around him.
RU

figures in various forms and sizes are frequently depicted, comprising more than 20 percent of the total number of figures (*ibid.*).

Images of deer are found throughout the entire rock art area, on both wide rock-faces and boulders, on outcrops and on smaller rocks, as single motifs and also in combination with other motifs. On a couple of the largest stone surfaces, deer are practically omnipresent, for example on the steep ridge facing north at Vehammaren, located at the western end of the locality, where there are about 200 deer images on one surface alone. At the far eastern side, at the inner end of Vingepollen, there is also a locality – Elva – with only deer images: on the sheer northern side of the ravine where the Vingefossen (waterfall) descends, there are 70–80 images of deer. On the other side of the ravine – facing the rock with the deer images – is a steep stone wall that is virtually covered with some 140 hook-shaped figures and a few deer. On the flatter brim of land between these two extremities, there is more variation in motifs. Here are deer, humans, hook-shaped images and geometric patterns in various combinations (Hallström 1938).

Intentional compositions?

Since the most abundant motif in Vingen is the deer image, we can assume that these animals represented a very important aspect in the lives of the people who created the rock art. Red deer were of course an important resource for the coastal population throughout the Mesolithic. Moreover, it is highly likely that it was also a central symbol in their world-view. The large variation in shapes suggests that it was not only important to illustrate the species of animal, but that there was a conscious desire to depict different behavioural aspects of the animal. Many of the animals appear to be in motion; some of them have their heads turned back, as if they are alert to an impending danger. Some have their heads lowered, as if they are grazing. A group of red deer with their heads turned in the same direction may depict a herd in migration, or maybe in flight from a pursuing hunter. Studies of the behaviour of animals living today – knowledge of how animals react in given situations – could perhaps help us to understand what these depictions were meant to represent (Lødøen 2009).

The fact that deer images occur together with other motifs supports the idea that they had a symbolic meaning beyond their mere use as wild game. In several cases animals and humans are placed in relation to one another in such a way that they appear to be part of a scene or story. For example, a group of large and smaller deer are arranged in a tight ring around a long, narrow human figure. The human has no head – instead, its neck extends into several wavy lines – and its arms and legs are depicted by means of zigzagging lines, giving the impression that the figure is dancing (see Figures 126-127).

In other places human figures seem to be sitting astride deer, and there are examples of images that appear to be half man and half animal. It is tempting to imagine that these depictions – where people and animals seem to be interacting in a kind of cooperation or symbiosis – imply a deeper significance than merely to illustrate the hunter's wish to kill his prey (Mandt 1998).

Hook-shaped images also occur in scenes comprising both animals and humans. On an elongated stone surface, for example, a large group of hook-shaped images are placed between – and almost framed by – deer images at either end of the surface. In other places the hook-shaped images appear to be growing out of the body of an animal. In some instances the human figures are depicted

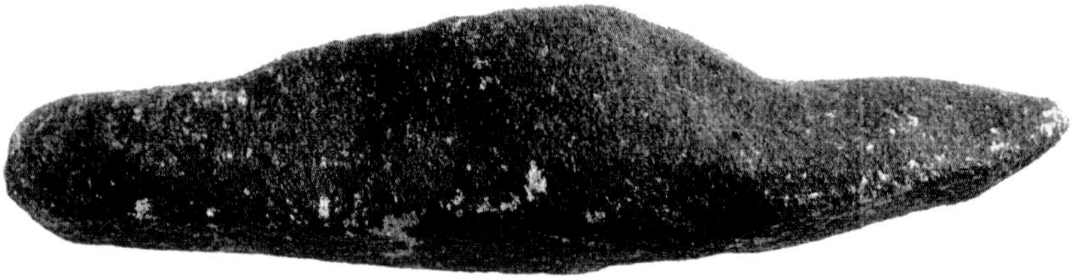

FIGURE 122.
Investigations of the subsoil unearthed an object probably used as a tool for pecking the rock images. The tool is pointed at one end, measures more than 10 cm in length, and the size of the tip tallies with the pecking marks forming the rock art images.
TL

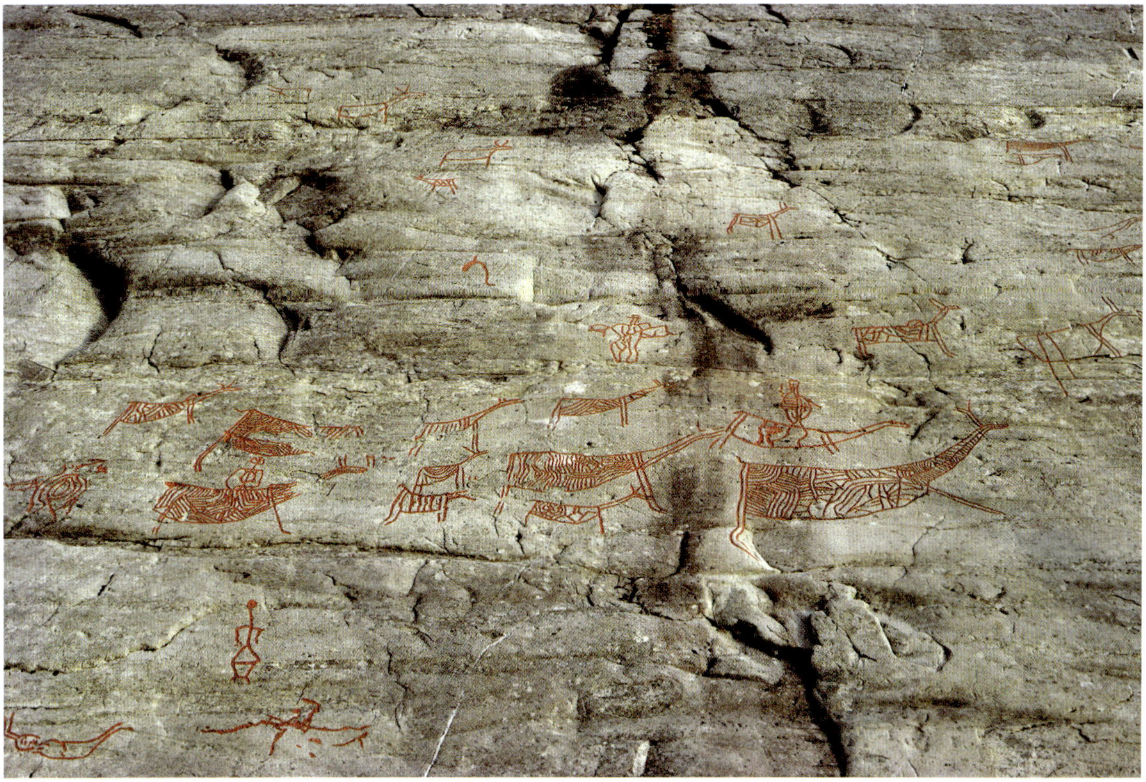

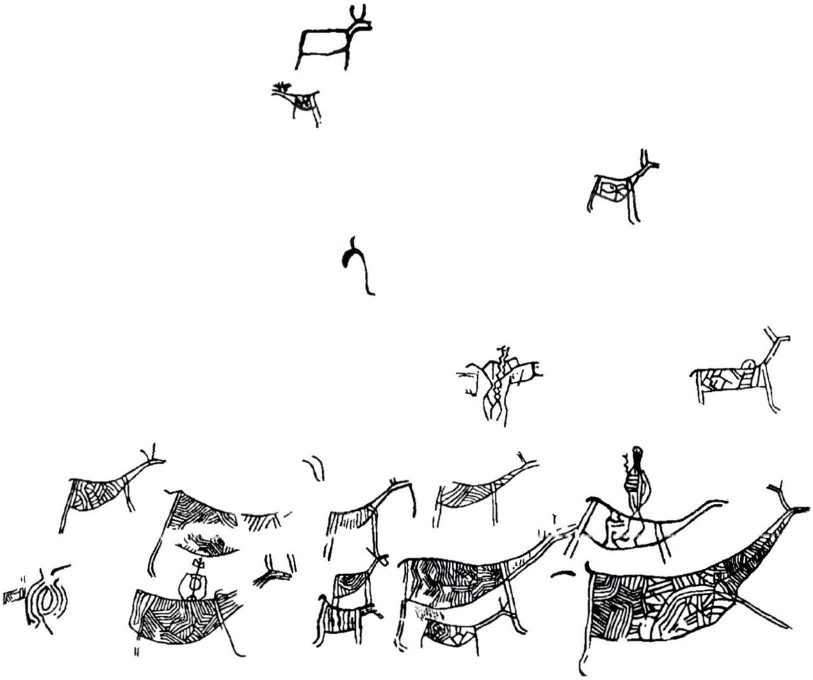

FIGURES 123–124.
Animals of the deer family are the predominant motif found in the rock art at Vingen. On this section of rock, called Brattebakken, is a concentration of deer images that appear to depict an entire herd. There are also a few human figures here, including two examples of a human apparently sitting on a deer's back. To the far left in the photo is a linear pattern interpreted by some scholars as depicting a vulva. Lying just below the rock panel is an expansive plain that may have been a suitable gathering place for large numbers of people.

PHOTO GM, TRACING EB

beside hook-shaped images that appear to be as tall as them. While hook-shaped images occur together with both animals and humans, they are just as frequently depicted alone – sometimes as individual lines on small stones, sometimes in great numbers, such as the panel near the waterfall ravine on the southern side of the Vingen waterfall. Perhaps they represent some kind of item – many are shaped like a shaft with a blade; several also have one or two ears (Carpelan 1975; Gurina 1956; Zagorskis 1973). In several places in Northern Europe, particularly in Russia, objects made of horn, bone or wood that may be used for comparison are found. These are simple representations of animal heads, where the prolongation of the neck resembles a shaft. They occur in contexts dating to the Mesolithic, from the same period as the activity in Vingen. The reason why such artefacts are not found in our geographic area is that they are made of organic material which only rarely has survived the ravages of time. The animal heads have been found, among other places, in the graves of people who undoubtedly had religious status (*ibid.*). Typically, these artefacts are very simply designed. It is nonetheless possible to identify them either as elk, deer or reindeer. Another typical trait is that the ears of the animals are clearly emphasized, a fact that provides an important parallel to the many hook-shaped images in Vingen. Therefore, it is tempting to interpret these images as animal heads of this kind, for use in rituals. At the same time, the hook-shaped images – which occur in so many different contexts – may also be understood as an ambiguous symbol that has no connection whatsoever to the physical world.

Before we can interpret the meaning of the many, varied rock art images, we

FIGURE 125. On the southern side of the gorge where the Vingefossen (waterfall) descends at the far eastern end of Vingepollen, there is an area called Nedste Lægda. On a wide rock-face extending down towards the river, there is a concentration of some 140 curved figures. In 1913 Hallström photographed three of these figures just after the turf was removed from the rock. Against the smooth, weathered rock surface we can clearly see every single peck mark in the images.
GH

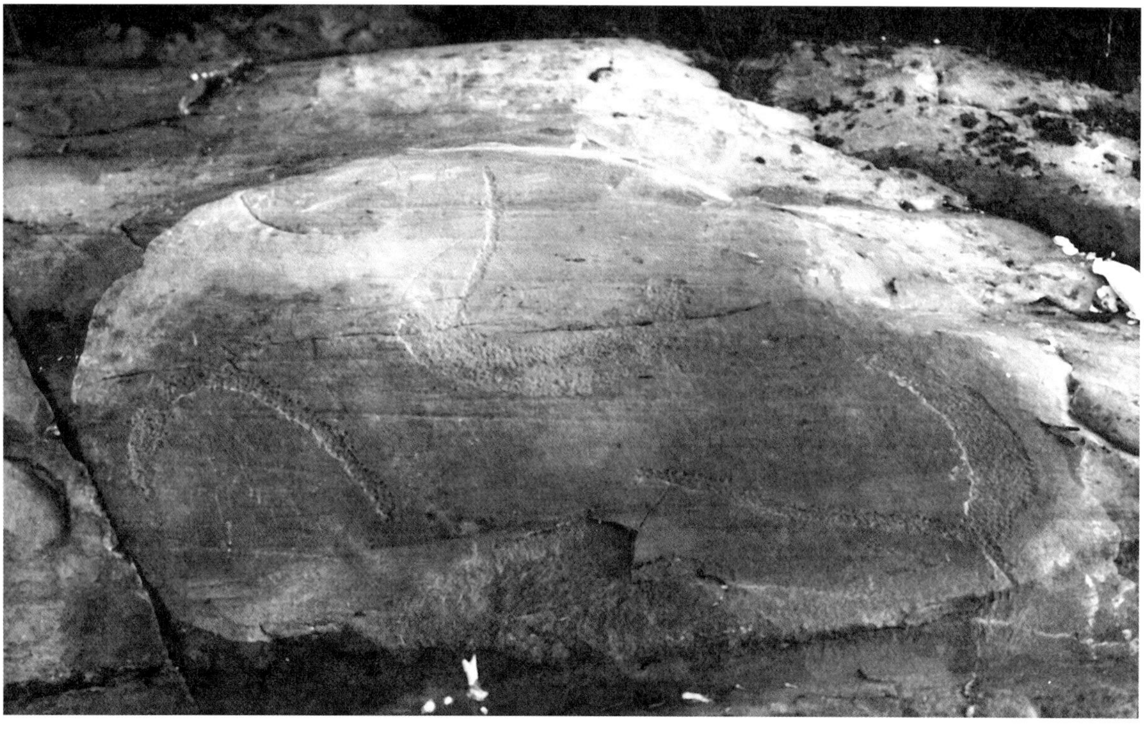

need to understand something of the society and the people who created them. In order to establish links between the rock images and other archaeological traces of human activity – such as dwelling sites, graves or artefacts – we need to know when the images were created.

Difficulties in dating

The many deer images in Vingen clearly define the rock art as part of the Northern Tradition, associated with hunter-gatherers of the Stone Age. But since this period stretches over many thousands of years from about 9000 to 2000 BC, covering both the Neolithic and the Mesolithic, we are in need of a more accurate dating of these images. Despite detailed knowledge of the chronology of stone tools and artefacts from these periods, its equivalent for rock art is not so well developed. While artefacts are often found in charcoal layers that can easily be dated by radiocarbon methods, rock art is most often documented above the soil or under thin layers of turf. This in turn makes it difficult to determine a more exact date for the rock art of the Northern Tradition. In contrast to the rock art of the Bronze Age, the motifs of the Northern Tradition offer few clues that make it possible to define dates: they do not occur in other dated contexts, such as graves, and few or none of the figures can be compared with dated artefacts such as weapons. Typological studies of similarities and differences in the design of the rock art images can, however, provide some indications that allow us to establish time differences between the figures themselves. The figures that have common features are considered to be contemporary to one another, while the figures that are dissimilar are regarded as being from different periods. The deer in Vingen are organized in this kind of chronology, where the figures west of Vehammaren are estimated to be the oldest and the figures in Elva the youngest. However, the analysis does not help us to place the rock art within a defined period of years, or into an absolute chronology (Bakka 1973; 1979).

One of the methods that has been used for a more absolute dating is post-glacial changes in the relationship between land and sea after the last Ice Age. These changes resulted in newer landmasses gradually being lifted up out of the sea, and we are able to date the stages, or shoreline levels, in this process. The dated shoreline levels can thus provide the oldest possible date for rock art that is located at the same level above today's sea level. The prevailing idea has been that the rock art was produced at the shore and that dating of shorelines could date the rock art (*ibid*). This method of dating is based on the prerequisite that the image must have been made immediate after the rock was part of dry land mass. The method that has been frequently used to date art of the Northern Tradition in various places in Norway is to analyze each panel in relation to the shoreline level. It is however of limited value in Vingen, because the level of the sea during the period the rock art was created lay below the lowest figures.

Another method for dating the rock art in Vingen is to excavate in the

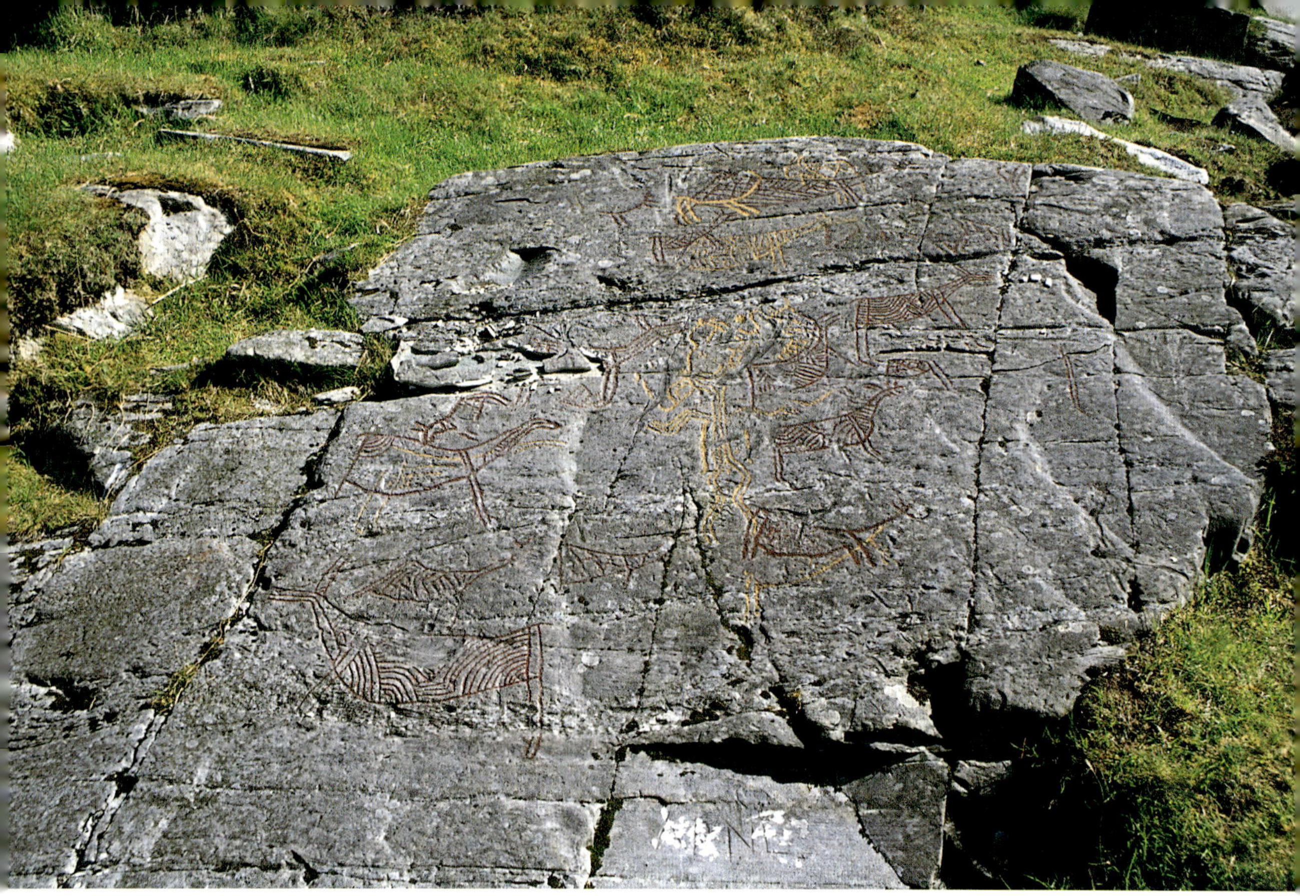

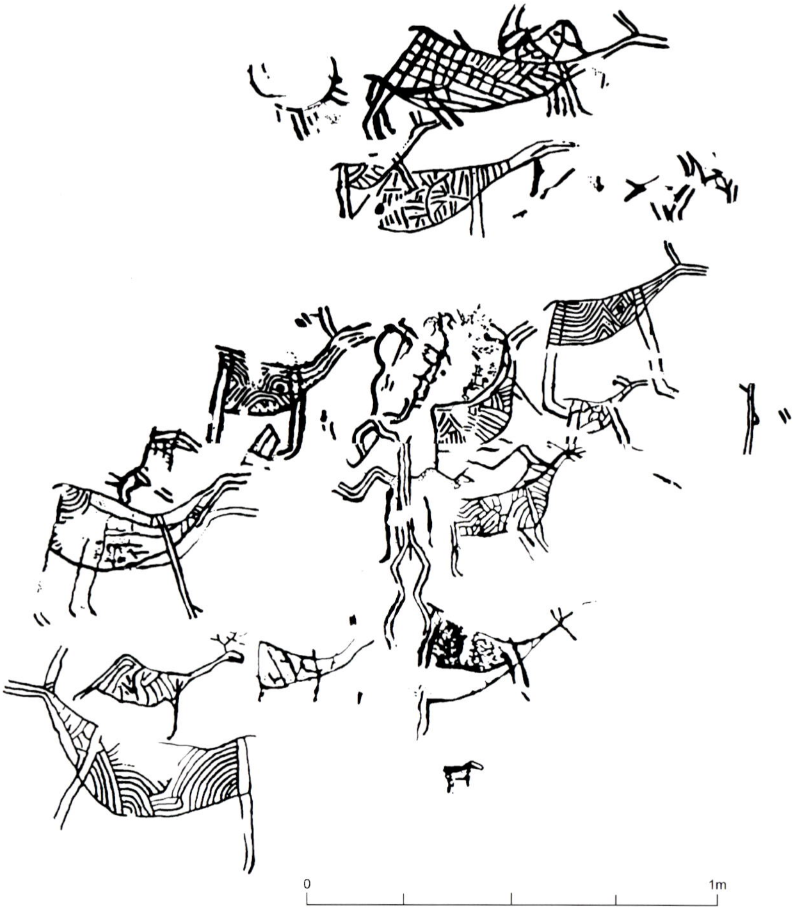

FIGURES 126–127. Ever since the first rock carvings were discovered in Vingen in the early 1900s, more and more have been found, either because slanting sun-rays have brought figures to light that were not previously visible, or because they were uncovered when turf was peeled away from the rock. In 1973 a large amount of turf was removed from an area called Leitet, and a panel with nearly 30 figures was uncovered on the grassy slope. The photo shows a group of animal figures gathered around a tall and thin, headless human figure. This was probably an intentional composition, perhaps depicting a mythical tale illustrating the relationship between animals and humans.

PHOTO GM, TRACING EB

vicinity of rock art panels and try to trace artefacts or remains of human activity that were contemporary to the period the rock art was created. Datable archaeological artefacts that are found in the sub-soil nearby and between the rock art panels can therefore help to date the images themselves.

Traces in the sub-soil

Rock art does not represent the only traces of the prehistoric people in Vingen. Concealed in the soil, beneath thin layers of peat, there are numerous remains left by human activity. Of particular interest are the dwelling features of small houses – or rather huts – that lie in groups between the rock art panels on the southern side of Vingepollen. To date, at least ten such dwelling features have been recorded (Lødøen 2001; 2003; 2007). They are visible in the terrain as round or oval depressions bordered by low banks of stone or soil, and they are about four to five metres in diameter. Around or in the banks of several of these dwellings there are stones of various sizes with rock carvings that may have once been part of the features. Sporadic archaeological investigations in some of the dwelling features and in the vicinity of the rock art have revealed a number of artefacts that have been dated, along with charcoal from the thin cultural layers, to the Mesolithic – primarily to the period between 5000 and 4000 BC (*ibid.*). Throughout the entire area and over the years there have also been more or less random discoveries of flint and stone material and waste flakes from tool production. These have been dated to the same time period. Some of the remains were found in old drainage trenches, and some were uncovered in conjunction with the removal of turf covering the rock art panels.

Traces of activity in the sub-soil on the southern side of Vingepollen appear to form a pattern. They were found close to the rock art, and all of them are dated to the end of the Mesolithic, while no cultural traces from more recent periods, such as from the Neolithic and later, have been found in the area. Therefore, it is very likely that the traces of activity are associated with the production of the rock art, thereby dating the rock art to around 5000–4000 BC.

We cannot, however, discount the possibility that the traces of activity in the sub-soil originate from a time long before the rock art was created. There may have been activity at Vingen during the transition at the end of the Mesolithic that was associated with the small dwellings. At a later point in time, the area may have been used by the creators of the rock art. This said, it seems less likely that the many rock art images would have been produced without this activity leaving behind a single datable trace. The additional fact that the rock art is found on stones surrounding the dwelling features, and that a pecking tool was found among the datable remains in the sub-soil, tends to support the conclusion that the various cultural traces in Vingen are essentially contemporary. We do not know, on the other hand, the span of the time period during which the production of rock art took place. One explanation for the great variety of designs seen, for example, in the deer images, may be that the

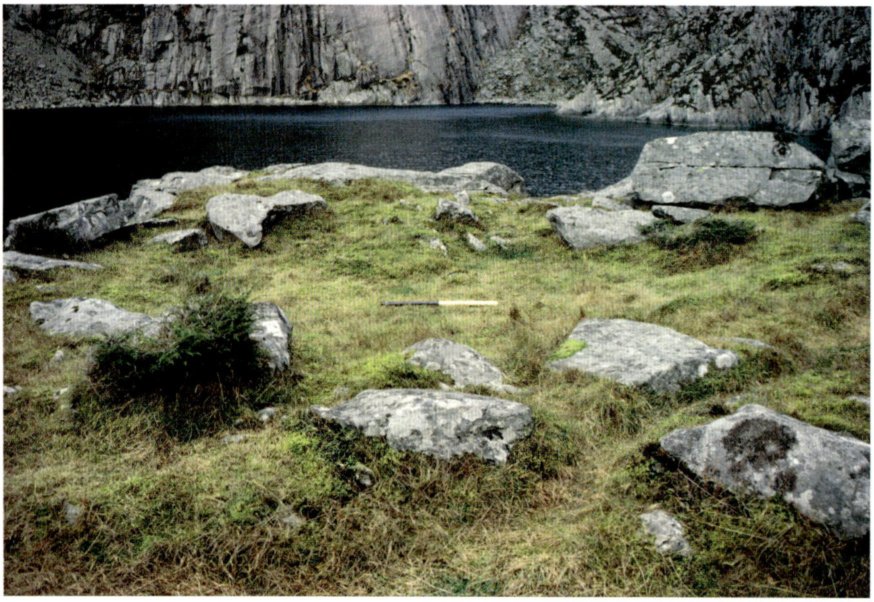

FIGURE 128. In Vingen around ten dwelling features from small huts have been found – circular or oval depressions with low mounds of stone and loose earth surrounding them. In an area called Bakkane, there is a group of several dwelling features, some of them flush with large stones with rock carvings. The black and white measuring stick, one metre in length, marks the centre of one of the dwelling features.
TL

figures were carved at different times – perhaps over several hundreds of years. Based on the knowledge we possess today, we believe that the beginning of rock art production in Vingen coincides with the dates for the traces in the sub-soil – that is, towards the end of the Mesolithic – and that rock art was created there for several hundred years afterwards.

And so, who were these people that began to peck images in stone at Vingen during the end of the Mesolithic, and where did they come from? Traces of activity in the sub-soil are so scarce that they do not reflect any lengthy or continuous settlement here. The answer may be found in the area of the nearest neighbourhood to Vingen – at Skatestraumen, which is located only one hour to the northwest by paddle boat.

Settlement at the tidal current

Skatestraumen is a tidewater stream between Bremangerlandet and Rugsundøy, at the intersection between inner Frøysjøen and the Nordfjorden outlet.

During 1989–1995 a number of dwelling features were found, recorded and excavated on both sides of the stream, dating from the Stone Age, Bronze Age and Iron Age (Bergsvik 1999a). It was primarily due to the stable fishing resources in the tidewater stream that people were attracted to the area in different prehistoric periods. The abundance of fish also attracted large numbers of different bird species, documented by the excavation of the dwelling features. The area is also strategic for expeditions in all directions along the fjords and in the adjoining mountain regions westward towards the Ålfot Glacier. Today the Ålfoten area is one of the best red deer territories in the country – as perhaps it also was in prehistoric times?

Several of the dwelling sites along Skatestraumen have been dated to the same time as the cultural traces in Vingen, between 5000 and 4000 BC (*ibid.*). Archaeological remains at other tidewater streams along the Western Norwegian coast suggest that there was a change in the settlement pattern and in the exploitation of marine resources during this period. The nomadic life that characterizes the Early and Middle Mesolithic – with small bands of people chasing wild game – appears to have gradually been reduced. Along the tidewater streams, stable marine resources created the basis for permanent settlement lasting through much of the year, or perhaps all of the year, while smaller groups were out fishing and hunting in other places.

Permanent settlement undoubtedly developed a strong sense of place for people in terms of the sites, the immediate area and the landscape surrounding them. One natural formation that is particularly visible and dominating for those who lived at Skatestraumen is Hornelen, which rises majestically above the small strip of land on the southern side of the stream. This is the same mountain that towers over the shipping channel and the approach to Vingen. It is not unlikely that the people who lived along Skatestraumen some 6000 years ago spun myths and tales about this mountain.

Several features of the archaeological material found here suggest that there was close contact between the people who lived at Skatestraumen during the Late Mesolithic and those who created the rock art and left behind traces of

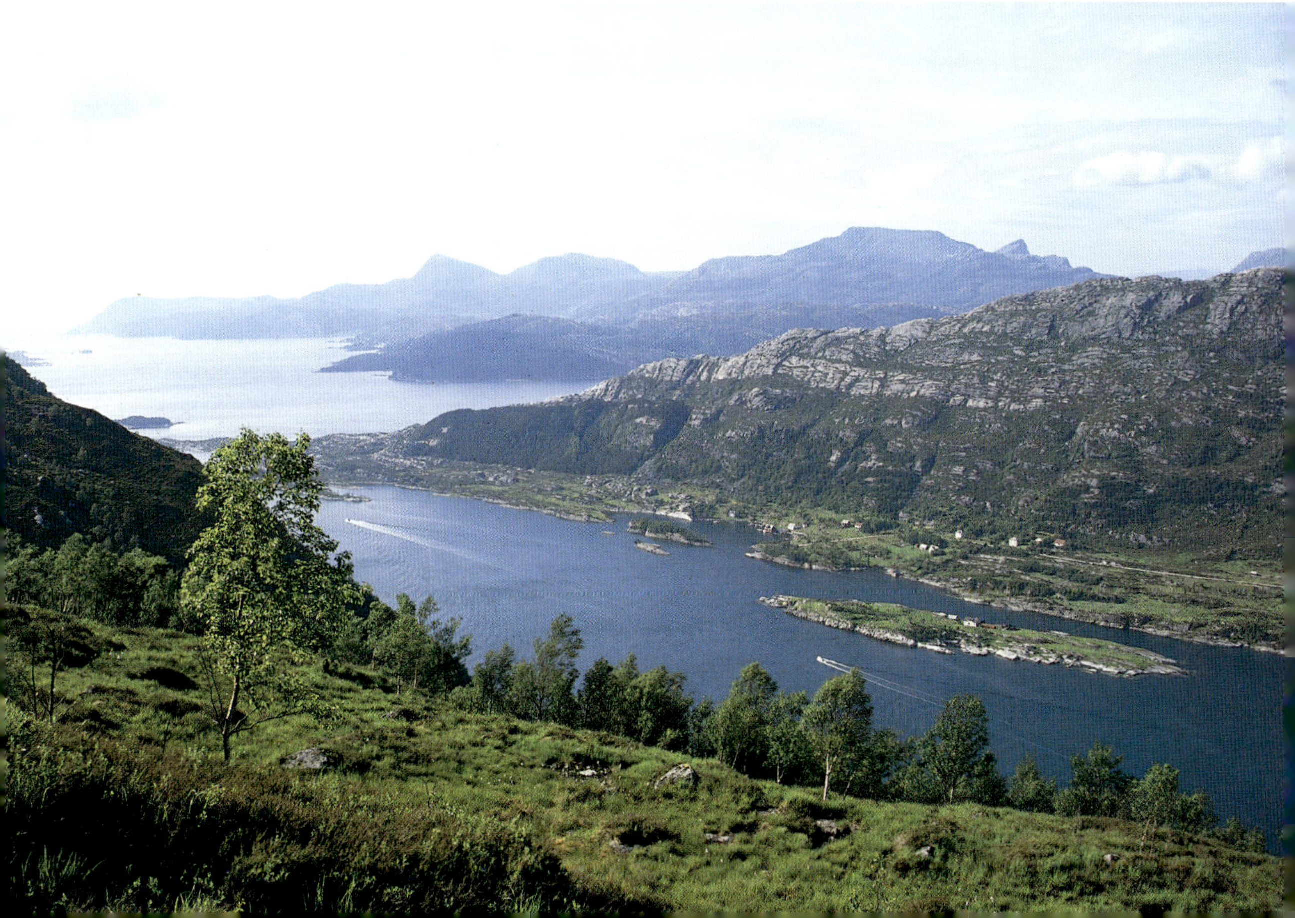

FIGURE 129. View towards Skatestraumen to the northwest, seen from Hornelen. On both sides of the tidal current there are remains of Stone Age settlements dating, amongst others, to the same era as the discoveries in Vingen. TL

their activity at Vingen. For example, the same bedrock used as a raw material for making tools was found in both places, and similar tools are found both at Vingen and at Skatestraumen. This suggests that the people living on the shores of the fishing stream were participants in – or perhaps even responsible for – the creation of the rock art (Bergsvik 1999b; Lødøen 2003). In contrast to the abundant archaeological material found at the settlement sites along Skatestraumen, only relatively scant remains have been recorded at the dwelling features in Vingen. This may suggest that the latter were not regular dwelling sites, but that they were used for shorter stays, perhaps while the rock art was being made, or in conjunction with rituals involving the rock art.

Rock art rituals and changes in society

The change in living and subsistence from an itinerant to a settled existence was hardly unproblematic. When people remain in a delimited geographic area over a lengthy period of time, such as the habitation area in Skatestraumen confirms, the stage is set for interpersonal conflicts. Ethnographical studies of societies with which it is natural to make comparisons show that rituals may have served as a means of resolving conflicts arising from new and changed forms of society. The act of creating rock art may have been a ritual designed to alleviate or resolve crisis situations – for example between women and men, or between young people and the older generation. Through the rituals of rock art, social order was maintained, independent of changes in the code of human coexistence that the changeover in life styles must have entailed.

What kinds of rituals were performed around the rock art panels at Vingen, who participated in them, and what was the meaning of the many images? In all

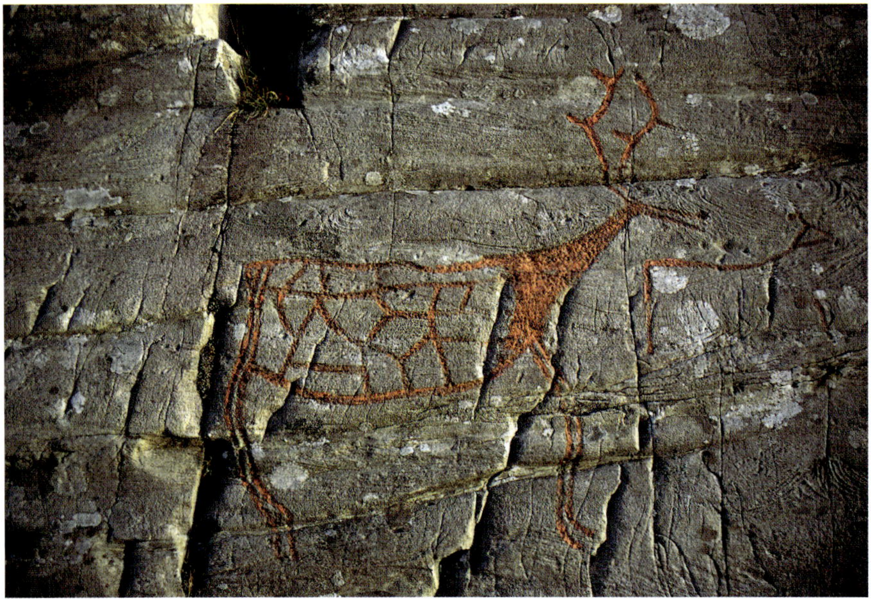

FIGURE 130. Were members of the deer family, such as those depicted in Vingen, merely regarded as game – as prey representing exciting hunting trips, plentiful and tasty food, hides for clothing and tents, sinews, antlers and bones for making tools? Or could these animals have held a deeper, more symbolic meaning? Perhaps the deer played a role in the worldview and myths of the humans who created the rock art – as a symbol of strength and community.
GM

likelihood, the key to understanding the rock art lies in the patterns that seem to emerge: in the diversity of motifs, the composition of figures and the way in which the images are arranged in the landscape (Mandt 1998). By comparing these patterns with what we know about hunter groups living today or groups we know from our recent past, we can approach an interpretation, or perhaps offer several possible interpretations.

Vingen as a hunting trap?

The earlier interpretation, put forward during the first half of the 1900s, is that the rock art at Vingen would have served as an invocation for sympathetic magic (Gjessing 1936; Frazer 1967). In hunting societies from the Christian era, including the Native Americans, we know of rituals whereby depictions of the game animals would give the hunter power over his prey and also ensure that the stocks of animals would be plentiful. This kind of hunting-magic applied to the Vingen rock art was supported not only by the images of the animals, but also by topographical features. The narrow passage from the mountain down to the fjord arm and the sheer mountain inclines were seen as a natural trap for hunting herds on a grand scale. Here a group of hunters could have stampeded the deer over cliffs and down into the water below, where other hunters would wait in boats, clubbing to death the animals that were not killed by the fall (Bøe 1932).

In the course of time, less focus has been given to the interpretation of rock art as sympathetic magic. Deer were certainly an important resource for the coastal people in Western Norway, even though subsistence was based on fish and other marine resources that they could depend on the year round. Venison was important and a welcome food supplement, as well as providing hide for clothing and tents, and the antlers, bones and sinews for tools and weapons. At the same time, the deer perhaps was far more than just a game animal and physical resource. The desire to kill game was without a doubt only part of the reason for depicting deer.

The mythical dimension of deer

Ethnographical studies tell us that animals which were important to the survival of society were attributed symbolic meaning. In many societies, certain species of animals have been central in myths about the creation of the world and of human beings – what we call myths of origin – and animals of a certain species have frequently been the origin itself (e.g. Willis 1990). There are examples showing that important game animals are associated with the world-view that people had. The animal is included in rituals designed to ensure life and family lineage and to guarantee that the rules of society are followed. The animal is a central symbol in rituals marking the passage of the young into adulthood – for example upon the first menstruation, or when the young hunter sets out to kill his first game – and the animal is also represented in marriage rituals (Lewis-Willians 1981).

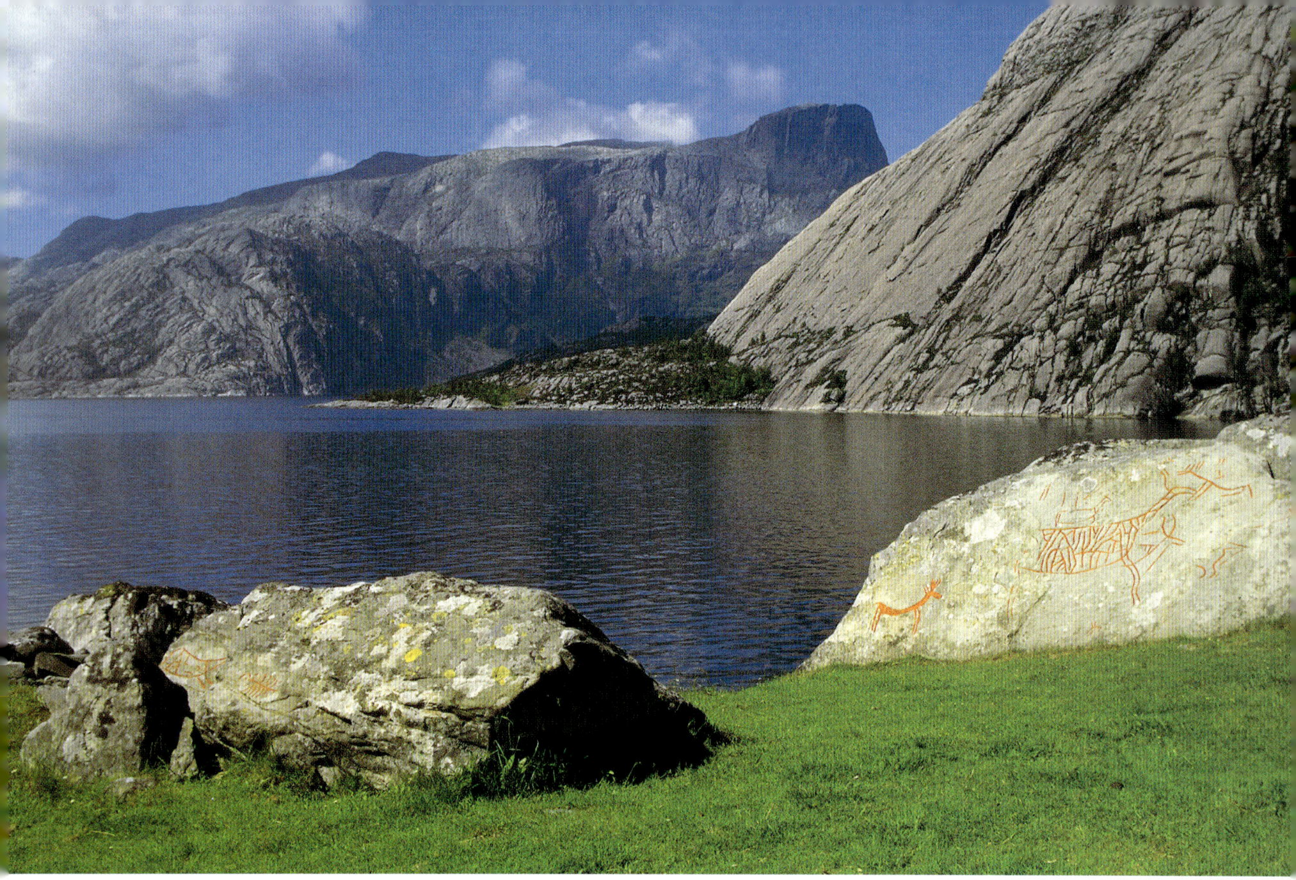

Perhaps the deer had a similar role for the people who depicted red deer at Vingen? In its capacity as an originator, the deer may have been attributed an important role as a mechanism for social maintenance. It may have been a powerful symbol for the community and the group's ability to survive and ensure future generations – a way of guaranteeing that society continued.

But why was Vingen in particular chosen as the setting for these important rituals? It could not have only been the deer in the mountains that attracted coastal people during the Mesolithic. What qualities does this isolated fjord arm have that made it so sacred, powerful and different from any other place in the secular world?

FIGURE 131. The Hornelen mountain mass – a landmark on the shipping route between Florø and Måløy – is visible from most points in Vingen. From ethnographic studies it is known that natural formations such as conspicuous mountains are often attributed special power and meaning in religious or cult contexts. It is tempting to wonder whether Hornelen held such significance for the people of Vingen during the Stone Age, although this is something we will never know for certain. GM

Sacred landscape

To the modern, western viewer, the landscape in Vingen evokes dramatic, perhaps inhospitable but also intriguing features because of its wild and pristine state. This was hardly how Mesolithic people saw Vingen. The landscape surrounding Vingepollen has not changed to any great extent in the 6000–7000 years since the rock art was made. We see the same mountains, the same fjord and the same sloping rock surfaces, knolls and boulders that were seen by people in the Mesolithic, and we experience the same changing natural phenomena that must have been experienced in earlier times. But the way in which people perceive and interact with the landscape today has undergone substantial

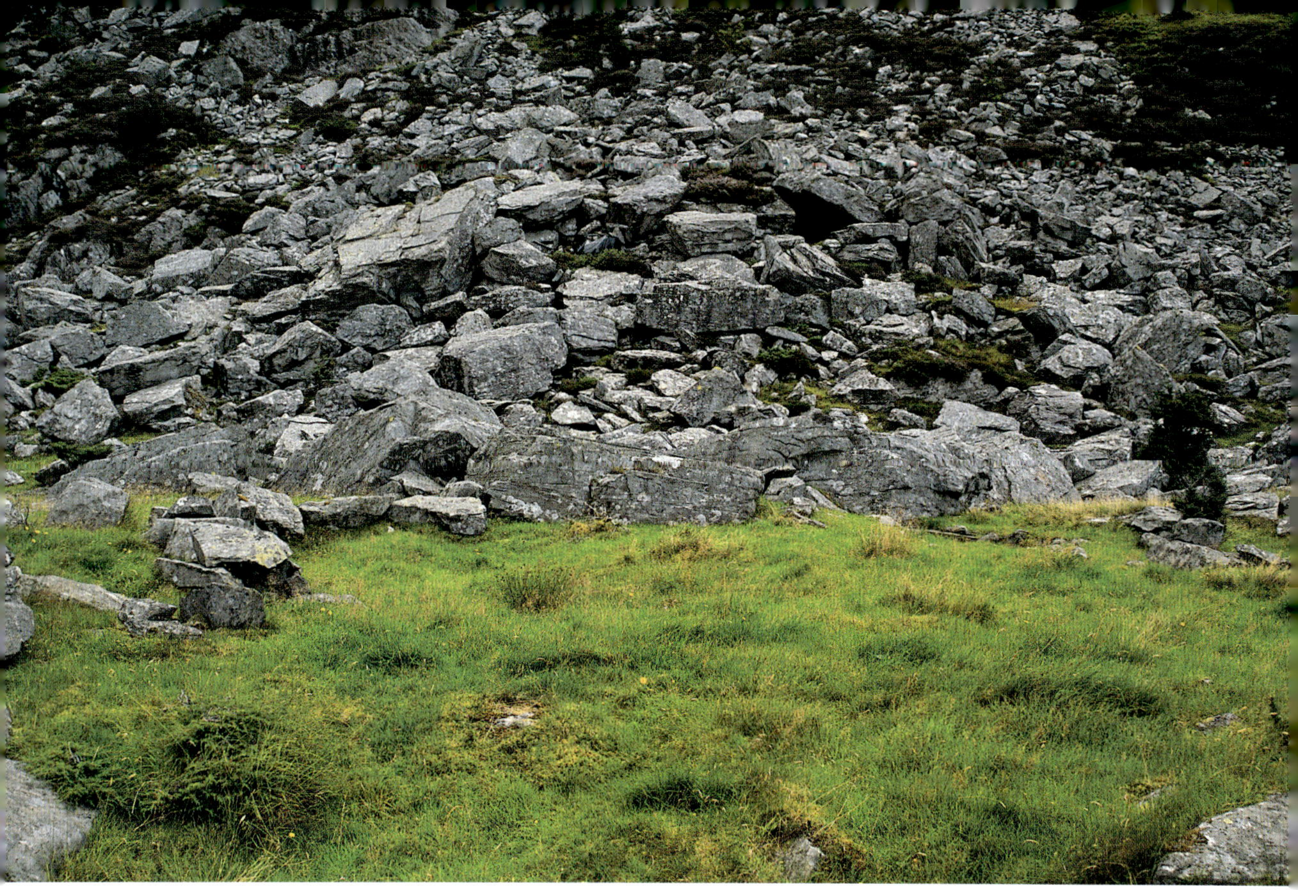

FIGURE 132. At the easternmost point on the strip of land along Vingepollen is a large hillside covered with scree where rock carvings are pecked on the enormous boulders as well as on smaller stones. Some of the surfaces with carvings face out towards the fjord; others are concealed between stones in the scree. In several places there are narrow passages between the stones where it is possible to crawl inside. On some of the stones in these passageways there are rock carvings – usually concentrations of peck marks or more abstract patterns that are difficult to identify.
TL

changes since the age when the Vingen rock art was created. It is people themselves who create and attribute meaning to nature and the environment, based on their own world-view, basic values and cultural identity (Tilley 1994, 2008; Bradley 2000). Ethnographical studies show that people of pre-modern societies attribute symbolic and mythical qualities to the landscape. Places in nature are assigned special powers and significance in a religious and cultural context. These may include natural formations such as conspicuous mountains and stones with special shapes, or places where real or mythical events have taken place. In this way, the landscape is filled with events from the past, it is populated by forefathers and thus provides the framework for a mythological system that defines social groups and their sense of belonging in terms of geographic areas and resources that are present there (Bradley 2000).

Is it possible to interpret the Vingen landscape in this way? The creation of images on stone is one way to commemorate special places, by marking them with symbols. Perhaps the natural features of Vingen hold some of the answers to why precisely this place was chosen as a backdrop for the rock art – the fjord and mountains, the boulders and sloping surfaces, the changing light, weather and wind, the echoes and other sound phenomena – and not least the towering, sheer mountainsides on three sides that form an enclosure, a type of sanctuary that appears to be created for the performance of rituals that occasionally were kept secret from the rest of the society.

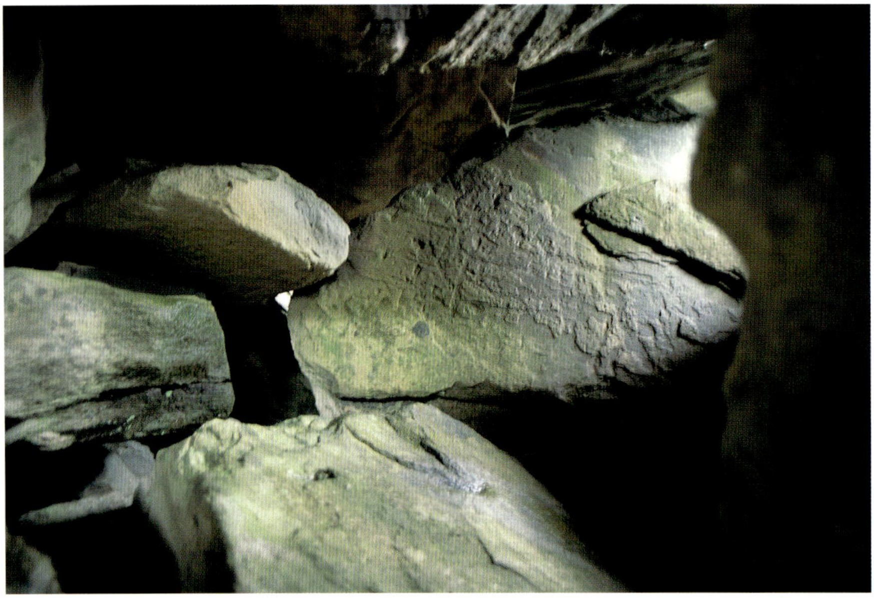

FIGURE 133. About midway in the scree, a large boulder serves as the roof above a small overhang in which carvings are found on both the stone walls of the overhang itself and in a passageway leading from the overhang and ending at a point farther up in the scree. On one large stone inside the cave passageway there is a concentration of pecked lines that are difficult to identify. Perhaps these were meant to depict an animal, or maybe an abstract pattern whose meaning is unknown. RU

Natural phenomena endowed with meaning?

The mountain of Hornelen may have been considered the centre of the world – an *axis mundi* – for the people of the Mesolithic. We know that in more recent times the peak was even taller – in the shape of an extended, pointed horn – and that it broke off and collapsed during the 1800s (Aaland 1909). The mountain literally juts up out of the underworld and soars skywards, and the sounds of the fjord and water currents beneath Hornelen reverberate as echoes far through the Vingen basin. The inlet to Vingepollen was perhaps considered as a portal – a passageway into a sequestered, sacred sanctuary (Mandt 1998). In this outdoor space there is no sunlight during wintertime, because the sun does not rise above the mountain crests. During the rest of the year, shifting light and shadows allow the sun's rays to illuminate some rock art panels during the morning hours, while others are illuminated during the evening, when the sun lays low over Hornelen. Perhaps the rock images were placed intentionally either on morning-panels or evening-panels, for example in relation to different rituals. The sheer mountainsides that enclose the narrow fjord arm also create other peculiar natural phenomena. When thunderbolts reverberate off the mountain walls, one has the impression of "being in Hell itself", as one local fisherman put it. And during the dreaded south-westerly storms, Vingepollen fjord seethes with foaming waves that crash in over the shoreline. The place name Vingen – or Vengjane, as it is known locally – literally means "the windy place" (Bøe 1932; pers. comm. Helga Vingelven).

We do not know whether – or how – these landscape features were important for the placement of the rock art (Walderhaug 2000). It is likely that there is no single reason why the Vingen area was chosen for creating images in stone.

Perhaps the isolated location was important, or the proximity to one of the most conspicuous landmarks along the coast. The place may have stood out as an ideal area for hunting and fishing. It is probable that the location also was influenced by non-material factors associated with ancient world-views and mythology – aspects that we will never be able to trace fully.

A ritualistic landscape

Was Vingen a place for the elite few – a sanctuary that was to be kept secret from the rest of society – or was the area a sacred meeting place where many people congregated? The location of the rock art in the landscape, along with the activities that may have gone on around them, may provide answers.

Some of the large rock art panels lie in relatively flat and open terrain with ample space below the mountainside. Here it would have been possible for a large number of people to gather. Other panels are practically isolated on the outskirts of the rock art area, amongst these the two large panels on either side of the ravine at the eastern end of Vingepollen. The steep mountainsides were barely negotiable for the persons who created the rock art, let alone crowds of cult worshipers. Other smaller panels are more or less concealed in the environment. These include rock art that was carved into stones beneath larger boulders and the images on stones and in cavities beneath the expansive scree at the eastern end of Vingen.

The variations in the way rock art was placed in the landscape may suggest

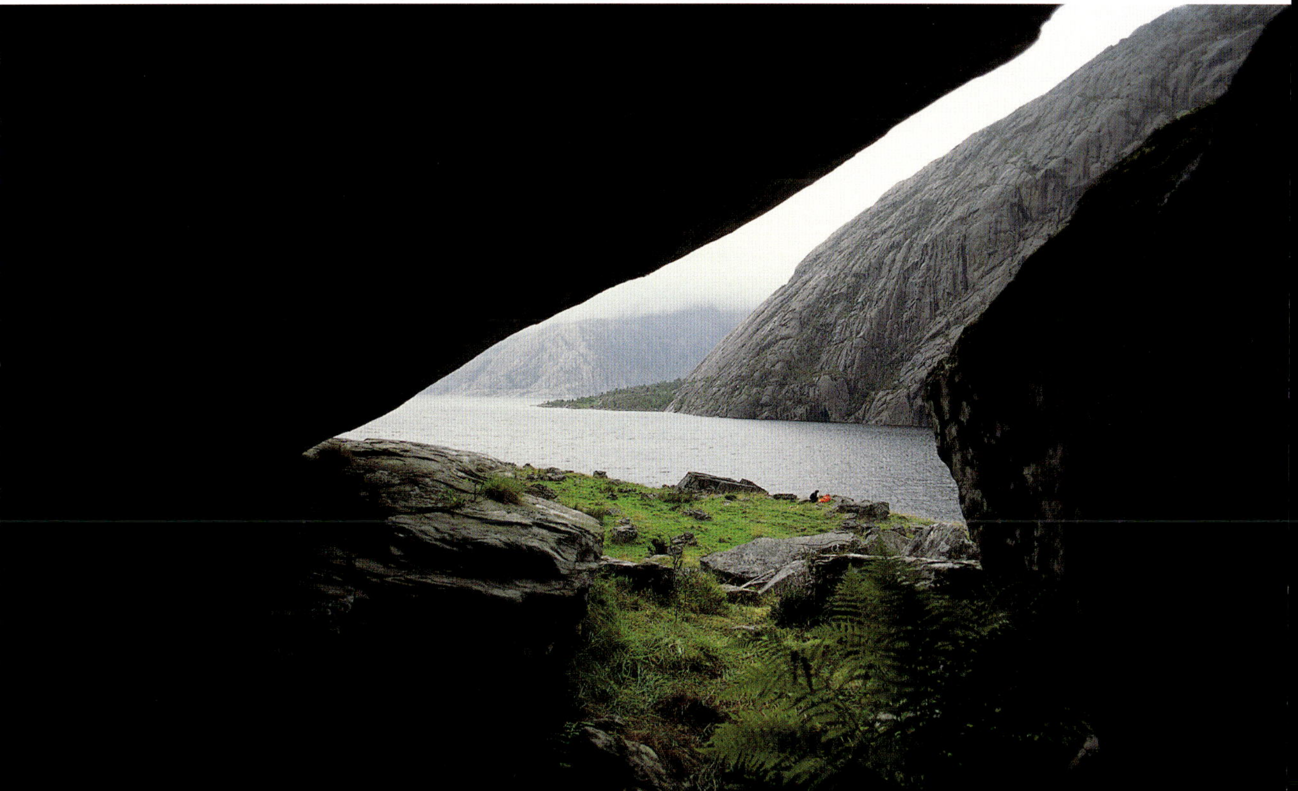

FIGURE 134. From this natural shelter in the scree field, there is an open panorama across most of the rock art area in Vingen.
RU

that it formed a part of different ritualistic contexts. The large sloping surfaces with. ample space around them may have been used for rituals in which many people participated, possibly at fixed times of the year. The small panels and those that are difficult to access were very likely reserved for smaller groups of perhaps only a few participants. Many of these panels appear to have been intentionally concealed – perhaps because they represented occult knowledge that was shared by only the chosen few? The images that are found inside and around the outlets from narrow passages in the scree were possibly used in rituals associated with initiation and transition to newly bestowed roles in society. The passages, which it is possible to crawl through, may have been the physical symbol of a birth canal through which the individual had to pass on the way to a new existence. Most societies have rituals associated with transitions in human life, for example when the younger members of the group enter adulthood, or when a new spiritual or religious leader is ordained (Turner 1967).

The many small, loose stones containing rock art found spread across large areas in Vingen may also have had some connection with ritualistic activities. A large number of these stones appear in the walls of the dwelling features of the small huts presumably used for short stays in Vingen. It was perhaps here that the religious leader stayed during the periods when the annual rituals were prepared, or when special secret rites of initiation were performed.

Religious leader – rock art specialist – shaman?

Who was this religious leader who had contact with ancestors through rituals and who served to maintain social order? It certainly had to be a person who possessed the necessary knowledge about and insight into what the rock art meant, how it was to be created, and the kinds of rituals that were to be performed in conjunction with the creation and use of the images. Through rituals the leader kept the contact open with the mythical deer, using the rock on which they were depicted, or with other forces of nature. This religious leader – a specialist in rock images – was probably also responsible for initiating new followers in the mysteries of rock art. Common carving techniques and ways of depicting images in Vingen suggest that there was a generally accepted artistic idiom. Many of the figures must have been created by the same person, or by apprentices who had received guidance from the same master artist. Perhaps we can see in this the contours of a rock art tradition passed from generation to generation.

In many societies it is the medicine man or shaman who possesses the necessary qualities that we can ascribe to what we call the rock art specialists in Vingen. Shamanism is a religious practice known from the hunter-gatherer societies found in many parts of the world, particularly in the northern and central areas of Asia, but also in Northern Europe (Price 2001). Among others, we are familiar with the *Noiades* in the Sami culture (Pollan 1993). In these societies the shaman has a large number of religious and social functions. They are both spiritual and secular leaders, and they have thorough knowledge of the history and mythology of their society. They know the attributes of plants and the behaviour of animals, and they often have animals as helping spirits, with deer, birds and fish as well-known examples. They heal the sick, can see into the future, and they have contact with the divine world and the spirits of ancestors.

A number of features in the rock images in Vingen – both the combination of motifs and the location of the images – can perhaps be interpreted as traces of shamanistic activity (Viste 2003). One of the hallmarks of shamans is their ability to travel in different astral planes. The soul or spirit of the shaman is able to move between different cosmic levels – the underworld, the earth and the sky. A journey to the underworld is usually set in the passageway of a cave or similar site. Perhaps the many concealed rock images in Vingen were places the shaman visited to prepare a journey to another cosmic level? The shaman's journey into the underworld may also be symbolised through the numerous depictions of the human skeleton. Another characteristic of shamans is their ability to enter into trances. When the shaman is in a trance, he or she is able to see patterns and figures with an "inner eye", and they experience bodily phenomena, such as being able to fly or being transformed into an animal. Some of the rock art images in Vingen appear to be a combination of a human and an animal. These are perhaps portrayals of the shaman in the process of being transformed.

Vingen as a sacred place

We do not know whether the religious leaders – the rock art specialists – in Vingen during the Mesolithic were shamans in the sense we understand the term today. However, those who were responsible for creating the images must have known all of the mythical tales and accounts about their ancestors. These were the same people who had the expertise concerning rituals and the sacred acts that needed to be performed in order to hold society together, and they were the people who were able to communicate with the spiritual world. We know from studies of currently living social groups that the individuals who are chosen to have close contact with higher powers represent an institution and a power factor in society.

In our opinion, Vingen was a sacred place that was important for the fjord society on the Norwegian west coast during a period of time in the Mesolithic. It is likely that many different types of religious and ritualistic practices were performed in and around the rock art. Some of these activities were perhaps reserved for the chosen few who had – or were ordained to – the knowledge associated with the images. In other respects, Vingen may have served as a gathering site for groups of people who lived along the coast, on the islands or inside fjord valleys. Here at Vingen they could have met, at fixed seasons of the year – either annually or at other intervals – to consolidate their sense of belonging to society, to share information and to acquire new knowledge.

Kårstad in Stryn – An Encounter Between Two Cult Traditions

At the end of the 1800s, foreign tourists began to visit the Norwegian fjords and mountain ranges. The first tourist hotels were built during the 1850s, and the rise in tourism brought the demand for better communications – not least for passable roads. By 1898 a new road had been built along Innvikfjorden, in Nordfjord's Stryn municipality in the county of Sogn og Fjordane. The terrain is steep and rugged, particularly between the small communities of Innvik and Utvik on the southern side of the fjord, where the sheer mountainsides descend vertically into the sea below. In former times the road between the neighbouring communities was a footpath that rose steeply from the Kårstad farm on the Utvik side of the fjord, crossing the protruding crag of Kleivane then descending steeply down again towards Innvik. Along the foot of Kleivane, the roadway had to be blasted out of the rock, and the loosened boulders were used to build retaining walls for the road along the shoreline. What was unknown at the time was that there were rock art images and runes on the stones that had been part of the steep mountainside at Kårstad, and thirty years would pass before the secrets concealed in the wall along the roadway would be revealed.

A chance discovery

One summer day in 1927 a schoolteacher who was on summer holiday in Stryn was out rowing on the fjord near Kårstad (Shetelig 1927). Over the years, stormy weather and winds had churned up sea spray, washing the stones in the retaining wall clean of lichens and moss. The diagonal rays of the sun undoubtedly helped to illuminate the relief on the surface of the stones at exactly the moment the rowing boat was at an optimal angle. These chance circumstances made Taraldset, the teacher, the first person to discover that there were figures and other images engraved on one of the blocks of stone. The account is one of many examples illustrating how chance plays a role in the discovery of prehistoric rock art. In many cases, optimal lighting is the necessary condition for being able to see the shallow and often heavily weathered lines of images. Therefore it is most frequently the local inhabitants, walking through the area during various times of year and with changing light conditions, who become aware of markings on rock, or otherwise as in Kårstad: a random summer tourist with the time to ponder the unexpected.

Bergens Museum was immediately informed of the find, and during the autumn of the same year, the curator of the Antiquities Collection, Haakon

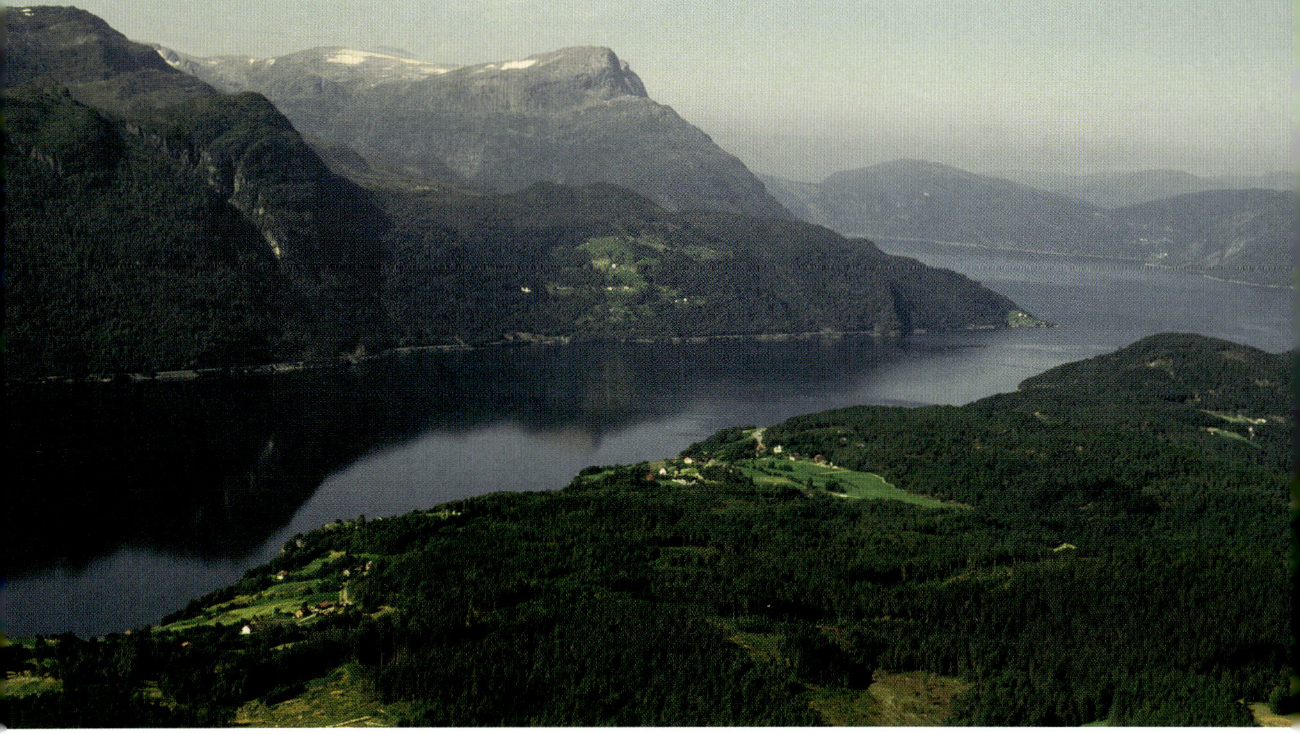

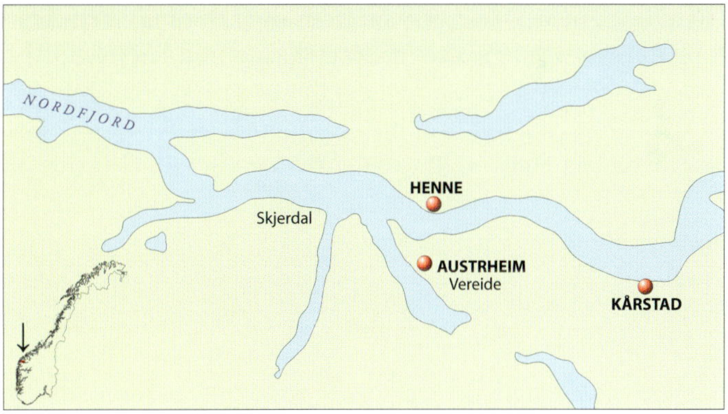

FIGURES 135–136. Nordfjorden, a long and many-branched fjord, stretches from the outermost edge of the sea at Bremangerlandet to the foot of the Jostedal glacier far to the east. Rural communities with lush green hillsides and fields are found along the slopes of the fjord arms, crowned by sheer white-capped mountain peaks with gushing rapids running down the mountainsides. Between the fjord and the watershed in the east, the mountain range with its peaks and plateaus, glaciers, waterfalls and fishing lakes towers to the east.
MAP AI, ILLUSTRATION TH

Shetelig, went to Kårstad. Because there was a danger of the rock art being damaged if it remained as part of the retaining wall, Shetelig decided, in consultation with the Public Roads Directorate, that the road should be re-excavated so that the blocks containing rock art could be removed (*ibid.).* This resulted in the discovery along the wall of three more large stones and a couple of smaller ones with rock carvings.

The sections of broken stone were reassembled like pieces in a puzzle, and a startling image appeared. Seven complete boat images were depicted on the panel, along with five or six boat fragments, eighteen runes and one large swastika (Mandt 1973, 2000). The combination of rock art images and runes

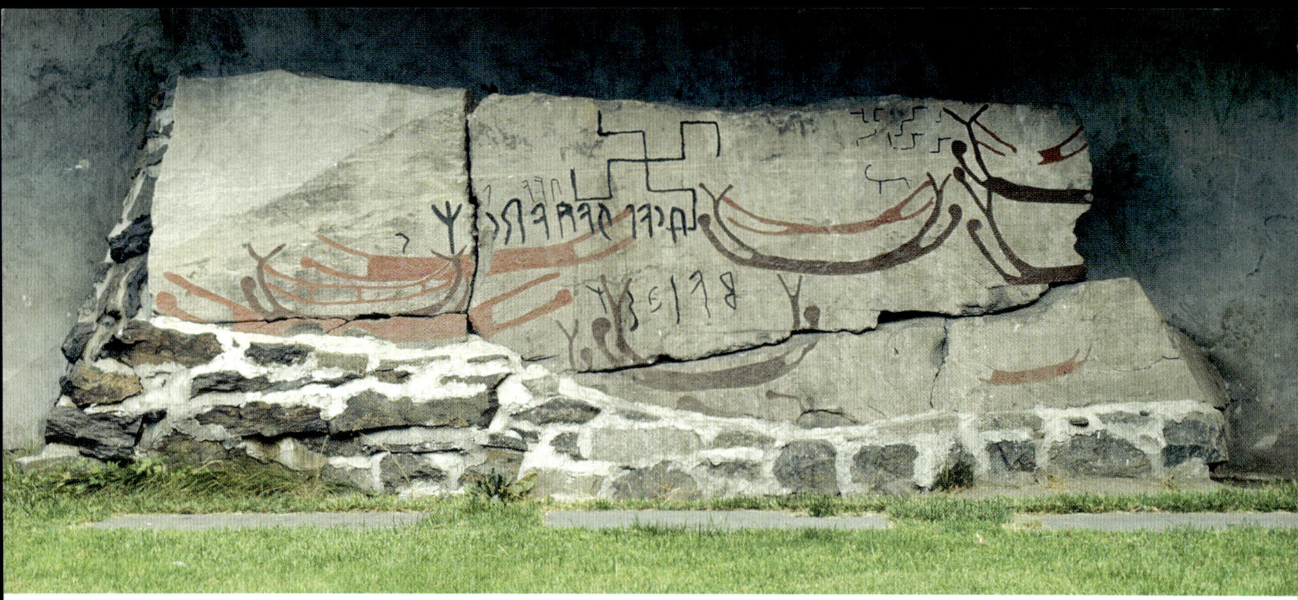

FIGURE 137. All of the boulders with rock art images that were found in the retaining wall along the road to Kårstad were transported to Bergens Museum. They were assembled there like pieces of a giant jigsaw puzzle and are still on display today in the museum's garden. The individual pecking marks of the figures are distinct and visible, and some of the figures are superimposed. In the 1970s the rock carvings were highlighted in paint to make them more easily visible to the public, and various colours were used to differentiate the time periods when the figures were created.
AMO/BM

on the same surface makes the Kårstad discovery unique, and it received a great deal of attention when it was made known to the public. In Scandinavia only a few places are known to exist with examples of runes alongside rock art images, such as Himmelstadlund in Sweden (Nordén 1932). The normal consensus is that the custom of carving images on stone ended when runes came into use during the Early Iron Age (Malmer 1989).

It is not only the combination of motifs that makes the Kårstad figures intriguing, but also their location. The stones with the images were blasted out of the Kleivane crag, and Shetelig believed that these huge, heavy blocks of stone could not have been transported very far from their origins when they became a part of the retaining wall along the roadway (Olsen and Shetelig 1930). It is not possible to establish the exact point where these figures were originally located. However, as the sheer cliff wall was blasted high above where the roadway was laid, some four metres above the waterline, Shetelig assumed that the images were made at a uniform elevation a good distance up on the cliff wall, with a broad panorama out across the fjord.

Boat images originating in the Bronze Age

The boat images at Kårstad belong to the rock art tradition that was in its prime during the millennium prior to, and the first centuries after, the birth of Christ. All of the boats have double prows, a trait that is known from boat images dated to the Bronze Age. The shape of the hull and stems in the Kårstad boats, however, suggest that they were made in the Early Iron Age (Mandt 1973). Four of the boats, which have extended, almost flat hulls, are comparable to the outline of a boat that was sacrificially buried in a moor in the mid-300s BC in Hjortspring, Southern Jylland, Denmark (Solberg 2000). The other boat images at Kårstad have strongly curved hulls and split or V-shaped stem tips and resemble the boat image that was carved into a memorial stone from Austrheim in Gloppen that was raised over a small mound dated to 400 AD (Skjelsvik and Straume 1957).

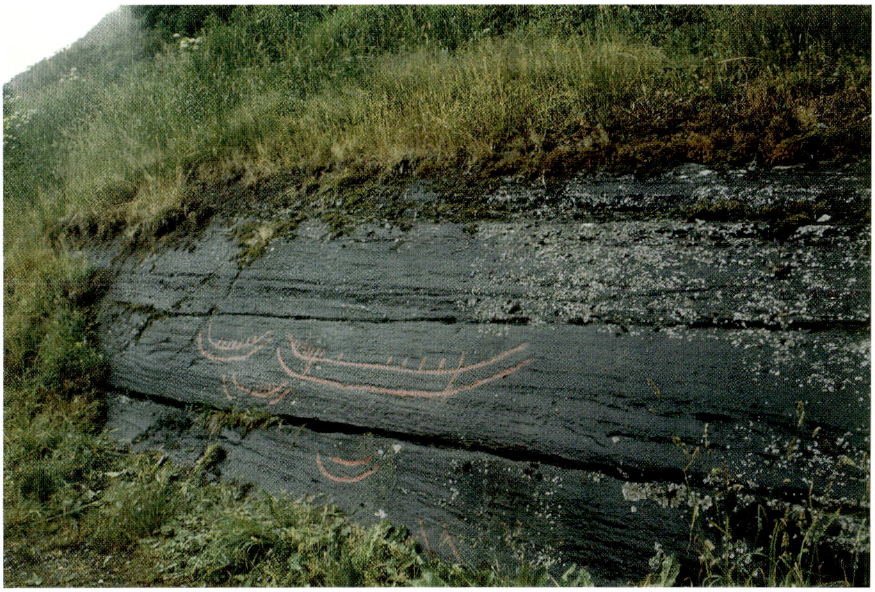

FIGURE 138. At Hennebygda in Gloppen, Nordfjord, two panels with boat figures were found with a similar shape to the outline of a boat found in the Hjortspring moor in Southern Jylland. As well as the boat, weapons and tools were found that date from the 300s AD. The objects are interpreted as votive offerings deposited in a sacred site in homage to the god of war after a victory. The boat from Hjortspring is considered the oldest preserved vessel in the Nordic countries. The shape differs from the images of the Bronze Age boats in that the stems are not tall and curved, but instead low and flattened.
GM

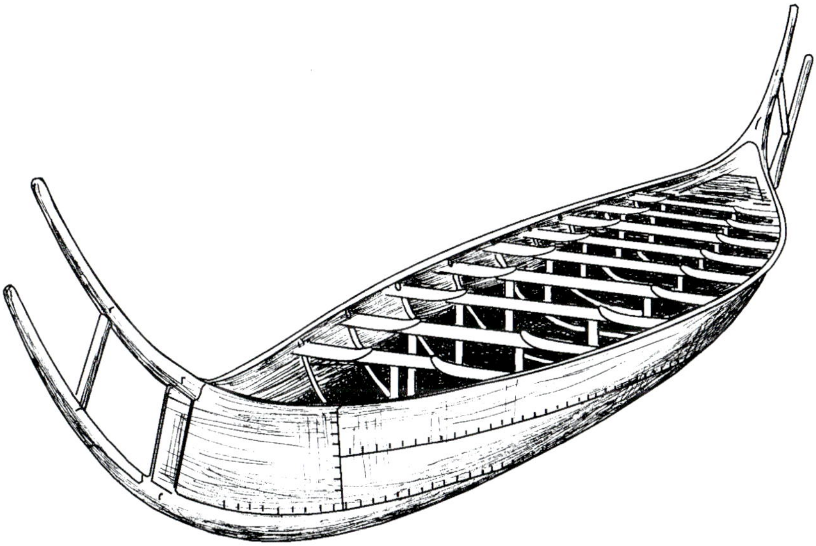

FIGURE 139. Reconstruction of the ship from Hjortspring in Southern Jutland, Denmark, sacrificially buried in a moor during the mid-300s BC. This is the oldest ship that is preserved in Northern Europe. It is 19 metres long and two metres wide with a hull made of broad strakes that are sewn together. It has no regular keel and was not equipped with sails, but was paddled by a crew of 22–24 men. Both the gunwale and bottom planks are sticking out from the hull in much the same manner as seen on rock carving boats of the Kårstad type. (Drawing after Hygen and Bengtsson 1999).
EH

A little further west in the fjord, at Hennebygda in Gloppen, two rock art panels with boat images similar to the four oldest Kårstad boats occur (Mandt 1991). A similar boat type is also depicted at a grave slab from Smiss on the island of Öland in Sweden dated 250–300 AD (Nylén 1978), and a comparable rock art boat is even found on an island in the Sunnmøre archipelago – this one with split stem tips such as the younger Kårstad boats (Mandt 1991). It would therefore seem that a certain rock art custom with roots in the Bronze Age existed during the Early Iron Age – in the period between 200–300 BC and 400 AD – in the communities around the inner parts of the fjord system in

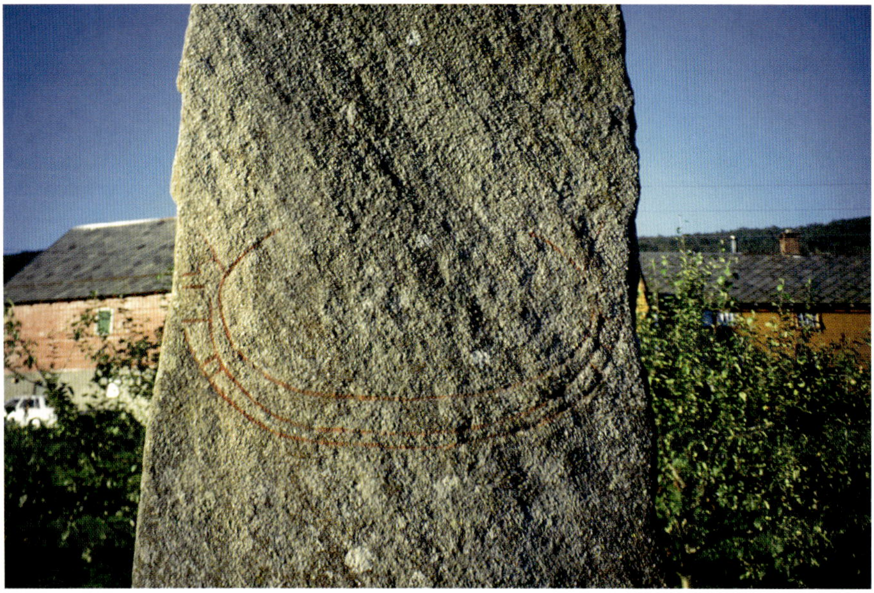

FIGURE 140. On a menhir raised on a small mound at Sandane in Gloppen, an image of a boat is depicted with a curved hull and a cleft stem. The boat figure must have been made after the menhir was put in place, and since the mound has been dated to 400 AD, both the image itself – and by extension, the other similar boat images at Kårstad – are from this same period.
GM

Nordfjord (Mandt 1991, 2005). Rock art from the Stone Age and Early Bronze Age is practically non-existent in the inner fjord districts, while several panels of various sizes from the older periods occur along the outer coast of Nordfjord and further south. There may be many reasons why older and younger rock art is found in different geographic areas, and here only one possible explanation will be suggested, namely the differences in settlement patterns and exploitation of resources. The concentration of more recent rock art deep inside in the Nordfjord basin may suggest that the inner fjord areas were exploited more intensively during the Early Iron Age than in earlier periods of history.

Runes and a swastika from the Iron Age

The runes in the Kårstad inscriptions belong to the oldest known runic alphabet, known as the *Futhark* – which takes its name from the first six of the 24 characters in the sequence of symbols. The *Futhark* was in use in Scandinavia from about 200 to 600 AD (Høst 1976). In order to decipher and date runic inscriptions, researchers rely on the shape of the runic characters, their placement in relation to one another and an analysis of Proto-Norse, which is the language form of *Futhark*. The longest Kårstad inscription is found just below the swastika and cuts across the prow of one of the oldest boat images (Mandt 1973). Read from right to left, it reads "*ek aljamarkiR*". The first scholar of runes who studied the find was Magnus Olsen, and he interpreted the inscription to mean "I, who am from a foreign land" or "I (am) the foreigner"(Olsen and Shetelig 1930). There appears to be general consensus both of the deciphering and interpretation – that this is probably the rune master presenting himself (Knirk 2000). The short row of runes at the lower section of the panel, which are placed between

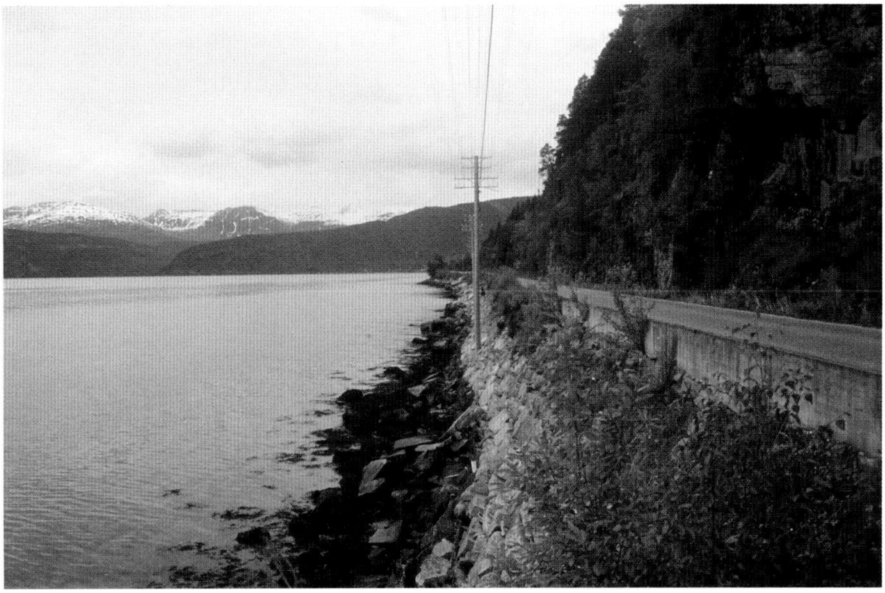

FIGURE 141. The rock carvings were found in the road fill along Innvikfjorden, but according to Haakon Shetelig they originally "were located on a sheer mountain wall resembling a picture board facing the fjord, where traffic passed close by daily".
GM

the split stems of the youngest of the boat images, is read right to left as "*baij (x) R*". Because the last rune but one (symbolised here with an x) is illegible, scholars on runes do not have a consensus on how the inscription is to be interpreted. One interpretation claims that the characters are the name of a tribe that lived in Bohemia up until 60 BC, and is translated as "I who come from the land of the Bohemians" (Olsen and Shetelig 1930). Others are of the opinion that the word means "warrior" (Krause 1966). Magnus Olsen assumed that the Kårstad runes were from a period between 200 and 400 AD, among other reasons because this period coincided with what he thought was the dating of the rock art. The most common opinion among scholars now seems to be that the inscriptions – based amongst other things on the shape of the runes – are older than the 400s AD (Knirk 2000).

The swastika at the top of the panel is a foreign element in Scandinavian rock art. In many parts of the world, however, the motif has been used as a religious symbol, magic sign and decorative element for thousands of years (Kostveit 2004). In Northern Europe the motif appears during the 200s and 300s AD, partly in the shape of fibulae (Dommasnes 2003), and partly as a decorative element on various objects. The special form of the swastika from Kårstad, with its double, extended angles, is known from gold bracteates dated to the end of the 400s or the early 500s BC (Nordén 1932). Many of them have runic inscriptions around the edge, and were probably worn as amulets.

Different ways of communicating messages

Within a period of 500–600 years, from about 200–300 BC to 400 AD, people made their marks on the mountain walls at Innvikfjorden. It appears that the

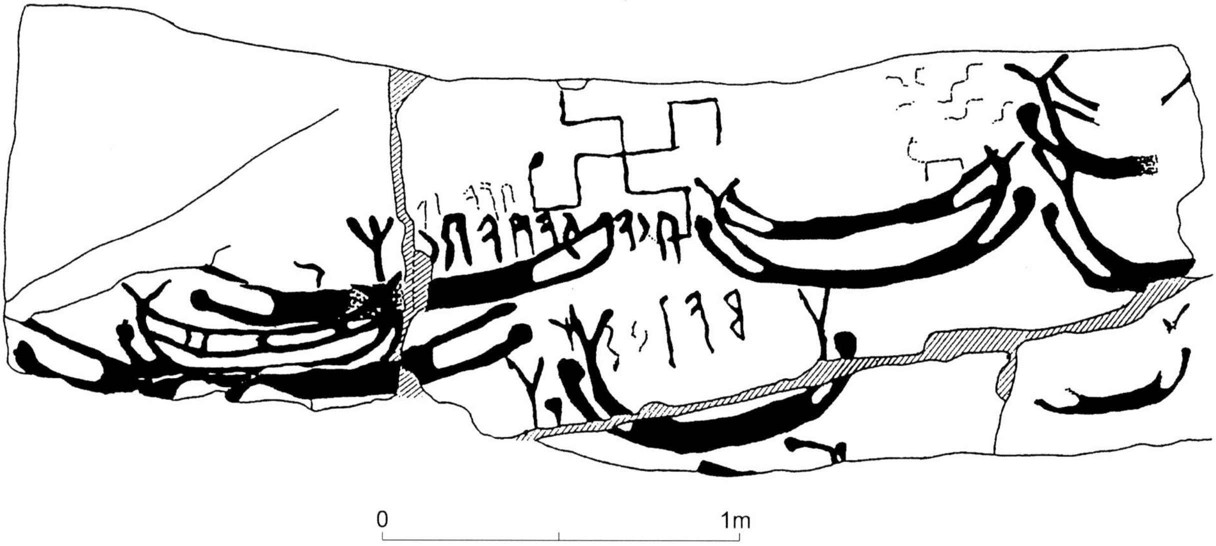

FIGURE 142. At the top of the preserved panel of images from Kårstad a large swastika has been pecked into the stone, with double broken arms in the cross. Directly below it is a dense cluster of boat images, some of which are partially superimposed. Above and between the boats, and partially pecked over them, are two rows of runes. Above the right side of the top row of runes are five vague lines that may be an imitation of the runes underneath. These have not been interpreted. In the upper right part of the panel are some faintly carved staircase-like patterns. GM

panels were engraved in three phases: two phases of boat images, marking the end of the thousand-year rock art tradition in the Bronze Age, and one final phase of *Futhark* runic inscriptions and the swastika dating from about 400 AD.

The images and the runes represent two different ways of communicating a message. Although both were designed to express and tangibly record thoughts and images, and although both probably shared religious and cultic meanings, they are essentially different. The world of rock art images is a symbolic system of references, wherein the individual motifs or groups of figures have a deeper, more complex meaning than what meets the eye. The rock images posses a narrative quality that was probably developed in conjunction with an oral tradition, thus passing on the content of a mythical universe (Fredell 2003).

As opposed to rock art, runic symbols are phonetic transcriptions, not unlike our own modern alphabet (Høst 1976). They are a graphic system in which each character denotes a sound – a phoneme – in a phonetic system. In this way the runes replicate words and sentences in what was the language of the day, while the rock art images impart a complex world of ideas through a diversity of portrayals. During the Early Iron Age the images were gradually transformed to mere passive illustrations, while the written sound-based language took over as a communicative medium (Fredell 2003).

What could be the reason explaining the coincidence of two disparate forms of communication, images and runes, occurring on the same rock wall in Kårstad? Is the content in the messages just as different as the way in which it is represented?

Boat images – bearers of meaning

Rock art images from the Bronze Age and Early Iron Age are found on stone surfaces and exposed rocks as well as on stone slabs and stones in graves. A multitude of different motifs are depicted – humans and animals, man-made objects and abstract symbols – and are often interpreted as part of religious and ritualistic practices, such as depictions of mythological tales, and associated with the ideology and world-view of the society at the time. One of the most common motifs is the boat in various shapes, a motif that also occurs on metal objects found in graves and sacrificial deposits from the Bronze Age. The boat symbol appears to permeate both the life and death of people in this era (Hauptman Wahlgren 2002).

Boats were undoubtedly indispensable as means of transport and contact between groups of people along the coast and inside fjords, not to mention the need to transport the glittering prestige metal of the day, bronze, which could not be extracted locally, but had to be brought in from the outside. In this way the boat motif can be understood as a symbol for journeys, for fellowship and contact. The Bronze Age rock art in Western Norway also lies along the most important communication arteries: the coastal waters and the long fjords. The rock images may have been markers denoting the borders between communities or signifying ownership or access rights to important resources. The boat images on the Kårstad mountain wall – placed in full view above the fjord leading into the hunting grounds and pastureland in the alpine areas around Jostedalsbreen (the Jostedal Glacier) – may have served as signposts, announcing an important territory.

The boat as a symbol of communication and transport may also carry with it a deeper meaning than that with which it is associated in the secular world. In many religions the notion existed that the deceased needed a boat in order to cross a river on their way into the realm of the dead. Another widespread notion was that the sun was pulled across the sky by a boat (Kaul 1998). Seen in this context, the boat may have been a symbol for passing time, for the seasons and cycles of nature, and for notions linked with life, death and rebirth – the very order of the world. Since boats are among the very few rock art images that lived on into the Early Iron Age, it is tempting to think that the boat figures from the end phase in rock art tradition carry with them the core of what was the complex world-view of the Bronze Age.

Runes for magical or practical purposes?

Inscriptions made with the oldest runes appear on personal property – for example on jewellery, knives, bone combs and amulets – on stones that are often from gravesites, and in some cases on stone walls, such as in Kårstad (Høst 1976). Many linguists believe that the *Futhark* is a direct or indirect development of the classical alphabet, while others claim that it is a uniquely

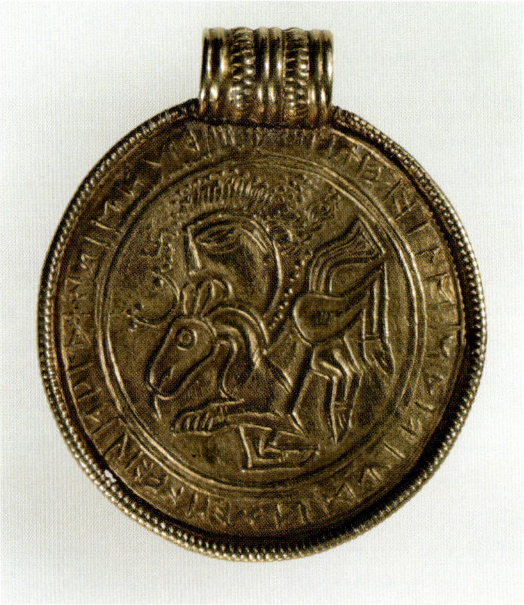

FIGURE 143. In 1879 the grave of a rich woman was found in Ytre Ågedal, Vest-Agder, the contents of which included two bracteates, one of them with a swastika and a runic inscription. The tomb, an incineration grave, is dated to about 500 AD. The runic bracteate has a mounted setting with a pearl ring around the edge, and measures 29.4 mm in diameter. The image on the front side is the depiction of a human head – probably a male – shown in profile, as well as an animal that probably depicts a horse. The swastika is placed in front of the man's forehead. The runes run in a circle inside the pearl ring, so that they encircle the entire centre area containing the pictorial motif. There has been much debate concerning the interpretation of the more than 40 runes on the Ågedal bracteate. The most recent interpretation suggests that the runic text repeats some of the verses of a mythical poem about a cremation describing how the deceased chieftain arrived in the realm of the dead after a successful journey.
SS/BM

Scandinavian, Proto-Norse alphabet that was created during a short time before it was taken into use (Grønvik 1996).

In old Germanic dialects, the term rune signifies "secret, mystery, esoteric religious knowledge", and it was not until later that the term was used to denote the characters themselves (Høst 1976). It is likely that runes, in the same way as other old types of writing and alphabets, were originally sacred symbols rather than letters, and were associated with certain religious and mythological notions. Writing in general was regarded as religious knowledge created by divine powers and imparted through religious tradition to the initiated. In Norse mythology, knowledge of runes was considered as knowledge associated with the gods, especially the god of sorcery, Odin.

Runes appear to have spread quickly through Scandinavia. Since the knowledge of runes was able to prevail throughout several hundred years, there must have been a strong tradition for teaching them to subsequent generations. The runes were a neutral system of writing that could be used for various purposes. Many of the older runic inscriptions that refer, among other things, to power relations and inheritance rights, suggest that the art of writing was a privilege reserved for the elite in society (Grønvik 1996). A large number of the inscriptions written with the older runes are interpreted as religious documents. They reflect rites and formulas associated with funeral processions and cults and record thoughts and notions that the people of the era held concerning the dead and their relationship to the living. Several inscriptions have a purely secular content, and some runes may have been perceived as magical signs for the purpose of providing protection or/and happiness, but that also could disarm evil spirits. Runic inscriptions on objects, for example on gold bracteates, may have been magic formulas. The swastika is also used as a religious symbol, magical sign and ornament in many parts of the world.

A meeting place for different traditions

Runes and rock art images appear to differ not only in visual, formal expression, but also in content as well as the entire underlying world of concepts. The runes very likely represent a new, different world of ideas, values and attitudes towards life and death than that which was expressed in the rock art traditions stemming from the world-view of the Bronze Age. One example of this difference is the abundance of runic inscriptions that begin with the pronoun "ek" (= "I"), often followed by a name or nickname that characterizes the rune master. This emphasis on the individual subject represents a clear departure from the way rock art depicted the human being – as an anonymous symbol of the human presence, where there was frequently no indication of gender (Hedengran 1991).

While these two cultural traditions are brought together at Kårstad, it is tempting to wonder whether this encounter was a peaceful one, or if the meeting represented a power struggle at the time or later on. For example, perhaps the runes superimposed over the stems of one of the boat figures are meant to demonstrate graphically that the thousand-year-old ideology is dead and powerless. The swastika, which is nearly contemporary to the runes in time and content, can perhaps also be understood in this perspective. On the Kårstad panel, the large swastika looms over both the boat images and the runes. It appears to be intentionally placed above the other figures as a symbolic accreditation of a new ideological order.

Continuity or recycling?

Was there a new group of people who brought with them new beliefs and symbols to the Western Norwegian fjord settlements, or was it the permanent dwellers who embraced new knowledge and ideas? Was the Kårstad mountain wall used as a holy place or border marking continuously over a period of five to six hundred years, or was there an interval between the three phases of usage, perhaps not limited to one, but several phases? Perhaps the people who created the boat images belonged to the same group, even though the boats they depicted changed in appearance over time. But if the people who knew of the runes came from a distance and had other beliefs and customs than those who lived there already, the question is why they felt the need to mark the mountainsides where they found traces of the distant past. In order to find answers, our attention should be turned away from Innvikfjorden to the surrounding communities, to seek out other indications of human activity in the period during which the Kårstad mountain was used for cult purposes.

Tradition and change

In the vicinity of Kårstad, in the communities along Innvikfjorden, there are few visible traces of settlement dating from the time the Kleivane mountain wall was in use (Shetelig 1932; Fett 1960, 1961). But some kilometres further west, at Gloppenfjord, which is an arm of Nordfjorden, archaeological remains have been

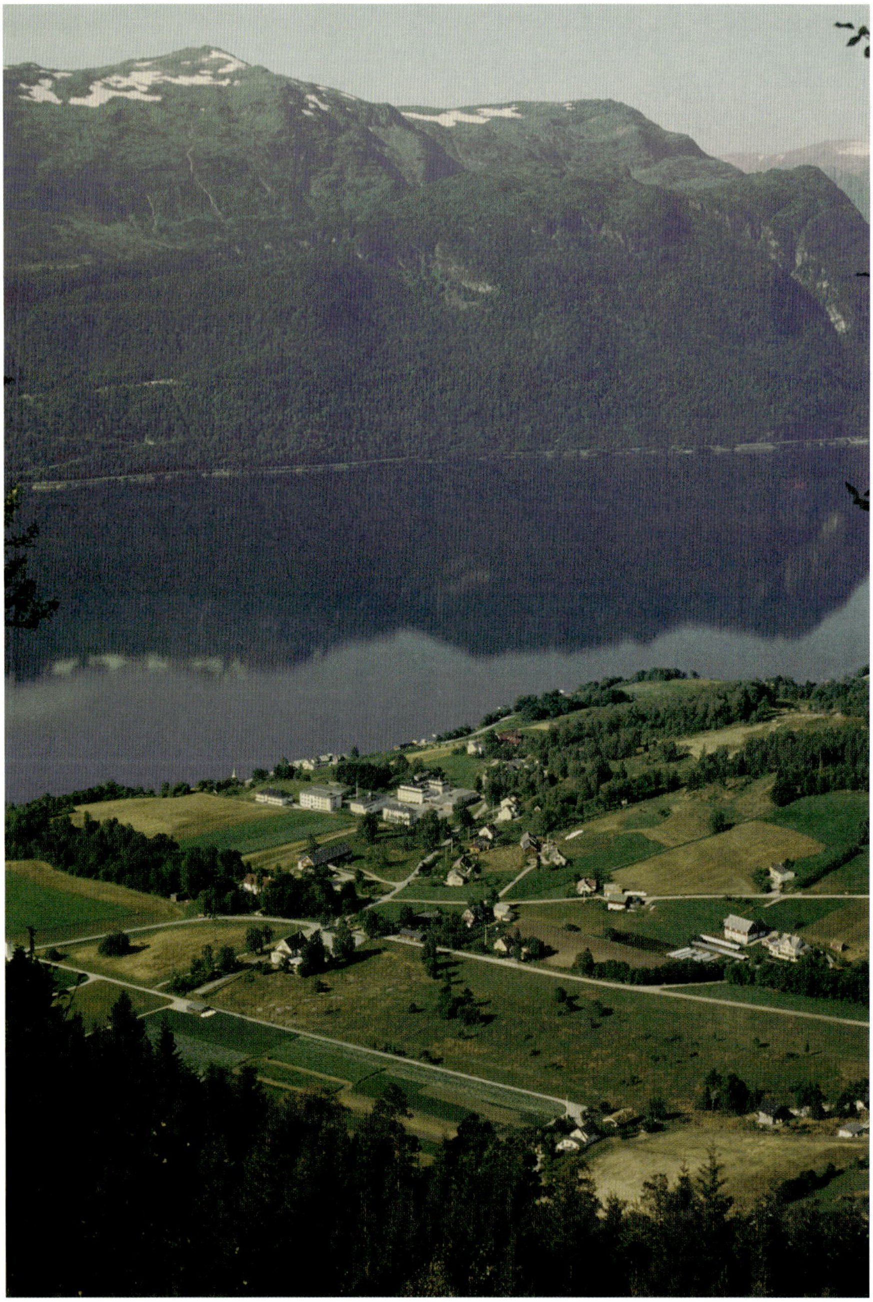

FIGURE 144. The Vereide terrace is a wide, slightly sloping surface on the northern side of Gloppenfjord, about 70 metres above sea level. Fertile farmland is abundant here, and the many monuments from the past found on the terrace bear witness of intensive agriculture over many centuries.

TH

uncovered that may shed light on the societal relations and living conditions in the centuries prior to and following the advent of the Christian era. On the eastern side of the fjord, on a wide sandy terrace at Vereide, Sandane, a large gravesite from this period was investigated in the 1990s, resulting in a number of finds (Dommasnes 1997, 2001). More than 200 funerary monuments were recorded, and in this material two different customs for burying the dead were revealed, one coming after the other.

The oldest graves at Vereide are dated from the last millennium before the birth of Christ, until 200 AD. These are narrow, low mounds concentrated in the gravesite towards the rear of the terrace at the foot of the mountain. The only remains of the dead are a few bone fragments, and the sparse items in the tombs consist of a little iron slag and burnt clay (Dommasnes 2001). Around 200 AD a new type of grave came into use, characterised by tall mounds situated at the edge of the terrace with a wide panorama out over the settlement and fjord. The abundant items that were buried with the dead were for personal use, often things that originally came from other parts of Scandinavia.

The two burial customs on the Vereide terrace reveal clear differences in terms of both symbolic expression and religious content. The oldest tradition is collective in nature, based on group fellowship and local traditions with roots in the Bronze Age. The younger tradition, which suddenly appears without any local prototype, emphasizes the individual, power and ownership and bears witness to a widespread contact network (*ibid.*). These essentially different ways of burying the dead suggest that great changes had occurred in both social structure and religion in the Nordfjord communities during the centuries before and after the beginning of the Christian era. By comparing the burial finds from the Vereide terrace with images and inscriptions on the Kårstad panel, along with other archaeological remains from a wider peripheral area, the outlines of a society in change emerge.

Vereide and Kårstad – two sides of the same coin?

The oldest boat figures at Kårstad and the two rock art panels in Hennebygda coincide in time with the early use of the Vereide terrace. The remnants of the dwelling places from this phase are not found in the immediate vicinity of Vereide, but traces of cultivation and crop fields have been registered (*ibid.*). Physical evidence of permanent farm settlements in the millennium before the birth of Christ has also been sparse in other parts of Nordfjord. However, along the coast and in the mountainous areas there are traces of human activity during this period. The finds have been interpreted as evidence of an itinerant living pattern based on a mixed economy of grazing and nomadic agriculture, in addition to the hunting of game and marine animals and fishing (Dommasnes 2001; Solberg 2000). One discovery that bears witness to contacts outside the local area is a collection of women's jewellery that originates in Southern Scandinavia. They were deposited as votive offerings around 500 BC in Skjerdal

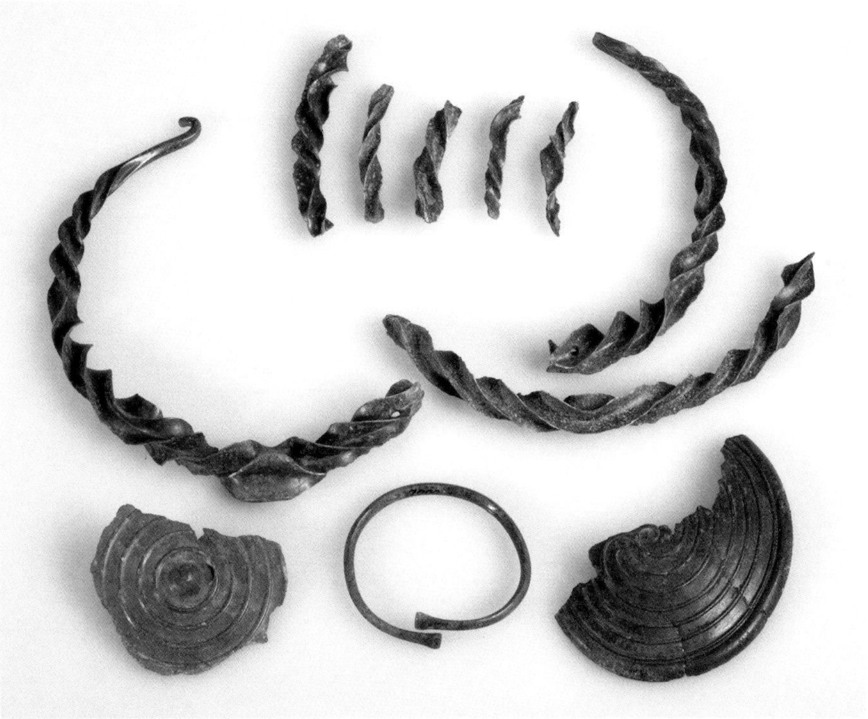

FIGURE 145. Throughout the entire Bronze Age it was the custom to offer precious objects of bronze to higher powers, often in inaccessible and remote places. In the earliest part of the period mainly weapons were offered, but in the later Bronze Age it became increasingly common to sacrifice women's jewellery. The offerings from Skjerdal found at the outer edge of Hyenfjord included two necklaces of a type called Wendelrings, one of them only fragments, a piece of a fibula, a fragment of a belt plate and a small bracelet. The Wendelrings were particularly common towards the end of the Bronze Age, with two or more frequently found together and often interpreted as attributes of a female divinity. The items were found in 1918, buried 30–40 cm deep in a moraine ridge, and were probably originally packed in cloth or leather.

at the mouth of Hyenfjorden, a parallel fjord arm to Gloppenfjord (de Lange 1920; Magnus 1978).

From this perspective, the gravesites at Vereide can be interpreted as sacred grounds for a wide area in Nordfjord. The burial custom is collective in nature, where the essential purpose does not appear to be burial of individuals, but rather the consolidation of an entire society through shared ceremonies (Dommasnes 2001). The large rock art sites from the Bronze Age are often interpreted in the same way: as collective sacred places and rallying grounds for groups of people living throughout the area. Several features of this burial custom can be seen as symbols of fertility and the transition between life and death. The features include traces of hearth and flagstones arranged in rings and wheel-like patterns – well-known motifs from Bronze Age rock art. All of this indicates that the oldest burial custom at Vereide was part of a religious tradition with roots in the Bronze Age world of ideas, in which concepts of the cycle of life – death – rebirth are central.

Old customs and new ideas

At about the same time that the new burial customs became commonplace at Vereide, the youngest of the boat images were engraved on the Kårstad wall, between 200–300 AD. Both the boat images and the Vereide graves from this time combine features from the older and the younger traditions (*ibid*). It is tempting to interpret this as gradual acceptance and adoption of new ideas and customs in the Nordfjord settlements. The rituals from ancient times may have incorporated elements from the new beliefs, and the visual symbols from the essentially different traditions gradually merged into one.

After 400 BC the new grave customs were established at the Vereide terrace (*ibid.*), and runic inscriptions and the swastika symbol were added to the Kårstad panel. The symbolic expression that emerged in the younger grave custom suggests that it was grounded in a different social and religious world of ideas than that of the older tradition. The burial rituals appear to be adapted to a society with social stratification based on individual power and status. The large graves are very visibly located in places that would later become part of the fields of an established farm, and this is perhaps a first sign of individual property rights (*ibid.*). Through the burial items, the individual is given precedence – they represent the personal items, necessities and status that the deceased is to take into a material existence in the afterlife.

The individual is also rendered visible in the runic inscriptions from Kårstad. The rune master writes about himself – *ek* – and tells where he comes from. In the word *aljamark(i)R*, the prefix *alja-* signifies "foreigner" or "of foreign origin". The second segment, *mark(i)R*, may mean "country" or "borderland". Other runic inscriptions from the 400s AD also refer to a "foreigner" who came from another "land" or "forest" (*ibid.*).

Both the younger burial tradition at Vereide and the runes from Kårstad suggest that people with new customs and distant contact networks came to the Nordfjord settlements in the first centuries after the birth of Christ. One can only speculate as to their origins. Perhaps the runic segment "*mark(i)R*" refers to a forested area east of the long mountain range. People may have migrated from here in search of new hunting grounds and fertile pastureland in the Western Norwegian mountains and fishing grounds along the fjord and coast. The newcomers and the original population most likely lived side by side over a period lasting some two centuries, but after 400 AD there are no longer traces of rock art or the earlier collective burial tradition.

Why only Kårstad?

In the course of the first century AD, changes appear to have occurred in terms of society and the way of living in the Nordfjord settlements. These are reflected in the grave material found on the Vereide terrace, where the practice of burying the dead underwent great changes in terms of both procedure and symbolic meaning. The interpretation of the archaeological remains at Vereide supports the hypothesis that the mountain wall at Kårstad served as a sacred place during three different phases, where changes in form and content also can be demonstrated.

It still remains an open question why rock art images and runes – each so different in aspect and content from the other, and both practically never occurring together – meet exactly at Kårstad. Why was this place so important that the rune master found it necessary to engrave his runes on precisely the same rock surface where others before him had carved the archetypical rock art symbols of the Bronze Age – the ambiguous boat motif? Apparently the cliff wall at Kårstad held a particular significance not only for the indigenous inhabitants but even for the succeeding population in the region – much in the same way as images of the Southern Tradition in Trøndelag occasionally were carved into panels with the more ancient rock art of the Northern Tradition.

In the case of Kårstad, if the images and the runes on the panel actually represent an encounter between two cultural traditions in the Early Iron Age, then why are there so few examples elsewhere of this kind of contact?

Perhaps a partial explanation may be found in the topographical location of Kårstad. High and open above the fjord strait, the engraved wall was situated at the gateway to the rich hunting and grazing lands surrounding the large glacier. This must have been an important resource area for the people who lived in Nordfjord during the millennium preceding the birth of Christ – a population that undoubtedly led a seasonally nomadic existence as they moved from place to place to exploit the resources. The mountain areas must have been equally important for the people who settled along the fjord at the beginning of the Christian era. Their graves reflect a concept of society based on power and status, with considerable importance given to ownership and rights to resources. Therefore they had reasons that were just as strong as those of the earlier population to protect their assets in the inner regions and to mark them with their own symbols.

Whether these "postings" were accepted peacefully, we do not know. Throughout history there are countless examples of religious fanaticism or political demonstrations of power that have led to the destruction of old cultural monuments by adherents of a new faith. In this perspective, the rows of runes that partially cover the older boat images may have been the newcomers' way of claiming their own sovereignty. On the other hand, there is much to suggest that the original population and the newcomers, through several centuries of co-existence, adopted one another's customs and incorporated them into their own world-view. Perhaps the boat images – as symbols of travel, contact and fellowship – were by no means a radical break with older beliefs and customs and were accepted by the people from the forests, who customarily buried items from distant places together with their own dead.

Leirvåg in Askvoll – Boat Images Reflecting the Spirit of the Time

In the summer of 1823, Jacob Neumann, the newly ordained Bishop of Bergen Diocese, embarked on his first visitation to the Sogn og Sunnfjord rectory in the northern part of his office that included Hordaland and Sogn og Fjordane counties. The bishop was born and raised in Eastern Norway and was unimpressed by the craggy, barren landscape along the Western Norwegian coast. However, as he wrote in his journal: "The historical monuments must be said to provide it (the coast) an Interest that it lacks from Nature" (Neumann 1834). With Snorre Sturlason's Saga of the Kings as a travel guide, he followed in the footsteps of the many heroes of the sagas who had accomplished great feats in these areas. One saga relates the account of a battle in Outer Sunnfjord between "two of Antiquity's greatest Warriors" (*ibid.*), both of whom perished in the battle. According to the Saga one of them, Atle Jarl, was buried on the island that bears his name – Atløy. It was here that the bishop heard about a highly unusual monument: carved images of ships had been seen on some rock faces along the shore at the Leirvåg Farm.

A "curious" ancient monument

During a visit to Bohuslän on the western coast of Sweden a few years before his journey to Sunnfjord, the Bishop had already seen rock art depicting boats (Brunius 1868). In his journal he nevertheless describes the Leirvåg carvings as "more curious than I had imagined" (Neumann 1824).

The rock art is located at the southern tip of Atløy, which looms conspicuously above the shipping channel just west of the community and municipal centre of Askvoll. The southern and southeastern portion of the island contains flat farmland and handsome farmhouses, and the church of Vilnes from the 1600s as well as the trading centre and waystation at Sauesundet bear witness to longstanding settlement and maritime traffic. Along a sandy belt south of the fields belonging to the Leirvåg farm, there are some rugged patches of land with scraggy vegetation, where smooth shoreline rocks are interspersed between heather-covered knolls and marshy hollows. In this shoreline terrain, five or six metres above the waterline (Bakka 1973), and with an open view out across the shipping channel, there are some fifty rock art images, along with several small grave mounds in immediate proximity to the rock art panels (Mandt 1975; Wrigglesworth 2000, 2002).

The images are distributed over four separate rock surfaces. Deep inside a

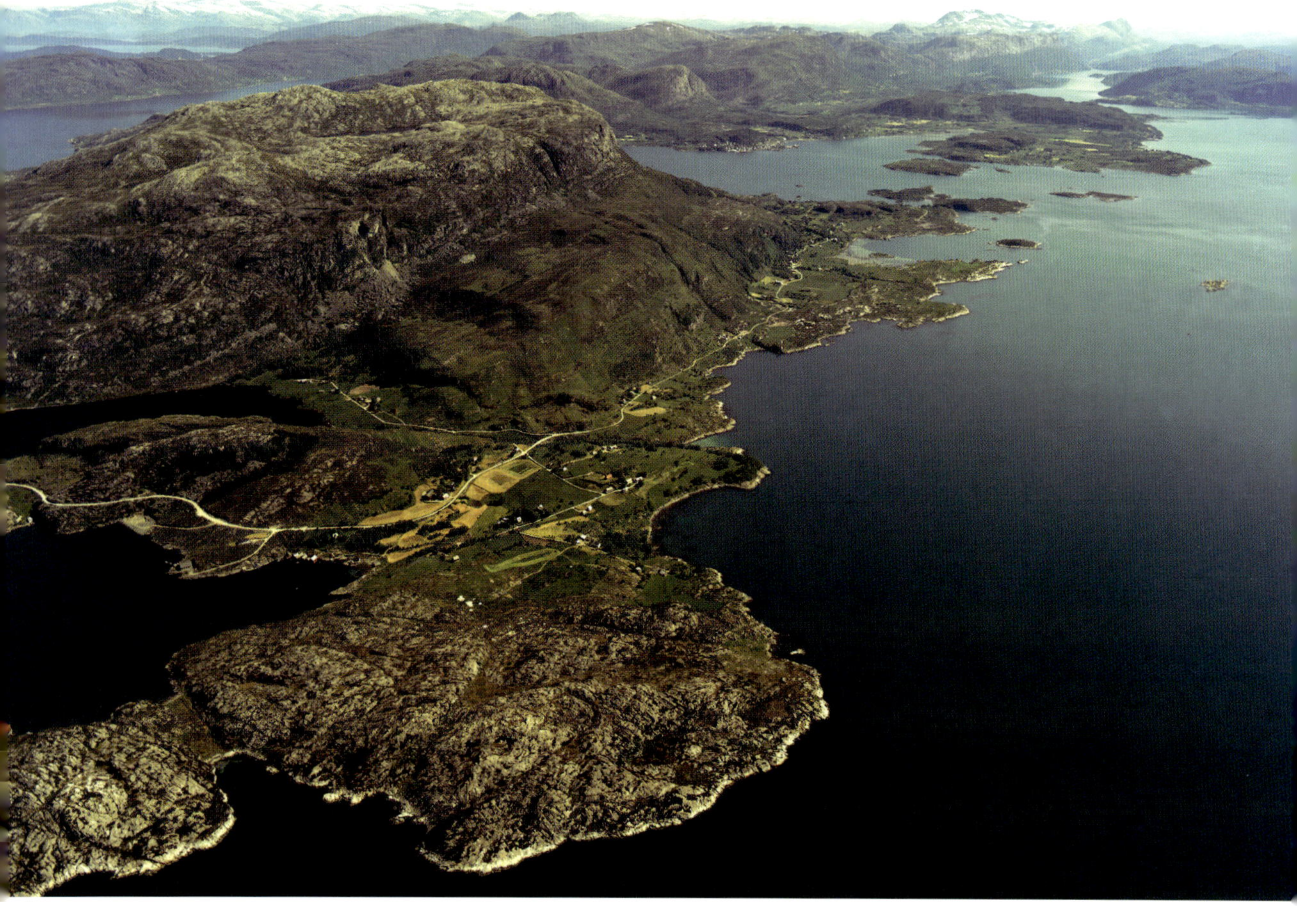

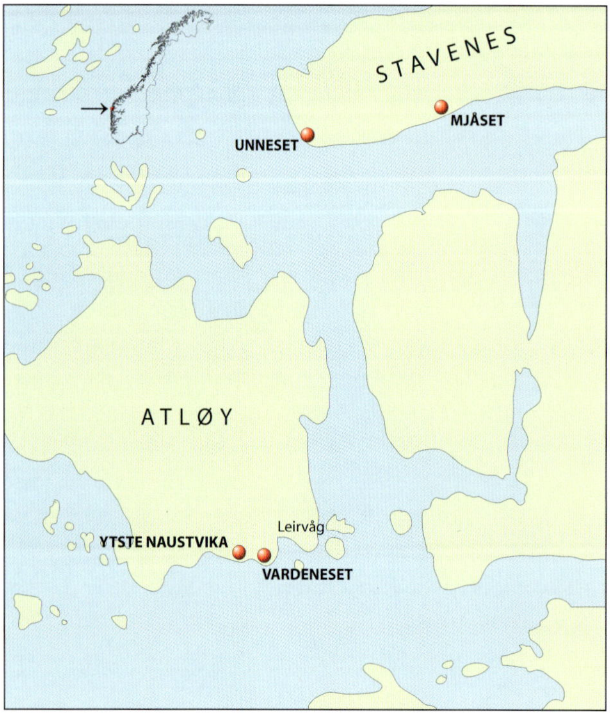

FIGURES 146–147. Nearly half of the inhabitants of Askvoll municipality in Sogn og Fjordane live on islands – more than 800 in all. The largest and most densely populated island is Atløy, located due west from the municipal centre at Askvoll. The island is shaped like a gigantic hat towering more than 636 metres tall, and people mainly live along the shoreline, where the land is cultivatable. The rock carvings at Leirvåg are found on the long promontory that juts out into Sauesundet, slightly above the centre of the photo.

MAP AI, ILLUSTRATION © FJELLANGER WIDERØE FOTO AS

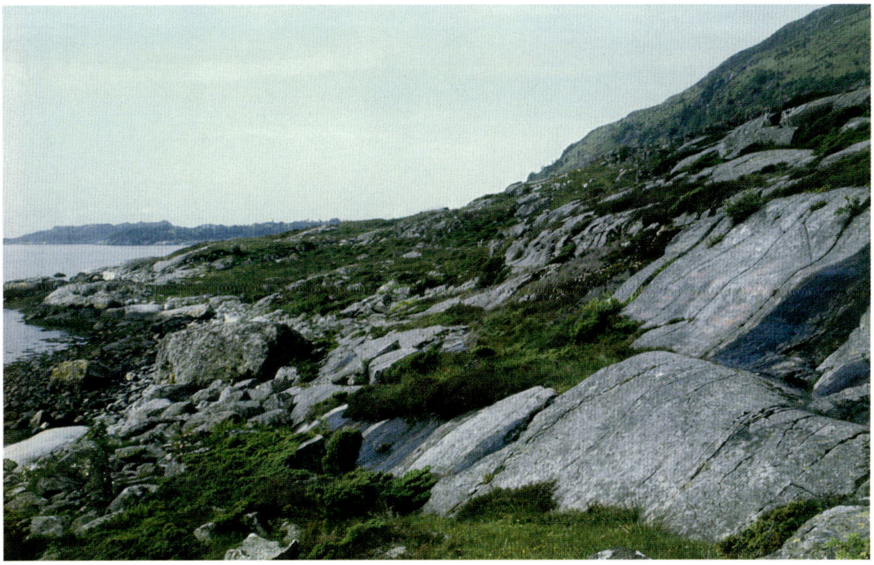

FIGURE 148. Proximity to the sea seems to have been an important factor in the choice of location for rock carvings in the Bronze Age. In many parts of the country it is necessary to imagine a higher sea level in order to properly see the relationship between the sea and the images on the stone outcrops. Along the West Norwegian coast, however, where the relationship between sea and land has changed very little since the Bronze Age, rock art sites are frequently found as far down as the waterline, such as here in Ytste Naustvikja at Leirvåg.
GM

sheltered bay, Ytste Naustvikja, there are figures on two steep rock surfaces lying about 150 metres apart. A few hundred metres further west there are images at several points along the sheer and smooth promontory of Vardeneset. Many are engraved on its outer edge, where the sea spray washes ashore and scours the rocks clean of moss and lichens, while another group of images is located on a broad mountain wall that juts vertically up from the shore. Just next to one of the groups of images is a large natural pothole filled with water – a geological phenomenon that may have been a factor in the location of the images.

Most of the figures depict boats with tall, steeply or softly curved prows, many with long "spears" extending from the stern keel. Vertical lines connect the keel and the gunwale, probably representing ribs. Several of the boat images are fitted with a row of parallel lines extending upwards from the gunwale – usually called crew lines and interpreted as the boat's crew. In addition to the boats, there are a couple of small, ring-shaped images and some line figures that probably represent humans. Some of the images have been carved with deeply cut lines and are very distinct, while others are so heavily weathered that they are only possible to make out when slanting light creates a relief effect in the grooves.

The sagas as a travel guide

At the beginning of the 1800s, knowledge about rock art in Scandinavia was scant, and the images at Atløy were among the very first to be discovered in Norway. Most of the rock art known to exist at that time was found in Sweden, where the first panels were discovered in the early 1600s (Suhm 1784; Ohlmarks 1963). One of the earliest known Swedish localities is situated near a mediaeval church, and antiquarians found no other explanation than that the

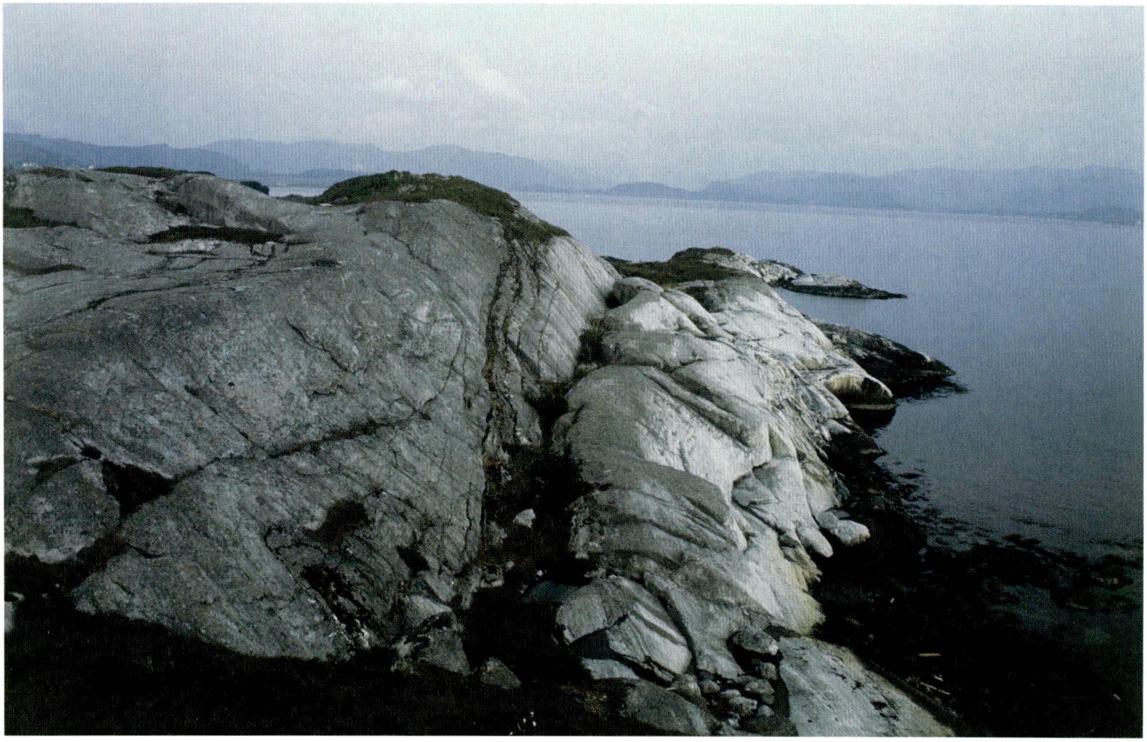

stonemasons must have carved the images as a mere pastime – what we would probably refer to as graffiti today (Mandt 1991, Mandt 2009). But throughout the 1700s increasingly more panels were discovered, and the scholars of the day – "*fornälskare*" [lovers of antiquity], as they preferred to call themselves – considered this to be much too banal an explanation (Tham 1794). Instead they interpreted the rock art images as depictions of historic events from the time before the advent of writing (Sjöborg 1822, 1830).

Around 1800 a new interpretation was proposed, focusing particularly on the boat images, which are one of the most common motifs in Scandinavian rock art. This was a time when nationalism was on the rise in the Nordic countries, supported by the major political upheavals caused by the Napoleonic wars. The nationalistic movement resulted, among other things, in a growing demand for a local identity rooted in historical events (Baudou 2004). In order to explain the ancient monuments, the antiquarians began to look to the Norse Sagas and their tales of a glorious Nordic past. They found that the many descriptions of Viking raids, plundering and bold exploits represented a clue to the interpretation of the rock art boats. The clusters of boat images were explained as fleets of Viking ships, either in battle or on raids, and the people and animals depicted together with the boat images were seen as loot plundered by the Vikings.

In Norway the antiquarians embraced these interpretations enthusiastically. In 1814, in the wake of the Napoleonic wars, the 400–year-long union between Denmark and Norway came to an end, and with their own constitution,

FIGURE 149. The rock carvings at Vardeneset are spread over the entire seaward side of the promontory, from the southernmost point where some human-like figures are found and in across the plateau and along the sides of the promontory where there are several images of boats. A large concentration of boats have also been pecked into the sheer mountain wall at the innermost part of the promontory, and at the summit, where the mountain flattens out, there is a group of cup marks.
GM

Norway gained a more independent position in union with Sweden. For the generation who had been part of this process it was particularly important to reinforce the new sovereign identity of the young nation by linking the present day with the glory of the past – a period in Nordic prehistory when Norsemen, according to the Sagas, were unrivalled on the sea and won fame and power far and wide through their exploits (Mandt 1991; Mandt 2009).

Building a nation

In the 1820s Bishop Neumann belonged to a group of officials and prominent businessmen from Bergen with a common interest in history and ancient cultural monuments. One of the most important members of this circle was Wilhelm Frimann Koren Christie, the former President of Parliament and later Customs Inspector in Bergen. Both Christie and Neumann had played an important role in the national political events of 1814. As part of the construction of Norway as a nation, Neumann worked to enlist the interest of the pastors of his foundation in antiquities and local rural history. In 1825 Christie took the initiative to found Bergens Museum, which was a unique institution in Norway at that time (Haaland 1996). Both Christie and Neumann travelled far and wide on official business in the region, where they collected information on legends, folk traditions and cultural monuments from the recent and distant past. It was as a result of this activity that the rock art at Atløy was discovered.

This led to the rock art images becoming tangible evidence of the grand deeds of the nation's forefathers, and stood as a symbol of Norway's golden age. In keeping with the general mood of the time, Christie and Neumann argued that the boat images on the sheer and smooth rock surfaces at Atløy represented Viking ships (Christie 1837). Based on narratives in the Sagas, they maintained that Viking warriors had depicted their fleet as a lasting and powerful monument to commemorate their heroic chieftain, Atle Jarl, who had been killed during the battle fought in these waters.

From Viking ships to cult vessels

Throughout the 1800s many new rock art images were discovered in all of the Scandinavian countries, and the debate concerning their age and meaning involved a large number of scholars. It was not until the middle of the century that it was determined that the boat images, as well as the other motifs depicted on the same surfaces, must be from the Bronze Age, 1800–500 BC, a period when the cultivation of crops and the domestication of livestock had become important modes of living in many places in Scandinavia (Holmberg 1848). During the second half of the 1800s, the rock art images were usually explained as a means of depicting folk traditions, where everyday activities and festive occasions were documented (Brunius 1868). During the last decades of the century, however, some scholars began to claim that the rock art had a religious

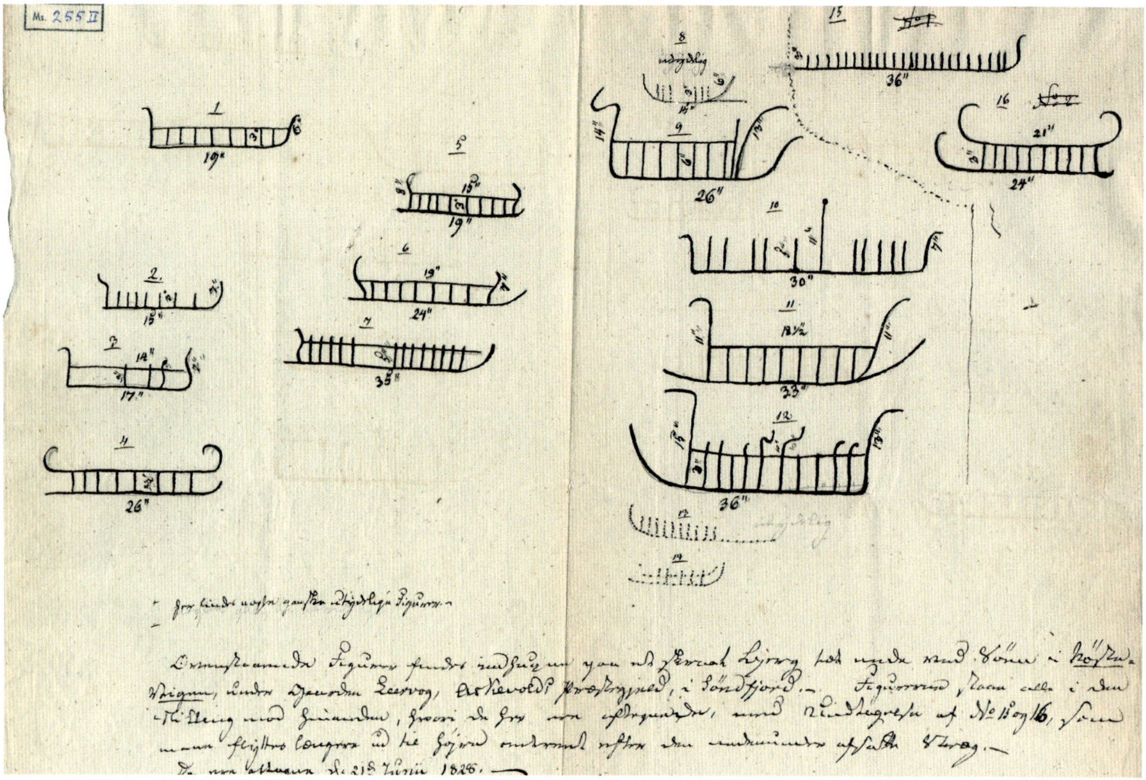

FIGURE 150. "Some very indistinct Figures are found here. The Figures above are carved on a slanting Stone incline all the way down to the Sea at Nöste-Vigen, subsidiary of Leervog Farm, Askevold Parish, in Söndfjord. The Figures all stand in this Position facing one another, such as they are all drawn here, with the Exception of No. 15 and 16, which must be moved farther to the right following the inserted Line below. The [drawings] were made d. 21st of June 1828." This was Christie's description of his first encounter with the rock carvings at Leirvåg that Bishop Neumann had seen a few years earlier. The original drawings, reproduced here, show that Christie first drew the figures in pencil and later highlighted the outlines in India ink. The drawings are the first scientific documentation of a rock carving in Norway. Although they were drawn freehand, they provide a very accurate picture of the panel. The figures are numbered and placed correctly in relationship to one another. The size of each boat is indicated in the drawing: the length of the boat, height of the stems, etc. In some cases comments are given indicating that the figures are indistinct, and these are frequently drawn using broken lines. Further down on the page, Christie cited literature in which the rock carvings of boats are mentioned or illustrated. (UB Bergen MS 255.8)

significance (Müller 1897; Montelius 1900). This was a time of upheaval in the fields of art and science, as well as politics, philosophy and theology. In a political sense, the Scandinavian countries were in the crucible. Innovations in technology and the natural sciences fused together with the somewhat incompatible spiritual currents of the day. The objective, scientific ideal that marked the century was challenged by currents of thought that placed emphasis on imagination and intuition (Schelderup 1958). The neo-romantic poets sought inspiration in their experiences of nature and exotic mysticism, and undogmatic religiousness opened the way for new value systems (Nettum 1975).

These currents also affected the study of prehistory. *Ex Oriente Lux* – from

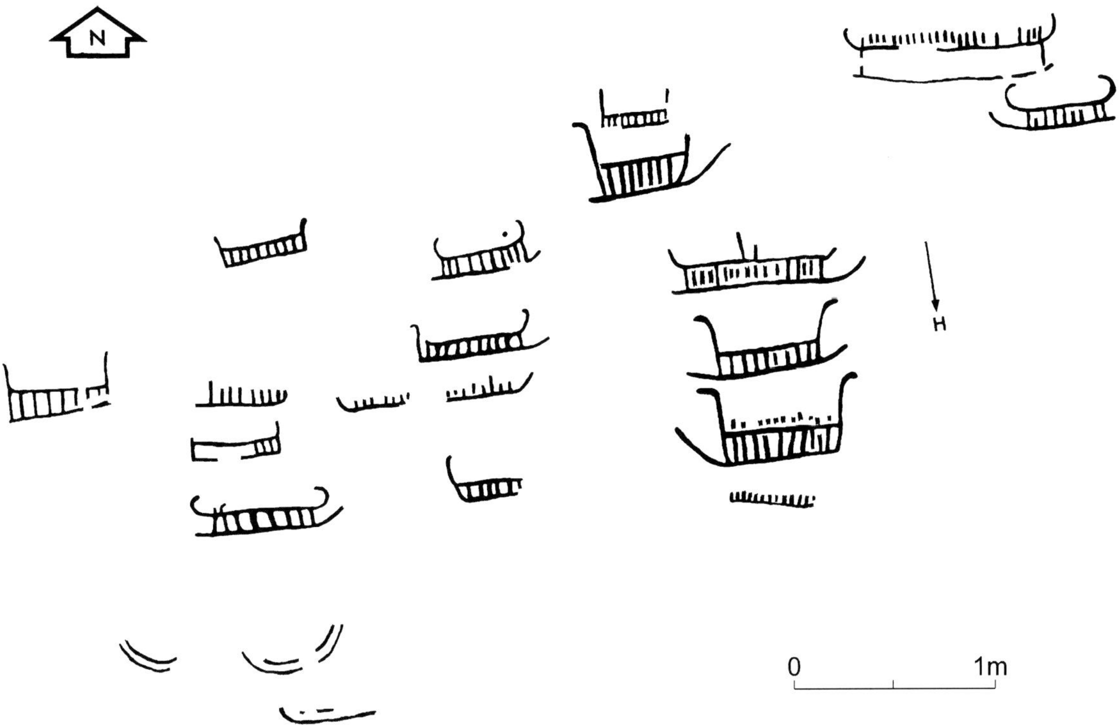

FIGURE 151. 150 years after Christie made the drawings of the figures found at Naustvikja in Leirvåg, they were re-documented. This time the panel was covered with transparent plastic foil and the carvings were outlined on the plastic using a black felt-tip pen. This results in a 1:1 reproduction of the images, which are then photographically reduced to a more manageable size. The method is called tracing, with reference to the original practice – from the early 1900s and before the advent of plastic – entailing the use of tracing paper. A comparison of Christie's freehand drawings with the modern tracing reveals a striking likeness between the two versions! GM

the Orient comes the light – became the motto of many scholars. Concepts of fertility and the eternal cycle of growth became the basis for interpreting prehistoric rock art within a religious/magical framework. The building blocks for this interpretation were found by researchers partly in the religions of the Orient and the Mediterranean countries, and partly in old myths and legends from different areas of Europe. Many rock art images depict scenes with a clearly narrative content. Boat images are often depicted together with humans and with circular or spiral-shaped figures that are interpreted as symbols for the sun. These scenes were explained as depictions of rituals or mythological tales and were intended to ensure fertility and increase harvests, and to provide both people and livestock with prosperity and happiness (Almgren 1927).

The mythical Drama of the Seasons was central in this interpretation. The myth associates the boat motif with a fertility deity known from both Norse mythology and the mythology of other regions. During spring, the God of Fertility came sailing in on a ship and wandered across the land awakening nature from its winter slumber. The coming of spring was celebrated with the ritualistic marriage of the gods. During the autumn, when the vegetation withers and dies, the god of fertility also dies. There are often notions that he is killed by a rival. The dead god is carried aboard his ship and taken to an island far in the west, and here he remains until he awakens the following spring, and the drama of the seasons is repeated. In this perspective, the scholars were able to redefine the countless boat images from the battleships of the Vikings to cult vessels for the fertility god.

The ecological perspective

After the middle of the 20th century, objections were raised against interpreting the rock art images based on a one-sided religious frame of reference. The field of archaeology at that time was influenced by new theoretical currents that can be seen in the light of the political, economic and spiritual attitudes of the time (Baudou 2004). The post-war years in the Western World bore the mark of revolutionary technological developments. Technical innovations in most areas of society made life easier and brought increased wealth to most people. At the same time, people became more aware of environmental problems, and ecology was established as a science. Scholars within a number of fields were convinced that it was possible to produce absolute knowledge and to find universal laws that could explain both natural phenomena and human behaviour (Trigger 1989).

In the field of prehistoric research, ecological adaptation became a watchword. The relationship between technology and the environment was seen as decisive for the development of society. The ability to renew oneself and to innovate was written off as a possible factor in cultural and social change. Human culture was seen as an eco-system – as the means by which the human being adapts to the environment. Studies of prehistoric societies were focused on the basis for existence, the subsistence models and patterns of adaptation, and the widespread view was that researchers lacked the prerequisites for being able to comprehend the concepts and world-views of the prehistoric human being. Based on this rationale, there was little room for studies of religion and cult.

From an adaptational perspective, the rock art images were interpreted as expressions designed to demonstrate power and to mark borders between resource areas or groups of people. The interpretation of the images as symbols for invoking fertility was still valid and acceptable, in the sense that the purpose for creating the images was to ensure wealth and prosperity for people and livestock. But the function of the boat images as a symbol for a fertility god was toned down (Mandt 1991; Mandt 2009). They were seen rather as a means of transport or trading vessels, or as status symbols for the social elite.

Interpretations at the turn of the millennium

Towards the end of the 20th century, attention once again focused on the religious potential of the images. Whereas the fertility-cult interpretation had practically reigned supreme during the first half of the 1900s, the debate at the turn of the millennium fragmented into an entire spectrum of interpretations in which the images were seen in an extended religious, ideological and cosmic frame of reference. Some of the same mechanisms, however, may still have been present. Like the turn of the previous century, the turn of the new millennium is characterized as a period of upheaval in most areas of society. The multicultural reality in which we live today is a mixture of diversity and uniformity. Alternative faiths abound, while at the same time society is becoming increasingly secular.

Moral customs are continually changing and traditional taboos are being debated. Art has become experimental, and technological development advances at an incredible pace. Political and ideological revolutions occur overnight. The busy humans of today seek direction and overview and meaning through alternative lifestyles, and there is increasing interest in naturopathy, astrology and the supernatural. Many different forms of communication link the world together, and national perspectives are quickly being replaced by an international perspective.

This complex world view also affects the approaches used in interpreting rock art images today, where new theoretical perspectives replace older ones at a steadily increasing rate. Today's scholars do not reject the idea that the boat images may have some connection with power factors and rights to property and resources. But perhaps the interpretations that are most enticing are those that link the images to the mystical and arcane. The images are seen as a product of rituals and ceremonies – a visual system of communication through which a human's view of the world, of the self and of the relationship to the sacred is expressed (i.e. Fredell 2003; Hauptman Wahlgren 2002; Wrigglesworth 2000; Fuglestvedt 1999).

The boat and the symbolic journey

The boat motif is central in most interpretations. The boat is one of the commonest motifs in the rock art tradition of the Bronze Age. Whether the boat is depicted as an isolated motif or together with others, it frequently dominates the panel. Boats are also engraved on slabs in coffins and on bronze items that have been buried with the dead or offered as votive sacrifices. It is reasonable to think that the boat motif played an important role in the world-view during the Bronze Age (Hauptman Wahlgren 2002). Most interpretations place emphasis on the boat as a vessel – as a symbol of a journey (Kaul 1998).

The symbolism of travel comprises a whole spectrum of notions about travelling or carrying cargo from one place to another, both on the concrete level and in a metaphorical sense, often simultaneously. Whereas the boat was a practical means of transport, it may at the same time symbolise contact and fellowship with other people as well as the imparting of new ideas. The places where the images were created on stone surfaces – such as at Leirvåg – may have been sacred grounds, where groups of people living scattered throughout the area may have come together at designated times of the year to participate in rituals, to exchange knowledge or to find marital partners. The boat may also be a symbol for long journeys to distant and exotic destinations – for which the purpose was to acquire the coveted bronze items or to build status in a wide-ranging barter network.

In a metaphorical sense, the boat may have been a symbol for the journey that every human takes in the course of a lifetime, through various stages beginning with birth and ending in death (Hauptman Wahlgren 2002). In a number of societies throughout the world it is common to perform rituals at certain stages or transitions in life – when a child joins the ranks of adult society (such as our own religious confirmation, for example), when marriages are performed, and when a person dies. The very transition from one state to another can be seen as a journey. A person abandons a secure and customary existence, continues through a phase of uncertainty and anxiety, and finally emerges with a new identity and a changed status. The rituals performed in conjunction with these transitional phases are often heavily symbolic in terms of life–death–rebirth.

In many different religions there are examples where the boat and the journey motif are associated with notions of death and renewal of life. To enter the realm of the dead, for example, the deceased must be carried across a river by boat; the body is either buried in a boat, or in a grave shaped like a boat. Another widespread belief is that the sun is carried aboard a boat or assisted by a boat – across the sky during the daytime and through the underworld or realm of the dead at night (Kaul 1998). In this way, the boat ensures that the sun once again rises over the horizon each day, and that nature awakens after the slumber of winter, and the boat thereby becomes a symbol for life-giving power. The many boat images appearing across the rock surfaces are perhaps meant to illustrate a mythical account of the sun's journey between day and night, and summer and winter.

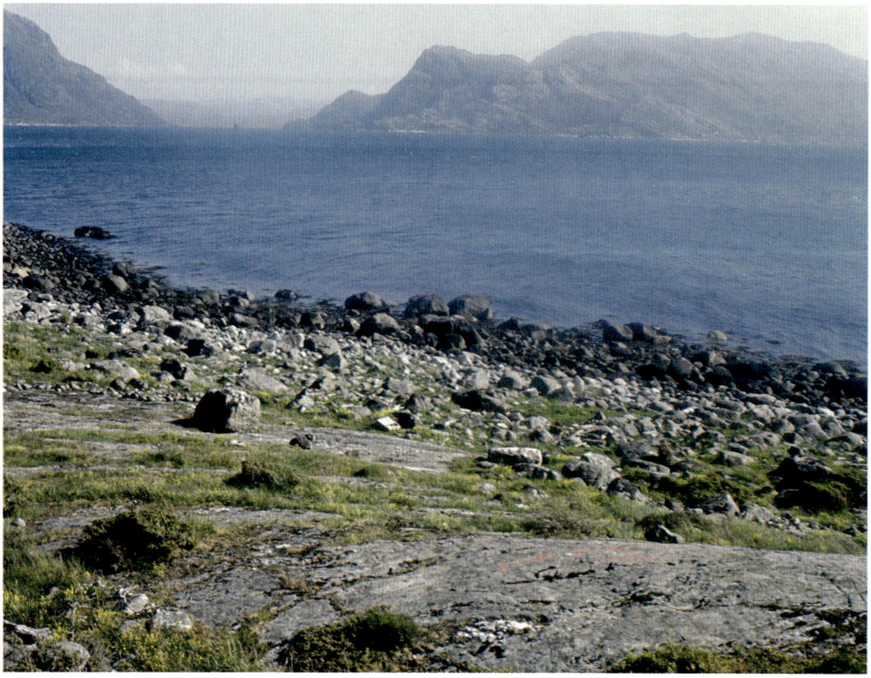

FIGURE 152. Since the 1940s, many small rock art sites and burial mounds have been found on the farms Unneset and Mjåset at Staveneset in Askvoll. The rock carvings and mounds are spread along the pebble beach located on the southern side of the promontory, facing Stongfjord and with a view towards the northern side of Atløy. GM

Abundant and different

More than a century after Bishop Neumann first saw the images on the Leivåg panel, several more boat images were discovered in Askvoll. They are located on the southern side of the long and narrow promontory Staveneset on the mainland, which faces the sheer northern incline at Atløy. Some 10–12 rock art panels and about thirty gravesites of various sizes are found on rocks and knolls along an extended pebble beach (Mandt 1991; Wrigglesworh 2000). In the early 1800s Christie and Neumann would undoubtedly have considered the boat images at Staveneset from a nationalist perspective, and explained them as yet another corroboration of the description in the Sagas of Viking hordes at battling in these waters.

For the scholars of today, the people of the past, their culture and their way of living are so different from ours and from the present time that it is impossible to trace affinities between the two (Kyvik 2002). Instead, a large number of potential interpretations emerge to explain the dissimilarities from the past. From this perspective, the interpretation of the boat images on the rocks in the Sunnfjord fjord landscape has changed once again. Today they are no longer Viking ships or cult vessels for a god of fertility, but rather complex and equivocal symbols of the human journey through life and into death, and of nature's eternal cycle and the passage of time.

Cup Marks in the Sub-Alpine Regions of Southern Norway – Traces of Ancient Animal Husbandry

On a lovely summer's day some 70–80 years ago, a group of young girls made their way up into the mountain summer farm areas of Luster in Sogn og Fjordane county to pick berries. During the ascent they stopped to rest at "Kvilesteinen" ("the Resting Stone") – an enormous boulder on the cattle track with a wide vista out across Lustrafjord – where people usually stopped for a rest on their way to the top. On the flat upper surface of the stone, they saw a concentration of small engraved depressions. The girls had heard that in the old days people made offerings in these "holes", as they were commonly known, and they agreed that they should perhaps also make an offering on their way home later in the evening. The mountainsides were red with berries, and the girls quickly filled their pails. On their way home they stopped at Kvilesteinen, and as agreed earlier in the morning, they filled the "holes" with berries. One of the girls, however, said she was unwilling to waste her berries on superstition of this kind. On her way further down the steep incline, she fell head over heels and spilt all of the berries she had gathered – perhaps a punishment for not making an offering as the others had done! At least, this was the opinion of her friends (Talle-Søvde 1912; Bøe 1944).

The puzzling rock art motif

The anecdote about the girls on a berry-picking trip vividly illustrates a unique group of ancient relics. The "holes" in which they laid offerings are the rock art motif called cup marks. They are round, semicircular shaped – occasionally oval – depressions that vary in diameter from two to three up to as much as 10 to 12 centimetres, and from a couple of centimetres deep to very shallow. Sometimes there is only one on a rock surface; at other times more than a hundred. Cup marks are most often randomly distributed over surfaces, but they also occur in groups, rows or other patterns; some are linked with shallow grooves, and many of them are incorporated into a more complex motif, for example the head of a human image.

Cup marks are the simplest motif in Scandinavian rock art; they are also the most common motif in most of the areas where rock carvings are found, and they appear to have been used over several thousands of years. Cup marks are also found in other parts of the world and over an extended period of time, either as single motifs or together with other figures. The simple shape, the widespread distribution and the lengthy period of use make cup marks the most puzzling of

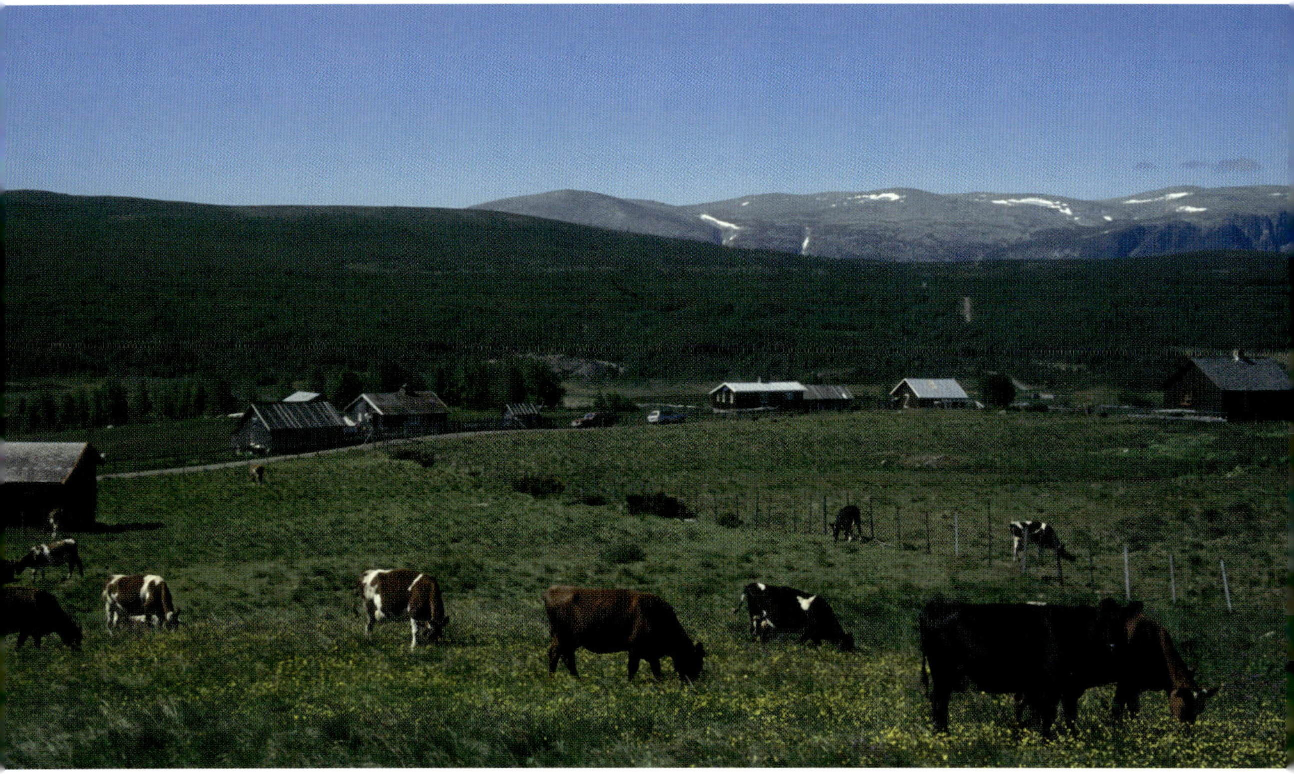

FIGURES 153–154. The number of dairy farms in the mountains has decreased drastically in most parts of Norway during recent generations. In Valdres, however, many of the mountain farms are still in use, such as Haugostølen, with its lush pasturelands, illustrates.

MAP AI, ILLUSTRATION SES

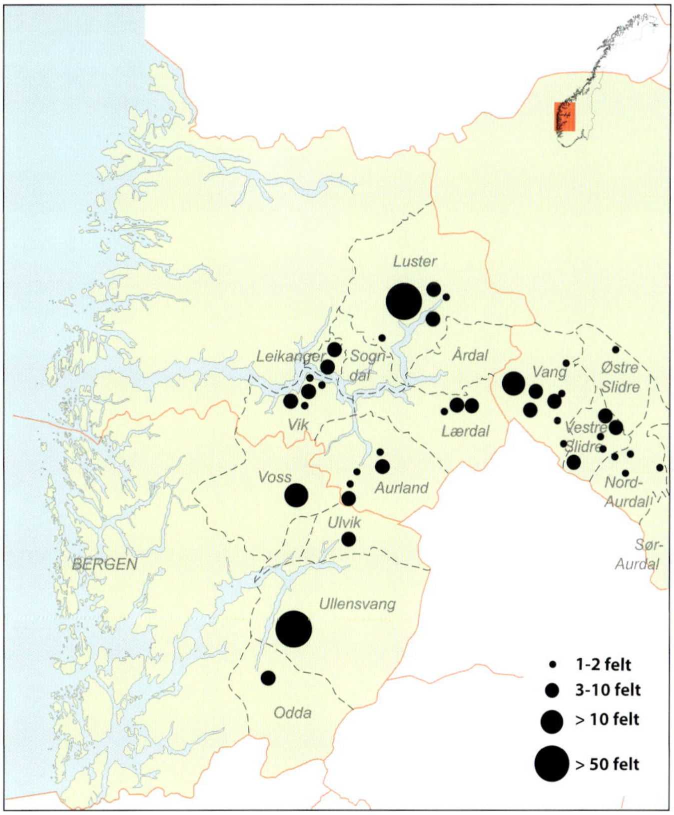

all rock art motifs (Innselset 2005; Mandt 1991). In contrast to motifs that depict images of more or less recognizable subjects or things we know and can compare them with, the cup-shaped depressions can represent just about anything at all.

Cups for votive offerings or symbols of fertility?

A widespread and longstanding notion has it that cup marks were used as receptacles for offerings, as illustrated in the anecdote about the berry pickers in Luster (Bøe 1944). Votive offerings were, for example, the blood of newly slaughtered animals, or butter to be melted by the first rays of sunshine in the spring. In Setesdal, the milk of a white goat was supposed to be poured into the cup mark of a specific stone (Hodne 1999). "Offersteinen" (the Offering Stone) is a common name in many rural areas for a stone with cup marks. In several places the tradition of votive offerings is also associated with stones without cup marks, particularly in conjunction with the annual return to the remote mountain summer farms. It has been said that the custom of making offerings in cup marks at Kvilesteinen in Luster was still practiced as recently as 1943 (Bøe 1944), but how far back in time such traditions extend is hard to determine. Perhaps it is people in recent times who have ascribed the function of offering receptacles to the cup-shaped depressions – long after their original purpose had been forgotten. But it is also possible that the idea of making votive offerings in the cup marks is a remnant of a thousand-year-old cult tradition.

In the second half of the 1800s, Swedish and Danish archaeologists advanced an interpretation of the cup mark motif that has survived the critical scrutiny of time. On the rock art panels from the Bronze Age, cup marks are sometimes placed near – usually between the legs of – human figures identified as women. Scholars came up with one explanation for this phenomenon by comparing the cup marks with the ancient Lingam-Yoni symbols in India, where Yoni – the ring, or pit – is the metaphor for the female genitalia, the vulva, and by extension for life and fertility (Innselset 1995). The cup marks were thus explained as a symbol for fertility – primarily female fertility – and in the broadest sense for life, death and rebirth.

It will probably never be known whether or not this is the original meaning of the cup mark motif. But the very concept of cup marks as a symbol for fertility presents an alluring perspective for understanding why, in popular beliefs, they are associated with votive offerings – that is, with acts intended to invoke bountiful years, safe travel at sea or in the mountains, or to offer thanks for the harvest. This may be an example of what the Rumanian historian of religion Mircea Eliade calls a degradation process (Eliade 1961). Symbols that were once part of a system of religious ideas and ceremonial cult acts will retain some of their sacred power in people's consciousness even in other contexts, and over time will be used in other magical activities designed to bring luck or avert evil.

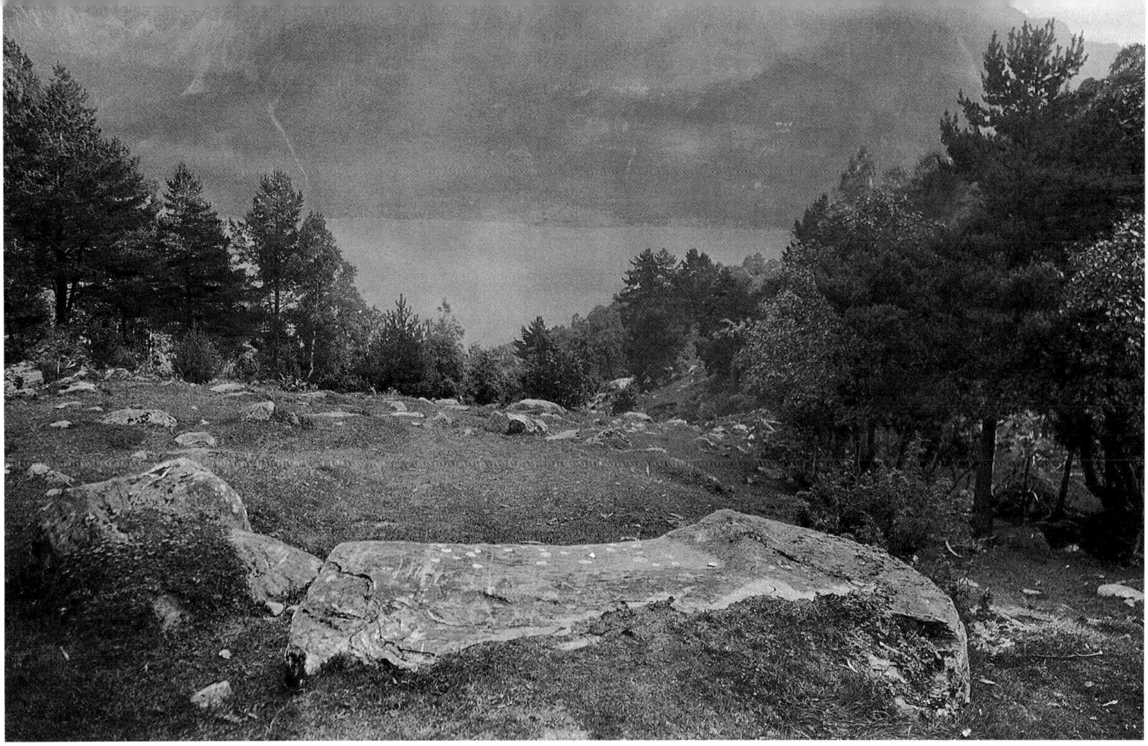

FIGURE 155.
"Kvilesteinen" (The Resting Stone) – or "Holesteinen" (The Hole Stone), as it was also known – is located directly on a mountain path leading from Hæri Farm in Luster and upwards to the Jøng mountain farm, situated at about 500 metres above sea level. The stone is oblong, 3 × 1 metres, and has 23 holes (cup marks) aligned in two rows. The photograph was taken by Johs. Bøe in 1932 at the time he investigated the cup marks in Luster. The spectacular view of Lustrafjord at the time is now almost entirely blocked by increasingly denser vegetation
JB/BM

Cup marks as isolated motifs

When trying to explain the meaning of the cup marks for the people who created them, it is necessary to study them within the context or environment in which they occur, such as other motifs found together with them, their location and the time period when they were made.

In Scandinavia, cup marks have been associated for some time with the world of ideas and religious practices of the Bronze Age, partly because the cup mark is the most frequently occurring motif in Bronze Age rock art, and partly because stones with cup marks have been found in many Bronze Age graves. However, cup marks have existed both in earlier and more recent contexts. They occur on panels of the Northern rock art tradition (Mandt 1998), on stones in and around Iron Age graves (Slomann 1971; Hougen 1947), and even on some gravestones from the Middle Ages (Mandt Larsen 1972). In addition there is a large and widespread group of rock art panels where cup marks are the only motif present. These are located on the outer coast, along fjords and in inland valleys, and in sub-alpine areas (Innselset 2005). The absence of other rock art motifs with which to associate the cup marks makes it extremely difficult to date and interpret them.

"Sub-alpine rock art"

An important piece in this interpretational puzzle is Kvilesteinen, with all of the "holes", on the cattle track in Luster. It serves as a typical example of a rock art panel that has only – or almost only – cup marks as motifs, and as one of many of its type found in the sub-alpine regions of Southern Norway. The first archaeologist who focused attention on this type of rock art was Johs. Bøe. In the 1930s he surveyed a large number of cup mark sites in the mountain farm regions of Luster in Sogn, and based on their location, he called them "sub-alpine rock art" (Bøe 1944). The people in these rural areas, who regularly went into the mountains, had seen the cup marks on boulders and stones, and they attributed their own meaning to them. For professional researchers this represented a new perspective concerning the interpretation of the cup marks than had been made by comparing them with rock art containing a diversity of motifs. The new interpretation model was reinforced during the subsequent decades by the gradual discovery of more, similar cup mark sites in other sub-alpine areas, notably in Indre Sogn, Valdres and Hardanger (Hougen 1947; Bakka 1963).

Mountain pastures – an important element in the farming economy

The rural areas of Valdres, Indre Sogn and Hardanger, which are on the outskirts of the Southern Norwegian mountain plateau, share a number of common features in terms of their landscape, settlement pattern and economy. Narrow and confined patches of arable land squeezed in between towering mountainsides naturally restrict the size of fields and pastures. Large portions of Valdres are barren mountains, particularly in the inner valley, while the lower part of the valley basin is heavily wooded, and settlements are located on the steep or more gently sloping inclines rising from the valley floor (Innselset 1996, 2005). In Indre Sogn and around Sørfjorden in Hardanger, the farms stand on narrow strips of land and marine terraces along the fjord, some of them quite elevated and hilly, or on sandbanks at the mouth of rivers at the head of the fjord (Bakka 1963; Mandt Larsen 1982; Mandt 1991). In all of these areas, good grazing land in the hillsides all the way up to the mountain plateau has represented a highly invaluable resource and an integral part of the economic basis for farming in historic times. During the summer, farmers moved their livestock to the mountain areas in order to take advantage of the lush pasture, to make hay and gather forage. By doing so, the farmers were able to reserve the grass cut at the farmstead for winter use, and were therefore able to keep more animals. In the sub-alpine areas, small huts were raised as shelters for the people who tended the animals at pasture and who did the milking.

In Western Norway and in Valdres these mountain summer farms are called "støler", while "seter" is the term normally used in Eastern Norway and in other parts of the country (Reinton 1955, 1957, 1961). Both words are used interchangeably, although the original meanings have been different. Støl, from the Old Norse *stodull*, meaning an open place in the field where the livestock is milked, is probably the earlier variant, while seter, from the Old Norse *setr* or *sætr* is a place where one tends the animals at summer pasture. A farmstead normally had several types of støler or setre, both heimestøler or melkestøler [near the farmstead, for milking the animals] and fjellstøler [mountain dairy farms] up near the mountain plateau, where hunting and fishing were important supplements to the farming economy.

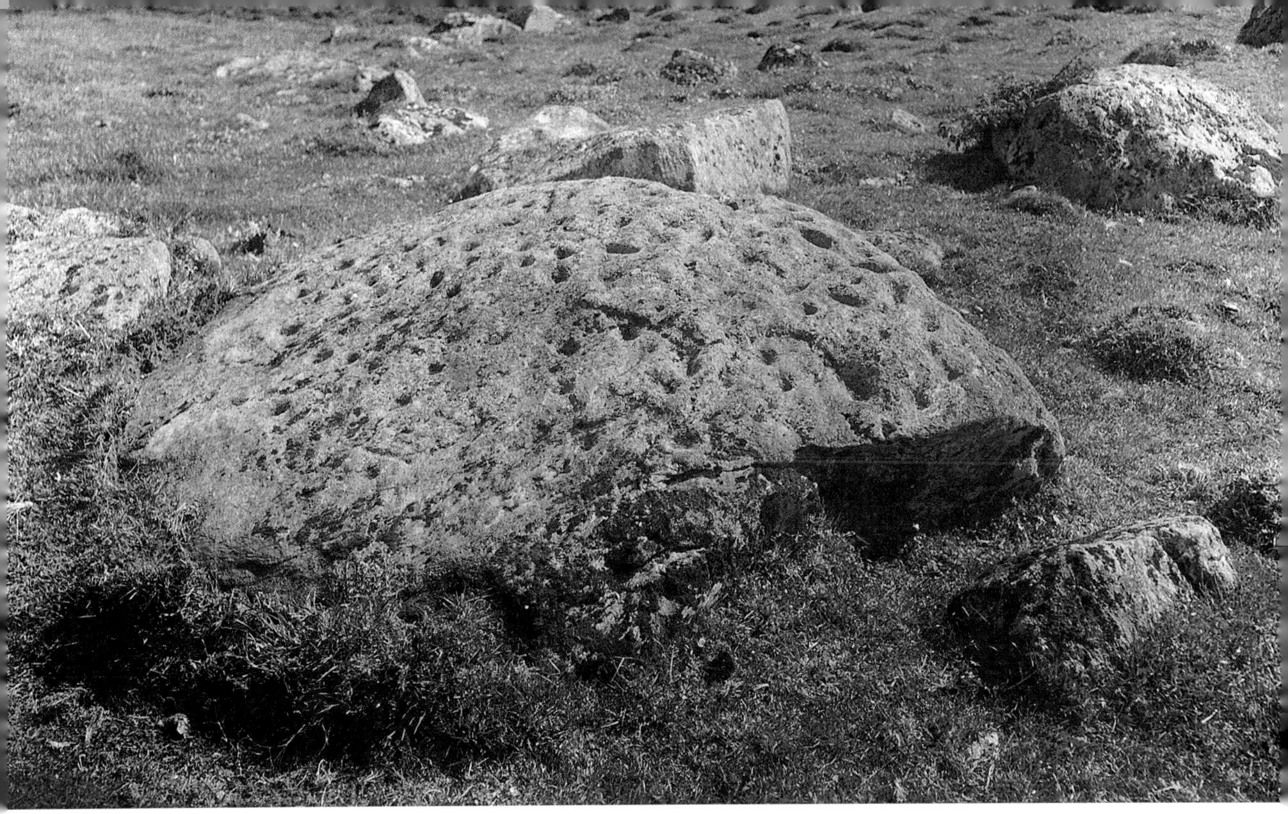

FIGURE 156. This large stone outcrop, completely covered with cup marks, is located on the Hodnane mountain farm in Luster, 600–700 metres above sea level. Several of the cup marks are linked together by small grooves in the stone. The outcrop lies at the edge of the field on the shores of the lake Kringlevatnet, near an old trail leading to Fortun. The photograph was taken in 1932 by Johs. Bøe.
JB/BM

Cup mark sites in the sub-alpine areas of western Norway

It is in these mountain farm areas – between the permanent farmstead and the bare mountaintops at an elevation of some 1000 metres above sea level – where the majority of the cup mark sites are found. In Valdres, all of the cup mark engravings are located in the four northernmost municipalities: Vang, Vestre Slidre, Øystre Slidre and Nord-Aurdal (Innselset 1996). In Indre Sogn cup mark sites occur in the municipalities of Aurland, Leikanger, Luster, Lærdal and Vik, with the greatest number in Luster (Mandt 1991). In Hardanger, cup marks are found in the municipalities of Odda, Ullensvang and Ulvik, the majority of them on the hillsides around Sørfjorden in Ullensvang (Bakka 1963).

The cup mark sites lie almost without exception in lush, mountain pastureland with ample access to fresh drinking water. In many cases the places have served as støler in living memory, or place names and remnants of mountain huts show evidence of mountain dairy farming in earlier times. In mountainous farm meadows and hamlets, concentrations of rock surfaces or earthbound stones are literally covered with cup marks. Luster in particular has several examples of such concentrations (Bøe 1944; Mandt 1991). Cup marks are also found along the paths between mountain farms or on the cattle tracks from the permanent farms up to the mountains, such as Kvilesteinen in Luster. They are also the most recurrent motif. Only rarely are others depicted, for example around Sørfjorden in Hardanger, where a single ring, a few foot soles and, in very rare cases, a boat image is depicted along with the cup marks (Bakka 1963).

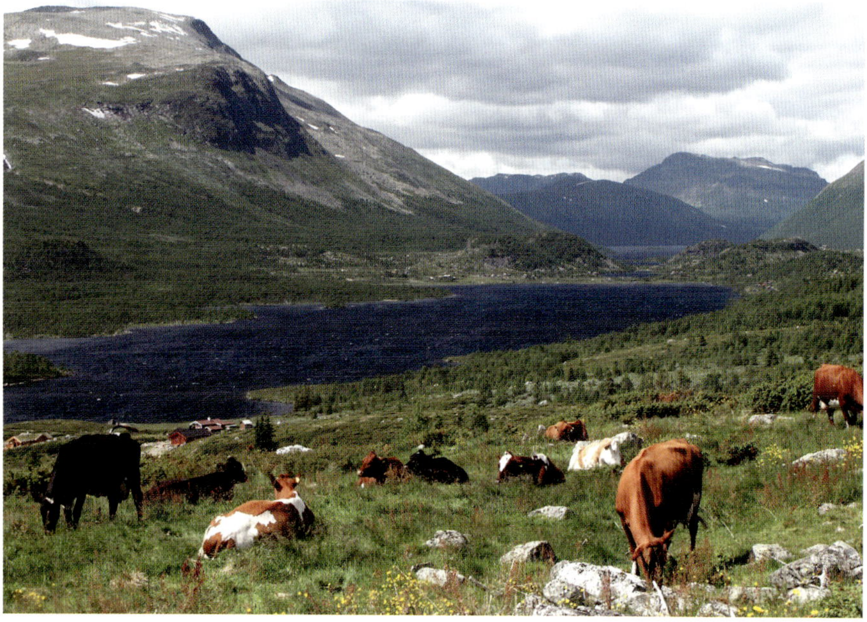

FIGURE 157. In the mountain grazing areas of Jaslangen in Vestre Slidre, Valdres, mountain dairy farms are still in operation for a few weeks each summer. The mountain farm at the bottom of the incline at the edge of the lake belongs to Solheim Farm. Some smaller rock carvings have been found near the farmyard at Solheim.
SES

Valdres – an extended valley of western Norway?

Despite the similarities between Valdres, Indre Sogn and Hardanger – in terms of topography, exploitation of resources and location of the cup mark sites – there is a conspicuous difference. Valdres is an inland valley, while the settled areas of inner Sogn and around Sørfjorden in Hardanger are situated at the intersection of mountains and fjord waters. However, if we consider Valdres as an extension towards the east of the settled areas in the innermost part of Sogn, the difference is not so pronounced. In both written sources and common tradition there are indications that the mountains separating Valdres and Sogn were not considered as a barrier, but instead as a link between the communities. During the Middle Ages, Valdres was under West Norwegian control, under the jurisdiction of the Gulating legal codes and the ecclesial administration of the Selja bishopric. The so-called Kongevegen [King's Road] over Filefjell has long been the most viable eastward communication trail for both Sogn and the greater part of Hordaland. Also, for the upper rural communities in Valdres, Lærdalsøyri in Sogn, situated in the inner part of Sognefjorden, was the most important marketplace, at least as far back as the 1500s. The similarities in dialect between Sogn and the upper Valdres districts also demonstrate that contact between these areas must be longstanding. Linguist Magnus Olsen has pointed out that the very name of the valley – Valdres – means "woodland grazing (-valley)", which may suggest that the valley in earlier times was a grazing area for the remote settled areas in Lærdal (Beitrusten 1983). If the upper portion of the Valdres valley is perceived as the extended arm of Lærdal, the similarity between the areas with cup mark sites becomes particularly striking: their location in the two large fjord systems of Western Norway, Sognefjorden and Hardangerfjorden.

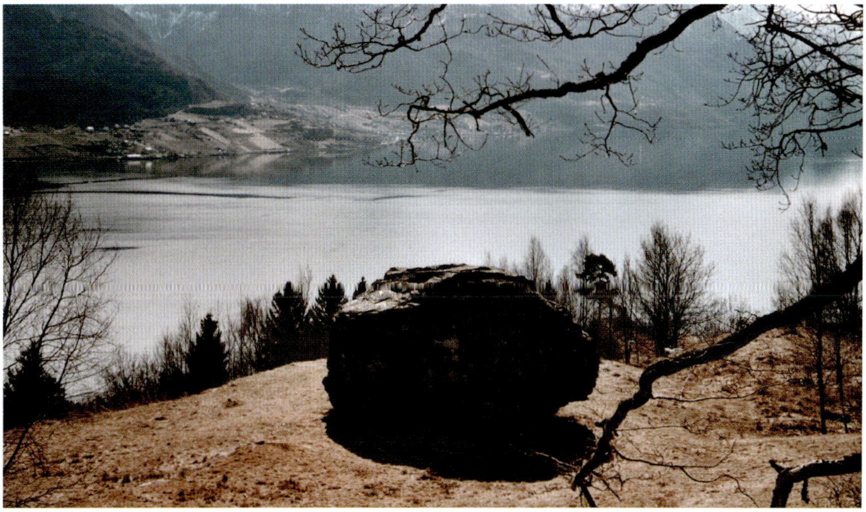

FIGURE 158. On the Haustveit farm located on the eastern side of Sørfjord in Hardanger there is a wide, open terrace on the hillside some 250–300 metres above sea level called "Håhaug". Rock carvings are found on a boulder located a distance from the edge of the plateau. The boulder, called "Håhaugsteinen", measures 7 × 4 × 4 metres, and has nearly vertical sides. The carvings occur on three of the sides, and they are of an entirely different type than those normally found in mountain farm areas.

HH

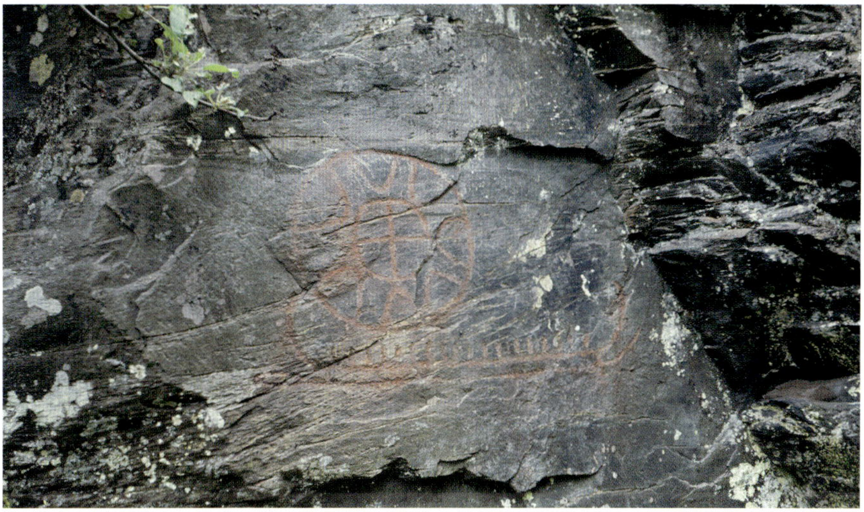

FIGURE 159. The motifs on "Håhaugsteinen" include both boats with high, curved stems and circular figures of rarely found shapes. The ring motifs consist of concentric and radial lines, and some of them have a loop or ring, as if they were to be worn as ornaments.

GM

The earliest mountain dairy farming?

The apparently close connection between the cup mark sites and the mountain farms provided the basis for Johs. Bøe's interpretation in the mid-1900s of the carvings in the alpine areas. In Hardanger and inner Sogn, between 60 and 65% of the high-lying cup mark sites are located on mountain farms or paths between them. In Valdres the figure is a little over 50%, but here many of the cup marks are found on high-lying farmsteads that may have been mountain summer farms in earlier times (Innselset 1996). Using the Bronze Age as the most probable time frame for the cup mark motif, it was easy to explain its location on mountain farms as the earliest evidence that the Bronze Age farmers turned to the rich mountain pastureland as an important resource for farming in the fjord regions (Bøe 1944). Thus the places with cup marks in the sub-alpine regions were explained as precursors of the *støl* or *seter* farming tradition known from historical time. This interpretation was in tune with the notion of Bronze Age rock art as an element in fertility rites to ensure good crop yields. The cup marks in the mountain farm regions were regarded as a simplification of the more comprehensive fertility cult – as a magical, protective symbol in cult ceremonies associated with everyday concerns, animal husbandry and mountain farming practices.

Alternative interpretations of the sub-alpine cup marks?

The origins and age of mountain farming practices in Norway have been the subject of long and vigorous debate among historians and archaeologists (Reinton 1955, 1957, 1961). Because the Vikings on their raids towards the west brought with them the practice of mountain summer farming to the North Atlantic islands, this system of farming must have existed in Norway earlier than 800 AD, and towards the end of the Middle Ages it was a fully established practice. Many researchers, however, claim that mountain farming in Scandinavia has much older traditions. Animal husbandry based on secondary animal products (milk, wool etc.) in an extensive, nomadic grazing regime, has been known to exist for thousands of years in both Europe and Asia. It has also been claimed that knowledge of this method of subsistence came to Norway with migrant groups some time around the Middle or Late Neolithic – about 2000 BC – as an integral element of the farming system in the earliest agricultural tradition (Prescott 1995).

Although more than half of the cup mark sites in the Western Norwegian sub-alpine areas are located on or near mountain farms, it is nonetheless uncertain whether the cup marks can be linked to mountain dairy farming rooted in the permanent farms of the Bronze Age. It has been pointed out that if cup mark production was a tradition in the historical use of mountain farms, the custom should necessarily have had greater repercussions. It would have become more widespread, and more traces would have been found in folklore (Innselset 1996, 2005). Mountain farms occur in woodland communities, flatland settlements, along the coast and on the islands, as well as in sub-alpine areas. Nevertheless, the majority of the high-lying cup mark sites are concentrated in Western Norway and Valdres. In the other Southern Norwegian mountain farm areas, only a few scattered localities with cup marks exist in the upper portion of Gudbrandsdalen, in Østerdalen and in Vest-Telemark. The location of cup marks in what are today defined as sub-alpine farming areas, can therefore be misleading in terms of the prehistoric situation.

The shared feature for the localities with cup marks in Valdres, inner Sogn and Hardanger is the good pastureland – open spaces where the animals can eat their fill of moist mountain grass and have unlimited access to fresh water. In all likelihood, these factors were paramount for those who adopted mountain grazing. The reason why so many cup marks are located in or around the mountain farms of today or earlier times may be that livestock farmers of later years were attracted by the same rich grazing resources and built their mountain huts there. But if the cup marks have no connection with earlier mountain farm practices linked with permanently established farms on the lowland during the Bronze Age – who then were the pioneers who carved cup marks in the stones and rock surfaces in the lush pasturelands?

Livestock pioneers during the Neolithic

The answer is perhaps found in the Årdal mountains in inner Sogn, where settlement sites have been found left by people who kept livestock for a living already by the end of the Neolithic (Presott 1995). The mainstay of their economy consisted of secondary animal products, such as milk, blood, wool and tractive power, but not meat. The subsistence model was based on maximal exploitation of the grazing resources through a seasonal nomadic pattern, where stays in the mountains during summer and in the lowlands during winter were balanced sides of the economic structure. This subsistence model – pastoralism – differs from the historical farming structure, where a permanent farm is the primary element, and the mountain farm the secondary element in the economy.

The archaeological remains in Årdal are associated with the first farmers who came to Western Norway with their animals at the end of the Neolithic, and they represent a way of living and exploitation of resources we find traces of in archaeological remains from large areas of the country. Fields used in prehistoric times and radiological datings of seeds and pollen provide evidence that the coastal and fjord areas of Western Norway and the inland valleys to the east were settled by people who grew grain and kept animals as early as around 2000 BC, during the transition between the Neolithic and the Bronze Age (Solberg 2000).

Perhaps the cup marks in elevated areas can be linked with the livestock pioneers from the end of the Neolithic, as an integral part of the new farming practices (Innselset 2005). The livestock herders who came to the West Norwegian mountains needed to establish their ownership rights over the new territory they took into use. The cup marks on the rocks and stones in the vital grazing grounds may have served as physical, visible markings to demonstrate the connection between these people and the landscape, as well as their temporal links to their ancestors. Perhaps the carving of cup marks was also a means of inaugurating the

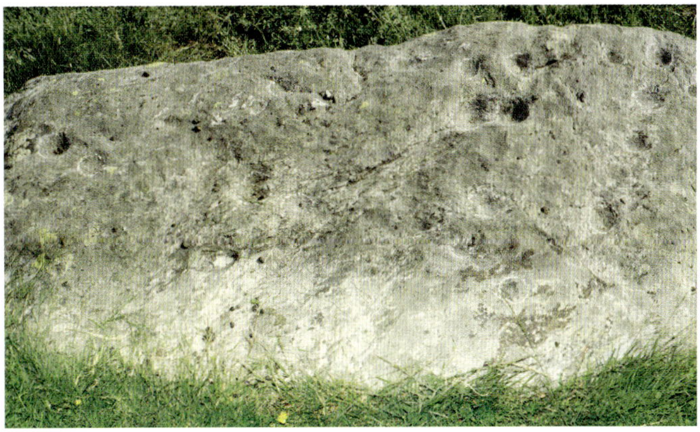

FIGURE 160. Not all rock art images are spectacular, and not all consist of varied motifs. Many are more modest in terms of choice and composition of motifs, and this includes the many rock carvings in which cup marks are the sole or dominant motif – such as this stone from the Navarsete mountain farm in Luster, Sogn, with a total of 19 cup marks scattered over it. Many secrets are concealed in this simple motif used over a period of several thousands of years, and found in rock art areas in different parts of the world.
SI

new area and to make it sacred in their own ritualistic domain (Tilley 1994). At the same time, the cup marks may have served to underscore the property rights of the newcomers in relation to the people who had exploited the resources in the mountains before their arrival.

Agricultural expansion in the Early Iron Age

The linking of the sub-alpine cup marks to the earliest agricultural phase – the end of the Neolithic and the Early Bronze Age – can be substantiated by cup marks found on panels dating from these periods. However, cup marks found in graves show that the motif was also used during the Iron Age and in the Middle Ages. Another approach to studying the sub-alpine engravings, therefore, is to see them in context with traces of intensified mountain grazing as identified in several places in Western Norway and dated to the transition between the Bronze Age and the Early Iron Age, around 500 BC. Although Johs. Bøe and his contemporaries interpreted the cup marks first and foremost as a phenomenon of the Bronze Age, they did not dismiss the possibility of a later dating (Bøe 1944; Hougen 1947). The problem then as now, however, was that the cup marks in themselves do not offer any clues for determining dates. They must be studied in context with other traces of human activity.

One such association between cup marks and other traces of activity has been discovered during recent decades in the mountain farm regions of Sogn, particularly in Leikanger and Luster. Cup marks are spread across the meadows of the summer farms, between and often close to features of old mountain huts, and archaeological registrations have also revealed many charcoal depressions that were probably used for cooking. Radiological datings and pollen analyses show that the mountain farms were in use over the entire time period from the Late Bronze Age and into the Middle Ages, and that the most intensive period of activity was from the middle of the Iron Age, around 200–300 AD, until well into the 1300s (Solberg 2000).

The clearest link between the cup marks and other ancient cultural traces was demonstrated at the mountain farm of Svolset in Leikanger (Skrede 2002). Svolset is located at the head of Friksdalen at the far upper end of a valley beneath an arm of Jostedalsbreen (the Jostedal Glacier), 700–800 metres above sea level and about 150 metres above today's tree line. There are sixteen or seventeen dwelling features registered in the area, fifty charcoal pits and ten earthbound stones with cup marks. Pollen analyses have revealed traces of extensive grazing from the Late Bronze Age, while dated dwelling features and charcoal pits give evidence of intensive use from the middle of the Late Iron Age until the Viking era, from about 200–300 to 1000 AD. Most of the cup marks appear so close to one or more dwelling features – among other places, just outside the entrance – that it can hardly be considered coincidental. It therefore seems logical to see the cup marks and the dwelling features in context, and one of the conclusions is that the cup marks were made during the time the buildings at Svolset were in use, during the Iron Age.

The archaeological remains at Svolset are not unequivocal proof of a concurrence in time between the production of the cup marks and mountain farming practices during the Iron Age or Middle Ages. Mountain grazing was a practice during the Bronze Age, and the first cup marks may have been made at that time. The livestock farmers who came to Svolset during the Iron Age may have chosen to place their dwellings close to the stones marked by what they recognized as powerful and possibly protective carvings made by their ancestors. Perhaps they kept the tradition alive, as well, by performing rituals associated with the cup marks and by carving new ones whenever they were needed. Regardless of the period of time we may determine, the purpose of the cup marks could have been to safeguard people and animals and to ensure good fortune and bountiful harvests.

The ambiguous cup marks

The long period of use and the diverse contexts in which the cup marks occur make interpretations equivocal, and there is little reason to doubt that the meanings have changed over time. We are not the only ones who have noticed these traces that ancestors have left on the landscape. Countless generations before us have done the same, and like us they have read their own meaning into the relics of the past.

The cup marks on the mountain hillsides and along high trails have given rise to many different explanations for why the concave depressions were created. Many folk notions concerning natural forces to be dealt with are also connected with sub-alpine farm life in historical time (Hodne 1999). The farms were often difficult to access, and the rugged and inhospitable surroundings far away from the warmth and safety of the home farm often harboured dangers for people and livestock. Not only did the mountain farmers have to be wary of beasts of prey, but it was also important to remain on good terms with the underworld and to appease the spirits. Mountain farms have thus been the scenes of many kinds of rituals designed to protect animals and harvests – traditions that may be rooted very far back in time.

We do not know the kinds of rituals that were performed around the cup mark sites. In the popular world of ideas, emphasis was placed on making offerings, such as illustrated by Kvilesteinen in Luster. Perhaps the motif – the cup mark itself – was not of prime importance, but rather the very act of carving out a section in the rock (Marstrander 1963). Neither do we know who might have performed these acts and rituals, or when it happened. It could have been the livestock pioneers during the Neolithic, signalling their ownership and property rights in a new landscape by carving marks in stone panels and boulders. It could also have been the fjord dwellers during the Bronze Age, demonstrating their interests in the mountain grazing areas their ancestors had learned about through generations of long hunting forays. The sub-alpine cup mark sites could even be precursors of the mountain farms that were developed during the Iron Age and Middle Ages. In any event, the debate is far from over.

Berge in Strandebarm

For the second time during the summer, he was cutting the grass around the farm buildings. He knew each of the small depressions in the ground, having swung his scythe here for many years. The work was an accustomed routine offering no surprises other than those of his own meandering thoughts. This summer's day, however, would be out of the ordinary. By chance a well-concealed relic from the ancient past would surface here on what is today the Berge farm. It was early afternoon and warm, very warm. The sun was still high in the sky. The Hardanger fjord lay calm and mirror-like, and there was not so much as a gentle breeze in the air. He swung his scythe with even strokes up across the field towards the cool, shaded rock wall above the buildings. The sheer cliff frequently offered welcome shade, although today the sun's slanting rays had begun to enter from the side. He longed for a cool spot to rest and frequently glanced towards the rock wall. How much longer would he have to wait? When would he be able to enjoy the shade? Again he glanced up from the blade of the scythe, but stopped dead in his tracks. He took a couple of paces forward. He groped for his handkerchief, quickly wiping the perspiration from his forehead. There on the mountain wall he saw the distinct outline of a boat. Where did that come from? He had never seen anything like this before, and he had worked here under the rock wall many, many times before. He was able to make out deep and clear grooves in the stone, illuminated by the slanting light of the sun that made the lines on the wall distinct and clearly visible. The grooves formed the outlines of tall ship stems linked together by other lines representing the keel and the gunwale. Extending above the gunwale was a series of short vertical lines. Surprised, he returned to his work, thinking to himself: It must have taken a long time to chip or carve that into the wall! He swung his scythe into the grass again, filing away the thought in the recesses of his mind. His discovery would remain his personal secret for the next 60 years. During that time, he never told a soul (The story of the discovery of the Berge rock carvings was told by property owner Leidolv Berge, and dramatized by the author).

The discovery

In January of 1998, the present owner of Berge farm was visited by his grandchildren, who were out playing amongst the trees that had grown tall in front of the rock wall over the period of the past 60 years. The low winter sun shone brightly at an angle, its rays striking the portion of the wall that had not been veiled with icicles. In this light, the children were able to make out a broad

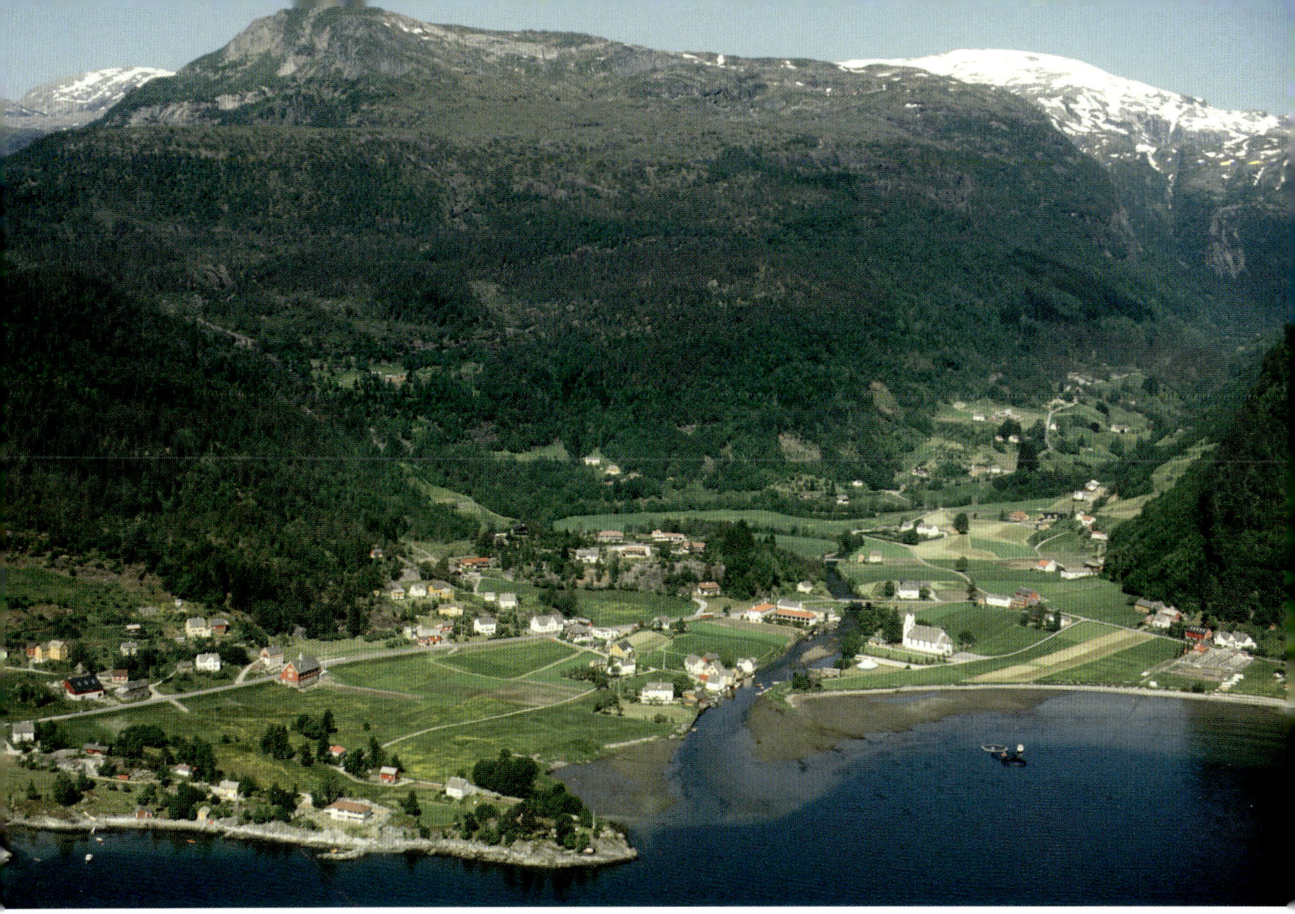

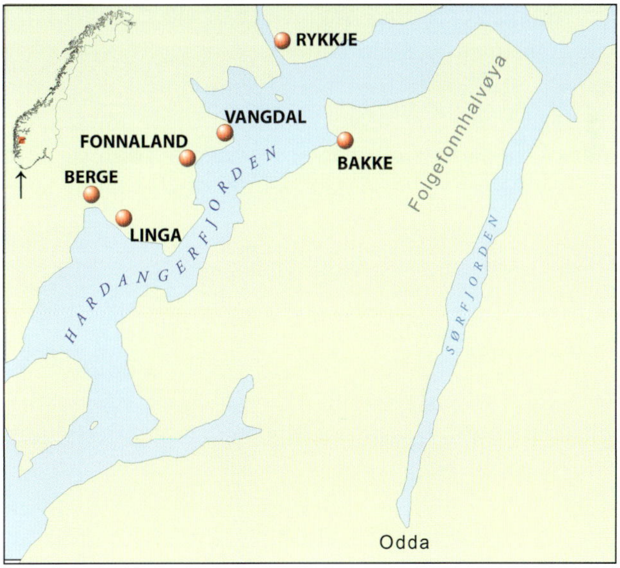

FIGURES 161–162. View of Strandebarm. Berge Farm is on the far right in the photo.

MAP AI, ILLUSTRATION HELGE SUNDE/SAMFOTO

circular figure on the wall, about 30 cm in diameter! They went closer and saw several boat images. As the sun changed position in the sky, still more outlines became more or less clearly visible, and the otherwise cold and hard surface of the rock wall seemed to come to life. Ring figures and ships formed a panorama of images across the wall. Could this really be true? Were there rock engravings

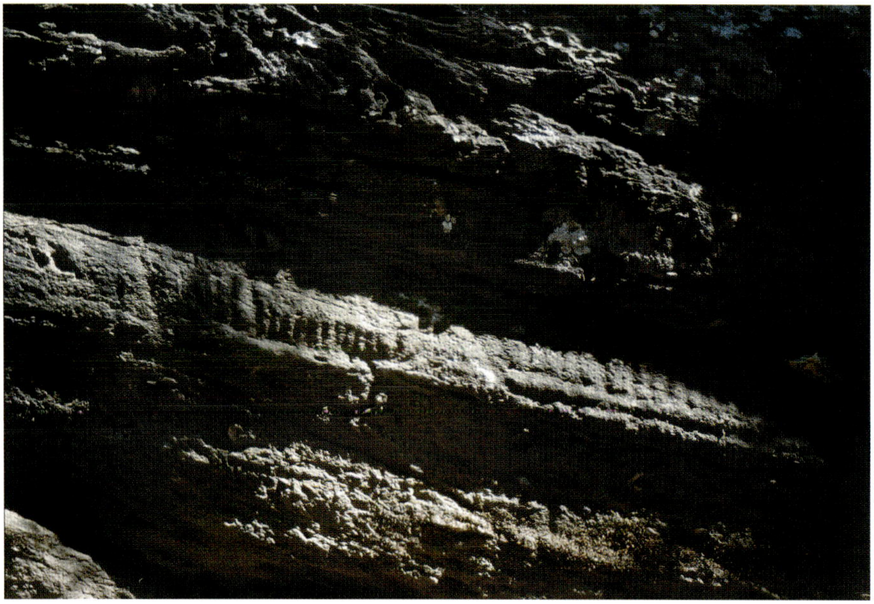

FIGURE 163. Slanted light is needed in order to bring out the figures on a stone surface. Even with proper lighting, they may be difficult to see when the rock surface is heavily weathered.
TL

here on the farm? Everyone at home was summoned, each one as astounded as the others at the discovery. Archaeologists and other rock art scholars were immediately notified. Only a few days after visiting the farm on the northern side of the Hardanger fjord, they triumphantly announced the discovery of what were determined to be rock engravings of the Southern Tradition. The conclusion was unequivocal. From all appearances the majority of the figures dated from the Bronze Age (Mandt 1991; Østmo 1990) and perhaps from the Early Iron Age as well. The incredible thing was that the images were discovered on the grounds of the farm itself, only a few metres from the farm buildings. The discovery was heavily publicised, and eventually the elderly uncle who had grown up on the farm revealed that he had seen the figures more than a generation earlier.

Difficult documentation

The fragile and weathered surface of the rock wall was a challenge for researchers. Carved lines, which were damaged and indistinct after centuries of weathering, had to be distinguished from natural cracks and glacial striations covering the wall. Culture had to be distinguished from nature. Sunshine and slanting light, which had coaxed the rock images out from the surface for the early discoverers, was obstructed by heavily overcast skies during this initial documentation procedure. At intervals the work was postponed indefinitely because of heavy rainfall and water leakage from the rock ridges above. The documentation did provide results, however, and when it was completed two seasons later, more than one hundred figures had been sketched, photographed and described. Most of them are boat figures, but there are also spirals and circles. All of them

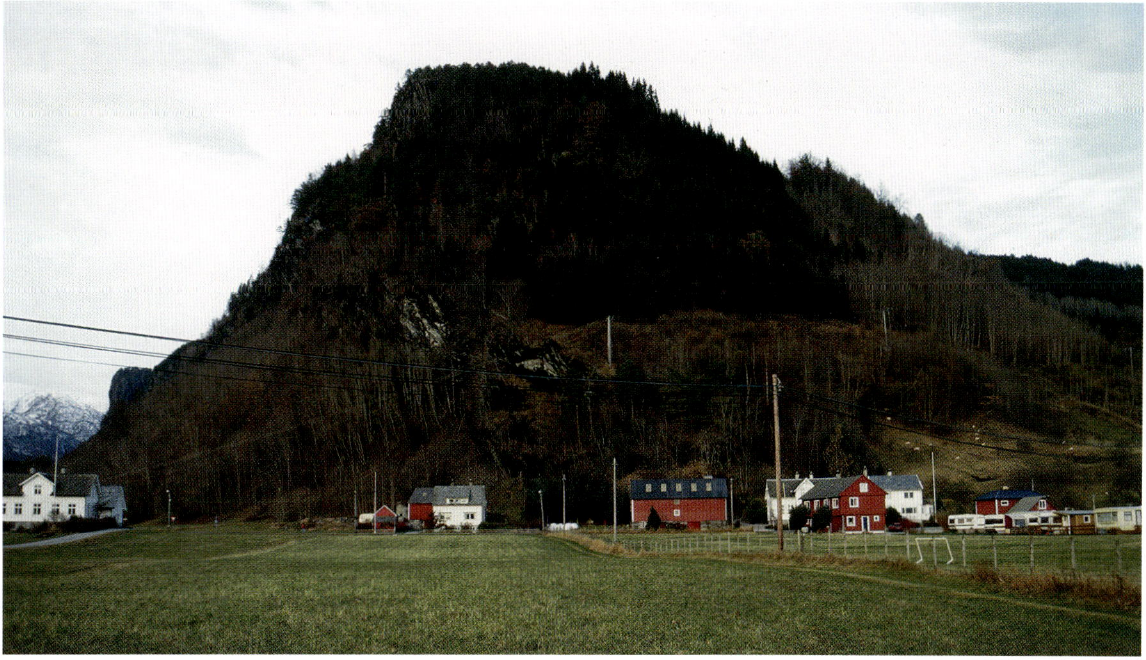

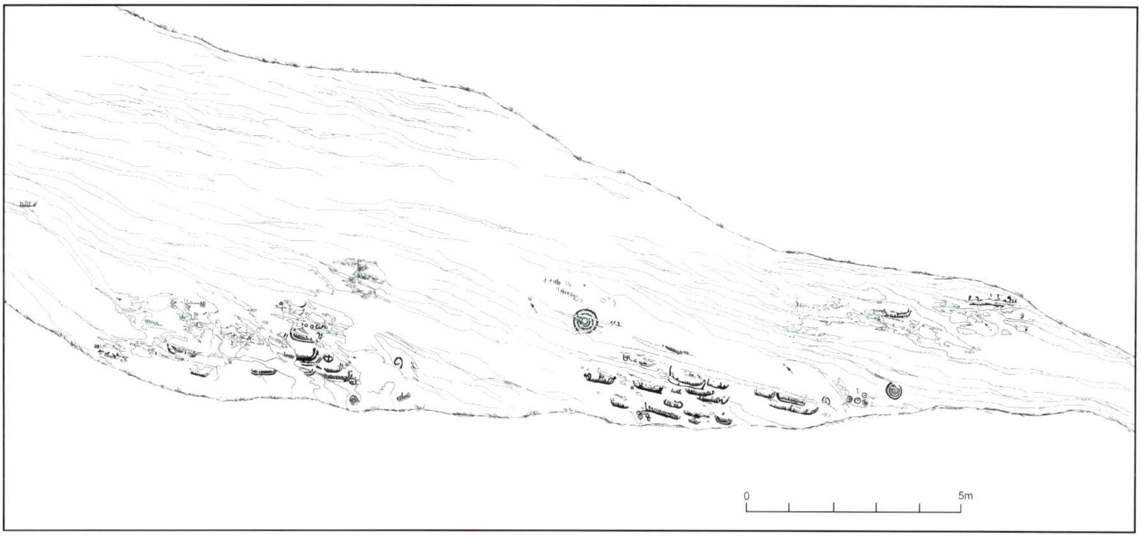

FIGURE 164 *(above)*. The rock wall with images is located at the foot of this landmark, Fløyen.

TL

FIGURE 165 *(below)*. The figures are distributed over a 15-metre-long area on the heavily weathered rock wall.

BM

are found inside a 15-metre-wide area on the wall surface and are distributed from just above ground level to nearly four metres further up. The lines of the figures are created by the chipping technique, probably with a pointed, hard type of stone, although it cannot be discounted that a metal tool may have been used. In any case, it must have been easy to chip lines into the phyllitic slate. Considering the abundance of figures and the short distance to the farm buildings, it is difficult to understand how the rock art could have remained undetected for such a long time. One explanation is probably that the rock wall today is concealed behind a large number of tall spruce trees. Erosive leakage and weathering can also be included as factors, although both the property owners and the researchers were perplexed that the images went undiscovered and unpublicised for such a long time.

The boat figures as clues for dating

Further research remains to be carried out in order to ascertain the age of the images, although differing styles and varying forms of expression suggest that they were created successively over a long period of time. Suggested dates are based on comparisons with motifs and stylistic elements from other rock art panels or comparisons with depictions on other archaeological material. The images at the top of the wall may have been carved as far back in time as the early part of the Early Bronze Age (Mandt 1991) or even earlier (Lindqvist 1994). While a scaffold or ladder is needed today to reach the higher images, local land uplift, which has continued ever since the last Ice Age, indicates that the images may have been at sea level some 3000–4000 years ago, making it possible to carve the images from a boat. Land upheaval and shoreline displacements also suggests that the lowest-lying figures are no more than some 2000 years old, provided they were created at shoreline level at the time. It is also possible that there are figures even further down the wall, but which are now concealed by soil deposits.

Even if additional figures are found, it is still a fact that boat images are the predominant motifs. They are depicted in various shapes, probably in line with

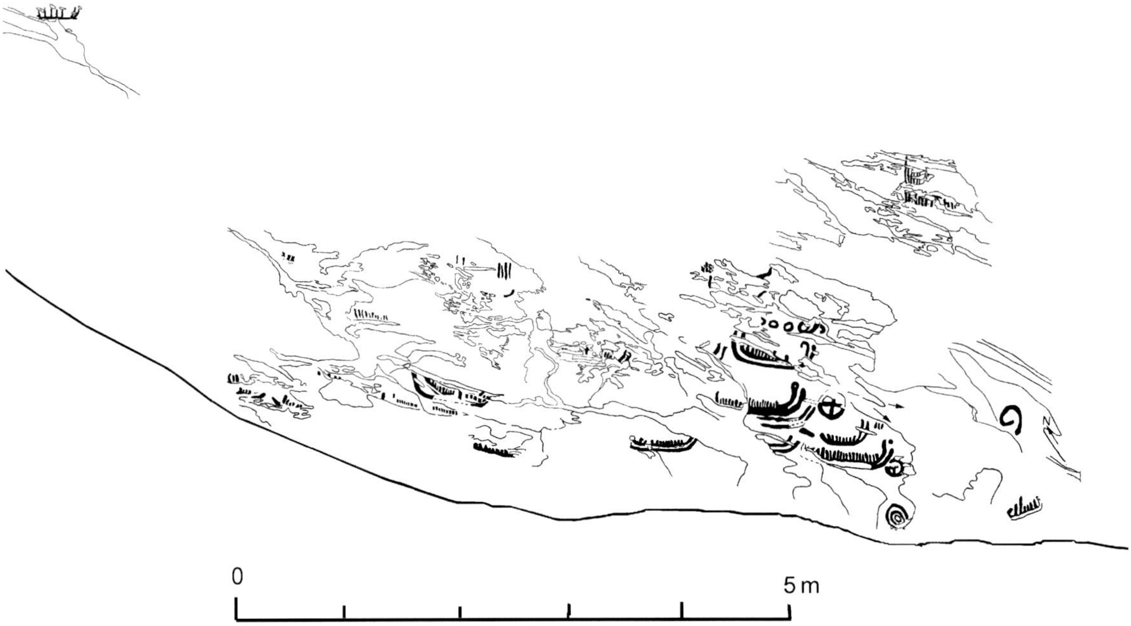

FIGURE 166. The westernmost section of the rock wall, showing several spirals, and sun wheels, along with boats of various types.
BM

changing trends in prehistory. The images that are present on the rock wall may therefore span over a period of many centuries. Studies of style have suggested that the earliest boat images are depicted with straight keels, straight gunwales and stems that are practically vertical, while the youngest images have curved keels and gunwales and a smoother transition between the keels and stems. On many of the boat images at Berge, the stems are capped with shapes resembling animal heads. Another characteristic trait is the series of parallel, vertical lines between the stems, normally extending directly up from the keels and gunwales. These are most often termed crew lines and are interpreted as depicting the rowers or paddlers, although they are also possibly renderings of the rib construction of the boat. The smallest boats are only about 30 centimetres long from stem to stern, while the longest are nearly a metre in length.

There are far fewer circles, spirals and sun wheels than there are boats. On the other hand, the former are located on central and prominent sections of the wall surface, making them all the more conspicuous. In some places there are circles and other sun wheels aligned in rows containing as many as four between the stems of a boat. This can perhaps be understood as an illustration of the notion that the sun was carried across the sky by a ship or boat (Kaul 2004).

Prototypes for rock art boats

As far as can be determined, the interpretations of boat types that are recurrent in rock art of the Southern Tradition, and which we find in large numbers at Berge, range from outrigger canoes to light, hide-covered constructions. If they were hide-covered boats, the ribs would have been visible from the outside, even at a great distance, and it would therefore have been natural to include the ribs when the boats were depicted. The keel and gunwale are supporting structures in a hide-covered boat, and are recurrent in the majority of the images. The

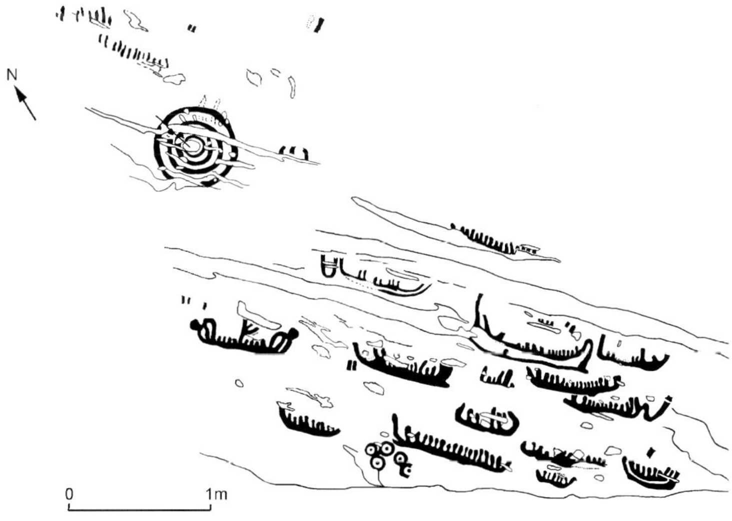

FIGURE 167. The boats clearly follow the stratification of the rock, even though it slants downward.

BM

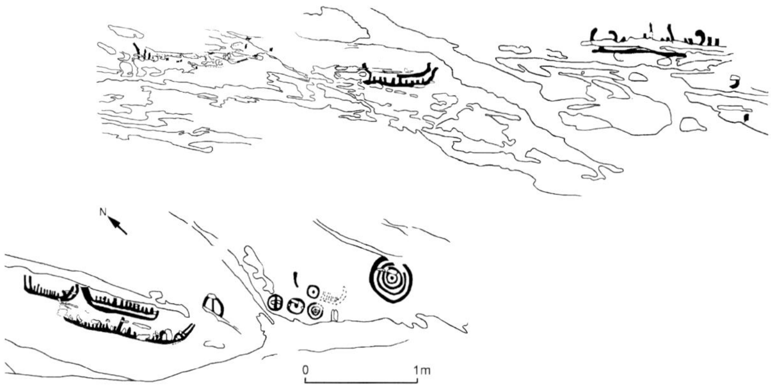

FIGURE 168. Weathering has deteriorated the stone; in many places the images are almost obliterated.

BM

stems extend from the keel in either direction, both fore and aft, and served to help the boat slice through the water. We cannot discount the possibility that they were capped with animal heads, a feature we know was common on vessels in later times (Østmo 1990).

From historic sources we know that hide-covered boats, which can be considered as a continuation of the boat-building tradition of the Bronze Age, were used for long ocean voyages as late as the beginning of the Iron Age (Kahl and Kristiansen 1976). However, we cannot overlook the possibility that wooden boats may have been the models for the images at Berge. At Hjortspring in Als, Denmark, a boat was found in a bog during the 1800s that is easily comparable to the rock art images (Crumlin-Pedersen and Trakadas 2003). It was constructed of thin lime-tree planks that were bound together and caulked with resin to make a round-bottomed vessel. The boat was built without a keel and was almost 20 metres long and 2 metres wide. It was pointed fore and aft, and like the images on the mountain wall, it had pronounced stems at both ends. The boat was constructed with a ten-ribbed frame that also served as the support for ten rowing benches. This means that the vessel may have had a crew of more than 20, including the lookout and helmsman. Oars found with the boat reveal that it was paddled instead of rowed, but was hand steered with a tiller. The large crew and the sleek shape allowed it to navigate at great speed. As a large number of swords, spearheads, mail armour and other war equipment were found on board, it is logical to assume that the boat was a warship fitted out for battle. The equipment suggests that it was in use during a time in the 300s BC, before it was buried in a bog far from the ocean, probably as a votive offering to the gods. The find seems to further clarify the relationship people of bygone eras had to boats, above and beyond their function as a means of transportation. In one place, boats were buried as offerings; in another, they are found engraved on stone, but both were elements in religious practice.

Clear visual similarities between the Hjortspring vessel found in Denmark and the boat images on the rock wall at Berge reinforce this impression, and may well have played a role in the creation of the rock art images.

Archaeological surveys of the sub-soil

Surveys of rock art sites are often limited to studies of the images alone, through comparisons of style and expression with other images from other sites. It has not generally been common practice to investigate the immediate surroundings of the rock art through excavations. Since the content and meaning behind the engravings is not easily accessible, the ground beneath the images can conceal important traces that help to tell us more about the contexts in which the rock art occurred. Artefacts and charcoal remaining from the same time as the images were created can be very helpful in identifying what went on around these sites. It also helps us to date activity here and enables us to more easily determine the social setting of the rock art. In this respect, however, we must add that some excavations carried out around rock art panels have yielded disappointingly few results, where not a single artefact, trace of charcoal or other cultural item has been unearthed. It is impossible to say with any certainty whether this is simply the result of no traces having been left, of obliteration when fields were cultivated or perhaps of deterioration due to natural processes. It should also be noted that the sub-soil around the rock art images may have remains of activity that are both earlier and younger than the rock art itself. Therefore, archaeological material from excavations of this kind must be thoroughly assessed before conclusions can be drawn about its relevance to the rock art images. To date, so few excavations in adjacent areas of rock art have been carried out that it is difficult to discern any clear pattern of possible activity on the sites during the time when the images were created.

As a remedy for the lack of excavations, parallel investigations were conducted of both the rock art at Berge and the sub-soil beneath the rock wall. A small plot was excavated, only one metre wide and three metres long, but large enough to retrieve any archaeological material that may have been present (Lødøen 2000). Based on earlier experience, or more precisely, on the lack of such experience, there was no clear idea as to what might be unearthed. This meant that it was even more important to proceed as cautiously as possible in order to avoid damaging any potential prehistoric remains that may have held the key to the world that is only vaguely insinuated by the rock art images. An atmosphere of excitement and curiosity reigned, and questions concerning the meaning of the images abounded: why were they created? How old might they be?

Many layers with traces of activity

It was quickly discovered that the upper layers of soil that were excavated contained items of a more modern nature. Apart from gravel and large amounts of detritus, there were fragments of glass, pottery and brick. These finds were not surprising, however. After all, the site was very close to the farm buildings. The upper layer was almost half a metre thick, somewhat thicker than expected, although waste matter in the layer revealed that it must have accumulated here over a period of some two hundred years. It immediately seemed probable, if these soil accumulations were equally as thick along the entire rock wall, that more rock art images may still be buried in the soil. Future investigations will be able to answer these questions. As the excavation continued, several clearly separate layers of soil were discovered, each of which was able to reveal activity beneath the rock wall. A compact layer of soil and stony detritus clearly revealed that a section of the mountain wall had broken off and fragments had been strewn across the flat stretch of land. A series of fractured areas towards the top of the mountain wall made it easy to see where the falling mass had come from.

Beneath the landslide detritus, characteristic traces of cultivation in former times were found. They revealed that far back in time there must have been two periods when fields had been cultivated all the way up to the mountain wall. The layers were mixed with bits of charcoal, indicating burnt wood and underbrush, or that ashes had been strewn over the field, possibly to improve the soil. Charcoal deposits are particularly decisive for our investigations as they allow us to date prehistoric activity likely to be associated with the production of the rock art. More layers and strata were uncovered further down, before the excavation work came to an end, more than one and a half metres below the ground surface, well into the layer of old shoreline gravel. Not a single artefact was found, although a series of soil strata was uncovered, revealing that the soil bore traces of both natural processes and human activity.

Traces of open fires from the time of the rock art

Some of the most surprising finds were the remains of three ancient hearths that were located almost on top of each other at the transition to the shoreline gravel. By pure chance, the outer edge of the excavation site had cut cleanly through all three and clearly revealed half of the two hearths and a section of the third. The halves that remained in the soil outside of the excavated area were clearly visible in the excavated wall against the yellowish-grey shoreline sand, appearing as three dark, oblong layers, pointed at both ends and thicker in the centre. The ends were marked with stones in places, suggesting that they may have had stones around them. The hearths were separated from one another by thin layers of shoreline gravel, which clearly indicated they were also separated by intervals of time. It is tempting to conclude that the hearths were in use at the time the images were made. The intervals that are reflected in their location one above the other are mirrored in the positions of the images on the mountain wall, where the temporal aspect is reflected in the gradual changes in the shape and stylistic expression of the boat images, descending from the uppermost images to those at the bottom. This means that the remains of the hearths and the rock art images can be seen together, as part of a whole. The fact that the hearths are separated by thin layers of sand also provides important information as to what occurred between each fire. Since the fires were made just below the rock wall, the shoreline sand

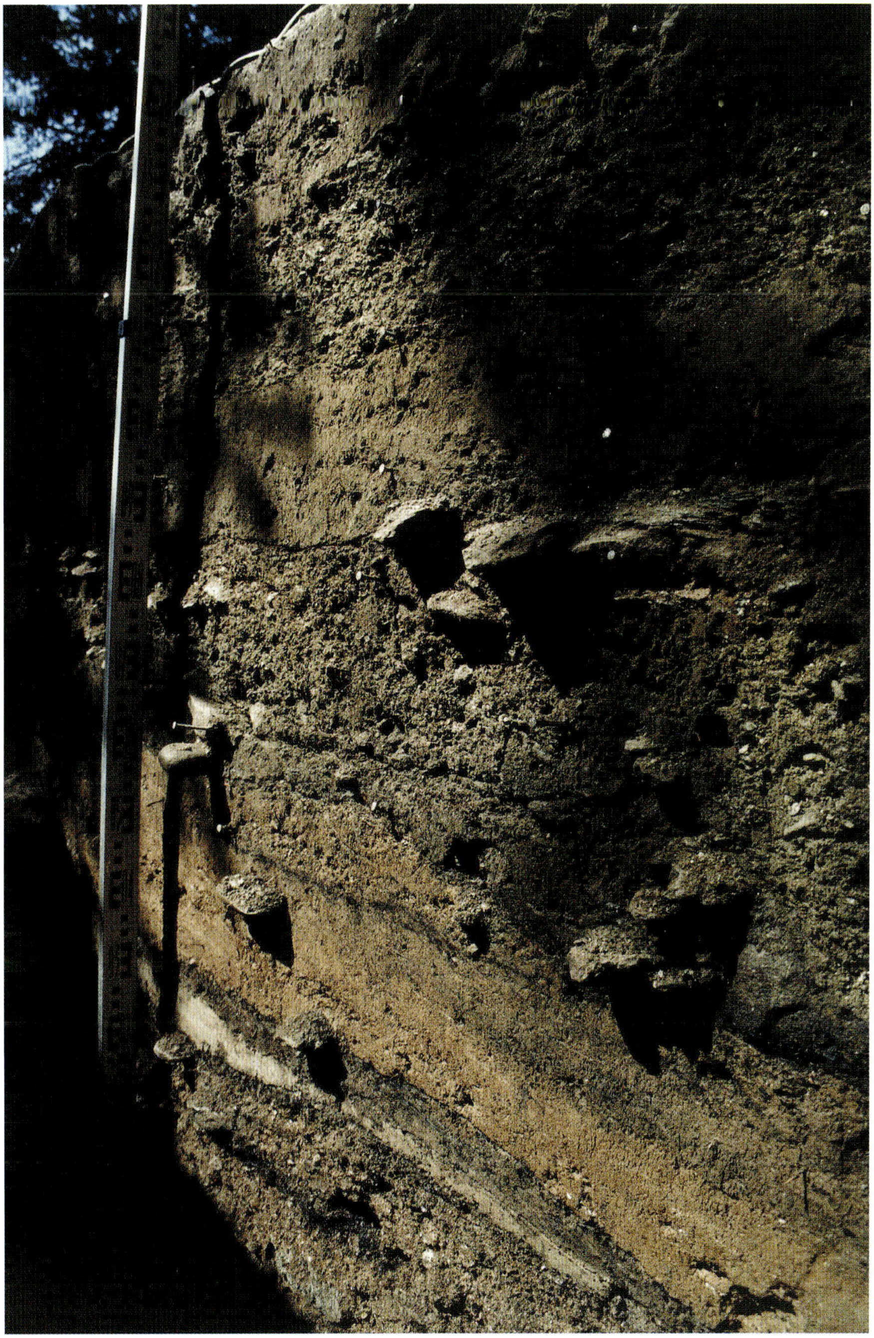

FIGURE 169. We can see the various soil strata descending along this profile from an excavation. At the bottom are several deposits from fires, appearing as dark layers against the greyish-brown beach gravel.
TL

surrounding them is an indication that the Hardanger fjord stretched up almost to the wall itself. Geological surveys show that we have to go as far back as the end of the Bronze Age in order to place the shoreline this far inland (Romundset 2005; Vasskog 2006). We may therefore conclude that the rock wall at the time was a cliff that rose directly up from the shoreline. If the fjord came up to the base of the mountain wall, or perhaps even some distance up the wall itself, it is easy to imagine that the wall was most easily accessed at low tide. This would also have made it easier to carve images on the wall without working from a boat. If the images were carved during periods of low tide and this included building fires, then the conclusion is that tidal waters flooded the hearths afterwards and gradually covered them with shoreline sediment. If the activity was seasonal or part of an annual ceremony, the spring or storm surges would have covered them with sandy sediment between each time they were in use.

Radiological dating of charcoal taken from the hearth sites shows that all three are prior to the Christian era, more specifically from the period between 400 and 100 BC. It is interesting to note in this respect that the Hjortspring boat (see Figure 139) and the rock art images are similar not only in appearance, but the shoreline fires were made during the same centuries when the boat was in use. No other relics older than this time were found. Another argument for a close connection between the fireplaces and the rock art can be drawn from a few less focused images on the rock wall. In between ships, in the lower middle section of the wall two interesting figures can be found. Today one of them is highly fragmented but both have probably consisted of three circles arranged in a triangular form, unified by a central hub.

The images probably represent triskeles, a classical form associated with both the Celtic La Tene period and the Pre-Roman Iron Age (Klindt-Jensen 1950:110p; Filip 1956). They are known from several rock art sites in Scandinavia and is a common motif on many archaeological artefacts, in particular bronze objects. A strong relation between triskeles and dated bronzes from the latter part (period V) of the Bronze Age has been suggested (Mikkelsen 1998), but their presence are far more common in the Pre-Roman Iron Age. The fireplaces, the triskeles and the lower images are probably parts of the same process, implying that the rock art can be pushed some centuries up in time (Lødøen 2007).

Future excavations may unearth other hearths, artefacts or man-made cultural layers and structures. However, there is much to suggest that no remains will be found for any activity older than the period of the hearths. The fjord's water line in earlier times came all the way up to the rock wall. It is possible in the future that the age of the hearths, structures and soil layers may be used as a basis for differentiating between the different phases in the creation of the many images on the mountain wall. Furthermore, a closer determination of the age of the images will make it easier to relate them to other archaeological material from the same time period and thereby create a better basis for understanding and interpreting the images, their location and their meaning. All of the indications we have suggest that the earliest figures highest on the wall were created from on board a boat, and that land uplift gradually made it possible to stand on the shoreline when the lowest and youngest of the engravings were made.

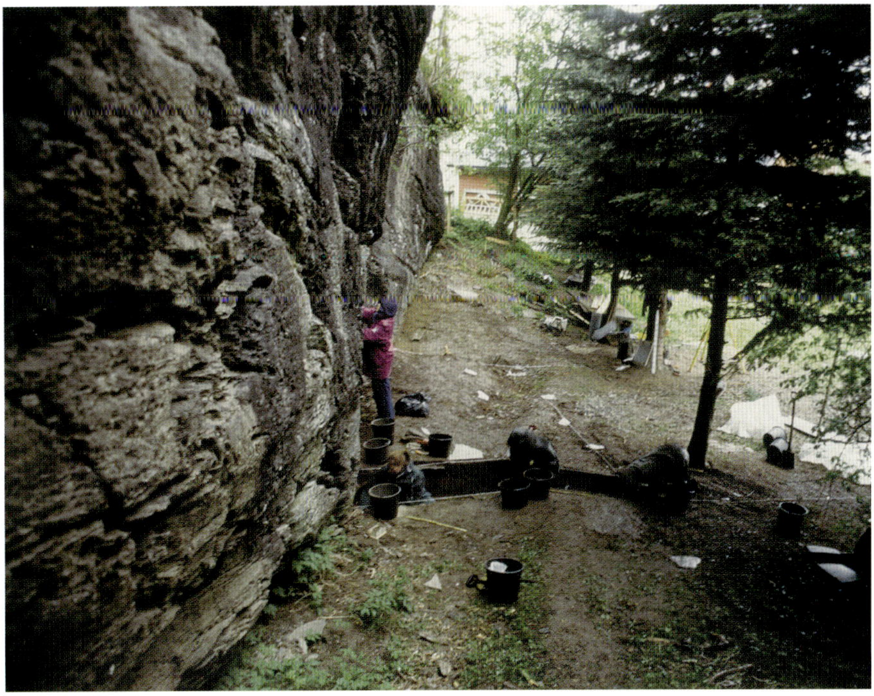

FIGURE 170. Documentation of excavation showing how the shaft was dug out perpendicular to the mountain wall.
TL

Religious rites

It is tempting to think that the images were made in conjunction with religious rites. However, exactly what kind of rites and how they were performed is currently unknown. Ethnographic studies show numerous examples of the importance of rites. When society undergoes changes and people's rank or status is altered, rites emerge and become important in order to promote acceptance and legitimacy for the new or changed social roles. In the same way, changes in society and rearrangements in prehistoric power structures through battles and feuds between groups and clans also created a need for legitimizing rituals. Through rituals, various aspects, even fragile aspects, of social norms and world-views were carved in stone in order to make them more tangible, more understandable. It is nevertheless quite difficult to understand the symbolism that may have been expressed. There are numerous, almost countless alternatives. What role did the boat play in these contexts? Apart from being an essential means of transportation and an important war vessel, and perhaps precisely because of these attributes, they were undoubtedly important power symbols that were naturally associated with religious contexts. In these contexts, is it possible that they also served as symbols for journeys into the afterlife? We are unable to comment on these aspects of past society with any degree of certainty. For the time being, we can perceive only a vague outline of what may have occurred. If rituals were performed in the distant past at this site, then it is highly likely that it entailed the use of open fires, which would explain the hearths that we have uncovered so far. Archaeological surveys have revealed that during both funeral processions and offering ceremonies, the use of open fires was quite common, particularly from the later years of the Bronze Age and on into the Iron Age. However, we lack an explanation as to why so many boat images were depicted together with the other figures here at Berge. It is interesting that the mountain wall was used for the same purpose at different periods of time, perhaps separated by many hundreds of years. This may be a tradition involving boat images that stretched from the beginning of the Bronze Age approximately 3000–4000 years ago until the beginning of the Iron Age, in the five hundred years before the birth of Christ. This coincides with the dating of the hearths.

A recurrent pattern

On promontories, sheer rock walls and overhanging ledges along the northern side of the Hardanger fjord, there are several panels that are more or less contemporary with the Berge site, and where boats are the central motif. The Vangdal site and the outermost boat images at Hamarhaug are found further inside the fjord. There are also a few rock images of the Northern Tradition with similar locations, as if the motive for choosing sites for rock art has remained the same for thousands of years. On the other side of the fjord is Bakke in Jondal, discussed separately in the following chapter. The uniform location of rock art images along fjords is curious and contrasts with the other areas of Western Norway, where the images are distributed on sloping rock faces, large blocks and earthbound stones. As if to illustrate this uniform location, two new panels of boat images were found recently at Linga and Aksnes, a few kilometres farther in along the fjord from Berge. Judging from available information, the discovery was a consequence of the finds at Berge, which had spurred the interest of others in the area who wanted to make discoveries.

Bakke in Jondal – A Sacred Site and Meeting Place in the Bronze Age

In the late autumn of 1903 Bergens Museum received a letter from Pastor Olafsen from Ullensvang, who wrote concerning "a couple of previously unknown Ancient monuments" that had been discovered a few years earlier by the rural bailiff at Jondal. At two places in the small rural community of Herand on the eastern side of Hardangerfjorden (the Hardanger Fjord), the bailiff had seen rock engravings depicting ships that resembled "the Images that are present in several other Places" (Olafsen 1903). Unfortunately one of these had been damaged as a result of roadworks at the steamship quay. The bailiff thought, however, that the other engraving, on the Bakke farmstead, could be found if the area was thoroughly searched. The next mention of the rock art in Herand is in 1910 in the natural science journal "Naturen", in which government geologist J. Rekstad described some rock carvings he had been told of by the landowner at Bakke (Rekstad 1910). On a sloping, ice-scoured rock surface, five or six indistinct boat images, a ring and some cup marks were seen. According to the landowner, there were more figures on a portion of the rock that he had covered with soil a few years earlier. During the century that has passed since the local pastor had announced the discovery of the rock art at Herand, a large number of rock art images have been discovered at Bakke, making this locality unique both locally and in a regional context.

The rock art at Kalhaugen

The Bakke farmstead – colloquially known as *Bokkå* – is located on a sloping hillside in Herandsbygda, a couple of hundred metres from the fjord and with a wide panorama out over the rural area and the sea. The rock carvings seen by the bailiff from Jondal and later by the geologist Rekstad is located in a sheltered hollow in the terrain called Kalhagen – a flat, grassy depression framed by two low, elongated slopes of bare rocks. The majority of the images – 123 in all – cover almost the entire surface of the southernmost rock-face that lies more or less flush with the ground. It was known in the past as Mariskarvet (Kolltveit 1954), and the earlier footpath down to the fjord ran across it, causing damage to many of the images at the top of the rock. On the other side of the grassy slope is Loftarskleivi, which is a somewhat taller ridge with a sheer edge facing south-east. Groups of images – 38 in all – are carved into the top and sides of the ridge. In addition to these two rock art panels, another panel with around twenty cup marks was recorded some decades ago, but it has not been found in recent years.

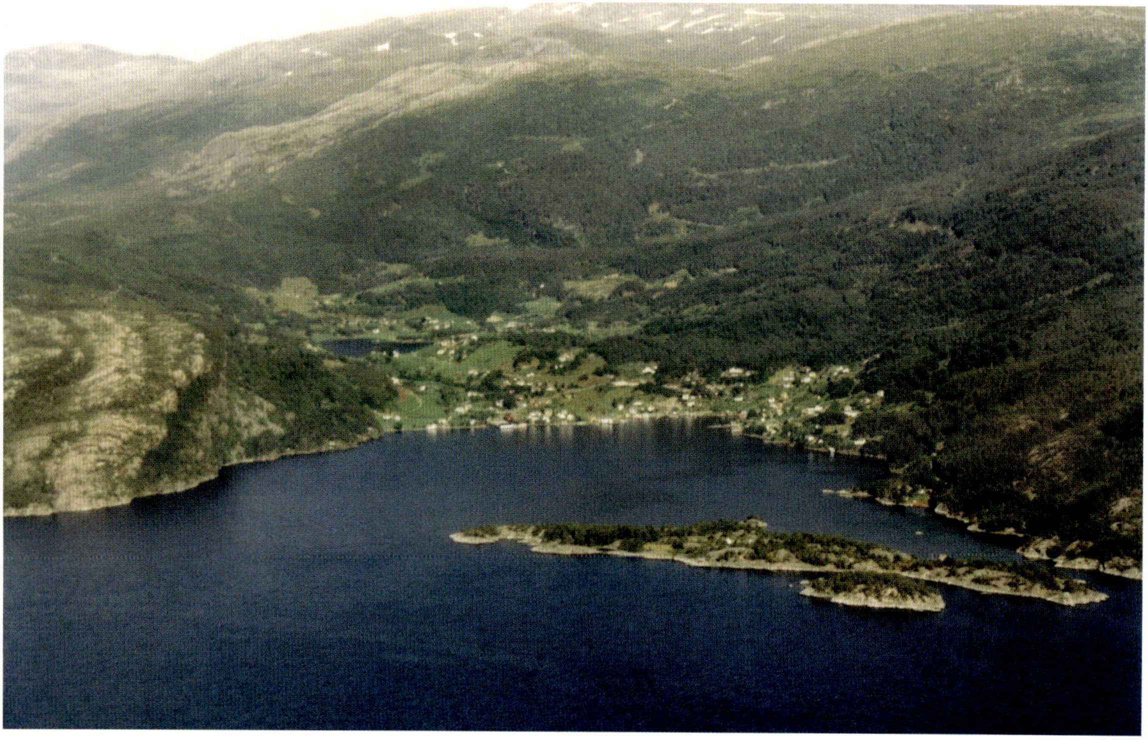

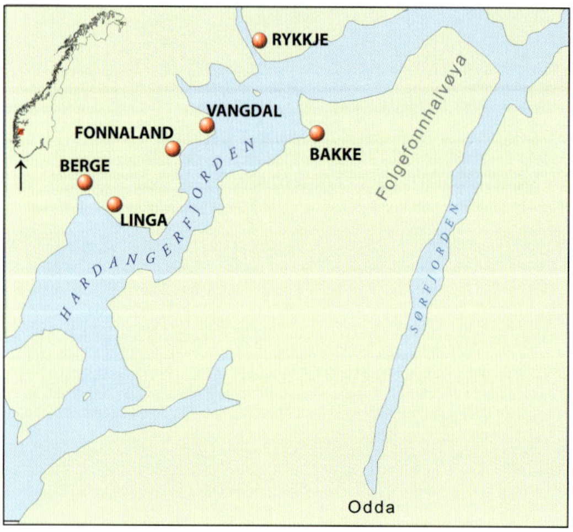

FIGURES 171–172. The aerial photograph shows Herandsbygda with the long and narrow Herandsholmen in the foreground. To the left of the photo is the steep, 700-metre-tall Samlanuten. Bakke, where the rock carvings are located, is in the centre of the photo, slightly to the right of a large green field some distance up from the seashore. In the background is the mountain range of the Folgefonn Peninsula, which rises to a height of 1300–1400 metres.

MAP AI, ILLUSTRATION MW

The images carved on the rock surfaces at Bakke are dated to the Bronze Age or Early Iron Age (1800 BC–500 AD). These include boat images in varying shapes, large and small circular shaped figures, foot soles and cup marks – all motifs that are amongst the most common of the Southern rock art tradition. One of the motifs at Bakke, however, belongs to the less commonly found motifs – namely depictions of humans. There are twenty-three human images on Mariskarvet and nine on Loftarskleivi.

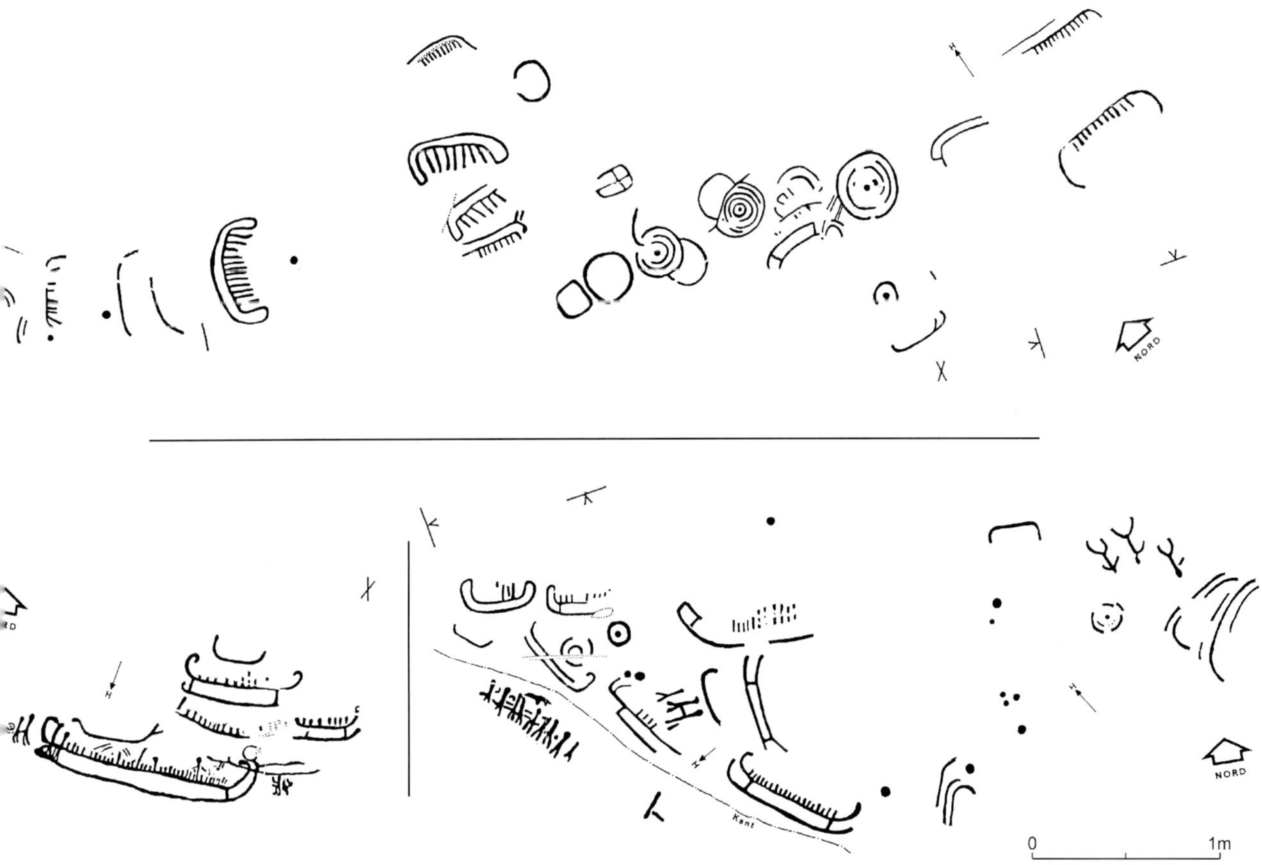

FIGURE 173. The rock carvings at Mariskarvet comprise a complex world of images that were probably created through continual use over a period of several hundred years. The rock-face is 12–14 metres long and more than three metres wide. The tracing, made in 1970, is divided in two in order to show the entire extent of the surface covered with images. At the end of the 1990s several more figures were discovered on the panel, but they do not appear in this tracing.
GM

The rare motif

Anthropomorphic images occur sporadically in Scandinavian rock art of the Southern Tradition. In many areas the motif is not present at all, and in other places only a few human figures appear on individual panels. Normally less than ten percent of rock art images in any given area are interpreted as representations of human beings (Coles 2003). The largest number of anthropomorphs occurs in Bohuslän on the west coast of Sweden, where the motif amounts to more than 20 percent of the total number of rock art images in this region. Of the total of 170 sites with rock art of the Southern Tradition in Hordaland, only Bakke and two or three other sites have depictions of humans: Bruteigsteinen in Etne, Sledasteinen at Voss and perhaps Berge in Strandebarm (Mandt Larsen 1972; Wold 2002). At Bakke, the human representations amount to one-fifth of the images on the two panels, thus setting the Bakke panels apart from the majority of rock art sites in both Hardanger and the adjoining region.

Despite the fact that depictions of humans are a rare motif in Bronze Age rock art, these images are central in the discussion concerning the meaning of rock art of the Southern Tradition. However, before discussing these images further, we will turn to Herandsbygda, and try to find out more about this tiny rural community, and why people during the Bronze Age carved motifs that were not in common use – and perhaps scarcely known to exist – in the surrounding settled areas.

The rural settlement at the foot of Samlanuten

Herand is situated on the western side of the peninsula Folgefonnshalvøya, named after the glacier Folgefonni – the third largest glacier in Norway – that crowns the mountain summits of inner Hardanger. A part of the settlement – the oldest according to place names – is located some distance uphill from the fjord, around a lake called Herandsvatnet, while the more recent farms are closer to the sea, nestled inside a deep, wide bay just south of the promontory Samlanes (Kolltveit 1954). Here the mountain Samlanuten – or Samlen, as it is also known – rises to a height of almost 700 metres, having withstood the ravages of the inland glacial ice. Along the foot of Samlanuten is a continuous range of overhanging cliffs and rock shelters, reaching all the way from the sea and up to about 150 metres above sea level.

The name Samlanuten – a pyramid-shaped mountain – is reflected in the names given both to the promontory on which it is located, the section of Hardangerfjorden to which Herand belongs – Samlafjorden – and the large valley basin, Samladalen, which stretches from Herand and eastward across the Folgefonni Peninsula to Aga at Sørfjorden in Hardanger. The prefix *samn-* in this nomenclature also occurs in the earlier name of the community, Samlandaherad, dated to the Middle Ages (1300–1400s) (*ibid.*). Both the prefix and the current community name, Herand, belong to a group of place names that scholars have not yet been able to explain. Some names of this type may date back to prehistoric time, although it is not possible to determine a more specific date for them (Olsen 1926).

The natural conditions were already favourable for settlement in Herand in prehistoric times. Southward along the fjord between Herand and the community centre of Jondal, the bedrock consists of granitic gneiss, and the entire shoreline and mountainsides are steep and barren, offering few suitable places for collective settlement and land cultivation. When reaching Herand, however, a lush and green landscape opens up around the Herand bay. The bedrock here is phyllite and mica schist, which yields reasonably good arable soil. The Herand bay is one of the few natural harbours in the inner part of Hardangerfjorden, with the elongated Herandsholmen at the outermost point of the bay as a buffer against the open fjord, which can be unpredictable during north-westerly gales. In the 1700s an inn for seafarers was established on this little islet (Kolltveit 1954). This meant that in the past, Herand was an important crossroads for travelling and communication on the route along the extensive, many-branched Hardangerfjorden, as well as across the mountainous peninsula to Sørfjorden, giving easy access to mountain grazing, hunting resources and fishing lakes.

Until a few years ago, the only physical evidence of human activity in Herand during the Bronze Age were rock carvings, some burial cairns and a few axes. Apart from the two rock art panels at Bakke, some smaller panels containing cup marks occur at a couple of farms closer to the fjord – Sævarhagen and

Tveiten (Mandt Larsen 1972; Wold 2002). Along the shore at Samlanes and on the eastern tip of the Herandsholmen islet are three or four burial cairns of a type normally dated to the millennium prior to the Christian era, although no datable artefacts have been found in them.

This picture changed when, as part of an interdisciplinary research project on rock shelters in Western Norway called the "Hellerprosjektet", excavations were carried out in rock shelters at the foot of Samlanuten in 2005–2006 (huin.uib.no/hellerprosjektet/index.spy). In some of the shelters cultural layers dated to the Bronze Age and Early Iron Age were uncovered, containing charcoal, ceramics and slag from metal production, as well as bones from sheep, pigs and cattle. Although the remains from the rock shelters have still not been fully analysed, the material presents new evidence on the way of life in Herand during the Bronze Age. The leader of the project, Knut Andreas Bergsvik, suggests that Herand may have been one of the earliest agricultural communities in the Hardanger region. While the rock shelters were probably used as places for working or in relation to ritual activity, he assumes that the farmhouses were located near today's courtyards (*ibid.*).

In an attempt to identify some of the activities that occurred in Herand, and in particular in relation to the rock art at Bakke, the human motif in Bronze Age rock art will be more closely examined – its design, the context in which it is found, its relationship to other rock art motifs, compositions and interpretations.

FIGURE 174. Along the foot of the 700 metres tall Samlanuten is a continuous range of overhanging cliffs and rock shelters called Sævarhellaren, reaching all the way from the sea and up to about 150 metres above sea level. Excavations in cultural layers in the shelters have disclosed archaeological remains from a wide time span, stretching from the Early Mesolithic to the Early Iron Age.
KAB

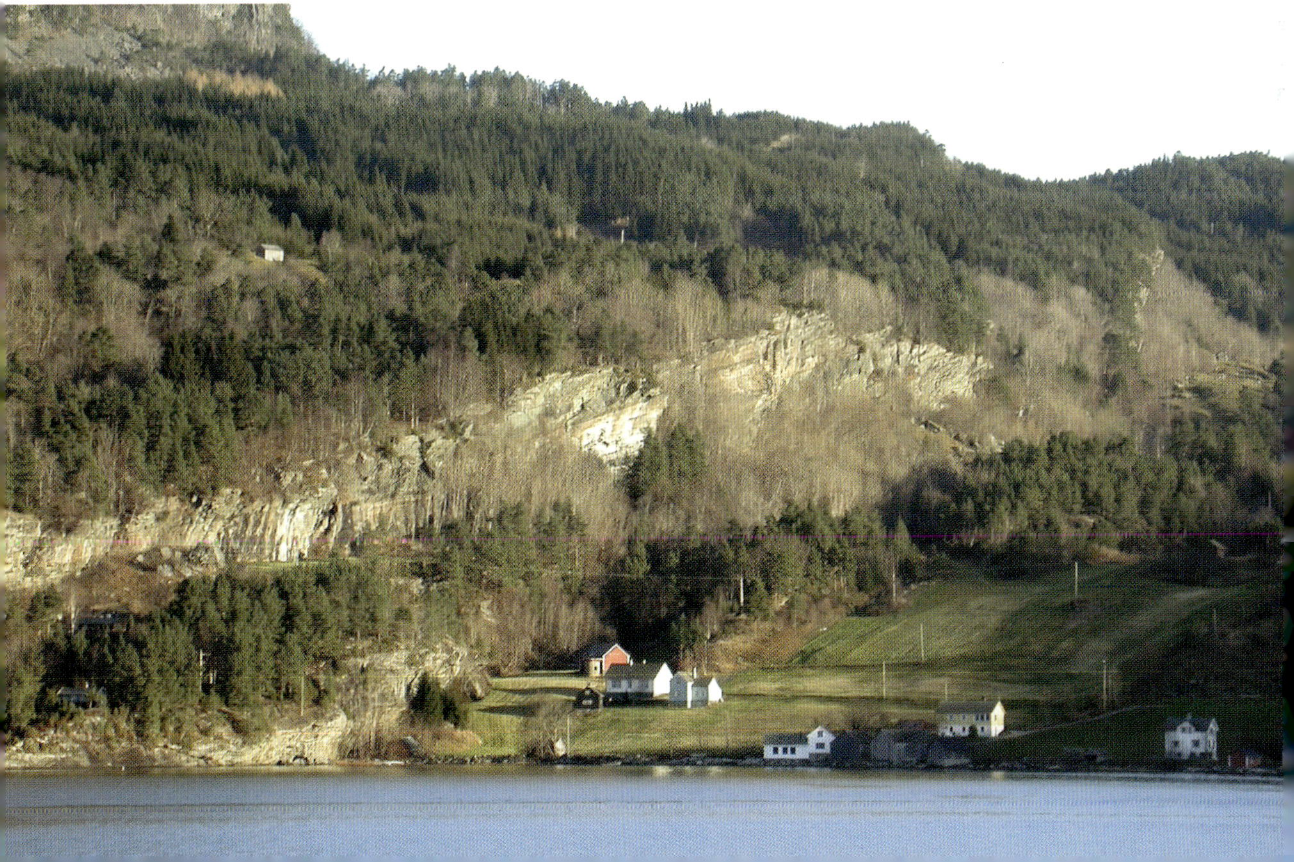

Human images in Bronze Age rock art

The human representations in the rock art of the Bronze Age are very schematic. Anatomical details such as the body and head, arms and legs, and in some instances the sex organs, are rendered using simple lines. The human representations frequently resemble the stick figures typically drawn by children, rather than flesh-and-blood humans. Despite the simple linear shapes, however, many of the figures have an elegance and lifelike quality that parallels the grace of human figures created by modern artists (Mandt 1991). The human figures at Bakke closely resemble the images of people found from other rock art panels in Scandinavia. A simple line denotes the body, and a circular, small depression symbolizes the head. Some of the figures are seen face-on and have their arms and legs extended out from the body. Most of the Bakke images, however, are depicted in profile, with straight or slightly curved legs. A few appear to have short arms, and the majority have straight lines extending outwards perpendicular with the body at about hip level. Most of the humans seen in profile are presented in pairs and are connected by this perpendicular line fragment. Several of the couples are lined up in a row, along with individual humans seen in profile.

In many rock art regions, the human figures are depicted in a much more lifelike manner than at the Bakke panels. They hold things in their hands; several raise spears or axes against one another as if in battle. Some appear to be dancing, or raising their arms as if worshipping. Some perform acrobatic exercises, and others play instruments similar to lures. A number of figures

FIGURE 175. The feature that distinguishes the Bakke panel from other rock carvings both in the immediate vicinity and in an even wider radius is the presence of numerous human figures. Above all, the depiction of humans in procession is a rarity – such as this group at Loftarskleivi, where the rows of human figures are also surrounded by boats.
GM

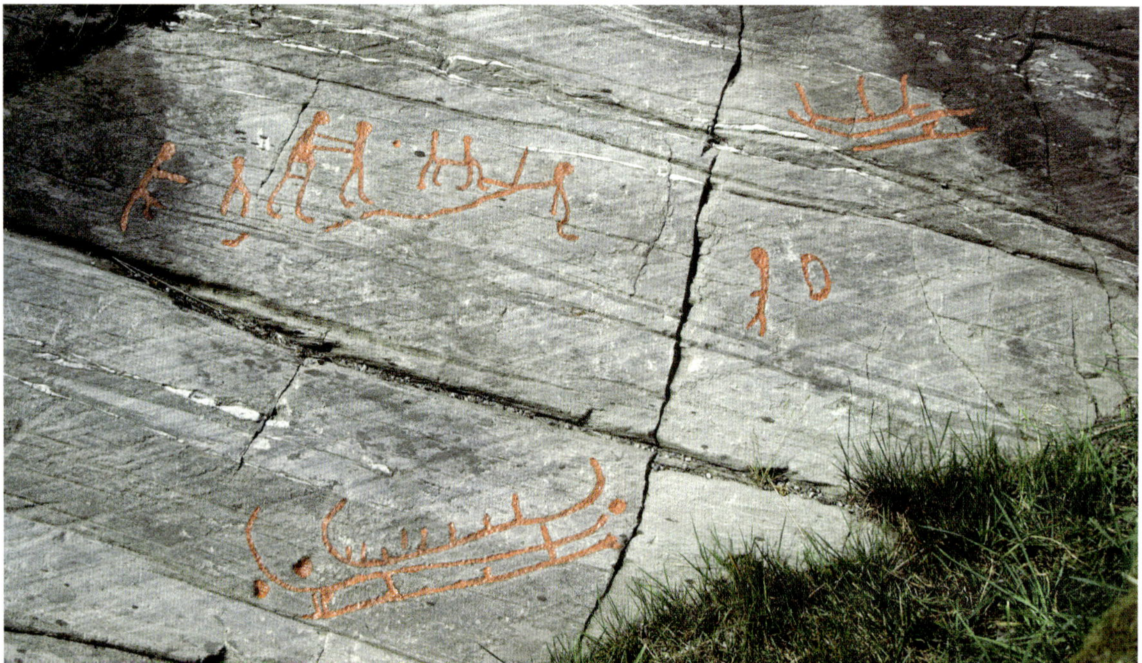

appear to be clad in a long robe or mantle, and a few wear headdresses (Hygen and Bengtsson 1999). It is reasonable to imagine that these presumably active humans are depicted as performing specific tasks. The rock art humans have been alternately interpreted as participants in cult rituals, as gods or as mythical creatures. Quite frequently, one human figure is much larger than the others, and these are commonly considered as depicting deities, heroes or religious leaders. In many cases several humans stand in a row, or in groups together with other rock art motifs, particularly boats and rings, and sometimes also with animals – for example horsemen and hunting parties accompanied by dogs. These scenes have been interpreted partly as illustrations of mythical tales, and partly as depictions of actual ritualistic acts.

Myths and rituals

In all religious and social systems there are myths explaining how the world was created, the relationship between people and deities, the order of nature and the values of society (Hygen and Bengtsson 1999; Wold 2002). Because the myths are considered as sacred and true, they legitimize the social and cultural system of which they form a part. From time immemorial people have affirmed and recreated the mythical events through ritualistic acts. The actual reaffirmation of the myths represented by the rituals serves to perpetuate the society's existence. Importance is attached to performing the rituals in exactly the same manner, and at the same intervals – otherwise the world as it is perceived faces the risk of collapse.

The depictions of humans performing acts of a ritualistic or mythical nature are to a great extent the features that have led to the interpretation of Bronze Age rock art as expressions of creed concepts and religious practices. This is illustrated most explicitly in an interpretation that was put forward in the 1920s – namely that the rock art of the Bronze Age was part of rituals performed in order to ensure the fertility of fields and pasturelands and to invoke good health and fortune for people and livestock (Almgren 1927). One central group of images includes the paired human figures that are also found at the Bakke engravings. The couples are interpreted as depictions of the sexual act: two human figures seen in profile and close to one another, the one apparently with an erect penis (the line fragment at hip level), the other frequently – but not always – with long hair. These scenes – popularly called "bridal couples" – were seen as illustrations of the god of fertility and his consort in the act of intercourse. The motif – the sacred wedding – is well-known from the myth of the seasonal drama: the tale explaining how vegetation germinates, flowers, withers and dies in correlation with the ever-changing seasonal cycle. By engraving the mythical tale in stone – and perhaps by practicing it ritualistically – the fertility myth is reaffirmed and the crop yield is ensured.

Men or women?

The erect penis occurs not only in scenes where couples are depicted, but also in a number of the individual human images, and all of these have commonly been considered to be males. The interpretation has been reinforced by the fact that many of these figures are involved in acts that are normally considered to be masculine – for example, battles and hunting scenes – and the figures which are frequently larger than average often have oversized penises.

Very few of the rock art humans can be identified as women based on physical traits (Engelstad 2001). It has been common to see one of the partners in the scenes depicting sexual intercourse as female, and the long hair that these figures have – apparently ponytails – has normally been seen as a distinctive trait denoting a female (Mandt 2001a). However, since there are also examples of human images with both a penis and long hair, the amount of hair can scarcely be used as a trait for determining gender. The issue has also been raised as to whether the "bridal couple" actually depicts intercourse between a male and a female, or whether both figures represent men in the same situation (Yates 1990). Moreover, the couple might even be perceived as ambiguous. It is conceivable that the viewer was meant to see the figures as male and female at certain times, while at others (or perhaps at the same time?) as two men (Mandt 2001b).

The majority of human images in Bronze Age rock art, however, lack gender attributes, making it impossible to determine with any certainty whether they depict men or women (Hedengran 1991). Despite the fact that human figures without penises outnumbers those with penises, the consensus is that the rock art humans are mainly males, and that the rock art as a whole is connected with an affirmation of male status, power and ownership rights (Engelstad 2001). Part of the explanation for this masculinisation may be that the figures with penises, and the activities in which they appear to be involved, are strikingly conspicuous on the rock surface. In a non-literal sense, we might say that they are "noisy" – we can almost hear the clashing of weapons and the din of battle. In this respect the active figures with penises are more easily noticed and focused on in the interpretation process than the simpler, genderless human images (Mandt 2001b).

The disproportion between the number of human figures with and without penises becomes particularly conspicuous when we take into account the stylized, almost anonymous human images populating the numerous boats – the so-called crew lines. The overwhelming majority have no individual characteristics, and they lack heads and bodily features such as penises. If these figures are taken into account, genderless, apparently passive humans dominate the rock surfaces, overshadowing the active individuals with erect penises (Hedengran 1993).

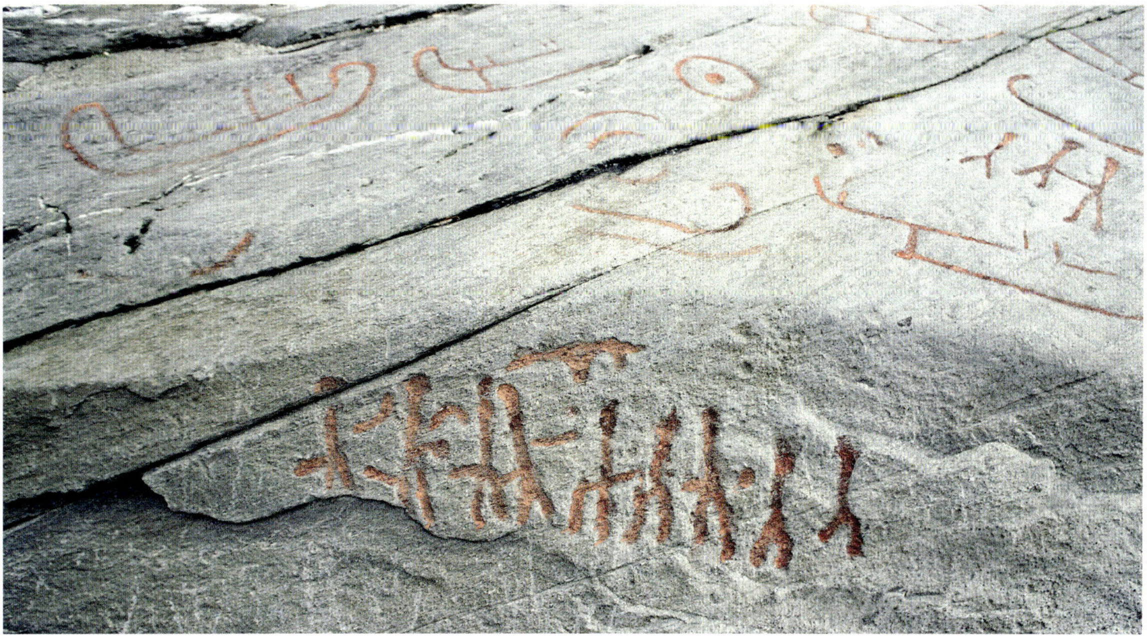

FIGURE 176. In the Mariskarvet procession, there are several examples showing individual, stick-figure humans arranged in pairs and linked at the hip by a line segment. These pairs have normally been interpreted as "bridal couples" and are associated with rituals involving the myth of the seasonal drama.
RU

Signs of gender or symbols of vitality?

Perhaps it is time to ask what the erect penis in rock art actually represents. Is it so certain that the male sex organ should be perceived as a specific sign for biological gender? In religious systems in different parts of the world, the phallus represents the power and fertility of nature, particularly in conjunction with religious celebrations with the purpose of increasing the fertility of people and animals as well as of nature as a whole (Fuglestvedt 1999). When this cultic, fertility-oriented interpretation of Bronze Age rock art was first proposed, the phallus as an attribute of the god of fertility was a central argument (Almgren 1927). But seeing the phallus as a symbol of something beyond a way of denoting a deity's gender or expressing male sexuality opens a much wider interpretive landscape.

For the people of the Bronze Age, carving images in stone was an important and meaningful act. We infer that the images are closely interrelated with the world-view of the people of the age, their outlook on life and their own place in existence. People experience the world through their own bodies and through their own sexuality. Human sexuality is not only a matter of reproduction: it is also self-realization and an expression of creative power in the widest sense of the term. Creativity and vitality are both masculine and feminine traits. The male body, however, permits a depiction of virility and zest for life in an extremely visual and concrete manner (Fuglestvedt 1999). In this respect, the phallus motif may represent potency in the common sense of the word, and can also be a symbol for the forces that were to be activated through the rituals involving the rock art. The scenes depicting intercourse should perhaps be interpreted within

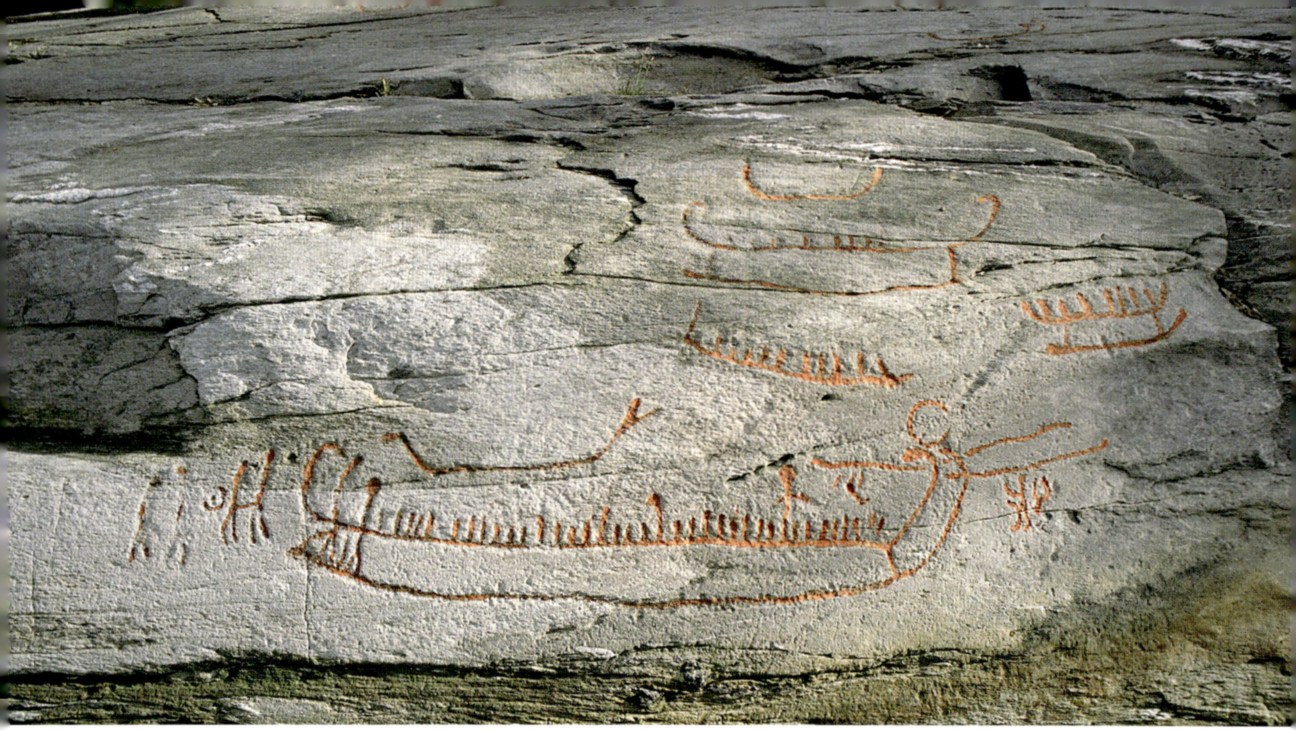

a similar frame of thought. The erotic illustrations may represent the vitality and forces that were necessary for the recreation of the myths expressed in the rock art carvings.

FIGURE 177. The largest boat figure at Bakke is found at Mariskarvet. It is more than 1.2 metres long, and among the many crew lines there are both human-like figures and several long lines that may depict bronze trumpets. Human figures are also placed on either side of the boat, some of them depicted in pairs – so-called "bridal couples".
RU

The interpretative context

If the intention of the phallic illustrations was not merely to identify gender, then how is it possible to explain the fact that some of the human images have phalli, while the majority lack any gender attribute? Perhaps it is the qualities that the human figures demonstrate and the context in which they occur that are essential – rather than their gender (Hedengran 1991, 1993). The phallic figures involved in lively activities – for example hunting and fighting, or dancing and lure-playing – can be associated with personal qualities such as vigour, boldness and strength. These are characteristic traits of the principal players in mythical tales or of active participants in rituals. The passive body language of the genderless individuals offers no clue as to the function they may have had in the rock art rituals. If we are to interpret the meaning of these figures, we must resort to the contexts, or situations, in which they occur: namely, the other images and rock art motifs with which the figures are depicted. Human images both with and without phalli often occur in complex groups of figures in which the boat image appears to be a central symbol. The genderless, almost anonymous crew lines in these boat images are the most typical example. But even human images with more clearly defined bodily elements – such as the bridal couples, and rows of paired individuals – are frequently depicted together with boats, in compositions that might be interpreted as representations of ritual activities (Hauptman Wahlgren 2002).

Conscious compositions

Compositions including boats and simplified humans in a procession occur on both of the rock art panels at Bakke in Herand. The most striking group of figures is found on the Mariskarvet panel. Approximately in the centre of a low, almost vertical surface of the rocky incline facing south is a boat image measuring a little more than one metre in length, with tall, curved stems. Above the boat image, where the incline flattens out, there are five or six densely grouped smaller boats. Some of the compactly drawn crew lines on the larger boat have distinct arms and heads, and a couple of the figures appear to be engaging in sexual intercourse. Human figures are situated on both sides of the boat: On the left side are two couples – apparently having intercourse – standing on either side of a small concentric circle, and on the right side is a single human figure with a phallus. A little further to the right – on the opposite side of a crevice in the rock – is a procession of eight or nine humans. Above this group is a small figure that perhaps represents an animal, although the species is impossible to identify.

The other human images on the Mariskarvet panel – a scene with a couple and some dancers – are located at the almost horizontal top of the rock surface, which is otherwise covered with images of boats, rings and foot soles. At Loftarskleivi there is also a composition including a procession of eight or nine humans surrounded by two or three boat images. The group is situated on a steep shelf along the edge of the ridge facing east, and just above this group, on the horizontal summit of the ridge, there is a row of foot soles and several boat images.

Amongst the several thousand rock art sites known from the Bronze Age in Scandinavia, only thirty panels with processions of human figures have been recorded (Coles 2003). Most of these sites occur in southern Sweden – in Bohuslän, Östergötland and Uppland, along with one in Skåne. In Norway, apart from the two processions at Bakke, one procession has been found at Leirfall in Trøndelag and two that are less clear in Østfold. The processions are most frequently placed alongside or between boat figures, in the same way seen as in Bakke. Although these compositions are not among the most common depictions during the Bronze Age, they occur so frequently and have so many common features that it is reasonable to assume they illustrate specific rituals involving processions of cult participants. It is likely that such processions were an important aspect of the activities that went on in the area around the rock art panels. Neither can it be discounted that the boat was an integral part of the rituals and myths of the Bronze Age.

The polyvalent boat symbol

In the world of Bronze Age images, the boat appears to have been a central and polyvalent symbol (Hauptman Wahlgren 2002). After cup marks, the

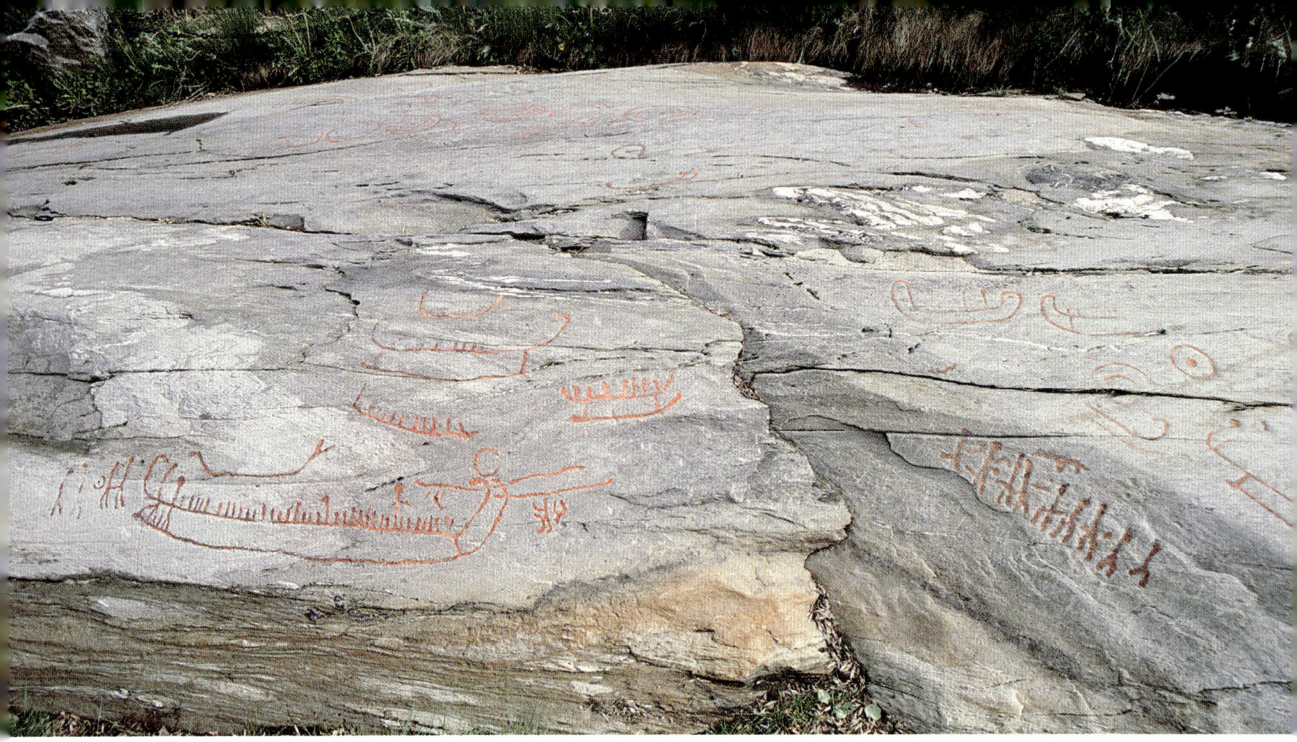

boat is the most common motif in Bronze Age rock art. It occurs on stones in burial chambers and is engraved on bronze artefacts. The boat is interpreted in a religious/mythological frame of reference, where the common denominator is symbolism for life – death – rebirth. The motif is associated with the journey into the realm of the dead and the underworld. However, it is also seen in connection with life-giving forces, with the sun's trajectory over the heavens (Kaul 1998, 2004) and with the renewal of nature after laying dormant throughout the winter. As a symbol for a journey, the boat can also be seen as an expression of communication and contact between people, and as a bearer of new ideas. In this respect, the boat is a basic symbol in the world-view of Bronze Age people, and it serves as a link between other symbols. The question is, what role did the boat play in the rituals where images of boats and people in procession appear to be a part of a fixed and continually recurrent relationship with one another?

FIGURE 178. The large boat figure and the procession at Mariskarvet are positioned on either side of a large cleft in the rock. The figures appear to have been intentionally placed in relation to this cleft, and it is tempting to interpret it as part of the composition. If the depiction is interpreted as a tale of the transition from one phase of human life to another, the cleft can perhaps be understood as the perilous liminal phase that humans must undergo before their newly acquired identity is assumed.
RU

The coming of age and acquisition of wisdom

An important quality of the boat is that it moves from place to place, it carries cargo – or people – and it crosses borders. In the course of their lives, all people go through a series of changes: from childhood to adulthood, from being single to marriage, from life to death (Hauptman Wahlgren 2002). When people experience crises, their existence must be given new meaning, and in order to achieve this, they must acquire new knowledge. Each of the changes or crises in human life entails the individual adopting new roles in the society in which they live, or put another way, it involves their "coming of age and acquisition of wisdom". Transitions in life are likened to shedding a skin – the individual acquires a new identity, perhaps a new status or a new social position. In most societies, the transitions that occur during life are accompanied by rituals which ensure that change occurs in a prescribed, orderly manner. The metamorphosis from one status to another can be a disturbing or frightening experience for a person. In the transition between the old and the new identity, the individual is in a kind of limbo – neither child nor adult, neither living nor dead. In this liminal stage, an individual is vulnerable, and the transitional rituals are designed to alleviate the harmful effects and to help the individual to cross to the other side.

The journey through life

The compositions including boat images and people in procession can be interpreted as depictions of the transitional rituals through which people enter a new stage of life. The use of images is associated with the boat as a symbol of a journey. In a non-literal sense, the boat may be seen as a metaphor of the journey made by a person between the cradle and the grave. The boat is the vehicle that carries the individual from one phase to the next on the journey through life. The human figures in and around the boats represent individuals in various phases of life: childhood, puberty, adulthood, old age and death (*ibid.*). Neither the humans in processions nor the stylized lines representing human figures aboard the boats are renderings of specific women and men. They are collective symbols for the group, for the people who are initiated into a new status, or for people who will help in the initiation process. Or perhaps they represent ancestors who will receive the deceased in the hereafter. The phalli seen on some of the human figures do not symbolize the male gender, but are rather a metaphor for the power and initiative that is necessary to accomplish the hazardous journey through life. The rituals depicted – and which were possibly performed around the rock art – can be seen as a part of the initiation to a new role in society, whereby the initiated has also acquired new qualities, such as wisdom and strength.

The individual's journey through the various phases of life can also be likened to the eternal cycle of nature: germination, growth, maturity, deterioration and withering. In nature just as in human life, the transitions between the phases can often be associated with hazards: a frosty night, a hailstorm or drought. From this perspective, the transitional rituals linked to the course of human life can be seen as rituals to safeguard the course of nature.

A sacred site for the chosen few or for the congregation?

If rituals and myths associated with the transitions and crises in human life really were important aspects of Bronze Age beliefs, then it is reasonable to wonder why depictions of these rituals are not more widespread. One explanation may be that it was not always necessary to depict all of the elements of a ritual, as one image that was more potent than the others – such as the boat

– would suffice. Another possibility is that the rituals were only intended to be performed in special places. Whichever answer we choose, in all likelihood the rock art sites represent sacred places that were carefully selected with a specific purpose in mind.

The type of transitional rituals that are depicted in the rock art may have been reserved for only a few participants, perhaps individuals with special ritualistic roles in society. The sites used for rituals of this kind were possibly mythical places holding knowledge reserved for the chosen few. The site may have been a no man's land where participants were neither inside nor outside the tangible world – a liminal space that can be likened to the liminal stage in the transitional rituals. The rituals may have been performed at intervals spanning many years, and the depictions of the rituals may have been used repeatedly for generations.

The places where the transitional rituals are depicted may also have served as meeting places where people from the scattered settlements surrounding the rock art site would assemble to perform rituals together as a group. This may have occurred when new groups of young people were to be initiated into adulthood, when special wedding ceremonies were to be performed, or when an important member of society was to be helped across into the world of the ancestors. The reason why the transitional rituals were depicted in only a few places in a given region may be that these sites had special qualities making them suitable for precisely this type of ritual. Perhaps the rock art depicting transitional rituals belongs to an earlier rock art tradition, and subsequent generations saw the places where the rituals were carved in stone as particularly sacred places, sites to be used for special occasions.

A scenario for Bakke

By way of conclusion, we will retrace the features in the tale of Herandsbygda at Samlafjorden in Hardanger that may perhaps explain why rock art that is unparalleled in Western Norway was created at this spot.

In the rural areas surrounding the extensive Hardanger Fjord, a rock art tradition in which boat images were the dominant motif had existed since the early years of the Bronze Age (Mandt Larsen 1972). A number of large and smaller rock art panels concentrated on the western side of the fjord bear witness to this fact, among them Berge, as seen in the previous chapter. Towards the middle of the Bronze Age a new rock art tradition took root in the region, most clearly demonstrated in Herandsbygda on the eastern side of the fjord, with compositions including boats and people in procession. The open space between the two rock art panels at Bakke where these motifs were engraved was highly suitable to ritual performances. The rituals portrayed in the scenes on the rock faces were perhaps designed for select social circles, a small group of people who were to be endowed with important social tasks, perhaps of a ritualistic nature. Herandsbygda – or perhaps Samlandaherad – may have been chosen because they were junctions for sea and land communications, located at an easily recognizable landmark in the district – Samlanuten – the pyramid-shaped mountain that shares its name with important areas of resources and communication lines in the region.

Throughout the latter portion of the Bronze Age, more and more rock art panels were created in Hardanger, both along the western side of the great fjord and in the areas around Sørfjorden on the eastern side of the Folgefonni Peninsula. Rock art at this time was often created near settlements and along roads and fjord waterways. The most frequent motifs are boats, rings, foot soles and cup marks. The earlier rock art sites probably remained in use. At the Bakke panels, foot soles, ring motifs and boat images of later types bear witness to the fact that new figures and different motifs were added to the old symbols. When the rituals associated with transitions in human life were performed, people from the other rock art settlements gathered at Bakke. These important rituals had to be performed according to specific rules and at the proper place. Because the ancient rituals had been carved in stone at Bakke, where ancestors had placed their marks, the place was revered as sacred and was associated with powerful forces. This was the reason why people found it necessary to come here to perform the sacred acts.

Etne in Sunnhordland – A Small and Diverse Rock Art Region

One fine late summer's day about 50 years ago, a ten-year-old schoolgirl named Halldis set out on her way up the steep escarpment rising from her home at the lowland farm Flåte at the far end of Stordalen in Etne, in the southern part of Hordaland County. She looked forward to a peaceful respite at the summit, where she could daydream and give free rein to her thoughts. The afternoon sun was hot, and on the precipice overlooking the farm below, she came to a large boulder that seemed to be a suitable place for taking a rest. The vantage point offered an open panorama out over the surroundings, including the expansive Stordalsvatnet (Lake Stordal). The boulder was almost entirely overgrown with turf – only the surface at the very top, where she was sitting, was bare. In the diagonal rays of the sun that fell on the rock surface, she became aware of some circular depressions and ring-shaped grooves. She quickly concluded that these must be man-made, rather than the work of nature, because she had seen similar markings on stones elsewhere in the local area. Her schoolteacher had told the pupils about these images from the prehistoric past – "offering cups" and "sun signs", as he called them (Vinje 1953). She happily ran along the path to the teacher's house to share the news that she, too, had discovered exactly the same type of symbols on her own homestead, on the large boulder that was later named Bruteigsteinen [the Bruteig Stone].

FIGURES 179–180. Bruteigsteinen is located in steep outland terrain some 40 metres above the lake Stordalsvatnet. The huge boulder is situated at the top of a steep gravel ridge facing northwest, at the edge of a small plateau that is said to have been cultivated in earlier times, but which is now used for grazing. There is an open panorama from the boulder, and the 13 × 11 metre-wide, flat rock surface is conspicuous and highly visible from most parts of the valley. To the north and west of the boulder, the river Floteelva cascades down the sheer mountainside. During winter the boulder is shaded by a tall mountain peak, and from the farms on the other side of Stordalsvatnet, people have noticed that Bruteigsteinen is illuminated by the first rays of sunlight in spring.
MAP AI, ILLUSTRATION GM

Variations on a theme

The type of rock art that Halldis and her schoolmates had been taught to identify as sun signs and offering cups were discovered in Etne already in the 1860s, on the Stødle farm in the main settlement along the fjord (Nicolaysen 1862). In the middle of the Stødle terrace – one of several wide, flat moraine terraces in Etne that were formed by the sea and glacial ice – there is a low-lying, elongated rock face called Helgaberg ("Holy Rock"), with about 350 rock art figures. The most eye-catching of these is a multitude of some 300 cup marks. Some are large and deep, others quite small; some are double, and some are linked together by grooves in the stone. In addition, there are a number of ring-shaped figures – some concentric, others with four or more radial lines like spokes in a wheel, and most of them with a central hollowed-out depression. There are even some oval or U-shaped figures (Mandt Larsen 1972).

When the rock art at Stødle was first mentioned in 1862, antiquarians were of the opinion that they were natural marks in the stone (Nicolaysen 1866). But a

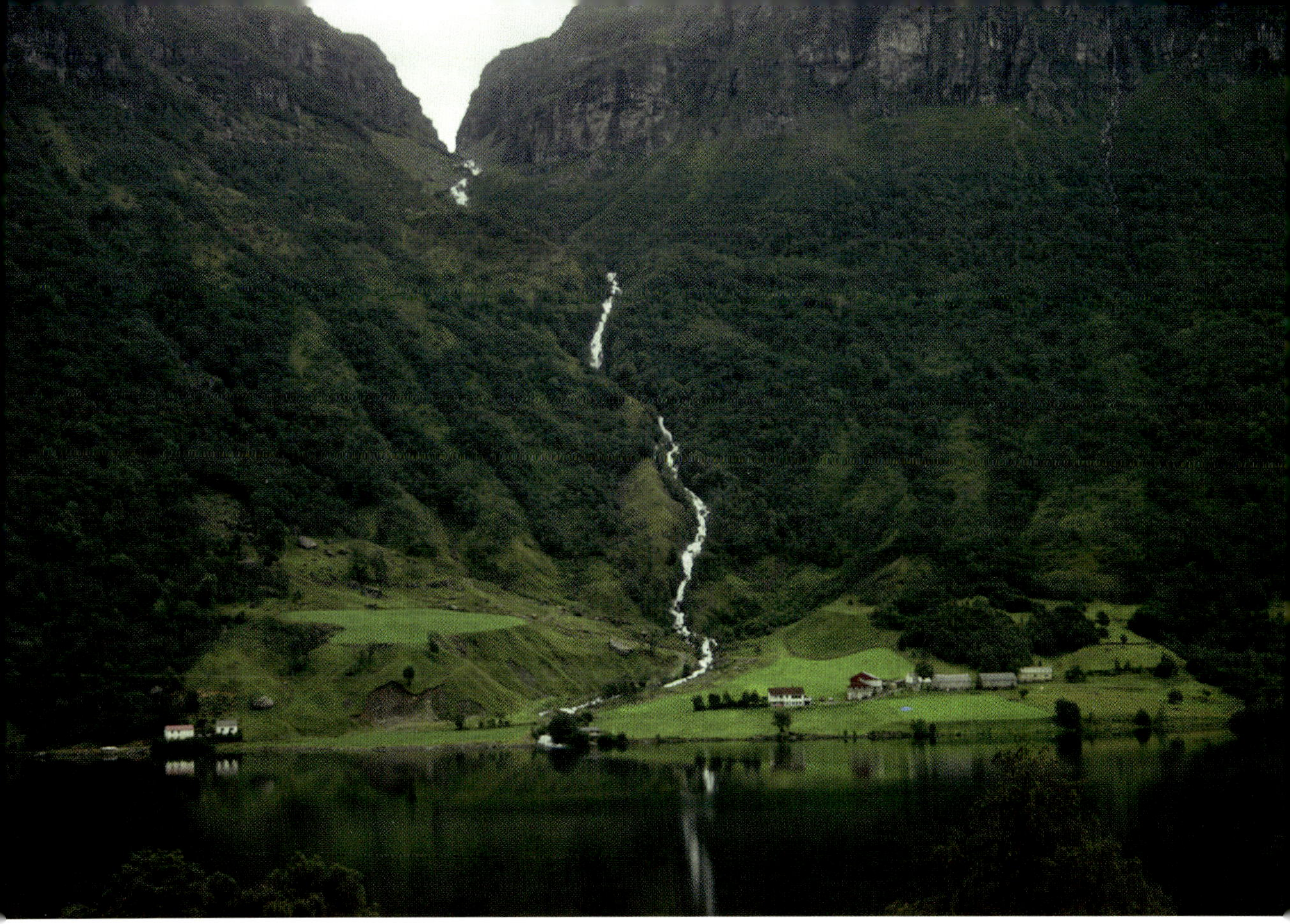

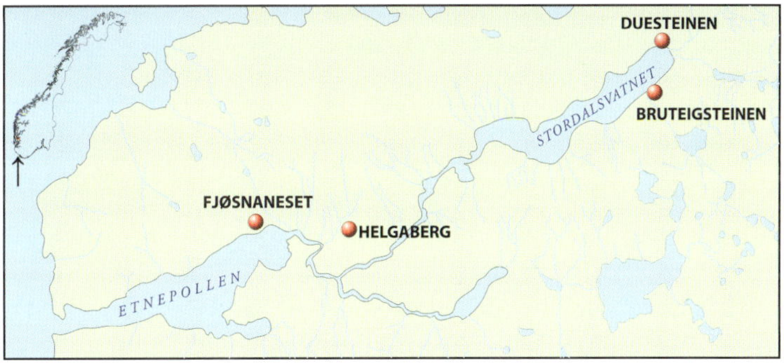

few decades later the consensus changed, and the ring figures and cup marks on the Helgaberg slab were considered to be Bronze Age rock art (Bendixen 1899).

Professionals who came to examine the carvings that Halldis had discovered on Bruteigsteinen all agreed that this was undoubtedly rock art from the Bronze Age (Bøe 1953). But when the turf was peeled away from the stone, the images proved to be more remarkable than expected. More than seventy figures are carved on the wide, flat surface, including both cup marks and rings – several of the latter with a kind of loop or eye above them – although a number of other motifs are also present. There are several boat images with high stems and crew lines, and on board some of the boats are long, curved lines interpreted as bronze trumpets (lures), an artefact that has been found primarily at votive offering sites

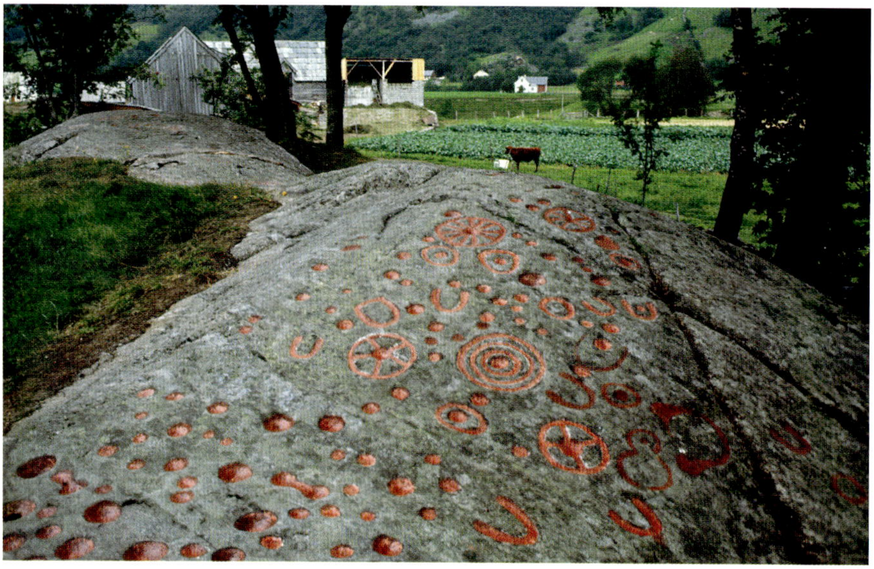

FIGURE 181. The rock carvings on Helgaberg have been public knowledge ever since the 1860s, but local people undoubtedly knew about the figures on the stone outcrop in the centre of the Stødle terrace long before that time. The rings and cup marks are so deeply engraved that it is reasonable to believe that people have seen them for generations, perhaps even as early as the Middle Ages or even earlier. It is unknown how far back in time the name "Helgaberg" – the holy rock – can be traced. Archaeologists from the museum in Bergen have highlighted the figures in paint to make it easier for visitors to see them.
GM

in Denmark. Other images include axes, some figures that probably depict horses or dogs, a single human image, as well as the outline of two large foot soles and single and double spirals. The most unusual figures on the stone, however, are six or seven depictions of trees (Mandt Larsen 1972; Vevatne 1997) – a motif that occurs sporadically in the rock art of both Sweden and Denmark, and in other places in Norway (Hygen and Bengtsson 1999), but never in such a large number in any single site as on Bruteigsteinen in Etne.

The numerous rock images

The rural community where these two very diverse – and individually distinctive – rock art sites were discovered is in the far south of Sunnhordland, bordering on Rogaland County. The Etne Valley cuts northeast through mountains and hills from the fjord arm Etnepollen in the west, and eastwards to Stordalen and the large lake Stordalsvatnet, once known as Laug. At the eastern end of Stordalen is a neck of land leading across to the long fjord Åkrafjorden, from where there is easy access to the mountain ranges of the Hardanger mountain plateau and the peninsula named after the large glacier Folgefonni. The rural area of Etne has large areas of rich, arable soil, and is considered one of the best agricultural areas in West Norway (Sund 1963). The more elevated areas offer abundant grazing land and are good hunting and fishing grounds. Many types of cultural monuments bear witness to the fact that Etne has provided the basis for livelihood throughout countless generations (E. Fett 1968).

One outstanding feature of the Etne area is the abundance of rock carvings. Helgaberg and Bruteigsteinen are only two out of a concentration of 30–40 rock surfaces, or large and small stones, with rock art. Most of these have cup marks as their sole motif. In some sites the motifs that characterize Helgaberg and

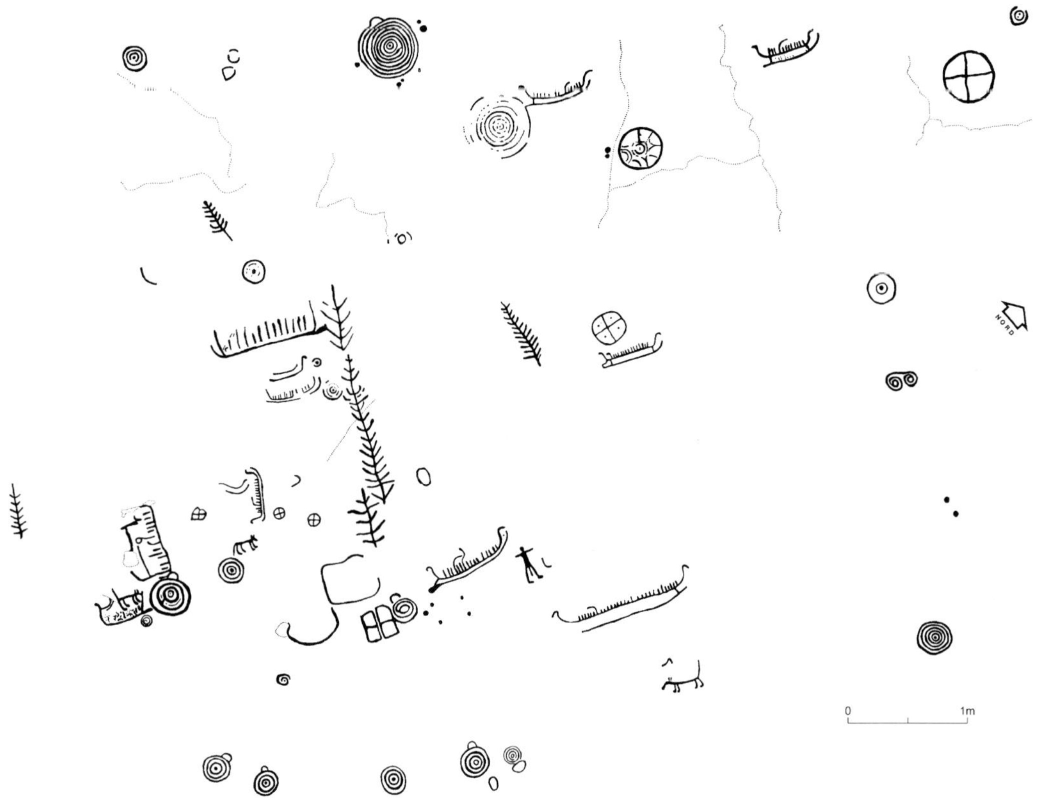

FIGURE 182. The diversity of motifs at Bruteigsteinen makes the site unique in West Norway. Several motifs characteristic of the Southern rock art tradition are present here: boats, rings, spirals, weapons, foot soles, humans, horses (or dogs?), cup marks and, not least of all, the rare tree motif.
GM

Bruteigsteinen are also found, consisting partly of individual, abstract symbols, and partly of more concrete motifs such as boat images, foot soles and human and animal figures in addition to cup marks and rings (Mandt Larsen 1972; Vevatne 1997).

The majority of the rock carvings are found deep inside Stordalen at the small community of Frette, located at the eastern end of Stordalsvatnet. Cup marks are the most numerous – loose stones and embedded boulders with cup marks are scattered throughout the farms on the valley floor and higher up on the hillsides surrounding Stordalsvatnet. Apart from Bruteigsteinen, there is only one other site with varied motifs in Stordalen: On the Vinja farm there is a rounded boulder, Duesteinen [the Dove Stone], which is covered with cup marks and about thirty ring figures and U-shaped motifs.

In the community centre on the western side of the fjord there are two prominent panels with varied motifs, while only two or three small cup mark sites are known to exist. As well as Helgaberg at Stødle, there are five larger or smaller panels at the Fjøsnaneset promontory on the southern side of Etnepollen. Boat images, foot soles and a few ring figures are carved into parallel rock faces stretching upwards from the water's edge.

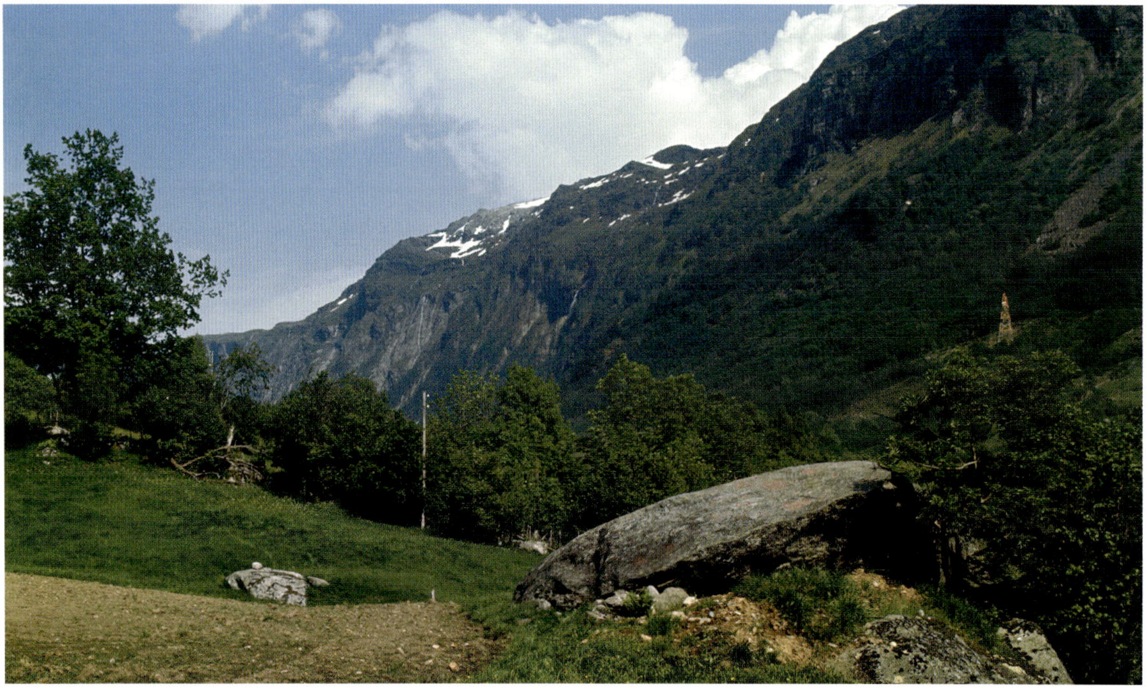

FIGURE 183. Duesteinen [The Dove Stone] at Vinja is a huge earthbound boulder lying on the southern edge of a field. The stone measures 15 x 7 metres, and is 10 metres tall on the lower side and two to three metres high on the upper side. On the upper side of the stone is a flat, cultivated field, where a minor excavation was carried out next to the stone in the 1950s. In a black layer of charcoal and ashes, a triangular flint arrowhead was found, along with several flint chips and charred stone. The flint arrowhead can be dated to the Late Neolithic, and it is possible that the remains stem from a fire made beneath Duesteinen at the time the rock carvings were in use.

AMO/BM

Contributions of a local enthusiast

Much of the credit for the discovery of so many rock carvings in Etne is due to the efforts of a truly dedicated schoolteacher by the name of Trygve Vinje, who lived and worked in Stordalen. Almost a third of the rock art sites in Stordalen were first reported by Vinje. In a letter to the Historisk museum [today's Bergen Museum] in the early 1950s, he commended the pupils and their parents and wrote that they "show great interest in such things and report back when they see something they wonder about" (Vinje 1953). Nevertheless, it is thanks to the teacher that this interest was aroused in the local population. Through the knowledge about cultural monuments he passed on to generations of schoolchildren, he taught them what to look for when they were out in the fields. And so it comes as no surprise that students of Trygve Vinje have been the most frequent discoverers of the largest and most varied rock art sites in Stordalen. Almost at the same time as Halldis' discovery of the images at Bruteigsteinen, two observant schoolboys – the twins Lars and Ståle who were born and raised at Vinja – discovered cup marks and other motifs on Duesteinen in their own farmyard. In this respect, the community of Frette in Stordalen is a shining example of the fact that people in the local environment – those who are in the area all year round in all kinds of weather and light conditions – are most often those who find rock art.

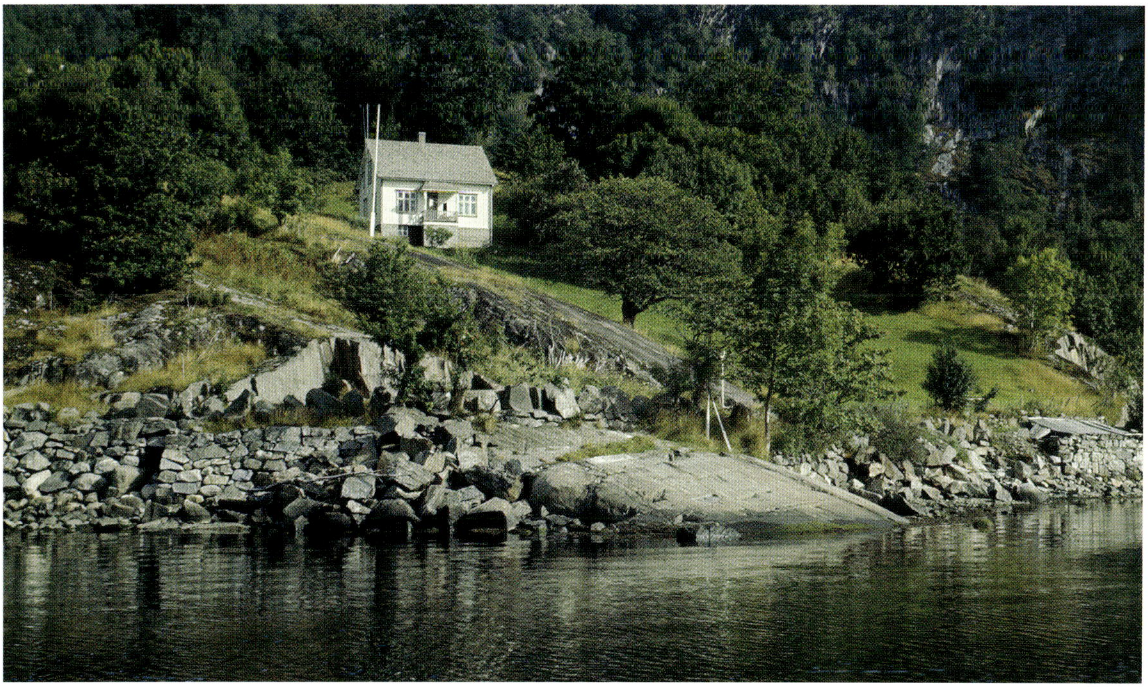

FIGURE 184. At the outermost point of the promontory Fjøsnaneset, a pair of round, ice-scoured ridges descend in parallel to each other down towards the sea, with rock carvings found on the flat section of these ridges. The largest concentration is on the long, rocky escarpment that slopes downward from the house near the road. The rock is schistous, and when the sun's rays shine directly against the dark stone surface, it is not easy to make out the carvings.
GM

Broad time frames

All of the rock art in Etne belongs to the type of motifs that are characteristic of the Southern Tradition – usually dated to between 1800–500 BC. It is more uncertain when this rock art tradition began. Some researchers claim that several of the motifs were already in use at the end of the Neolithic, perhaps around 2300–2000 BC (Vevatne 1996, 1997).

The motifs found on Helgaberg and Duesteinen – cup marks, rings and oval and U-shaped figures – can probably be dated to this early phase. The dating is based, among other factors, on a comparison with rock art in Denmark, Ireland and the British Isles. In the western islands in particular, simple, abstract symbols, such as combinations of "cups-and-rings" are dated to the end of the Neolithic (Fett and Fett 1979; Vevatne 1996). It is more uncertain whether the cup mark sites in Etne also belong to the earlier rock art phase. Examinations of cup marks located in areas where mountain farms were established in historical times suggest that mountain grazing in Western Norway was in use, and cup marks created, already by the end of the Neolithic (see chapter on the sub-alpine carvings). This tends to support an early dating of the cup mark sites in the grazing areas of Stordalen. However, it seems that the custom of carving cup marks in conjunction with grazing grounds continued for a long period of time after the establishment of the historical mountain farming. This may suggest that at least some of the cup mark sites in Etne are a recent phenomenon, while the cup marks on loose stones and boulders in the home fields – like the carvings on Helgaberg and Duesteinen – were perhaps created in the early part of the Bronze Age.

As the Bronze Age progressed, rock art became more and more visually illustrative. The abstract symbols were complemented with figurative motifs depicting known physical models, with boats, weapons, animals and humans occurring in different variants (Vevatne 1996). This is the tradition to which the rock art of Fjøsnaneset and Bruteigsteinen belongs, dated to the Late Bronze Age. The boat motif at the two sites displays great formal variation, and many of the boat images on Bruteigsteinen can be compared with depictions of boats in Østfold in South-eastern Norway and neighbouring Bohuslän in Western Sweden. Even other motifs on Bruteigsteinen – the trees – suggest that contact existed with eastern areas during this late phase of the Bronze Age.

Over the long period of time that people in Etne carved images in rock, the society changed as much in terms of vocations and technology as it did in political, social and religious affairs. The question is whether there are any other features in the rock art at Etne, apart from differences in the use of motifs, which may mirror these changes.

Changes in society and rituals

Towards the end of the Neolithic, people in many areas of Scandinavia had begun to cultivate the soil and keep livestock. Trapping in the mountains and fishing in the fjords and rivers were still important for subsistence, but in rural areas with arable soil, such as Etne, the new type of economy quickly took hold. The earlier rock art, dominated by abstract motifs, is located in the current collective farm yard, surrounded by farmlands. Helgaberg sits like an inland island in the centre of the terraced fields of Stødle, and the Duesteinen is located at the edge of a broad, cultivated area of flat land at the mouth of Stordalselva (Stordalen river). Although the soft, rounded stone formations characterizing these two panels are visible in the flat and open landscape, they are not easily seen from a distance. They give the impression of being sheltered, perhaps a little secluded, and intended for the closest surroundings, maybe for the settlement or the immediate family group (Vevatne 1996, 1997).

Already by the end of the Neolithic, there are traces of a nascent class distinction in the society of the time, as a result of which some people had more power and prestige than others. When bronze began to be used, people in positions of authority enjoyed a golden opportunity to affirm and increase their status, a development seen in burial monuments and votive offerings from the Early Bronze Age too (Hygen and Bengtsson 1999). Several large burial mounds from the Early Bronze Age have been found in Etne and serve to support this impression. The burial mounds are located on the moraine terraces in the main settlement area, one of which is just to the west of the rock carvings on Helgaberg. In an era when boundaries and personal claims to land were new concepts, the rock carvings may have served as property markers – a way of punctuating the landscape for the purpose of marking and proclaiming the local inhabitants' right to use the fields and pasturelands. The carvings could also have been part of rituals that supported the new social structure entailing higher status and increased power for certain individuals.

The more recent rock art sites have quite different locations than the rock carvings with abstract motifs. They are usually located on the periphery of the best agricultural land, at distinctive places in the landscape that are easily seen from every direction (Vevatne 1996, 1997). Bruteigsteinen is situated in the outlying fields, on a steeply sloping gravel ridge offering a wide panorama, and is readily visible from most areas in Stordalen. Fjøsnaneset is strategically located at the mouth of the fjord with a view in all directions, and was probably even more distinctive before the outermost portion of the promontory was blasted away when the road along the fjord was constructed. From both sites there is a view of the important communications arteries – Stordalsvatnet in the eastern part of the community and the fjord arm Etnepollen farthest west leading into the main settlement.

In the Late Bronze Age the power structures in society were further reinforced. Major differences in terms of social equality can often give rise to discontentment and more or less open conflict. In order to quell unrest and opposition, those in power may have used mythological and ritualistic effects. By emphasising equality in religious rituals, they achieved solidarity and support from the rest of society. The figurative and easily visible rock art panels may have contributed towards achieving a shared feeling of interdependence and security, while at the same time supporting the power positions of the elite (Vevatne 1996). The large scale and easy accessibility of the sites suggest that they were collective monuments as well as unifying measures designed for use by larger groups, and not merely by individual families. The expanded range of motifs, including a mixture of old and new symbols, served to prevent potential conflicts, and the power structure acquired a religious validation.

Memorials of bygone times even in the distant past

In the course of the last few centuries before the birth of Christ, the tradition of carving images in rock gradually came to an end in most parts of Scandinavia. One notable exception is cup marks, which are often found in conjunction with graves dating from the first centuries AD. It is unclear why people stopped using the old symbols, myths and rituals. It was perhaps due to social, economic and technological changes that occurred in many parts of continental Europe at the time – circumstances that had a knock-on effect for societies in the Nordic countries as well (Hygen and Bengtsson 1999).

For many generations after the custom of carving images in rock had been abandoned, the rock images must have remained visible in the landscape, as they still are for us today. People in the past have also been curious and have pondered these physical traces left by their ancestors. Like us, they have tried to explain the monuments of the past, and interpreted them in their own ways (Varenius 1994). Although the original meaning of the symbols and the myths they illustrated had long been forgotten, the rock carvings served as a link with the ancient past and with ancestors (Wriglesworth 2000). The re-use of the earlier symbols and monuments by linking them to existing, more modern myths and rituals may in turn have re-energized and reactivated them (Bolin 1998). In Etne, evidence of the re-use of monuments may be seen on the Stødle terrace, where cultural monuments from different eras co-exist side by side (Mandt 2006).

A site for worship over thousands of years?

The cultural monuments on the Stødle terrace represent a period spanning from the beginning of the Bronze Age or earlier, about 2000–1800 BC, up to the Middle Ages, 1100–1200 AD. The nature of these traces of human activity implies that the area may have been used as a site for cultic and ritualistic observances throughout this entire period of time.

Today, the most conspicuous landmark on the Stødle terrace is a small medieval church, located at the outermost edge of the wide terrace plain. The church was probably built sometime during the 1100s as a private rural chapel for the Earl Erling Skakke, who owned the family farm at Stødle, probably one of the largest in the local area (Dyrvik 1968). In his capacity as guardian for his young son, King Magnus Erlingsson, Erling Skakke acted as the representative of the monarch, and in several of Snorre Sturlasson's Sagas of the Kings, he is mentioned as one of the most powerful of the gentry in his day (Ingvaldsen 1996). According to the land register for taxes from 1547, Stødle was the fourth largest farm in the local area (Madsen 1998). The uncompounded place name Stødle probably dates back to the Early Iron Age while the two neighbouring farms on the terrace – Sørheim and Austrheim ("Southern and Eastern homesteads") – became separate properties, divided from Stødle sometime during the Late Iron Age (Fett 1968).

On both sides of the church, extending some 700 metres along the terrace ledge, there was once a large burial site with 40–50 grave mounds from which artefacts from the early and late Iron Age have been unearthed. The graves, which are located on the infields of Stødle and Sørheim, reveal that the area was continuously settled from 500 BC until 1000 AD (Madsen 1998). When graves from the Iron Age and a Medieval church site are found together on the same farm property, it is seen as an indication of a certain continuity in cult tradition (Ingvaldsen 1996).

Burial mounds containing artefacts from both the early and late Bronze Age have also been found on the Stødle terrace. They are located on the outskirts of the Iron Age burial site – one just west of the rock carvings on Helgaberg, at the edge of the terrace and with a panorama out over the main settlement area and the fjord, and two others farther inland on the terrace (E. Fett 1968). These grave monuments, which are located in the immediate vicinity of the graves from the Iron Age, suggest the Stødle terrace was settled at a much earlier time than the artefacts dated to the Early Iron Age would indicate (Madsen 1998).

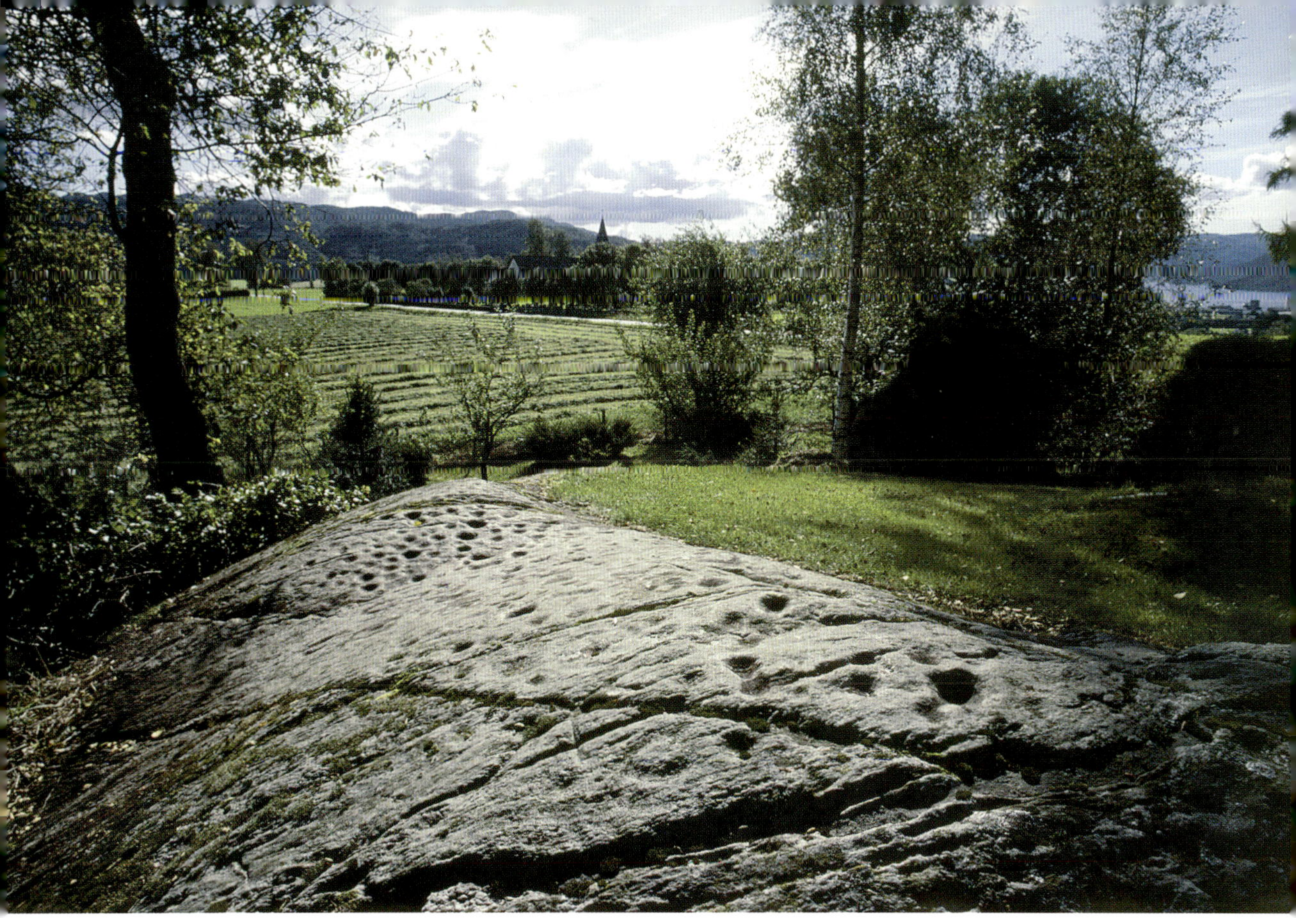

FIGURE 185. From the Helgaberg rock carvings the spire of the medieval church located at the edge of the terrace is clearly visible among the trees. Between these extreme points in time, additional cultural monuments from various periods are known, all within the relatively limited space of the Stødle terrace. Ever since the rock art was pecked into the rocky knoll, cult rituals have been carried out here; their form and content has changed over time, but the site has remained the same.
RU

Both the nature and the spatial context of the cultural monuments at the Stødle terrace – traces of cultic and ritual actions performed within a constricted area – indicate that the place itself has been important. With the exception of an offering site from the Bronze Age – a bronze necklace ring from the Late Bronze Age found at the northern edge of the terrace (E. Fett 1968) – all of the cultural monuments on the Stødle terrace are located in close proximity to one another. As a whole, the archaeological remains also represent a continuous period spanning from the Bronze Age through the Iron Age to the Middle Ages. Grave mound was added to grave mound along the edge of the terrace, and the church was built as a continuation of the row of graves, in the vicinity of the ancient farmyard of the Stødle farm. Perhaps the most curious feature is that the rock art at Helgaberg from the Early Bronze Age is virtually adjacent to the earliest farmyard of the Stødle farm – considered to be the site of Erling Skakke's family estate, and from Helgaberg there is visual contact with the spire of the Medieval church. Here we may be seeing the outlines of a process in which a monument that was once a sacred site in the distant past was recreated and reactivated continuously in subsequent generations, over a period lasting thousands of years.

Re-actualization of mythical time

For centuries the rock carvings at Helgaberg must have been visible to people who lived on the Stødle terrace. During the Late Bronze Age, when large grave mounds were built on the terrace and a votive offering deposited, the custom of carving images in rock was still active other places in Etne, and rituals may still have been performed at Helgaberg. But how did the mound builders during the Iron Age and the Medieval church builders explain the markings in the rock? And how did the church builders look upon the grave mounds that were probably much more monumental during the Middle Ages than they are today (Mandt 2006)?

Meaning is not an immanent quality of a monument or a place. By means of observations and associations, and based on their own historical context, people ascribe meaning to the things surrounding them (Barrett 1999). Although the ancient rituals were no longer performed, the monuments to a bygone time remained as concrete symbols of a mythical past. Monuments that were sacred sites in the distant past were recreated and made active again in subsequent generations (Barret 1999; Bradley 1993). Religious ceremonies recreate sacred events that were observed in a mythical past, and by creating new cultic monuments alongside the older ones, it was possible to once again participate in the mythical past. The vestiges of the past may have been seen as tokens – signs indicating the special, appointed, perhaps sacred nature of the sites. Therefore the rock images from the distant past served as tokens legitimizing the use of the area and its resources in contemporary periods.

Modern re-use of ancient monuments

Contemporary use of ancient monuments can also be seen as a re-activation of the mythical past (Mandt 2006). Even for people of today, the traces of prehistoric human activity represent links to a past that fascinates us, a past we want to grasp a piece of, in spite of – or perhaps because? – it is different from our own time. Thus both scholars and the public interpret the ancient monuments in line with the general mood of the time. An illustrating example is the multiple interpretations of rock art.

Revheim at Hafrsfjord – a Unique Context in the Rich Rock Art Region of Rogaland

In early July 1894 local workers at the Revheim farmstead at Hafrsfjord in Northern Jæren, Rogaland, were digging soil drainage trenches on the large lowland moor below the farm-yard. As they were laying a pipe next to a brook that ran through the moor, they came across an unusual and – as it would turn out – unique discovery. Near the bottom of the bog they found a number of bronze pipes and some smaller pieces of bronze. An agricultural engineer who was present at the site drew a sketch of the position in which the items were found and recorded the observations he made at the site (Grimes 1894). The engineer identified the items discovered as parts of two bronze horns, consisting of two large and two smaller pipes, in addition to one bell plate. One of the larger pieces as well as the two smaller ones were located parallel to one another, about 13 cm above the sandy bottom. The second large piece, which is also the best-preserved, was situated diagonally across these three with the curved portion facing up and the ends turned downwards. The wider end was approximately 8 cm above the sandy bottom, and 16–18 cm from it was the bell plate, standing on end.

In honour of the gods

The horns found in the Revheim Moor turned out to be parts from two prehistoric bronze trumpets (lures) from about 800 BC, disassembled before they were laid on the sandy bottom. Bronze lures are large trumpet-like instruments, the only type known from the Bronze Age (Johansen 2000). Altogether, 60 prehistoric bronze trumpets have been found – most of them in Denmark and Southern Sweden, a few in Northern Germany and one in Latvia. In Norway only one other pair of lures has been found in addition to those at Revheim, deposited in a moor at Brandbu in Hadeland in eastern Norway. About a third of all lures found have been pairs, most often in moors and disassembled like the ones at Revheim. The earliest lures are dated to the middle of the Bronze Age, but the majority come from the Late Bronze Age.

The bronze trumpets are assumed to have been cult objects used in various rituals, perhaps during burial processions or rituals designed to ensure solidarity and order in society. The depositing of costly ritual objects in moors or marshy areas was a custom throughout the entire Bronze Age, interpreted as votive offerings to the forces of nature or to deities (Hygen and Bengtsson 1999).

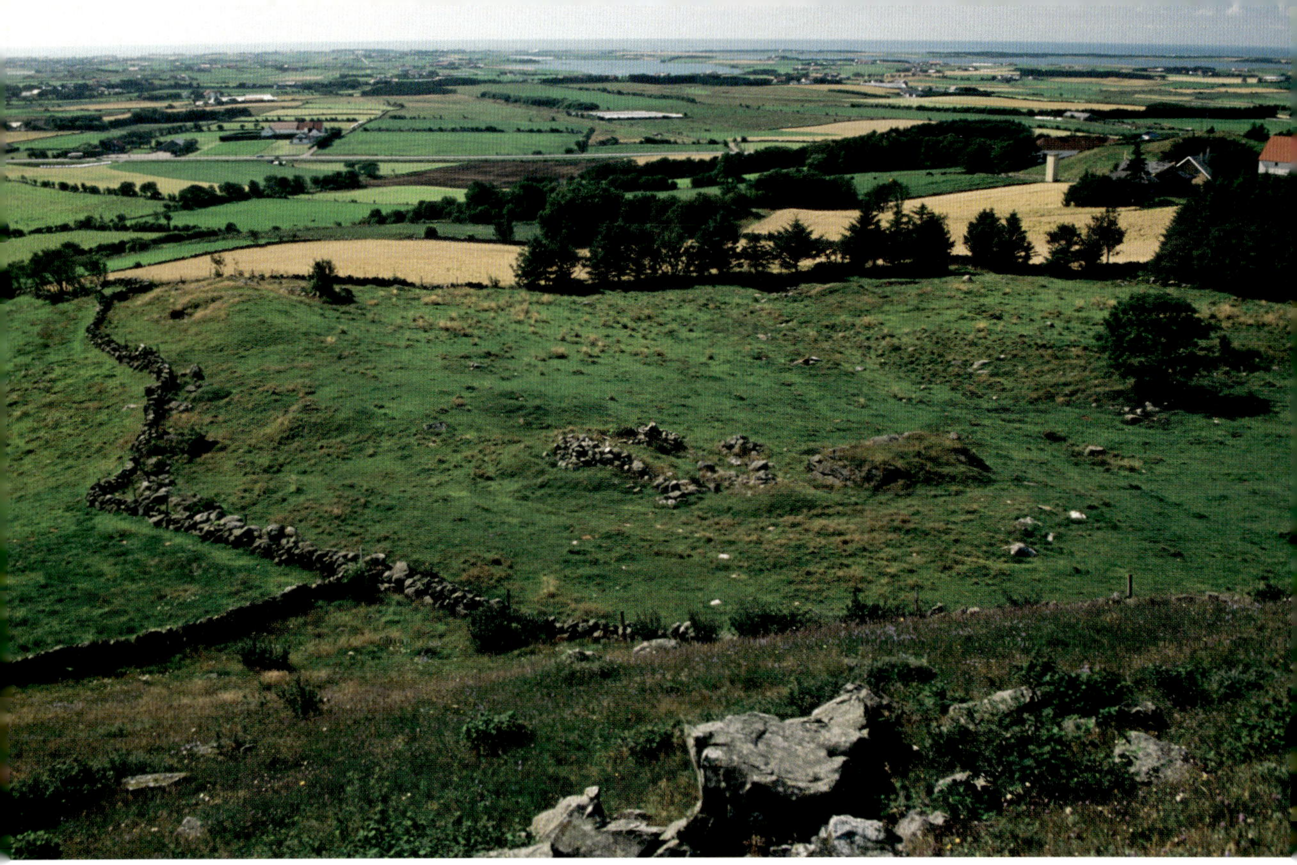

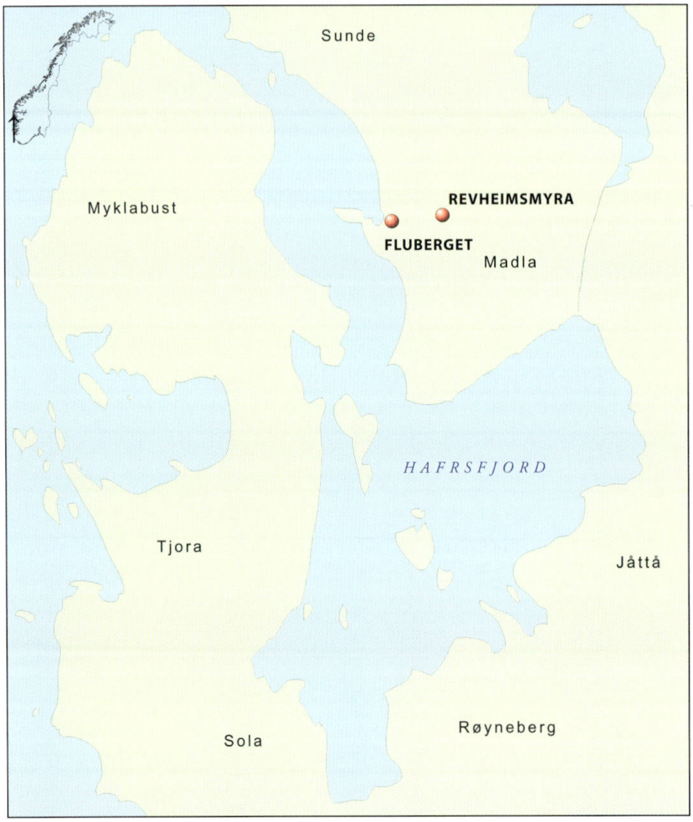

FIGURES 186–187. Jæren is a continuous moraine shaped into a rolling landscape, framed to the south and east by hills and mountains, and with the open sea as its western border – or in the words of Arne Garborg (1892): "Outside in the west, the sea crashes against a seventy-kilometre-long sandy shoreline. This is the open ocean itself: The North Sea wild and free... Spanning it all is a heavenly ceiling wide and grey, stretching from mountain farms to the open sea and beyond as far as the eye can see...". Seemingly endless stone walls and cultural monuments of many types bear witness to the active use of the Jæren landscape for countless generations.

MAP AI, ILLUSTRATION HELGE SUNDE/SAMFOTO

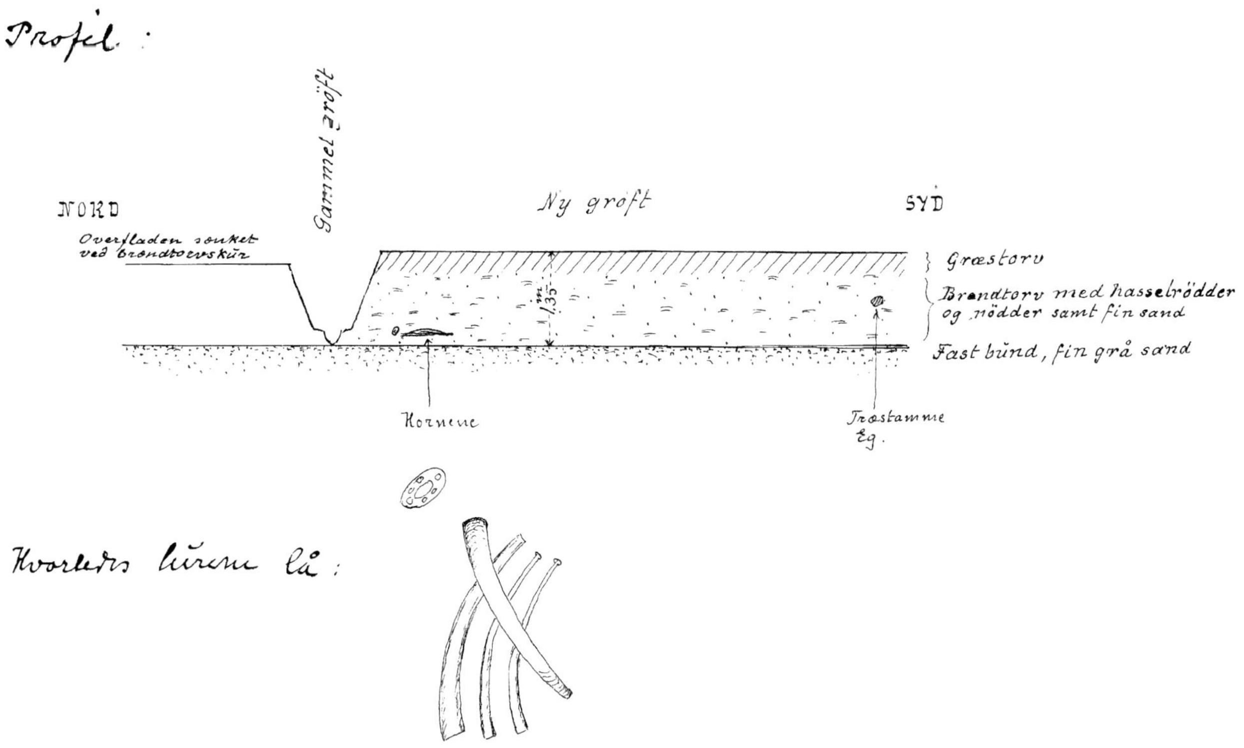

FIGURE 188. It was an agricultural engineer, A. Grimnes, who first became aware of the artefacts that were uncovered while digging trenches on the Revheim moor. The drawing he made is preserved in the archives of the Archaeological Museum of Stavanger.
AMS

The bronze trumpets can still be played, but as they lack valves, only so-called natural tones can be played, in the same way as a modern bugle. The size of the instrument determines the number of different tones that can be played. On the largest Danish lures, fourteen tones can be played over a five-octave range. The lures in a set of two not only resemble one another in appearance, but are also tuned to the same key, making it impossible to play them in harmonic intervals with one another (Johansen 2000).

There is no way of knowing what kind of sounds the people of the Bronze Age made with their instruments, but we do know that the tones that can be produced are clear, deep and sombre. It is easy to imagine ceremonies with the tones of the glittering golden bronze trumpets resounding across the landscape. In the Revheim area itself, it is likely that scenes of this kind took place on a recurrent basis. Only 200–300 metres from the moor is a conspicuous rock formation called Fluberget, where the second largest collection of Bronze Age rock art in Northern Jæren is located.

A curiosity of nature

The rock carvings at Fluberget were discovered in the late 1870s (Fett and Fett 1941). The site is a high, 70 metre-long elongated outcrop, which has been compared to an upturned boat when seen from the shore of Hafrsfjord (Bradley

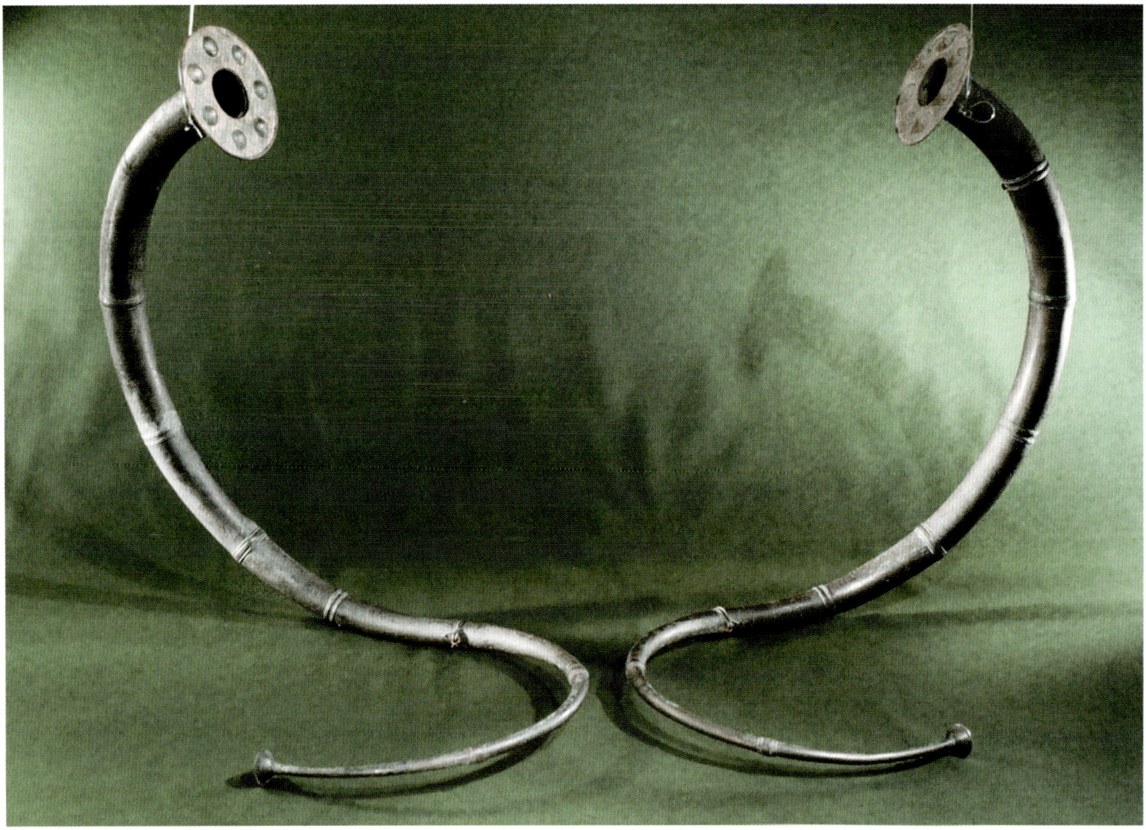

FIGURE 189. The bronze trumpets from Revheim are in very good condition after lying buried in a moor for several thousand years. They were cast by a complicated method requiring great technical expertise. Each trumpet consists of six thin-walled pipes that are connected to one another by sleeves and clasps. Fully mounted, they measure 176 centimetres in length. They are symmetrical and curved in an S-shape, one of them with its bell turned to the right, the other to the left. The bell end is capped with a round ornamental plate 14.7 centimetres in diameter, decorated with a bulb and seven nodules, and the neck is fitted with a mouthpiece.
AMS

et al 2002). It is visible over a considerable area, and from the top there is a broad panorama over the flat landscape of Northern Jæren and the entrance of Hafrsfjord. The close relationship with the sea must have been even more distinctive during the Bronze Age when the water level was 4–5 metres higher than it is today (Nordenborg Myhre 2004; Prøsch-Danielsen 2002).

One of the most striking features of Fluberget is the sheer, nearly 15-metre-high southern wall, shaped by nature as a rolling, vertical mini-landscape. On the glaciated rock surface, riddled from end to end with cracks and crevices of various sizes, ice and water have chiselled out several deep, wide depressions. They can be compared to concave potholes raised on end and separated by protruding ridges. It is no wonder that this strange natural formation attracted people and inspired them to put their own marks on the rocky surface.

About 250 rock carvings have been recorded at Fluberget, although originally

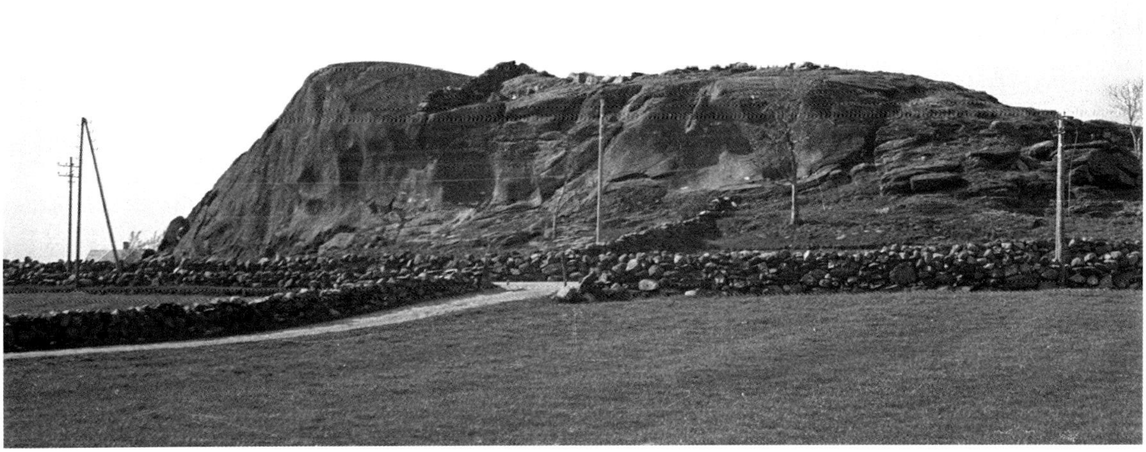

FIGURE 190. The sheer, rolling southern wall of Fluberget is an impressive sight. A large number of the rock carvings have been pecked into the deep depressions in the rock wall, especially in the large hollow at the centre of the wall.
HEL/AMS

there may have been many more, now weathered away (Fett and Fett 1941). There are 170 figurative images and eighty cup marks. The majority of the images are boat figures – most of them with curved stems and crew lines – although there are also rings and spirals; four-sided frames or lattice figures filled with dense, parallel lines; some Y-shaped figures that may represent humans; foot soles and two hand imprints – a motif that occurs only sporadically elsewhere in the rock art of the Southern Tradition. The majority of the carvings are carved into the undulating southern wall, many of them inside the depressions. In several places it seems that the figures were consciously placed in relation to one another in a type of composition. As a result of the alternating hollows and protruding ridges, some parts of the rock face are concealed, while the positions of other parts are emphasized, so that different sections can only be viewed in sequence. Water running from the top of the rock to a basin below, washing over some of the carvings, also creates an axis of movement across the surface (Nordenborg Myhre 2004).

In contrast to the images on the southern side of Fluberget, the motifs on the northern side are largely abstract, comprising frame- and lattice figures, a large spiral and a number of what may be foot soles, arranged in an almost horizontal sequence at the base of the outcrop where it meets the flat, surrounding fields.

A unique context

A context of this kind – where a large rock art panel and a votive offering site lie within visible proximity to one another – is rare. It is possible that both the rock art and the offering site have been in use as sacred places at the same time throughout most of the Bronze Age. Some of the motifs at Fluberget – such as cup marks and ring figures – may have been carved during the entire period, and the boat images are of types known from both the Early and Late Bronze

Age. In addition to the bronze trumpets from the Late Bronze Age in the Revheim moor, artefacts dated to the Early Bronze Age have also been found: a flint dagger and axe, and a spear made of bronze (Myhre 1981).

The area surrounding Revheimsmyra and Fluberget has been described as a closed landscape situated within a wider topographical unit, limited by the sea to the north, Hafrsfjord to the south and two, now partly drained, lakes to the east. Fluberget is situated at the entrance to Hafrsfjord, and appears to be aligned with the largest Bronze Age barrow of Rogaland, called Sothaug (Nordenborg Myhre 2004). Two other figurative rock art sites are located along the shoreline north of Revheim, and a number of boulders with cup marks are found on higher terraces. Excavations of burial mounds on the moraine heights around the Revheim moor have unearthed artefacts from both the Early and Late Bronze Age (Myhre 1981).

A maritime distribution pattern

The rock art repertoire in the remainder of Rogaland also presents fascinating scenarios. A total of some 150 small and larger sites are located within the coastal zone from Hafrsfjord and south towards the Boknafjord basin, the Stavanger peninsula and the central agricultural districts of the middle part of Jæren. Most of the rock art appears to be orientated towards a maritime environment, being situated less than 0.5 km from the present shore or close to lakes, wetlands and drained waterways, with easy access to the sea. In contrast with the rock art regions further north in West Norway, no rock carvings have been found in the inner uplands and mountain farm areas in Rogaland (Prøsch-Danielsen 2002).

It has been possible to distinguish two main concentrations, or core areas, of rock art in Jæren, partly based on the amount of sites and carvings and partly on variations in the motif repertoire, where different motif groups seem to coincide with different types of landscape (Syvertsen 2002, 2003; Nordenborg Myhre 2004; Prøsch-Danielsen 2002).

The largest concentration of rock art in Rogaland is found in Northern Jæren. The sites are dominated by figurative motifs – such as boat figures, foot- and handprints, some human and animal figures, and circles. They are mostly on the Stavanger peninsula, where Fluberget is the most prominent site, and on the southern islands in the Boknafjord basin. One of these islands is Austre Åmøy, where the largest collection of rock art in Rogaland is found, with more than 1000 figures spread over fifteen different panels. Also, sites with cup marks and cup marks in combination with grooves, ring figures or ovals – although common all over the county – are the most numerous in the central parts of the Boknafjord basin (Prøsch-Danielsen 2002). The carvings in this area are found on solid rock, on sloping rock faces and outcrops situated close to the sea, near protected harbours where central passages and waterways meet. The maritime aspect of these carvings is underlined by having boat figures as the dominant motif (Nordenborg Myhre 2004).

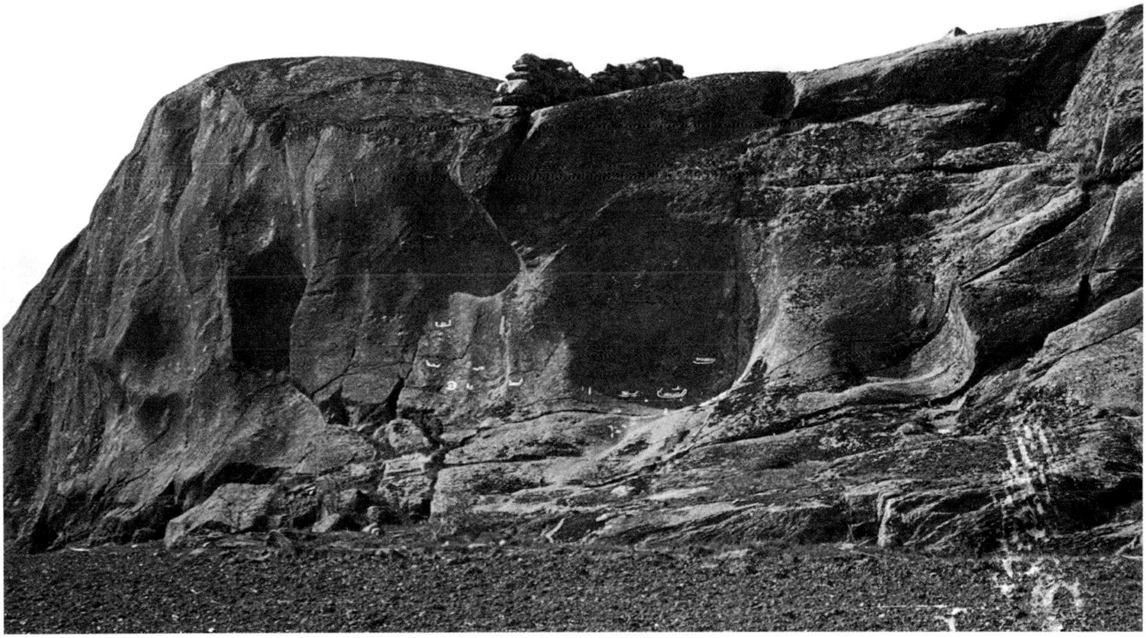

FIGURE 191. It is not surprising that the undulating formations of Fluberget attracted attention during the Bronze Age.
HEL/AMS

While the rock art in Northern Jæren is chiefly found in open air sites, the rock art in Middle Jæren is mainly characterized by a concentration of more than 100 decorated grave slabs. Most of them come from around 40 barrows or cairns dated to the Bronze Age, and a few from the Iron Age.

The number of decorated grave slabs in Rogaland is therefore much higher than elsewhere in Norway, where only twenty-five have been recorded (Syversten 2002). The majority of the slabs are decorated with cup marks, and a few with boats and footprints, although a number of the slabs have more conspicuous motifs consisting of abstract-geometric patterns, such as wavy lines, zigzag and fishbone patterns and multiple bows. These are motifs that only sporadically occur on open-air sites. The decorated slabs are placed inside the grave monuments; many of them as part of grave cists – either as end or side slabs or capstones – and the decorations face inwards into the cists (Syvertsen 2002, 2003). The grave slabs are all found in the rural districts and coastal communities of Middle Jæren, in an area with rich and easily tillable soil, well suited for Bronze Age cultivation (Prøsch-Danielsen and Simonsen 2000; Prøsch-Danielsen 2002).

The Bronze Age society of Jæren

The open landscape characterizing Jæren had already been created by the Late Neolithic as a result of forest clearance and extensive grazing, a process that continued in the Early Bronze Age. It has been suggested that in the rich agricultural area of Middle Jæren this led to economic changes that triggered a hierarchical society, based on surplus products from agriculture and animal husbandry, foreign alliances and exchange networks (Prøsch-Danielsen 2002). The large burial mounds located on the moraine heights tower above the flat surrounding land. It is possible that each of the large burial mounds was built by a single family, who thereby wanted to affirm their ownership and rights to the cultivated land, the low-lying pastures and beaches on the ocean and fjord (Myhre 1981). It is easy to interpret these monuments as a demonstration of power, as a way of announcing to wayfarers from near and far that this was the domain of powerful chieftains. The best arable soil was found in this area, there was a wide vista out across the land and sea, and the area was criss-crossed by communications routes.

Before 800 BC Middle Jæren was completely deforested, heathlands had taken over, and the soil was probably exhausted as a result of intensive farming (Prøsch-Danielsen and Simonsen 2000). This may have led to an ecological crisis, and from the middle of the Bronze Age onwards the centre of power seems to have been moved from Middle Jæren to Northern Jæren. The grave mounds in this area are located along the coast, on points and headlands with a good view over the fairway, and near sheltered harbours with easy access both to the sea and inwards into the fjords (Prøsch-Danielsen 2002).

Recent research has demonstrated that the monuments in Northern Jæren, rather than being central places in an agricultural landscape, instead highlight movement and mobility by accentuating lines of communication both on land and sea (Nordenborg Myhre 2004). Almost all of the areas where the richest bronze artefacts have been found are oriented towards Hafrsfjord or the seaports on the North Sea, and the wealth mirrored by the artefacts indicates close contact with Jylland in Denmark and further south on the continent (Nordenborg Myhre 1998). During an era when the sea was the natural link between people, Jæren may therefore be considered a gateway for ideas and goods.

The differences seen between the two main rock art concentrations in Jæren, with respect both to landscape types, motif variations and their contextual situation, indicate that two types of agricultural societies existed in Jæren, probably one after the other. In Middle Jæren, where the soil is suitable both for cultivation and animal husbandry, the grave monuments from the Early Bronze Age are mainly situated on the moraine ridges, organized along natural lines of overland movement. In the Mid and Late Bronze Age there is a shift in the location of grave monuments from the open moraine landscape in the south to the hilly fjord landscape of Northern Jæren, an area that was primarily suited for animal husbandry, hunting and fishing, as well as small scale agriculture (Prøsch-Danielsen 2002). At the same time as the location of the grave monuments changed, there was a shift from feminine grave goods, mainly jewellery, in the south to masculine related objects, such as swords and spearheads, in the north. These changes also coincide with the increase in number and complexity of rock art sites in the coastal districts of Northern Jæren, strengthening the maritime aspects of society (Nordenborg Myhre 2004).

The religious dimension

The votive deposits and rock art in the Revheim area were created by a society characterized by material wealth and contacts with the world around them. For the settlements in Jæren it must have been important to maintain the production of essential goods and surplus products – the very basis for the stable and sustainable wealth of the society that had developed. Rituals were undoubtedly performed to ensure good crops and increased harvests, but only as part of a much more complex and comprehensive religious practice. Religion played many other roles in human existence other than to merely guarantee subsistence. It structured and organized existence, provided explanations for life and death and defined people's relationship to one another and to the supernatural powers. In all faiths there are myths that explain how the world and humans were created, and how divine events have affected people's lives. Through ritual observances, people were able to take part in and recreate these events, thereby reaffirming the world order and the state of things (Hygen and Bengtsson 1999).

Fluberget at Revheim revisited

It is within the frame of this complex world-view – even though it is not fully comprehensible – that Fluberget and the Revheim moor should be interpreted. With its conspicuous geological shape and number and variety of motifs, Fluberget stands out in relation to the smaller rock art sites found in the surrounding area. This position is emphasized by the votive deposits in the Revheim moor, thus indicating that Fluberget was an important sacrificial and cultic site during the Bronze Age. In addition to attributes such as acting, portraying and relating, music and dance were also associated with religious rituals. In several rock art sites in other parts of Scandinavia, humans are depicted playing bronze trumpets, often in pairs – a portrayal that coincides with the fact that lures are normally found in pairs (Hygen and Bengtsson 1999). Lures are also depicted individually on rock art panels, and among the crew lines on boat images there are often long, curved lines assumed to illustrate lure players on board the boats.

An altar consecrated to the sun?

Through the rock art imagery and the ornate artefacts from burial mounds and sacrificial sites, it is possible to glimpse the outlines of Bronze Age ceremonies and cult observances. However, the meaning of these religious rituals is elusive, and many alternative explanations exist. A strongly supported theory is that sun worship was a central element in the religious observances of Bronze Age people. Already in the mid 1800s it was suggested that the ring figures depicted in rock art were symbols for the sun (Brunius 1868), an interpretation that received considerable backing in the early decades of the last century (Helander 1906; Almgren 1927). The ring motif occurs in many variations: one simple ring,

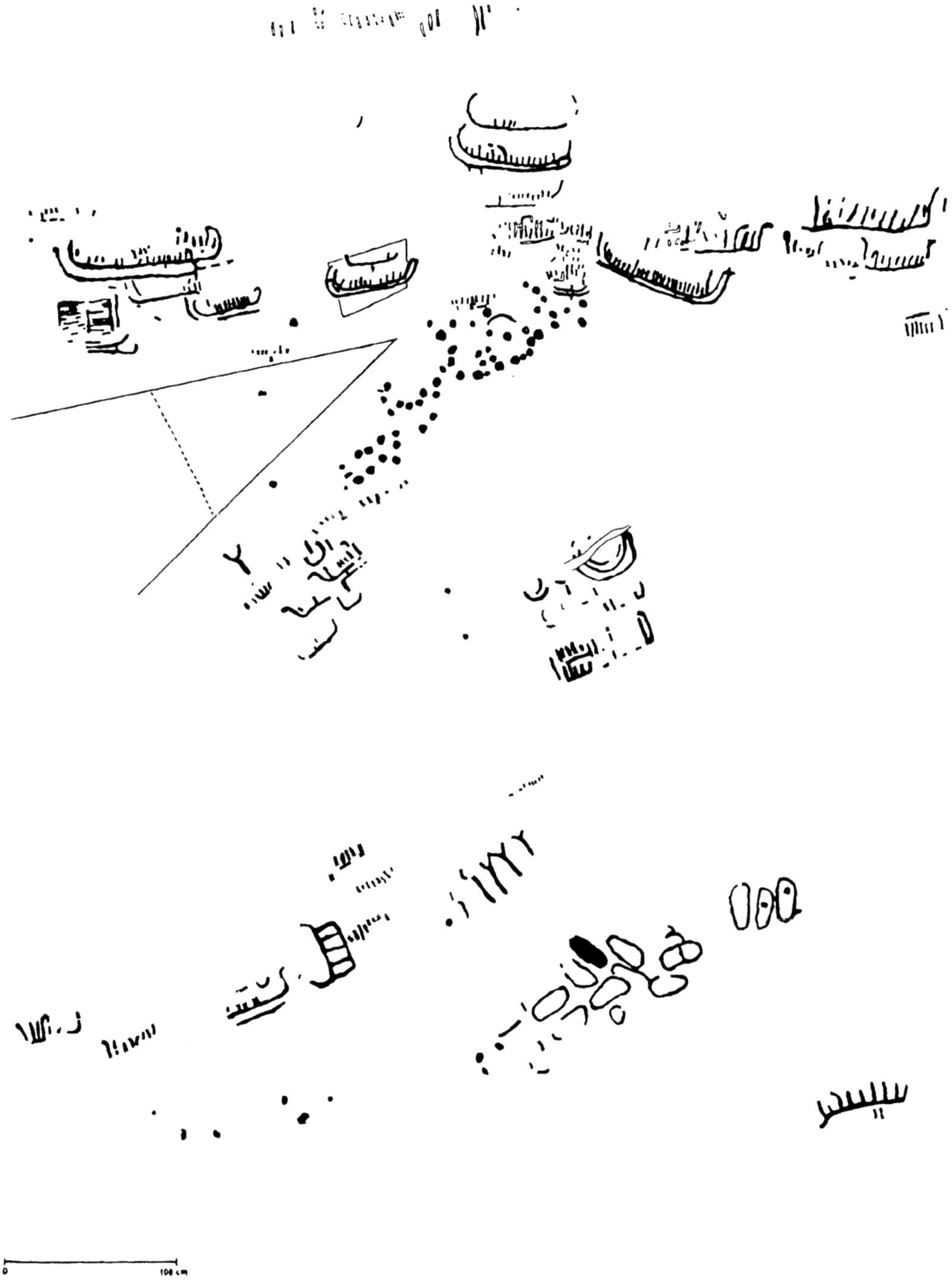

FIGURE 192. Tracing of the rock carvings in the largest hollow of the southern wall of Fluberget – the so-called "sun altar". About midway in the hollow, where the rock wall vaults outwards on three sides, there is a row of boat images. On a ledge just below the boats is a group of cup marks, and on an overhang beneath the cup marks are two large, concentric ring figures. Just below the rings is a row of Y-shaped images, interpreted as stylized human figures. At the bottom of the hollow, on a horizontal ledge at about ground level, there is a row of foot soles, apparently placed in a natural position for viewing the figures above – or when climbing up to the top of the cliff.

EPF

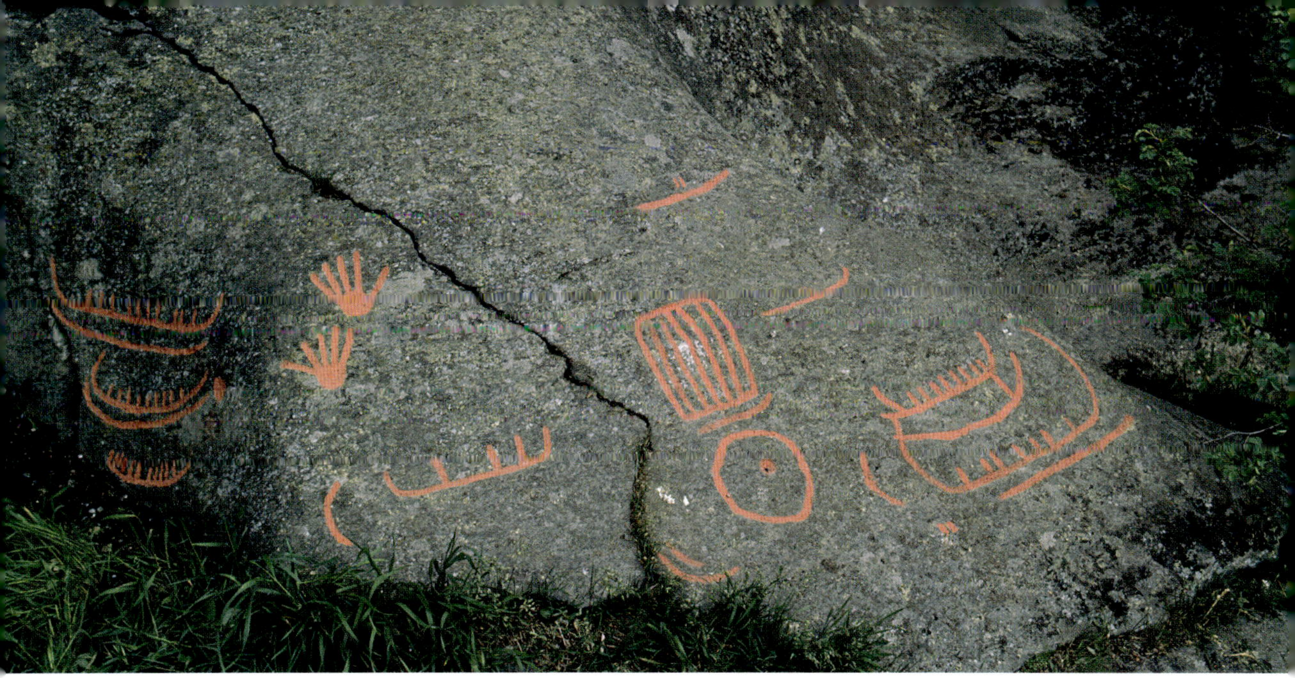

FIGURE 193. In the body of Scandinavian rock art material, particularly in Bohuslän, there are many examples of human figures depicted with large, raised hands and spread fingers. It is much less common to find only the hands depicted, as seen in Fluberget. There are a few isolated examples in Østfold, among other places on one of the Solberg panels at Skjeberg, and a few in Trøndelag. Elsewhere in Europe and Asia, the hand motif has been associated with a visualization of strength and power. The outstretched or raised hands played a role in rituals, among others in the Oriental sun cult. RU

multiple concentric rings, rings with radial lines or combinations of a number of these elements. The symbols occur alone or together with other motifs: carried by people, drawn by horses, or mounted on boats.

In the 1930s Eva Nissen Fett and Per Fett proposed an interpretation of the rock art at Fluberget, in which the sun symbolism is central (Fett and Fett 1941). The point of departure for this interpretation was the largest of the pothole-like depressions in the centre of the south wall. Here the figures are placed in relation to the natural topographical features of the crag such as recesses, protrusions and flatter surfaces. Fett and Fett saw this as a conscious composition based on a general plan, even though perhaps not all of the figures were carved at the same time. They believed that the dominant mid-point in the composition was the pair of rings placed below a row of boat images and a group of cup marks. The larger ring symbolized the sun, and the row of Y-shaped figures beneath the sun symbol was seen as "worshippers" – people with their arms raised as if they were venerating a deity. They interpreted the composition as a whole as an altar consecrated to the sun, and in subsequent years Fluberget has often been referred to as the "sun altar" (Skjølsvold 1961).

Time reckoning and the calendar year

The sun is also central in more recent interpretations of the rock art at Fluberget – not the symbol on the stone surface, but the actual sun disc and its trajectory across the sky. The premise is that the society of Northern Jæren during the Bronze Age must have had some sort of system for reckoning time based on the calendar year. In order to farm profitably, more was required than just good tools. It was necessary to be able to foresee the best times for sowing and harvesting, for sending the cattle to the grazing grounds, and for setting out on long journeys in search of costly metal. To do so, it was necessary to be able to correctly calculate the passage of time throughout the year (Vinsrygg 1982).

The basis for constructing and maintaining calendars is primarily the movements of the heavenly bodies – the stars, the moon or the sun. At northern latitudes, the sun's movement across the sky throughout the year is the most noticeable and easily-observed phenomenon. The most conspicuous features of this movement are during the solstices that occur around 21 December and 21 June. At the solstice, the sun appears to stand still for a short period of time, before it resumes its natural course across the sky. Solstices are the benchmarks for all solar calendars, and it is necessary to be able to fix the times for these events as precisely as possible. Observations made from the summit of Fluberget show that the location is well suited for studying the sun's positions during the winter months. Sunrise during the winter solstice is particularly eye-catching. On the shortest day of the year, the sun appears behind a mountain gorge on the horizon and appears to roll across the horizon before ascending (*ibid.*). The location of the rock art crag at Revheim therefore appears to be favourable for the observation and marking of significant occurrences in the sun's movement throughout the year. This knowledge was not only important for material and economic interests. The creation of calendars also appears to have had a religious importance.

Public festivals, votive offerings and religious ceremonies were associated with the annual cycle and had to be observed at fixed times in order to maintain order in society. Yearly calendars and official celebrations were interdependent, and they

FIGURE 194. Through the so-called "sun altar" – from the summit of the cliff and down past the rows of foot soles at the foot of the mountain – there is a deep fissure with distinct signs of water seepage along the crack.
RU

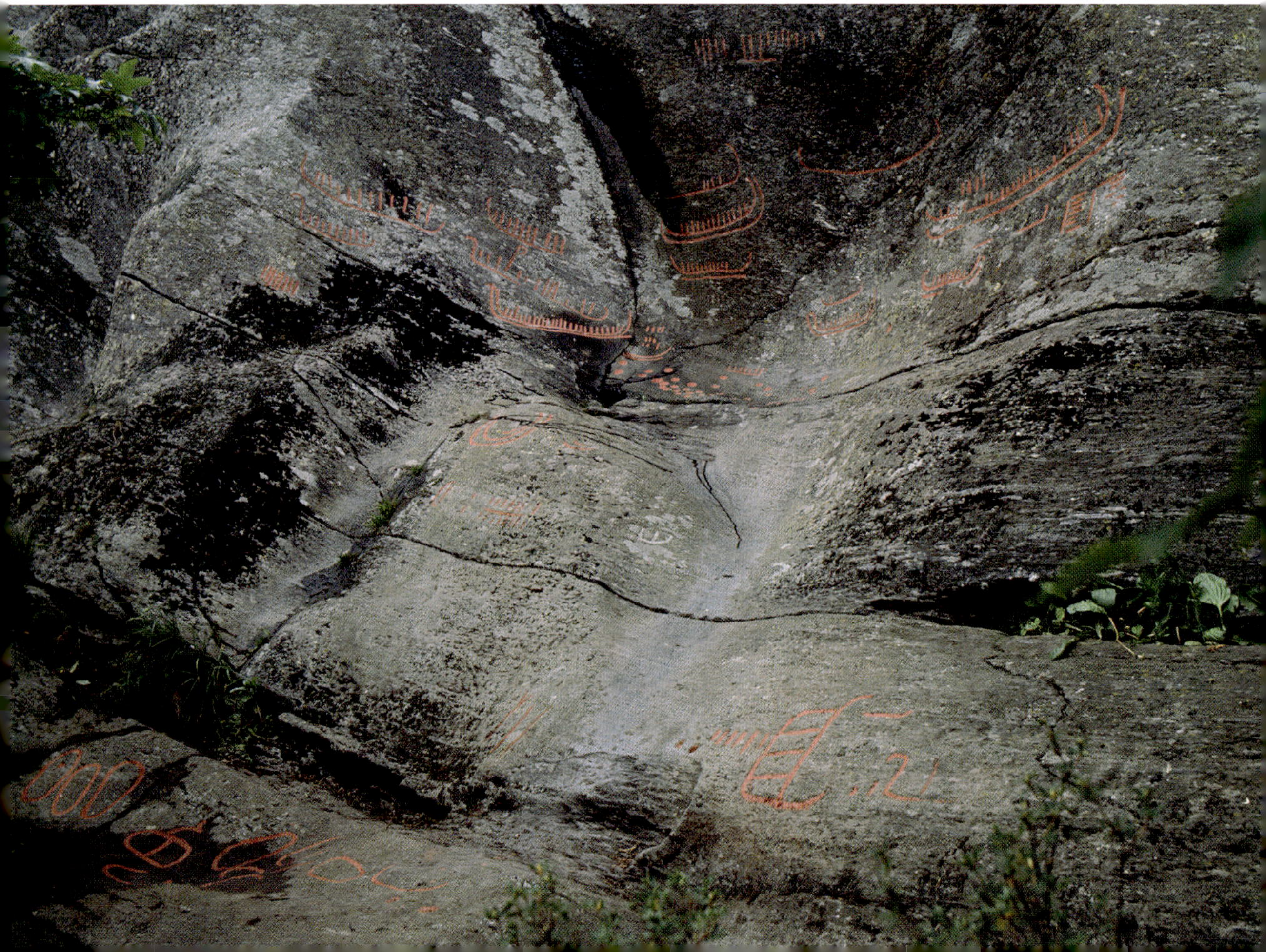

influenced the economic and cultural activities of society. The deeper the insight into the annual cycle the chieftains possessed, the more prestige they enjoyed.

The importance of astronomical calendars to Bronze Age society is also revealed by a number of objects originating from Middle Europe (Solheim Pedersen 2008). The so-called Nebra Sky Disc, found in central Germany, is a 30 cm-wide bronze disc with celestial bodies made of gold welded on it. A total of 32 small gold plates representing stars, placed in between a moon crescent and the full moon, form the astronomical constellation the Pleiades. In the area where the disc was discovered, this constellation marked the beginning and end of the farming season. One aspect of particular interest in relation to Fluberget is that the Nebra disc was found inside a walled structure situated on a hill aligned with a mountain where the sun sets at the summer solstice.

Four tall gold cones, probably also related to astronomical observations, have been discovered in France and Germany. They are made of paper-thin hammered gold foil and are decorated with sun and moon symbols. Their function is disputed, but one interpretation is that they were ceremonial headgear worn by chosen persons on special occasions. The decorations are interpreted as a type of calendar or a visualization of the cosmic order in order to calculate time.

Life, death and rebirth

If the rock art site at Revheim really was a place where Bronze Age people made solar observations, it is reasonable to consider this as a kind of concrete rendition or elaboration of the interpretation from the 1930s of Fluberget as an altar consecrated to the sun. Research from recent decades also supports the view of the sun as a central element in the beliefs of Bronze Age peoples. The sun is seen as the very genesis in the shaping of the cosmology during the Bronze Age, and one of the original myths is the tale of the daily rebirth of the sun (Kaul 1998, 2004).

The basis for this interpretation is an analysis of imagery in the Bronze Age as it appears on bronze artefacts, primarily on the razors that appear in grave finds. The razors are decorated with engravings similar to some of the motifs occurring in rock art – rings, boats and horses. The central motif is the ring – the symbol for the sun. The myth describes the course of the sun over a 24-hour period. Each morning the sun disc rises above the horizon in the east and journeys across the sky towards the west, where it disappears at the end of the day into the realm of the dead, only to be reborn again the following morning. On its journey across the sky and down into the underworld, the sun is drawn along by boats or horses. The sun, the horse and the boat are thus seen as three important and closely related components in the mythology and world-view of the Bronze Age.

The sun's journey across the firmament may also serve as an image for the cradle-to-grave human life cycle as well as the perennial growth cycle, from the first buds of spring and on until winter once again regains its iron grip on nature. Traces of symbolism and notions regarding birth, life, death and rebirth are found both in Bronze Age burial rituals (Linge 2007; Syvertsen 2003;

Goldhahn 1999), and in cult rituals intended to promote fertility (Almgren 1927).

The rock images in the large depression at the centre of the sheer mountain wall at Fluberget, with the ring figures as the centrepiece, perhaps portray mythical events from the ancient past – from the time when the world was created. It is true that the rock images at this site comprise only two of the components in the myth relating to the daily rebirth of the sun – the sun itself and the boat. Nonetheless, it is possible that the myth may be used as an explanatory model, especially in terms of the composition that was the source of referring to it as "the sun altar". Perhaps it was not always necessary – or desirable – to depict all the parts of a myth. It may have sufficed to illustrate some of the highlights in the mythical tale in order to evoke the essence of the subject matter (Hauptman Wahlgren 2002). At Fluberget, the most important factor may have been to render visible the relationship between the sun and the boat. Furthermore, it has been pointed out that in addition to solar symbolism, there is also aquatic symbolism in the mythological world of ideas from the Bronze Age. Water symbolism is found in the motif of the boat in the rock art, in the location of the sites near the seashore or fjord and the depositing of offerings in bogs or wetlands (Nordenborg Myhre 2004). In this respect, the entire cult arena at Revheim falls into a mythical universe of symbols where the sun and water are central elements – the rock art site by the fjord as an observation post for designing a solar calendar, the rock art as a means of illustrating the mythical tale of the sun being drawn by boats, and the wet bogs where the ceremonial bronze items were offered.

Towards a new era

Towards the end of the Bronze Age, the cult site at Hafrsfjord gradually became less important. Changes in society may have resulted in a devaluation of the old myths. A new metal appeared – iron. The venerable rituals of the past were succeeded by new customs, and new symbols and concepts of life and death were introduced (Fredell 2003). No further rock carvings were added to Fluberget, and the foremost symbol of the Bronze Age – the glittering bronze trumpets – were disassembled and laid deep in a moor as a final, reverential offering. Or could it be that the trumpets had been disassembled after each time they were used – and at some point, something occurred that caused them never to be retrieved?

Analyses of pollen from some of the places where bronze trumpets have been found suggest that they were not buried in the moor, but rather laid on the surface, and that overgrowth on the moor later concealed and surrounded them (Johansen 2000). They must have lain exposed to the elements for a long period of time, but were left untouched by passers-by. Although ceremonies in which the instruments had played an important role were no longer performed, the place where they were laid must have been perceived as sacred. The bronze trumpets had been offered by ancestors to higher powers as an expression of gratitude, or as an invocation for health, wealth and good harvests, and the sacrifice itself was not to be touched by mortals.

The Rock Art of Lista – the Southernmost Outpost

The Lista Peninsula at the southern tip of Vest-Agder County has been referred to as "Norway in miniature". Facing the open ocean is a wide, barren plain of moors and lakes. Shoreline skerries exist only on the far eastern side, around the small town of Farsund. To the north, the coastal plain landscape gives way to rolling terrain with heath-covered hills, knolls and crags up to about 350 metres above sea level, incised by narrow valleys (Prøsch-Danielsen and Simonsen 2000). The lowlands in the south and west comprise Lista in the true sense of the place name – it means brim, edge or brink. This three or four kilometre-wide coastal zone is called Listalandet, located on the open sea and exposed to the forces of nature – a rugged and weather-beaten shoreline that many seafarers through the ages has encountered with tragic consequences. It is an undulating moraine landscape, most of which is lower than 20 metres above sea level. The entire area is covered by large masses of glacifluvial deposits, with a varying sand and clay content. The low-lying part of Lista is dominated by eluviated sandy ground, and by shifting sands on the outermost edge (*ibid.*). Bird life abounds in the many large lakes that are dammed up by the moraine. Although the landscape of Lista is windy, barren and boggy, agricultural conditions are good, mainly due to the favourable climate with mild winters and early springs (Prøsch-Danielsen 1995). The place names and numerous archaeological discoveries and monuments bear witness to the fact that this landscape provided attractive living conditions for people in prehistoric times. The most visible traces of human activity on the flat, largely cultivated landscape of Lista are burial mounds and stone cairns from the Bronze and Iron Ages, as well as the rock art panels from the Bronze Age.

Limited motifs – time frame of several centuries

Fewer than 100 rock art panels have been recorded at Lista. Although the range of motifs is limited to boat figures, foot soles and cup marks, the imagery depicted is undoubtedly part of the Southern rock art tradition. Cup marks are the only motif found on the majority of the panels, and only nine feature boat figures and foot soles in addition to cup marks (Fett and Fett 1941).

The boat images vary in shape, revealing that not all of the panels were created at the same time. Comparisons with similar figures in other parts of Scandinavia indicate that the boat images at Lista were created in the middle and latter part of the Bronze Age – probably in the period between 1500–1000

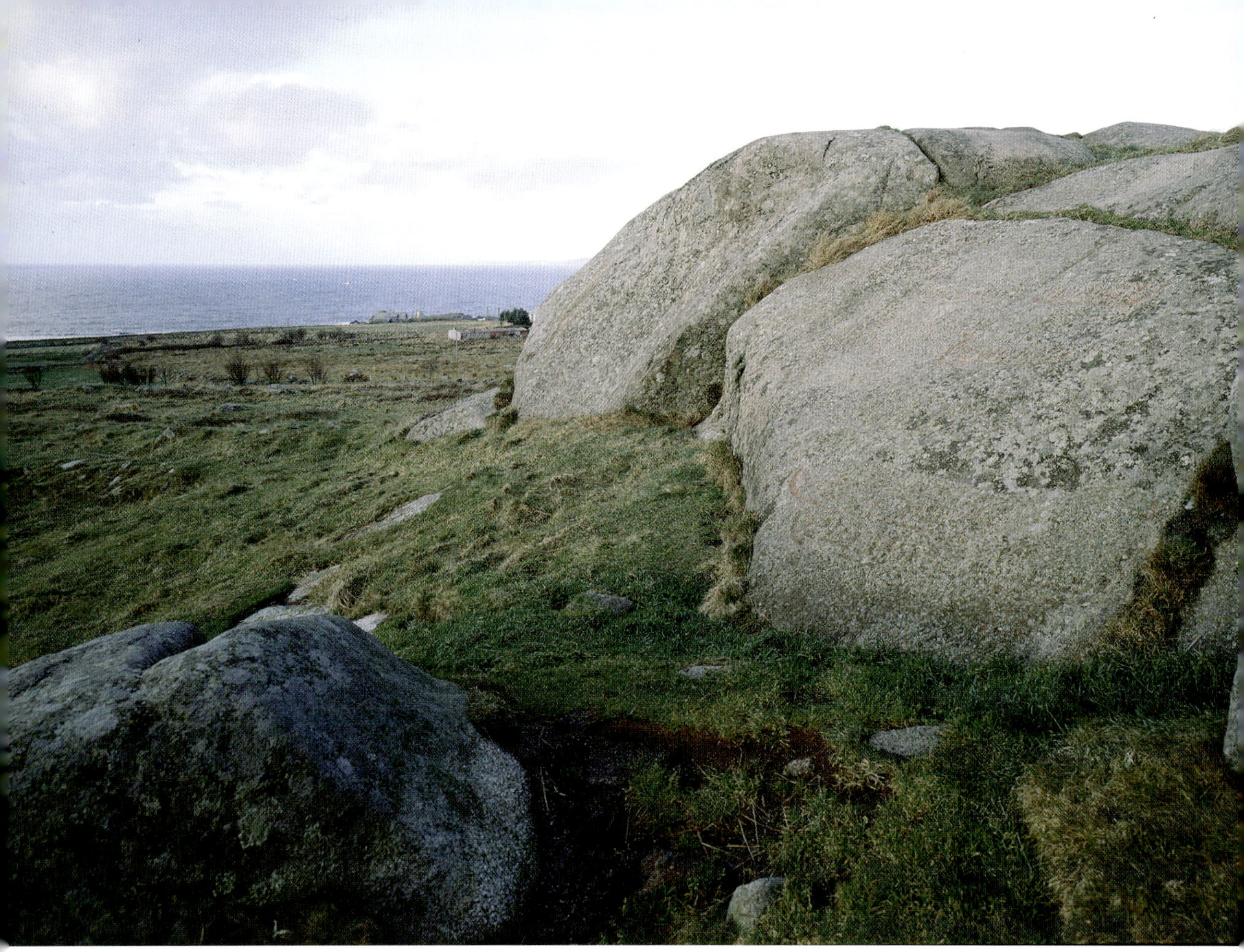

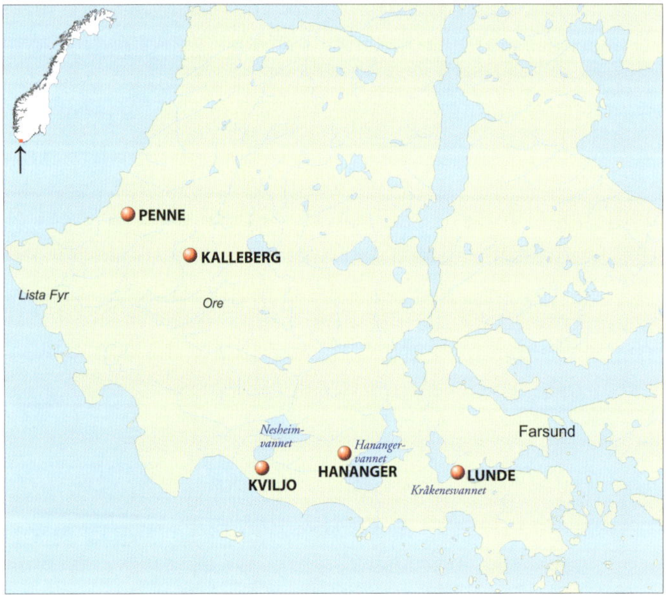

FIGURES 195–196. The rock carvings located at the highest point in Lista are on Gjerdberget, a 30-metre-tall knoll. Boat figures and other motifs are pecked into the summit of the knoll, from where there is a panorama of the flat landscape below and out towards the open ocean.

MAP AI, ILLUSTRATION AK

and 700–500 BC. The foot soles, most of which are completely carved out, are usually found in pairs. In a few cases it is difficult to determine whether the carvings illustrate foot soles or oval depressions/double cup marks. The cup marks are most frequently 4–8 cm wide and 1–1.5 cm deep, but there are others of both smaller and greater dimensions. The cup marks are almost always found at the top of the panels, often densely clustered. Many are linked with narrow grooves, and on some panels there are longer grooves leading out from the cup marks and extending all the way to the edge of the panel (*ibid.*). The cup marks and foot soles cannot be dated more precisely than to the Bronze Age. As mentioned in the chapter on the sub-alpine regions of Southern Norway, cup marks may have been created as early as the end of the Neolithic (around 2000 BC), and the tradition seems to have been maintained throughout the entire Bronze Age and until the Early Iron Age (500–600 AD).

All of the cup marks and most of the boat and foot sole images at Lista are carved into the surfaces of large embedded boulders and smaller stones – the natural choice in this rocky landscape. Only three larger panels with boat figures are found on solid rock, at the Penne, Lunde and Hananger farms. Two other larger panels with boat images – Kalleberg and Kviljo – appear on large, embedded rocks.

Penne – rock art with a view

In 1917, local residents discovered the rock art at Penne, which is one of Lista's largest panels in terms of numbers of images. At the most westerly point of Listalandet, the terrain rises evenly from the sea to the hills in the north. On a large knoll called Gjerdberget, about 30 metres above sea level, rock carvings are found in several separate groups. From here there is a wide panorama out across the flatlands towards the sea and the endless horizon beyond, with Lista lighthouse as a conspicuous landmark on the western tip of Listalandet. The summit of the knoll is a plateau, and the bedrock is cracked and exfoliated over a large area as a result of Midsummer Eve bonfires in earlier times. There are remains of an old stone wall surrounding the knoll that possibly once enclosed the rock art panel (*ibid.*).

The largest group of carvings are located on a flat, sloping surface facing to the southwest. The group comprises twenty-two boat images and sixty to seventy partly scattered, partly clustered cup marks. Most of the boats have double hulls, with parallel longitudinal grooves denoting the gunwale and keel, and vertical lines terminating the hull at each end. The boats have double, tall and curved stems and crew lines. Two of these are more than a metre long, and the largest one has a loop at the end of the prow, interpreted as a "pennant". At the top of the knoll is a deeply carved pair of foot soles surrounded by scattered cup marks and several cup mark clusters. On the north-western side of the knoll, on the slope below the site of the bonfires, is another fully carved pair of foot soles and several clusters of cup marks, and far down on the surface facing

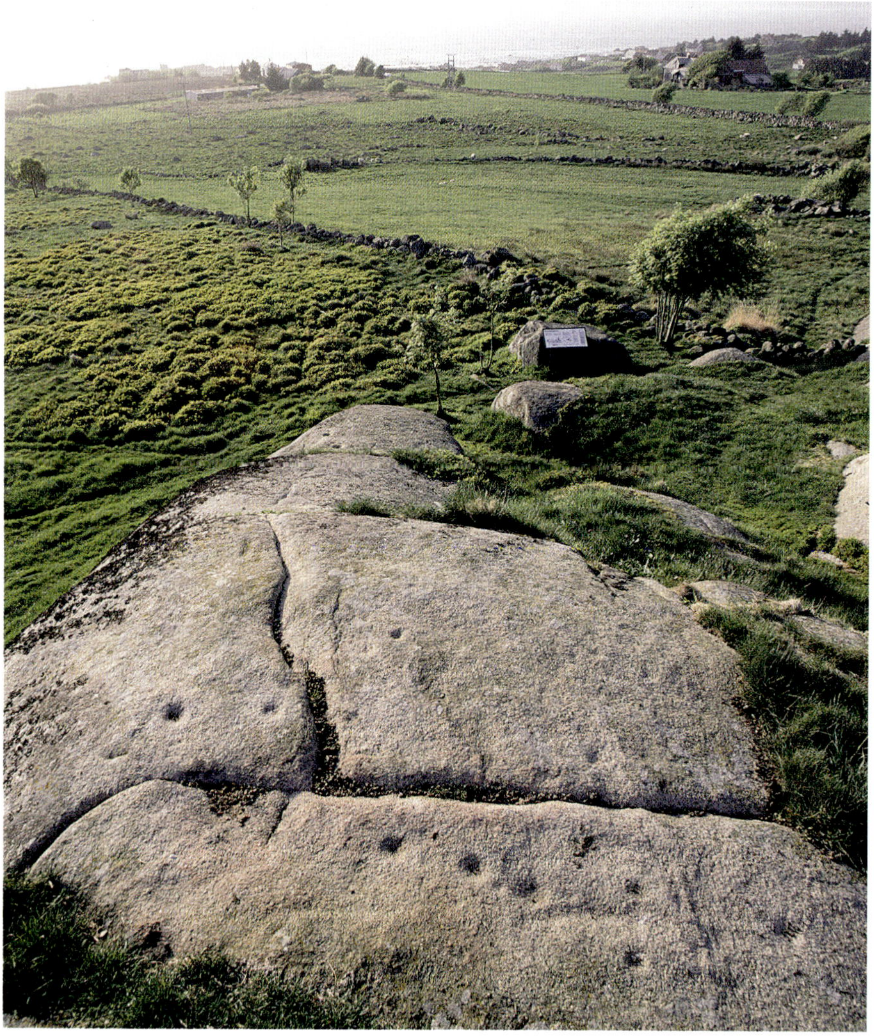

FIGURE 197. There are groups of rock carvings in several places on Gjerdberget, including many cup marks.
RU

southwest are two boat images, one with crew lines. The Penne boat images probably date the site to the earlier part of the Bronze Age, perhaps around 1000–900 BC. During an excavation in front of the panel in 2007, a bronze fragment dated to the Bronze Age and some flint and pottery were uncovered. Traces of agricultural activity from around 2000 BC onwards were also found (hf.uio.no/iakh/for-ansatte/avis/2007/august/feltkurs-oppf.html).

At Penne, in addition to the rock art on Gjerdberget, a glacial boulder with a pair of cup marks on the top has been found.

Kalleberg – the earliest discovered boat images

The Kalleberg boats have been known since the 1880s, although it was not until 1913 that antiquarians were officially notified of their existence (Fett and Fett 1941). On the flat terrain near the farm buildings there is a large, embedded

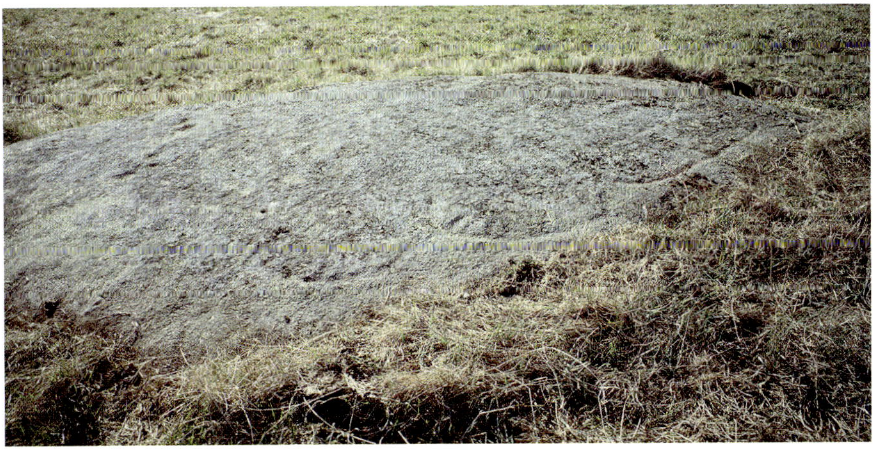

FIGURE 198. At Kalleberg there are rock carvings on a flat stone outcrop lying flush with the ground. Several single-lined boat images are arranged in a row and extending all the way to the edge of the turf.
GM

stone almost flush with ground level. Halfway up the stone there is a group of fourteen circular and oval cup marks, and down across the northern side are six boat images arranged in two rows. The hulls and stems are carved using one continuous, curved line, and five of the boats have crew lines. Two boats have a "pennant" on one of the two stems, similar to that depicted on one of the Penne boats. These simply shaped boat figures are difficult to date, apart from the fact that they belong to the Southern rock art tradition.

In the fields surrounding the panel of boat images, five embedded rocks with cup marks have been found, one of which also has what may be a pair of foot soles.

Kviljo – surrounded by an elevated ridge

Some two hundred metres southeast of a lake called Nesheimvatnet, at the edge of an expanse of shifting sand, a large glacial boulder with rock carvings was discovered in 1919. The terrain is quite hilly, with flat fields stretching southwards towards the ocean. The stone measures 4 × 6 metres and is two metres tall and flat on the top. In earlier times it was surrounded by an artificial ridge around 13–15 metres wide that rose some distance up the sides of the stone. During the first examination of the rock art in 1921, the artificial ridge was investigated, but nothing was found inside it (*ibid.*).

Altogether there are fifteen or sixteen boat images, two foot soles – one of which is completely carved out and the other as an outline – and sixty to sixty-five cup marks, some linked together with grooves. Most of the rock carvings are on the top of the stone, with some around the sides. The flat section on top slopes toward the north-west, and all of the boat figures are arranged vertically in relation to the slope of the stone. Like the Penne boats, more than half of these have double-line hulls, high curving stem lines and crew lines, with the longest measuring some 1.5 metres. The double-lined boats are carved using deep and distinct lines, while the boats with single-line hulls are shallower. The rock art at Kviljo probably belongs to the same time period as the Penne images, the earlier part of the Bronze Age.

Hananger – the oldest boat images?

In 1932, a panel with boat images was discovered at the south-western end of a lake called Hanangervatnet. The figures are carved into a low-lying, rounded knoll located in a field near the farm buildings (*ibid.).* Like Penne, this knoll is damaged by exfoliation that was possibly caused by bonfires. Some twelve to fifteen cup marks and twelve boat figures are carved on this panel. There are two different types of boats, one which resembles those on the Penne panel, but lacks crew lines. The other boat type is almost quadratic in shape, and the hull is filled in with parallel lines between the lines indicating the gunwale and keel. These boat figures also lack crew lines. The boat images belong to an earlier phase of the Bronze Age than the Penne boats. They are of the same type as the boat images found on slabs covering the burial cists in the large grave mound of Mjeltehaugen at Giske in Sunnmøre. The Mjeltehaugen boat type is dated to the Early Bronze Age, meaning that the boats at Hananger must have been made at some time during the same period, perhaps around 1700/1500–1300 BC.

On another flat stone in the farmyard area, a single boat image of the oldest type was found, together with a group of cup marks. Five more stones with only cup marks have been found in the surrounding area.

Lunde – the most easterly boat images

In 1917, the same year when the rock art at Penne was discovered, a young student notified the University Museum of Antiquities in Oslo that there were also rock carvings at Lunde, at the easternmost edge of Listalandet. The student had taken part in the first investigation of the Penne panels, and this was probably the reason why he notified the authorities about the rock art at Lunde, which people in the local area had known for some time (*ibid.*).

Lunde is situated just southeast of a lake called Kråkenesvatnet. About 50 metres from the lake there is a 2 × 5 metre-wide, 1.75 metre-tall granite boulder. The rock art was carved into a flat surface that slopes towards the northwest. The images comprise five boat figures and twenty to thirty cup marks. Three of the boats have double hulls, tall and curved stems and crew lines. They are of the same type as the boat figures at Penne, and probably date from the same period. The larger of the boats is well over one metre long. About 100 metres from the boulder with the boat images, another stone is said to have been found, containing a few cup marks.

Cultural traces on the landscape

The largest concentration of rock art panels is located at the western edge of Listalandet, in an area where the soil consists of clay-rich moraine gravel (Prøsch-Danielsen 1995). Here the two large panels with boat images at Penne and Kalleberg are found, as well as two smaller panels with boat figures and one with foot soles and cup marks. In addition there are no fewer than sixty or seventy stones with cup marks as their only motif, with up to sixteen panels being found on the same farm property. To the east, across Listalandet, the rock art sites are more scattered. Most of them are located in or adjacent to smaller areas with clay-rich moraine gravel, although some of the panels are also found on sandy ground, among others many of the cup mark stones. The three large panels with boat figures – Kviljo, Hananger and Lunde – are relatively close to one another, at the edge of the best farmland, and bordering the large wetland areas.

Burial mounds and artefacts from the Bronze Age are also generally found in the same areas as the rock art, on or in close proximity to the clay-rich moraine gravel. Towering earthen mounds and stone cairns, many of them 20–30 metres in diameter and some three metres tall, are found individually or in groups from the most westerly promontory and heading east along the coast

FIGURE 199. The two-metre-tall curved stone outcrop at Kviljo is distinctly visible on the flat landscape in the southernmost area of Listalandet. There was once an artificial, raised ridge around the stone, the remains of which are still visible.
GM/BM

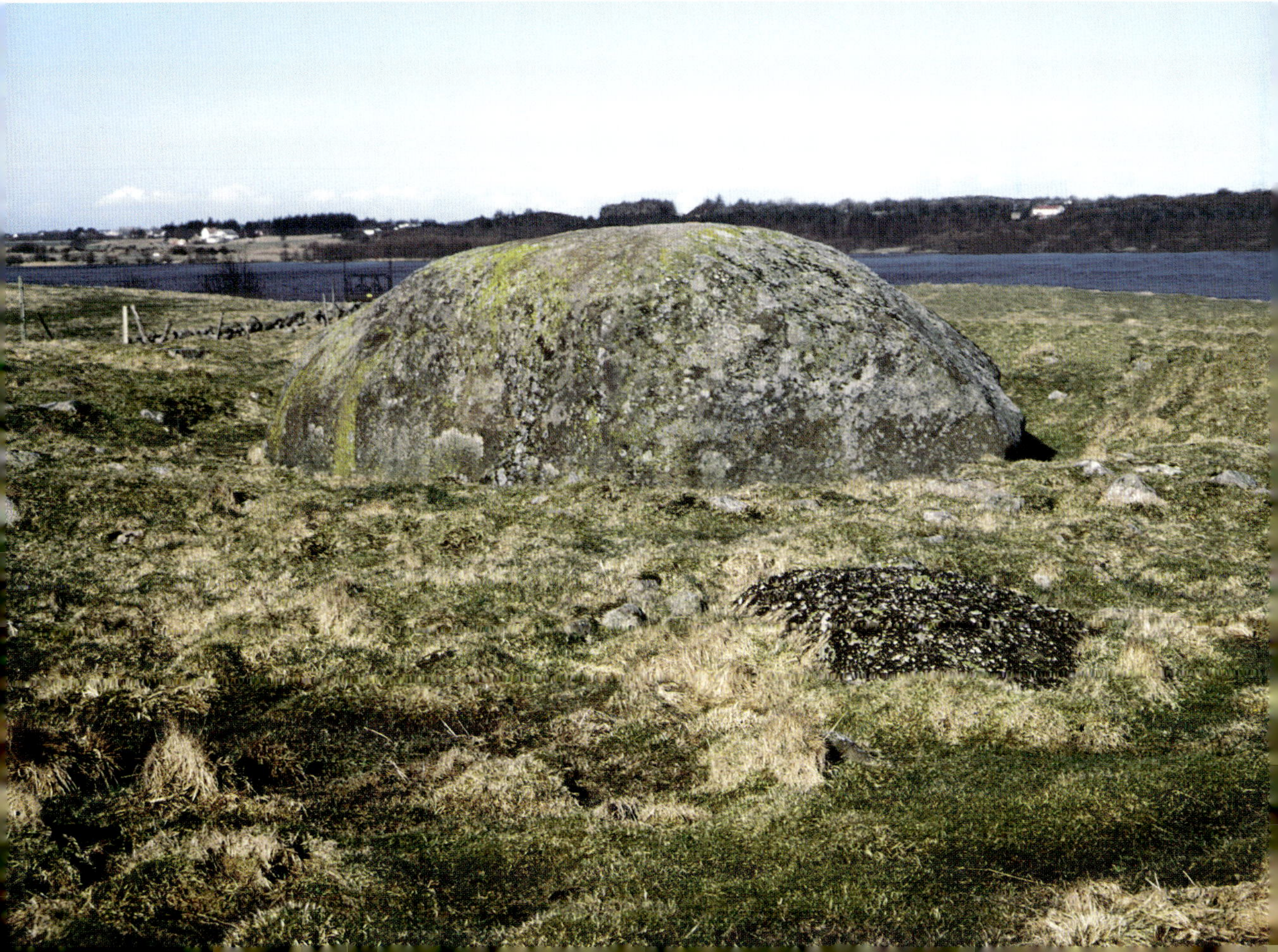

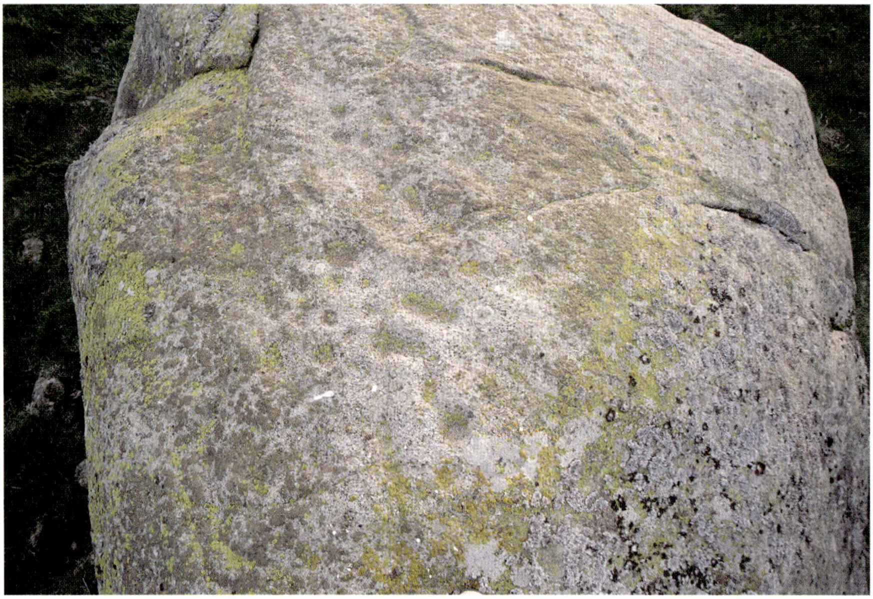

FIGURE 200. On the top of the Kviljo stone is a group of cup marks, some of which are linked by narrow grooves. On both sides of the cup marks boat images can be seen in bright, slanted lighting.
RU

(Johansen 1986). Several of them once contained grave goods from the Early and Late Bronze Age. Votive offerings have also been unearthed, as well as several so-called isolated finds – artefacts for which there is no known determination of their origin.

The remnants of material culture at Lista – the rock carvings, the graves and the bronze artefacts – are not the only coinciding indicators of the past. Place names also support the distribution patterns of the material remains. At Listalandet there are many farms with names that may date as far back as the Bronze Age (Fett and Fett 1941). These include short, inexplicable names such as Penne and Kviljo, and uncompounded natural names containing "berg" (mountain or crag), such as (Kalle)-berg, (Med)-berg and "hassel"(hazel), such as (Nord)-Hassel. In all likelihood, Hananger also belongs to the former nomenclature. The majority of Bronze Age discoveries are found on the farms with these early names.

The meaningful distribution pattern

The distribution of archaeological remains and place names indicate that two localization factors were crucial when the Bronze Age settlers at Lista selected their dwelling sites: arable fields and the sea. The concentrations of the cultural monuments reveal that the nutrient-rich and easily tillable moraine gravel must have been the most attractive, probably because it was the most suitable for cultivation using the agricultural tools of the age. Also, just below the fields was the open ocean: a supply of food, communications artery and link with neighbours near and far who were the source of goods and new ideas.

So what was the function of the rock art in the Bronze Age society at Lista?

The boat motif, the foremost symbol for travel and communication in the Bronze Age, was undoubtedly essential for the people living on these ocean shores. However, no single site stands out for its size or its location as a central, common sacred site for all of Lista. The location of the boat images in two main areas perhaps reflects that Listalandet was divided into two major settlements – the "western settlement" and the "eastern settlement" – each having its own sacred rock art site.

On the western side (or the "western settlement"), Penne – with its open vista out over the ocean and perhaps surrounded by an enclosure – is the natural choice for a central holy place. Kalleberg, which lies almost concealed at ground level, may have had another function, perhaps reserved for the "chosen few", or only for use on special occasions. The cup mark panels can probably be interpreted as sacred sites for the individual farm. This area, where the largest deposits of clay-rich moraine gravel in all of Lista are found, was most likely the largest agricultural settlement in Lista during the Bronze Age.

To the east (or the "eastern settlement"), Kviljo is a prominent landmark in the centre of the undulating flatland, a large, rounded stone boulder surrounded by a man-made embankment. In this settlement area, the holy place may have moved from one spot to another over time. The rock art of Hananger appears to be from an earlier phase than the other boat images, which were probably made in the middle or later part of the Bronze Age. This coincides with the dates for the bronze artefacts found, which are largely from the Late Bronze Age.

The Bronze Age society at Lista

The favourable conditions for farming and animal husbandry probably laid the foundation for surplus production that surpassed what was needed for daily subsistence. Traces of Bronze Age farms, with houses and collective farmyards, have not yet been found in Lista. On the basis of the distribution of bronze objects, it has been proposed that in the Bronze Age, Listalandet may have been sub-divided into ten to fifteen farms, each with its own relatively large surrounding property (*ibid.*). However, it is uncertain whether this kind of settlement division applies to the entire period of time. Regardless of how many farms there were, the archaeological remains indicate that a stable and well-organized society existed on the flat, windy coastal stretch of land. This structure made it possible to recruit enough manpower to build the monumental burial sites and to obtain the much-coveted metal items that are so abundant at Lista.

Nearly 90% of the bronze artefacts found in all of Vest-Agder County come from Lista, with the majority concentrated on the narrow coastal shelf (Johansen 1986). Although this amounts to only about thirty objects, the number is surprisingly high if we consider that the artefacts are found in such a limited area. Swords, axes and jewellery have been found, often several in the same grave or votive offering. Many of the objects are rare and precious,

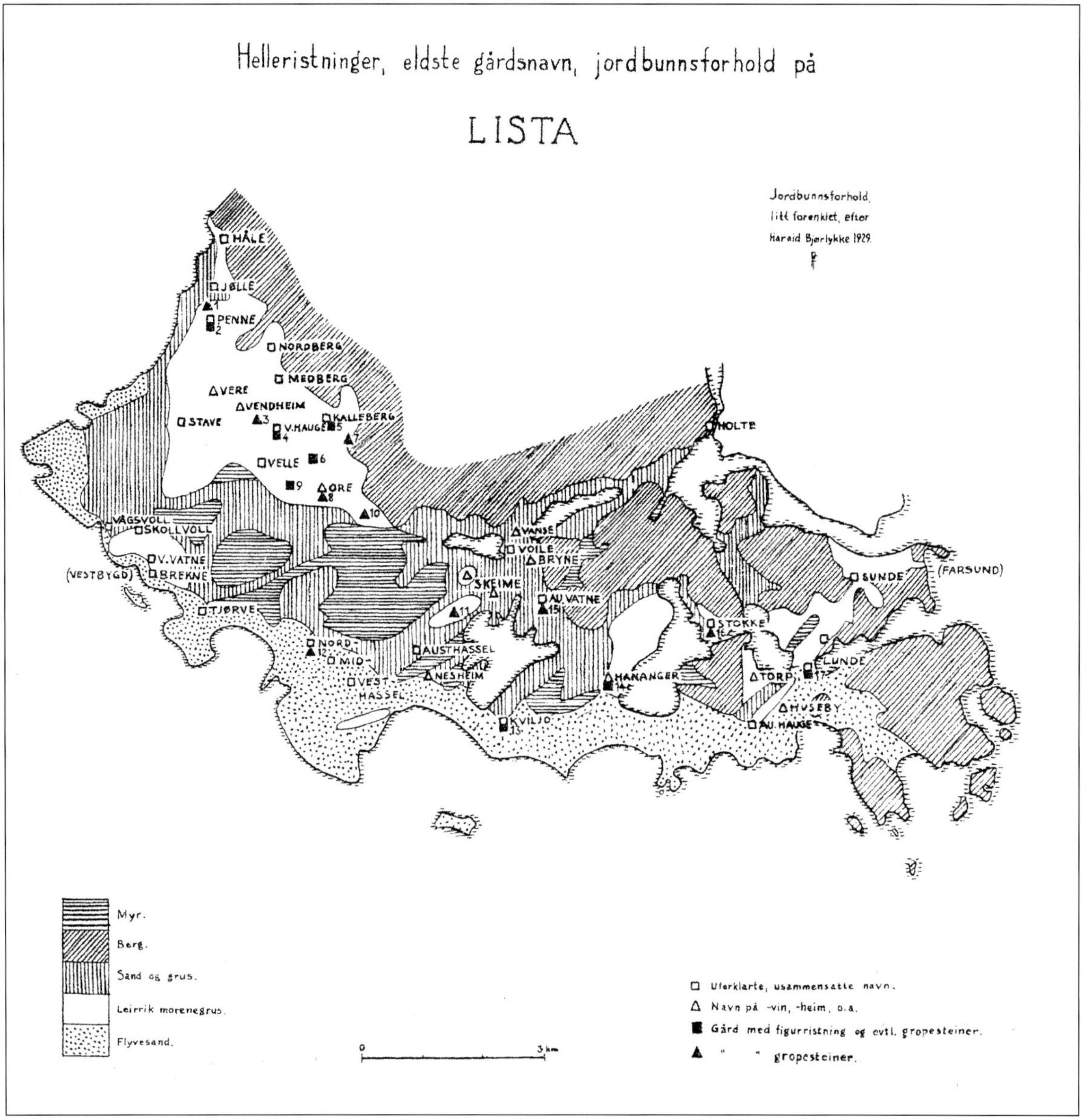

FIGURE 201. The overview made by Eva and Per Fett in the 1930s showing the distribution of rock carvings, old place names and topography at Listaland.

including a spiral arm ring made of gold of which only three others of the same type have been found in Norway, all from the neighbouring county of Rogaland.

Resources other than fields and pasturelands undoubtedly contributed to the wealth and surplus production needed to maintain this society. With the ocean on one's doorstep, so to speak, fishing must have been an important source of food. Another attractive resource was probably the teeming bird life in the wetland areas around the large moraine lakes, areas which were much more expansive in ancient times. In all likelihood, hunting and trapping in the inland area were also carried out. Due to the favourable location of Lista at the junction of two large fjord systems, it must have been easy to penetrate into the surrounding hills and mountain regions.

Gift exchanges and prestige networks

The abundance of bronze at Lista bears witness not only to material wealth. It also suggests that the society had a widespread social network that enabled steady and stable access to metal products throughout the greater part of the Bronze Age (*ibid.*). The practical utility value of the metal objects was not the only reason that made them so sought-after in the Bronze Age. Bronze was most likely part of a system of ceremonial gift exchange, the purpose of which was to reinforce the social prestige of both the giver and the receiver, and to establish bonds of kinship and other alliances. As a rule, the objects exchanged in this system were rare and precious. The items were often spread over great distances, so that they ended up in places far away from where they were made. In this way, the prestigious gifts were intended to ensure stability and maintain social structure in the society.

Most of the bronze objects found at Lista were probably made in Denmark or in Northern Germany and Poland, and they must have been brought to Lista by ship, primarily from the bronze-rich societies of Northwest Jylland (Marstrander 1950). The demands of transport across the open ocean must have required expert seamanship and precise planning, probably organized by the leading families at Lista. Prestigious objects were then carried further north along the West Norwegian coast to the rich agricultural settlements at Jæren (see previous chapter). The burial customs, artefacts and rock art tradition all bear witness to the close ties and lasting cultural collaboration between Lista and Jæren in the Bronze Age. The contact network between the Bronze Age societies in South-western Norway and Jylland was probably already in place by the end of the Stone Age – a dating that is corroborated by finds of flint and amber originating in Denmark but discovered in southwestern coastal settlements in Norway (Marstrander 1950; Johansen 1986).

However, the rock art tradition in these settlements cannot be considered to have resulted from contact across the Skagerrak Strait. In particular, the boat images at Lista and Jæren are quite different in comparison with the few, scattered rock art sites, mainly with cup marks, that are found in Northwest Jylland, in Denmark. In order to trace the contact route for the boat motif in Southwestern Norway, one undoubtedly has to look to the north and east. But that is another story.

Sporaneset in Rauland and other Rock Art Sites in Telemark

A rock carving site in the upper region of the county of Telemark has captured the imagination of visitors for many generations. The carvings are located in the small community of Rauland, bordering on the wide mountain plain of Hardangervidda. They appear on the north-eastern side of the great lake of Totak, on the low-lying promontory of Sporaneset (lit. Tracks Promontory), named after the most abundant motif – depictions of foot soles. Legend has it that King Olaf the Holy (king of Norway at the beginning of the 11th century) came ashore at this point after he had risked his life on the lake, and it is said that the king's followers left their footprints on the stony outcrop at the edge of the water. In gratitude for his life being spared, the king promised that "many are they who will be in mortal danger, but few will lose their lives on Totak" (Kostveit 1999). The rock carvings at Sporaneset have been known to professionals since the mid-1870s. The first investigation was conducted by Martin Arnesen, the same schoolteacher who recorded and documented rock carvings in Østfold during the 1860s.

Footprints and other figures on the shoreline

From its outermost tip, Sporaneset slopes upward and inland from the water in an even arc. Due to the development of hydroelectric power in the watercourses of upper Telemark, the water level of Totak fluctuates between 680 and 690 metres above sea level, and at high water the lake engulfs a large portion of the promontory, covering many of the figures. The rock species is mica schist, which is extremely weathered, with many cracks, glacial striations and depressions. Despite this the figures are relatively easy to make out, with the carving marks appearing clearly as black indentations in the shallow grooves.

Altogether there are some sixty figures on the panel, and more than half of these are outlines of foot soles, several of them arranged in pairs. Some have a transverse line near the heel, and some have the marks of toes. Five small animal figures are drawn in profile, most with humped backs, suggesting that they depict elk. There are also three small carvings of human figures, two of whom are seen in a frontal position – one in outline and the other only with lines – while the third is portrayed in profile. The human figure in profile seems to have an erect penis, while it is not possible to determine the gender of the other two. A few rectangular/square figures – some with parallel transverse lines – have often been interpreted as depictions of herd-hunting pits. Even a pair of

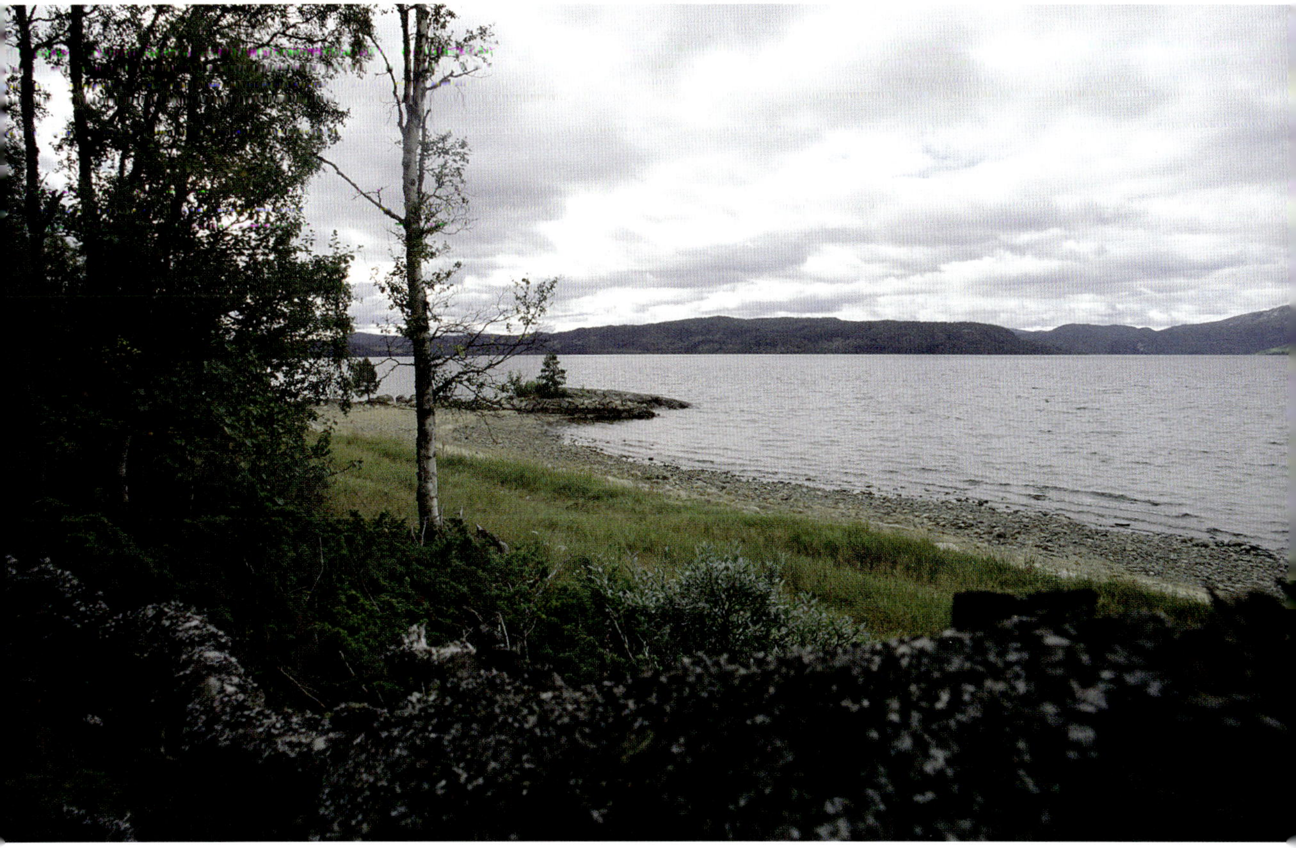

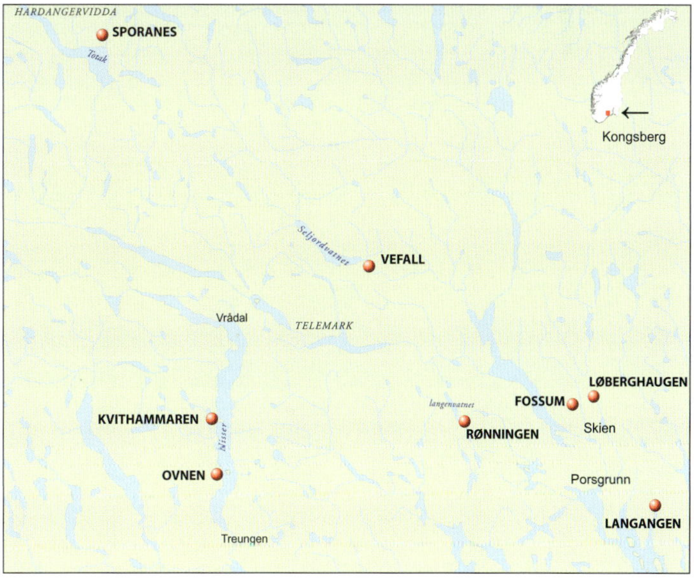

FIGURES 202–203. The promontory Sporaneset juts out into the bay between Haddlandsgrend and Raulandsstrand on the northeast side of the great lake Totak.

MAP AI, ILLUSTRATION RU

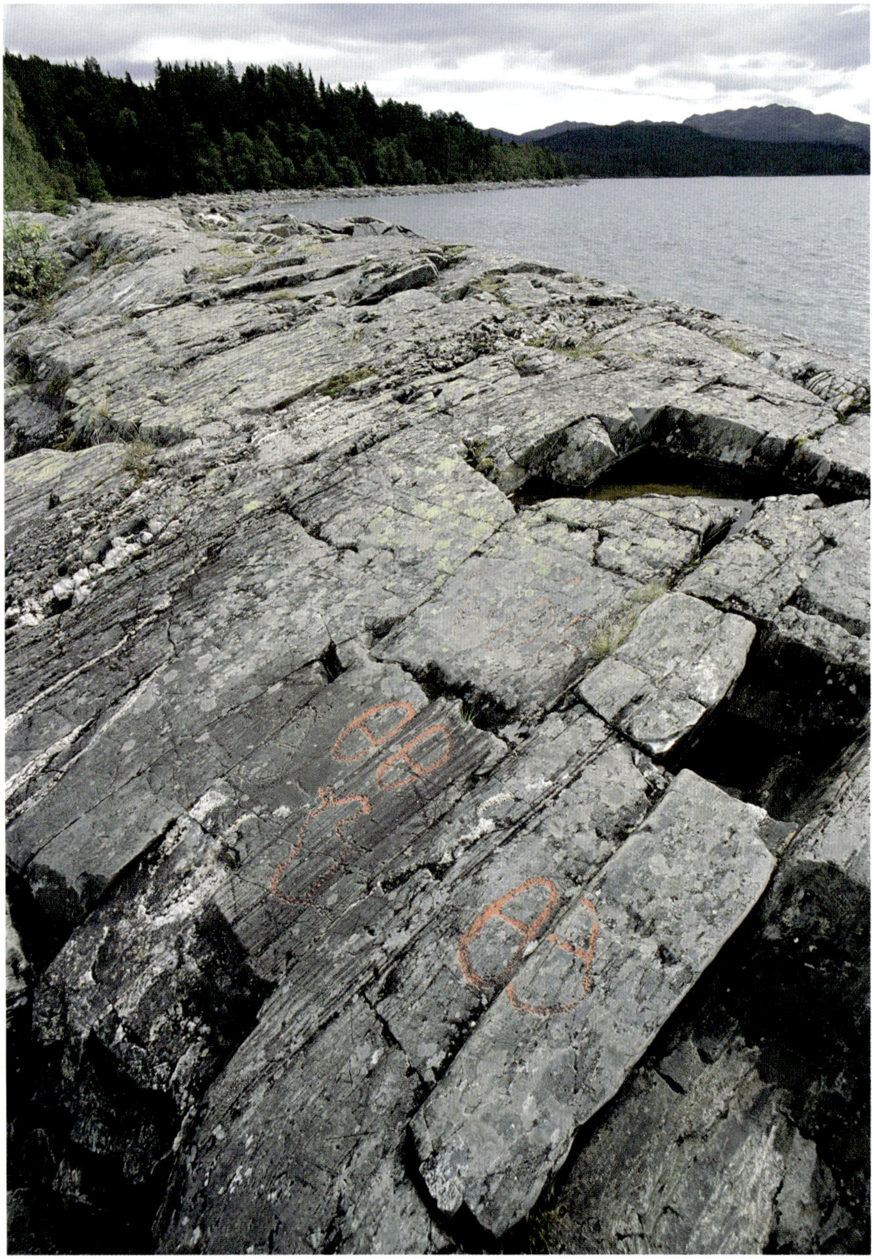

FIGURE 204. The part of the promontory on which rock carvings are found measures about 60 square metres. The highlighted figures seen in the photograph – an elk and two pairs of foot soles – are on the northernmost end of the rock art panel.
RU

horseshoe-shaped figures, a four-spoked wheel and a boat figure with seventeen crew lines are found. The foot soles are spread over the entire panel, while the human figures, the boat, most of the animals and quadratic figures are clustered densely around the middle of the panel, with the circular figure nearby. The footprints point in all directions, some towards the lake and some towards the land, while many appear to be in procession across the promontory, past the cluster of figures in the middle of the panel.

A mixture of rock art traditions?

Both the interpretation and the dating of the Sporaneset rock carvings have been a major headache for scholars. The motifs appear to represent an assortment of images from two different rock art traditions. On the one hand, depictions of the game and hunting methods of the hunter-gatherers – the elks and the rectangular "hunting-pits" – are normally associated with the Northern Tradition. The presence of hunters in the area is testified by a small habitation site uncovered on the inner side of the promontory, containing arrowheads and flint chips amongst other items (Martens 1975; Kostveit 1999). On the adjacent mountain plateau, there are numerous remnants of prehistoric hunting activity, such as habitation sites, hunting pits and look-out points (Indrelid 1994; Martens 1975). On the other hand, the rock art at Sporaneset incorporates motifs that belong to the Southern Tradition – above all the circular motif and the foot soles. A likely explanation is that the markings on the rock-face were made by different groups of people living in this mountainous region in separate periods of time.

Contrary to this hypothesis, however, several features suggest that the various carvings are part of a unified whole. Both the carving technique and the stylistic expression indicate that all the images were made by the same group of people (Hagen 1990).

Exchange of knowledge?

If the motifs at Sporaneset are seen as an amalgamation of symbolic expressions from the Northern and Southern rock art traditions – as a concrete visualization of a medley of ideas – the key question is how and why this happened in a remote location at the edge of Hardangervidda. Where did the knowledge of Southern rock art symbolism and possibly of rituals come from? Through what channels did it reach the mountain people? The explanation may be found partly in the natural conditions of the region, and partly in the occurrence of rock art in other parts of the county.

The mountain areas of upper Telemark are connected with the coast of southern Norway by an extensive system of branching watercourses. A wide array of rivers and large and smaller lakes – the so-called Skiensvassdraget (The Skien Watercourse) – flows all the way from Totak to the small towns of Porsgrunn and Skien situated at the bottom of a system of small fjords that flows into the sea (Dons 1975). Rock carving sites belonging to the Southern Tradition occur sporadically along some of the lakes in the woodlands and low mountain areas of the interior (Groseth 2001; Vogt 2006a). However, the most prominent occurrence of Southern rock art in the county is a cluster of sites by the outflow of the Skien watercourse. Undoubtedly the waterways facilitated access between the northern and southern parts of the county during prehistoric times, as they have in historic times. Easy access between different rock art areas may explain how knowledge was procured, but in order to understand the exchange of ideas that appears to have taken place at Sporaneset, it is necessary to look more closely at the Southern rock art along the watercourses, and the Skien sites in particular. Before turning to these sites, however, yet another rock art tradition found in the interior parts of the county should be examined.

Painted images along the Telemark watercourses

A group of rock art sites located along the watercourses in the interior woodland areas of Telemark differs considerably from both the carvings at Sporaneset and the sites belonging to the Southern Tradition. The most obvious difference is the production technique. While the majority of the rock images in the county are carved into the stone, the images on lakeshore panels are painted in shades of red and rust-brown colours. There are a total of five sites with painted images, all situated on lakes. The number of figures on the individual panels varies between five and nineteen, and the motifs include human images, boats, four-legged animals – elk, deer or reindeer – and geometric patterns (Engelstad 1934; Slinning 2002).

FIGURE 205. The rock art site Kvithammaren at Nisser were probably named after the place where the images are painted: in a white niche in the mountainside, three or four metres above the surface of the lake, at the foot of a 50–metre-tall cliff, easily visible from a distance. Such natural phenomena were perhaps seen as openings in the earth and a link to the underworld. GM

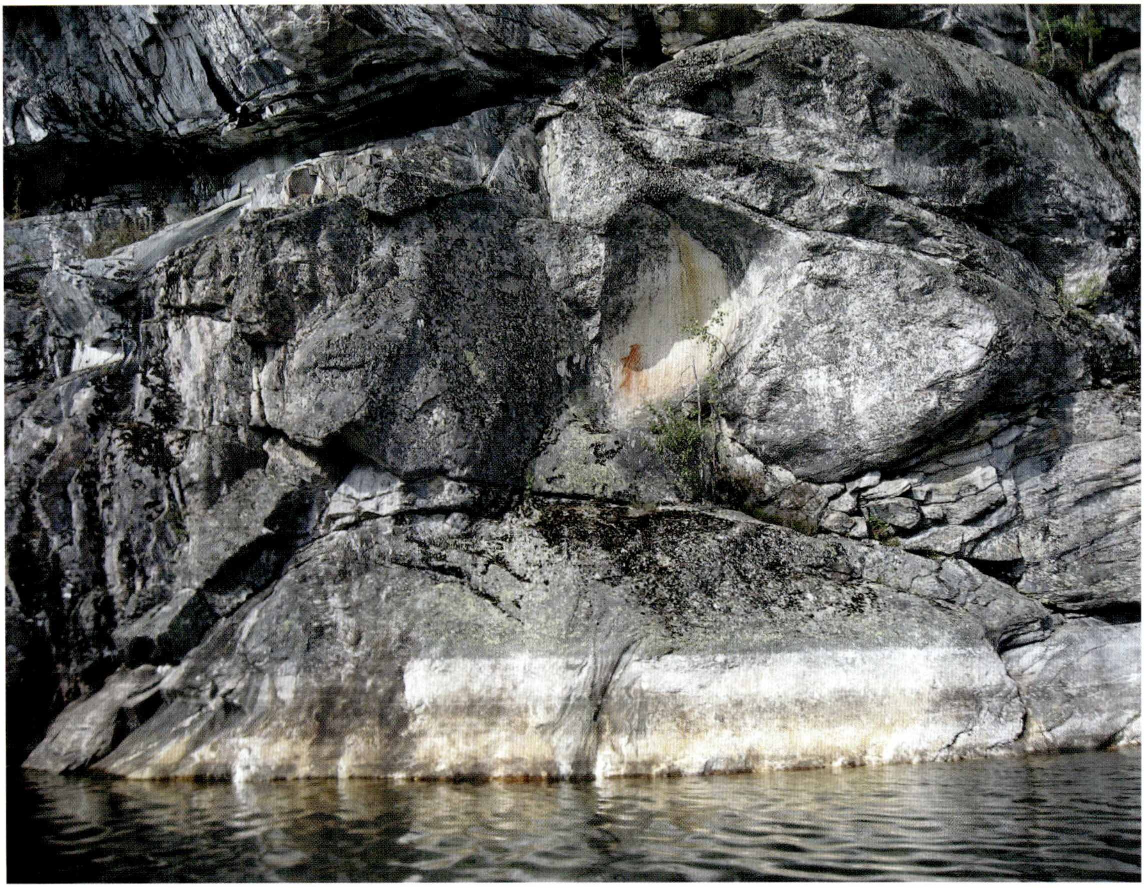

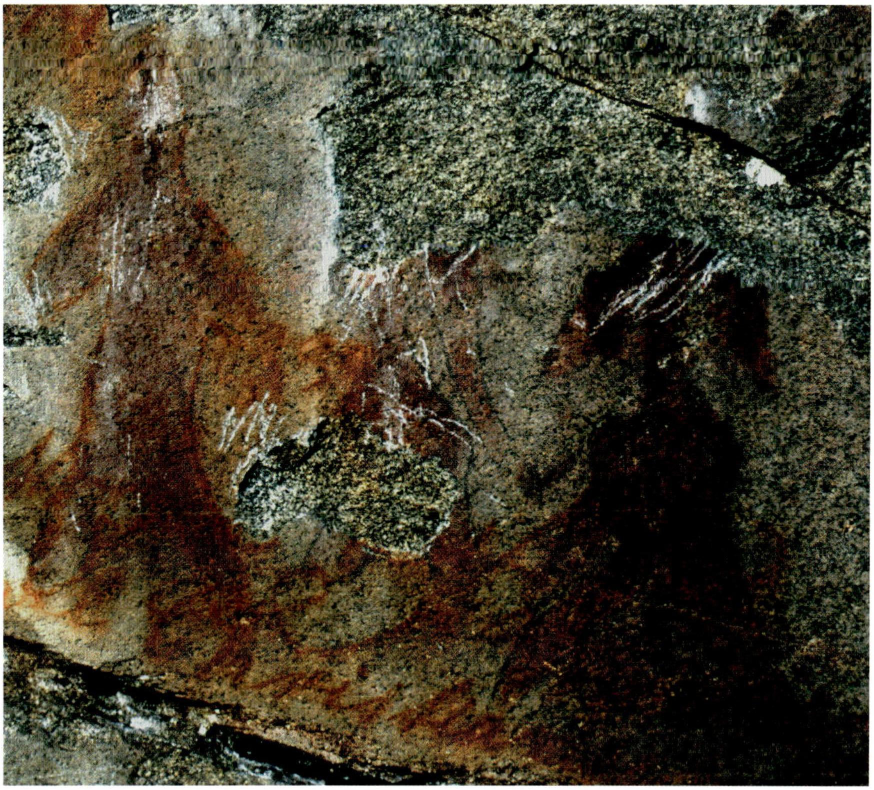

FIGURE 206. For many years there have been discussions concerning how figures painted on exposed rock surfaces could remain preserved for several thousand years. One theory has been that they were created on surfaces where there were natural colours present – for example, sections with iron oxide deposits that have the same reddish-brown hue as the paint used to create figures. However, recent investigations indicate that the red colour was applied to the rock. This is the case in Rønningen, a sample section of which is shown in this photograph. Here there are several examples of figures being painted over other, earlier figures. The red pigment most probably derives from earthen colours containing iron, for example ochre. It is less certain whether a binding agent was used, and if so, what type.
TS

Two of the painted sites are found on the western shore of the 35 kilometre-long Lake Nisser, surrounded by sheer mountainsides rising to a height of almost one kilometre. From the northern end of the lake a series of rivers and lakes stretch all the way up to Totak, and from the southern end the lake feeds a watercourse that flows southwards to the coast. One of the two sites, Kvithammaren (The White Crag), was most probably named after the place where the images of a few animals and humans are painted, in a white niche in the mountainside, three or four metres above the surface of the lake, at the foot of a 50-metre-tall cliff. The other site on Nisser – Ovnen (The Oven) is situated at the foot of a 20-metre-tall escarpment that originally jutted up directly out of the water, although in modern times a road was constructed in front of the panel. It features a long row of human figures, an animal image and a pattern of zigzagging lines. In the early 1800s, both sites on Nisser were visited by a group of clergymen. One of them, a local priest, claimed that the row of human figures at Ovnen had been drawn by a monk in memory of a bridal procession that had drowned on their way to church. Their colloquial name – "Munkeskrifta" (Monk's Drawings) – is a reference to this story (Slinning 2002).

The tale of a bridal party who lost their lives on their way to church may be an itinerant story, because a similar tale is associated with a site called Vefall located on the northern side of the lake Seljordvatnet – otherwise famous for its Sea Serpent! The five figures of Vefall are painted in a triangular depression in the mountainside at the foot of a 60-metre-tall cliff wall, two or three metres above the surface of the lake. Together with the promontory Ulveneset (the Wolf's Rock) on the opposite side of the lake, the cliff forms a strait, and the spot has long been known locally as "Bruredynni" (the Bridal Door). From Seljordvatnet, the waterways and other communications arteries run northward to Hardangervidda, and to the southeast there are waterway connections all the way to the coast.

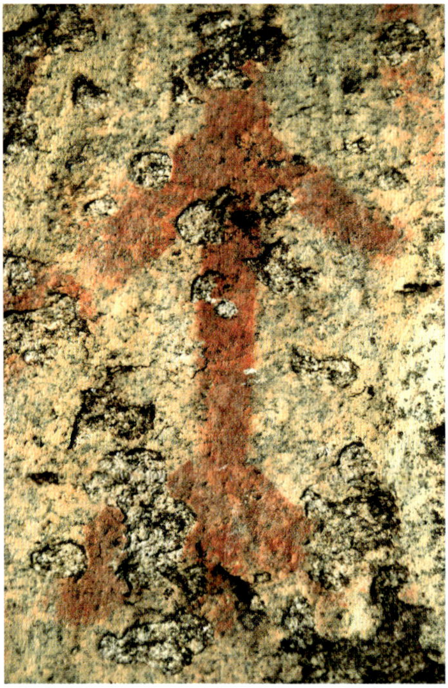

FIGURE 207. A small human figure found at Rønningen.
TS

The largest site with painted images is Rønningen, located on the eastern side of Lake Langen, which is part of the Lower Tokke watercourse that flows through hilly landscapes towards the coast. Part of the Rønningen site was documented in 1919, although during a new investigation in 1998 a total of nineteen paintings of humans, animals, boats and geometric patterns were discovered (*ibid.*). The figures are situated under an overhanging rock bordered at the front by a narrow shelf, and located three or four metres above the surface of the lake.

The only painted site found along the coast is Langangen, some 10 kilometres southeast of the town of Porsgrunn. The site occurs at the outlet of a watercourse that stretches northward towards forested inland regions. Discovered at the end of the 1990s, the figures are on a sheer mountain wall under a prominent overhang, with the current national main road passing just beneath them.

Cult sites along communications arteries?

One distinctive feature of the sites with painted images is their location: the figures occur on steep precipices at the foot of tall cliff walls that rise directly out of the water. Today the panels are remote, located in places where people scarcely travel. With the exception of Ovnen and Langangen, where roads have been constructed in front of the sites, the paintings are not easily accessed from the inland. They are more easily reached by boat, or by walking across the ice when the lake is frozen, and even the people who painted the red figures on the precipices along the waterways most likely came by boat. The images are facing what was once the common artery for the people who hunted and fished in the lakes and rivers that cover the forested interior regions.

The places marked with red paint may be seen as sacred sites for the hunter-

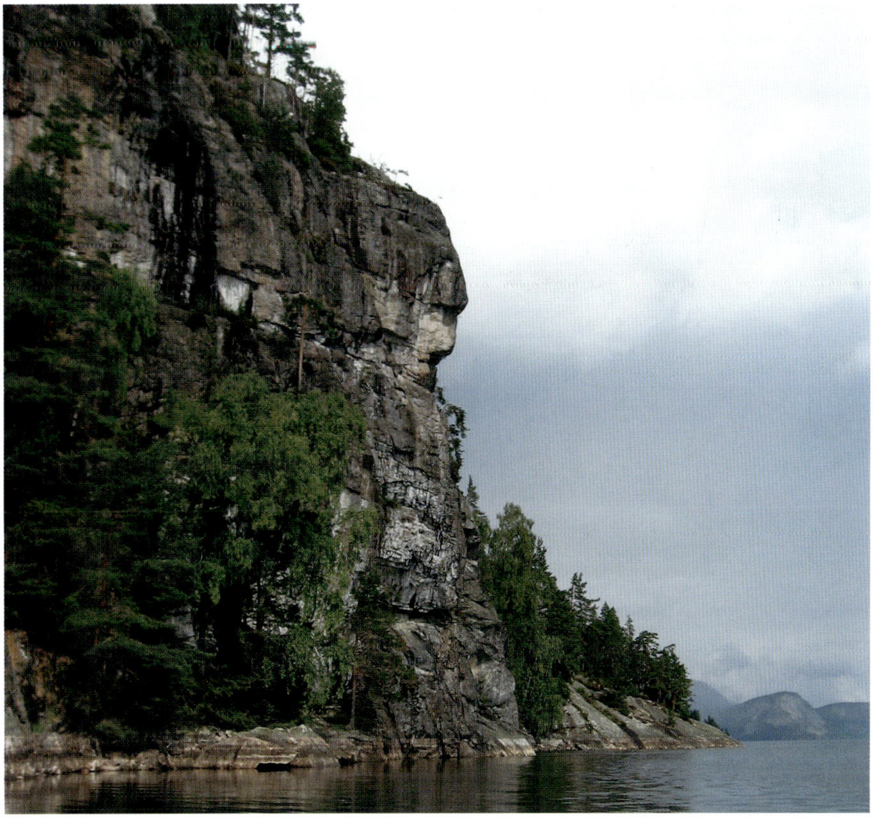

FIGURE 208. It is known in many cultures that prominent places in the landscape have been associated with cultic observances. For example, Sámi cult sites are often associated with large stones or distinctive cliff formations, some shaped like the bodies of animals or human faces. All of the painted rock art sites in Telemark are located at the foot of towering cliffs, and a few of these cliff-like formations resemble faces in profile – among others, Kvithammaren at Nisser.
GM

fishermen, perhaps used as cult or offering sites by passers-by. The towering, cliff-like formations on which the images are painted are prominent points in the terrain, and from certain angles some look like faces in profile (*ibid.*). Could this have been a factor in the original choice of the spot? In some instances the figures are painted inside a depression or niche in the mountain wall, easily visible from a distance, such as Kvithammaren at Nisser and 'Bruredynni' at Vefall in Seljord. Perhaps these natural phenomena were seen as openings in the earth, a link to the underworld, to places that are normally inaccessible to humans.

Both the stylistic traits of the figures and their location in the terrain reveal so many similarities that the paintings should be seen as a cultural and temporal unit. However, it is not easy to date these images. The most reliable indications for dating are probably provided by the only one of the five sites located on the coast – Langangen – where the figures are situated some 25 metres above current sea level. Based on shoreline datings for this area, it is possible to conclude that the paintings were made at the earliest some 4000–5000 years ago (*ibid.*). This indicates that the rock paintings along the Telemark watercourses were most probably created at the end of the Late Neolithic or the beginning of the Bronze Age.

Bronze age images in the Gjerpen Valley

As mentioned above, the largest group of rock art in Telemark belonging to the Southern Tradition occurs in the vicinity of Skien, in the Gjerpen valley to the north of the town. With forty sites and close to 2000 individual figures, this is considered one of the largest and most important rock art regions in Eastern Norway (Vogt 2006b). The first description of a rock carving in Gjerpen – the Fossum site – dates from 1857. For a long time this was the only known rock carving in Telemark. During the 1900s, however, scattered sites were discovered, but the real boom in rock art discoveries in Gjerpen occurred in the early years of the 21st century (*ibid.*).

The main body of the rock images consists of ship figures, various circular motifs, cup marks, foot soles and representations of humans and animals. Both in terms of their style and their choice of motifs, the carvings of Gjerpen are in keeping with the symbolic expressions of Bronze Age rock art in Scandinavia. In particular, considerable similarities with the carvings of Østfold and Bohuslän may be seen. Various elements in the Gjerpen material, however, indicate a local individuality, a kind of dialect within the overall traditional expression of the Southern Tradition. A number of images are unique for the Gjerpen valley – such as animal tracks, probably of red deer; a large ship figure depicted only using cup marks, and human figures with shapes that differ to those found in Østfold (*ibid.*).

Despite the great variety of motifs and all of the details they display, the Gjerpen rock carvings contain few indigenous elements that contribute towards a positive dating. However, similarities with motifs in Østfold and Bohuslän indicate that the Gjerpen carvings belong to the same period of time, during the Late Bronze Age, around 800–500 BC (*ibid.*).

FIGURE 209. The ring motif is found in many different shapes in the Southern Tradition of rock art, from simple circles to more complex figures. The ring is often interpreted as a symbol for the sun, but it may have an even deeper meaning as a symbol for the cyclical order of the world: all things move in a perpetually revolving cycle. At the Fossum site in Gjerpen there are depictions of so-called "sun wheels" – circular figures with spokes. These kinds of wheel-shaped rings are perhaps meant to symbolize the cart, a motif that is found on some rock art panels. In some religions, the cart is associated with deities, and in this perspective the wheel motif can perhaps be interpreted as a sign of power.
TL

Images from different eras or for different uses?

Although all of the rock art in the Gjerpen valley dates from the Bronze Age, there are differences in the choice and design of the motifs on the individual panels. This may be exemplified by the two sites of Fossum and Løbergshaugen, both of which have between forty and fifty figures (Hagen 1990).

Fossum is the most distinctive of the panels. About half of the figures are large and small ring motifs of a type known as "cross-wheels" This is a relatively common motif in Scandinavian Bronze Age rock art, although the design of the figures at Fossum is practically unrivalled in other parts of the country. The rings – several of which are double or triple – have four spokes rendered with double lines. There is a concave depression in the centre of the cross and a depression in each of the quadrants. In addition to the dominant ring figures there are five ship figures and some foot soles, several with transverse lines.

At Løbergshaugen, some five kilometres northwest of Fossum, an entirely different combination of motifs occurs. Here the central symbol is represented

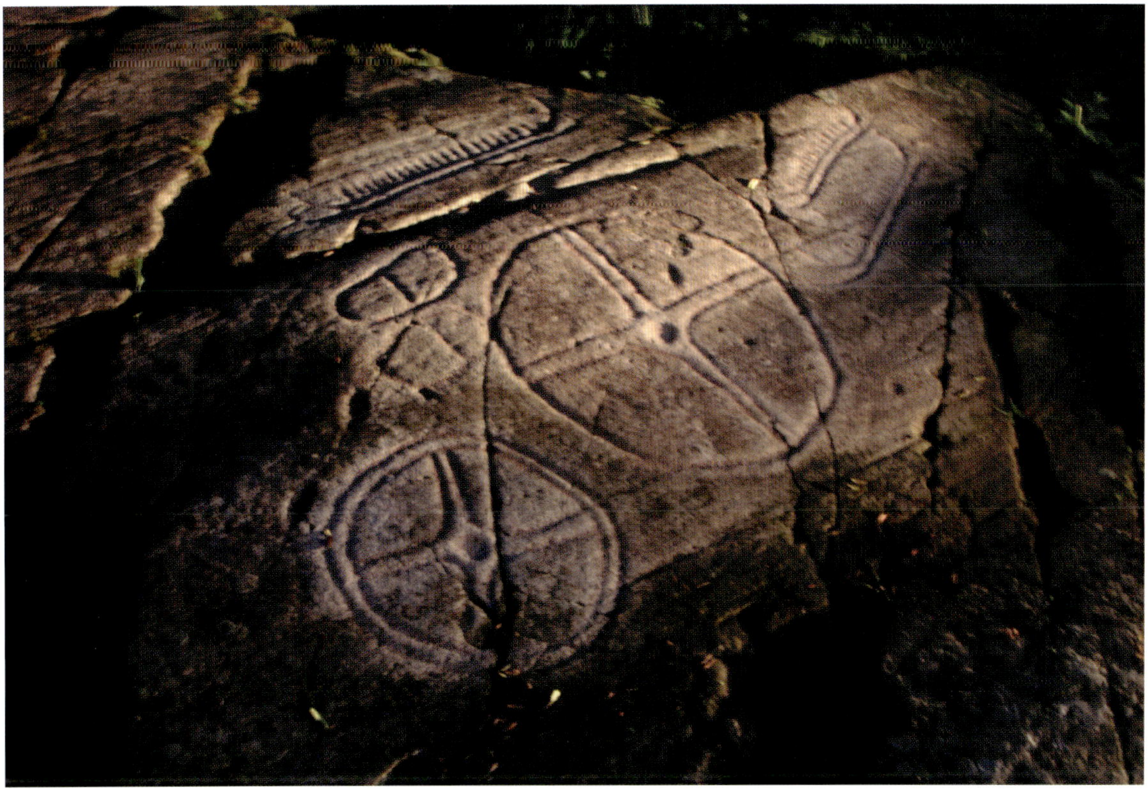

by ship figures. About half of the more than forty figures are ships with single or double hull lines, curved stems and crew lines. There are also many small animal figures – fourteen in all – illustrated by single lines. It is difficult to determine what kind of animal they are intended to depict, but a reasonable guess is that they represent horses. There are even some concentric rings and foot soles.

What explanation is possible for the differences in the choice of motifs at these two sites located so close to one another? One explanation may be that they were created at different times. It is tempting to draw an analogy to Etne in Sunnhordland, where rock art panels dominated by ring motifs and cup marks are dated to an early stage of the Bronze Age, while panels with a varied repertoire of motifs belong to a later phase (Vevatne 1996). Another explanation is that the sites were made by separate groups of people (Groseth 2001). One of the sites may, for example, have been used by women for their rituals and drawing on their repertoire of symbols, while men may have performed their ceremonies at the other site, as seen in Australia, where separate rock art sites were used by men and women respectively (Smith 1993).

The assumption that differences between individual sites are due to group affiliation and not to chronology, indicates that there was a common notion of the landscape as being special, not only for its grazing potential, but also for its mythological and ritual memory (Groseth 2001).

The rock art landscape

The rock carvings are located at the outlet of the small fjord of Frierfjorden that forms the southernmost part of the Skien watercourse. They are concentrated along the eastern shore of Skienselva (the Skien river), flanked to the east and north by steep hillsides. The valley floor between the sea and the forested hills is interspersed with low outcrops known as "åkerholmer" (Field Islets) where the rock art is found (Groseth 2001; Vogt 2006b). All of the carvings are situated in the northern part of the valley, while a number of votive deposits from the Bronze Age have been found further south on the same, eastern, side of the river. On the western river bank the ancient monuments are of a different type, consisting of a number of burial mounds, most probably dating from the Bronze Age, and various positive settlement indicators have been found in close vicinity to the graves. Based on this distribution pattern, the two sides of Skienselva have been interpreted as different activity zones during the Bronze Age: the area on the eastern shore is seen as a *ritual space*, while the western side is explained as a *settlement space* (Groseth 2001). This interpretation appears to be supported by variations in the natural conditions. The main space for rock art and votive deposits is found in an area that seems to be unsuitable for Bronze Age cultivation, but well suited for grazing. The grave mounds and settlement indicators, on the other hand, are found in an area with a greater potential for agriculture, and grave finds from later periods even indicate a continuous pattern of settlement in this area (*ibid.*).

This pattern coincides with similar scenarios from other areas in Southern Norway and Sweden, where Bronze Age fields and settlement sites are located on sandy ridges, while the clayey low-lying areas where the rock carvings are found were used as grazing land (Vogt 2006a, 2006b; Groseth 2001).

The Bronze Age society of the Gjerpen area

The extent and nature of Bronze Age settlement in the Gjerpen valley has not yet been sufficiently clarified. However, the area has favourable conditions for cultivation and animal husbandry, and the distribution patterns of artefacts, rock art, burial mounds and scientific analyses (soil, pollen and charcoal) indicate continuous settlement from the Late Neolithic to the Bronze Age and Early Iron Age. Throughout the Bronze Age, cultivation and animal husbandry were probably equally important elements in the economy. However, while agricultural activity appears to be more intensified in the Late Bronze Age in the Skien region, it is assumed that animal husbandry was more important during the Late Neolithic and Early Bronze Age (Groseth 2001).

Although no towering burial monuments are found on rocky outcrops in the fields, as is the case in Northern Jæren and Lista, other archaeological remains are indicative of a society in which its leaders had the wherewithal to acquire prestigious objects. One of the richest votive deposits in Norway, dated to the Late Bronze Age, is found at Nystad in the Gjerpen valley. Hidden in a rocky scree, it contained 11 bronze objects: two ring necklaces, four garment clasps, a belt pouch, an earring, a cup, a knife and an adze (Johansen 1993). The items probably originate in North Jutland or even further south (Groseth 2001). Together with other archaeological remains in the area, the Nystad deposit demonstrates that Gjerpen was a fully developed community during the Bronze Age, possessing considerable wealth and power, and probably holding a prominent position on the western side of the Oslofjord region (Vogt 2006b).

FIGURE 210. The rock carvings in the Gjerpen valley are situated at outcrops in the low-lying valley floor between the sea and the forested hills. Although there are considerable similarities between the rock art of Gjerpen and Østfold, some motifs are unique for the Gjerpen valley – such as this large ship figure from Ås depicted only using cup marks. TL

Movement as a way of life

Apart from maintaining a network of alliances with more southerly parts of Europe, the Bronze Age community of Gjerpen seems to have also had contact with communities in the interior. This is seen in the sporadic rock carvings of the Southern Tradition occurring along the watercourses in the more peripheral parts of Telemark. They all display elements similar to those found in the Gjerpen area, particularly with regard to the distribution patterns of rock carvings and votive deposits (Groseth 2001). The most intriguing indication of contact between the coastal and inland areas, however, is the amalgamation of motifs on the Sporaneset panel.

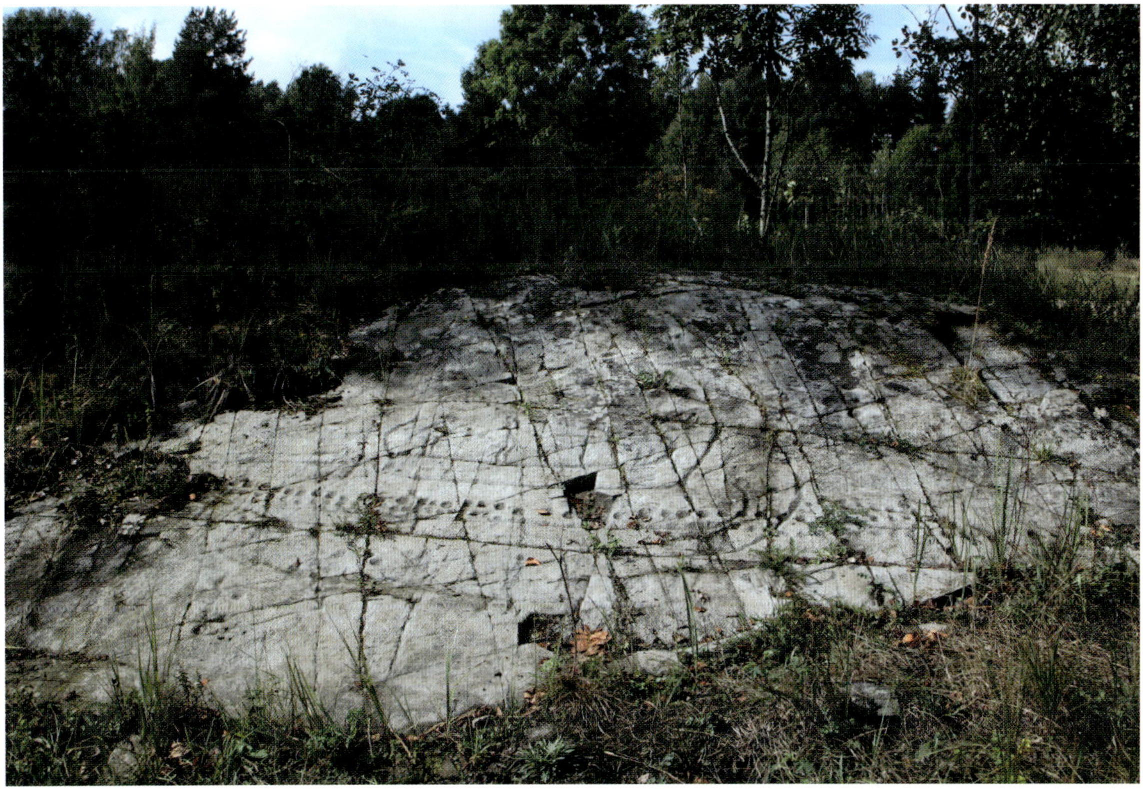

If we consider the Gjerpen community as having initiated these contacts with more northerly areas, what was it that prompted the inhabitants to share their symbolic repertoire with the inland communities and the remote mountain hunters? One likely explanation is that the coastal travellers on hunting expeditions to Hardangervidda were instrumental in the process, and that the mountain people incorporated the foreign – and potentially powerful – symbols into their own world-view. Another and more profound explanation, however, may be sought in the very basis of existence in the Bronze Age society of Gjerpen.

As previously mentioned, animal husbandry appears to have been the most important economic activity in the area during the Late Neolithic and Early Bronze Age. The grazing potential of the pastureland where the rock art is located was probably not sufficient for intensive use. Therefore, larger grazing areas in the surrounding countryside would be required. In the same way as dairy farming in the mountains in historic times, it is assumed that the area surrounding the rock carvings was used for grazing and most likely for rituals, before the animals were taken inland or up into the mountains, where the animals were herded in a seasonal pattern between different pastures (*ibid.*).

This process of following livestock is seen as a legacy from earlier times, when hunting, fishing and gathering were vital aspects of life, while migrating from area to area following natural arteries of movement, such as, in this case, the many-branched waterways connecting the northern and southern regions of Telemark.

It has been argued that this so-called "movement-habitus" (*ibid.*), was an integral part of people's lives and an important aspect of the cosmology that existed during the Late Neolithic and Early Bronze Age. Moreover, movement also appears to be a recurrent theme in the rock art motifs of Gjerpen, with foot soles indicating the migration of people or animals, ships symbolising travel – whether physical or spiritual – and circular figures representing wheels or the sun's journey across the firmament (Groseth 2001; Kaul 1998).

Re-contextualizing ideas: Sporaneset revisited

The "movement-habitus" may also be a clue to the symbolic repertoire of the Sporaneset carvings. The establishing of long-lasting transit routes along the watercourses, as well as the similarities in symbolic expressions that initially suggested influence from southern rock art at Sporaneset, support the possibility that the mountain people and the coastal dwellers must have been in contact with each other in prehistoric times. One likely explanation why such contact was established in the first place is related to the demands of the Bronze Age society of Gjerpen for valuable exchange objects. To maintain a widespread southbound network for gift exchanges and alliances, the Gjerpen community no doubt had to rely on resources other than low-land fields and pasturelands in order to enable steady and stable access to prestigious metal objects. The

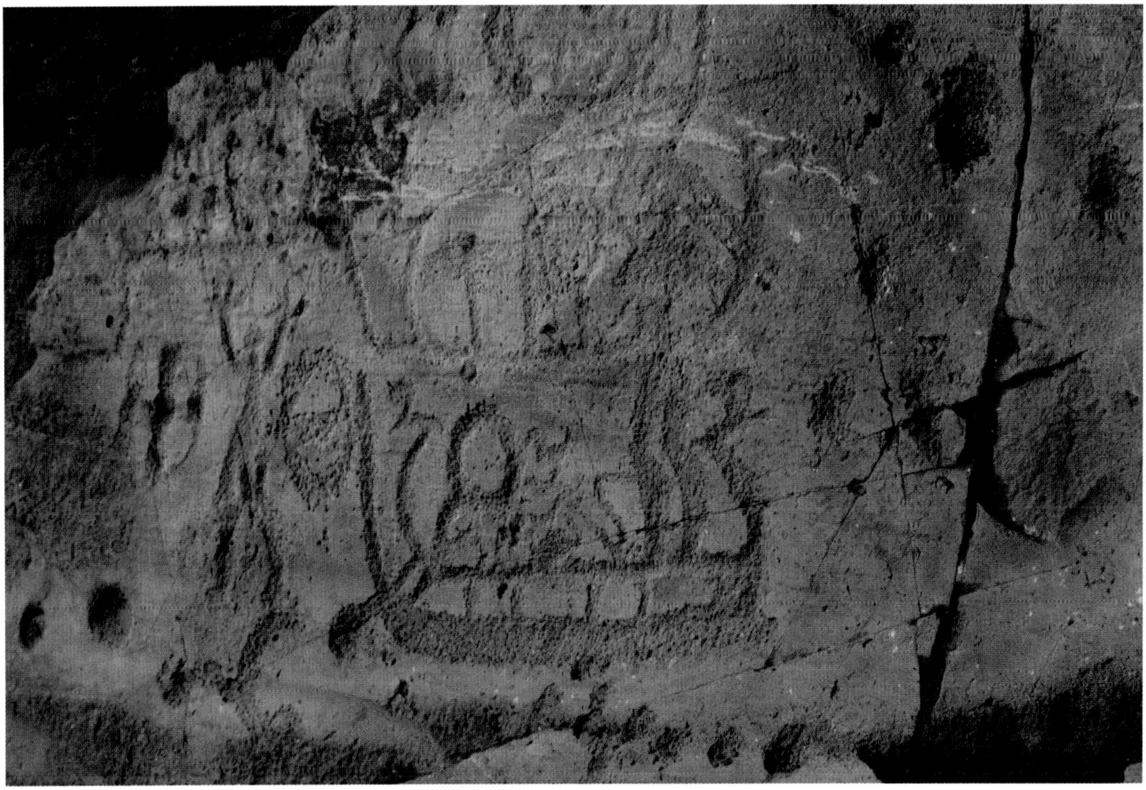

FIGURE 211. Section of a panel from Hoppestad with a total of four ship figures, a number of humans, two of them possibly carrying round shields, a foot sole, two ring figures and more than 100 cup marks.
TL

abundant wildlife in the woodlands and mountainous regions of the interior, and in particular the horned animals of the mountain plateau, were probably considered essential contributions to maintain the prestige networks to the south.

The routes to the north were well known after centuries of herding the livestock between various pasturelands along the inland watercourses, and perhaps even from earlier periods when hunting was an integral part of life. One scenario for the contact is that scouts or hunters from the rural community came all the way up to the edge of the mountain plateau, either to barter products supplied by the mountain people or to exploit the highly prized resources in that area themselves. Another scenario is that contact between the south and the north was maintained through a number of intermediaries settled along the rivers and lakes of the interior. Whether the contact network was kept up solely by people responsible for the Southern carvings along the watercourses, or if the rock painters were also involved, is an open question.

In any event, contact between groups of people in order to barter or exchange goods is often accompanied by ritual actions. The passing on and acquisition of religious and ritual knowledge may have been a prerequisite for establishing alliances and achieving successful transactions. Knowledge was passed on in both directions, and new ideas were incorporated into the world-view of each of the participants. Thus religious ideas and concepts would be spread, but at the same time the content and expressions of the ideas were changed. In the process of passing on knowledge, visual communication became an important medium. Through figurative expressions and symbols, such as the rock art motifs, knowledge was visualised and re-contextualised, perhaps accompanied by oral transmissions (Groseth 2001). At Sporaneset, then, the symbols of movement passed on from Gjerpen – the foot sole, boat and ring – represented perhaps a concrete visualisation of the ideas behind the southbound contact and potential transactions taking place at the beach of Totak.

A melting pot for different traditions

From mountain to fjord, the rock art of Telemark reflects different traditions, from the hunter-gatherers' rock carvings and paintings to the farmers' world of symbols. The sites appear to span a wide range of time from the end of the Late Neolithic up to the end of the Bronze Age. The painted rock art along the watercourses most likely dates from the Early Bronze Age, but it may also partly concur with the rock art of the mountain settlements on Hardangervidda. In this case, the paintings and rock carvings perhaps constitute two groups of hunters who based their livelihood on different resources of the interior – on the one hand the upland mountains and plateaus, and on the other hand the forested lower-lying areas with lakes and rivers. At the same time, at least part of the rock art in Rauland probably dates from about the same period as the rock carvings of Gjerpen, representing a totally different style of life based on easily tillable land and favourable grazing conditions, good harbours that facilitated southbound contacts and people depositing valuable bronze objects. The easy access between the northern and southern region of the county provided by the numerous watercourses no doubt facilitated contact between groups of people, a theory supported by similarities in the repertoire of rock art motifs. However, the nature and extent of this contact is difficult to ascertain, and for the time being remains an open question.

Rock Art of the Northern Tradition in Eastern Norway

We find a group of rock carvings of the oldest type, clearly associated with rivers and lakes, in a limited area of Eastern Norway. We cannot refer to them as a concentration as such, because these rock images are separated by many tens of kilometres. In any event, there are a total of ten sites between the upper lowlands in the north and Oslo Fjord in the south, where the rock images bear great similarities to each other in terms of design, technique and location. The rock carvings probably date from the Late Mesolithic period, some 6000–7000 years ago, and are traces of a hunter-gatherer population that was active in this area. The sites within this general area where the rock art of the Northern Tradition was found are closely associated with the Gudbrandsdalen and Drammen watercourse, and are situated in the counties of Buskerud, Hedmark, Oppland and Oslo. In some places only one isolated figure or small groups of figures are

FIGURES 212–213.
(left) Rock art of the Northern Tradition at Kløftefoss in Geithus; *(right)* Distribution of Northern tradition rock art in Eastern Norway. It mainly follows the waterways along the Gudbrandsdalen and Drammen watercourses
MAP AI, ILLUSTRATION RU

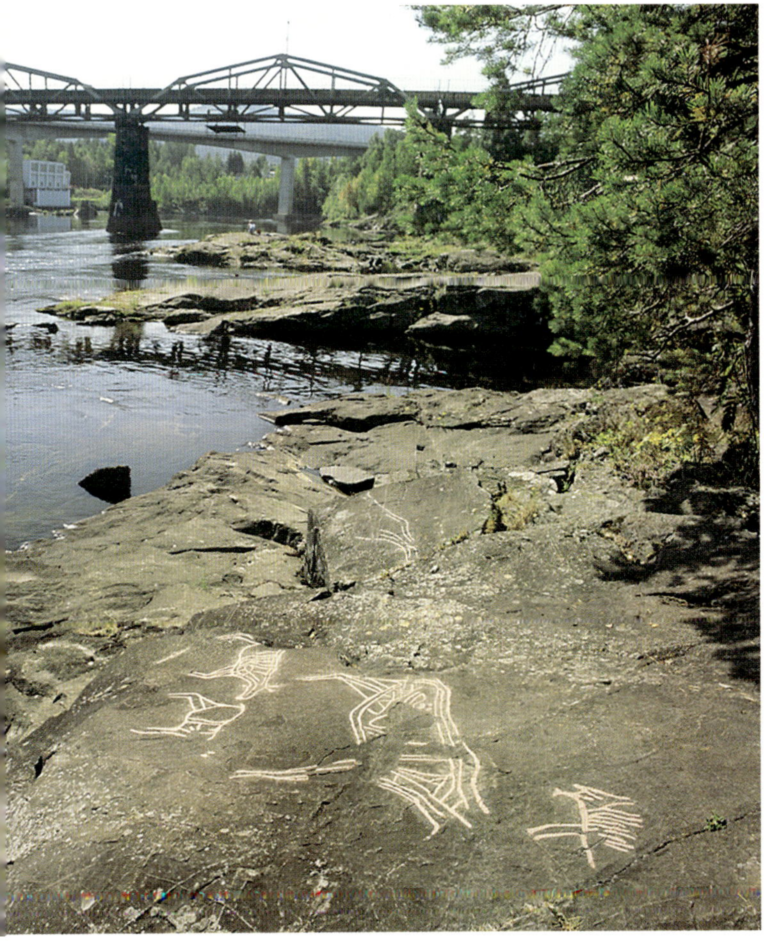

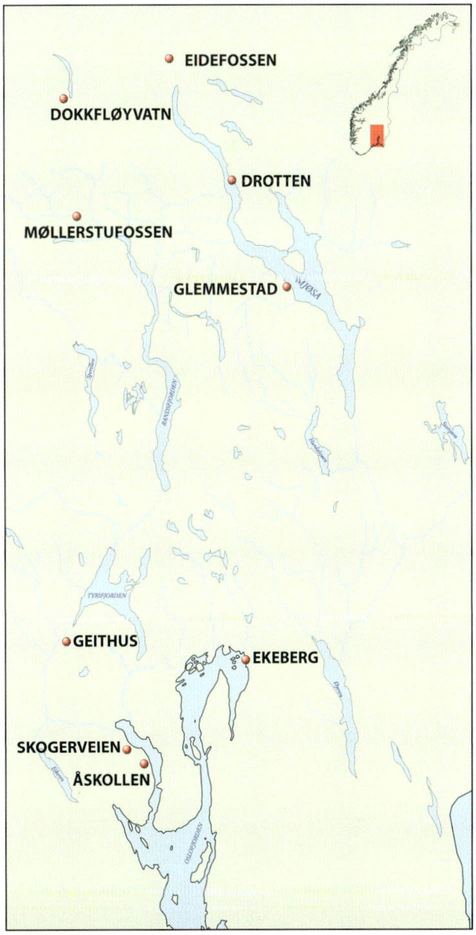

carved on the coastal rock slopes or on stones, while in other places there are larger numbers of figures. The motifs are mainly elk and deer, with depictions of other animals or humans as exceptions to this rule. In addition, striking resemblances in technique and design between several of the rock art panels suggest the possibility that they may have been carved by the same person.

From hunting magic to mythological explanatory models

All of the lines seen in these figures were made using the 'pecking' technique, and as in most of the other sites, the lines must have been created using a hard type of stone as a tool. The depth of the lines varies depending on the type of stone surface on which the images are carved and the degree of subsequent weathering. A typical trait of the figures in this area is that they are four-legged animals, with quite characteristic and distinctive body decorations, especially the line that runs from the muzzle of the animal, through the neck and often ending in a circular design inside the body (Mikkelsen 1977; Haukalid 1999). Based on ethnographic studies of Native American groups in North America, this trait is often referred to as the life-line in archaeological literature (Gjessing 1936). In order to ensure a catch during the hunt, it was important to attack the game along this line, which coincided with the vital respiratory organs and arteries, ending in the heart. In order to invoke a successful hunt through magic, depictions of the game were drawn in the sand, and the life-line was included as a target. From the beginning of the last century until 1930, many rock art panels of the Northern Tradition were found in Norway. For historians and archaeologists who set out to understand why the animal figures were depicted, the analogy to Native American practices was a welcome model to explain the oldest rock art. The images depicted were then considered to be a self-evident confirmation that hunting magic was practiced already as far back as prehistoric time (*ibid.*).

We cannot discount the fact that the animals were depicted in order to gain control and to ensure a successful hunt. However, the biased reference to hunting magic is simplistic. The contexts the animals form a part of suggest that there may have been entirely different explanations for their use, factors taken into account in other chapters of this book. Archaeological investigations and new explanatory models provide increasingly more knowledge about older societies, while at the same time we try to make use of ethnographic studies from comparable societies in which the production of rock art has been commonplace even up until the modern era. This knowledge indicates that mythology-oriented explanations are equally plausible. Even in present-day societies, various animal species play central roles in creation myths (e.g. Willis 1990). For this reason, it is no less common that when societies of this kind experience crises and attempt to solve them, they invoke certain chosen animals or animal spirits. The premise that circumstances of this kind may explain the origin of the numerous images along the watercourses provides an acceptable explanation that is in line with the location and interpretation of rock art elsewhere in Norway. There is no written documentation or evidence amongst societies that still create rock art that suggests any association with hunting or control over game.

Despite an ever-growing amount of new and interesting knowledge, we still only have a vague notion of the form of prehistoric societies. Research continues to reveal new aspects from many different eras, so that an increasingly large number of patterns emerge allowing us to postulate the contexts within which rock art was included. Nevertheless, we know little about how common a practice rock art was in the periods when it was produced, or how often it was necessary to produce it. Nor do we know, obviously, how many panels and figures have been lost, nor how many may still be concealed beneath layers of moss, lichens and soil. We have no set answers. It is a striking fact that most of the rock carvings discussed in this chapter, as well as many of the sites discussed in previous chapters, were discovered purely by chance, not by archaeologists or other scholars of prehistory, but in most cases by observant laymen.

Ekeberg on the grounds of the Oslo Seamen's School

One of the first places where rock art of the Northern Tradition was discovered in this main area was at Ekeberg in Oslo, in the autumn of 1915 (Engelstad 1934). One of the technical assistants from the Museum of Antiquities (now the University Museum of Oslo), who had years of experience surveying rock carvings in Østfold, had sat down on a tree stump and, purely by chance, spotted an animal figure carved on the slope of a stone outcrop. Closer investigation over the following years revealed no fewer than ten animal figures, although the rock surface and the images themselves were extremely worn from pedestrian traffic. The animal figures are mainly elk and deer, depicted standing next to one another. Moreover, it seems that the figures may be part of two groups of animals, each moving in a different direction. The figure at the far south end can also be perceived as a bird. Beneath the most distinct of the four-legged animals, there is an individual human figure, and beside it is a strange, oblong figure that is difficult to identify. It is tempting to compare this latter figure with similar ones found on one of the Drammen panels, which have been interpreted alternatively as both boats and hunting pits. Most of the animals are portrayed as if emerging from the sea. The shoreline zone was probably just below the rock when the image was created. Because the figure is relatively indistinct, the body decorations are somewhat difficult to see. Many of the figures also lack heads, probably the result of weathering. Nonetheless, several of the figures have decorations in the body where the life-line and heart are visible. There appear to be two types of animal depictions. Two of the animal images differ markedly in technique and character from the others by their more naturalistic style, more rounded shapes and the representation of the fore and hind legs using only a single leg, in contrast with the others, where all four legs are depicted. Typically, the latter type of animal has leaf-shaped ears.

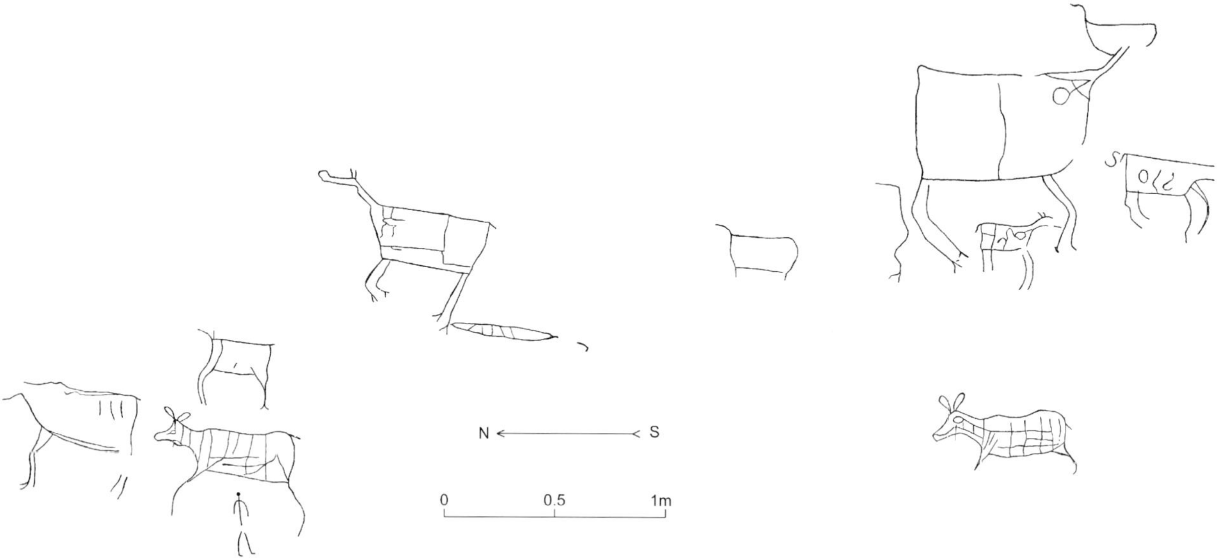

FIGURE 214. Two groups of animals at Ekeberg moving in separate directions.

One interesting common feature in many of the figures is that the belly and back lines use natural glacial striations, which were then carved more deeply. We also find this feature in other panels in the area, as if the images were latent in the stone surface and at some point were made visible to the human world by enhancing and completing them through the creation of rock art, a feature mentioned in many of the other chapters.

Many people were surprised to discover that rock carvings actually existed in Oslo City itself, and that they had not been found earlier, particularly as a footpath ran directly across the stone outcrop. The discovery was treated as a sensation, and several newspapers ran stories on the Ekeberg find.

The rock art along the Drammen watercourse

In the same way as with other discoveries of rock carvings in Norway, this event led to the discovery of even more carvings in other locations, as if information of this type heightened the awareness of hikers, farmers and other people, or served as a reminder of the importance of reporting findings. Shortly after the rock art at Ekeberg became public knowledge, a property owner at Åskollen, located south of the city of Drammen on the Nordby Farm, learned that rock art supposedly existed on his property (*ibid.*). The rock carving had been known to exist since the 1850s and was mentioned in several written sources from the 1860s and later. Scholars of the day, however, had been in doubt as to whether the carving was authentic, as similar carvings were not known to exist elsewhere. Until the beginning of the 1900s there was little or no knowledge about the type of rock art that would later be referred to as from the Northern Tradition. At the time researchers were mainly familiar with the ship images from the Bronze Age, and this uncertainty detracted attention from the rock carving at Åskollen. As a result, it was quickly forgotten, abandoned and overgrown. Spurred on by the surprising discovery at Ekeberg, the property owner made it a point of honour to find the forgotten panel. After removing large amounts of earth and overgrowth from several stone outcrops, the rock art of the Northern Tradition at Åskollen once again saw the light of day on an early August morning in 1916. Today we are no longer in doubt that this is a prehistoric rock carving. In addition, two smaller animal images were subsequently found in and around the area of the first rock carving. Also, the Åskollen rock carving enjoys a special status among those that are dealt with in this chapter because of its size and the distinctly accentuated and developed body decorations of the figure (Mikkelsen 1977). In this case, both the life-line and heart are clearly emphasized, in addition to several intricate body lines. The head is large and has a distinct cleft that was undoubtedly meant to depict an open mouth, and the animal has large and well-defined antlers. The animal is also quite corpulent, with several partitioned areas carved deeply into both the belly and body. We also see only one foreleg and one hind leg, as if the other

FIGURE 215. The elk figure at Åskollen has a very well developed body decor that has led many to wonder if the lines are meant to indicate the animal's internal organs. RU

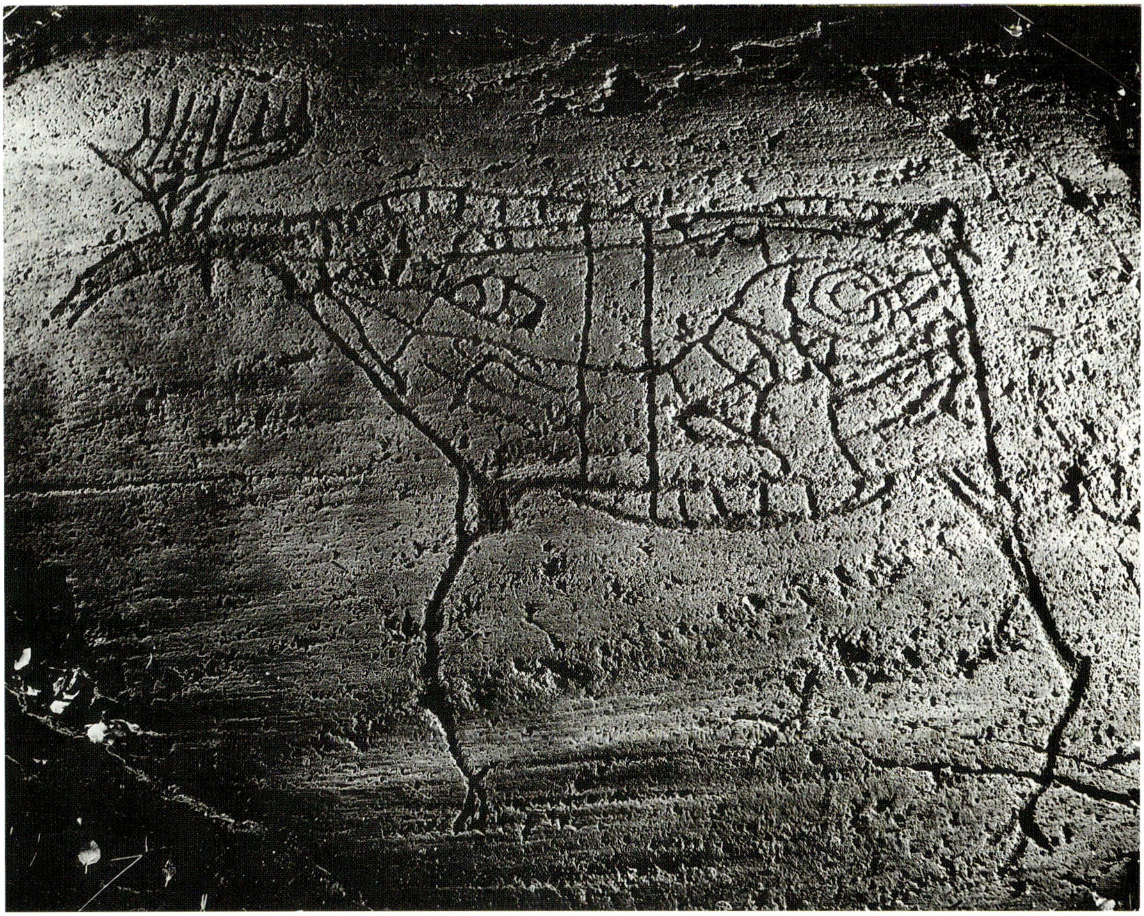

two are concealed behind them. One of the other figures probably depicts a bird, simple and angular in appearance, with a distinctly carved head and neck. The remaining figure, a small triangle, is difficult to identify in terms of what it may represent (Engelstad 1934).

When the Åskollen rock art was mentioned in the Buskerud newspapers, it was only a short time before new information concerning other rock art came to light. Already in the same year, news was received of similar images in two other places in the Geithus area, a little farther north along the Drammen watercourse. One of these panels was at Djeveløya, or Katsundholmen, as the island is also called, located in the rapids of the Drammen River, where two elk figures with body decorations were found next to one another (Engelstad 1934; Hallström 1938). The other panel is at Kløftefossen, about a kilometre farther up the river, where a total of seven more or less distinct figures were found in at least two places. Among these are two elk figures depicted in the act of mating, and both with distinct life-lines and hearts shown in the bodies. Local people had long

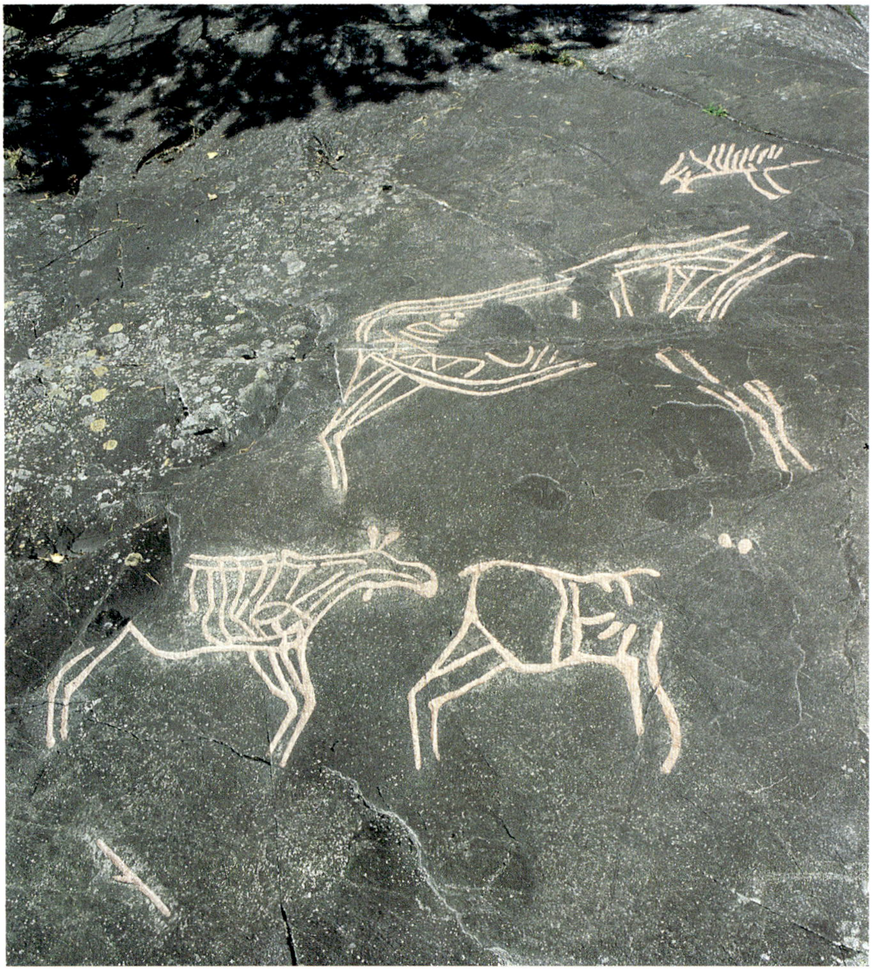

FIGURE 216. Detailed view of the rock carvings found at Kløftefoss.

RU

known of the existence of the rock art at Djeveløya, but it was the discovery at Åskollen that led to them being made known to the public. During the 1970s even more figures were discovered on many of the small islands in the river. A total of ten rock carvings were found in different points, taking the total number of finds to 20 (Paasche 2000), and there can be no doubt that there are other figures in the area. Unfortunately many are extremely weathered, in some places almost eradicated by water erosion after thousands of years of water flow across the panel surfaces at regular and irregular intervals, during floods and high water levels. On the figures that are still relatively distinct, there are well-developed body decorations, and many of them include clear-cut life-lines and hearts.

Skogerveien in Drammen

A series of chance discoveries in 1930 revealed a number of rock carvings in the city of Drammen itself, at Skogerveien. A heavy rainstorm put an end to digging in a garden and ultimately resulted in the underlying bedrock being washed clean and dry when the property owner returned to resume his work. It was at this point that he noticed the numerous carved lines in the rock. During the commotion while uncovering the animal figures on the rock surface, assisted by local museum workers, the owner of the neighbouring plot on the other side of Skogerveien became interested. He remembered that he had seen similar figures on the stone outcrops on his land in 1913, when his house was built (Engelstad 1934). A short time after receiving this information, the excavation work in the neighbouring garden was extended to include his garden as well. The question raised was how many figures might exist beneath Skogerveien itself, which ran between the two gardens and the currently known rock art panels. Therefore, the earth beneath the street was investigated. Unfortunately the result was merely a confirmation of the fact that the bedrock had been blasted away. It is reasonable to conclude that a large amount of the rock art panel was lost, although we will never know how many images it contained. However, at a later date it was discovered that not all of the bedrock had been blasted away after all. A pair of figures were discovered beneath the road fill, and on both sides of the road, a total of at least fifteen deer images and some distinct whale figures with ornate body decorations.

On the south side of the road is one of the whale figures, with the tip of its tail fin distinctly carved and its entire body filled in with a dense chequered pattern. On the same panel there are two relatively large flatfish, probably halibut, with what must be the skeleton clearly depicted (Mikkelsen 1977). The lines of both the whale and the halibut are extremely clear-cut, and the tails of the halibut are deeply carved. Apart from these, there are two animal figures that are less skilfully outlined, some disjointed lines and a spindly, possibly human figure, suggesting that a different artist created these images.

On the northern side the animal images are more conspicuous, with thirteen in total. Four have clear-cut antlers, and twelve are carved next to each other

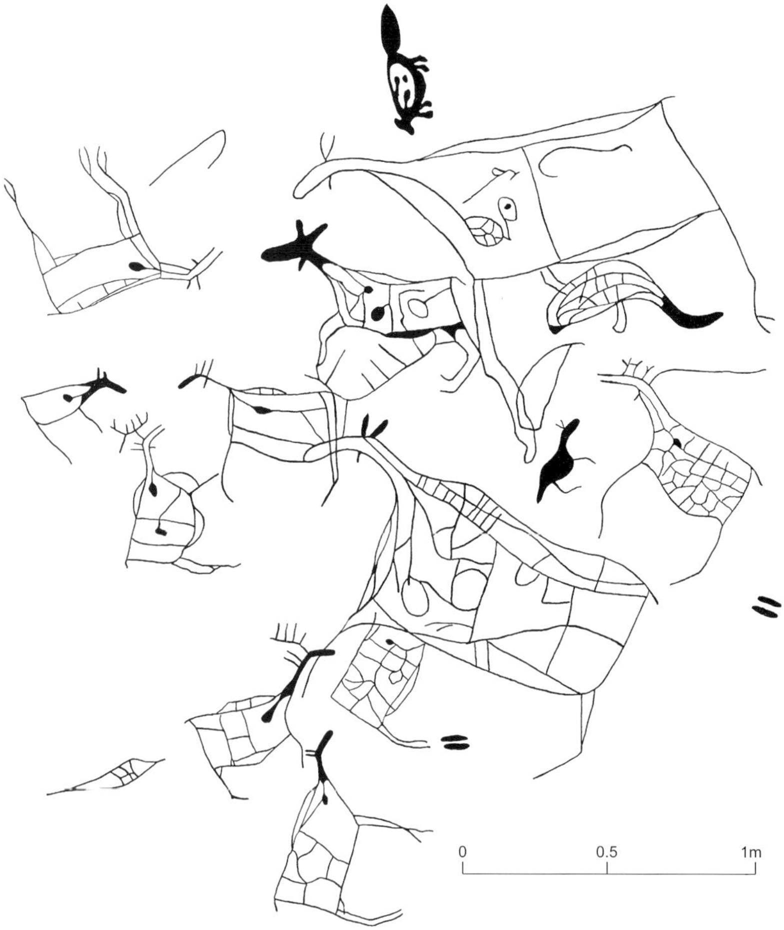

FIGURE 217. Tracing of images at Skogerveien. It seems as if the smaller animals are arranged in a circle around the two larger ones.
EE

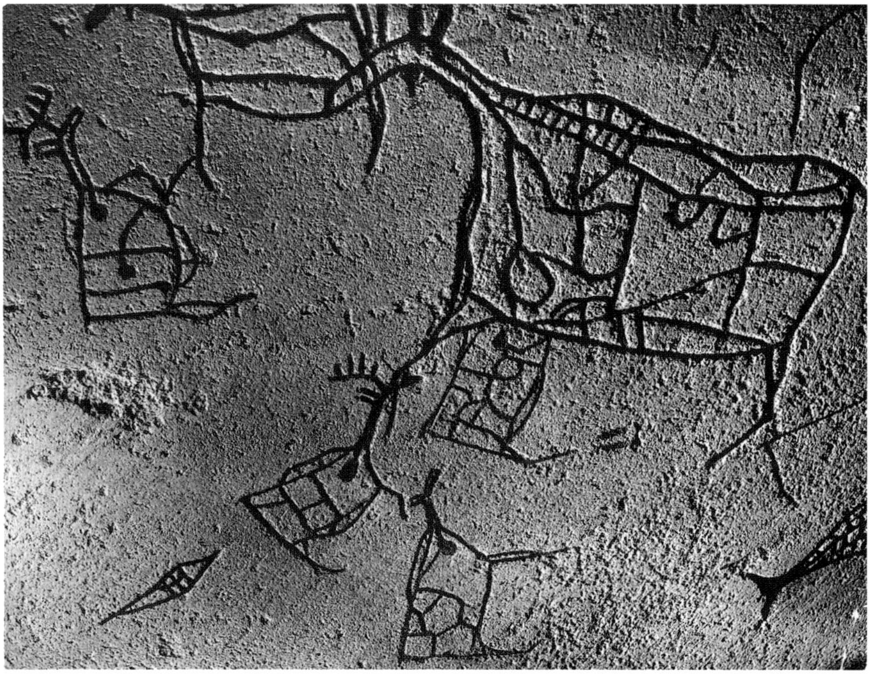

FIGURE 218. Detail of the panel shown above. The contours became clearly visible using night photography and artificial light.
RU

in a cluster, and they appear in at least three different sizes, arranged in varying positions on a limited section of the panel (Engelstad 1934). What seem to be two large elk are placed in the centre, and are surrounded by the others. All of them have clearly marked life-lines and hearts. On this side of the road there is also a whale figure, slightly larger than the one on the other side, but with a similar body decor and with a clear-cut tail and tailfin, like the halibut images. Between the elk there is a carving of a bird and two smaller four-legged animals, one of them possibly depicting a fox. Due east from the concentration of animal figures there are about ten images that we are unable to identify. They are arranged in a row and lead away from the concentration of four-legged animals. They have been interpreted as boats or hunting pits, but neither of these interpretations has been substantiated in any way. The row ends at the far eastern side with a single animal figure.

A large amount of soil was removed from around the rock art during the 1930s. There was a limit, however, to the quantity of material that could be removed, as by then the area was already a well-developed residential neighbourhood. Glacial striations are uncommon in the bedrock here, and we see no tendencies to incorporate lines for the back, belly and other body lines with natural lines in the rock, as is the case at Ekeberg. There is a striking resemblance between these figures and the Åskollen images, and it is likely that both were created by the same person. Most of the deer images have a distinct life-line ending in a

FIGURE 219. The whale at the innermost end of the panel south of Skogerveien. A number of pecked lines divide the entire body into small, irregular squares. Some parts are entirely chipped away, for some unknown reason, including what is probably the heart, in the centre of the body, and the tip of the dorsal fin, together with some other parts.
RU

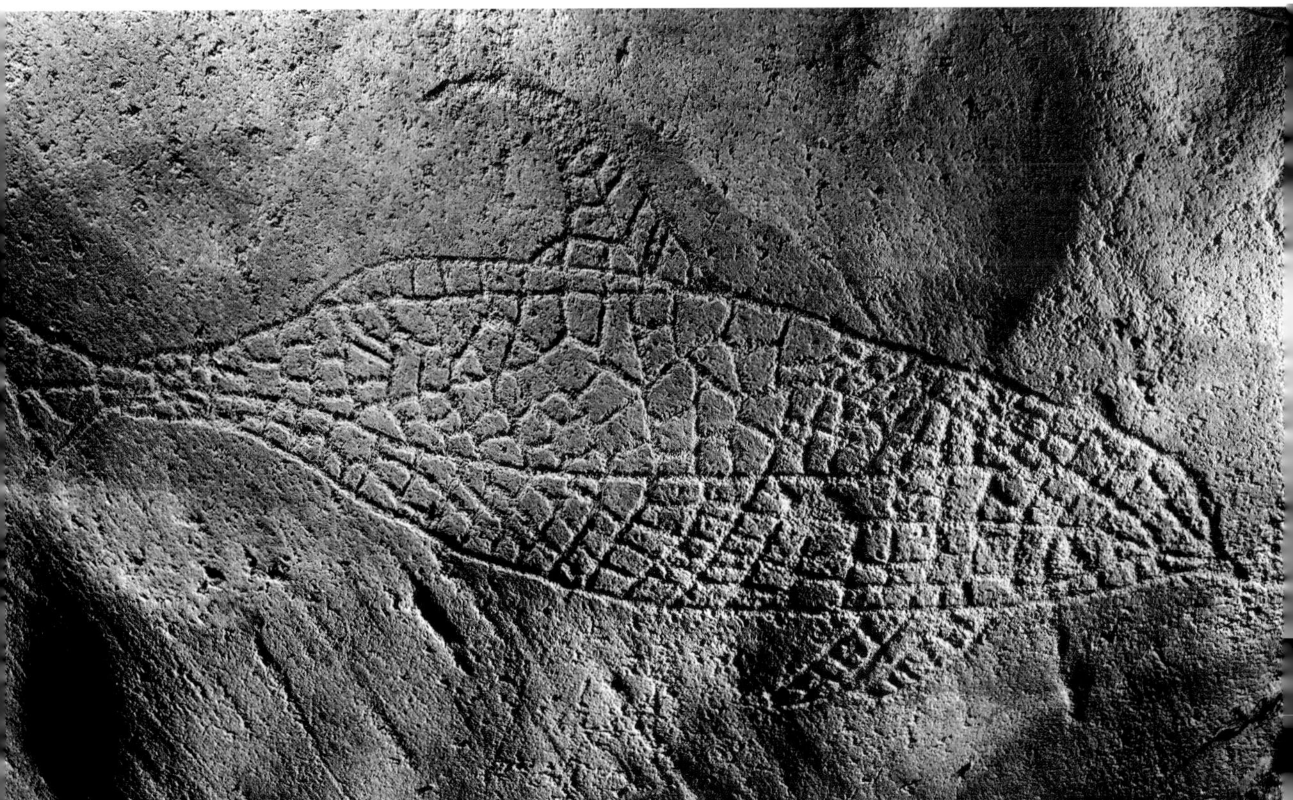

circular design inside the body of the figure. It is also interesting that this same feature is present in most of the whale figures.

Møllerstufossen at Etna

If we continue up the Drammen watercourse past Tyrifjorden and Randsfjorden, we arrive at the rock carvings that were the last to be discovered along this body of water. From Randsfjorden we need to follow the Etna River to Dokka and then westward to Møllerstufossen, where one of the concentrations is located. The other is reached by following the Dokka watercourse north to Dokkfløy Lake.

The Møllerstufossen rock carvings at Nordsinni were discovered in 1961 on a series of rock surfaces on the Etna shoreline. Here the river rapids are turbulent and flow close to the figures. The site has the largest concentration of rock art of the Northern Tradition in Southern Norway's inland region. The images are distributed among three limited areas of rock surfaces that lie beneath one another on the slope leading down towards the Etna River. Here there are a total of fourteen figures, eleven of which depict either deer or elk (Mikkelsen 1977). Some of the figures are so small that it is difficult to identify what they represent.

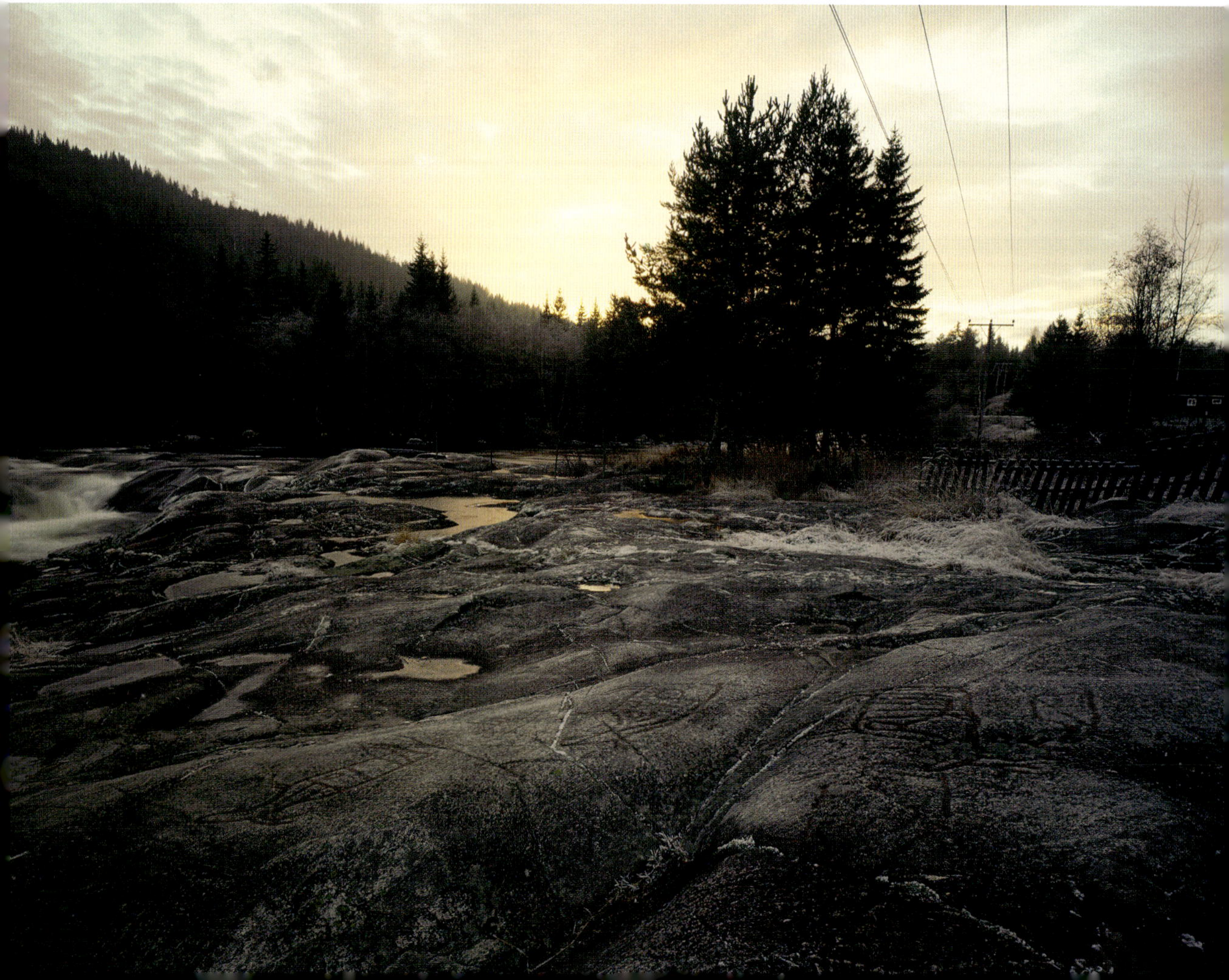

FIGURE 220. Hoarfrost over Møllerstufossen. Freeze-thaw processes are deteriorating factors for rock art.
AK

It has been suggested that they are beavers, while others have interpreted them as human figures. Most of the animals have their heads turned towards the river, while at least two have their heads turned away from it. The animal images are created both with and without body decorations, and at least four of them have life-lines that end in circular bulges inside the body. One feature of some of the figures is that they have tufts of hair beneath their chins, allowing us to identify them as elk. Some of the figures are carved with broad, deep lines, while other lines are less strongly accentuated. Weathering has taken its toll, and in many places it is difficult to recover the figures. During flood periods along the Etna, some of the panels have been covered by the rapids, meaning that the images have been exposed to severe erosion.

Dokkfløy Lake

The last place along the Drammen watercourse where we find rock art of the Northern Tradition was discovered on the western side of Dokkfløy Lake, some 200 metres north of the outlet (Haukalid 1999). Three small animal figures were found here, slightly less than 30 cm long and carved into a small rock outcrop on the shoreline of the lake. The three figures are quite different from one another, as one of them is carved along the outside edge and is created by what we call the contour technique, while the other two have the full bodies of the animals pecked into the stone surface. Also, one of the figures is a little smaller than the other two. The large figures have their heads turned towards the south, while the third, smallest animal is in the middle with its head facing north. It has been suggested that the animals represent migration directions, with the two larger animals representing the spring migration, and the autumn migration symbolised by the smaller figure. The figures are simple and quite stylised. They are most likely elk, although none of the figures have distinct antlers. Their location is very similar to that seen with other rock carvings along the Drammen watercourse (Mikkelsen 1977).

The rock art here has also suffered from weathering, and there may have originally been more figures at this location. Parts of the rock surface have been blasted away in conjunction with timber floating. Before Dokkfløy Lake was regulated in the 1980s, the stone surfaces with rock carvings were cut out of the bedrock as large stone blocks in order to prevent them from being destroyed by wave impact, ice scouring and erosion. The preserved sections can be seen at the Kittilbu Wilderness Museum located on the north-eastern side of the lake.

We do not know of any other rock carvings farther north or west along the Drammen watercourse or tributaries. It is difficult to predict whether more will be discovered in time, but it is a fact that people have travelled up and down through the valleys as long ago as the Stone Age. How often they did so and their number remains an open question. Hundreds of settlement sites have been found in the mountains, including raw materials and objects that must have been carried here from the coast. Flint is one of these raw materials that is not native to the bedrock in Norway. It is found only in uncompacted deposits near today's shoreline belt or along prehistoric shoreline belts, meaning it must have been carried from here and probably up through the valleys. Other raw materials and objects were also brought to the mountains. Recently a stone axe of the Nøstved type was found at Tyin in Jotunheimen, at a height of almost 1100 metres above sea level (Lødøen 2003). The axe is typical of the Olsofjord area, and was undoubtedly produced in this area. We estimate it to be about 6000 years old, perhaps from the same period when the rock art images mentioned above were created. It is possible that the axe was carried here by the same people who created the rock art.

Rock carvings along the Gudbrandsdalen watercourse

In the summer of 1933, the first Northern Tradition rock art in Gudbrandsdalen was revealed to the public. News arrived that rock art of the hunter-gatherer type had been discovered in Hedmark, more specifically at Stein in Ringsaker (Gjessing 1937). On a promontory on the north-western side of the Mjøsa Lake, a large glacial boulder with a number of figures on all four sides was found by chance. The promontory had previously been heavily forested. Timber clearing had opened the landscape and brought the more than three-metre-tall boulder into view, while at the same time good light conditions had made it possible to discover the rock art. Although the stone had been well sheltered by the surrounding trees for a long period of time, it was nonetheless heavily weathered. Today there are many places on the weathered, schistous stone surface where we can only find fragments of lines from what once were images. In total, fourteen animal figures can be made out, although there is no way of telling how many it originally contained. There

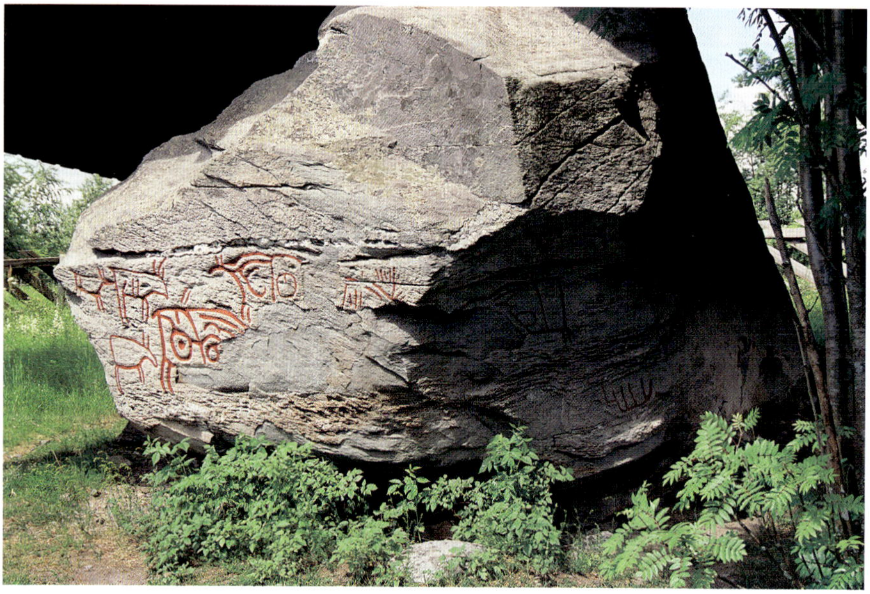

FIGURE 221. The glacial boulder at Stein in Ringsaker has a row of figures on all four sides. Many of the rock carvings are so weathered that the stone has been placed under cover.
RU

are also numerous fragmented lines that probably were parts of figures that have been weathered away. Today the stone is covered by a shelter, designed to protect the rock art from further deterioration.

The images were possibly meant to depict deer and elk, but many are so simplistic in style that it is impossible to distinguish the various animal species from each other. On the northern side of the stone, however, there is an animal that contrasts sharply with the rest. Created in an almost naturalistic style, the image leaves little doubt that it was meant to depict an elk. It is reasonable to believe that the other animal figures were also meant to portray elk. Most of the animal images have body decorations in the form of lines and circular markings inside the body. The life-line and heart, however, are not as clearly marked as in the figures found along the Drammen watercourse.

Drotten in Fåberg Municipality

In the 1940s, less than a decade after the rock art was discovered at Stein, a legal dispute over boundaries led to the discovery of rock art of the Northern Tradition farther north in Gudbrandsdalen, at Drotten in Fåberg municipality (Gjessing 1944). As people searched for a boundary marker on a sheer cliff that partially towers over a section of the Lågen river valley in Gudbrandsdalen, they found at least seven animal images. What originally had been a dispute over property boundaries was transformed into a discussion of whether the rock carvings were of the same type as those at Stein, and ended in notification being sent to the University Museum in Oslo. The rock art is located approximately 2.5 metres above Lågen and faces towards the river, which like several of the other rock art sites in Eastern Norway, runs very

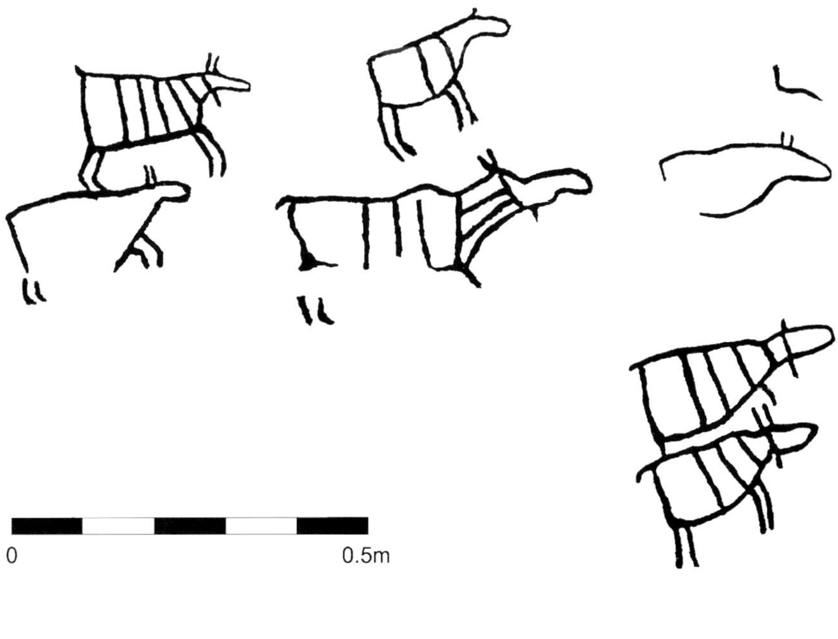

FIGURE 222. Rock carvings found at Drotten in Fåberg municipality. The figures are very simply depicted, but several of them have distinctive tufts of hair under their chins, making them identifiable as elk.
EM

close to the carvings. Four of the figures have tufts of hair beneath their jaws, suggesting that the images depict elk. The other figures are also probably elk, although many of them are so indistinct or simplistic it is impossible to identify the species. There are also numerous line fragments on the panel, but it is difficult to determine the carvings they were once a part of, probably animal images that have been weathered away. Most of the figures have simple body decorations with vertical lines running from back to belly, not unlike the pattern in several of the images at Stein. This panel is also similar to the one in Stein in that one of the animals differs markedly from the others, as if it has some special quality. All of the animal images that can be identified are facing in the same direction. They are also depicted so close together that we get the distinct impression that they are a herd of migrating animals. The stone surfaces on which the images are engraved are heavily fractured, and in somc spots there is a real danger of whole sections with rock art images breaking off completely.

Glemmestad in Østre Toten

Rock carvings were later found along this watercourse at Glemmestad in Østre Toten and further north along the Lågen Valley in Gudbrandsdalen, specifically at Eidefossen in Fron, Oppland County. These sites represent the southern and northern limits for the rock art known to date that is distributed along the Gudbrandsdalen watercourse.

A total of three boulders with rock art have been found at Glemmestad. The first of the boulders was discovered in 1969, while the others were found in 1973 (Gihle 1975). All three are nearly two metres long, approximately one metre wide and have two distinctly carved animal images. Two of the boulders also have the remains of what may be a third animal on one of the stones, and possibly a human figure on the other. They differ from each other in rendition and technique. The boulders were discovered along the shoreline of Lake Mjøsa, where the combination of river containment and dashing waves had washed the rock surfaces clean, making the figures visible to passers-by. They must have been originally created slightly above the shoreline zone. Two of the boulders show very simplistic depictions of deer, while the third has more distinct, but still simple body lines, like those in the images at Drotten and Stein. Several of the figures are clearly marked with tufts of hair beneath the chins, while one of them has antlers with clear-cut tips. A common feature for all of the boulders is that the animals appear to be emerging from the water, with their heads turned more or less away from the lake. The boulders were found relatively near to each other, two of them only three metres apart, while the third was at a distance of some 15 metres from the others. All of them were surrounded by a large number of other boulders. Despite persistent searches over the past 25–30 years, no other figures have been found. It is of course difficult to determine why the images were carved at precisely this location, but a common denominator

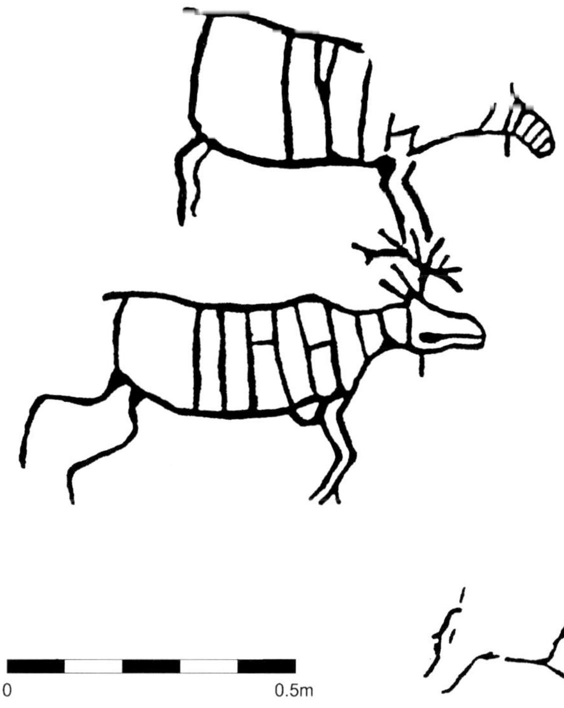

FIGURE 223. Three figures depicted on one of the boulders at Glemmestad.
EM

is that all were found inside an area where tributaries to the Mjøsa have flowed continuously, at times violently. Due to the imminent danger of ice-scouring and frost erosion, all of the boulders were moved indoors during the mid-1970s and are now on display in Toten Museum.

Eidefossen in Fron Municipality

Until recently, the last panel in this group of Northern Tradition rock carvings was located at Eidefossen, but was moved during the 80s to the centre of Vinstra (to just outside of the town hall). Originally, two animal figures were pecked into the surface of a large boulder that partially jutted out into the Lågen River, which has strong rapids at this point (Mikkelsen 1977). We cannot discount the possibility that the boulder may have been moved down the watercourse by strong currents, and that there may be still other rock carvings in the area where the boulder originally came from. However, to date no others have been found. The rock carvings are located high up on the boulder, on a smoothly scoured surface. The distinct chin tufts on both figures leave no doubt that they were meant to depict elk. Both have a similar, simple form of body decoration, a vertical line running through the entire body. Both figures have their heads turned landwards. In its original location, the stone was submerged during flood periods. The original location of the rock art is similar to both Møllerstufossen

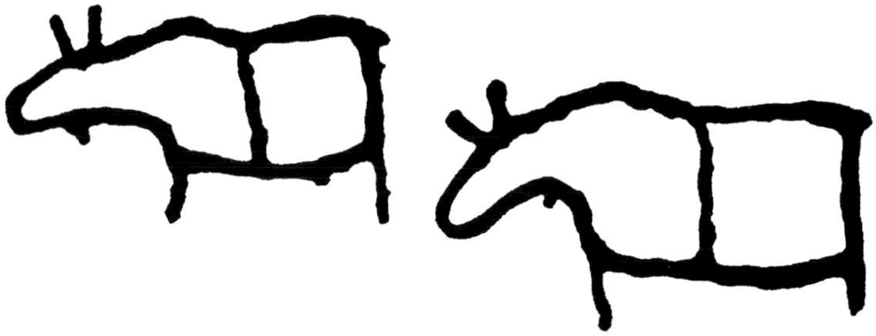

FIGURE 224. These figures from Eidefossen were found on a boulder that was located out in the Gudbrandsdal watercourse.
EM

and Drotten, and would seem to be a clear indication that the rapids, together with other related factors and qualities, played a decisive role in the choice of the original site for the rock images.

Differences and similarities

So far, no other rock carvings have been found in this main area. The numerous figures and rock art panels described here are often considered to be a group. This said, we would point out that the boundary to the east is less evident, as we find similarly depicted images of elk further inside Sweden. At the same time, some of the figures have counterparts both further west and to the north. It is difficult to deduce what this may mean in terms of earlier contact networks. In any event, the body decorations that we find among these Eastern Norwegian figures is a distinctive feature, where a number of animals show traits that may have been meant to be schematic depictions of the internal anatomy such as the heart, stomach, gullet and lungs. As a result, these images are also known as "x-ray style" depictions. Farther west and north, where body decorations are also common, the images are carved in more abstract styles.

We are able to identify many interesting similarities and differences between the rock carvings in the two watercourses. Along the Drammen watercourse, all of the figures are carved into low-lying outcrops, while the figures along the Gudbrandsdalen watercourse are created on stones of various sizes and glacial boulders. In the rock art along the Drammen watercourse, the feature that closely links most of the figures and panels is the rendering of the life-line and heart, while this trait is not as predominant in Gudbrandsdalen. In the latter area the figures are more simplistic and most frequently have simple body decorations. In any case, it seems that for both watercourses, the further north they are located, the fewer body decorations they contain. A feature that closely links all of the inland panels and figures is that all of them are located just above the water surface, or only a few metres above the level of rivers and lakes. A similar, water-related factor also seems to have played a role for the figures produced in coastal areas at Åskollen, Skogerveien and Ekeberg

(Mikkelsen 1977). However, the substantial land uplift that has occurred along the Oslo Fjord has led to them being displaced, and explains their present-day location, high above the water level. A comparison of the figures at Møllerstufossen, Drotten and Eidefossen has convinced us that strong water rapids were a decisive factor for their location. However, if we include the figures at Glemmestad, Stein and Åskollen, we do not see such a strong association (Haukalid 1999). The one parallel we are able to draw is that many of these individual sites were relatively conspicuous in the past, in an era when it may have been imperative and compelling to create rock carvings.

Age

As in the case of the rock art of the Northern Tradition discussed in previous chapters, the use of the shoreline dating system has been applied to determine the age of the rock carvings. This method is directly related to land uplift that began towards the end of the last Ice Age. Based on the rate of land uplift, we are able to calculate how long ago a figure, now located high on a stone outcrop, was once at the water's edge. The method offers a good approximation of the rock art's age, but nevertheless has a number of weaknesses. Firstly, we do not know if the figures were originally carved on the shoreline, at low tide, mean water level or low tide, or if they were created above the wave impact zone or higher up, with the different conditions leading to major time differences. Secondly, the precision of our calculations depends on reliable geological data. In this case, there are a large number of local variables. However, this method is very helpful for calculating when a rock surface emerged out of the water and became available as a surface for rock carvings. Before this time, it would have been covered by water.

Land uplift along the entire coast has varied from place to place, depending on the amounts of ice that covered the land mass during the last Ice Age. Land uplift was most extensive in the inner fjord regions, as the ice was thickest in these areas. Further out towards the coast, the ice was thinner and therefore compressed the land mass to a lesser extent. When the ice began to melt, land uplift began, and continued at varying rates in different points. Although we do not know exactly where the Northern Tradition rock art was produced in relation to the shoreline, the link to watercourses for all of the inland figures discussed in this chapter offers a good indication of where the images were carved, within a few metres from the rivers and lakes where they are located (e.g. Bakka 1973). The inland area has been basically unaffected by land uplift. Images that were carved here are in the same positions today, in relation to the watercourses on which they are located, as they were in ancient times. And since the Northern Tradition rock art throughout all of this main area displays a number of common traits, it is very likely that what applies to the inland rock carvings of the hunter-gatherer tradition also applies to those located on the coast. The location in relation to inland lakes and rivers thus serves as an indicator for us today, as we seek to determine the original places where the coastal hunter-gatherer rock art was produced, and which we find today at varying elevations above sea level. It is also likely that the coastal rock art was created just above the water level, although in this case, it was sea water.

The locations that were situated on the coast during the Stone Age were the Northern Tradition rock carvings at Ekeberg, Åskollen and Skogerveien, all of which are between 50 and 60 metres above sea level (Mikkelsen 1977; Haukalid 1999). The rock carvings at Geithus must also be considered to be coastal, as a 50 to 60 metre rise in the water level resulted in the Oslo Fjord extending much farther north. According to land uplift studies of the Oslo Fjord, we need to calculate some 6000–7000 years back in time in order to establish the era when the carvings were at approximately shoreline level. As further support for this dating, we would add that a number of Stone Age settlements have been found at approximately the same elevation as the rock art, and often in its immediate vicinity, settlements that we know were located near the shoreline when they were in use during the Stone Age and which have been dated radiologically to the same time period suggested for the rock art (*ibid.*).

It is easy to understand why the rock art was created near water. At the time, the inland regions were heavily wooded with virgin forests, making them difficult to cross. The waterways were much better suited for travelling, particularly in summer and autumn, when the water level was low. Along the waterways it was possible to pick and choose between exposed rock surfaces on which messages could be carved, or to be drawn to the surfaces for the purpose of creating images of a spiritual or mythological nature. Similarly, it was easier to cross open terrain along the shoreline or by boat, where exposed low-lying rock surfaces were readily available. The question still remains as to why one particular rock surface was chosen over another. This is an issue that is addressed in other chapters of this book.

At present, we are unable to determine whether the rock art images in Eastern Norway represent two separate groups, or whether they are the products of individuals who wandered between the coast and the valleys along two different watercourses. Perhaps these people had sporadic contact with one another, which might explain some of the similarities between the watercourses, despite the fact that there are also numerous differences. Detailed studies of both the carving techniques and linear patterns may help us to reveal features that can more closely link the rock carvings in the different locations. Neither can we discount the possibility that in the area of the rock art there may be other traces left by the people who created the images, traces that may help us to understand why they were created and allow us to discover contact networks. Hopefully, future archaeological excavations will help us to discover this material.

Skjeberg in Østfold – an Abundance of Rock Carvings

In late January 1875, a teacher at Fredrikshald School in Halden, Martin Arnesen, sent a report to the Senate of the University of Oslo about his ongoing project, stating among other things that: "As a rule, all year round, weather permitting, I spend every Saturday Afternoon and all of Sunday for these Investigations; when I have additional Days off, my Wanderings take me to even more Distant Areas" (Marstrander 1963).

The investigations to which the teacher had devoted his weekends and holidays over the preceding eight to ten years involved searching for rock carvings in his local surroundings, more specifically the coastal communities in the south-eastern part of Østfold County. Arnesen's great interest was local history, and in the mid-1860s, when he became a member of The Association of Norwegian Fortidsminnesmerke ("Ancient Monuments") Preservation (Fortidsmindeforeningen), his eyes were opened to cultural heritage and ancient monuments. In particular, he became curious about rock carvings. During the 1800s a number of previously unknown rock art sites had been discovered in the neighbouring district of Bohuslän in the south-western part of Sweden, where the very first documentation of a rock carving in Scandinavia was carried out as early as 1627. Close cultural and social ties have always existed between these two bordering districts, which resemble one another in terms of both their natural surroundings and climate. The national boundary between Sweden and Norway is an artificial, political division, established in 1658 as a result of the peace settlement between Denmark-Norway and Sweden, leading to Norway having to give up Bohuslän (Hygen and Bengtsson 1999). It therefore comes as no surprise that Arnesen looked to Bohuslän for inspiration when searching for rock carvings in Østfold as well.

An ardent amateur

Arnesen's task was not an easy one. He began his investigations at about the same time as documentation of the abundant Bohuslän rock art started in earnest. In Norway, however, only a few sites were known to exist in the 1860s, such as those at Tennes in Troms, Leirvåg in Sogn og Fjordane and Fossum in Telemark, and most people were barely aware that rock carvings existed at all. This meant that Arnesen had a scant basis for comparison, and so he decided to personally investigate all of the rock-faces where, in his opinion, carvings might be found (Gjessing 1939). He must have had a keen eye and informed

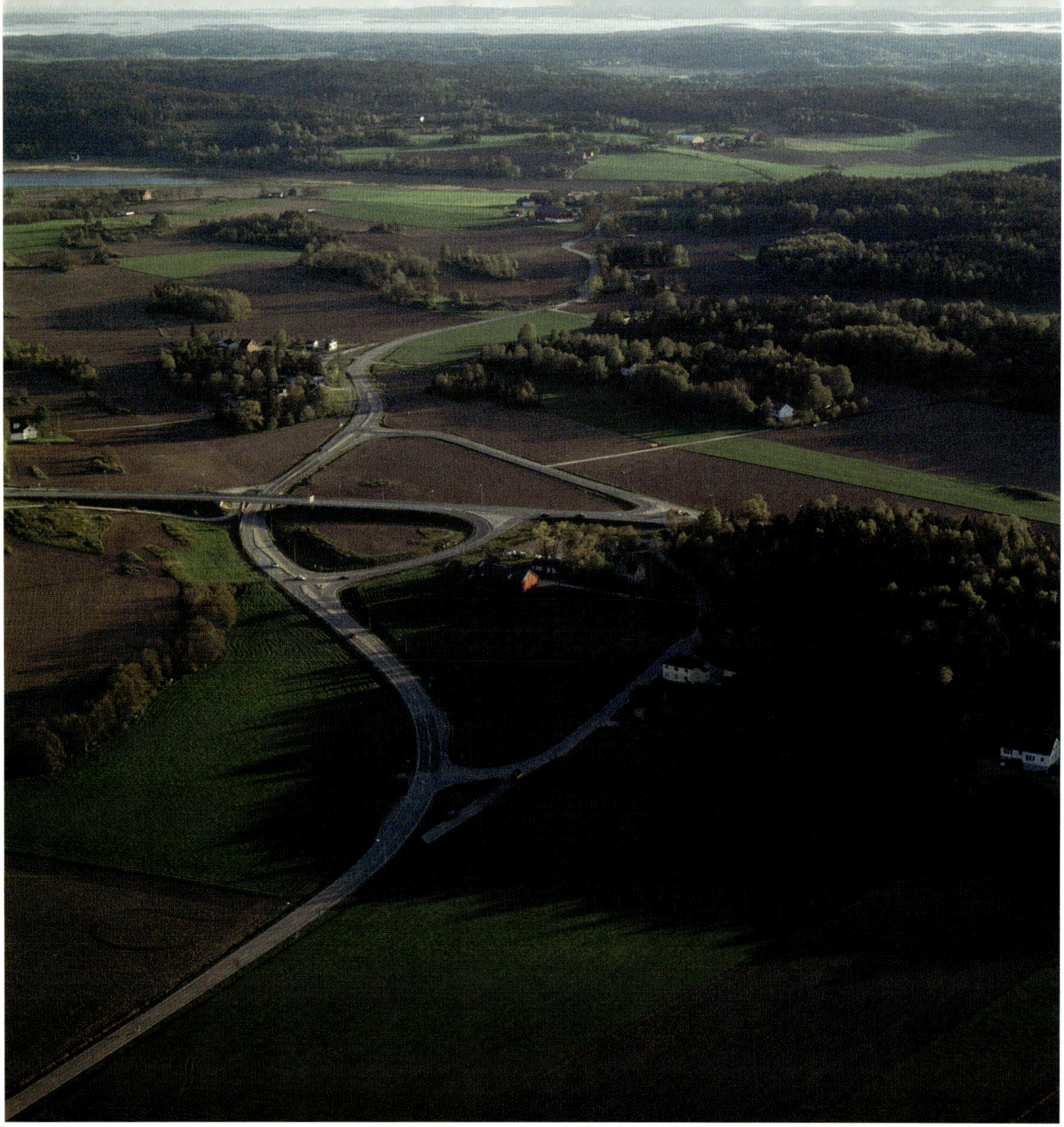

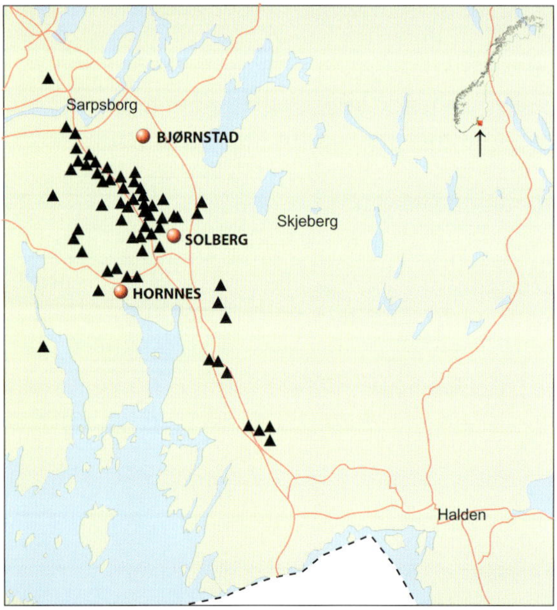

FIGURES 225–226. Aerial photo of parts of Skjeberg. This is a gently sloping landscape with loose deposits between the hills down along the coast. Near the house to the right in the photograph, at Solberg, there are three panels with rock carvings, and several more nearby.

MAP AI, ILLUSTRATION RU

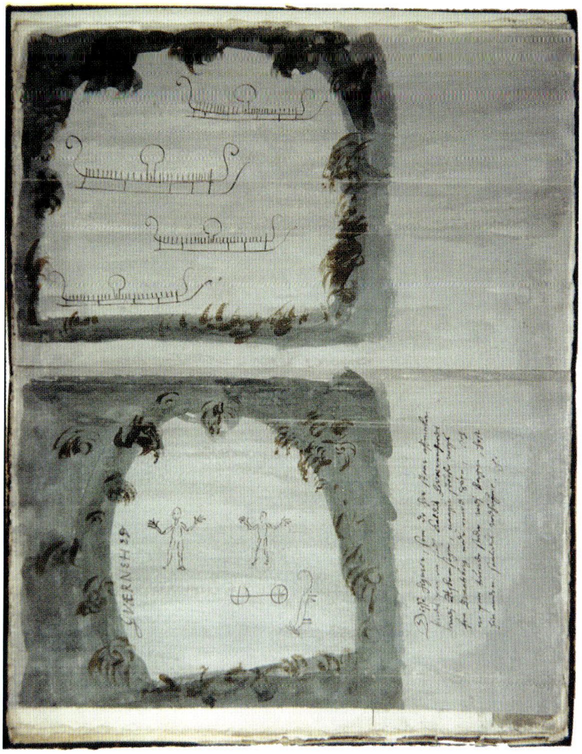

FIGURE 227. In 1627 Norwegian schoolteacher Peder Alfsson painted a watercolour of the rock art site at Backa in Brastad, Bohuslän. This is the oldest preserved depiction of a Scandinavian rock art site. It was drawn freehand, and the figures do not appear in relation to one another in the same manner as they occur on the rock surface. The human figures are depicted without gender, with the exception of the largest figure, given breasts – despite the fact that the figure actually has a penis. It is possible that Alfssön found it less offensive to depict a woman with breasts than a man with a large, erect penis!

intuition in order to distinguish between man-made lines and natural cracks and fissures in the surfaces. His voluminous, handwritten catalogue, which is in safe keeping at the University of Oslo's Museum of Cultural History, bears witness to his success beyond all expectations (Gjessing 1939; Marstrander 1963). He described the rock carvings he found, and used a quill to make meticulous drawings of the most important sites. Before Arnesen began his investigations, only nine rock art sites were known to exist in all of Østfold County. By the end of the 1870s he had raised this number to about 200 (Gjessing 1939). For the many researchers who followed in Arnesen's footsteps in the study of Østfold's rock art, the drawings he made have been an invaluable guide and basis for further studies (Marstrander 1963). It has also been established in retrospect that Arnesen was correct in claiming that rock carvings in Østfold would be of the same type – although not as abundant – as those found in the neighbouring region of Sweden.

Rock art in the borderland

More than 2700 rock art panels belonging to the Southern Tradition have been found in the border region of Østfold and Bohuslän (Vogt 2006a), and this area constitutes the largest concentration of Bronze Age rock carvings in Northern Europe (Hagen 1990; Hygen and Bengtsson 1999). In 1994, part of the rock art area of Bohuslän, Tanum, with its abundance of rock carvings, was included on UNESCO's World Heritage List, thereby defining it as one of the world's irreplaceable cultural monuments.

The majority of the rock carvings in the border region occur in the southern part of Østfold and the northern part of Bohuslän. The area does not represent one coherent, homogeneous landscape. On the contrary, the rock art sites are interspersed with forests, straits and bays, or are located on islands, with each rock art area, whether small or large, appearing to constitute a separate space in the landscape, framed by hills, woods or bays. These spaces, however, have been linked geographically and culturally by common ideas about rock art (Vogt 2006).

The rock carvings displayed on the smooth, glaciated granite in the border region reflect a plethora of motifs and intentions, combined into a figurative language that is unparalleled anywhere in Northern Europe (Hagen 1990). Boat and ship images occur in countless variations, as well as two- and four-wheeled carts, swords, spears and axes. Human-like figures are found in great numbers, and there are depictions of hands and foot soles. Wild and tame animals abound: red deer stags and wild boar, horses, dogs and oxen. Here and there are tree and plant motifs. Various abstract and geometric shapes, such as rings, spirals and chequered patterns occur in great numbers, and there is an abundance of cup marks, either depicted individually or in groups and long rows, scattered among the other motifs or depicted as a single motif on several panels (Hygen and Bengtsson 1999).

Although the variation in motifs in Østfold is not as great as in Bohuslän, the two neighbouring districts display so many similarities in choice of motifs and stylistic expression, indicating cultural unity, that it is justified to consider them as one continuous rock art region.

During the years following Arnesen's pioneering work, new panels were continually discovered in various parts of Østfold (Vogt 1998, 2000, 2006a). However, continuing the task he began has not been easy. During the years 1905–1909 Gabriel Gustafson conducted rock art research in Østfold (Marstrander 1963), and from the 1930s Gutorm Gjessing (1939) and Sverre Marstrander (1963) invested a huge effort in recording and documenting the extensive body of rock art that emerged. Special mention goes to Erling Johansen, as he spent his entire life as an active field archaeologist in Østfold (Johansen 1944, 1948, 1953, 1976, 1978). Drawing on his superb knowledge of the local area and his passion for the Østfold landscape, he was instrumental in the discovery and preservation of a large number of rock art sites. Through his contributions he was also influential in awakening an interest and fondness for cultural heritage among the local population. From the late 1990s onwards, recording and research on Østfold's rock art have been carried out, among others, by Anne-Sophie Hygen and Lasse Bengtsson (1999) and David Vogt (2000, 2006a).

The manifold Skjeberg Plain

The largest and most varied concentration of rock carvings in Østfold is found in Skjeberg, which is part of the municipality of Sarpsborg, a small town in the south-eastern part of the county. This is the very same area that was Martin Arnesen's most important field of activity (Marstrander 1963). Unfortunately, it has not been possible to recover many of the carvings Arnesen described, either due to weathering or because they are overgrown with moss and turf.

The majority of the rock carvings of Skjeberg are located on Skjebergsletta (Skjeberg Plain), a stretch of clayey soil that runs from the outskirts of Sarpsborg to the inner part of Skjebergkilen (Skjeberg Bay), framed by granite ridges to the east and west and bordered to the north by an immense glacial end moraine called Østfoldraet. The rock carvings are located at the transition zone between the higher rocky uplands and the arable lowlands. They are carved on low-lying, glaciated rock-faces at the foothills, or on partially embedded rocks and outcrops that stick up as islets in the flat terrain.

When the rock carvings were made during the Bronze Age, the landscape was quite different, as a result of the changes caused when the ice cap covering Northern Europe began to melt some 10,000–12,000 years ago. The clayey plains, consisting of fine sediment deposited under the water in front of the glacial apron, gradually became dry land as the weight of the ice masses lifted. The moraines – long ridges of sand and gravel – were formed where the glacial ice remained motionless during the melting process. During the Bronze Age, the ocean level was 15–20 metres higher than it is today, and Skjebergsletta was a rocky landscape with countless bays and sounds, and small islands off the ocean shoreline. At that time, the well-drained, fully cultivated clay plains we see today were open, grassy marshlands (Johansen 1953, 1978).

The people in the landscape

There are few physical remains of Bronze Age settlement in the Skjeberg area. However, based on the sparse remains and their distribution in the landscape, as well as research in other areas of Scandinavia, it is possible to make some deductions about how the people who made the rock carvings lived. Investigations in Denmark and Southern Sweden suggest that Bronze Age dwellers took advantage of a wide array of resources (Hygen and Bengtsson 1999).

Especially during the Early Bronze Age, the climate was warmer than today, the growing season was longer, and deciduous trees were predominant. Archaeological remains, such as habitation sites and graves, as well as scientific analyses of pollen and traces of cultivation, indicate that fields and settlements were located on sandy ridges, while the clayey low-lying areas, often marshlands, were used for grazing. It appears that the grazing territory was sizeable, which in turn suggests that animal husbandry was the most important economic activity of the period (Groseth 2001).

These investigations may serve as an analogy for the Skjeberg area during the

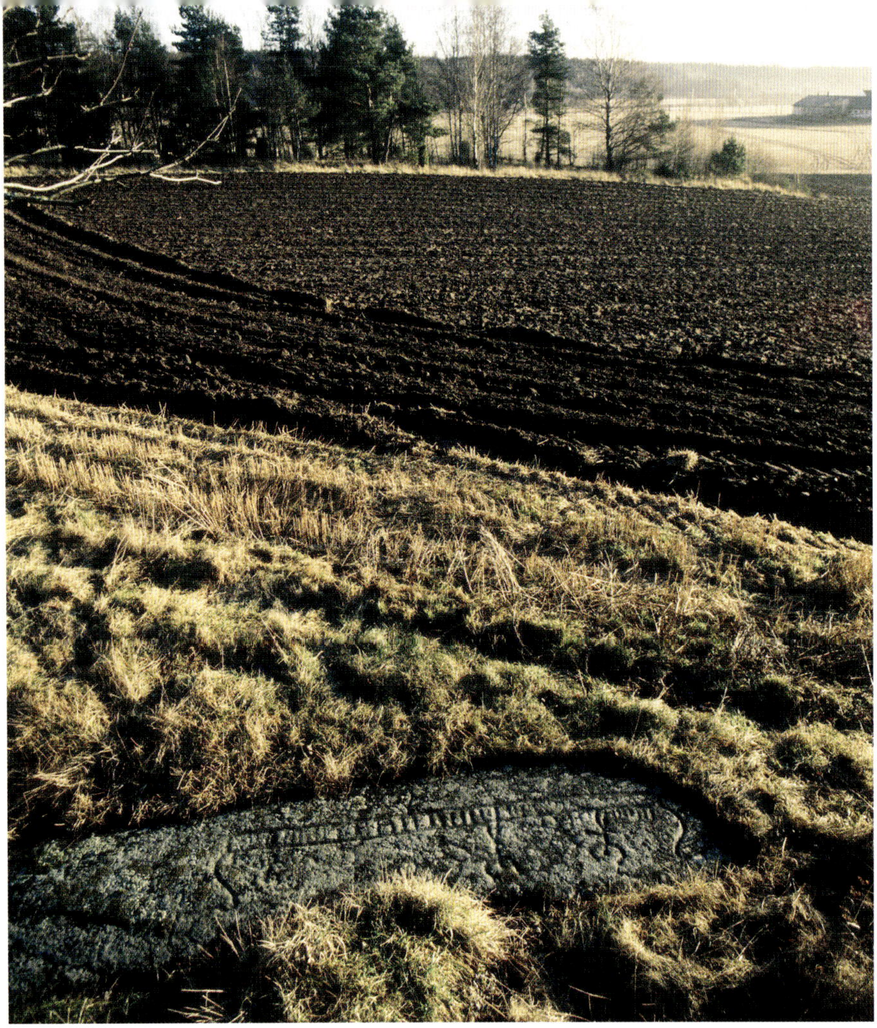

FIGURE 228. Many of the rock carvings in Skjeberg occur on low-lying knolls in the centre of flat country, such as this boat at Bakkehaugen. The stem is shaped like a horse's head with a long, flowing mane. On board are several human figures – one doing a somersault, three with their arms raised as if they are worshiping or dancing. There are also three circular figures, one attached to the boat by a rod.
RU

Bronze Age. Skjeberg's landscape is characterized by gravel slopes, wetland areas, valleys and low crests. Considering the agricultural tools people in the Bronze Age had at their disposal, the low-lying fields with heavy, waterlogged clayey soil were poorly suited for cultivation. While these areas offered favourable grazing conditions, the dry and self-draining sandy soil of the moraines aligned in a southerly direction was most likely used for tilling. Whereas the rock carvings are located in lowland areas, with dwellings and fields probably on the adjacent moraines, the burial mounds from the Bronze Age are found on the crests as well as on islands along the coastline of that time (Hygen and Bengtsson 1999). It seems that the lower-lying settlement areas, with dwellings, pastureland and rock carvings, were the domain of the living, while the dead were ushered to higher ground, removed from the world of the living (Nordbladh 1980).

The proximity to the sea and the waterways seems to have been an important factor in the choice of settlement location for the people of the Bronze Age. The ocean was both a natural source of food and a communication artery, and the sea route was the most important link with the outside world, and a highway for the exchange of goods and ideas. Perhaps the numerous boat images on the rock art panels represented the very symbol of the journey, in the broadest sense of the term – of contact and interaction with people from other areas, but also of the journey to the other world.

The myriad of figures

The majority of the rock carvings at Skjeberg were probably made during the final centuries of the Bronze Age – between 700–800 and 500 BC (Vogt 2006a). There are indications that the Bronze Age rock art tradition continued into the Early Iron Age (after 500 BC), as seen for example in Bohuslän and parts of Western Norway. It is also possible that some images were created in the Early Bronze Age, around 1800–1500 BC, indicating that certain panels may have been in use over a long period of time (Hygen and Bengtsson 1999). At first glance, the numerous and varied rock art images appear confusing, almost chaotic. However, on closer examination it becomes possible to recognize motifs that reflect realities of the Bronze Age – people, animals and man-made objects. Although these figures appear recognizable, there is more than meets the eye: in the Bronze Age they were perhaps symbols of something entirely different. The premise that the motifs can be seen as symbols is supported by the fact that the human figures are involved in activities not immediately associated with everyday tasks. In addition, interspersed between depictions thought to represent objects from the material world, there are also motifs that cannot be identified as anything specific or recognisable. On panel after panel, combinations of this type of motifs are repeated, as if they are meant to illustrate certain tales. Perhaps this is how the groups of figures are meant to be understood – as scenes in which the concrete and the abstract depictions form part of a symbolic whole – the world-view of the Bronze Age.

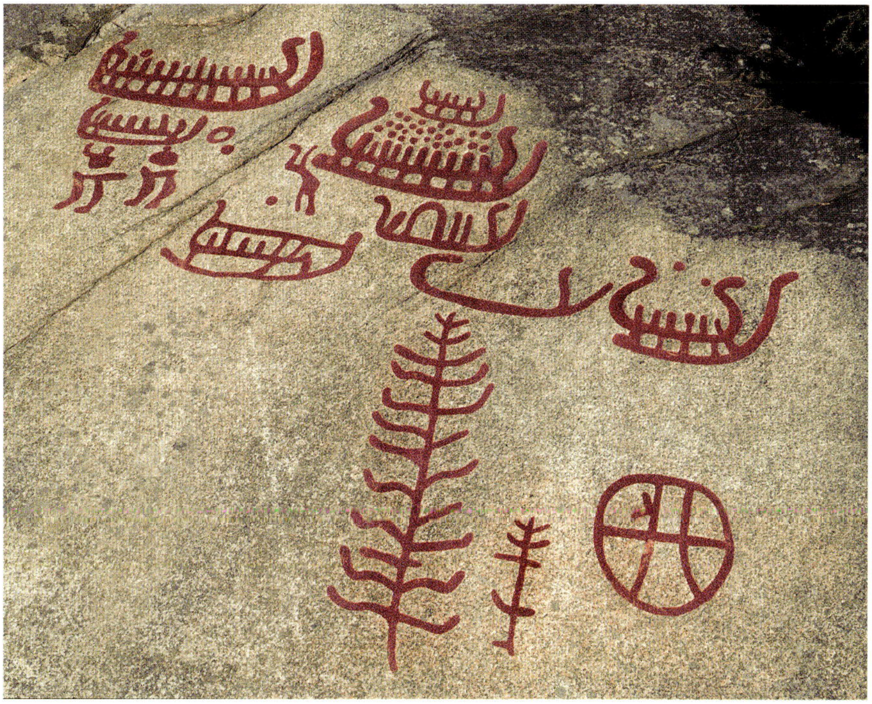

FIGURE 229. On many of the rock art panels at Solberg Farm, as well as boats, humans and rings, there are also depictions of trees. As illustrated in the chapter on Etne in Sunnhordland, this is a rare motif in the Southern Tradition, but it is used as a symbol in many religions. In Norse mythology we have Yggdrasil – the World Tree that spans from the underworld to the heavens, and which is said to be eternally green. The tree is also a symbol for death and rebirth, for the eternal cycle of life. The images of trees in the rock carvings demonstrates that already by the Bronze Age, our area of the world was part of a major religious and cultural context that extended across all of Europe and into parts of Asia.
RU

In Bronze Age society, the transmission of customs and knowledge was based primarily on the oral tradition, and the rock carvings may have served as a means of communication supplementing the spoken word (Fredell 2003). The images may have been intended to bring to life the oral transmissions of myths, legends, rituals and other traditions through the durable medium of stone. As a result they became a means of recording memories, a way by which a society lacking a written language could preserve important knowledge and information and pass it on from generation to generation. It perhaps sufficed to illustrate the highlights of the myths or rituals in order to recollect all of the minute details of the stories that were retold around the rock art panel.

The ritual universe

The stories that were told are now long forgotten, and no myths or rituals that could be linked with the rock carvings have been transmitted down to us through the ages. Some conclusions may be drawn, however, based on the composition of the images that seem to describe certain events – people dancing, playing bronze trumpets or taking part in processions. These kinds of ritual activities may have been performed around the rock art panels, perhaps on the ground immediately in front of them.

Written references from the same time period and from other areas may also be used as analogy for interpreting the rock carvings. The people of the Bronze Age in Norway most likely had contact with people from other areas of Continental Europe, not least in order to procure the coveted metals. The Nordic people probably gained knowledge about bronze casting from eastern Mediterranean areas. Numerous written sources have been preserved which suggest that bronze smelting and casting were closely related to religious faith, symbols and myths (Larsson 1997). It is reasonable to assume that the use of symbols and rituals was transmitted to the Nordic countries along with this metal technology, as suggested by the similarities in the types of materials and visual depictions used (Hygen and Bengtsson 1999; Larsson 1997).

Even the location of the rock carvings in the landscape may be an important source for understanding their meaning. Many of the panels in Skjeberg are located in open, easily visible places, indicating that they were meant to be seen (Hygen and Bengtsson 1999). Frequently there are flat fields below the sloping rock-faces were carvings are found, and the images are positioned so that they are relatively easy to be seen by people standing in front of the panels. Other rock art sites are more concealed, with many of the images carved on low-lying outcrops almost at ground level, making it difficult to see them from a distance. Variations in location are perhaps indications of other intended uses. The broad, open and easily visible outcrops with rock art may have been part of a ritualistic system that included and communicated with all members of society. The more secluded sites may have represented more esoteric knowledge, places and rites that were reserved for only the select few. Whatever the case, the important act

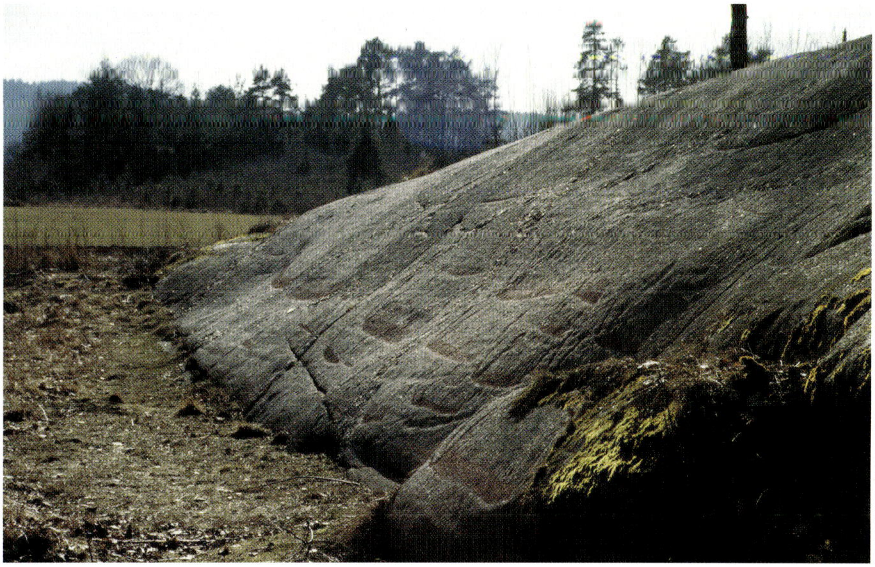

FIGURE 230. There are often flat, open spaces in front of rock art panels where it is possible to imagine that people would gather for ritual purposes during the Bronze Age.
RU

of creating rock carvings was not delegated to common members of society. The privilege would only have been granted to specially selected individuals with the necessary knowledge and experience.

Neither were the images made on randomly selected stone surfaces. The sites were most likely chosen with great care. Why certain rock surfaces were chosen over others is an open question. Perhaps the rock contained powers with which it was important to come into contact. Maybe ancestors were thought to be present there, or perhaps an important event had taken place on these sites. By carving symbols and signs into the stone, the memory of the event was kept alive, and the place was made sacred. This memory would affect the routines and activities of the people living in the landscape (Tilley 1994). Through the symbols and their location in the landscape, world order was given visual form, and the mythical tales transmitted notions about life and death and the relationship between people and higher forces.

Myths and rituals are closely related. Through the rituals, the timeless mythical realities were retold and recreated. By observing and taking part in ritual acts, people are initiated in the myths. Ritual and cult observances are located in places where people and higher powers encounter one another (Hygen and Begtsson 1999). By observing the cult, they participate in the knowledge associated with the sacred place and the rituals performed there. Rituals that serve higher powers in maintaining social order in the human world often accompany important events in a society.

Context as a source of knowledge

In an attempt to obtain greater and more tangible information about the activities that went on around the rock art sites, a number of excavations

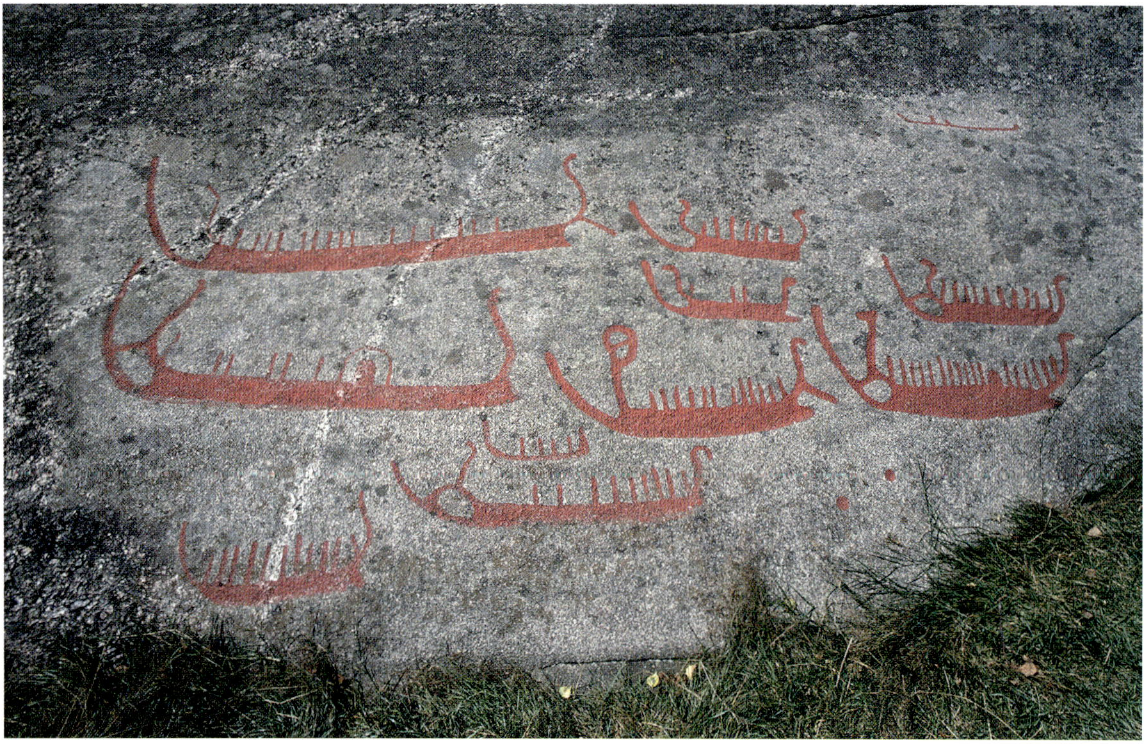

FIGURE 231. The numerous boat figures at Hornnes have the same shape, and all face in the same direction – towards the coast and the open ocean. Excavations were carried out in the mid-1970s in front of this "Bronze Age fleet" panel. RU

have been carried out in recent years in the areas next to the rock carvings. In the mid-1970s finds were made in front of the two largest panels in Skjeberg – Hornnes and Bjørnstad – which may provide information about the events that occurred in the Late Bronze Age (Johansen 1979).

The Hornnes panel consists of an almost vertical rock face on which 21 ship figures are carved, together with one or two humanlike figures doing back-flips over a ship, and some cup marks. All of the ships are sailing in the same direction – towards the coast and the open ocean. Excavations immediately in front of the panel, at the edge of the rock wall, unearthed a low-lying row of stones arranged in a semicircle. They frame the area of the rock face on which the carvings appear. Several of the stones had been exposed to heat, and the lowermost portion of the rock wall also had traces from an open fire: the granite was rust-coloured and flaking off. Inside the row of stones, several kilograms of sherds of coarse, undecorated pottery were found, together with large amounts of burnt clay clumps, varying quantities of both burnt and unburnt flint, and a small stone with pecked lines of the same type seen in the grooves of the rock carvings.

Similar remains were found during excavations next to the so-called Bjørnstad Ship, one of the largest rock art ship images in all of Norway. One metre tall at the stem and 4.5 metres long, it is located on an almost vertical rock wall along with two smaller boats. The excavation unearthed a nearly semicircular arrangement of stones directly in front of the large ship figure, and within this

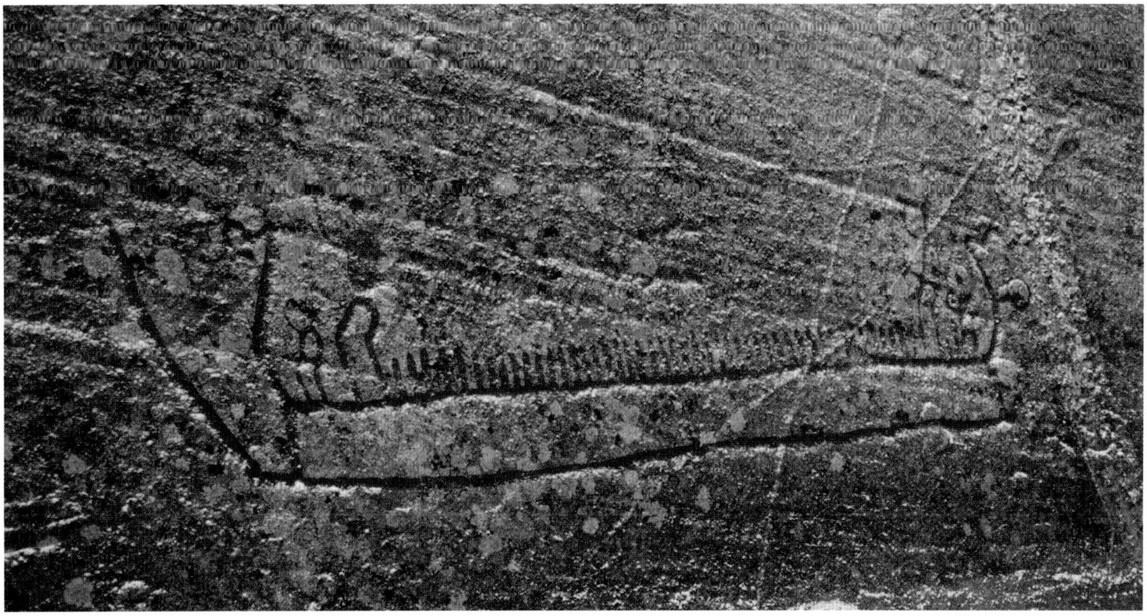

FIGURE 232. The boat figures at Skjeberg feature a wide variety of shapes and sizes. The largest is the so-called Bjørnstad ship, 4.5 metres long and located on the Navestad Pyntelund farm at the edge of a wide valley. Some 50 vertical lines represent the boat's crew. At both stem and stern, the tallest figures amongst the crew lines are two with raised axes. Archaeological remains excavated in front of the rock art panel suggest that rituals had taken place at this spot.
RU

half circle of stones burnt clay clumps, flint flakes, a potential hammer stone and a small amount of charcoal were found. However, the site contained a smaller number of artefacts than the Hornnes site.

The arrangement of the stones suggests that the rock carvings were cordoned off with a fence-like enclosure. The clumps of burnt clay may also be the remains of structures made of the material in the area. Constructing physical enclosures around sacred sites is known to be a common practice in many societies, in order to separate them from the secular world (*ibid.*). This interpretation also explains why the majority of the remains are found inside the stone enclosures, as it was the place where the sacred acts were performed. The burnt stones, layers of soot and charcoal all indicate that open fires were made near the rock carvings. Bonfires and the use of fire are common elements in festive and cult acts, in conjunction with ritual feasts. The large amount of ceramic sherds may be the remains of rituals during which the pottery that was used for food and drink was broken on site at the end of the ceremony.

Fragments of reality

The location of the rock art in the terrain, the large number of figures and the physical remains recovered in front of the panels, represent only fragments of the reality of which the rock carvings formed a part. It will never be possible for people of today to know exactly why the carvings were made and what really happened around the panels.

The interpretation of rock images as depictions of mythical tales or ritual observances is based on knowledge about the religion and cults of other societies and other time periods than the Nordic Bronze Age. It is possible to justify comparisons and inferences of this kind because the act of expressing oneself through images and actions in order to ensure the existence of a given society are associated with basic human characteristics and needs (Hygen and Bengtsson 1999). Despite the similarities, there are infinite variations in human forms of expression in terms of time and space. For this reason, the interpretations merely provide a concise and incomplete notion of what the rock carvings meant at the time they were created. However, it seems reasonable to suggest that Bronze Age rock art provides us with an indication of how humans of that time perceived themselves, their surroundings and their relationship to higher powers. The images in stone provide a glimpse of another world, in which people who resembled modern man in many ways nonetheless lived another kind of life, with other concepts of life and death, good and evil and their relationships with each other.

Fading Images

> "In terms of weathering, the process has advanced so far in some places that large sections of the panel are wholly or partially obliterated. This is a matter partly of an overall weathering of the surface and partly of exfoliation of large sections of the rock" *(Author's translation)*
>
> Hagen 1969

This is a description of the state of the rock carvings of Ausevik in the early 1960s. The rock carvings located in Flora municipality in Sogn og Fjordane County, had been discovered in 1934 and were then recorded and documented by Johs. Bøe of Bergens Museum. Ausevik is one of the largest and most distinctive rock art sites of the Northern Tradition in southern Norway, comprising about 350 figures: various abstract or geometric patterns, images of deer, depictions of humans, some plant motifs and scattered cup marks. Bøe's reports from the investigations were never published, and when Anders Hagen was appointed Professor of Archaeology at the University of Bergen in 1961, he decided to resume Bøe's studies of the rock carvings in Ausevik (Hagen 1969). A disheartening spectacle awaited him out in the field. When Hagen compared Bøe's tracings with the actual situation in the 1960s he resignedly noted that the rock art had deteriorated dramatically over the thirty years that had passed.

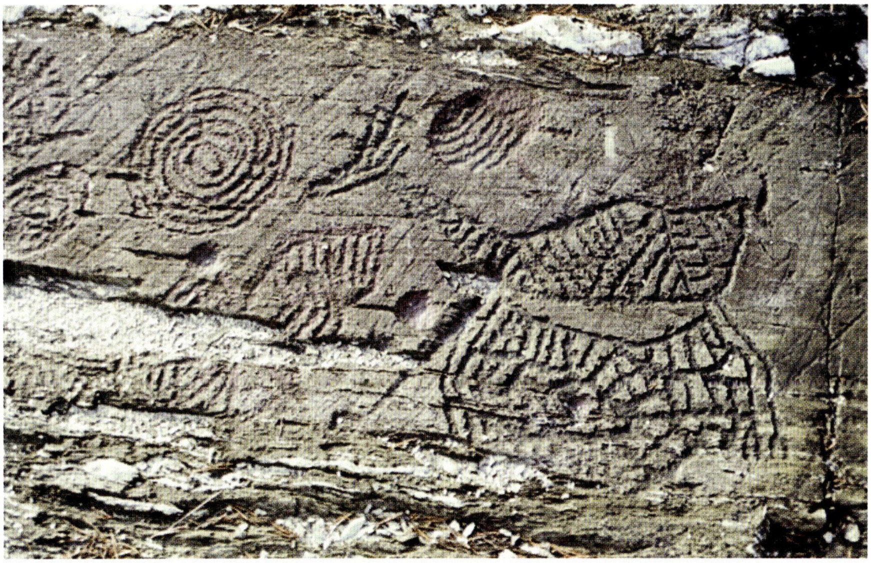

FIGURE 233. The rock in Ausevik is fine-grained slate with the stratification running perpendicular to the surface of the stone. When the rock deteriorates, it breaks off in thin flakes that are 0.5–2 mm thick, 1–2 cm wide and 1–5 cm long. The deterioration results in disintegration of the upper 1–2 centimetres of the rock – what we call the weathering zone. The result is that both the details of the images and even the entire rock art figure are obliterated over the course of thirty years. GM

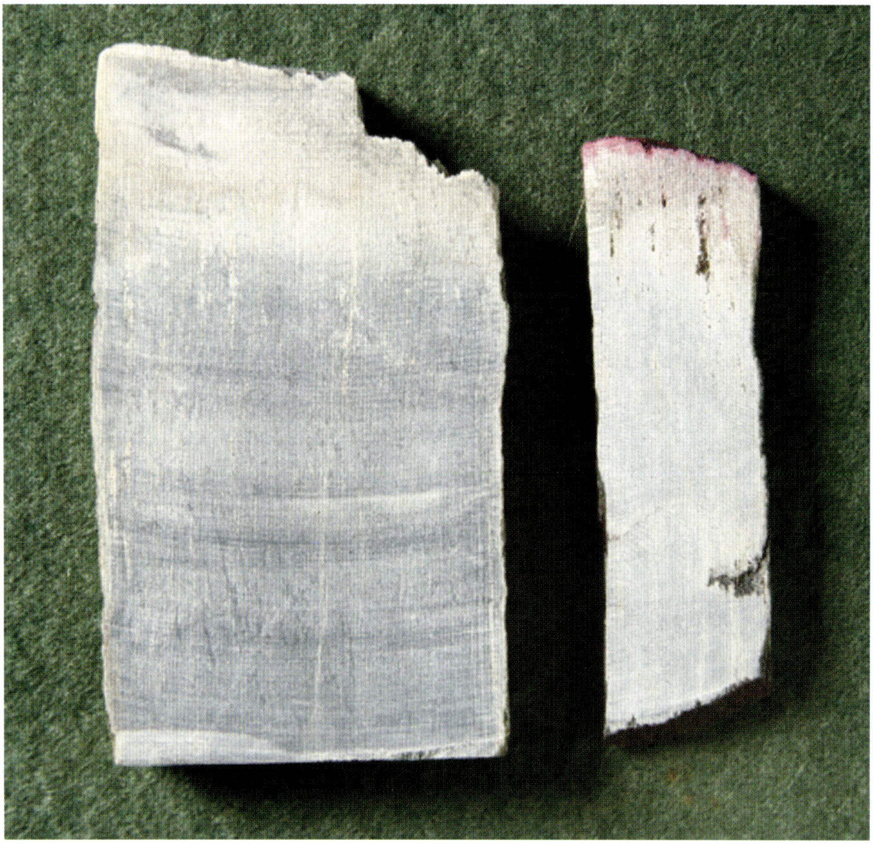

FIGURE 234. The thickness of the weathering zone can vary from a few millimetres to 2–3 centimetres. On this enlarged cross-section of a rock, the surface appears as a light grey zone, while the healthy rock beneath it has a darker colour. This results from a number of minerals leaching out of the surface and leaving cavities or pores in the weathering zonc. This makcs thc surface very porous and vulnerable, particularly to physical and biological degradation processes. At the transition between the weathering zone and the healthy rock, a system of fine fissures is created, explaining why the surface layer has a tendency to loosen and flake off.
KM

The details of the images, entire figures and large sections of the stone surface had been obliterated.

Continuous disintegration

Archaeologists had long been aware that rock art panels were susceptible to damage. Ever since the end of the 1800s both Swedish and Norwegian rock art researchers had experienced how difficult it was to find and document rock carvings and recover panels that previous researchers had described (Mandt *et al.* 1992). Many panels were so overgrown with vegetation that it was difficult to make out the figures, and in other cases, previously recorded rock carvings had wholly or partially disintegrated. In addition, many panels were damaged or vandalised by passers-by who had painted or marred the figures and scratched names or dates around them. Throughout the 1930s, researchers described the state of rock art as precarious. However, it was only when Hagen was able to compare the state of the rock art at Ausevik in the 1960s with its condition 30 years earlier that he became aware of the extent of the damage. It became imperative to implement measures aimed at discovering the causes of the deterioration, and hopefully find ways of repairing the damage. The dramatic deterioration suffered by the Ausevik rock carvings over a period of 30 years was caused by natural weathering, a process that had already begun at the time the rock art was created. When the ice cap that covered Scandinavia during the last Ice Age receded some 10,000 years ago, the weathering process began to disintegrate the rock surfaces, which were constantly exposed to the elements. This is a slow process that continues uninterruptedly (Lødøen *et al.* 1997). Natural weathering was accelerated several thousand years after the end of the Ice Age when people began to carve images into the exposed stone surfaces. The carving process created a kind of "wound" in the surface of the rock, resulting in accelerated weathering as water and vegetation could penetrate cracks and cavities in the stone more easily. Deterioration of stone is a normal process: the problem facing cultural heritage management, however, arises when the deterioration obliterates large portions of the rock art.

The weathering processes

One of the major causes of the disintegration of rock images is associated with changes over time in the mineral composition of the stone surface. Some of the minerals are weathered away and leave pores in the upper layer of the stone, the layer we call the weathering zone. On many rock art panels, the weathering zone varies in thickness from a few millimetres to 2–3 centimetres. To the bare eye it appears as a light-grey zone, while the unweathered or "healthy" rock beneath it is darker in colour. The images are no longer on solid rock, but rather on a porous and brittle stone surface that has different properties to healthy, solid stone (Mandt *et al.* 1992; Lødøen *et al.* 1997).

The porous weathering zone is highly vulnerable to all kinds of external factors. Water penetrates the pores left by the washed-out minerals and enters

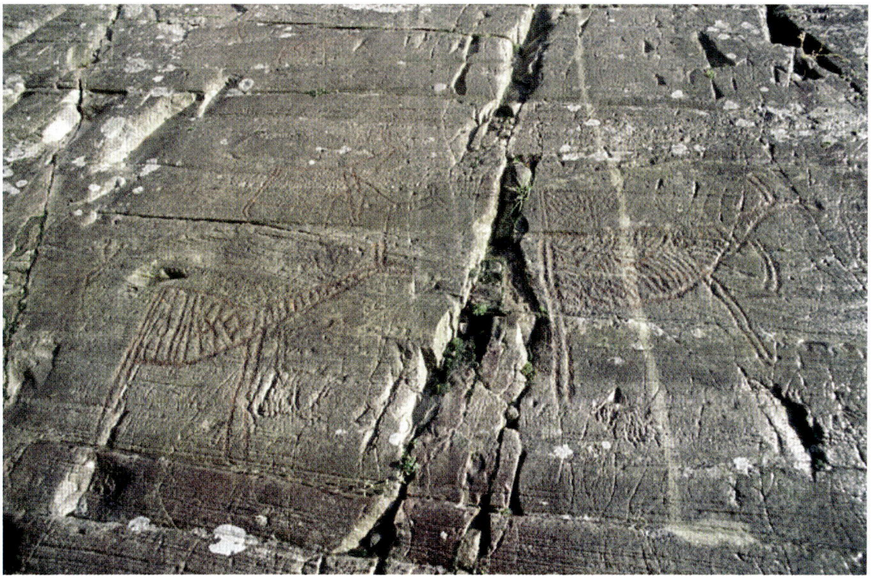

FIGURE 235. In many places there are large cracks in the stone surface, such as in this panel at Vingen. As grass and heather gradually begin to grow in the cracks, the roots can penetrate deep into the rock and cause larger portions of the rock surface with carvings to break off.
RU

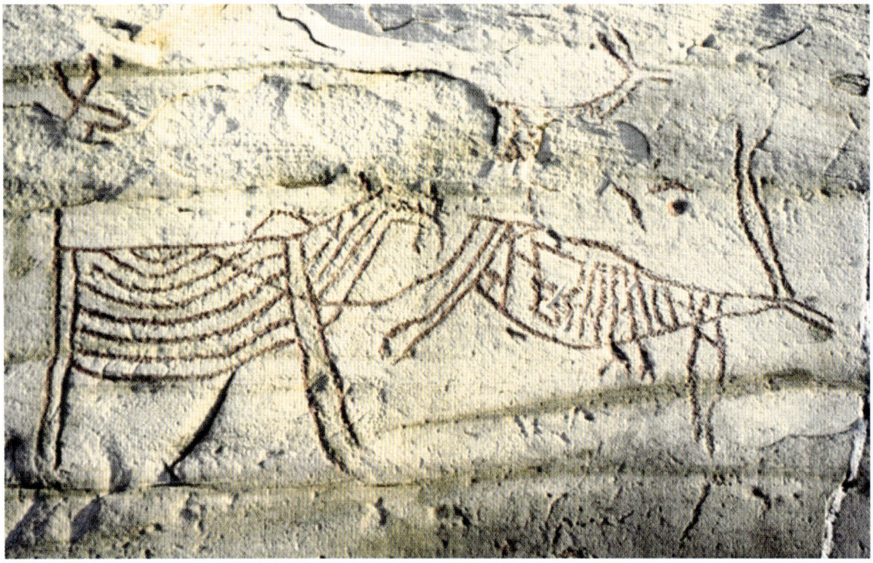

FIGURE 236. On the sandstone at Vingen there are many instances where the weathering zone flakes off in thin chips, taking parts of the rock art with them.
GM

the microscopic cracks in the rock. In damp climates the weathering zone can be completely saturated with water, almost like a sponge, and this in turn leads to an even higher rate of mineral depletion. In coastal climates, frost erosion is a serious problem. Surface water collects in hollows and cavities in the rock, and during the course of a damp winter the water that has penetrated the surface will alternately freeze and melt several times in succession. This process then causes large sections of the surface, along with the rock art images, to loosen and flake off. Cavities are often formed between the weathering zone and the healthy rock beneath it. When this occurs, the surface is particularly prone to disintegration from external factors, such as when passers-by step or stand on the images themselves.

Vegetation on and around the rock art is also a factor in disintegration. Grass and heather growing in cracks in the rock tend to widen the cracks and eventually to rupture whole sections of rock containing figures. Lichen growth appears to accelerate, although we are uncertain as to why. Plausibly, a rock surface that has reached a certain stage in the deterioration process provides favourable growing conditions for lichens, and they can then proliferate in the weathering zone until nutrients are depleted. Certain lichen species eat into the rock and cause it to crumble, a process known as gravel weathering.

The vulnerable rock

Weather conditions, wind, precipitation and vegetation are all factors that result in varying degrees of damage to rock art. The damage is caused in different ways, depending on the climate and the type of stone. Not all rock types weather at an equal rate. The most vulnerable rocks are the mica slates of Western and Northern Norway (Mandt *et al.* 1992; Lødøen *et al.* 1997).

The Ausevik rock carvings are particularly vulnerable because the rock is a fine-grained slate with stratification that is perpendicular to the surface. Stratification can be compared to a deck of cards standing on end. The various weathering processes cause the edges of the "cards" to peel off in thin flakes. This in turn causes the upper centimetres of the rock surface – where the rock art images are engraved – to crumble, and the images are lost (Mandt *et al.* 1992; Lødøen *et al.* 1997).

Damage from various types of weathering has also been reported in Østfold granite and sandstone in Finnmark and Sogn og Fjordane (Thorseth *et al.* 2001). Large sections of the rock surface loosen from the base – flaking off in chips that are as thick as the weathering zone itself – or the surface crumbles as a result of depleted mineral grains that have fallen out.

Man-made damage

The forces of nature are not the only cause of disintegration. Even human activity is a threat to rock art. Most people know that stones used in buildings gradually disintegrate, often as a result of acid rain or air pollution. It is perhaps less well known that Norwegian bedrock, the very symbol of stability and solidness, is so weathered and fragile that all types of external wear and tear are harmful to it, not least of all the comings and goings of the interested public. Damage frequently occurs simply because visitors to the rock art panels are not aware of how vulnerable the images are. In addition, there are cases of deliberate vandalism in many rock art sites. People make scratches inside and across figures, or deface the images with felt markers and spray paint (Mandt *et al.* 1992).

A dilemma without solution?

In the 1990s, the Directorate for Cultural Heritage conducted a survey to assess the state of preservation of rock art throughout Norway (Riksantikvaren 1995). The results revealed that more than 90 percent of the sites were damaged in one way or another, partly due to natural weathering and partly as a result of vandalism. Sites that have been known to exist for a number of years – many of them since the early 1900s – are almost nonexistent today. We are able to document this because – as in the case of Ausevik – we can compare the condition of the sites today with their state twenty, thirty or fifty years ago, by examining tracings, mouldings, photographs and illustrations in journals. In some cases, even older documentation exists.

If the rock art is already as damaged as these surveys suggest, and if the extent of this damage is constantly increasing, then what are the chances of us preserving these cultural monuments for future generations? We will never be able to stop the effects of natural forces on rock, but we can hopefully delay deterioration, and we can probably repair some of the worst damage. The prerequisite for this is that we regard and treat rock art images in the field in the same way as archaeological artefacts in a museum (Lødøen *et al.* 1997). In museums, artefacts are preserved and exhibited in display cases or kept in museum vaults under controlled climatic conditions. Moving rock art indoors to a museum can only be done in exceptional cases – such as with decorated burial slabs or other loose stones engraved with figures. Our foremost objective is to preserve rock art at the site where it was created. For this reason, we have to consider the rock art sites as outdoor museums, where we can create an environment that will contribute towards diminishing natural deterioration, at the same time as preventing people from unwittingly or intentionally damaging the rock art images.

Safeguarding rock art

The preservation of rock art has been on the archaeological agenda of the Directorate for Cultural Heritage since the mid-1990s. The majority of the causes of deterioration have been identified, and efforts have been made to develop methods that can help reduce and slow down the harmful processes. The phrase "safeguarding rock art" can be understood in several ways. Many people believe that sufficient safeguarding entails describing the rock art images and documenting them with photographs, drawings, mouldings and the like, so that subsequent generations will be able to study them in museum archives. Documentation is, of course, important and one objective is to document all rock art as thoroughly as possible. However, studying rock art images based on archive materials will never be able to replace the actual experience of examining it in its proper environment – in an ancient cultural landscape or in context with other cultural monuments. Safeguarding rock art also involves preserving the rock art as source values and knowledge potential, and this is best done by preserving it on the site and in the context within which it was created (Lødøen *et al.* 1997).

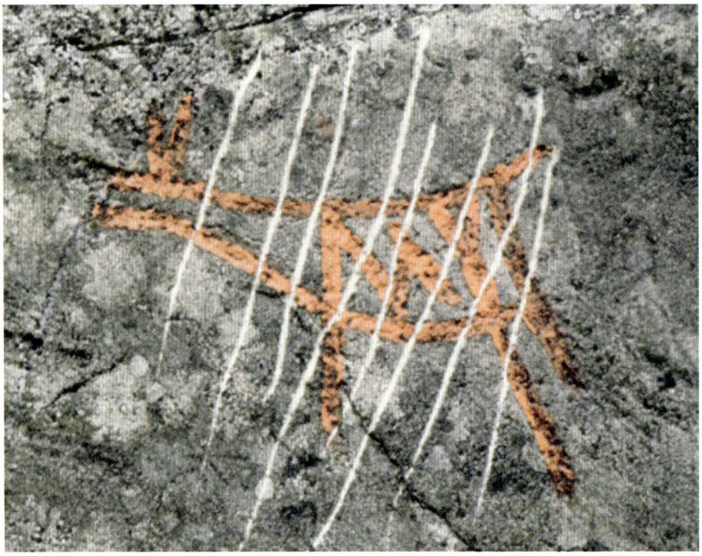

FIGURE 237. A major problem at many of the rock art sites is vandalism, such as here in Vingen, where deep gouge marks were scratched over several figures. There are also examples of spray-painting over figures, or graffiti drawn over them with felt-tipped pens. It is often difficult to repair the figures after this kind of vandalism.

GM

The effort to preserve rock art involves both preventive measures and conservation. Preventive efforts entail taking every precaution to effectively reduce the risk of damage to a minimum: leading water away from the rock surfaces, keeping the surfaces clear of vegetation growth, preventing large fluctuations in temperature, reducing the effects of frost erosion and controlling public traffic through the site (Thorseth *et al.* 2001)

It may be necessary to "warehouse" portions of the rock art, covering panels for longer or shorter periods of time, mainly in order to limit physical and biological degradation. Placing covers over severely damaged panels will also prevent the public from more or less consciously causing damage to the figures. At the same time we must take care to avoid damaging or destroying archaeological artefacts and traces in the subsoil around the rock art panels. These are important materials for understanding, dating and interpreting the rock art (Lødøen *et al.* 1997; Thorseth *et al.* 2001). Conservation entails directly treating the cultural monuments themselves, and is only performed if the situation is so precarious that the figures are in danger of being lost for ever. A guiding principle in all conservation efforts is that measures must be reversible, meaning it must be possible to alter the measures or start afresh. As a result, research continues with the aim of identifying and adopting the most appropriate and prudent methods for conservation. We are still faced with major problems in terms of preservation, and this will be costly in terms of time, money, commitment and work. It is heartening to see that there appears to be genuine interest and willingness to make an effort amongst politicians, administrative authorities, friends of cultural heritage preservation and interested members of the general public. The effort implemented by the Directorate for Cultural Heritage during the past decade to preserve rock art, with funding from the Department of the Environment, is tangible proof of this. There are also significant cooperative efforts across national boundaries, as rock carvings and rock paintings all over the world are at risk of being lost. The effort to safeguard rock art for posterity will remain a priority at research institutions all across the globe.

Long-term conservation

An important preventive measure for conserving rock art in the long run is to define the endurance limit for each site. A cultural monument has a limit to what it can endure without becoming reduced, damaged or destroyed. These limits vary depending on the type, age and size of the cultural monument. The simplest preventive measure is to determine what the cultural monuments, considered separately, are able to withstand in terms of physical stress factors. What types of preservation measures can be implemented by conservation authorities without causing more harm than good for the rock art images? We cannot, for example, use the same type of documentation techniques for painted images as for rock carvings, when the painted figures are unable to withstand

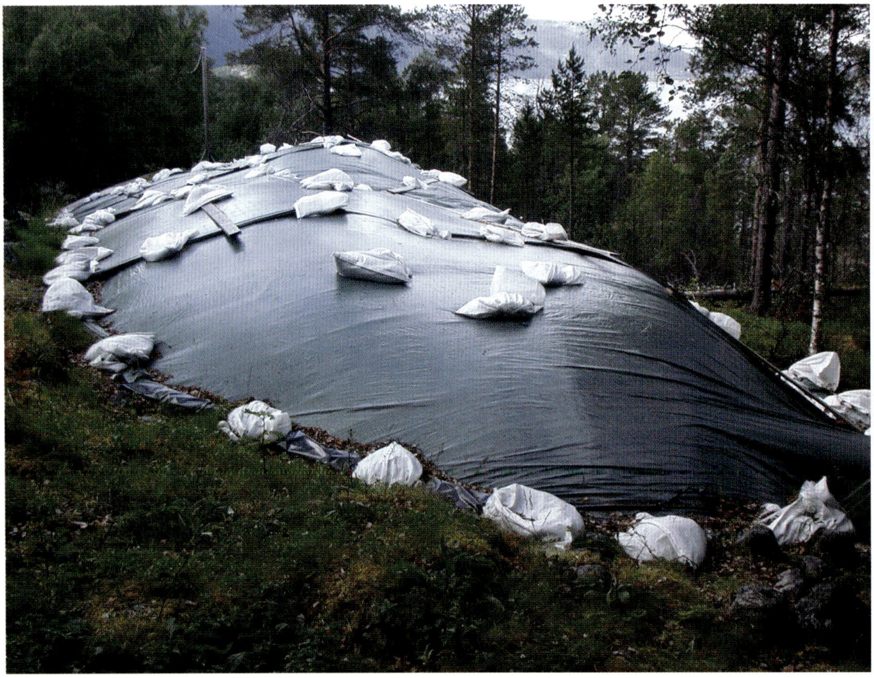

FIGURE 238. The rock carvings at Forselv in Skjomen, Nordland, were overgrown with lichen and other micro-vegetation, making them difficult to see. Researchers have reached the conclusion that the gentlest method for cleaning a rock art panel is to cover it for a period of time with insulated, opaque material, thereby slowing down the physical and biological processes.
TL

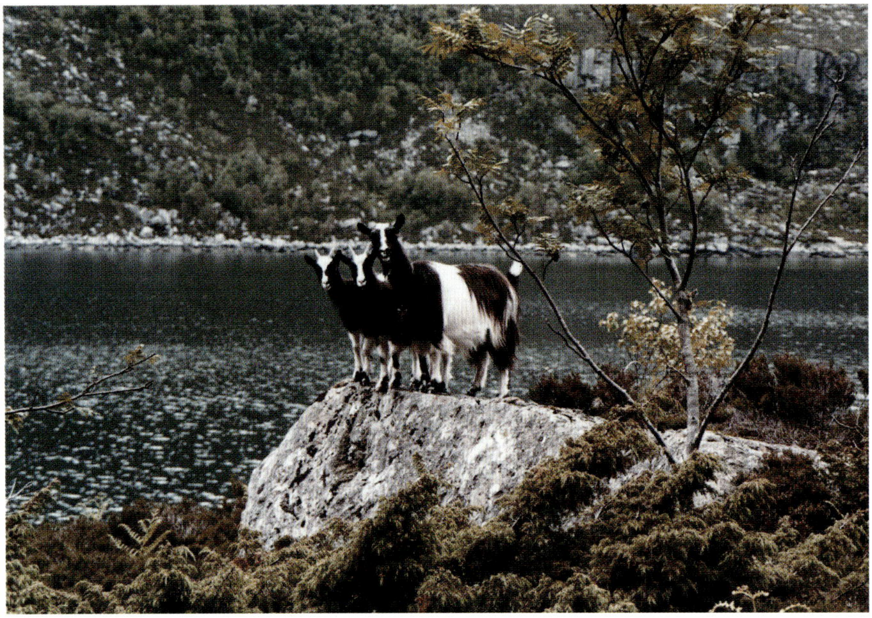

FIGURE 239. Rationalization of traditional means of farming has also had an effect on a number of rock art sites. Many sites are located in cultural landscapes in which old grazing land and hay fields are increasingly turning into woodlands and undergrowth. In order to prevent heather and other vegetation from engulfing the rock carvings, the best allies of cultural preservation workers are grazing animals, such as these curious goats in Vingen!
GM

even being touched by human hands (Thorseth *et al.* 2001). We need to assess limits to the number of visitors a site can withstand per day, per week or per year, in order to avoid excessive deterioration. Is it wise to remove lichens from rock surfaces, or will it be more damaging to the rock when lichens continually re-establish themselves on surfaces that have been cleaned? How much turf around a rock art panel can be removed without interfering with or destroying archaeological remains in the subsoil, traces that could perhaps reveal when and how the rock carvings were used?

A cultural monument also exists within a context, whether it is located in an ancient cultural landscape, near a river or seashore, or in an urban area. The surrounding environment also has limits of endurance. How many alterations can the local environment withstand without being spoilt? How many footpaths, fences, information signs and commercial booths can be constructed around a rock art site without overshadowing the magical charm of the site and without losing its value as a monument to be experienced? How many visitors can the rock surface and the vegetation withstand? How can tourism be harmonized with grazing animals needed to maintain the cultural landscape around the rock art?

The images and the public

Tourism is a growth industry in many local areas, and there is widespread interest in developing cultural monuments in order to attract tourists. Rock art is a particularly inviting tourist attraction. The images carved in stone are spectacular; they stimulate the imagination and aesthetic sense of visitors. For this reason, the tourist industry and local authorities wish to make rock art available both to individual visitors and tourist groups. The problem is that rock art is one of our most vulnerable cultural treasures. In terms of conservation, rock images are poorly suited to tourism on a grand scale. In the eyes of the tourism industry, they will be worn out and consumed in just a short time. In all tourist-oriented undertakings, the user is normally the centre of attention, but where rock art is concerned, we must be prepared to give priority to other factors. If the surface of a burial mound is worn down a couple of centimetres, the mound will still look the same, and the monumental shape will be maintained at the same time. If a rock carving site is exposed to similar wear and tear, for example from visitor traffic, fragile parts of the rock may be broken or flaked off, and the entire cultural monument – the images – may be lost. In order to preserve rock art for the long term, conservation of the images and the natural surroundings must be the guiding principle. This principle is in line with the Norwegian Cultural Heritage Act, where the primary concept prescribes an overall protection of cultural monuments (http://www.regjeringen.no/en/doc/Laws/Acts/Cultural-Heritage-Act.html). If we wish to preserve the rock art, conservationists of cultural monuments must be willing to make decisions that will be unpopular amongst tourists, local residents and others wishing to take advantage of the potential that the rock art represents. Among other things, this means that only certain selected sites will be made available to the public, visitors will be limited and regulated, and certain panels will be covered over lengthy periods of time. We are not used to thinking along these lines in Norway. But if we are to preserve the rock art, these kinds of measures – regardless of how drastic they may seem – may be the only viable alternative.

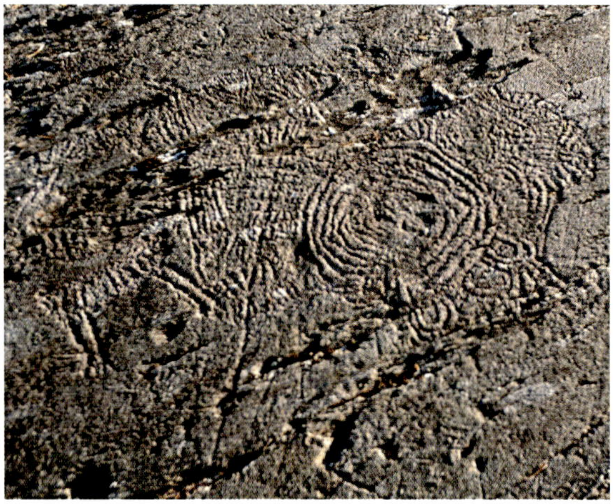

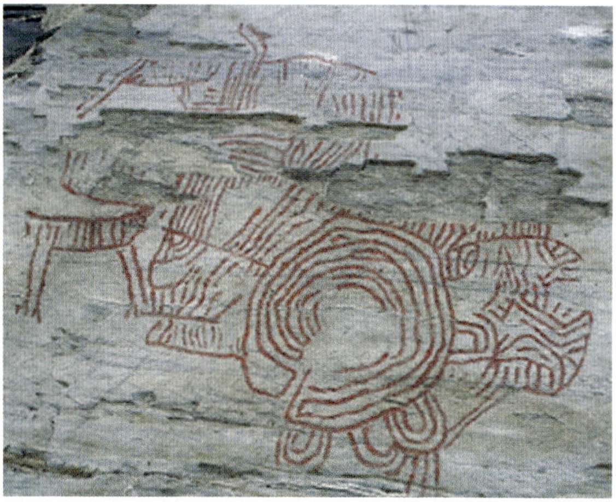

Highlighting rock art with paint?

In Scandinavia there is a long tradition of highlighting the lines of carved images with paint, despite the fact that we do not know if the images were highlighted at the time they were created (Lødøen *et al.* 1997). Normally a reddish-brown colour is used, similar to the colour of many of the original rock art paintings. The highlighting is done for the benefit of the public, partly so that indistinct figures are easier to see and photograph, and partly to prevent people from "freshening up" the figures by chalking, scratching or painting them on their own. Non-Scandinavian researchers strongly disapprove of this practice, and many characterise highlighting – even when done by professionals – as deliberate vandalism. In recent years, there has also been increased opposition to highlighting in Norway itself. Highlighting cultural monuments is undoubtedly a drastic measure. It has also been proved that certain types of paint have damaged the rock carvings, and frequently paint has been applied so thickly that the peckmarks in the grooves of the images have been hidden from view. There are also examples of figures being highlighted incorrectly. Furthermore, highlighting diminishes the experience of observing the carved figures. When a rock art image is painted, it becomes as if it were "frozen" on the rock surface, meaning that the public is deprived of the magical experience of seeing how the rock images emerge and disappear under changing light conditions. When rock carvings are highlighted, we are left with only one interpretation, or one person's perception of how the figures appear. Today we are of the opinion that highlighting with paint should only be a final recourse to be used when rock art images open to the public are so indistinct that the viewers would have extreme difficulty making them out.

FIGURES 240–241. In recent years it has been discussed whether rock art should be highlighted with red paint in order to enhance its visibility. Applying paint to the grooves of the rock art images is a drastic measure that can result, at worst, in damage to the figures if the wrong paint is used. It is also a drastic measure in terms of the viewer's experience of the rock art. In the photo above, we see how an untouched group of figures with a labyrinth as its central motif stands out clearly in slanted sunlight. In the photo below the same group of figures is shown after they were highlighted in paint. Some of the magic and excitement in these engraved figures seems to be lost when they become trapped in the lines of red paint.

GM AND RU

Irreplaceable cultural heritage

In the chapters of this book we have attempted to show that rock art – images in stone – provide us with a glimpse of another reality. We are given an idea of the way people thought, felt and believed thousands of years ago, rather than merely what they ate, how they lived and how they buried their dead. This is a reality we can never fully fathom. Nonetheless, the images are enriching and provide us with a better understanding of what it means to be human. The experience of seeing rock art must not be reserved for the privileged few. In principle it should be made available to everyone, both for the inhabitants of Norway and visitors from other countries. However, it must be made available in a way that best preserves the images and the information potential they represent. When making rock art accessible to the public, the guiding principle must be the conservation of the images themselves and their surrounding environment. Only then can we hope that our generation will not be the last to experience the rock art images in the places where they were carved, polished or painted thousands of years before our own era.

Key to Caption Credits

Initials underneath photo and illustrations refer to the following individuals/institutions:

AI	Arkikon
AK	Arve Kjersheim
AMS	Arkeologisk museum i Stavanger
AS	Arvid Sveen
BHH	Bjørn Hebba Helberg
BM	Bergen Museum
CO	Camilla Olsson
EB	Erik Bendixen
EE	Eyvind Engelstad
EH	Ellinor Hoff
EM	Egil Mikkelsen
EPF	Eva and Per Fett
GG	Gutorm Gjessing
GH	Gustaf Hallström
GM	Gro Mandt
HEL	Harald Egenes Lund
HH	Heidi Handeland
JB	Johs. Bøe
JMG	Jan Magne Gjerde
KAB	Knut Andreas Bergsvik
KH	Knut Helskog
KM	Kristen Michelsen
KS	Kalle Sognnes
MW	Marit Wold
NTNUV	NTNU Vitenskapsmuseet
OMD	Olav Magnar Dikkaneen
PS	Povl Simonsen
RU	Ragnar Utne
SES	Svein Erik Ski
SI	Sonja Innselset
SP	Sunnmørsposten
SS	Svein Skare
TEL	Trond Eilif Linge
TH	Tom Heibreen
TL	Trond Lødøen
TM	Tromsø Museum
TN	Terje Nordsted
TS	Tore Slinning
ØV	Ørnulf Vorren

Bibliography

Aaland, Jacob (1909) *Nordfjord fraa gamle dagar til no. (Del 2) Dei einskilde bygdene*. Nordfjordeidet. Brødrene Totland.

Almgren, O. (1927) Hällristningar och kultbruk. Bidrag till belysning av de nordiska bronsåldersristningarnas innebörd. *Kungl. vitterhets historie och antikvitets akademiens handlingar* 35, 1926–1927. Stockholm.

Askvik, H. (1983) Petrography of the Mjeltehaugen slabs. *Norwegian Archaeological Review* 16:1, 33. Oslo.

Bäckman, L. (1975) Sájva. Föreställningar om hjälp- och skyddsväsen i häliga fjäll bland samerna. Acta Universitatis Stochholmiensis. *Stockholm studies in comparative religion* 13.

Bäckman, L. and Å. Hultkrantz (1977) *Studies in Lapp shamanism*. Stockhom studies in comparative religion. Stockholm.

Bakka, E. (1963) Forntida i Odda, Ullensvang og Kinsarvik. In Kolltveit, O. (ed.) *Odda, Ullensvang og Kinsarvik i gamal og ny tid*. Bygdesoga 1, 1:47–205. Bergen.

Bakka, E. (1973) Om alderen på veideristningane. *Viking* 37, 151–187. Oslo.

Bakka, E. (1979) On Shoreline Dating of Arctic Rock Carvings in Vingen, Western Norway. *Norwegian Archaeological Review* 12:2, 115–122.

Bakka, E. (1987) Bronsealderristningane på Bogge i Romsdal. *Guneria* 57. Trondheim.

Barnes, F. A. (1982) *Canyon County. Prehistoric Rock Art*. Wasatch Publishers, Inc. Salt Lake City.

Barrett, J. C. (1999) Chronologies of landscape. In Ucho, P. and R. Layton (eds) *The archaeology and anthropology of landscape*. Routledge.

Baudou, E. (2004) *Den nordiska arkeologien – historia och tolkningar*. Kungliga Vitterhets Historie och Antikvitets Akademien. Stockholm.

Beitrusten, G. (1983) Valdres. Daler, fjell og fjordbygder i Sør-Norge, 65–92. *Norge vårt land*. Gyldendal Norsk Forlag AS. Oslo.

Bendixen, B. E. (1899) Fornlevninger i Søndhordland. *Foreningen til norske Fortidsmindesmerkers Bevaring*. Aarsberetning for 1899. Kristiania.

Berglund. B. (1993) Nyfunne hulemalerier på kysten av Sør-Helgeland. *Spor* 2, 36–37. Trondheim.

Berg, B. (2003) *Bergkunst på Amtmannsnes II – Spor etter sjamanisme*. Unpublished thesis in archaeology. University of Tromsø.

Bergsvik, K. A. (1999a) Steinalderundersøkelsene ved Skatestraumen, Sogn og Fjordane. *Arkeologiske skrifter fra Universitetet i Bergen* 10, 1–26.

Bergsvik, K. A (1999b) A new reference-system for classification of lithic raw materials. A case-study from Skatestraumen, Western Norway. In Boaz, J. (ed.) *The Mesolithic of Middle Scandinavia*, 283–298. Universitetets Oldsaksamlings skrifter, Ny rekke.

Bergsvik, K. A. (2002) Arkeologiske undersøkelser ved Skatestraumen Bind 1 Med bidrag av Kristin Senneset og Anne Karin Hufthammer, Kari Loe Hjelle og Einar Alsaker. *Arkeologiske avhandlinger og rapporter fra Universitetet i Bergen*.

Bing, K. (1912) Helleristningsfund ved gaarden Vingen i Rugsund, Ytre Nordfjord. *Oldtiden* 2, 25–39.

Bjerck, H. B. (1995) Malte menneskebilder i «Helvete». Betraktninger om en nyoppdaget hulemaling på Trenyken, Røst, Nordland. *Universitetets Oldsaksamlings Årbok* 1993/1994, 121–150.

Bjerck, H. B. (2008) Norwegian Mesolithic Trends: A Review. In Bailey, G. and P. Spilkins (eds). *Mesolithic Europe*. Cambridge University Press. Cambridge.

Bloch, M. and J. Parry (1982) *Death and the regeneration of life*. Cambridge University. Cambridge.

Bøe, J. (1932) Felszeichnungen im westlichen Norwegen I. Vingen und Hennøya. *Bergens Museums Skrifter* 15. Bergen.

Bøe, J. (1942) Fra ledens fortid – et forsøk. *Viking* 6, 175–194. Oslo.

Bøe, J. (1944) Høgfjellsristninger i Luster i Sogn. *Viking* 8, 169–181. Oslo.

Bøe, J. (1953) *Innberetning. Flaate, Grindheim s, Etne p., Hordaland gnr 65, bnr 1. Eire; Knut Flaate. Helleristninger*. Report Topographical files, University Museum Bergen.

Bolin, H. (1998) Activating monuments. The ritual use

of cairns in Bronze Age Norrland. *Current Swedish Archaeology* 6, 7–16.

Bradley, R. (1993) *Altering the Earth*. Society of Antiquries of Scotland Monograph Series 8. Edinburgh.

Bradley, R. (2000) *An archaeology of natual places*. Routledge. London.

Bradley, R., A. Jones, L. N. Myhre and H. Sackett (2002) Sailing through stone: carved ships and the rock face at Revheim, Southwest Norway. *Norwegian Archaeological Review* 35:2, 109–118.

Brøgger, A. W. (1925) *Det norske folk i oldtiden*. Aschehoug and Co. Oslo.

Brøndsted, Johannes (1961) *Vikingene*. Gyldendal Norsk Forlag. Oslo.

Brunius, C. G. (1868) *Försök till forklaringar över häll-ristningar*. Lund.

Carpelan, C. (1975) Älg och björnhovudföremål från Europas nordliga delar. *Finskt Museum* 82. Finska Fornminnesforeningen. Helsingfors.

Chippendale, C. and P. S. C. Tacon (1998) The many ways of dating Arnhem Land rock-art, north Australia. In Chippendale, C. and P. S. C. Tacon (eds) *The Archaeology of Rock-art*, 90–111. Cambridge University Press. Cambridge.

Christie, W. F. K. (1837) Om Helle-Ristninger og andre Indhugninger i Klipper, især i Bergens Stift. *Urda* 1:91–94. Bergen.

Christie, W. F. K. (1847) *Indberetning til Directionen for Det Bergenske Museum*. Universitets-bibliotekets manuscriptsamling nr. 227.

Christie, W. F. K. and Hagerup C. (1847) *Kontrakt om retten til å grave i Mjeltehaugen. Signert på Gidskøegjerdet den 19*. August 1847. Universitets-biblioteket i Bergens manuskripsamling nr. 193.

Clottes, J. and D. Lewis-Williams (1998) *The shamans of prehistory. Trance and magic in the painted caves*. New York.

Coles, J. (2003) And on they went ... Processions in Scandinavian Bronze Age rock carvings. *Acta Archaeologica* 74, 211–250.

Crumlin-Pedersen, O. and A. Trakadas (ed.) (2003) *Hjortspring. A Pre-Roman Iron-Age Warship in Context. Ships and boats of the north*. Volume 5.

Dahl, R. (1993) Skjomen. In Eriksen, M. G. and P. Holmlund (eds) *Skjomen och Riksgränsfjällen*. Til fjällklubbens årsbok 63–64. Stockholm.

Dommasnes, L. H. (1997) *Tradisjon og handling i førkristen gravskikk1. Undersøkelser på et gravfelt på Vereide i Gloppen, Sogn og Fjordane*. Arkekologiske rapporter 21. Bergen.

Dommasnes, L. H. (2001) *Tradisjon og handling i vestnorsk gravskikk 2. Fra Vereide til vikingtid*. Arkeologiske avhandlinger og rapporter ved Universitetet i Bergen. Bergen.

Dommasnes, L. H. (2003) Minne fra et kulturmøte?: ristninger og runer fra Kårstad i Styn. *Årbok for Bergen Museum*, 65–69.

Dons, J. A. (1975) Telemarks geologi – fylket som har alt. In Johan E. Holand (ed.) *Bygd og by i Norgen Telemark*, 34–70. Gyldendal Norsk Forlag. Oslo.

Dyrvik, S. (1968) Mellomalderen 1000–1500. In Dyrvik, S. (ed.) *Etne-soga. Frå dei eldste tider til 1660*, 257–327. Etne bygdeboknemd.

Eliade, M. (1961) *Images and symbols*. London.

Engelstad, E. S. (1925) Arkeologiske undersøkelser i Troms og Finnmark sommeren 1925. *Tromsø Museums Årshefter* 1.

Engelstad, E. S. (1934) *Østnorske ristninger og malinger av den arktiske gruppe*. Instituttet for sammenlignende kulturforskning. Oslo.

Engelstad, E. (2001) Desire and body maps: all the women are pregnant, all the men are virile, but ... In Helskog, K. (ed.) *Theoretical Perspectives in Rock Art Research*, 263–289. Novus forlag. Oslo.

Fett, E. N. (1968) Førhistorien i Etne. In Dyrvik, S. (ed.) *Etne-soga. Frå dei eldste tider til 1660*, 124–256. Etne bygdeboknemd.

Fett, E. N. and P. Fett. (1941) Sydvestnorske helleristninger. Rogaland og Lista. Stavanger.

Fett, E. N. and P. Fett (1979) Relations West Norway – Western Europe. Documented in Petroglyphs. *Norwegian Archaeological Review*, 12:2, 65–92.

Fett, P. (1950) *Borgund Prestegjeld*. Førhistoriske minne på Sunnmøre. Historisk museum, University of Bergen.

Fett, P. (1960) *Innvik prestegjeld*. Førhistoriske minne i Fjordane. Historisk museum, University of Bergen.

Fett, P. (1961) *Stryn prestegjeld*. Førhistoriske minne i Fjordane. Historisk museum, Universiy of Bergen.

Fillip, J. (1956) Keltove ve stredni Europe. *Monumenta archaeologica* 5. Praha.

Flood, J. (1990) *The Riches of Ancient Australia. A Journey into Prehistory*. University of Queensland Press. Queensland.

Frazer, J. G. (1967 [1922]) *The Golden Bough. A Study of Magic and Religion*. MacMillan and Co. London.

Fredell, Å. (2003) Bildbroar. Figurativ bildkommunikation av ideologi och kosmologi under sydskandinavisk bronsålder och förromersk järnålder. Gotarc Serie B. *Gothenburg Archaeological Thesis* 25. Göteborg.

Fuglestvedt, I. (1999) Adoranten, voltigeuren og andre dødelige. In Fuglestvedt, I., T. Gansum and A. Opedal (eds), Et hus med mange rom. Vennebok til Bjørn Myhre på 60–årsdagen, 83–102. *AmS-Rapport 11A*. Stavanger.

Garborg, A. (1951 [1892]) *Fred*. Oslo.

Gihle, P. (1975) Helleristning på Glemmestadstranda. *Totn* (tidsskrift for Toten historielag) 5:331–2. Gjøvik.

Gjessing, G. (1931) The Skjomen Carving in Northern Norway. *Acta Archaeologica*. København.

Gjessing, G. (1932) *Arktiske helleristninger i Nord-Norge*. Instituttet for sammenlignende kulturforskning. Oslo.

Gjessing, G. (1936) *Nordenfjeldske ristninger og malinger av den arktiske gruppe*. Instituttet for sammenlignende kulturforskning. Oslo.

Gjessing, G. (1937) Veideristningen på Stein i Ringsaker (Hedmark). *Universitetets Oldsaksamling Årbok* 1935–1936, 52–68. Oslo.

Gjessing, G. (1938) Nyopdagede veideristninger i Nord-Norge. *Viking* 1938, 137–144.

Gjessing, G. (1939) *Østfolds jordbruksristninger*. Idd, Berg og delvis Skjeberg. Instituttet for sammenlignende kulturforskning. Serie B. Skrifter 37. Oslo.

Gjessing, G. (1944) Veideristningen ved Drotten i Fåberg. *Universitetets Oldsaksamlings Årbok 1941–1942*, 103–108. Oslo

Goldhahn, J. (1999) Sagaholm – hällristningar och gravritual. *Studia Archaeological Universitatis* Umensis 11. Umeå.

Goldhahn, J. (2004) *Från Sagaholm till Bredarör – hällbildstudier 2000–2004*. Göteborgs Universitet. Gotarc Serie C. Arkeologiska Skrifter 62. Intellecta DocSys, Västra Frölunda.

Grimes, A. (1894) *Skisse av lurfunnet fra Revheim, Rogaland*. Topographical archive, Archaeological Museum of Stavanger.

Grønvik, O. (1996) *Fra Vimose til Ødemotland. Nye studier over runeinnskrifter fra førkristen tid i Norden*. Universitetsforlaget. Oslo.

Groseth, L. (2001) Å finne sted. Økonomiske og rituelle landskap i Telemark i sen-neolitikun og bronsealder. *Varia* 53. Universitetets kulturhistoriske museer. Oldsaksamlingen. Oslo.

Gurina, N. N. (1956) *Oleneostrovski Mogilnik*. Materialy i Issledovaniya po Arkheologii SSSR 47. Nauka. Moscow.

Haaland, A. (1996) Bergen Museums historie 1825–1845. *Universitetet i Bergens historie* 1, 10–186.

Hagen, A. (1969) Studier i vestnorsk bergkunst. Ausevik i Flora. *Årbok for Universitetet i Bergen*. Humanistisk serie 3.

Hagen, A. (1983) *Norges oldtid*. 3. Utg. Cappelen. Oslo.

Hagen, A. (1990) *Helleristningar i Noreg*. Det Norske Samlaget. Oslo.

Hagen, A. (1997) *Gåten om Kong Raknes grav*. Hovedtrekk i norsk arkeologi. J. W. Cappelens forlag. Oslo.

Hallström, G. (1938) *Monumental Art of Northern Europe From the Stone Age. I. The Norwegian Localities*. Stockholm.

Hansen, L. J. and B. Olsen (2004) *Samenes historie. Fram til 1750*. Cappelen Akademisk forlag. Oslo.

Hauglid, M. A., B. Helberg and A. Hesjedal (1991) Strekfigurene i Kollhellaren på Moskeneøya, Vest-Lofoten. *Tromura*, Kulturhistorie 19, 157–169. Tromsø.

Haukalid, S. (1999) *Menneskenes bilde*. En studie av 10 veideristningslokaliteter i Øst-Norge. Unpublished MA thesis, University of Oslo.

Hauptman Wahlgren, K. (2002) Bilder av betydelse. Hällristningar *Stockholm Studies in Archaeology* 23. och bronsålderslandskap i nordöstra Östergötland. Bricoleur Press.

Hedengran, I. (1991) Att synliggöra människor. Figurer eller gestalter? Kring hällristningsforskingens förutsätningar. *K. A. N. Kvinner i arkeologi i Norge*, 12, 104–126.

Hedengran, I. (1993) Att synliggöra människor, figurer eller gestalter? Kring hällristningsforskingens förutsätningar. In Forsberg, L. and T. B. Larsson (eds) *Ekonomi och näringsformer i nordisk bronsålder*, 177–193. Rapport från det 6: e nordiska bronsåldersymposiet, Nämforsen 1990. Studia Archaeologica Universitatis Umensis 3. Umeå.

Helander, J. (1906) Den svenske solguden och den svenske Tyr. *Ord och Bild*, 177–194. Stockholm.

Helskog, K. (1988) *Helleristningene i Alta. Spor etter ritualer og dagligliv i Finnmarks forhistorie*. Alta.

Helskog, K. (1999) The Shore Connection. Cognitive Landscape and Communication with Rock Carvings in Northernmost Europe. *Norwegian Archaeological Review*, 32:73–94.

Helskog, K. (2000) Changing Rock Carvings – Changing Societies? A Case from Arctic Norway. *Adoranten*. Scandinavian Society for Prehistoric Art, Tanum Hällristningsmuseum, Underlös.

Hesjedal, A. (1990) *Helleristninger som tegn og tekst. En analyse av veideristningene i Nordland og Troms*. Unpublished MA thesis, University of Tromsø.

Hesjedal, A., C. Damm, B. Olsen and I. Storli (1996) Arkeologi på Slettnes: dokumentasjon av 11.000 års bosetning. *Tromsø Museums skrifter.*

Hodne, Ø. (1999) *Norsk folketro*. Oslo.

Holmberg, A. E. (1848) *Skandinaviens hällristningar.* Forläggaren P. G. Berg. Stockholm.

Holmboe, J. (1916) En «arktisk helleristning», omtalt av Martin Vahl. *Naturen.*

Hougen, B. (1947) *Fra seter til gård.* J. Chr. Gundersens Boktrykkeri. Oslo.

Høst, G. (1976) *Runer.* Våre eldste norske runeinnskrifter. Aschehoug. Oslo.

Hygen, A.-S. and L. Bengtsson (1999) *Helleristninger i grensebygd. Bohuslän og Østfold.* Warne Förlag. Göteborg.

Indrelid, S. (1994) Fangstfolk og bønder i fjellet. Bidrag til Hardangeviddas førhistorie 8500–2500 år før nåtid. *Universitetets Oldsaksamlings Skrifter. Ny rekke* 17. Oslo.

Ingvaldsen, L. M. (1996) *Kirkene i søndre Sunnhordland i tidlig-og høymellomalder. Hvor ble kirkene bygget, hvorfor ble de bygget her og av hvem?* Unpublished MA thesis, University of Bergen.

Innselset, S. (1995) Skålgropa – kvinnesymbolet i bergkunsten. *K. A. N. Kvinner i arkeologi i Norge* 19–20, 73–82.

Innselset, S. M. (1996) *Skålgropristningar. Ein analyse av helleristningane i Valdres – distribusjon, kontekst og tid.* Unpublished MA thesis, University of Bergen

Innselset, S. M. (2005) Skålgropene i Valdres og indre Sogn – ikkje berre "stølsristningar"? In Bergsvik, K. A. and A. E. jr. (eds) *Fra funn til samfunn. Jernalderstudier tilegnet Bergljot Solberg på 70–årsdagen,* 67–89. UBAS. Universitetet i Bergen Arkeologiske Skrifter. Nordisk 1.

Johansen, E. (1944) Nyoppdagete helleristniger ved Begby i Borge (Østfold). *Viking* 8, 99–120.

Johansen, E. (1948) Nyoppdagete helleristninger i Østfold. *Viking* 12, 63–88.

Johansen, E. (1953) *Skjebergs forhistorie. I: Bakke, Harald.* Skjeberg bygdebok. Del 1, 77–188. Skjeberg kommune. Halden.

Johansen, E. (1976) Sarpsborg før 1839. *Bygdebok for Sarpsborg,* Sarpsborg kommune. Sarpsborg

Johansen, E. (1978) Den lengste historien. In Evensberge, E. and Mykland, R. (eds) *Bygd og By i Norge, Østfold,* Gyldendal Norsk Forlag. Oslo.

Johansen, Ø. (1979) New results in the investigation of the Bronze Age rock carvings. *Norwegian Archaeological Review,* 12:2, 108–114.

Johansen, Ø. (1986) Tidlig metallkultur i Agder. *Universitetets Oldsaksamlings Skrifter. Ny rekke.* 8.

Johansen, Ø. (1993) Norske depotfunn fra bronsealder. *Universitetets oldsaksamlings skrifter. Ny rekke,* 15.

Johansen, Ø. K. (2000) *Bronse og makt.* Andresen and Butenschøn AS. Oslo.

Kahl, H. and K. Kristiansen. (1976) Bronsealderskibe. *Hikuin.* Moesgård.

Kaul, F. (1998) Ships on bronzes. A study in Bronze Age religion and iconography. *Publications from the National Museum Studies in Archaeology and History* 3:1–2. København.

Kaul, F. (2004) *Bronzealderens religion. Studier af den nordiske bronzealderens ikonografi.* Det kongelige nordiske oldskriftselskab. København.

Kjeldstadli, K, (1997) Hva er symboler? En introduksjon. *Dugnad* 3, 3–25.

Klindt-Jensen, O. (1950) *Foreign Influences in Denmark's Early Iron Age.* København.

Kloster, R. (1957) Borgund kirke og Giske kapell. In *Borgund og Giske bygdeboknemnd* (ed.) Borgund og Giske 1:353–420. Bergen.

Knirk, J. (2000) Kårstad. § 3: *Runologisches. Reallexikon der Germanischen Altertumskunde.* Bd. 16, 324. Walter de Gruyer. Berlin/New York.

Kolltveit, O. (1954) *Jondal i gamal og ny tid.* Jondal bygdeboknemnd. Bergen.

Kostveit, Ø. (1999) *Kulturhistorisk vegbok for Vinje, Rauland, Haukeli.* Det Norske Samlaget. Oslo.

Kostveit, Å. Ø. (2004) *Kors i kake, skurditre.* Landbruksforlaget. Oslo.

Krause, W. (1966) *Die Runeninnschriften im Älteren Futhark.* Mit Beiträge von Herbert Jahnkuhn. Göttingen.

Kvamme, S. (1994) Eigedomstilhøve på Sunnmøre. Giskegods og anna gods. In Ugelvik Larsen, S. and J. Sulebust (eds) *Sunnmøres eldste historie.* I balansepunktet, 267–275. Ålesund.

Kyvik, G. (2001) *Begrepet Livsverden – Fenomenologiske perspektiver. Borum Eshøj og den kosmologiske død.* Unpublished MA thesis, University of Bergen.

Kyvik, G. (2002) Hjemmeverden, fremmedverden og arkeologisk refleksivitet. Med kommentarer av H. Karlsson. In Fuglestvedt and B. Solli. *Primitive tider.* 5. årgang: 127–160. Oslo.

de Lange, E. (1912) Ornerte heller i norske bronsealdergraver. *Bergens Museums Årbok* 1912, 2, 3–36. Bergen.

de Lange, E. (1920) Et nytt funn fra Vestlandets yngste bronsealder. *Bergens Museums Årbok* 1919–20, 1–14.

Lahelma, A. (2008) A Touch of Red. Archaeological

and Ethnograpic Approaches to Interpreting Finnish Rock Paintings. *Iskos* 15. The Finnish Antiquarian Society. Helsinki.

Larsen, A. J. and E. Reimers (1994) De nyoppdagede mellomaldermurene på Giske. Har man funnet hovedsetet til Giskeætta? In Ugelvik Larsen, S. and J. Sulebust (eds) *Sunnmøres eldste historie.* I balansepunktet, 281–291. Ålesund.

Larsen, C. (1996) *Haugene fra eldre bronsealder på Jæren – en religionshistorisk analyse.* Unpublished MA thesis in archaeology, University of Bergen.

Larsson, T. B. (1997) Materiell kultur och religiösa symboler. Mesopotamien, Anatolien och Skandinavien under det andra førkristna årtusendet. *Arkeologiska studiar vid Umeå universitet* 4. Umeå

Lauritzen, S. E., H. Nese, *et al.* (1996) "Interstadial/interglacial fauna from Norcemgrotta, Kjøpsvik, north Norway." *Karst Waters Institute Special Publication* 2:89–92.

Leroi Gourhan, A. (1982) *The Dawn of European* Art. Cambridge.

Lewis-Williams, D. (1981) *Believing and seeing: Symbolic Meanings in Southern San Rock Paintings.* Academic Press. London.

Lewis-Williams, D. (2004) *The Mind in the Cave. Consciousness and the Origins of Art.* Thames and Hudson. London

Lewis-Williams, J. D. and T. Dowson (1990) Through the veil: San rock paintings and the rock face. *South African Archaeological Bulletin* 45, 5–16

Lindgren, B. (2002) Hällmålningar – ett uttryck för materiella och immaterialla dimensioner. In Klang, L., B. Lindgren and P. H. Ramqvist (eds) *Regional Arkeologi* 2 – Hällbildar and Hällbildarnas rum. Örnsköldsvik.

Lindqvist (1994) *Fångstfolkets bilder. En studie av de nordfennoskandinaviska kustknutna jäger-hällristningarna.* Theses and papers in archaeology. N.S.A. 5. Stockholm.

Linge, T. E. (2007) Mjeltehaugen – fragment frå eit gravritual. *UBAS* – Universitetet i Bergen Arkeologiske skrifter. Hovedfag/master 3.

Lødøen, T. (2001) Interpretation of Stone Age ideology based on rock art, structures and artefacts in the Vingen area, Western Norway. In Helskog, K. (ed.) *Theoretical Perspectives in Rock Art Research.* Novus forlag. Oslo.

Lødøen, T. (2003) *Kulturminneregistreringer Tyin. Årsrapport Fase 1A – 2002.* Report Topographical files, University Museum Bergen.

Lødøen, T. (2003) Late Mesolithic Rock Art and Expressions of Ideology. In L. Larsson, H. Kindgren, D. Loeffler and A. Åkerlund (eds) *Mesolithic on the Move. Papers presented at the Sixth International Conference on the Mesolithic in Europe.* Stockholm 2000, 511–520. Oxbow Books. Oxford.

Lødøen, T. (2007) Exploring the Contemporary Context of Rock Art. *Adoranten*, 54–18.

Lødøen, T. (2009) Confronting important animals. In McCartan, S., P. Woodman, R. Schulting and G. Warren (eds), *Mesolithic Horizons*, 576–582. Oxbow Books. Oxford.

Lødøen, T. and G. Mandt (in prep.) *Vingen "...et naturens kolossalmusæum for helleristninger".*

Lødøen, T. K. (2000) Bergbildene på Berge i Strandebarm. *Hardanger* – Tidsskrift for Hardanger historielag. Utne.

Lødøen, T. K., G. Mandt and K. H. Riisøen (1997) Sikring av bergkunst: problemer – metoder – tiltak. *Bergkunstrapporter fra Universitetet i Bergen* 1. Arkeologisk institutt – Bergen Museum.

Lorange, A. (1879) Indberetning om arkæologiske Undersøgelser i 1878. Mjeltehaugen paa Gidske. Foreningen til norske Fortidsmindesmerkers Bevaring. *Aarsberetning* 1878–79.

Madsen, O. (1998) *Fra Tor til Kristus. Overgangen fra hedendom til kristendom, belyst utfra det arkeologiske materialet fra Etne i Sunnhordland.* Unpublished MA thesis, University of Bergen.

Magnus, B. (1978) De eldste tider i Gloppen og Breim. In *Soga om Gloppen og Breim*, 103–227. Sandane.

Malm, T. (1995) Excavating submerged Stone Age sites in Denmark – the Tybrind Vig example. In Fisher, A. (ed.) *Man and Sea in the Mesolithic. Coastal settlement above and below present sea level.* Oxbow Monograph 53. Oxford.

Malmer, Mats P. (1989) Bergkonstens mening och innehåll. I Bertilsson, U. (ed.) *Hällristningar och hällmålningar i Sverige*, 9–28. Stockholm.

Mandt, G. (1973) Kårstad-feltet. Kronologiske betraktninger omkring en nyundersøkelse. *Viking*, 103–126.

Mandt, G. (1975) Helleristninger gjennom 150 år. En funnhistorie i forskningshistorisk sammenheng. *Viking* 39, 61–93.

Mandt, G. (1983) Tradition and diffusion in West-Norwegian rock art. Mjeltehaugen revisited. *Norwegian Archaeological Review* 16:1, 14–33. Oslo.

Mandt, G. (1991) *Vestnorske ristninger i tid og rom. Kronologiske, korrologiske og kontekstuelle studier.*

Bd. 1–2. Unpublished PhD thesis, University of Bergen.

Mandt, G. (1998) Vingen revisited. A gendered perspective on 'Hunters' rock art. In Larsson, L. and B. Stjernquist (eds) *The Worldview of prehistoric man. KVHAA* Konferenser 40:201–224. Stockholm.

Mandt, G. (2000) Kårstad. §2: *Archäologisches. Reallexikon der Germanischen Altertumskunde*. Bd. 16, 323–324. Walter de Gruyer. Berlin/New York.

Mandt, G. (2001a) Women in disguise or male manipulation? Aspects of gender symbolism in rock art. In Helskog, K. (ed.), *Theoretical Perspectives in Rock Art Research*. Instituttet for sammenlignende kulturforskning. Serie B: Skrifter. Vol. CVI, 290–310. Novus forlag. Oslo.

Mandt, G. (2001b) Manipulasjon – Metafor – Kontekst. Om kjønnsperspektivet i bergkunsten. *Tidsperspektiv. Tidskrift för Samhällsanalys* 1–2, 22–39.

Mandt, G. (2006) *Kultsted gjennom generasjoner? Et eksempel fra Etne i Sunnhordland*. In Glørstad, H., B. Skar and D. Skre (eds) Historien i forhistorien. Festskrift til Einar Østmo på 60–års dagen. Kulturhistorisk museum. *Skrifter* 4, 329–336. Oslo.

Mandt, G. (2009) Streiftog i bergkunstforskningens virkningshistorie. In Brattli, Terje (ed.) *Vitark* 6.10.Nordiske bronsealdersymposium. Trondheim 5.-8. Okt. 2006, 48–63. Tapir akademisk forlag. Trondheim.

Mandt, G., K. Michelsen and K. H. Riisøen (1992) (eds) Conservation, Preservation and Presentation of Rock Art. *Arkeologiske skrifter* 6. Historisk museum. Universitetet i Bergen.

Mandt Larsen, G. (1972) Bergbilder i Hordaland. En undersøkelse av bildenes sammensetning, deres naturmiljø og kulturmiljø. *Årbok for Universitetet i Bergen. Humanistisk serie* 1970, 2.

Marstrander, S. (1950) Jylland – Lista. *Viking* 15, 63–85.

Marstrander, S. (1963) *Østfolds jordbruksristninger*. Skjeberg. Instituttet for sammenlignende kulturforskning. Universitetsforlaget. Oslo.

Marstrander, S. (1965) Fingalshulen i Gravvik, Nord-Trøndelag, *Viking* 29. Oslo.

Marstrander, S. (1978) The problem of European impulses in the Nordic area of agrarian rock art. In Marstrander, S. (ed.) *Acts of the international symposium of rock art*, 45–67. Universitetsforlaget. Oslo.

Martens, I. (1975) Fra veidemark til bondebygd. In Holand, Jn. E. (ed.) *Bygd og by i Norge, Telemark*, 94–119. Gyldendal Norsk Forlag. Oslo.

Mikkelsen, E. (1977) Østnorske veideristninger. Kronologi og øko-kulturelt miljø. *Viking* 40, 52–201. Oslo.

Mikkelsen, E. (1998) Et bidrag til datering av bronsealderens bergkunst i Østfold. In Østmo, E. (ed.) Fra Østfolds oldtid. Foredrag ved 25–årsjubileet for Universitetets arkeologiske stasjon Isegran. *Universitetets Oldsaksamlings Skrifter Ny rekke*. No 21.

Montelius, O. (1900) Solgudens yxa och Tors hammare. *Svenska fornminnesföreningens tidskrift* 10, 277–296. Stockholm.

Mulk, I.-M. and T. Bayliss-Smith (2001) Anthropomorphic Images at the Padjelanta Site, Northern Sweden. Rock Engravings in the Context of Sámi Myth and Ritual. *Current Swedish Archaeology*, 133–162.

Mulk, I.-M. and T. Bayliss-Smith (2006) Rock Art and Sami Sacred Geography in Badjelánnda, Laponia. Sweden. Sailing Boats, Anthropomorphs and Reindeer. *Archaeology and Environment* 22. Kungl. Skytteanska Samfundets Handlingar 58.

Müller, S. (1897) *Vor Oldtid. Danmarks forhistoriske arkeologi*. Det Nordiske Forlag. København.

Myhre, B. (1981) Sola og Madla førhistorisk tid. *AmS-Småtrykk* 10. Stavanger.

Nettum, R. N. (1975) Generasjonen fra 1890–årene. *Norsk litteraturhistorie* 4. Fra Hamsun til Falkberget. J. W. Cappelens forlag. Oslo.

Neumann, J. (1824) Bemærkninger paa en Reise i Sogn og Søndfjord 1823. *Budstikken* 5. Aargang. 67–73:529–84. Kristiania.

Nicolaysen, N. (1866) Norske Fornlevninger. *Foreningen til norske Fortidsmindesmerkers Bevaring*. Aarsberetning for 1866, 54–78. Kristiania.

Nordbladh, J. (1980) *Glyfer ock rum. Kring hällristningarna i Kville*. Akademisk avhandlilng. Utgiven vid Institutionen för arkeologi. Göteborgs universitet. Göteborg.

Nordén, A. (1932) Hällristningstraditionen och den urnordiska runskriften. *Arkeologiska studier tilägnade H. K. H. Kronprins Gustaf Adolf*. Stockholm.

Nordenborg Myhre, L. (1998) Historier fra en annen virkelighet. Fortellinger om bronsealderen ved Karmsundet. *AmS-Småtrykk* 46. Stavanger.

Nordenborg Myhre, L. (2004) Trialectic archaeology. Monument and space in Southwestern Norway 1700–500 BC. *AmS-Skrifter* 18. Stavanger.

Norsted, T. (2008) Maleriene i Fingalshula, Gravvik i Nærøy. *Niku* Rapport 23. Oslo.

Nylén, E. (1978) *Bildstenar*. Barry Press förlag. Visby.

Ohlmarks, Å. (1963) *Hällristningarnas* gudar. Stockholm.

Olsen, A. B. and S. Alsaker. (1984) Greenstone and Diabase Utilization in the Stone Age of Western Norway: Technological and Socio cultural Aspects of Axe and Adze Production and Distribution. *Norwegian Archaeological Review*, Vol. 17, No. 2. 71–103.

Olsen, B. (1994) *Bosetning og samfunn i Finnmarks forhistorie*. Universitetetsforlaget. Oslo.

Olsen, M. (1926) *Ættegard og helligdom. Norske stedsnavn sosialt og religionshistorisk belyst*. Instituttet for sammenlignende kulturforskning. Serie A. Oslo.

Olsen, M. and H. Shetelig (1930) Kårstad-ristningen. Runer og helleristninger. *Bergens Museums Årbok* 1929. Historisk-antikvarisk rekke 1.

Østmo, E. (1990) Helleristninger av sørskandinaviske former på det indre østlandet. Fylkene Buskerud, Akershus, Oslo, Oppland og Hedemark. *Universitetets Oldsaksamlings Skrifter. Ny rekke* 12.

Paasche, K. (2000) Nye helleristninger på Geithus: dokumentasjon, motiv og kunst: Knut Paasche. *Universitetets oldsaksamling. Årbok 1999*, 25–37

Petersen, T. (1914) Solsem paa Leka. En boplass fra arktisk stenalder. Foreløpig meddelelse. *Oldtiden* 4 24–41.

Pollan, B. (1993) *Samiske sjamaner. Religion og helbredelse.* Oslo.

Prescott, C. (1995) *From Stone Age to Iron Age. A Study from Sogn, western Norway*. BAR International Series 603. Oxford.

Prøsch-Danielsen, L. (1995) *Lista i støpeskjeen – landskapsendringer gjennom 15 000 år*. Fylkeskonservatoren i Vest-Agder i samarbeid med Direktoratet for naturforvaltning. Trondheim.

Prøsch-Danielsen, L. (2002) Jordbruksristningene i ulike landskapsrom. *Fra Haug ok Heidni* 1, 5–12.

Prøsch-Danielsen, L. and A. Simonsen (2000) The deforestation patterns and the establishment of the coastal heathland of southwestern Norway. *AmS Skrifter* 15. Museum of Archaeology in Stavanger. National research centre for paleostudies and conservation.

Qvigstad. J. (1927) *Lappiske eventyr og sagn*. I. Lappiske eventyr og sagn fra Varanger. Instituttet for sammenlignende kulturforskning. Oslo.

Ramstad, M. (2000) Veideristningene på Møre. Teori, kronologi og dateringsmetoder. *Viking* 43, s. 51–89. Oslo.

Randsborg, K. (1993) Kivik: Archaeology and iconography. *Acta Archaeologica* 67 (1). Munksgaard. København.

Reinton, L. (1955, 1957, 1961) *Seterbruket i Noreg*. Bd. 1–3. Instituttet for sammenlignende kulturforskning. Oslo.

Rekstad, J. (1910) Helleristninger i Herand i Hardanger. *Naturen*. Illustrert maanedsskrift for populær naturvidenskap. 34. årg., 2:48–50.

Riksantikvaren (1995) Tiltaksplan for sikring av bergkunst. Stencil, 45 c. Oslo.

Romundset, A. (2005) *Strandforskyving og isavsmelting i midtre Hardanger*. Unpublished MA thesis, University of Bergen.

Rydving, H. (1993) The end of Drum-Time. Religious Change among the Lule Saami, 1670s–1740s, *Acta Universitatis Upsaliensis*, Uppsala

Schaafsma, P. (1992) *Indian Rock Art of the Southwest.* School of American Research. Southwest Indian Arts Series. University of New Mexico Press. Albuquerque.

Schanche, A. (2000) *Graver i ur og berg. Samisk gravskikk og religion fra forhistorisk til nyere tid*. Davvi Girji OS. Karasjok.

Schelderup, H. K. (1958) *Filosofiens historie. Fra renaissancen til nutiden*. Gyldendal norsk forlag. Oslo.

Shetelig, H. (1927) *Ristninger og runeindskrift paa Kårstad, Utvik sogn, Innvik pgd., Norfjord*. Undersøkt av Shetelig 23. og 24. Oktober 1927, B 7975. Innberetning, Bergen Museum.

Shetelig, H. (1932) Funn og minner fra oldtiden. In Aaland, J. (ed.) Nordfjord. *Fraa gamle dagar til no*. Innvik-Stryn, 33–66. Sandane.

Simonsen, P. (1955) Helleristninger ved Tromsø. *Ottar*. Populære småskrifter fra Tromsø Museum 5. Tromsø.

Simonsen, P. (1958) *Arktiske helleristninger i Nord-Norge II*. Institutt for sammenlignende kulturforskning; B 49. Oslo.

Simonsen, P. (1969) *Ottar*. Populære småskrifter fra Tromsø Museum 61. Tromsø.

Simonsen, P. (1970) *Fortidsminner nord for polarsirkelen*. Tromsø.

Sjöborg, N. H. (1822) *Samlingar för Nordens fornälskare*. 1. Stockholm.

Sjöborg, N. H. (1830) *Samlingar för Nordens fornälskare*. 3. Stockholm.

Skjelsvik, E. and E. Straume (1957) Austrheimsteinen i Nordfjord. Et nytt bidrag til dateringen *Universitetet i Bergen Årbok. Historisk-antikvarisk rekke* 1, 1–21.

Skjølsvold, A. (1961) "Solalteret" på Revheim i Madla. *Frå Haug ok Heidni*. Tidsskrift for Rogalands arkeologiske forening 1, 37–40.

Skrede, M. A. (2002) *Utmark og gard. Nærstudie av tufteområde i Friksdalen i Leikanger, Sogn og Fjordane.* Upublished MA thesis in archaeology, University of Bergen.

Slinning, T. (2002) *Bergmalingene i Telemark. Kultstedenes tidfesting og sosiale sammenheng.* Unpublished MA thesis, University of Bergen.

Slomann, W. (1971) Gravfeltet omkring Einangsteinen i Slidreåsen, Valdres. *Viking* 35, 11–88.

Smith, C. (1993) The negotiation of gender through Western Desert Art. In De Cros, H. and L. Smith (eds) Women in Archaeology. A Feminist Critique, 161–172. *Occasional Papers in Prehistory* 23. Department of Prehistory, Research School of Pacific Studies. The Australian National University. Canberra, Australia.

Søborg, H. C. (2006) Mannen i mitt liv og mennes-kefigurene i Alta. In Barndon, R., S. M. Innselset, K. K. Kristoffersen and T. K. Lødøen (eds) Samfunn, symboler og identitet – Festskrift til Gro Mandt på 70–års dagen. *UBAS*. University of Bergen.

Sognnes, K. (1983) Prehistoric Cave Paintings in Norway. *Acta Archaeologica* 53 (1982):101–118. København.

Sognnes, K. (1999) *Det levende berget.* Trondheim.

Sognnes, K. (2001) *Prehistoric imagery and landscapes: rock art in Stjørdal, Trøndelag.* BAR international series. Oxford.

Solberg, B. (2000) *Jernalderen i Norge.* Ca. 500 f.Kr. –1030 e. Kr. Oslo.

Solheim Pedersen, E. (2008) (ed.) Solens reise. Rogaland i europeisk bronsealder. *AmS Småtrykk* 80.

Suhm, P. F. (1784) *Samlinger til den Danske Historie.* Andet Binds Tredie Hæfte. København. Gyldendals Forlag.

Sund, T. (1963) Vestlandet. In Norge bd. 1. *Land og folk*, 115–162. Oslo.

Svarstad, P. (1983) Sogn og Fjordane. Daler, fjell og fjordbygder i Sør-Norge, 233–262. *Norge vårt land.* Gyldendal Norsk Forlag AS. Oslo.

Sveen, A. (2003) *Mytisk landskap. Ved dansende skog og susende fjell.* Stamsund.

Syvertsen, K. I. J. (2002) Ristninger i gravcer – graver med ristninger. In Goldhahn (ed.) Bilder av bronsåler – ett seminarium om förhistorisk kommunikation. Rapport från ett seminarium på Vitlycke Museum 19.e–22.e oktober 2000, 151–184. *Acta Archaeologica Lundensia. Series in 8*, 37. Almquist and Wiksell International. Stockholm.

Syvertsen, K. I. J. (2003) *Ristninger i graver – graver med ristninger. Om ristningers mening i gravminner og gravritualer. En analyse av materiale fra Rogaland.* Unpublished MA thesis, University of Bergen.

Talle-Søvde, A. (1912) *På Bærplukking.* Report in topographical files, Kulturhistorisk samling, Bergen Museum.

Tansey, R. G. and Kleiner, F. S. (1996) *Gardner's Art Through the Ages.* New York.

Tham, P. (1794) *Göthiska Monumenter; Samlade och Beskrifne.* Langeska Tryckeriet. Stockholm.

Thorseth, I. H., T. K. Lødøen, T. Torsvik and G. Mandt (2001) (eds) Sikring av bergkunst. Forvitrings-faktorer og bevaringstiltak. Undersøkelse av hellerist-ningsfeltene Vingen, Bremanger kommune og Hjemmeluft, Alta kommune. *Bergkunstrapporter fra Universitetet i Bergen* 2. Arkeologisk institutt – Bergen Museum.

Tilley, C. (1994) *A phenomenology of landscape. Places, paths and monuments.* Oxford.

Tilley, C. (2008) *Body and image. Explorations in landscape Phenomenology* 2. Left Coast Press. California.

Trigger, B. (1989) *A history of archaeological thought.* Cambridge.

Turner, V. (1967) *The Forest of Symbols. Aspects of Ndembu Ritual.* Cornell University Press. Ithaca and London.

Turner, V. (1970) Betwixt and Between: the liminal period in Rites de Passage. In Hammel, E. A. and Simmons, W. S. (eds) *Man Makes Sense.* Little, Brown and Co. Boston.

Tveit, N. (1983) Sogn og Fjordane – kyststripa. In Evensberget, S. (ed.) *Norge vårt land. Tusen fjorder og tusen fjell*, 160–182. Gyldendal norsk forlag. Oslo.

Vanberg, D. (1988) *Vingen. Frå gardssamfunn til landskapsvernområde.* Bremanger kommune. Stryn. Fjordingen.

Varenius, B. (1994) Monument och samhällelig re-produktion. *Kulturmiljövård* 5, 56–63. Stockholm.

Vasskog, K., (2006) *Strandforskyvning på sørlige Bømlo.* Unpublished MA thesis, University of Bergen.

Vevatne, K. (1996) *Ristningar i Etne. Ein analyse av tid og rom.* Unpublished MA thesis, University of Bergen.

Vevatne, K. (1997) Helleristningane i Sunnhordland. *Arkeo.* Nytt fra Arkeologisk institutt, University of Bergen 1, 13–18.

Vinsrygg, S. (1982) Helleristningar og tidsrekning. *AmS-Skrifter* 9, 75–86.

Vinje, T. (1952) *Brev til Bergens Museum, datert 29.09.52.* Top.ark., Kulturhistorisk samling, Bergen Museum. Ref. Nr. 1201 1952, 29/9/1202, 040903.

Viste, S. (2003) *Bildene forteller – sjamanistiske elementer i helleristningene fra Vingen og Ausevik?* Unpublished MA thesis, University of Bergen.

Vogt, D. (1998) *Dekonstruksjon – rekonstruksjon. Helleristninger og landskap i Østfold.* Unpublished MA thesis, University of Tromsø.

Vogt, D. (2000) Helleristninger i Onsøy. Fredrikstad kommune, Østfold. *Varia* 50. Universitetets kulturhistoriske museer, Oldsaksamlingen. Oslo.

Vogt, D. (2006a) Helleristniger i Østfold og Bohuslän. En analyse av det økonomiske og politiske landskap. *Acta Humaniora.* Det humanistiske fakultet. Universitetet i Oslo. Unipub AS. Oslo.

Vogt, D. (2006b) *Helleristninger i Skien.* Designtrykk: Wera AS. Porsgrunn.

Vorren, Ø. and H. K. Eriksen. (1993) Samiske offerplasser i Varanger. *Tromsø Museums skrifter* 24. Stonglandseidet.

Vorren, Ø. (1998) Villreinfangst i Varanger frem til 1600–1700–årene. *Tromsø Museums skrifter* 28. Stonglandseidet.

Wahlgren, K. H. (2002) Bilder av betydelse. Hällristningar och bronsålderslandskap i nordöstra Östergötland. Bricoleur Press. *Stockholm studies in Archaeology.* 23.

Walderhaug, E. (2000) Some reflections on the implications of form, context and function in rock art studies. In Olausson, D. and H. Vandkilde (eds) Form, Function and Context. Material culture studies in Scandinavian archaeology. *Acta Archaeologica Lundensia. Series in 8*, 31, 59–70. Almquist and Wicksell International. Stockholm.

Willis, R. G. (1990) Signifying animals. Human Meaning in the Natural World. *One World Archaeology* 16. London.

Wold, M. (2002) *Bergkunst som levninger etter ritualer. Motivbaserte tolkningsforsøk av lokaliteter i Hordaland.* Unpublished MA thesis, University of Bergen

Wrigglesworth, M. (2000) *Ristninger og graver som sted. En visuell landskapsanalyse.* Unpublished MA thesis, University of Bergen.

Wrigglesworth, M. (2002) Ristninger og graver i landskapet. In Goldhahn (ed.) Bilder av bronsåler – ett seminarium om förhistorisk kommunikation. Rapport från ett seminarium på Vitlycke Museum 19.e–22.e oktober 2000, 185–200. *Acta Archaeologica Lundensia. Series in 8*, 37. Almquist and Wiksell International. Stockholm,

Yates, T. (1990) Archaeology through the Looking-Glass. In Babty, I. and T. Yates (eds) *Archaeology after Structuralism*, 153–204. London.

Zagorskis, I. (1973) Das Spätmesolitthikum in Lettland. *The Mesolithic in Europe.* Warsaw.

Ziegler, R. (1901) Arkæologiske undersøgelser i 1900. *Det Kongelige Norske Videnskabers Selskabs skrifter* 1900, No. 7. Trondheim.

Zwelebil, M. (2008) Innovating Hunter-Gatherers: The Mesolithic in the Baltic. In Bailey, G. and P. Spilkins (eds) *Mesolithic Europe.* Cambridge University Press, Cambridge.

Index

Numbers in bold refer to figures.

Åfjord 98
Aga 216
Åkrafjorden 230
Aksnes 212
Aldon Ridge 27, **28**, 29, 33, 34, 35, 38, 40
Alta **16**, 41
Altafjord 15, **16**, 17, 21, 25
American continent, the 3, 7
Åmøy 71
Åmøya 71
Amtmannsnes 15, **16**, 17, 19, 24–5
Amtmannsneset 15, 24–5
Angsneset 29
Apanes 19
archaeological excavation 20, 23, 31, 59, 124, 126, 128, 217, 232
  at rock art sites 9, 149, 151, 207–8, **211**, 256, 285, 306–7
archaeological monuments 29, 124–7, 236, 253
  re-use of 236, 238
archaeological remains 8–9, 14, 123, 151, 172–3, 197, 237, 253, 260, 274–5, 306–7
  Bronze Age 89, 123, 130, 131, 152, 217, 256
  dating of 9, 38, 95, 149, 151, 173, 197, 198, 208, 210, 212
  flint 151, 232, 244, 256, 267, 289, 306, 307
  links to rock art 149, 151, 153–4
  organic 9, 38, 95, 148, 197, 198, 207–8, 252, 274, 301
  regulations pertaining to 124
  pottery 207, 217, 256, 306–7
Arctic Circle 71
Årdal 197
Arnesen, Martin 264, 297, 299, 300, 301
art, views of 3
artefacts 88, 89, 148–9, 151, 169, 207–8, 236, 244, 246, 247, 260, 261, 263, 274, 315, *see also* metalwork; grave goods
  arrowheads 46–7, 59, 89, 95, 232, 267
  relationship with rock art 89
  tools 9, 23, 46, 143–4, **146**, 151, 154, 203, 216, 280, 280
Åskollen 282–5, 287, 294, 295, 296
Askvoll 177, 186, 187
Åsli 44, 47
Atløy 177, **178**, 179
Auran 104
Aurland 193
Auscvik 2, 19, 309, 310–11, 312
Australia 3, 7, 273
Austre Åmøy 244
Austrheim 164

Bakke 212–15, 218, 223, 226–7
  Loftarskleivi 213–14, 218, 223
  Mariskarvet 213–14, **215**, 223, 224
Bakkejordberget 55
Ballangen 76, 80
Balsfjord **42**, 43, 44, 50
Balsfjorden 42–3
Bardal 67, 98, 100, 103, 107–9
Beitstad 100
Beitstadfjord 101
Beitstad peninsula 105
Berg 100
Berge 200, 205–6, 212, 215, 226
Bergen 126
  Museum 124, 126, 128, 142, 164, 181
Billefjord 41
Bing, Kristian 139, 141–2
Bjørngård 104
Bjugn 98
boats 63, 83, 131–2, **165**, 169, 184, 186, 206, 223
Bodø 74
Bøe, Johs. 143, 145, 191, 195, 198, 309
Bogge 61, 112–23
Bohuslän, Sweden 17, 177, 215, 223, 234, 272, 297, 299–300, 303
Boknafjord 244
Bossekop 15, 19
Brandbu 239
Bredarör (burial mound) 129
Bremanger 142

Bremangerlandet 139, 152
British Isles, the 133
Brønnøy 91
Bronze Age, the 95, 116, 122, 129, 135, 168, 173, 191, 195, 197–8, 206, 216, 221, 239, 251, 263, 275
  beliefs 225, 251, 303
  Early 204, 226, 233, 234, 236, 237, 243, 244, 245, 246, 256, 258, 260, 271, 276
  farming 196–7, 245, 274, 276
  landscape 179, 242, 245, 301–2
  Late 209, 212, 227, 234, 235, 236, 237, 239, 243–4, 246, 260–61, 272, 274–5
  rock art 2, 4, 114, 149, 164, 165–6, 169, 174, 176, 181, 185, 190, 196, 202, 214–15, 217–20, 223, 229, 253, 255, 278, 299, 303
  settlement 274, 301–2
Brusteinhola 93
Bruteigsteinen (the Bruteig Stone) 215, 228–32, 234–5
Bryggen 17
Bukkhammarn 43, 48–9, 50, 54
Bukkhammerhola 94
burial practices 130, 131, 135–7, 173–5, 234, 251, 263
burial sites 29, 123, 148, 173–4, 177, 186, 187, 191, 224, 246, 260, 261, 301, *see also* Mjeltehaugen (burial mound)
  boat burials 164
  Bronze Age 245, 253, 259, 274
  cairns 216–17, 245, 253, 259
  cist graves 130–31, 245
  mounds 1, 8, 123, 173, 178, 186, 234, 236–8, 244, 245, 246, 253, 259, 274, 203
Buskerud 279
Buvika 101
Bøla 98, 102
Bøla River 100

calendars 249–51, 252
cannibalism 88
caves 3, 4, 14, 84, 86, 88–97
  significance in spiritual world 97
Ceavccageadgi 29
central places 10, 246, 260
ceremonies 10, 190, 196, *see also* ritual, rituals
  sacrificial 27, 34–7, 38, 65, *see also* offering sites; spiritual world, the
    stones (*storjunkeren*) 34–6, 40
Christie, Wilhelm, Frimann Koren 124, 126–8, 135, 138, 181–2, 187
churches 104, 124, 177, 179, 236–8
climate 253, 301, 312
  change 53
communications 68, 83, 133, 162, 169, 194, 216, 227, 235, 246, 260, 267, 270, 277, 278, 302
  visual 6, 122, 168, 171, 185, 278, 304
cultivation 56, 59, 123, 142–3, 173, 181, 208, 216, 234, 245–6, 260, 274, 301, *see also* farming
culture 65, 80, 111, 171, 175, 176, 181
  oral 139, 168, 278, 304

decoration in rock art **51**, 52, 58, 67, 102, 144, 245, 280, **283**, 284, 285, 287, 289, 291–4
deer 146, 154, 155–6, 161
Denmark 63, 180, 230, 233, 239, 263, 301
depictions in rock art 1, 4, 97
  abstract 14, 22, 144, 231, 234, 243, 245, 309
  animals **1**, **3**, **5**, 14, 17, 18, 24, 27, 31, **36**, **39**, 44, 50, **51**, 58, 69, 98, **103**, 107–8, 118, **141**, **150**, 234, 244, 272, 285, **286**, 289, 290–1, 300
    bears 22, 26, 44, 46, 54, 60–61, 72, **73**, 74, 78, **81**, 82, 94, 100
    deer 4, 8, 31, 44, 52, 54, 91, 102, 110, 139, 144–6, **147**, 148–9, **154**, 268, 280, 281, 285, 287, 288, 309
    dogs 44, 144, 230, **231**
    eland **5**, 7
    elk 19, 44, 48, 49, 54, 55, **70**, 72, 74–5, 77, 78, 94, 100, **101**, 107, 109–10, 118–20, 144, 264, 268, 280, 281, 281, 284, 287, 288–9, 291–4
    goats 43, **49**
    hares **32**, 78
    horses **1**, 105, **106**, 110, 230, **231**, 273
    porpoises 44, 52, 62, 82, 108
    reindeer 19, 24, 26, **32**, 40, 44, 46, 48, 60–3, 65, 72, **73**, 74, 75, 77, 78, 80, 82, 100, 144, 268
    reptiles 91
    sea mammals 4, 8, 48, 52, 61, 66, 69, 72, 77, 78, 80, 82, 83, 101, 117, 144
    whales **48**, 52, 61, 62, 69, 72, 78, 80, 101, **102**, 107–10, 114, 117, 144, 285, 287
    wolves 144
  battles 220
  birds 69, 78, **79**, 80, 108, 110, 144, 281, 284, 287
  boats 22, 33, **34**, 62, 63–4, 65, 104, 115–16, 131, **132**, 164–5, **166**, 169, 176, 179, 180, 181, **182**, 185–7, **195**, 204–6, 212, **222**, 223–4, **248**, 253, 255, 257, 272–3, 300, **302**, 306–7
    crew lines 22, 110, 179, 205, 220, 222–3, 229, 243, 247, 266, 273
  carts **1–2**, 300
  ceremonies/rituals 22, **106**, 219, 223, 225–7, 304
  choice of motifs 16, 24–5, 58, 161, 164, 244, 246, 273, 275, 300

depictions in rock art, *continued*
circles and spirals 1, **106**, 107, 110, 116, 183, 205, 230, **231**, 243, 244, 272, 300
common motifs 4, 188, 191, 193
conjunctions of images 62–3, 69, 72, 74, 78, 80, 82, 83, 117, 146, **147**, **150**, 188, 223, 243, 249, 303
cross/spoked wheels 228, 266, 272, **273**
cup marks 4, 188, 190–99, 228–33, 235, 244, **248**, 253, 255, **256**, 258–9, **260**, 261, **275**, **277**, 300
diversity of motifs 231
fish 61–3, 69, 74, 77, 101, 109, 285, 287
foot soles 105, **106**, 227, **248**, 255, 264, 266, 267, 276, 278
geometric forms 18, 19, 54, 55, 58, 66–8, 98, 102, **103**, 105, 109, 144–5, 243, 245, 268, 270, 300, 309
hand forms 243, **249**, 300
hook shapes 144, 145, 146, 148
humans 18–19, 22, 24, **25**, 26, 45–6, 86, **87–8**, 92–3, 96, **104**, **106**, 144, 146, 215, 218–23, **248**, 269
"bridal couples" 219–20, **221**, 222
gender 86, 190, 219–22, 299
hunting and fishing 22, **33**, 62, 64–5, 219, 220, 264, 267
lures (trumpets) 105, 218, 229, 247, 304
phalli 46, 86, 219, 220–23, 225, 264, 299
rare motifs 4, 74, 215, 243
rings 104–5, 116, 193, 213, 223, 227, 228–9, 231, 233, 243, 244, **248**, 249, 273, 278, 300
runes 163–4, 166–8, 175–6
sexual intercourse 219–21, 223
size of 31, 44, 45, 49, 54, 60, 69, 74, 78, 100, 101–2, 104, 107, 118, 182, 222, 283, 287, 307
social interactions 22
superimposed **49**, **59**, 60, 61, 64, 78, 80, 83, 98, 114, 117, 119–20, 122, 176
swastikas 163, 167–8, 171, 175
traps 45
trees 230, **231**, 234, **303**
triskeles 210
use of natural features in 11, 40, 75, 116, 282, 287
weapons 231, 234, 300
Djeveløya 284–5
Dokka 288
Dokkfløy Lake 288, 289
Drammen 285
Drotten 291, 295
Duesteinen (the Dove Stone) 10, 231–4
dwelling features/sites 23, 29, 54, 59, 67, 74, 88, 151–4, 160, 173, 198, 260, 267, 301

Early Metal Period, the 38, 55, 89, 95, *see also* Bronze Age, the
economy 65, 173, 192, 197, 234, 245, 274
Efjorden 70, 76, 77, 80
Eidefossen 292, 293, 295
Ekeberg 281, 287, 294, 296
Elva 145, 149
Eresfjorden 112, 123
Etna 288
Etne 10, 215, 228, 230, 232–4, 236, 273
Etnepollen 230–31, 235
Evenhus 107, 110
exchange 185, 246, 263, 268, 276–7, 302

farmers 4, 123, 142, 192, 195, 197, 199, 278, 282
farming 4, 133, 141, 142, 172, 173, **189**, 192–9, 217, 234, 245–6, 249, 261, 274
arable 142, 192, 216, 230, 246, 260, 302, *see also* cultivation
animal husbandry 196, 197, 233, 246, 261, 274, 276, 301
farms 189, 190, 192–3, 196–7, 198, 199, 216, 231, 233, 260, 261
faunal remains 14, 88–9, 95, 217
Fauske 74
fields 173, 175, 197, 208, 274, 301
Filefjell 194
Fingalshola 17, 90, 94, 95, 97
Finland 31, 67–8
Finnmark 15, 27, 41
fishing 15, 37, 62, 65, 133, 141, 142, 152, 153, 159, 192, 246, 262, 275
Flåte 228
Fløyen **203**
Fjellvika 77
Fjøsnaneset 231, 234–5
Flora 2, 309
Florø 139, 144
Fluberget 241–4, **245**, 247–9, 251–2
Folgefonni (glacier) 216, 230
Folgefonn peninsula **214**, 216, 227
folklore 196
folk traditions 181, 199, *see also* culture
Fordal 104, 105
Forselv 56, **57**, 58–9, 62, 63, 64, 66, 67, 68, 103, 109
Fosen peninsula 98, 100, 101
Fossum 272, 297
France 3
Frette 231–2
Frierfjorden 274
Friksdalen 198
Frosta peninsula 110
Frøysjøen **140**, 142, 152

Gauldalen 105
Geirangerfjord 17
Geithus 284, 296
gender relations 8, 273
geology
  diabase 143
  gneiss 70, 115, 216
  granite 70, 115, 258, 300, 301, 306, 313
  mica schist 216, 264
  moraines 228, 234, 240, 244, 246, 253, 301, 302
  phyllite 115, 216
  slate 203, 309, 312–13
  sandstone 143, 313
  tillite 31
geological survey 70, 96
Germany 239, 263
Gildeskål 93
Giske (island of) 124–6, 133, 136
Gjerpen valley, the 272, 274–6, 278
Glemmestad 292, 295
Glomfjord 50, 72
Gloppen 164–6
Gloppenfjorden 172
grave goods **128**, 148, 169, **170**, 175, 236, 244, 246, 251, 260
Gravvik 90
Gråbergan 48, 49, 50, 52, 54
graffiti (modern) 72, 74, 93, 115
grazing *see* farming, animal husbandry; pastureland
Gudbrandsdalen 196, 290–2

Hælvete 83, 95
Hafrsfjord 239, 241–2, 244, 246, 252
Håhaugsteinen (boulder) **195**
Hallström, Gustaf 42–3, 50, 54, 114, 116, 141, 145
Hamarhaug 212
Hamarøy 75
Hammer 98, 107
Hamnøy 92
Hardanger 192–4, 196, 215–16, 226–7, 230
Hardangerfjorden 194, 202, 209, 212, 213, 216, 226
Hardangervidda 264, 270, 275
Hardbakken 141
Harstad 54
Haugostølen 189
Haustveit 195
hearths 9, 59, 98, 174, 208, **209**, 210, 212
Hedmark 279
Hegra 104
Helgaberg (the Holy Rock) 228, 230–31, 233–4, 236–7
Hell 67, 98, 102, 103, 109
Hennebygda 165, 173
Hennøya (island of) 141
Herand 213, 217
Herandsbygda 213, **214**, 215, 226
Herandsholmen **214**, 216–17
Herjangen 68
Hinnøya (island of) 76
Hjemmeluft 15, **16**, 17, 19, 20–22, 24, 25, 26, 46, 65
Hjortspring boat, Denmark 206, 210
Holtås 101, 102, 103
Hordaland 10, 177, 194, 215, 228
Hornelen massif 139, 142, 153, **156**, 158
human remains 88, 126, 128, 173
human sacrifice 135
hunting 37, 66, 153, 155, 159, 169, 192, 246, 262, 267, 280
hunting and gathering 149, 275
Hyenfjorden 174

Ice Age, the 14, 22, 63, 71, 83, 94, 96, 115, 149, 204, 295, 311
images, human interpretation of 2–3, 6
indigenous populations 3, 7, 176, 280
Indre Sogn 192–4
Innvik 162
Innvikfjorden 162, 167, 171
Ireland 233
Iron Age, the 29, 116, 123, 152, 191, 198–9, 236–8, 245, 253, 274
  Early 4, 122, 164, 165–6, 168–9, 176, 198–9, 202, 206, 212, 214, 217, 236, 255, 303
  Late 210, 236
Italy 17

Jæren **240**, 244–7, 263
  Middle 245–6
  Northern 239, 241–2, 244, 245–6, 249
Jämtland, Sweden 102
Jaslangen **194**
Jiebmaluokta see Hjemmeluft
Johansen, Erling 300
Jondal 212, 213, 216
Josarsaklubben 76, 77
Jostedalsbreen 169, 198
Jylland, Denmark 246, 263

Kåfjord 15, **16**, 17, 25–6, 41
Kanstadfjorden 76, 77
Kårstad 162–9, 171, 173–6
Kazakhstan 2
Kirkely 50–54
Kivik 129

Kjeøya (island of) 17, 55
Kleivane 162, 172
Klubba 61, 71, 80, 82, 83
Kløftefossen 284
Kollhellaren 92, 94
Komsafjellet 15, 24
Korsneset 77
Kvænangen 54
Kvaløya 43, 46, 47
Kvernavika 101
Kvilesteinen ("the Resting Stone") 188, 190–91, 193, 199
Kvithammaren **268**, 269, 271

Lærdal 193, 194
Lærdalsøyri 194
landscape, the 10, 27, 29, 71, 83, 143, 153, 155–6, 192, 194, 245–6, 253, 278, 300, 301
  meanings ascribed to 38, 40, 65, 156–8, 176, 273
land uplift 47, 49, 50, 53, 59, 71, 115, 117, 149, 204, 210, 295
Langangen 270, 271
Langfjorden 112, 123
Langnesholmen 15
language 1, 194
Lånke 102
Lappviktinden **64**
Lascaux 3
Latvia 239
Leikanger 193, 198
Leiknes 61, 76, 77–80, 82, 83
Leirfall 98, 104, 105, 106, 223
Leirvåg 177, 185, 297
Leka (island of) 84, 90
Levanger 101
life stages *see* rites of passage
Linga 212
Lista peninsula 253, 260–61, **262**, 263
  Gjerdberget **254**, 255, 256
  Hananger 255, 258–61
  Kalleberg 255, 256, **257**, 261
  Kviljo 255, 257–9, **260**, 261
  Lunde 255, 258–9
  Penne 255–6, 259, 261
Listalandet 253, 255, 258–9, 260–61
livestock 181, 197, 234, 277, *see also* farming
Løbergshaugen 273
Lødingaksla 76
Lødingen 76
Lofoten 85, 94
Lorange, Anders 128–30, 136
lures (trumpets) 239, 241, **242**, 244, 252
Luster 188, 190–3, 198, 199
Lustrafjord 191

Malangen 43, 44, 47
Måløy 139
material culture 7, 23, 38, 95, 260
Meløyfjorden 71
menhirs 166
Mesk River 27
Mesolithic, the 14, 123, 144, 146, 148–9, 151–3, 156, 158, 161, 279
metal production 217, 304
metalwork 167, 170, 173, **174**, 261–2, 275
  bronze 128, 210, 224, 237, 239, 244, 246, 251, 256, 261, 263, 275
Middle Ages, the 29, 34, 124, 191, 194, 196, 198–9, 236–8
migration 276
  animal 22, 44, 46, 47, 48, 60, 66, 82, 120, 146, 289
  human 71, 123, 175, 196, 276
Mjeltehaugen (burial mound) 124, **125**, 126–31, 133, 135, **136**, 258
  dating of 128–9, 130, 131
Mjåset 186
Mjønesfjellet 74
Mjøsa Lake 290, 292
Molde 112
Møllerstufossen 288, 295
Mortensnes 29
Moskenes 92
Murget 29
myth, mythology 3, 5, 7, 8, 15, 41, 66, 82, 96, 98, 107, 115, 116, 120, 150, 154, 161, 170, 183, 219, 225, 235–6, 237–8, 280, 304–5 *see also* spiritual world, the
  creation 247, 280
  animals in 22, 24, 62, 64–5, 74, 117, 155, 160
  boats in 115, 223–4
  landscape in 38, 153, 157, 159
  sun 251–2

Nærøyfjord 17
Narvik 56
natural resources 65, 133, 153, 155, 166, 175, 176, 192, 194, 197, 216, 227, 230, 260, 262, 276–7, 289–90, 301–2
Neolithic, the 14, 67, 149, 196–9, 232–4, 245, 255, 271, 274, 276
Nes 76, 77, 83
Nesaunet 104
Nesseby 27
Neumann, Jacob 177, 181, 187
Nisser 269

Nord-Aurdal 193
Nordby 282
Nordfjord 44, 139, 162, 165–6, 173–5
Nordfjorden **163**
Nordland 14, 18, 69, 70–71, 91, 92, 117, 119
Nordsinni 288
Nord-Trøndelag 17, 18, 84–5, 90
Northern Europe 17, 160, 167
North Sea, the 246
Norway 4, 7, 14, 179–81, 230, 297, 319
  Central 98, 102, 104
  chronology of 12, **13**
  Eastern 239, 272, 279–96
  Northern 41, 42, 59
  Southern 59, 142, 191–2, 196, 288, 309
  Western 131, 169, 192–4, 196, 197–8, 226, 230, 233, 303
Nyelv 31

Odda 193
Oddajohka 31
offering sites 29, 34, 38, 40, 120, 229, 237, 271, *see also* ceremonies, sacrificial
  proximity to rock art 243
Ofoten area 14
Ofotfjorden 56, 68, 76
Oppland 279
Osen 101
Oslo 279
Oslofjorden 295, 296
Østfold 1, 223, 234, 264, 272, 297, 299–301
Østerdalen 196
Östergötland, Sweden 223
Østre Homnes 110
Østre Toten 292
Øystre Slidre 193
Ovnen 269–70

Padjelante, Sweden 33
Paleolithic, the 14
pastureland 169, 175, 176, **189**, 192–3, **194**, 195, 196–9, 216, 230, 233, 249, 274, 275, 276–7, 302
place names 34, 194, 216, 236, 253, 260
politics 6, 136, 176, 180, 181–2, 184, 185, 234, 297
Porsanger fjord 41
Portugal 17
prehistory, study of 182–4, 280–81

Rafsbotn 17
Rauland 264, 278
raw materials *see* natural resources
reindeer 34, 36, 40, 44
  herding of 37
religion 7, 9, 15, 37, 65–6, 68, 96, 111, 120–22, 148, 157, 160–61, 169–70, 173–5, 181–2, 184, 186, 190–91, 206, 211, 219, 221, 247, 250, 277–8, *see also* spiritual world, the
  Christianity 34, 37, 111
religious practices 35, 37, 161, 169, 191, 219, 221, 235, 238, 247
Reshåla 93, 94
Revheim 239, 241, 244, 247, 250, 251, 252
Revheimsmyra 244
Ringsaker 290
rites of passage 66, 96–7, 155, 160, 186, 224–6
ritual, rituals 8, 36–8, 89–90, 96–7, 160–61, 211, 238, 247, 252, 305, *see also* ceremonies;
  associated with rock art 5, 8, 154–5, 157, 160, 183, 199, 211, 219, 221–7, 236, 304, 307
rock art
  access to 10, 68, 159–61, 235, 261, 304–5
    modern 26, 315, 316–17, 319
  age of 3–4, 14, 15, 18, 33, 38, 70–71, 94–5, 115, 166, 174, 181, 204, 210, 253, 255, 279, 295, 303
  cessation of 235
  choice of rock for 10, 115, 122, 131, 143, 255
  concentrations of 4, 10, 12, 17, 31, 99, 104, 107, 112, 166, 196, 230, 244–5, 246, 259, 288, 301
  condition of 10, 24, 30, 45, 48, 52–3, 54, 58, 66, 72, 74, 76, 92, 97, 102, 105, 110, 115, 117, 118, 162, 179, 202, 213, 264, 281, 285, 289, 290–1, 292, 309
  deterioration of 309–12, 313, 314
  weathering zone, the 309–10, 311–12
  conservation of 315, 317
  creators of 9, 11, 15, 24, 68, 74–5, 77, 80, 82, 102, 122, 151, 154, 160, 171, 176, 197, 199, 273, 278, 280, 287, 296, 305
  dating of 9, 12, 18, 23, 24, 26, 29–30, 34, 35, 47, 49, 50, 55, 59, 82, 94–5, 114, 117, 119, 130, 149, 151–2, 167, 191, 198, 233, 258, 267, 272, 278
    shoreline method 204, 271, 295, *see also* land uplift
  depictions in *see* depictions in rock art
  divorced from original context 71, 100, 115, 164, 293, 295–6
  on grave slabs 126–8, 129–30, **132**, **134**, 135, 137, 165, 169, 185, 245, 258
  historical context of 27, 122–3, 207
  interpretation of 6, 10, 12, 27, 82, 117, 148–9, 155, 180–7, 190, 196, 199, 221, 235–6, 238, 249, 267, 280, 308
  landscape context of 1, 4, 8, 10, 24, **70**, 74, **79**, **81**, **114**, **144**, 157–9, **167**, 169, 191, 244, 246, 259, 314, 317
    on *åkerholmer* (field islets) 274, 301
    in caves 3, 4, 17, 18, 84–97
    coastal 143, 244, 246, 275, 280, 295–6

rock art, landscape context of, *continued*
near communications 227, 270, 296
by fjords 21, 48, 52, 56, 68, 194, 212, 213, 227, 244
inland 194, 275, 295
in mountainous areas 27, 31, 44, 47, 54, 164, 176, 195, 212
near settlement 23, 50, 54, 107, 151, 227, 234, 261, 302
shoreline 22, 115, 209–10, 264, 288, 292
sub-alpine 191–3, 195–6, 199
in transition zones 49, 107, 301
by water 80, 177, 179, 186, 242, 244, 268–9, 275, 289, 291, 293–6
link with farming 195–8, 261
maintenance of 53–4, 119, 199
makers of 1
meanings of 3, 6, 8, 29, 58, 61, 65, 66, 111, 120–21, 137, 146, 154, 168–9, 181, 199
as safeguards 199, 225
demonstrating ownership 145, 169, 173, 197–9, 220, 234
demonstrating power 171, 173, 184–5, 211, 220
migration 276, 289, 292
portraying myth 19, 21, 168, 169, 183, 219, 222, 252, 303–4, 308
sun symbolism 247, 249, 251, 276
symbols of fertility 183–4, 187, 190, 219, 221
symbols of travel 176, 185, 261, 276, 302
water symbolism 252
methods of 1
carving/scratching 18, 34, 160, 164, 221
chipping 203
chiselling 16–17
contour method 289
engraving/cutting 102, **103**, 104
painting 17, 18, 67, 90, 94, 268–9
pecking 29–30, 34, 54–5, 58, 60, 67, 100, 115, 143, 151, 280
polishing 70, 80, 83
paintings 15, 17, **18**, 30, 31, 41, 55, 84, 86, 90–95, 98, 269–70
pecked 94, 98
polished 14, 61, 69, 71–2, 74–8, 82–3, 94, 117
preservation of 26, 291, 293, 300, 313–15, **316**, 317
spiritual significance of 40–41, 58, 75, 121–3, 271
stone used for 115, 122
style of 22, 25, 27, 50, 54, 58, 68, 69, 71–2, 94, 100, 110, 119, 123, 204, 205, 207, 208, 218, 267, 271, 272, 281, 294, 300
naturalistic 50, 54, 58, 60, 64, 69, 71–2, 74, 83, 98, 100, 111, 118, 119, 281, 291
stylised 31, 44, 48, 49, 52, 64, 91, 101, 102, **103**, **106**, 107, 117, 120, 220, 225, **248**, 289, 291
typological studies of 149
vandalism of 310, 313, **314**, 319 *also see* graffiti
visibility of 10, 11–12, 25, 36, 45, 58, 76, 118, 162, 179, 200–202, 235, 286, 292, 304, 319
rock art sites
choice of 179, 212, 271, 294–6, 305
connections between 29, 67–8, 80, 83, 275, 287, 300
use of 7–8, 154, 160, 174, 211, 223, 226
rock art traditions 4, 14, 33–4, 98, 107–8, 110–11, 112, 130, 160, 164–5, 168–9, 171, 174, 190, 199, 212, 226, 263, 267–8, 278
Northern tradition (*veidekunst*) 8, 43, 54–5, 69, 70–71, 74, 76, 80, 82, 100, 101, 102, 114, 123, 131, 149, 176, 191, 212, **279**, 280, 282–3, 288–91, 293, 295–6, 309
Southern tradition (*jordbruksristninger*) 104, 105, 123, 176, 202, 205, 214–15, 231, 233, 243, 253, 257, 268, 271, 275, 299, 303
rock shelters 217
Rogaland 130, 230, 239, 244, 245, 262
Rolla (island of) 54
Romsdalsfjorden 112
Rønningen 270
Røros Mining Town 17
Røst (island of) 93
Rugsundøy 152
Ruksesbákti 41
runes, runic alphabets 166, 169–71, 175
Russia 31, 148
Rystraumen 46

sacred places 7, 38, 40, 97, 159, 161, 174, 175, 185, 226, 227, 243, 247, 252, 260, 270–71, 274, 307
continuity in 236–8
meaning of 238
Sævarhagen 216
Sagas, the 139, 177, 179–81, 187, 236
Sagelva 75, 83
Salten area 14
Salten 74
Saltstraumen 74
Sami, the 20, 22, 29, 34, 37–8, 41, 160
Samladalen 216
Samlafjorden 216, 226
Samlandaherad 226
Samlanes 217
Samlanuten **214**, 216–17, 227
San, the 5, 7
rock art of 8

Sandane 166
Sandenhola 93
Sarpsborg 301
Sauesundet 177
Scandinavia 4
sea levels 53–4, 59, 94, 101, 149, 179
Sciland 21
Selenjárga 29
Seljord 271
Seljordvatnet 269–70
settlement 23, 25, 47, 112, 123, 152–4, 166, 172–3, 177, 192–3, 216, 236, 261, 263, 274, 289, 296
Simon Krane-hola 94
shamans, shamanistic practices 3, 5, 37, 41, 122, 160–61
Shetelig, Haakon 162–4
Skåne, Sweden 129, 223
Skardsfjorden 71
Skåren-Monsen cave 91
Skarnsundet 101
Skatestraumen 152–4
Skatval peninsula 104
Skavberget 43, 44, 47, 48, 64
Skjeberg 297, **298**, 301–2
  Bjørnstad 306–7
  Hornnes 306
Skjebergskilen 301
Skjebergsletta 301
Skjerdal 173
Skjerstadfjorden 74
Skjervøy (island of) 54
Skoddevarre 20
Skjomen 56, 65, 67–8
Skjomenfjorden 56, **57**, 68
Skogerveien 285, 294, 296
Skotrøa 107, 110
Sledasteinen 215
social conflict 10, 154, 176, 211, 235
social hierarchies 8, 246
social norms 111, 211
social order 136, 154, 160, 263, 305
social status 133, 135, 211, 234
societies 9, 111, 176
  agricultural 107, 261, 263, *see also* farmers
  Bronze Age 133, 136, 245–7, 249, 263, 276, 304
  changing 154, 173–5, 182, 184–5, 211, 234–5, 252
  contact between 2, 68, 83, 133, 169, 173, 175, 185, 194, 234, 246, 263, 275–8, 296, 304
  hunting 17, 37, 123
  hunter-fisher 123, 270–71
  hunter-gatherer 160, 279
  influences on 2
  nomadic 83, 123, 173, 196
  organisation 133
  relations within 8, 96–7, 156, 173, 235
  wealthy 247, 261–3, 274, 276
Sogn 192, 194, 196–8
Sognefjorden 194
Sogn og Fjordane 2, 162, 177–8, 188, 309
Solsem 84, 86, 90, 95
Solsemhola 17, **85**, 94, 97
Sørfjorden 192–3, 195, 216, 227
Sørheim 236
South Africa 3, 5
Spain 3, 17
spiritual world, the 15, 37, 40–1, 64–5, 69, 97, 120–21, 160–61, 199
Sporaneset 264, **265**, 267–8, 276, 278
Stadhavet (Sea)
Stadsbygda 100
Stavanger 244
Staveneset 1, 186, 187
Stein 290, 291, 295
Steinkjer 101, 110
Stjernøya 21
Stjørdal **99**, 102
Stjørdalen 104, 105
Stødle terrace 228, 230–31, 234, 236–7
Stone Age, the 4, 29, 37, 38, 46, 48, 53, 54, 59, 63, 65, 67, 74, 123, 130, 149, 152, 166, 263, 296, *see also* Neolithic, the
Stordalen 228, 230–33, 235
Stordalsvatnet 228, 230–31, 235
Storsteinen 15, **16**, 17, 19, **20**, 25
Strandebarm **201**, 215
Straumfjord 46
Straumfjorden 43
Straumsfjord 43
Struve Geodetic Arc 17
Stykket 100–101, 102
subsistence strategies 278, *see also* farming; hunting; fishing
  changes in 154, 234
  nomadic 4, 15, 153
Sunnfjord 131–2, 177, 187
Sunnhordland 230
Sunnmøre 124, 133, 165
Svolset 198–9
Sweden 68, 179, 181, 230, 294, 297
Sweden, *continued*
  Northern 18
  Southern 223, 239, 301

taboos 8, 66
Tamgaly 2
Tanum 17
Tapes transgression, the 53
Telemark 264, 267–8, 271–2, 276, 278
Tennes 43, 44, 48, 51, 297
Tessem 105
time reckoning *see* calendars
Tollevik 15
topography *see* landscape, the
Totak 264, 269
tourism 162, 317
trade, trading 3, 178, 184, 133
Transfarelv 17, 18
Transfarelvdalen 15, 16, 18, 30
trapping 15, 234, 262
Trenyken 93
Troillhåle 92
Troms 14, 17, 42, 43, 54
Tromsø 43, 55
  Museum 17, 19, 31, 44, 47, 50, 55, 68, 93
Trøndelag 67, 98, 104, 107, 119, 123, 130, 131–2, 176, 223
Trondheimsfjorden 98, **99**, 105, 110
Tussurfjellet 142
Tveiten 217
Tysfjord 76, 77

Ullensvang 193
Ulveneset (the Wolf's Rock) 270
Ulvik 193
UNESCO 17, 26, 300
Unjárga gielda 27
Unneset 186
Uppland, Sweden 223
Urnes Stave Church 17

Værøy (island of) 93
Vågan 74–5, 83
Vahl, Martin 42–3, 49
Valdres 189, 192–4, 196
Valle 70, 76, 77, 80, 82, 83
Valletindan 80
Vang 193
Vangdal 212
Varanger 31, 37, 38
Varangerbotn 27
Varangerfjord 27, 29, **39**
Vardeneset 179, **180**
Vefall 269, 271
Vega Archipelago, the 17
Vegaøyan 17
Vehammaren 142, 145, 149
Venset 48, 54
Vereide **172**, 173–5
Verdal 100
Vest-Agder 253, 261
Vestfjorden 76, 78
Vestre Slidre 193–4
Vest-Telemark 196
Vevelstad 92, 93
Vik 193
Vikings, the 34, 180–81, 187, 196
Vingelven 141, 142
Vingefossen 145, 148
Vingen 19, 121, 139, **140**, 141–2, 144–6, 148–61
Vingeneset 142
Vingepollen **140**, 142, 145, 148, 151, 156, 158–9
Vinja 231–2
Vinje, Trygve 232
Vistnesfjorden 93
Voss 215
votive offerings 121, 173–4, 185, 190, 199, 206, 234, 238, 239, 247, 250, 252, 260, 274–5, *see also* spiritual world, the
  of the Bronze Age 274

watercourses 56, 71, 75, 83, 116, 234, 267–71, 274, 276–7, 278, 279, 294, 295
  Dokka 288
  Drammen 279, 282, 284, 288–9, 294
  Gudbrandsdalen 279, 292, 294
Western Norwegian Fjords 17
woodland 27, 56, 104, 268, 270, 277, 296
  clearance 245–6
World Heritage 16, 17, 26, 300

Ydstines 104
Ytste Naustvikja 179

Ziegler, Reinhold 112, 114, 118